BACKGROUND READINGS
FOR
PHYSICAL EDUCATION

Background Readings
for
Physical Education

ANN PATERSON and EDMOND C. HALLBERG
SAN FRANCISCO STATE COLLEGE

HOLT, RINEHART and WINSTON
New York, Chicago, San Francisco, Toronto, London

DEDICATED TO THE MEMORY
OF
Gladys E. Palmer

FOREWORD

PERHAPS NO VOLUME in recent years has so effectively distinguished the significance of the ideas that have emerged in the wake of the activity experience as this volume does. Professors Paterson and Hallberg have sought both near and far for the selections in this anthology and thus have afforded the reader an opportunity to see their subject—the physical education experience—not merely through the eyes of enthusiastic twentieth-century advocates but also from the viewpoints of such venerable thinkers of other places and periods as Plato, Franklin, Rousseau, and Spencer.

It would be difficult to miss the message. Students who seek something more in physical education than performance alone, who may be concerned about games but whose concern goes beyond the score, as well as people who have some interest in those deep motivations of the human spirit that drive man beyond the mundane, will find in these essays many insights and answers to the perplexing contradictions of modern education.

Perhaps no element of today's curriculum is so readily considered suspect as is the program of physical education. And yet, teachers in physical education may, if they wish, think of themselves as descendants of an ancient legion whose mission it was to pass on some of the lore of living through the games, sports, and dance of the age in which they lived. Long before the Hellenic period, children had been taught the solemnities of worship through the ceremonial dance, the contest had been a means of determining leadership, and movement of any kind had been a means of exploration and revelation. Without movement man fails to learn. Without movement, man dies. The culture of man has been recapitulated through the centuries not merely through his art, or his music, or his spoken word but also through his play, his dance, and his great variety of kinesthetic communications. Movement has always been indispensable as a means of development—and of learning.

Today we recognize that modern physical education originated in Greece in the fourth century B.C. Thus the authors quite properly invite us first to read Homer and Plato early in the historical and philosophical sections. But whether physical education was an integral part of the Hellenic program of *education* is questionable. To be sure, the ancient Greeks were concerned with the character of general education, citizenship training, and the liberal arts. To be sure, they debated what subjects should constitute the fundamentals of an education. But the physical educator, if he reads carefully enough, will note that although the health of the body was a major concern of Hellas, it was valued only as a care-taking structure for the mind, which was to be developed principally through rhetoric, aesthetics, oratory, music, and drama. The Greeks had elaborate gymnasiums and sponsored contests of all kinds, and yet, there was something missing in their understanding of the physical education experience, as we now look at it. A search through ancient Greek philosophy does show some, but very little, appreciation of it as a valuable educational experience in itself. Physical education was considered useful occasionally to produce character qualities only nebulously defined, but mainly to develop strength for the military campaign or for slave labor, that is, mainly as a conditioning process whereby other tests could be well met. Rhetoric was all important as the method of education; other skills were valued in descending order so that the marathon runner, hero though he was, was not expected to have profited intellectually from his grueling test.

Nor did the Romans improve upon this situation. Although the Roman community was well supplied with athletic fields and swimming pools, the Romans of the first century A.D. established a pattern for liberal arts education that entirely ignored physical education. There is no place in the Trivium or the Quadrivium of Varro for the physical education experience.

But beginning with the Reformation, things began to change. The full thrust of the radical thought of Spencer, Herbert, Froebel, Locke, Pestalozzi and Basedow, and Montesorri opened the curriculum to activity. Their naturalistic individualism was a refreshing effort to encourage the use of all of man's senses for the realization of all of his potentialities. Motor development and motor experience became important in their own right as means of education—as ways of cultivating self-understanding, or self-realization. As well as means of creative expression, they were valued, too, as means of gaining an understanding of one's world, one's culture, or as ways by which one could redirect behavior to make it compatible with social purposes.

And, thus, today, one has a choice of three views from which to formulate a concept of physical education. The wide range of readings in this volume will stimulate the thoughtful student to make such a choice. Are schools today offering physical education as a means of conditioning young people for tasks imposed upon them by a demanding society? Or, do we "offer" physical education for custodial care only to ensure the brain a sound body to house it? Or is the experience of movement potentially educative in itself?

Which of these concepts will guide the physical education of the future? And must we distinguish in this rubric between physical education and physical training?

Only by raising such fundamental questions, can we find solutions, or at least some answers, to many "practical" problems. This may be a very critical decade for physical education in schools and colleges. Its continuance within the curriculum is at stake. There are those who would remove it as unrelated to the purposes of education and the educative process; and there are those who would keep it as central to such purposes. Political or financial factors may determine its fate in some places, but for the most part, it will be resolved in terms of the prevailing philosophical or theoretical views on the nature of man and his destiny in this life. The practitioner of physical education will have to come to grips with his purposes. He will have to re-examine many of his teaching practices. He will be compelled to develop a new format for his program in order to remain in step with the emerging "new education," which includes such developments as the nongraded curriculum, redistribution of teaching modules, the use of television, and master teachers.

He will have to make his peace with the seductive goal of "physical fitness" and in so doing will, we shall hope, remove the quack, the charlatan, and the opportunist from his ranks. He will have to carry out responsibly his role in a moral culture and decide whether this role should function to perpetuate the generally accepted ethic of this heterogeneous society. He will have to make his goals and values clear and demonstate his implementation of them through teaching and administration. He will not sit idly by and allow sport to be degraded as a phenomenon of the market place; where it has been so threatened, he will be willing to move to its rescue and place schoolboy sports, at least, on a higher level of experience.

But mainly he will have to decide whether the learning experience for which he is responsible shall be a means—or an end. It is fashionable now, in this decade, to say that the purpose of education is to cultivate the ability to think. Important people have said this is the central purpose to which the school must be oriented. In that context and with no clarification one can take exception to that statement. The ability to think? About what? John Dewey may be in disrepute with some modern

critics, but his particular brand of pragmatism challenges such direc-
tionless admonitions by remarking that the basic purpose of education is "social, and that the criterion to be applied in estimating the
value of the practices that exist in schools is also social. It is true that
the aim of education is development of individuals to the utmost of their
potentialities. But this statement in isolation leaves unanswered the
question as to what is the measure of the development. A society of free
individuals in which all, through their own work, contribute to the
liberation and enrichment of the lives of others, is the only environment in which any individual can really grow normally to his full
stature."

Norman Cousins, in an essay of 1960, "Education Against Help-
lessness," suggests that "there can be no more important education
today than education for personal effectiveness. . . ." This takes the
purposes of education one step beyond the development of the capacity
to think critically and requires that educators give some thought as to
how we may assist our students not only to develop but also to apply
their capacity for critical thought to bear on their world.

This involves a personal effort of the total personality. It does not
merely require the use of intellectual power. On the contrary, it forces
the educator to examine what the total individual *is*, how he is made,
what his metabolism is like, what the physiological forces playing upon
him are, and how the adversities of an adverse environment have been
met. A man makes his mark in and on the world, to be sure, but the
quality of that mark, the nature and extent of its benefaction, is not a
product merely of the man's worldly knowledge or, as Cousins puts it,
his ability to marry theory to technique. A man's mark in the world is
determined by his very fiber, his whole being, by the deep potentialities
in his genetic inheritance as well as by his manner of organizing and
administering his own life. Knowledge of his world is basic, of course,
but we venture to say it is no more basic than what he does with that
part of knowledge that shows him the way to make the other part
effective!

And so it is that people in physical education must take their program
one step beyond the development of physical strength and physical fitness. They must understand that mere health—or fitness—have *never*
been adequate motivations. As an end in itself, fitness lacks appeal;
rather, it is in reality a means, and a good one, to achieve purposes in
Dewey's context of the enrichment of society. Precisely as Cousins

asks for more than undirected critical thinking, we ask modern physical education to go beyond undirected physiological values.

In a brilliant essay on "The Depth and Magnitude of Human Nature," Ira Progoff makes it clear that "on almost every level of civilization, from the most primitive to the most complex, the pursuit of life is not merely physical but qualitative. More important than the life of the individual as such is the *way* that his life is spent. . . . The opposite side of this same coin is seen in the fact that people who do not have a sense of meaning in their lives tend to be unable to function even on the most simple levels."[1]

And this is the crucial issue for physical education in today's schools. What meaning does it have? What experience does it offer in the direction of that meaning? Does it make a contribution to man in his entirety? Or are the benefits directed only to his physiology? To survive, the physical education programs of the day must recognize the totality of man and be constantly mindful that man lives in a social setting, not in isolation. If we can picture a physical education program as a social system, we should be mindful of Alfred North Whitehead's remark that "the worth of any social system depends upon the value experience it promotes among individual human beings."

From this splendid collection of provocative readings, the student will receive great pleasure and stimulation. Surely the ingredients for the construction of a personal point of view towards the physical education experience are here. The editors are to be congratulated on the range and quality of their selections.

Delbert Oberteuffer
The Ohio State University
March 1965

[1] Ira Progoff, "The Depth and Magnitude of Human Nature," *Main Currents in Modern Thought*, Vol. 16, No. 5, May 1960, p. 98.

PREFACE

TODAY, in the time of the international struggle for survival and the desire for universal education, all areas of education are being scrutinized. Those maintained must constantly justify their curricular existence. Physical education is no exception. It can point with some satisfaction to a past of stable curricular positions despite its changing environment, and it wisely continues to re-examine its purposes in light of a long and venerable heritage.

Physical education is an outgrowth of the analysis and application of history, philosophy, psychology, biology, and sociology. If it is to be effective, this applied field cannot foster its own specialization; it must recognize that its origins lie in the liberal arts. The student all too frequently becomes so imbued with the necessity to master myriad, dissimilar motor skills that he may inadvertently overlook the broad nature of his profession. Thus, he becomes narrowly specialized, and he loses sight of the fact that physical education is, indeed, a component of general education, and that it has an important and impressive background.

This book of readings attempts to contribute to the understanding of the backgrounds for physical education. It is designed for students who have chosen this field as a career. It can be used as a supplementary readings book for courses in the "introduction" to and "principles" of physical education and for courses in research and current problems in physical education. It can help teachers already in service to deepen their thinking about their profession by reconsidering its origins. The book may suggest possibilities for future research, leading to the reformulation of principles and current practices.

This book limits itself to the elaboration of several specific concepts underlying physical education. For the most part, the representations are drawn from writings of specialists in history, philosophy, psychology, biology, and sociology. From his study of the works selected, the student may derive a point of view that will help him become an intelligent educator. The book is divided into five sections. Each is organized differently, for each discipline suggests its own grouping. This approach gives each section a unique character and interest.

Section I, Historical Backgrounds, is descriptive in nature and serves to illuminate two concepts: that down through the ages sports, games, dance, and exercise have been of vital concern to people in many cultures; and that they have not changed appreciably from epoch to epoch, although many of them had their origins in religious and military pursuits.

Section II, Philosophical Backgrounds, combines five major lines of philosophical thought, which the student can compare. Matched with classic philosophers are contemporary physical educators. The selections illustrate that the relationship between mind and body has long been a subject of philosophic inquiry. Specifically shown are Platonic idealism and the pragmatic idealism of Oberteuffer; naturalism (romanticism) of Rousseau, the dynamic idealism of Hegel, and the modern naturalism of Brightbill; realism of Locke, dualism of Descartes, and the contemporary realism suggested by McCloy; pragmatism (experimentalism) of Dewey and the social pragmatism of Williams; aesthetics of Spencer and the modern point of view of H'Doubler.

Section III, Psychological Backgrounds, organized on yet another pattern, gives the student an opportunity to examine research on the acquisition of motor skills. The concepts presented here concern the feedback in the learning of motor skills, the retention of motor skills, the training for transfer, and the effects of stress on performance. Also discussed are psychomotor and physical abilities and the relationship of physique to various physchological characteristics, for example, height and temperament.

Section IV, Biological Backgrounds, is presented around the unique contributions of physical education to the educative process. This section devotes itself to two important concepts; that exercise has a direct bearing upon growth and development and that exercise is needed for the maintenance of physical fitness.

Section V, Sociological Backgrounds, concerns itself with the following five areas: American values, the separate culture of the school, the individual within the society, social class, and social change. Each of these is elucidated by sociological articles dealing primarily with the role of athletics and play in the culture.

Most of the articles and essays in this book are classics in their field. They constitute a basis for critical analysis of current procedures and research in physical education. When practicable, complete works rather than fragments are presented to allow full acquaintance with the authors' material and to reveal ideas as the writers originally structured them. Whenever an essay is abridged, it is so indicated.

Comments to direct the student's progress and to emphasize relevant points introduce each section and reading. Questions focused upon the afore-mentioned concepts follow the readings. Suggestions for further reading appear at the end of the majority of the selections. No suggestions for additional reading, however, are supplied for many of the psychological and biological research studies because the numerous references cited in the works themselves provide sufficient bibliography to the subjects discussed. Relationships between articles in the various sections can be observed. For example, some of the same views expressed in the essays by Dewey and Spencer in Section II, Philosophical Backgrounds, emerge again in Soule's article in Section V, Sociological Backgrounds. These relationships are also indicated and emphasized in the introductions.

The readings are correlated with several physical education "introduction" and "principles" textbooks. A correlation chart (see pages xxii–xiii) offers a guide whereby the student may readily study the applicable sections in other works.

Hopefully, this book will provide a vehicle for further reading and thinking about the origins of physical education. It may help to bridge the gap between an understanding of the historical and theoretical foundations in other areas and what actually transpires in the gymnasium and the classroom.

We wish to thank all authors and publishers who have permitted us to use their works in this book. Special gratitude is due John P. DeCecco, Department of Psychology and the Center for Interdisciplinary Studies, San Francisco State College, for his generous assistance in the preparation of the entire manuscript, but particularly of the Philosophical and Psychological Backgrounds sections.

We are indebted, also, to other colleagues at San Francisco State College who offered many helpful suggestions: Ray A. Kelch and George D. Gibson, Department of History; Alfred C. Jensen, School of Education; Charles L. Earlenbaugh, Student Personnel Division; Douglas A. Fessenden, Mary E. Whitney, Anatole Joukowsky, Division of Health, Physical Education and Recreation; and Marvin E.

Weinberger, School of Language and Literature, for translating the Dally article from French to English. We also wish to thank Gabor Vermes, Department of History, Stanford University, and Thomas E. Shaffer, School of Medicine, The Ohio State University, for their contributions. Earle F. Zeigler, University of Illinois, very graciously read the first version of the manuscript, and his insightful and challenging comments have helped the authors tighten the rationale for the entire book. We are singularly pleased and honored that Delbert Oberteuffer, The Ohio State University, agreed to write the Foreword.

Our heartfelt thanks go to Veloris Hallberg whose penetrating questions aided immensely in the improvement of the book and to Patricia J. Quance for her interest and painstaking typing of the manuscript. We are grateful for the assistance of Adair Miller and Shirley Knipe. If there are errors or omissions, we alone are responsible.

ANN PATERSON
EDMOND C. HALLBERG

San Francisco, California
March 1965

CONTENTS

Contents

TEXTS IN PHYSICAL EDUCATION
LISTED IN THE CORRELATION CHART

BROWNELL, CLIFFORD LEE and PATRICIA E. HAGMAN, *Physical Education—Foundations and Principles*. New York: McGraw-Hill, Inc., 1960.

BUCHER, CHARLES A., *Foundations of Physical Education*, 4th ed. St. Louis: The C. B. Mosby Company, 1964.

COWELL, CHARLES C. and WELLMAN L. FRANCE, *Philosophy and Principles of Physical Education*. Englewood Cliffs, N.J.: Prentice-Hall, Inc., 1963.

COWELL, CHARLES C. and HILDA M. SCHWEHN, *Modern Principles and Methods in High School Physical Education*, 2d ed. Boston: Allyn and Bacon, Inc., 1964.

DAVIS, ELWOOD CRAIG and EARL L. WALLIS, *Toward Better Teaching in Physical Education*. Englewood Cliffs, N.J.: Prentice-Hall, Inc., 1961.

DUNCAN, RAY O. and HELEN B. WATSON, *Introduction to Physical Education*. New York: The Ronald Press Company, 1960.

JENNY, JOHN H., *Physical Education, Health Education, and Recreation*. New York: The Macmillan Company, 1961.

JOHNSON, GRANVILLE B., WARREN R. JOHNSON, and JAMES H. HUMPHREY, *Your Career in Physical Education*. New York: Harper & Row, Publishers, 1957.

NIXON, JOHN E., LANCE FLANAGAN and FLORENCE S. FREDERICKSON, *An Introduction to Physical Education*, 6th ed. Philadelphia: W. B. Saunders Company, 1964.

NIXON, JOHN E. and ANN E. JEWETT, *Physical Education Curriculum*. New York: The Ronald Press Company, 1964.

OBERTEUFFER, DELBERT and CELESTE ULRICH, *Physical Education*, 3d ed. New York: Harper & Row, Publishers, 1962.

SHEPARD, NATALIE MARIE, *Foundations and Principles of Physical Education*. New York: The Ronald Press Company, 1960.

VAN DALEN, DEOBOLD B. and MARCELLA M. VAN DALEN, *The Health, Physical Education and Recreation Teacher*. Englewood Cliffs, N.J.: Prentice-Hall, Inc., 1956.

WILLIAMS, JESSE F., *The Principles of Physical Education*, 8th ed. Philadelphia: W. B. Saunders Company, 1964.

CORRELATION CHART*

OTHER TEXTS	SECTION I HISTORICAL BACKGROUNDS	SECTION II PHILOSOPHICAL BACKGROUNDS	SECTION III PSYCHOLOGICAL BACKGROUNDS	SECTION IV BIOLOGICAL BACKGROUNDS	SECTION V SOCIOLOGICAL BACKGROUNDS
BROWNELL AND HAGMAN:	IV, V, VI	I, II, VII, VIII	X, XV, XVI	III	IX, XI
BUCHER:	XII, XIII, XIV	I, VI, VII, VIII	XVI	I, V, XV, XXV	II, IV, X, XVII, XXV
COWELL AND FRANCE:	XII	I	II, III, VI, VII, VIII	II	IV, VIII
COWELL AND SCHWEHN:	I	I, IV, VII, IX	II, III, X	II, VIII	I, V, VI
DAVIS AND WALLIS:	XI	I, VII, VIII, XI	II, III, IV, V, VI, X, XIII, XV	IV, V, VIII	VII, VIII, XVI, XVII, XVIII, XIX
DUNCAN AND WATSON:	I	II, III	VII, IX, X, XI	V, IX, XI	I, VI, XII, XIII
JENNY:	IV, VI	I, VII		VIII	XIV, XX

OTHER TEXTS	SECTION I HISTORICAL BACKGROUNDS	SECTION II PHILOSOPHICAL BACKGROUNDS	SECTION III PSYCHOLOGICAL BACKGROUNDS	SECTION IV BIOLOGICAL BACKGROUNDS	SECTION V SOCIOLOGICAL BACKGROUNDS
JOHNSON, G. B., JOHNSON, W. R., AND HUMPHREY, J. H.:	II	I, IV, V, VI, IX, XIII	X	XIV	XV
NIXON, FLANAGAN, AND FREDERICKSON:	VII	IV, V, VI	VIII, XV	VIII, XI	VIII, X, XII, XIII, XIV
NIXON AND JEWETT:		II, III, VI, VII	I, II, V, VI, VII, VIII	II	I, IV, V, IX, X
OBERTEUFFER AND ULRICH:	I, II	II, III, V, XII	III, IV, VII, XI	III, VII	I, III, VI
SHEPARD:	I, II, VI, VII, VIII	III, IV, IX, X	V, XII, XIV		I, V, XI, XV
VAN DALEN, D. AND VAN DALEN, M:	VI, VII	I, XII	XI, XIII	XI, XIII	I, IV, VI, X, XI, XII, XV
WILLIAMS:	I, VIII	II, III, IX	VII, X, XI	II, VI	IV, V

*Roman numerals refer to chapter numbers in other texts. In some instances only parts of chapters are relevant.

[SECTION I]

Historical
Backgrounds

The study of history gives the attentive student an appreciation of the vastness of man's struggle with his universe. It makes possible a critical understanding of where we were yesterday, where we are today, and where we hope to go in the future. Further, provision of an historical base for the interpretation of present problems enables the student to understand better his own position in relationship to his environment. A study of history and an application of the knowledge so derived can result in the enrichment of one's life through a fuller realization of the broad social issues of the day. What are the truths of our existence? What directions shall our lives take? What can we expect from life? How can the past give meaning to what we do every day? These questions certainly cannot be answered by this book alone, but perhaps through the readings some progress may be made toward their solution.

In presenting the history of physical education, one can take various historical approaches, such as Spengler's cyclical theory, Hegel's great-man theory, or a Toynbeean theory of challenge and response. We have chosen to devote this section not to any one approach but rather to a representation from the writings of and on the great eras.

Two major purposes govern the choice of material for this section. The first purpose is to acquaint the student with a description of the place of games and sports down through the ages. We include excerpts to show this from the earliest known record from China of the origin of several exercises. Next, we consider ancient Greece and the Olympic games and look at the Roman games and their importance in Roman culture. Then we view the medieval wars in England to show the importance of archers and their use of the longbow. Next, we examine the work of a great Italian humanist and educator, Vittorino da Feltre, to illustrate the development of schools and the place of exercise in the Renaissance. In the modern period we consider Jahn's work in Germany, and de Coubertin's description of the revival of the Olympic games. Next, from early America, we present a letter from Benjamin Franklin, which suggests his interest in swimming, and then a resumé of play activities from colonial times. The final selection is a graphic story of a football game, written by the late Grantland Rice, which was chosen to show how games and people really have not changed appreciably from early Grecian days.

The second purpose of the historical section is to illustrate how many ideas about the role of sports have not altered from epoch to epoch. The parallels that can be drawn, for example, between Homer's *Iliad* and the classic piece of Grantland Rice clearly remind us how persistent the problems are between historical periods, however remote. Other recurring historical themes concern the role of the spectator, the roles of amateurism and competition, man's desire for vicarious adventure, and man's effort to increase his social status. These concerns are just as evident at the funeral of Patroclos or in a medieval war as they are at Sunday's double-header today.

We are all products of our past. Whatever we are today is in part a consequence of tradition and past experiences. Even Sir Isaac Newton acknowledged his debt to his predecessors when he said, "I saw what I saw because I stood on the shoulders of giants." No one who would contribute to man's understanding of himself or his universe can deny such indebtedness to his forebears. Essential for any well educated person in any profession is a knowledge of what he owes to those who have gone before him.

N. DALLY

TRANSLATED BY MARVIN E. WEINBERGER

A Treatise on
Chinese Exercise: Cong-fou*

In this selection, Cong-fou is described as the "art of medical gymnastics of the Chinese." It describes the earliest known gymnastics (about 2700 B.C.). Physical therapy, prescribed calisthenics, and even the Western adoption of Yoga may be modern survivals of the Cong-fou. Cong-fou refers not to a person but to an ancient pattern of exercises.

It is anachronistic to describe Cong-fou as Platonic (see Section II). Both Plato and Cong-fou share the same objectives for physical education: the perfection of the self. Even the ancient Chinese dance had a moral and religious purpose. We base this assumption, however, on tertiary and secondary documents. The author of the following article is basing his conclusions partly on a short history of China by a Jesuit priest (Père Jean Joseph Marie Amiot, 1718–1793) who presumably examined and translated the "original" documents on Cong-fou. In addition, we know about the generally religious *Zeitgeist* of the ancient Chinese, and it would seem consistent to represent the primary purpose of Chinese exercises—as they were originally conceived and practiced—as primarily moral in nature. The modern enjoyment of sports and physical development for their own sake would seem alien to this older climate of opinion.

The first time that there is mention, in the annals of China, of a system of movements to conserve health and to cure illnesses, was in prehistoric times. This takes us back to the time of the one hundred families, who were still in Pamir. One reads in the *Short*

* Dally, N., *Cinesiologie au Science du Mouvement*. Paris: Librairie des Sciences Centrale. 1897, pp. 65–83.

Chronology of the Universal History of the Chinese Empire by Father Amiot. (1):

"Yn-Kang-Chi (the second emperor of fou-Hi). In his period, the air was almost always rainy and unhealthy; illness flooded, so to speak, the earth. The Emperor had his subjects do military exercises each day. The movements which they were obliged to do contributed not a little to curing those who were unhealthy and in maintaining the health of those who were in good condition."

The same tradition is also reported in the Research on the Time before Chou-King, by Father de Premare:

Yn-Kang-Chi. In his time, waters were not flowing; rivers followed their ordinary course. This caused much illness. The Emperor instituted dances called Ta-Vou. (Broad reels.)

The Chinese writer who speaks of their tradition states:

"The life of man depends upon the union of the earth and the sky, and upon the usage of all its creatures. A subtle matter circulates in bodies. If, therefore, the body is not in movement, the humors do not flow, matter gathers together, and illness results. All these come from some kind of obstruction."

It is in about the same way that the Greek doctors and philosophers—Hippocrates and Plato—explain the cause of most of the maladies—and modern nosology (classification of diseases) says just about the same thing.

But that which is especially remarkable in the Chinese tradition is that humidity and stagnant water are considered as the source of endemic and epidemic illnesses, and that a good means of preventing these consists in regular exercises of the body or in "turning dances." These movements tend in effect, to produce an effect (*sic*) of the center to the circumference, a centrifugal effect, which is very good for re-animating the functions of the skin, and for giving tone and vigor to the entire economy.

Modern Science does not disavow this doctrine, nor this preservative in similar pathogenic conditions.

These dances were part of the instruction of the Empire.

One also reads in Chou-King that the Emperor Yu, to whom China owes its great canals, tried to bring in good qualities and instigated dances with shields and standards.

These two types of dances were the first consecrated in the *Li-Ki,* or ritual of civil and religious ceremonies.

One can judge a reign, says this holy book, by the dances which are in use.† This shows to what extent ancient China gave importance to regular exercises of the body. Besides, this was also the case in Greece where to sing well and to dance well were the marks of a good education.

This same idea was maintained in China: still today, one notices that no people are more given to exercises which provide the body with the strength and agility of which it is capable.

This general taste of the Chinese for exercises of the body is born from the fundamental principle which, in China, has not ceased to be considered as the basis of all progress, of all moral development: the *Perfection of the Self.*

One reads in the life of Confucius, that this philosopher tried to perfect himself in all exercises.

Thus, the education of the soul and that of the body were, in China, organized into the unity of the human being. There were, therefore, principles and rules which applied themselves to the development of intellectual and body faculties. All this was done in order to conserve for generations a certain integral perfection. We have not been able to discover what these principles and rules are; but the certitude of their existence is seen in the very organization of public education in the Empire.

Among the movements which are in the domain of this method one finds the *massage,* the *friction,* the *pressure,* the *percussion,* the *vibration,* and many other passive movements, whose application,

---

† One can add, said M. Pauthier, that dancing was practiced in all of ancient China. One danced in order to evoke the spirits, one danced when an eclipse came, when a great calamity happened, or a great disaster, when a government officer died. In all the sacrifices to genies, in all civil ceremonies, one gave dances.

Among the most famous, one distinguished: *The Gate to the Clouds, The Grand-Turns;* the *All-Together,* the *Cadence,* one of the most graceful in ancient times, the *Virtuous One* (female), which was slow and serious, the *Benevolent,* the *Great Warrior, etc.*

Among the little dances, there was the dance of the *piece of silk, with many colors,* the *dance with the feather,* the *Phoenix dance,* the *Ox-tail dance,* the *shield dance,* the *man dance,* in which the dancers held no object at all in their hands.

There were also pantomime ballets. These ballets were, for the most part figurative and represented scenes which one finds in the choruses of Ancient Greece: *Work and Labor;* the *Toys of the Harvest,* the *Pleasures of Peace.*

As early as the year 1766 B.C. these ballets had become so licentious that they provoked severe laws.

brought about with intelligence, produces effects which are essentially hygienic and curative.

Now, these different movements have been in usage in China since the most ancient times. One employs them to relax the rigidity of muscles which is caused by fatigue, to relieve spasmodic contractions, rheumatic pains, pains after fractures, and in many cases of plethora of blood in the spot of the wound. These practices have today passed into the habits of the nation; and those who are given to practice them are usually the barbers, as was the custom in Europe in the Middle Ages, or people who walk the streets, advertising their skills to the people by means of musical instruments. Most travelers speak of these people and their salutary effects.

What then is the *cong-fou?*

The Art of Magnetism?

No.

The Cong-fou is the art of medical gymnastics of the Chinese. This word, composed of *Cong,* a worker or artist, and of *fou,* a man, *means a man who works with art.* This word is also used to represent the general idea of *working, bodily movement.* But here, the special meaning conveys the idea of *the art of exercises of the body applied to the treatment of illnesses.*

Let us listen to Father Amiot, who was initiated into this art by a neophyte who had practiced it while he was still a pagan.

"One calls *Cong-fou,*" said the scholarly missionary, "the particular postures in which some *Tao-Sse* hold themselves. Those who have more leisure have more time to practice *Cong-fou,* and they are generally able to understand it better than others."

"The thick clouds of superstition," he said, "and the frightful shadows of idolatry have hidden the true theory of *Cong-fou* from the multitude. It is really an exercise of religion which while curing the body of infirmities, frees the soul and the servitude of the senses; and prepares it (the soul) to enter into a relationship with the Spirits. It opens to it (the soul) some kind of immortality, to which it arrives without passing through the tomb." One could compose whole volumes, fables, stories, reveries, chimera and tall stories about the *Cong-fou.*

By resuming and coordinating these facts we have a general idea of the method of *Cong-fou.*

1. This art is a very ancient practice of medicine, founded on principles which were originally pure and free from all the superstitions which now surround it. It might go back as far as the time when the Priests of Tao formed an official religious caste, that is, at least to the time of Hoang-Ti, about the year 2698 B.C.

2. It consists of three essential parts:

One includes the essential parts of the body.

The other includes the art of changing the attitudes of these parts.

The third explains how, during the time of these positions and attitudes, the act of respiration should be brought about, according to certain rules, by varied inhalations and exhalations.

3. This method has its own scientific vocabulary.

4. It has really produced cures and relieved many illnesses.

5. Finally, all Chinese, no matter what order they belong to, resort immediately to this type of therapy when any other type of cure has been tried in vain.

Thus, the Cong-fou has really all of the characteristics of an ancient scientific method.

"This curious assertion," adds Father Amiot, "is supported by reasons which have caused us to ask physicians and doctors of Europe to find out whether the medical part of the Cong-fou of the Tao-Sse is really a practice of medicine which one can use to relieve and cure some illnesses. If this is the case, it would be well worth the trouble that would be caused for a person in our state, to whom such studies and occupations are so foreign. If we should be wrong in our conjectures, we should have no reason to be embarrassed for our sensitivity and for our attempts to cure the ills that afflict the lives of men. . . ."

Further Readings

EBERHARD, WOLFRAM, *Chinese Festivals*. New York: H. Schumann, 1952.

HU, CH'ANG-TU, ET AL., *China: Its People, Its Society, Its Culture*, edited by Hsiao Hsia. New Haven: Human Relations Area Files Press, 1960.

GOODRICH, LUTHER, *A Short History of the Chinese People*, 3d edition. New York: Harper & Row, Publishers, 1959.

LATOURETTE, K. S., *The Chinese: Their History and Culture,* 3d
edition. New York: The Macmillan Company, 1946.

VAN DALEN, D. B., ELMER MITCHELL and BRUCE BENNETT, *A
World History of Physical Education.* Englewood Cliffs:
Prentice-Hall, Inc., 1953.

WOODY, THOMAS, *Life and Education in Early Societies.* New
York: The Macmillan Company, 1949.

Questions for Discussion

1. For what purposes were Chinese exercises used in 2698 B.C.?
2. What are the similarities between Cong-fou exercises of the
   ancient Chinese and the ones we use today?
3. How do the purposes of dance today differ from its purpose
   in ancient China?

HOMER

The Iliad*

The Ancient Greeks. Although one may find the antiquated
literary style of Homer's *Iliad* perplexing, he should nevertheless see its special relevance to current sports events. This reading includes an interesting description of a chariot race, which
took place at the funeral of Patroclos, Achilles' comrade.

The death of a prominent man drew together all the chiefs
from neighboring cities, and the Greek funeral games provided
the entertainment for these guests. Sports were held at religious
festivals, also, because the crowds demanded some kind of
amusement. In addition to accompanying religious ceremonies
and funerals, sports and games were spontaneously organized
to honor returning heroes. The Greeks used games as divertisse-

* Reprinted with permission of the publisher from *The Iliad,* Book XXIII. Translated by W. H. D. Rouse. Edinburgh and London: Thomas Nelson & Sons, Ltd.,
from the Mentor edition, published by The New American Library of World
Literature, Inc., New York, 1964, pp. 265–282.

ments in the theatre to make the exhibitions more palatable to the common people.

In the next reading note how similar the actions of the crowd, the participants, and the coaches are to the behavior of these groups at games today. Observe the casting of lots for chariot places, just as we do in running races today. Look for the description of gambler's luck, which was very important to the Greeks. Note, too, how the Greeks revered the smart contestant. Contrast Antilochos' father's coaching with examples of coaching today. Observe the significance of planning to win at all costs. Find examples of poor sportsmanship in the false words used to constrain Antilochos.

Among the several prizes set forth for fleetness of foot were a silver mixing bowl and a half talent of gold; these were from the booty the Greeks took from the Trojans. Compare the importance of prizes then with today's attitudes toward rewards for winning.

While the Trojans were mourning within their city, the Achaians made their way to the ships beside the Hellespont. Most of them dispersed to their own vessels, but Achillês would not let the Myrmidons disperse until he had addressed them in these words:

"Your horses have done good service to-day, my brave comrades; but we must not unyoke them yet. Let us go, horses and chariots and all, to mourn for Patroclos, for that is the honour due to the dead. When we have consoled ourselves with lamentation, let us unharness them and take our meal."

Then he led the cavalcade three times round the body, all mourning and crying aloud; and Thetis lamented with them. The sands were drenched with their tears, their armour was drenched, so much their hearts longed for that mighty man. And Peleidês led their lamentations, as he laid his manslaying hands on his true friend's breast:

"Fare thee well, Patroclos, even in the house of death! See now I am fulfilling all that I promised! I said I would drag Hector to this place and give him to the dogs to devour raw; and in front of your pyre I would cut the throats of twelve noble sons of the Trojans, in payment for your death."

Then he did a vile outrage to royal Hector: he stretched the body
on its face in the dirt beside the bier of Menoitiadês.

After that all took off their armour, and unharnessed the loud-
whinnying horses, and sat down beside the ship of Achillês in their
thousands. There he provided a fine funeral feast. Many bellowing
bulls fell under the knife, many sheep and bleating goats; many
tusker boars bursting with fat were stretched out to singe over the
fire. Around the dead body the blood of the victims poured out in
cupfuls was running all over the ground.

Meanwhile Prince Peleion was being led by the Achaian chieftains to Agamemnon. They had trouble to persuade him, so deep
was his sorrow for his comrade. At the King's headquarters orders
were given to set a cauldron of water over the fire, that his body
might be washed clean of the bloodstains, but he flatly refused and
swore to it:

"No, by Zeus highest and greatest of gods! It is not lawful that
water may come near my head, before I lay Patroclos on the fire
and build him a barrow and cut off my hair! For no second sorrow
like this shall come upon me so long as I am among the living. Yet
for this present we must consent to the meal which we hate. Then
to-morrow, my lord King Agamemnon, shall be for bringing firewood and providing all that is proper to send the dead down into
the dark. The fire shall burn him quickly out of sight, and the people shall return to their work."

They did accordingly: the meal was prepared, and all partook
and found no lack. When they were satisfied, the others retired
to rest; but Peleidês lay with many of his Myrmidons, in the open
air on the shore of the sounding sea, while the waves washed on the
beach, lay groaning heavily until sleep fell upon him: a deep
sweet sleep that soothed the sorrows of his heart, for his strong
limbs were weary with that long pursuit after Hector about the
city of Ilios.

In sleep came to him the soul of unhappy Patroclos, his very
image in stature and wearing clothes like his, with his voice and
those lovely eyes. The vision stood by his head and spoke:

"You sleep, Achillês, and you have forgotten me! When I lived
you were not careless of me, but now that I am dead! Bury me without delay, that I may pass the gates of Hadês. Those phantoms hold
me off, the souls of those whose work is done; they will not suffer
me to join them beyond the river, but I wander aimlessly about

the broad gates of the house of Hadês. And give me that hand, I
pray; for never again shall I come back from Hadês when once
you have given me my portion of fire. Never again in life shall we
go apart from our companions and take counsel together; but I am
swallowed up already by that cruel fate which got me on the day
I was born; and you also have your portion, my magnificent
Achillês, to perish before the walls of this great city. One thing
more I say, and I will put it upon you as a charge if you will
comply: do not lay my bones apart from yours, Achillês, but with
them, as I was brought up with you in your home, when Menoitios
brought me quite a little one from Opoeis to your house, for man-
slaughter, the day when I killed Amphidamas' son—I did not mean
it, we had a silly quarrel over the knuckle-bones. Then Peleus received me, and brought me up kindly in his house, and named me
as your attendant. Then let one urn cover my bones with yours,
that golden two-handled urn which your gracious mother gave
you."

Achillês said in answer:

"Why have you come here, beloved one, with all these charges
of this and that? Of course I will do as you tell me every bit. But
come nearer; for one short moment let us lay our arms about each
other and console ourselves with lamentation!"

He stretched out his arms as he spoke, but he could not touch,
for the soul was gone like smoke into the earth, twittering. Achillês
leapt up in amazement and clapt his hands with solemn words:

"See there now! So there is still something in the house of Hadês,
a soul and a phantom but no real life in it at all! For all night long
the soul of unhappy Patroclos has been by my side, sorrowing and
lamenting and telling me what to do. And it was mightily like himself!"

All around were moved to lamentation when they heard his
words.

They were still mourning when Dawn showed her fingers of light.
Then King Agamemnon sent out mules and men from the whole
camp to bring firewood, under the charge of Idomeneus's man
Merionês. The company set out with their axes and ropes, driving
the mules in front: a long journey—upalong downalong offalong
and criss-cross. On the foothills of Mount Ida they felled the tall
trees busily, down came the trees with a crash, the men split them
and tied them on the mules, the mules tore up the earth, hurrying

to the flat land, scrambling through the bushes and over the plain. All the woodcutters had logs to carry, under the orders of Merionês. Down on the shore they laid their logs in order, in the place where Achillês designed a great barrow for Patroclos and himself.

When the logs were laid in their places, the men sat where they were, all together. Then Achillês ordered his Myrmidons to don their armour and harness their horses; they mounted the cars, both fighting men and drivers, chariots in front, a cloud of footmen behind, thousands, and in the midst was Patroclos borne by his comrades. They had cut off their hair and thrown it over the body like a shroud. Achillês came behind him clasping the head; his own unspotted comrade he was escorting to the grave.

At the place which Achillês had appointed, they laid him down and piled great heaps of firewood. Then Achillês did his part. He stood away from the pile, and cut off the golden tress which he had kept uncut among his thick hair for the river Spercheois, and spoke deeply moved as he gazed over the dark sea:

"O Spercheios! this is not for thee! That vow was vain which Peleus my father made,[1] that when I returned to my native land I would consecrate my hair to thee, and make solemn sacrifice, and that he would sacrifice fifty rams without blemish into thy waters, at the altar which is in thy precinct at the same place. That was my father's vow, but thou didst not fulfil his hope. Now therefore, since I am not to return to my native land, I would give the warrior Patroclos this to carry with him."

Then he laid the hair in the hands of his well-loved companion. All present broke into lamentation with all their hearts; and they would not have ceased while the sun shone, but Achillês drew near to Agamemnon and said to him:

"Atreidês, you are our lord paramount, and it is yours to command. There is plenty of time for the people to mourn, but just now I ask you to dismiss them from this place and tell them to get ready their meal. All this is the business of those who are nearest akin to the dead; and let the chieftains remain with us."

Agamemnon accordingly dismissed the people, while the mourners remained, and piled up the wood, and made a pyre of a hundred feet each way, and upon it they laid the body. They killed flocks of sheep and herds of cattle in front of the pyre, skinned

---

[1] A boy kept one part of his hair uncut and this he dedicated to his river-god at puberty: Aeschylus *Choephoroe* 6. Achillês had left home so young that the πλόκαμος θρεπτήριος [sacred piece of hair] was still uncut.

them and cut them up; Achillês took away all the fat, and covered the dead with it from head to foot, and heaped the flayed bodies about him. Jars of honey and oil he placed leaning against the bier. Four horses he laid carefully on the pyre, groaning aloud. Nine dogs the prince had, that fed from his table; two of these Achillês took, and cut their throats and laid beside him. The twelve noble young Trojans he slew without mercy. Then he applied the relentless fire to consume all, and with a groan he called on his comrade's name:

"Fare thee well Patroclos, even in the grave fare thee well! See, I now fulfil all that I promised you before. Here are the twelve noble sons of Trojans—the fire is eating them round about you! Hector Priamidês the fire shall not have to eat, but the dogs!"

But his threat was vain: no dogs were busy about Hector, for the dogs were driven off by the daughter of Zeus, Aphroditê herself, by day and by night. She washed the skin with rose-oil of ambrosia that it might not be torn by the dragging; and Phoibos Apollo drew down a dark cloud from heaven to earth, and covered the place where the body lay, that the sun might not scorch the flesh too soon over the sinews of his limbs.

But the pyre would not burn, and Achillês did not know what to do. At last he stood well away from the smouldering heap, and prayed to North Wind and West Wind promising them good sacrifices; many a libation he poured from his golden goblet, praying them to come and make the wood quickly catch fire, to burn the bodies.

Iris heard his prayers, and flew quickly to the Winds with her message.

They were all in a party at West Wind's, and having a fine feast, when in came Iris flying and stood on the doorstone. As soon as they set eyes on her, up they all jumped and shouted out, every wind of them, "Come and sit by me!" But she said:

"No thank you, no sitting: I'm bound for the Ocean stream. There is a grand sacrifice in the Ethiopian country for us immortals, and I want to have some too. But Achillês is praying to North Wind and West Wind; he wants them to come and promises a good sacrifice. He wants them to make the pyre burn, where Patroclos lies with the people all mourning around."

Her message given, away she flew, and the Winds rose with a devil of a noise and drove the clouds in a riot before them. They swooped upon the sea and raised the billows under their whistling blasts; they reached the Trojan coast and fell on the pyre till the flames roared again. All night long they beat upon the fire together blowing and whistling; all night long stood Achillês holding his goblet, and dipt into the golden mixer, and poured the wine on the ground, till the place was soaked, calling upon the soul of unhappy Patroclos. As a father laments while he burns the bones of his own son, newly wedded and now dead, to the grief of his bereaved parents, so Achillês lamented as he burnt the bones of Patroclos, stumbling up and down beside the pyre with sobbings and groanings.

But at the time when the morning star goes forth to tell that light is coming over the earth, and after him the saffron mantle of Dawn spreads over the sea, at that hour the flame died down and the burning faded away. Then the Winds returned over the Thracian gulf to their home, while the waters rose and roared.

And then Achillês moved away from the pyre, and sank upon the ground tired out: sleep leapt upon him and gave him peace.

Now the people were all gathering round Agamemnon. They made such noise and uproar that Achillês sat up and said:

"Atreidês, and you other princes, you must first quench the pyre with wine wherever the flames have touched. Then let us gather the bones of Patroclos Menoitidês, and be careful to find the right ones. They are easy to know, for he lay right in the middle and the others were on the edge, horses and men together. His bones we must wrap in a double layer of fat and lay them in a golden urn, until I myself shall be hidden in Hadês. But I do not wish any great mound to be raised for him, only just a decent one. Afterwards another can be raised both broad and high, by those of you who are left behind me."

They did his bidding at once. First they quenched the pyre with wine wherever it had burnt and the ashes were deep; then weeping they gathered the bones of their gentle companion, and laid them covered with fat in a golden urn, which they wrapt up in fine linen and put away safely in the hut. Round the pyre they set up a circle of stone slabs to mark the outside limit, and shovelled earth within.

As they were about to go after finishing this task, Achillês told them to stop, and made them sit in a ring while he sent back for prizes: cauldrons and tripods, horses and mules and fine cattle, women also and grey steel.

For the chariot-race he offered as first prize a woman skilled in women's work, and a tripod of two-and-twenty measures with handles to it. The second prize was a mare, a six-year-old unbroken, heavy with a mule-foal. The third was a cauldron of four measures, brand-new and still white. The fourth, two ingots of gold, and the fifth a brand-new basin with handles. Then he rose to his feet and addressed them:

"My lord King, and gentlemen all, here are prizes ready for the charioteers. If our contests were held in honour of any other I should be sure of carrying home the first prize, since you know how much the best my horses are; for they are immortal—Poseidon himself gave them to Peleus my father, and he lent them to me. But let me say that I and my horses will not come forward. Think of the glorious driver they have lost, how kind he was! How often he would wash their manes in pure water and pour soft oil upon them; and now they stand trailing their manes in the dust and mourning him, now they stand with sorrow in their hearts. The course is open to all the rest of you, whoever believes in his horses and car."

The competitors quickly came up, and first by a long way Eumelos Admetos' son, who was well known for horsemanship. Next came Diomedês Tydeidês, driving the two horses of Tros which he had taken from Aineias (when Apollo saved the man). Next King Menelaos Atreidês with a pair of quick goers, Agamemnon's mare, Sunshine Aithê, and his own horse Whitefoot Podargos. Agamemnon's mare was the gift of Echepolos Anchisiadês,[2] a very rich man who lived in Sicyon, which he offered because he wanted to stay at home happy instead of going to war. The mare was eager for the race. Antilochos was the fourth who brought a team. This was the son of Nestor Neleiadês, and the horses were Pylos-bred. As he was getting ready Nestor took the opportunity to give him some advice (although he was quite able to do without it), and this is what he said:

"Zeus and Poseidon were very kind to you, Antilochos, when you were quite young, and they taught you all the art of horsemanship. Then I don't think there is much need to teach you anything, for you know well how to wheel round the post. But your horses are the slowest of all, and so I fear you will find it

[2] Son of Anchises of Sicyon, not the Anchises of Troy. The old Greek annotator remarks, "The King preferred a good warhorse to a conscientious objector."

a bad job. Their horses are faster, true, but the men could not
be more knowing than you are. Well then, dear boy, rub up
every trick you can think of, or the prizes will give you the slip
and out of sight! The tricks of the trade—and a woodman's
made! He does not depend on brute force. The tricks of the trade—
and a pilot's made! The winds may blow but on he'll go. And
the tricks of the trade make driver beat driver. One man leaves
everything to horses and car, wheels wide to this side or that side
carelessly, the horses go roaming over the course, he does not
hold them in hand; but he that knows his tricks may have inferior horses to drive—yet he keeps his eye always on the post,
wheels close in, does not forget how much to stretch the horses
at first by the handling of the reins, but keeps them well in hand
and watches the man in front.

"Now I will tell you the mark—you can't miss it. There's a
dry stump at the turn of the road standing about a fathom above
the soil, oak or fir, which does not rot in the rain. Two white
stones are set against it, one on each side, and the land round
this is smooth for horses. It may be the mark of some man dead
long ago, or set up for a post in former days, and now Achillês
has fixed it for the turning-point of his race. Drive your car
close almost grazing the post, and yourself in the basket lean
gently to the left: give the goad to the off horse with a call and
let him have rein. Let the near horse almost graze the post, so
that the nave of the wheel seems almost to touch the surface of
the stone, but do not let it touch or you may wreck the car
and damage the horses. That will be a disgrace to you and a
pleasure to the others! But my dear boy, keep your head and
be careful, for if at the turning-post you can cut in and get
round in front, no man alive could catch you by a spurt or
pass you, even if he were driving Arion, Adrastos' divine thoro-
bred racer, or some of Laomedon's fine stock from this part of
the world."[3]

Then Nestor returned to his seat, after telling his son all the
ins and outs of the matter.

Merionês was the fifth.

When they were all ready, they mounted their cars and threw
in their lots. Achillês shook them, and the lot of Antilochos

[3] Of course the cars had to make a loop about the post. The cars were put in a line
at scratch, and the best place was on the left hand.

leapt out, next came Eumelos, after him Menalaos Atreidês, then Merionês, and last the best of them all got his place, Tydeidês. They took stand in a row, and Achillês showed them the turning-point in the distant plain. He posted his father's man Phoinix as umpire, to keep an eye on the running and report what happened.

They were all off together at once, whipping up the horses, flicking them with the reins, crying them on furiously: the ships were left behind, and away they galloped—their manes went flying on the wind and clouds of dust rose under their bodies. The cars now ran steady, now bounded high; the drivers stood in their baskets with hearts beating high in hope. Every man called to his horses, and the horses flew over the ground.

But when they had turned back seawards on the return course, then indeed each horse showed his mettle, then indeed they forced the pace. At once Eumelos' mares took the lead, followed by the stallions of Diomedês, the famous breed of Tros—not far behind, indeed quite close—they seemed ever on the point of trampling on Eumelos' car, and their breath warmed his back and shoulders as their heads leaned over his body.

And now Diomedês would have passed, or at least made a dead heat, if Apollo had not been annoyed at his success; so he knocked the whip out of his hand. Tears of anger filled his eyes, as he saw the mares going better than ever and his own team slackening without the prick.[4] But Apollo's cheating did not escape the eye of Athena: she picked up the whip and gave it back, encouraged the horses, ran after Eumelos furious and broke the yoke of his chariot. His horses ran away off the road, and the pole was left dragging on the ground[5]; the driver was rolled out over the wheel, and barked his elbows and mouth and nose and bruised his fore-head. Tears filled his eyes, he choked, and could not utter a word.

Tydeidês kept his team in hand and cleared them, galloping now far in front of the others, for Athena put spirit into the horses and made him win. After him came Menelaos; but Antilochos who was next shouted to his pair:

"Go it, you two! Pull away—there's no time to waste! I don't ask you to beat that pair in front; Athena has made them go like that, and she will make him win. But do catch up Atreidês, don't let his horses beat you. What a shame—let a mare beat a

---

[4] The whip was probably a long pliant rod with spurs at the end.
[5] They were fastened by the yoke only without traces.

pair of stallions! Why are you behind, my brave boys? I tell you
plainly and I shan't forget—there will be no more fodder for
you in Nestor's stable, he will just cut your throats at once if we
make poor sport by carelessness! After him—put on a spurt! I know
what to do—I'll head past him at the narrow way, he shan't escape me!"

They were fairly terrified by their master's shouts, and put
on a spurt for a short time until Antilochos saw the narrows.
The road here led through a gulley, and in one part the winter
flood had broken down part of the road and made a hollow.
Menelaos was driving in the middle of the road, hoping that no
one would try to pass too close to his wheel, but Antilochos turned
his horses out of the track and followed a little to one side. This
frightened Menelaos, and he shouted at him:

"What reckless driving, Antilochos! Hold in your horses. This
place is narrow, soon you will have more room to pass. You'll
foul my car and destroy us both!"

But Antilochos only plied the whip and drove faster than ever,
as if he did not hear. They raced about as far as the cast of a
quoit swung from the shoulder of a lusty young man who tries what
he can do, and then Atreidês fell behind: he let the horses go
slow himself, for he was afraid they might all collide in that narrow space and overturn the cars and fall in a struggling heap.
But he shouted angrily:

"That was a nasty trick, Antilochos! Damn you, why do we
say that Antilochos always plays the game! Far from it! Still
you shan't get your prize without taking your oath."[6]

Then he called to the horses:

"Now then, don't be slack, don't stand still there! It's hard
on you of course—but you'll see, their feet and joints will fail
before yours. Their young days are behind them!"

The horses took the hint and put on pace, until they caught up
the others.

Meanwhile the crowd were looking out for the horses. Soon
they came flying along in clouds of dust. Idomeneus the Cretan
prince was the first to see them: he was sitting away from the
rest on high ground. He heard a shout and knew the man's

---

[6] He must swear an oath that he had played fair.

voice, then he made out a horse clear in front; he was roan so far as he could see with a white full-moon on his forehead. He stood up and shouted to the spectators:

"Hallo, my lords and gentlemen! I spy horses—can you see them too? Another team appears to be in front, looks like another driver. The mares must have come to grief somewhere on the plain, but they were leading on the way out. I certainly saw them first at the turning, and now I can't see them at all—I have looked hard over the whole plain. Did he lose his reins, couldn't hold them and failed at the turn? That's it, I think he was thrown out and wrecked his car and the horses ran away at their own sweet will. Do get up and have a look too—I can't see clearly, but he seems to be that Aitolian prince, you know who, he has the city in Argos—Diomedês Tydeidês."

Aias Oïleus' son laughed scornfully and said:

"Cataracts of talk as usual, Idomeneus. There are the mares yonder, the old high-stepping racers! You are not the youngest man in the army so much as all that, those eyes in your head are not so much the sharpest of the whole nation. But always cataracts of words; you really should not be such a cataractorator before your betters. The same mares are leading that led before, and the same Eumelos holding the ribbons."

This brought an angry reply from Idomeneus:

"Quarrels are your best line, Aias, for you have not much sense, and for anything else we can all beat you easily. You are a stubborn one! Come along now—let us bet a tripod or a cauldron which team is first, and the umpire shall be my lord Agamemnon! You will learn something when you pay up."

Then Aias the Runner jumped up to make a retort with more angry words, and the quarrel would have gone on, but Achillês stopt them by saying:

"Don't abuse each other like that, you two, Idomeneus and Aias. It is quite out of place here. You would be the first to reprove any one else who did that kind of thing. Sit down in your places and see what happens. They will soon be here themselves, and then every one will know who is first and who is second."

While he spoke Tydeidês had come quite near, at the gallop, plying his whip down from the shoulder, and the horses were bounding along at full speed, kicking up clouds of dust over

their driver, and the car with its gold and tin plates gleaming
rolled behind: the tires left hardly a trace in the light dust, so
quickly they flew.—And now he was there, in front of them, the
sweat dripping from the horses' heads and chests! He leapt
down from the car and leant the whip against the yoke. Nor was
Sthenelos behindhand. He ran up and took the prize, and then
loosed the horses; the woman and the tripod were taken in
charge by his comrades.

Next Antilochos drove in, after beating Menelaos, by trick
not by merit; even so Menelaos was close behind, as near as a
horse to the wheel when he trundles his master along at full
speed—the tip of the tail touches the tire. That is pretty close,
there is not much space between! Menelaos had got as near as
that, and when he began there was a quoit's throw between them;
but Menelaos soon caught up, for Agamemnon's mare Sunshine
was in great form, and if the course had been longer she would
have passed and left no doubt as to the winner.

But Merionês was a spear's throw behind Menelaos, for his
horses were slowest of all and he was the worst driver for a race.

Eumelos came in last of all, dragging his car behind and driving the horses in front. Achillês was very sorry for him and made
no secret of his feelings:

"The best man comes last," he said, "but let us give him a
prize, as he deserves. He shall have the second, but Diomedês
must have the first."

There was a cheer at this, and he would have given him the
mare with general approval, but Antilochos Nestorides pleaded
his claim before Achillês Peleidês.

"Achillês, I shall strongly resent it if you do what you have
said. For you intend to rob me of my prize, and your only reason is that his horses and car came to grief, and himself too
though he is such a good man. Well, he ought to have made his
prayers to heaven, and then he would never have come in last
at all. If you are sorry for him and want to show your friendship, there is plenty in your quarters—there is gold, there is
bronze and sheep, there are captive women and horses: take
some of that and give him even a bigger prize by and by, or
even now, that every one may be pleased. But the mare I will
not give up. If any one wants it let him fight me for it."

Achillês smiled, for Antilochos was his very good friend and he was delighted with him. He answered:

"Very well, Antilochos, if you say I am to fetch out something more to give Eumelos, I certainly will. He shall have the corselet I took from Asteropaios, bronze with a slip of tin running round it. That will be a treasure for him!"

He directed Automedon to fetch it out from the hut. Automedon did so, and handed to it Eumelos, who received it with satisfaction.

And now Menelaos rose in high dudgeon, for he had not forgiven Antilochos. The herald placed the staff in his hand and called silence, and Menelaos proceeded to speak.

"Antilochos," he said, "you were always one for fair play, and now see what you have done: you have disgraced my reputation, and fouled my horses by throwing yours in front, when yours were not nearly so good.

"I appeal to you, my lords and gentlemen. Judge between us without favour, that no one may ever say—'Menelaos compelled Antilochos to give way by false evidence; he leads away the mare, because he is superior in dignity and power, although his horses were not nearly so good.' Or look here, I will decide the matter myself, and I don't think any man will ever reproach me, for it shall be justice.

"Come this way, Antilochos, my young prince, and observe the custom. Stand before your chariot and horses, and take in your hand the whip that you had in the race, lay your hand on the horses and swear by Earthholder Earthshaker that you did not foul my chariot with malice aforethought."

Antilochos, once more the man of fair play, made answer:

"Bear with me now, for I am much younger than you, my lord Menelaos; you are my elder and my better. You know that a young man always goes too far. His mind is too hasty, his wits are flighty. Then let your heart forgive me. I will give up to you willingly the horse I won. And if you demand something of my own besides, something greater, I will give it at once rather than be out of favour with you, my prince, all my days, and offend against heaven besides."

Then he led up the mare and gave her over to Menelaos; and the prince's heart was warmed, like growing corn with the dew upon the ears when the fields are bristling—so, Menelaos, your heart warmed within you!—And he said simply:

"Now, Antilochos, I will put away my anger gladly, for you were never perverse or light-minded before. Just for once boydom was too much for wisdom. Another time don't try to overreach your betters. Not every one, let me tell you, could have made me change my mind; but you indeed have suffered much and worked hard for my sake, and so have your excellent father and brother. Then I will grant your petition; and I will make you a present of the mare, which is my own, that all these here may know that my temper is not tyrannical and harsh."

So saying he gave Noëmon the mare to lead away, and took the cauldron himself.

Merionês took the two ingots of gold in the fourth place, as he came in fourth. The fifth prize was left over, the two-handled bowl; this Achillês carried through the company and gave it to Nestor, saying:

"Here, venerable prince, you shall have something too; let it be a treasure for you in memory of the burying of Patroclos. For you will see him no more in this world. I give you this prize for nothing: you will not box for it, or wrestle, or cast a javelin, or run a race. Already the years are heavy upon you."

He placed the bowl in Nestor's hands, and Nestor received it with pleasure and said with great simplicity:

"Aye, aye, my boy, that's true enough. My joints are not what they were, my dear boy, nor my feet, my hands do not shoot out from the shoulders right and left, touch and go! Ah, if I were young and strong as I was once, when the Epeians were burying my lord Amarynceus in Buprasion, and his sons set up prizes in the King's honour! There wasn't a man to match me, not an Epeian, not a Pylian, not an Aitolian of them all! In boxing I beat Clytomedês Enops' son, in wrestling Pleuronian Ancaios who stood up to me, I outran Iphiclos though he was a good man, with spear I overshot both Phyleus and Polydoros. I only lost with the horses. There the two Actorions beat me by force of numbers! They coveted victory because the biggest prizes were waiting. They were doubles, one took the reins and went bowling along, bowling along, one talked to 'em with the whip.[7]

---

[7] Twins, joined in one body. Thus they were "two to one," and they had four arms, two to drive and two to whip, which was not fair.

"Ah yes, once! that's what I was. Now it's the turn of younger men, let them tackle such tasks. Old age is my master now, worse luck, but then I was high among the heroes. Now go ahead, there's your comrade to honour with games like the others. This gift I accept with grateful thanks, and it does my heart good that you remember me your affectionate friend, and you do not forget the honour which is my due among our people. May the gods reward you according to your desire."

Peleidês listened to all the praises of the grand old man, and returned through the throng of spectators to his place.

Next he displayed the prizes for boxing. A hard battle that is! And the prize was a much-enduring mule, a six-year-old yet unbroken, the hardest age to break. The prize for the loser was a two handled goblet. Achillês rose in his place and said:

"Prince Atreidês and gentlemen all, we invite the two best men to put up their hands and box for these prizes. He to whom Apollo shall grant endurance before the face of the whole nation, shall lead away to his quarters this much-enduring mule; and the loser shall carry off this two-handled bowl."

At once a fine big man came forward, Epeios Panopeus' son, a good boxer. He laid a hand on the mule and said:

"This way for any one who wants the bowl! For the mule, no one else shall have it, for no one will beat me in the ring. There I claim to be the best man. I lack something in the battlefield, and is not that bad enough? A fellow can't be number one in every kind of work that's done—that is quite true. I tell you plainly and I will make good my words: let him come on—I'll tear his flesh and smash his bones to a pulp. He had better bring his friends and relations in a body to carry him out when I've done with him."

A dead silence followed these words. At last one man Euryalos rose alone, a splendid fellow; he was the son of my lord Longman Standfastson,[8] who came to Thebes for the funeral of Oidipus after he took his deadly dump, and there beat all the Cadmeians. Tydeidês got him ready. He put on his belt, gave him the gloves of good oxhide straps, cheered him up, and wished him luck.

The two men stept forward girt into the ring and put up their hands. They they fell to it with stout fisticuffs, lead and parry. You might hear their teeth gnashing, and the sweat poured

---

[8] Mekisteus Talaïonidês, a genuine name used with comic effect.

from their bodies! Euryalos watched warily for an opening, but
at last Epeios landed him one on the jaw and he did not stand
long after that. He was knocked clean off his feet and lifted into
the air, curving like a great fish that leaps out of the shallows
off the seaweed and through the ripples when Boreas blows, and
into the dark waves again. So he came down, but his generous
adversary helped him up, and his friends were ready to lead him
away, dragging his legs and spitting blood and drooping his head
to one side. So they led him away dazed and fainting, and came
back for the two-handled bowl.

Without delay Peleidês displayed the third set of prizes, for
the wrestling—and a hard bout that is! He showed the prizes
all round. For the winner, a large tripod to stand on the fire,
which the spectators valued at twelve oxen. For the loser, he
brought out a woman well skilled in women's work, valued at
four oxen. Then he stood up and said:

"Rise any who wish to compete for this prize."

Up rose that large man Telamonian Aias; up rose Odysseus,
the man who was never at a loss, who knew all the tricks of the
game. They girt them and stood forth into the ring, and their
strong arms took hold of one another with close grip. Their
bodies looked like a pair of baulks which a builder leans together to hold up a high roof. Their backs creaked as the hard
hands pulled steadily; drops of sweat came out, bleed-red weals
began to show on ribs and shoulders. Hard was the struggle for
that fine tripod; but Odysseus could not bring his man down, nor
could Aias, for Odysseus was too strong.

As the spectators began to be bored by this, the large man
Aias said to his adversary:

"Prince Laërtiadês, Odysseus never-failing! Either lift me, or
I will lift you, and as to the rest Zeus will provide!"

As he spoke, he lifted, but Odysseus knew the trick. He
knocked him behind the knee so that his leg gave way and threw
him backwards; Odysseus fell on his chest, to the admiration of
all. Then Odysseus took his turn and tried to lift Aias, but he
could not do it, only moved him a little from the ground. So
he hooked his knee round and both fell together in the dirt. Then
they would have tried for the third throw, but Achillês rose and
stopt them.

"That is enough," said he, "don't tire yourselves out. I declare both men winners. Receive equal prizes, and let us go on to the next event."

They were quite willing, wiped off the dust and put on their tunics.

Achillês now brought out prizes for the footrace. There was a silver mixing-bowl finely wrought, holding six measures. It was the most beautiful bowl in the world, for it was the work of Sidonian artists, and Phoenician merchants had brought it over the sea to the harbour of Lemnos and given it to Thoas as a gift; his grandson Euneos Iasonidês gave it to Patroclos as the price of Lycaon. This bowl Achillês offered as first prize, for the second a great fat ox, and for the last a half-nugget of gold. Then he got up and said:

"Rise any who wish to run for this prize."

Aias the Runner rose, Odysseus rose, then Nestor's son, Antilochos, for he was the best runner among the young men. They stood in a row, and Achillês pointed out the goal. The pace was forced from the start, but before long Aias was leading with Odysseus close behind him, close as the weaver holds the crossbeam to her breast while she pulls the spool across the warp— Odysseus trod in his footsteps before the dust had time to settle, and the breadth of Odysseus beat on his head as he ran; the spectators cheered his efforts, but he was doing his very best already. When they came to the last bit of the course Odysseus offered a silent prayer to Athenaia:

"Hear me, my goddess, give thy good help to my feet!"

Pallas Athena heard and made his limbs light, the feet and hands on him. And when they were just on the point to pounce on the prize, Athena tript Aias and made him slip, where the place was covered with offal from the beasts which Achillês had butchered in honour of Patroclos; and down he went, got mouth and nostrils full of the stuff. So Odysseus came in first and lifted the mixing-bowl, and then Aias took hold of the ox. As he stood holding the animal's horn and spitting out the dirt, he said:

"Damn it, that goddess tript me up! She's always by his side like a mother and helps him!"

All burst into a roar of laughter. Antilochos carried off the last prize smiling, and he said to the people:

"You know it quite well, my friends, but I will repeat it: The saying now is true agen, the immortals honour older men. Aias is a little older than I am, but this Odysseus is one of the ancient generation—a green old age is his, as they say. Yet it would be a hard job for any of us to beat him in running, except only Achillês."

So he ended with a compliment to Achillês, and Achillês responded:

"Thanks, Antilochos, your kind words shall not be said in vain. I will add half a nugget of gold to your prize."

He placed it in his hands as he spoke, and Antilochos received it with satisfaction.

Now Achillês brought out the armour of Sarpedon which Patroclos had taken in the field—the long spear and the shield and helmet, and said:

"We invite the two best men to contend for these. Let them arm themselves and take their blades, and try one another before us. Whichever shall first pierce through the armour to what is within and touch the flesh and draw blood, to him I will give this fine Thracian sword silver-bossed which I took from Asteropaios, but the armour both shall hold together; and we will make a good feast to entertain them."

At this invitation up rose Telamonian Aias, up rose Diomedês Tydeidês; and both donned their armour in the rear. Then they came forward to confront each other glaring terribly, to the admiration of all. They drew close—thrice they charged, thrice they attacked, then Aias pierced the buckler: but he did not reach the flesh, for the corselet held the blow. But Tydeidês reached over the great shield and touched the neck with his blade again and again. Then the people were afraid for Aias; they called them to stop and share the prize. But Achillês gave Diomedês the sword with sheath and sling.

Again Achillês brought out a lump of roughcast iron which that mighty man Eëtion used to hurl. When he killed Eëtion, he brought it away with the rest of the spoils. He rose now and said:

"Rise, you who wish to contend for this prize. Any man will have enough here to use for five revolving years, even if his fat fields are far away. No shepherd or plowman will need to visit the city for iron, there will be plenty at home."

At this challenge up rose that redoubtable warrior Polypoitês, up rose Leonteus the strong man, up rose Aias Telamoniadês and prince Epeios. They stood in a row, and Epeios took up the weight, circled it round his head and put it, and the people roared with laughter. Next to put the weight was Leonteus, that veritable sprig of Arês; third Telamonian Aias lifted it and hurled it. The cast from that strong man went beyond the others. But when Polypoitês raised the lump, he threw it as far beyond all the others as a herdsman sends his cudgel flying over the herds of cattle. There was a loud cheer, and his companions got up and carried away the prize to their camp.

Next for the archers Achillês brought forward blue steel—ten axes and ten half-axes.[9] Away on the sand he sat up a ship's mast, with a rockdove tied to the top by a string round its leg. He told them to shoot at this: "Whoever hits the dove shall have all the axes to take home; whoever misses the dove but hits the string shall have the half-axes."

Then up rose prince Teucros, and up rose Merionês that excellent servant of Idomeneus. They shook their lots in a helmet, and Teucros won first shot. He let fly at once a strong shot, but he forgot to vow that he would make due sacrifice of firstling lambs to the Lord. So he missed the dove, since Apollo grudged that to him, he cut through the string close to the bird's foot. Away flew the bird into the sky, and the string fell to the ground amid the cheers of the people. But Merionês instantly snatched the bow from his hand—his arrow had been ready in hand while Teucros aimed. He vowed quickly that he would make due sacrifice of firstling lambs to Apollo Shootafar. High in the clouds he could see the dove: there he shot her under the wing as she circled round. The arrow went right through, and fell down before the feet of Merionês, and stuck in the ground; but the dove settled on the pole, head hanging and wings drooping. Then the life left her, and she fell away from the pole, to the amazement of all who saw it. Merionês took away the ten axes, and Teucros had the half-axes.

9 "Dark violet-coloured iron" suggests tempered steel. If the meaning is axes made of this metal, possibly half-axes with one blade. But scholiasts tell us that "axe" meant a certain weight of iron. The axe may have been a sort of currency, when there was no coinage, and the name may have been transferred to a given weight. See Ridgeway, *Origin of Coin and Weight Standards*, 40; Rouse, *Greek Votive Offerings*, 389.

Again Peleidês brought out a long spear, and a brand-new cauldron ornamented with flowers, worth one ox; and the spear-throwers came forward. Up rose my lord King Agamemnon, up rose Merionês, the excellent servant of Idomeneus. But Achillês had something to say:

"My lord King, we know how high you are exalted above all, and how you are best in strength and in casting of spears. Very well, pray accept this prize and take it with you; but let us offer the spear to Merionês, if you approve; at least that is what I should like."

My lord King Agamemnon was content. He gave the spear to Merionês, and gave the prize into the hands of Talthybios his herald.

Further Readings

BOWRA, SIR CECIL MAURICE, *Homer and His Forerunners.* Edinburgh: Thomas Nelson and Sons, 1955.

FORBES, CLARENCE A., *Greek Physical Education.* New York: Appleton-Century-Crofts, 1929.

FORSDYKE, SIR EDGAR JOHN, *Greece Before Homer.* London: M. Parrish, 1956.

HADAS, MOSES, *Humanism: The Greek Ideal and Its Survival.* New York: Harper & Row, Publishers, 1960.

MIREAUX, EMILE, *Daily Life in the Time of Homer,* translated by Iris Sells. New York: The Macmillan Company, 1959.

ROBINSON, RACHEL SARGENT, *Sources for the History of Greek Athletics.* Ann Arbor, Mich.: Cushing-Malloy, Inc., 1955.

TOYNBEE, ARNOLD J., *Greek Civilization and Character.* New York: New American Library of World Literature, Inc., 1961.

Questions for Discussion

1. What persistent problems of athletic competition do you see in this tale?
2. Could this piece be used by prospective teachers to delineate some precepts for today's physical education programs? If so, which ones?

3. What is the significance of the "draw" in the wrestling match?
4. What was the category of games suggested by Nestor?
5. How do Nestor's words of advice remind you of the last-minute admonitions of a football coach today?
6. What are some examples of poor sportsmanship described in the chariot race?

E. NORMAN GARDINER

The Olympic Festival*

During the Homeric Age, the Delphian, Isthmian, Nemean, and Olympic games were held periodically. We have chosen to include a description of the Olympic games because they alone have survived.

The contests between city-states in Greece had their origin in formal, religious ceremony. They brought about a feeling of mutual brotherhood in the same way that public interest is engendered by the World Series in the United States. All wars between Greek cities and fighting among the Greek tribes ceased during the games, and, therefore, they became symbols of peace and Greek solidarity against the non-Greeks, all of whom the Greeks called "barbarians." With the decline of Greek political and economic power, the significance and excellence of the games changed as well.

The following selection depicts the Olympic festival which, according to tradition, had its beginning in 776 B.C. These ancient games continued to be held every four years. An early Christian Roman Emperor, Theodosius I, cancelled the games in 394 A.D. because they connoted the pagan past and had become almost wholly mercenary.

The Hellanodikai mentioned throughout this article supervised the preliminary training of participants in the Olympic

---

* Reprinted abridged and without footnotes by permission of the publisher from E. Norman Gardiner, *Olympia: Its History and Remains.* Oxford: The Clarendon Press, 1925, pp. 300–311. Textual omissions are shown by ellipsis marks.

games. They received reports of the contestants and verified
their country of origin and identification. Non-Greeks were rejected. The participants strictly observed the training rules.
This was in deference to the gods, for their performance was
an offering to these gods, and they wanted to curry favor by
doing as well as possible.

Note the recurrent significance of the religious meaning of
the Olympic festival. Observe, especially, sportsmanship's possible origins in ethics. These can be traced to the oath sworn
by contestants that no unfair means would be used during the
games.

N o work on Olympia would be complete without some account
of the festival itself. Yet to describe it is no easy task. Our information is fragmentary, derived from various periods, many of them
late, and the details are often obscure and disputed. Here I can
only attempt to describe it such as it appears to me to have been
in the middle of the fifth century, the most glorious period in the
history of Olympia.

Some months before the date of the festival the 'heralds of the
seasons, the truce-bearers of Zeus', left Elis. East and west they
travelled, and in every state they were welcomed. The magistrates
received them in the Prytaneion, and there on the Hearth of the
city they poured libation, proclaimed the Sacred Truce, and invited
the citizens to join in the festival. From that time the territory of
Elis was sacrosanct, none might bear arms within it, and whatever
wars were going on there was safe-conduct for all who travelled to
Olympia whether as private citizens or as representatives of the
states.

A month or more before the festival athletes and trainers, chariots and horses, owners and jockeys, began to gather at Elis. Competitors, it seems, had to give in their names a month beforehand,
and there, under the eyes of the Hellanodikai, they underwent their
last month's training. The training was especially severe, and the
Hellanodikai enforced their orders by means of the rod. This
month was a very valuable time for these officials. In it they had
the opportunity of testing the competitors, rejecting the unfit,
satisfying themselves of their parentage and right to compete, above
all of judging the claims of boys and colts to compete in these

classes. A few days before the festival the whole company of officials and competitors left Elis for Olympia. The procession followed the sacred road along the coast to the fountain of Piera, the boundary of Elis and Pisatis. There they halted and performed certain rites of lustration. They passed the night at Letrinoi and the next day made their entrance to Olympia.

Meanwhile crowds were gathering at Olympia. Along the coastal road from the gulf of Corinth poured a constant stream of visitors of every class, driving, riding, or on foot. Conspicuous among them were the state embassies, each striving to outdo the others. Up the Alpheios rowed barges bringing splendid equipages from the princes [the Greeks of Magna Graecia] of Italy and Sicily. Along every valley and over every pass came the hardy peasants from the Peloponnese. Some came from love of sport or to see their friends compete, others for profit or advertisement. There were princes and politicians, philosophers and rhetoricians, poets and sculptors, merchants and horse-breeders from Elis, and with them all the crowd of those who catered for the needs of the assembly, peasants loaded with wine-skins and baskets of fruit or fish, shepherds driving in victims for the sacrifices, vendors of wreaths and fillets, of amulets and votive offerings, tumblers, acrobats, mountebanks. Outside the Altis the plain was full of tents and hastily constructed booths, but for most of the crowd there was no shelter and they had to sleep under the open sky or in the corridors.

The festival lasted five days, from the 12th to the 16th of the month. The first day was given up to preliminary business. The chief event was the final scrutiny of competitors in the Bouleuterion. Between the two wings of this building stood the Altar of Zeus Horkios. In either hand he held a thunderbolt as a warning to evil doers. Before this awe-inspiring statue competitors, their fathers, brothers, and trainers took their stand. A pig was sacrificed, and with uplifted hand they swore that they would use no unfair means in the coming games. The competitors themselves further swore that for ten months they had strictly observed the rules of training. Next the judges, whose duty it was to decide on the claims of boys to compete as such, swore to give their decision justly and without bribes, and not to reveal the reasons of their judgement. Not till then could the final list of entries be made out. The heats and ties were drawn, the order of the runners was settled, and the names perhaps were pasted on a white board.

On this as on the other days there were various sacrifices both public and private, but of these little is known. The daily sacrifice to Zeus of course was duly offered, and we can hardly doubt that on this opening day special sacrifices were offered at the six double altars. In the evening of this day, or possibly of the day before, an offering of blood was poured on the mound of Pelops. The competitors, too, and their friends, would offer their vows and sacrifices to gods and heroes whose favour they hoped to win, and would try to obtain from the seers and soothsayers some omen of success. Some perhaps would go off to the Stadion for a last practice. Everywhere crowds followed them. But there were other attractions than the athletes. There were the temples and treasuries to be seen, the monuments and statues. In the opisthodome of the temple were orators, philosophers, poets to be heard. Elsewhere there were sculptors and painters exhibiting their works, and for the common folk the booths around the Agora provided all the attractions of a fair.

On the second day the games began. First came the chariot race. Early in the morning the low embankments of the Hippodrome were filled with an eager crowd who occupied every point of vantage, especially at the ends facing the pillars round which the chariots turned. Meanwhile the procession had been marshalled, probably at the Prytaneion. First came the Hellanodikai robed in purple with garlands on their heads, the herald, trumpeter, and other officials, then the competitors, the chariots, and the horses. Skirting the Altis they entered the Hippodrome at the west end by the Porch of Agnaptos. As the competitors passed before the spectators the herald proclaimed each man's name, the name of his father and of his city, and asked if any man had any charge to bring against them. Then in solemn terms he proclaimed the opening of the games, and the chief Hellanodikas or some other distinguished person addressed the competitors.

Now all was ready and the chariots took their places in the stalls along either side of the aphesis, their places being assigned by lot. Then the trumpet sounded, the ropes in front of each pair of chariots were withdrawn, and they moved forward slowly till they were level with the beak of the aphesis. Then from the altar in the centre a golden eagle rose, and the dolphin at the beak dropped and the race began. The fields were large, sometimes as many as forty, but the race was long, twelve times the length of the double course, 72 stades or nearly 9 miles, and the pace must have been slow at first. Yet even so the excitement must have been intense from start to finish. For the chariots had to negotiate twenty-three turns round the pillars, and skilful driving was sorely needed to avoid losing ground at the turn and to avoid collisions. Accidents were frequent, as we know from the *Elektra* of Sophokles. There in a field of ten only one reached the goal in safety, and Pindar tells us that Arkesilas of Kyrene was the sole survivor out of a field of forty. During the last lap the excitement of the spectators knew no bounds, they shouted, leapt from their seats, waving their arms or their clothes and embracing their neighbours in their joy.

When the race was over the owner of the victorious chariot came forward and bound a fillet round the head of his charioteer. Then, leading perhaps his chariot, he advanced to the place where the Hellanodikai sat. Beside them was set the gold and ivory table wrought by Kolotes, and on it were the olive crowns cut from the sacred olive-tree. Then the herald proclaimed the name of the victor, his father, and his city, and the chief Hellanodikas placed upon his brow the crown, while the people pelted him with flowers and branches. If the race was a dead heat, the crown was not awarded but was dedicated to the god.

After the chariot-race came the horse-race. It was started in the same manner, but the distance was only a single lap or 6 stades. The jockeys rode without saddle or stirrups. In the first half of the fifth century there was also a riding race for mares and a mule chariot-race, but both these events were discontinued in 444 B.C. The two-horse chariot-race was not introduced till the close of the century, and the various competitions for colts at a still later date.

No sooner was the last race over than the spectators hurried over the embankment to secure places to witness the pentathlon. This was the most characteristic of all Greek athletic competitions. Its object was to test the all-round athlete. The five events of which it was composed, running, jumping, throwing the diskos and the javelin, and wrestling, were the basis of all physical education among the Greeks. The three events which were peculiar to the pentathlon, the jump, the diskos, and the javelin required that rhythmical, harmonious movement which appealed especially to the Greek, and perhaps for this reason these exercises were performed both in practice and in competition to the accompaniment of the flute.

The competition must have taken considerable time, especially if the field was large, and three Hellanodikai were especially appointed to judge it. It is difficult to say how it was decided. It is certain that a competitor who was first in three events won outright, and it seems also that a victor in the pentathlon was commonly described as a triple victor. . . . But it must often have been the case that no one won more than two events or perhaps one. Thus Philostratos, describing the mythical origin of the pentathlon, narrates how five heroes each won one event, and the prize was awarded to Peleus because, having won the wrestling, he was second in the other four events. Further, it seems certain from a passage in Xenophon that wrestling was the last event and that some sort of elimination took place before the wrestling and only those who had qualified in the first four events were entitled to wrestle. What was the method of elimination and what the system of marking formerly seemed insoluble mysteries. A solution, however, has been recently put forward by a Finnish athlete, Captain Lauri Pihkala which seems to me to satisfy all the conditions. He suggests that in the first four events the performance of each competitor was compared with those of each of his fellow competitors individually, and that any competitor who had been defeated by any single other in three events was cut out of the contest. If any one was absolutely first in three of the four events, or if he had defeated every one else in three, not necessarily the same three events, he would be the sole survivor and therefore the winner of the pentathlon. More often it would happen that from two to four were left in who had tied by defeating all their rivals in two events. These alone were permitted to wrestle and the winner of the wrestling was therefore the winner of the whole pentathlon, 'the triple victor' who had defeated every rival in three events.

The pentathlon began with a foot-race, the length of which was a single stade. Then came the jump. It was a long jump and the jumpers used jumping weights, *halteres,* of stone or metal. Some of these may be seen in our museums. They vary in shape, and in weight from 2½ lb. to 10 lb. A stone *halter* was found at Olympia 11½ inches long and slightly over 10 lb. in weight. . . . The jumper seems to have taken a short, springy run, swinging the weights backwards and forwards once or twice as he ran. At the moment of taking off he swung them vigorously forward, so that in mid-air arms and legs were almost parallel. Just before landing he swung them sharply backwards, a movement which helped to lengthen the jump and also to secure a firm, even landing, a point of style to which the Greek attached great importance. The jump possibly took place at the end of the race-course, in which case the stone sills may have served as the take off. . . . In front of this a pit . . . was dug, the ground being carefully loosened and levelled. Each jump was marked by a peg, and when all had jumped the jumps were measured with a rod. . . . On a vase in the British Museum we see a jumper in mid-air, and underneath him are three pegs representing the jumps of previous performers.

Throwing the diskos was the next event. The diskos was a circular plate of metal or stone. Existing specimens vary from 6½ to 9 inches in diameter, and from 3 to 9 lb. in weight. The [ring], from which it was thrown, was marked out by lines in front and on the sides, which the thrower might not overstep. The object was to throw the diskos as far as possible. The drawings of the diskos thrower on vases show a considerable variety of style, but the principle of the throw is always the same; it is that represented in Myron's Diskobolos. The thrower, after rubbing the diskos with sand, took his stand a short distance behind the front line holding the diskos in his left hand with his right foot advanced. He then swung it forward and upward in both hands till it was on a level with or higher than his head, at the same time moving the left foot to the front. Next he swung it vigorously downward and backward, drawing the left foot back again till at the end of the swing he reached the position represented by Myron. Then with a vigorous lift the whole body was straightened, and as the diskos swung forward the left leg was once more advanced. The whole movement was backward and forward like that of a pendulum, and thereby differed from the circular swing of the modern diskos thrower.

The stone sills of the Stadion probably served as the [ring] for both the diskos and the javelin. In the pentathlon the javelin was not thrown at a target but for distance only. At the same time the thrower was obliged to keep within certain limits on either side, and a throw outside the lists, . . . was disqualified. The javelin was about 5 or 6 feet long, and was thrown by means of a short thong, . . . attached to the shaft near the centre of gravity.

The last event in the pentathlon, the wrestling competition, took place not in the Stadion but in the open space in front of the Altar of Zeus. Three falls were necessary to secure victory, and sometimes it happened that victory in the whole pentathlon depended on the last throw. Thus Herodotos tells us that Tisamenos of Elis 'came within a single throw of winning'. He and Hieronymos had each won two events, each had secured two falls, but he lost the last bout.

'Then in the evening, the lovely shining of the fair-faced moon beamed forth, and all the precinct sounded with songs and festal glee.' Victors and their friends wreathed with fillets and garlands held revelry. To the sound of flute and lyre they went in glad procession round the Altis, singing as they went the old triumphal hymn of Herakles written by Archilochos, or some new song written for them by Pindar or Bacchylides. Banquets followed given by the victors to their friends. Sometimes the victor would feast the whole assembly and the revels would last the whole night.

The third day, the day of the full moon, was the great day when the official sacrifice was offered to Zeus. Of the procession we can form some idea from the frieze of the Parthenon. First came the officials, the Hellanodikai in their purple robes, the seers and priests, the attendants leading the victims for the sacrifice: then came the Theoriai, the official deputations from the states of Hellas, bearing in their hands rich vessels of silver and gold: after them the competitors, chariots, horsemen, athletes, trainers, friends. The procession started from the Prytaneion. Following the processional road it moved southwards past the Temple of Zeus, then turning east passed between the temple and the council house, whence it made its way through an avenue of statues past the east end of the temple to the Great Altar. The priest of Zeus, the seers and their ministers, mounted the ramp that led up to the platform or prothysis, and there in the sight of all the people the victims were slain. The thighs were taken up to the top of the altar and there burnt; the rest of the flesh was removed to the Prytaneion.

The sacrifice took place in the morning. In the afternoon the competitions for boys were held, a foot-race, wrestling, and boxing. We do not know for certain what was the age limit for boys. At the Augustalia at Neapolis, which were modelled on the Olympic Games, boys had to be over seventeen and under twenty. But the Greeks had no registers of births, and the Hellanodikai doubtless exercised considerable discretion, taking account not merely of a boy's declared age but of his physical development. Thus we hear of a boy of eighteen who was disqualified from competing among boys, and who thereupon entered for the men's competition and won it.

Most of the athletic events were reserved for the fourth day. The programme began, in the morning with the foot-races. They were three in number, the stade race of 200 yards, the double stade race or diaulos, and the long race of twelve laps or approximately three miles. Each event was proclaimed by the herald. The finish was probably at the east end, near which were the seats of the Hellanodikai. The stone starting-lines have been already described. Each runner occupied one of the divsions. He took his stand with his feet close together, the position of the feet being determined by the two grooves cut in the stone sills, with his body bent slightly forward, but not, like the modern runner, starting off his hands. The start was given by the herald with the word 'go'. . . . Just as to-day, runners tried to poach at the start, but Greek discipline was drastic. 'Runners who start too soon', says Adeimantos to Themistokles, 'are beaten with rods.'

The starting-lines at Olympia provided room for twenty runners. If there was a larger number of competitors, preliminary heats were held, the winner of each heat running in the final. The stade race was a single length of the course. The diaulos or double race was so called because the course resembled a double flute. Hence each runner probably ran straight to the post opposite his starting-place, turned round it to the left, and returned on the parallel track. In the long race it seems probable that all the posts were removed except the centre one at each end, and that the runners raced up and down round these posts just as did the chariots in the Hippodrome. It is reasonable to conjecture that the posts were connected by ropes, but there is no evidence for this. The style of the Greek runners, if we may judge from the drawings on Panathenaic vases, did not differ much from that of the modern runner. The conventional drawing of the sprinters with the right arm and right leg working together has led writers who are not conversant with the conventions of Greek vases to infer that the Greek sprinter advanced by a series of awkward leaps, in fact that he did not know how to run. But as the same conventionality occurs in the drawing of horses, it would be equally reasonable to infer that the Greek horse did not know how to trot.

The foot-races were over before midday, and now there was a rush back to the Altis to witness the most exciting of all events, the competitions in wrestling, boxing, and pankration. These events took place in the open space in front of the Altar of Zeus. Here

the ties were drawn in the presence of the spectators and the Hellanodikai. Lots marked with letters of the alphabet were put into
a silver urn: there were two marked A, two B, two Γ, and so on
according to the number of entries. If there was an odd number of
competitors a single lot was put in for the bye. Each competitor,
after uttering a prayer to Zeus, drew a lot, holding it in his hand
but not looking at it until all were drawn. Then the Hellanodikais
went round and examined the lots, pairing off the competitors accordingly. To draw a bye in such a contest was naturally a great advantage, and it was regarded as an additional honour to win one
of these events without ever drawing a bye. The number of entries
probably rarely exceeded sixteen, requiring four rounds. Occasionally a famous athlete was allowed a walk over.

Wrestling was perhaps the most popular of all Greek sports, and
was an essential part of physical education. The very name
Palaistra signifies the wrestling school. The style of wrestling employed was described by the Greeks as . . . upright wrestling, as
opposed to ground wrestling, which was only allowed in the pankration. The object was to throw an opponent, and a wrestler was
considered thrown if he touched the ground with any part of his
body above the knees. Whether a wrestler who fell on his knee was
thrown is a point hard to determine. As a wrestler in throwing another over his head is sometimes depicted as sinking on one knee, it
seems to me probable that this did not count as a fall. Three throws
were necessary to secure victory, and if both wrestlers fell together
it appears that nothing was scored. A wonderful variety of grips
and throws are represented on the vases. All holds seem to have
been allowed, but from the nature of the competition there was little
opportunity for leg holds. Tripping was freely used. Among the
throws represented are the heave, the flying mare, and the cross
buttock.

Boxing came next. Neither in boxing nor in wrestling was there
any classification according to weight. This was one of the causes
that led to the deterioration of these sports, and especially of boxing. But we must not be misled by the descriptions of boxing in
Virgil and other Roman writers who knew nothing of athletics. The
deadly cestus of the Romans, heavy with lead and iron, had no
place in Greek sport, though the Greek gloves of the fourth century with their ring of hard leather round the knuckles were sufficiently formidable weapons. But the boxing thongs . . . repre-

sented on vases of the fifth century are merely strips of soft leather some 10 feet or more long, wound round the fingers and across the back of the hand and fastened round the wrists. They served rather to protect the knuckles than to decrease the force of the blow. Boxing scenes on these vases suggest that the young Greek boxer had considerable knowledge of foot-work, and used both hands with effect. But the absence of classification according to weight quickly led to deterioration, and this was hastened by two other causes. The Greek ring was large, and there were no rounds. The fight went on till one or other boxer acknowledged defeat by holding up his hand. Hence cautious tactics prevailed, the boxer adopted a stiff guard with the left hand and boxing became a matter on endurance. Perhaps with the idea of making it more lively, more formidable gloves were introduced. If so, the remedy was worse than the disease.

The most exciting of all the contests was the pankration, in which, as the name denotes, each competitor tried to force his opponent to acknowledge defeat by any means in his power. These means included boxing with bare hands, wrestling upright or on the ground, kicking. Twisting the arm, throttling, kicking in the stomach were some of the methods employed, and we should naturally regard it as mere brutality did we not know that the Greeks considered it to be a contest of pure skill and ascribed its invention to Herakles. Perhaps if we knew the laws that governed it we should find that it was no more brutal than the prize fight, or than jiu-jitsu. As it is, the only regulation that we know is one forbidding biting and gouging. . . . The latter expression seems to denote digging the fingers into the eye or other tender parts of the body.

The first usually began with sparring and attempts to secure a wrestling grip, especially a leg hold. But soon both competitors were on the ground and the contest consisted mostly in ground wrestling, though hitting was still allowed. Sometimes a wrestler would intentionally take to the ground with the intention of throwing his opponent heavily by a stomach throw, or of seizing his ankle and twisting it. The struggle went on as in boxing till one of the two acknowledged defeat. Occasionally it happened that a pankratiast died before he would give in. Thus it is related that one Arrhichion died at the moment when his opponent gave in, and thus though dead was awarded the Olympic crown.

The programme closed with the race in armour, a popular and picturesque event which afforded a welcome relief after the excitement of the fighting events. Like the modern obstacle race, it was a practical military exercise, and appealed to the citizen soldier rather than to the specialized athlete. The race was a two-stade race, and the runners wore helmets and greaves and carried round shields. The fields were large; twenty-five shields were kept at Olympia for use in this race. If, as seems probable, the whole field raced together up the track and turned round a single post, it must have been an amusing race to watch, and marking as it did the connexion between athletic training and real life, it formed an appropriate finish to the games.

The last day of the festival was spent in feasting and rejoicing. The victors paid their vows at the altars of the gods, and in the evening were entertained at a banquet in the Prytaneion. Already the crowd was beginning to disperse. All was hurry and confusion. The booths and tents were taken down. There were provisions to be bought for the journey, horses, mules, and vehicles to be hired, and the country folk did a roaring trade. Many who had no mule or vehicle of their own or could not hire them had to start off on foot or stay behind. But all were happy as a Derby crowd—all save the defeated. Greeks, we fear, had little sympathy with defeat. 'By back ways', says Pindar, 'they slink away sore smitten by misfortune.' 'No sweet smile graces their return.' As for the victors, rejoicing friends brought them to their homes, there to be received in triumph by their fellow citizens, and with dance and song to be escorted to the temple of their city to dedicate to god or hero their crown of victory. And so ended the Olympiad.

Further Readings

DURANT, JOHN, *Highlights of the Olympics from Ancient Times to the Present*, New York: Hastings House, Publishers, Inc., 1961.

EVANS, IDRISYN O., *Olympic Runner*. London and New York: Hutchinson & Co. (Publishers), Ltd., 1956.

HARRISON, JANE ELLEN, *A Study of the Social Origins of Greek Religion*, 2d ed., Cambridge: The University Press, 1937.

HENRY, WILLIAM M., *An Approved History of the Olympic Games*. New York: G. P. Putnam's Sons, 1948.

HYDE, WALTER W., *Olympic Victor Monuments and Greek Athletic Art.* Washington, D.C.: Carnegie Institution of Washington, 1921.

PARANDOWSKI, JAN, *The Olympic Discus.* London: Minerva Publishing Co., 1939.

Questions for Discussion

1. What was the place of the Olympic games in the early Greek culture?
2. In what way is this description of the Olympic games in the fifth century B.C. reminiscent of today's Olympic games?
3. Are there similarities between the administration of these ancient games and that of modern competitive sports? If so, what are they?
4. Compare the concepts of sportsmanship in ancient Greece with the ones we hold today.
5. What religious function did the ancient Olympic games serve?
6. What are some of the problems facing United States participation in the Olympic games today?

HORATIO SMITH

Games of the Ancient Romans*

The Ancient Romans. The early Romans were extraordinarily fond of splendor, amusements, feasting and their games. They spent much of their leisure time at the theatres where games and sports were part of the entertainment (as we also observed for the Greek period). Bloodthirsty and cruel spectacles provided much amusement in the various arenas. The Circus, the theatres, the naval war games, and the Colosseum, although more spectacle than sport, nevertheless testify to the importance the Romans placed upon sports of all kinds.

* Reprinted and abridged from *Festivals, Games, and Amusements* by Horatio Smith. New York: Harper & Row, Publishers, 1831, pp. 76–83.

The people of Rome participated in games, boat races, boxing matches, archery contests, foot races and cavalry movements.

Despite the intrusion of his own biased opinions, the author
of the following selection presents a lucid account of some
Roman games. The edile, to which he frequently refers, was an
official in charge not only of the games, but also of the public
buildings, streets, and markets.

At a very early period we find the games of the Romans regulated
with great order and method. Under the republic the Consuls and
Pretors presided over the Circensian, Depolinarian, and secular
games; the plebian ediles had the direction of the plebian games;
the curule ediles, or the pretor, superintended the festivals dedicated to Jupiter, Ceres, Apollo, Cybele, and the other chief gods. . . .

The scenic games, adopted from those of Greece, consisted of
tragedies, comedies, and satires, represented at the theatre in honour
of Bacchus, Venus, and Apollo. To render these exhibitions more
attractive to the common people, they were accompanied by rope-
dancing, tumbling, and similar performances. . . .

Besides these numerous festivals—for, though many of them pro-
fessed to be religious ceremonies, they were essentially merrimak-
ings and revels—there were the secular games, revived by Augustus,
and celebrated only once in a hundred years. Everything appertain-
ing to these games was calculated to impress the superstitious mind
with deep and solemn reverence. From the long interval between
the celebrations none could have seen them before, none could ever
hope to behold them again. Slaves and strangers [foreigners,
non-citizens] were excluded from any participation in this great
national festival; the mystic sacrifices to Pluto and Proserphine, to
the Fates and to the Earth were performed at night on the banks of
the Tiber; the Campus Martius, which was illuminated with innumerable lamps and torches, resounded with music and dancing,
and the temples with the choral hymns of youths and virgins, im-
ploring the gods to preserve the virtue, the felicity, and the empire
of the Roman people. While these supplications were tendered,
the statues of the deities were placed on cushions, where they were
served with the most exquisite dainties. During the three days
of the festival three different pieces of music were performed, the

scene being changed as well as the form of the entertainment. On the first, the people assembled in the Campus Martius; on the second, in the Capitol; the third, upon Mount Palatine. A full and beautiful description of these games is furnished by the Carmen Saeculare of Horace, who was appointed the laureate to celebrate their revival by Augustus, and whose ode, like those of Pindar upon the Olympic games, is all that now remains to us of the great and gorgeous spectacle that it commemorates. . . .

As superstition and cruelty seem to be inseparable, we find the ignorance of early Paganism, and perhaps of all religions, except the Jewish and Christian, stained with the blood of human sacrifices, more especially in the funeral rites. Allusion has been made to the twelve noble Trojans thus slaughtered by Achilles, as recorded in Homer; in Virgil, also, the pious Eneas sends his prisoners to Evander that they may be immolated upon the funeral pile of his son Pallas. The Greeks, however, becoming more humanized as civilization advanced, not only discarded these barbarous practices, but even in their public games gradually suffered all such as were of a cruel and perilous nature to fall into desuetude. . . .

Similar or greater atrocities are of frequent occurrence in the history of those sanguinary tormentors and butchers of the world, who appear to have been never happy unless they were shedding human blood in war, or slaughtering whole herds of animals as sacrifices to their gore-loving gods. So invincible was this propensity, that when there was no foreign enemy on whom to wreak their brutal ferocity, they could even delight in civil wars, and in witnessing the destruction of their fellow-citizens, of which a horrible example was afforded towards the commencement of the empire. . . .

That such a nation should be fierce and ruthless, even in their sports, was naturally to be expected; to the Romans accordingly belongs the disgrace, if not of inventing, at least of adapting, enlarging, and continuing, the gladiatorial and animal combats of the amphitheatre. A superstitious conceit that the souls of deceased warriors delighted in human sacrifices, as if they were slain to satisfy their revenge, originated and gave a sort of religious sanction to this cruel custom, which often proved fatal to prisoners of war. But as the inhumanity of such massacres became recognised, combats of captives and slaves were substituted at the funeral games, a practice which led to the subsequent introduction of regular gladiators, exhibited, not to appease the dead, but to amuse the living. Whether or not the Romans derived these cruel games from the ancient Etrurians, as some have maintained, they eagerly seized every opportunity for their exhibition, even upon occasions when such hideous spectacles would have been peculiarly repugnant to the feelings of any other people upon earth. . . .

Combats of wild beasts were first exhibited in the 568th year of Rome, when Marcus Fulvius treated the people with a hunting of lions and panthers: but as luxury and riches increased, and the conquest of Africa and the East facilitated the supply of exotic animals, it soon became a contest with the ediles and others who should evince the greatest magnificence in the Circensian games, and construct the most sumptuous amphitheatres for their display. Caesar, however, surpassed all his predecessors in the funeral shows which he celebrated in memory of his father; for, not content with supplying the bases and all the apparatus of the theatre with silver, he caused the arena to be paved with silver plates; "so that," says Pliny, "wild beasts were for the first time seen walking and fighting upon this precious metal." This excessive expense on the part of Caesar was only commensurate with his ambition. Preceding ediles had simply sought the consulate; Caesar aspired to empire, and was resolved, therefore, to eclipse all his competitors. Pompey the Great, on dedicating his theatre, produced, besides a rhinoceros and other strange beasts from Ethiopia, 500 lions, 410 tigers, and a number of elephants, who were attacked by African men, the hunting being continued during five days. Caesar, after the termination of the civil wars, divided his hunting-games into five days also; in the first of which the cameleopard was shown; at least 500 men on foot, and 300 on horseback were made to fight, together with twenty elephants, and an equal number more with turrets on their backs, defended by sixty men. As to the number of gladiators, he surpassed every thing that had been seen before, having produced, when edile, as Plutarch tells us, no less than 320 couples of human combatants. . . .

Further Readings

FOWLER, WILLIAM M., *The Roman Festivals of the Period of the Republic.* New York: The Macmillan Company, 1899.

GIBBON, EDWARD, *The Decline and Fall of the Roman Empire.* New York: Dell Publishing Company, Inc., 1963.

JENNISON, GEORGE, *Animals in Ancient Rome.* Manchester: Manchester University Press, 1937.

REINHOLD, MEYER, *Greek and Roman Classics.* Great Neck, New York: Barrons Educational Series, Inc., 1946.

VAN DALEN, D. B., ELMER MITCHELL, and BRUCE BENNETT, *A World History of Physical Education.* Englewood Cliffs, N.J.: Prentice-Hall, Inc., 1953.

Questions for Discussion

1. What characteristics of the Romans are clearly brought out in this account of their games?
2. What general cultural values held by the Romans were expressed in their games? What American values are exemplified at our football games?
3. What was the relationship between the ancient Greek games and those of the Romans?
4. What part did religion and superstition play in the presentation of the Roman games?

C. W. C. OMAN

The English and Their Enemies*
A.D. 1272–1485

The Middle Ages. We now reach the middle of the thirteenth century, which witnessed the rising popularity of chivalric tournaments. Even while the church held absolute control over the spiritual life of all Christians in Europe, physical exercise, as an integral part of making the medieval knight fit for battle, was not neglected. All this was closely interconnected; it was part of the medieval pattern, which set lofty demands upon the

* Reprinted from *The Art of War in the Middle Ages* (A.D. *378–1515*), by C. W. C. Oman. Revised and edited by John H. Beeler, Ithaca, N.Y.: Great Seal Books, Cornell University Press, pp. 116–128. Copyright 1953 by Cornell University. Used by permission of Cornell University Press.

knight, who ideally had to be both a pious Christian and a good soldier. Battles were fought not only for personal honor or for the king but many times, as during the Crusades, for the "only, true Faith." To live up to these high expectations, the knights were obliged to be constantly on guard, never to relax, and always strong and fit; the chivalric tournaments were organized for that purpose among others.

The age of Chivalry did not last very long, however. It declined because of the emergence of new values and social order of the Renaissance—a growing secularism concomitant with the gradual disintegration of the feudal socio-economic order.

In the next selection, observe how the longbow became an important asset to the English armies. Note that the pike, which the Swiss used, was a spearlike weapon; that archers formed the central part of the medieval army; and the knights in the tournaments utilized both the shortbow and the lance.

The use of the longbow is as much the key to the successes of the English armies in the fourteenth and fifteenth centuries as that of the pike is to the successes of the Swiss. Dissimilar as were the characters of the two weapons, and the national tactics to which their use led, they were both employed for the same end of terminating the ascendancy in war of the mailed horseman of the feudal regime. It is certainly not the least curious part of the military history of the period that the commanders who made such good use of their archery had no conception of the tendencies of their action. Edward the Black Prince and his father regarded themselves as the flower of chivalry, and would have been horrified had they realized that their own tactics were going far to make chivalrous warfare impossible. Such, however, was the case; that unscientific kind of combat which resembled a huge tilting match could not continue if one side persisted in bringing into the field auxiliaries who could prevent their opponents from approaching near enough to break a lance. The needs of the moment, however, prevented the English commanders being troubled by such thoughts; they made the best use of the material at their disposal, and if they thus found themselves able to beat the enemy, they were satisfied.

It is not till the last quarter of the thirteenth century that we find the longbow taking up its position as the national weapon of England. In the armies of the Norman and Angevin kings, archers were indeed to be found, but they formed neither the most numerous nor the most effective part of the array. On the English side of the Channel, just as beyond it, the supremacy of the mailed horseman was still unquestioned. It is indeed noteworthy that the theory which attributes to the Normans the introduction of the longbow is impossible to substantiate. If we are to trust the Bayeux Tapestry—whose accurracy is in other matters thoroughly borne out by all contemporary evidence—the weapon of William's archers was in no way different from that already known in England, and was used by a few of the English in the fight of Hastings.[1] It is the short bow, drawn to the breast and not to the ear. The bowmen who are occasionally mentioned during the succeeding century, as, for example, those present at the Battle of the Standard (A.D. 1138), do not appear to form any very important part of the national force. Nothing can be more conclusive as to the insignificance of the weapon than the fact that it is not mentioned at all in the Assize of Arms of 1181. In the reign of Henry II, therefore, we may fairly conclude that the bow did not form the proper weapon of any class of English society. A similar deduction is suggested by Richard Coeur de Lion's predilection for the arbalest; it is impossible that he should have introduced that weapon as a new and superior arm if he had been acquainted with the splendid longbow of the fourteenth century. It is evident that the bow must always preserve an advantage in rapidity of fire over the arbalest; the latter must therefore have been considered by Richard to surpass in range and penetrating power. But nothing is better established than the fact that the trained archer of the Hundred Years' War was able to beat the crossbowmen on both these points. It is, therefore, rational to conclude that the weapon superseded by the arbalest was merely the old short bow, which had been in constant use since Saxon times.

However this may be, the crossbowmen continued to occupy the first place among light troops during the reigns of Richard and John. The former monarch devised for them a system of tactics

---

[1] E.g., by the diminutive archer who crouches under a thegn's shield, like Teucer protected by Ajax.

in which the pavis was made to play a prominent part. The latter entertained great numbers of both horse and foot arbalesters among those mercenary bands who were such a scourge to England. It would appear that the barons, in their contest with John, suffered greatly from having no adequate provision of infantry armed with missiles to oppose the crossbowmen of Fawkes de Breauté and his fellows. Even in the reign of Henry III, the epoch in which the long-bow begins to come into use, the arbalest was still reckoned the more effective arm. In 1242, at the battle of Taillebourg, a corps of 700 men armed with this weapon were considered to be the flower of the English infantry.

To trace the true origin of the longbow is not easy. There are reasons for believing that it may have been borrowed from the South Welsh, who were certainly provided with it as early as A.D. 1150.[2] Against this derivation, however, may be pleaded the fact that in the first half of the thirteenth century it appears to have been in greater vogue in the northern than in the western counties of England. As a national weapon it is first accepted in the Assize of Arms of 1252, wherein all holders of 40*s*. in land or nine marks in chattels are desired to provide themselves with sword, dagger, bow, and arrows.[3] Contemporary documents often speak of the obli-gation of various manors to provide the king with one or more archers "when he makes an expedition against the Welsh." It is curious to observe that even as late as 1281 the preference for the crossbow seems to have been kept up, the wages of its bearer being considerably more than those of the archer.[4]

To Edward I the longbow owes its original rise into favor. That monarch, like his grandson and great-grandson, was an able soldier, capable of devising new expedients in war. Unlike them, he also showed considerable strategical ability. His long experience in Welsh campaigns led him to introduce a scientific use of archery much like that which William the Conqueror had employed at

---

[2] Gerald de Barri speaks of the Welsh bowmen as being able to send an arrow through an oak door four fingers thick. The people of Gwent (Monmouth and Glamorgan) were reckoned the best archers. Those of North Wales were always spearmen, not archers. *Giraldus Cambrensis Itinerarium Kambriae*, ed. James F. Dimock (Rolls Series; London, 1868), p. 54.

[3] William Stubbs, *Select Charters* (9th ed.; Oxford, 1913), p. 364.

[4] In the Pay Roll of the garrison of Rhuddlan castle, 1281, we find "paid to Geoffrey le Chamberlin for the wages of twelve cross-bowmen, and thirteen archers, for twenty-four days, £7 8*s*., each cross-bowman receiving by the day 4*d*., and each archer 2*d*."

Hastings. We are informed that it was first put into practice in a combat fought against Prince Llewelyn at Orwin Bridge (A.D. 1282), and afterwards copied by the Earl of Warwick in another engagement fought near Conway during the year 1295.

> The Welsh, on the earl's approach, set themselves fronting his force with exceeding long spears, which, being suddenly turned toward the earl and his company, with their ends placed in the earth and their points upward, broke the force of the English cavalry. But the earl well provided against them, by placing archers between his men-at-arms, so that by these missive weapons those who held the lances were put to rout.[5]

The battle of Falkirk (A.D. 1298), however, was the first engagement of real importance in which the bowmen, properly supplemented by cavalry, played the leading part. Its circumstances, indeed, bore such striking witness to the power of the arrow that it could not fail to serve as a lesson to English commanders. The Scots of the Lowlands, who formed the army of William Wallace, consisted mainly of spearmen, armed, like the Swiss, with a pike many feet in length. They had in their ranks a small body of horse, a few hundred in number, and a certain proportion of archers, mainly drawn from the Ettrick and Selkirk district. Wallace, having selected an excellent position behind a marsh, formed his spearmen in four great masses (or *schiltrons,* as the Scotch called them) of circular form, ready to face outward in any direction. The light troops formed a line in the intervals of these columns, while the cavalry were placed in reserve. Edward came on with his horsemen in three divisions; his archers were disposed between them. The foremost English "battle," that of the Earl Marshal, rode into the morass, was stopped by it, and suffered severely from the Scotch missile weapons. The second division, commanded by the bishop of Durham, observing this check, rode around the flank of the marsh in order to turn Wallace's position. At the approach of the English knights the small body of Scotch cavalry turned and rode off the field without striking a blow. Then the bishop's horsemen charged the hostile line from the rear. The squadrons opposed to the light troops succeeded in riding them down, as Wallace's archers were only armed with the short bow and were not particularly skilled in its use. Those of the English, however, who faced the masses of pikemen received a sanguinary check, and were thrown

[5] Nicholas Trivet, *Annales,* ed. Thomas Hog (London, 1845), pp. 335–336.

back in disorder. The bishop had therefore to await the arrival of the king, who was leading the infantry and the remainder of the cavalry around the end of the marsh.

When this had been done, Edward brought up his bowmen close to the Scotch masses, who were unable to reply (as their own light troops had been driven away) or to charge, on account of the nearness of the English men-at-arms. Concentrating the rain of arrows on particular points in the columns, the king fairly riddled the Scotch ranks, and then sent in his cavalry with a sudden charge. The plan succeeded; the shaken parts of the masses were pierced, and the knights, having once got within the pikes, made a fearful slaughter of the enemy. The moral of the fight was evident: cavalry could not beat the Scotch tactics, but archers supplemented by horsemen could easily accomplish the required task.

Accordingly, for the next two centuries the characteristics of the fight of Falkirk were continually repeated whenever the English and the Scotch met. Halidon Hill (A.D. 1333), Neville's Cross (A.D. 1346), Homildon (A.D. 1402), and Flodden (A.D. 1513) were all variations on the same theme. The steady but slow-moving masses of the Lowland infantry fell a sacrifice to their own persistent bravery when they staggered on in a vain endeavor to reach the line of men-at-arms, flanked by archers, whom the English commander opposed to them. The bowman might boast with truth that he "carried twelve Scots' lives at his girdle"; he had but to launch his shaft into the easy target of the great surging mass of pikemen, and it was sure to do execution.

[Bannockburn (A.D. 1314), indeed, forms a notable exception to the general rule. Its result, however, was not due to an attempt to discard the tactics of Falkirk, but to unskillful, almost insane generalship, which one might have expected of a campaign conducted by Edward II. The forces of Robert Bruce, much like those of Wallace in composition, may have amounted to 10,000 men and 500 picked horsemen. Bruce had taken up a strong position in the New Park, covering the town and castle of Stirling, which Edward had sworn to relieve. The Scottish king had made his dispositions to meet an attack along the old Roman road which ran from Falkirk to Stirling, but the English, who had made a strong reconnaissance on the afternoon of June 23, 1314, decided to try and turn the Scots' position under cover of darkness. They spent, therefore, the night of June 23–24 in crossing the Bannockburn between Bannockburn village and Crookbridge, an area which in the fourteenth century was extremely wet. Edward's army, numbering close to 20,000 men, spent all night in passing the stream, and dawn found them still a disorganized mass milling about on the flats below St. Ninian's church. Only the vanguard under the Earl of Gloucester had managed to get into some sort of order. This presented Bruce with a golden opportunity which he hastened to use. Facing his army to the new front, he launched them down the slope in echelon of *schiltrons* strikingly like the normal Swiss order of attack, and crashed into the weltering mass of English with devastating effect. A few of the English archers had got into position on their own right flank, but these were ridden down and chased off the field by a charge of the Scottish cavalry under the marshal Keith, the single noteworthy deed ever recorded of the Scottish knighthood.

[The battle developed into a confused melee between the spearmen of Bruce and Edward's knights. The latter, cramped for room, could make only partial and ineffective charges which failed utterly to break the lines of pikes. Meanwhile they suffered frightful casualties. The rear ranks could not get up to join the combat and stood helpless while their comrades were mowed down. Finally, either through exhaustion or through a Scottish stratagem, the entire English front broke to pieces, and the defeat became a rout. Behind them lay the marshy banks of the Bannockburn and the broad reaches of the river Forth. Hundreds were drowned in attempting to escape. King Edward himself eluded capture by taking a circuitous route which led him past Stirling castle, where the governor refused him admittance. Never before or since has such a dreadful slaughter of the English baronage taken place, nor has such a defeat been administered to an English army. Its lessons were obvious. Cavalry, no matter how brave or how determined, cannot defeat steady pikemen unaided, and archers unsupported by heavy troops are worthless.][6]

The next series of campaigns in which the English bowman was to take part were directed against an enemy different in every

---

6 These paragraphs have been rewritten by the editor for this edition. They are based in part on John Barbour, *The Bruce*, tr. Geo. Eyre-Todd (Glasgow, 1907), pp. 222–223, W. M. MacKenzie, *The Battle of Bannockburn* (Glasgow, 1913), and John E. Morris, *Bannockburn* (Cambridge, 1914).

respect from the sturdy spearman of the Lowlands. In France those absurd perversions of the art of war which covered themselves under the name of chivalry were more omnipotent than in any other country of Europe. The strength of the armies of Philip and John of Valois was composed of a fiery and undisciplined aristocracy which imagined itself to be the most efficient military force in the world, but which was in reality little removed from an armed mob. A system which reproduced on the battlefield the distinctions of feudal society was considered by the French noble to represent the ideal form of warlike organization. He firmly believed that, since he was infinitely superior to any peasant in the social scale, he must consequently excel the peasant to the same extent in military value. He was, therefore, prone not only to despise all descriptions of infantry but to regard their appearance on the field against him as a species of insult to his class pride. The self-confidence of the French nobility—shaken for the moment by the result of Courtrai—had reasserted itself after the bloody days of Mons-en-Pévèle and Cassel. The fate which had on those occasions befallen the gallant but ill-trained burghers of Flanders was believed to be only typical of that which awaited any foot soldier who dared to match himself against the chivalry of the most warlike aristocracy in Christendom. Pride goes before a fall, and the French noble was now to meet infantry of a quality such as he had never supposed to exist.

Against these presumptuous cavaliers, their mercenaries, and the wretched band of half-armed villeins whom they dragged with them to the battlefield, the English archer was now matched. He was by this time almost a professional soldier, being usually not a pressed man, but a volunteer, raised by one of those barons or knights with whom the king contracted for a supply of soldiers. Led to enlist by sheer love of fighting, desire for adventures, or hope of plunder, he possessed a great moral ascendancy over the spiritless hordes who followed the French nobility to the wars. Historians, however, have laid too much stress on this superiority, real as it was. No amount of mere readiness to fight would have accounted for the English victories of the fourteenth century. Self-confidence and pugnacity were not wanting in the Fleming at Roosebeke or the Scot at Falkirk, yet they did not secure success. It was the excellent armament and tactics of the yeomanry, even more than their courage, which made them masters of the field at Crécy or Poitiers.

The longbow had as yet been employed only in offensive warfare, and against an enemy inferior in cavalry to the English army. When, however, Edward III led his invading force into France, the conditions of war were entirely changed. The French were invariably superior in the numbers of their horsemen, and the tactics of the archer had to be adapted to the defensive. He was soon to find that the charging squadron presented as good a mark for his shaft as the stationary column of infantry. Nothing indeed could be more disconcerting to a body of cavalry than a flight of arrows: not only did it lay low a certain proportion of the riders, but it caused such disorder by setting the wounded horses plunging and rearing among their fellows that it was most effective in checking the impetus of the onset. As the distance grew shorter and the range more easy, the wounds to horse and man became more numerous; the disorder increased, the pace continued to slacken, and at last a limit was reached beyond which the squadron could not pass. To force a line of longbowmen by a mere front attack was a task almost hopeless for cavalry. This, however, was a fact which the continental world had yet to learn in the year 1346.

[At Crécy (A.D. 1346) King Edward III divided his army of approximately 11,000 men into the usual three "battles." The right wing was commanded by the Prince of Wales and occupied the hillside halfway between the river Maye and the village of Wadicourt. It consisted of 800 dismounted men-at-arms flanked on either side by archers, 2,000 all told, and about 1,000 Welsh spearmen. On the prince's left and somewhat drawn back lay the second corps under the joint command of the earls of Arundel and Northampton. It was somewhat smaller than the first, consisting of about 500 men-at-arms and 1,200 archers, arrayed in the same manner. Its right rested on the prince's left, and its left flank was protected by the village of Wadicourt. King Edward himself, with the reserve of 700 men-at-arms, 2,000 archers, and perhaps 1,000 Welsh spearmen, lay on the plateau in front of the wood of La Grange, behind the "battle" of the Prince of Wales.][7]

Nothing could be more characteristic of the indiscipline of the French army than the fact that it forced the battle a day sooner than its leader had intended. On observing the English position, Philip and his marshals had determined to defer the conflict till the next morning, as the troops had been marching since daybreak. When, however, the order to halt reached the vanguard, the nobles

[7] This paragraph has been rewritten by the editor.

at the head of the column believed that they were to be deprived of the honor of opening the fight, as they could see that some of the troops in the rear were still advancing. They therefore pushed on, and, as the main body persisted in following them, the whole army arrived so close to the English position that a battle became unavoidable. The circumstances of that day have often been described; it is unnecessary to detail the mishap of the unfortunate Genoese crossbowmen, who were shot down in scores while going through the cumbrous process of winding up their arbalests. The fruitless charges of the cavalry against the front of the line of archers led to endless slaughter, till the ground was heaped with the bodies of men and horses, and further attempts to advance became impossible.

[The main assault of the French seems always to have been directed against the dismounted men-at-arms, rather than against the archers, and sometimes pressed them severely, but in no instance did the English line yield a single foot. The knights fell before the line of lances, which they were unable to break, and fared no better than their comrades in the center. At nightfall the French fell back in disorder, and their whole army dispersed. The English had won the day without stirring a foot from their position; the enemy had come to them to be killed.] Considerably more than a third of his numbers lay dead in front of the English line, and of these far the greatest number had fallen by the arrows of the bowmen.

Crécy had proved that the archer, when adequately supported by dismounted men-at-arms, could beat off the most determined charges of cavalry. The moral, however, which was drawn from it by the French was one of a different kind. Unwilling, in the bitterness of their class pride, to ascribe the victory to the arms of mere peasants, they came to the conclusion that it was due to the stability of the phalanx of dismounted knights. . . .

Further Readings

LOT, FERDINAND, *The End of the Ancient World and the Beginnings of the Middle Ages.* New York: Harper & Row, Publishers, 1961.

OMAN, SIR CHARLES W. C., *The Dark Ages.* London: Rivingtons, 1923.

William Harrison Woodward 55

PAINTER, SIDNEY, *A History of the Middle Ages.* New York: Alfred A. Knopf, Inc., 1960.

SLESSER, SIR HENRY H., *The Middle Ages in the West.* London: Hutchinson and Co. (Publishers), Ltd., 1949.

TAYLOR, HENRY, *The Emergence of Christian Culture in the West.* New York: Harper & Row, Publishers, 1958.

Questions for Discussion

1. What is the historical significance of the longbow for physical education?
2. How did the French soldiers differ from the English ones?
3. Identify and distinguish the uses of the longbow, the pike, and the arbalest?
4. What were the tactics employed by the English to win wars? Are similar strategies used today?
5. How was feudal society represented on the battlefield?

WILLIAM HARRISON WOODWARD

Vittorino da Feltre*

The Renaissance. For a long time the values of ancient Greece and Rome were forgotten. But by the fourteenth and fifteenth centuries, scholars and the educated populace of new growing urban centers—especially in Italy, but to a lesser degree also in France, England, and Germany—were developing a renewed interest in secular culture in general and in the full realization of human potential in particular. This new outlook was reflected in formal education.

In order to provide some understanding of ideas about education that developed the early Renaissance, we have included an article about an interesting Italian humanist and educator, Vittorino Rambaldoni, or as he was popularly called, Vittorino

* Reprinted and abridged from *Vittorino da Feltre and Other Humanist Educators: Essays and Versions* by William Harrison Woodward. Cambridge: The University Press, 1897, pp. 34–36, 65–67.

da Feltre (1378?–1446?). He believed that physical exercise and the development of a personal physical style had a definite place in the education of young men, and he worked to encourage such development along with their studies so that they would grow into well educated and successfully adjusted adults. This concept of education was in harmony with the ideal of the Renaissance man, who was expected to be interested and active in all aspects of life. You will want to note the relationship of this concept to the point of view expressed by Plato in the following section on Philosophical Backgrounds. The remarkable combination of training in the humanities and physical education has existed many times in the past, and perhaps is emerging again today.

Vittorino definitely held himself the father of his scholars. It was with him no formal claim. His school entirely absorbed him. He watched the youngest with affection and hope, the elders with pride and confidence. Himself moving always amid the larger things of life, the power that went forth from him insensibly raised the tone of thought and motive in those around him. His singleness of purpose was quickly felt, and a word or even a glance of disapproval was, with the keenly sensitive Italian youth, often sufficient to bring tears of shame and repentance to the eyes of a culprit. Living a common life with his scholars in meals, in games, in excursions, always sharing their interests and pleasures, his control over the sixty or seventy boys under his charge was such that harsh punishments were not needed. Naturally quick-tempered, he had schooled himself to a self-control which never gave way except in face of irreverence or looseness. Corporal punishment was very seldom resorted to, and then only after deliberation, and as the alternative to expulsion. For ill-prepared work the penalty imposed was the compulsory re-learning of the task after school hours. But it was part of Vittorino's purpose to attract rather than to drive, and to respect the dignity and the freedom of his boys. So he refused, after fair trial made, to force learning upon an unwilling scholar, holding that nature had not endowed all with taste or capacity for study. It is characteristic of the time that Vittorino could appeal with confidence to the personal and family distinction conferred by excellence in the study of Letters. It was a motive to which most youths of spirit eagerly responded.

We are told that Vittorino watched carefully habits of self-indulgence in eating and drinking,[1] and by discipline in these matters eradicated even gross faults: whilst he was equally attentive to those whose appetite seemed deficient. Like other educators of the time, he discouraged resort to artificial heat, even during the severe cold of the Mantuan winter. He never stood near a fire, though his hands and feet were often numbed with cold. Clapping the hands, stamping the feet, or, better still, discussion and reading aloud were the proper remedies for anyone in health: for cold was generally the result of idleness of mind or body. The healthy activity of childhood was always encouraged, and skill in games was cultivated in all his pupils. Two little boys were overheard by him talking earnestly apart; hearing that they were discussing their lessons, he exclaimed, 'That is not a good sign in a young boy,' and sent them off to join the games. Regular exercise in all conditions of weather he regarded as the foundation of health, and health as the first necessity of mental progress. The health of the boys under his charge was a matter to which Vittorino paid much attention; in this respect again we feel how remote he was from the mediaeval standards. In the excessive heats he made provision for sending or accompanying parties of his scholars to the villas owned by the Marquis at Goito, or at Borgoforte, or to the Lake of Garda, or the lower Alps of the Veronese. If any fell ill his care was unremitting. Indeed the tie of personal affection which united him with his pupils was manifest in all relations. His keen desire for their progress, and his pride in it; his peculiar insight into individual character; the absence of all considerations of self, so affected the methods of discipline that in the truest sense La Giocosa was an ideal school, and, so far as a school ever may be, an ideal home.

What is here written may seem a fancy sketch based on the adulatory method of criticism common to the fifteenth century. But we have the correspondence, fragmentary but most significant, of Vittorino himself, the unvarying testimony of scholars who spent their youth and early manhood under Vittorino; the indirect evidence afforded by those of his pupils who became famous schoolmasters in their turn; and the respect of men of so wide experience and such ample opportunity of information as Guarino, Ambrogio, Filelfo and Poggio,—a respect due not only to his attainments but to the noble temper by which Vittorino gained and kept his unique

[1] The use of wine, though discouraged, was not actually forbidden. It was always diluted. He himself drank very sparingly a light and sweet wine.

authority. We may trace the characteristics of this new discipline, if we will, to the study of Plutarch's Treatise, and of Quintilian. Something no doubt was due to the revolt of the Humanist against the doctrine that the body is the enemy of the mind and of the spirit. But most of all do we feel that Vittorino could dispense with harshness just because he was intensely sympathetic with the young, was master of his task in all its detail, and pursued it with an undivided mind. Moreover, we know that he was aided by able colleagues, men of like mind with their Master; for most of them had been trained by Vittorino himself. But the last word that can be said is after all just this: the secret of his authority lay in the genius of the man himself.

The aim of Vittorino, the aim of the true humanist educator, was to secure the harmonious development of mind, body, and character. . . . The important place which games and bodily exercises occupy in Vittorino's scheme of education is readily accounted for. For Vittorino was in one sense a continuator of the Court training which had held its place beside the municipal or ecclesiastical schools of the Middle Age. He was, we remember, preceptor in the first place to the family of a Condottiere prince; and a not inconsiderable proportion of his pupils were, like Frederic of Urbino, called to follow a career of arms. On the other hand Vittorino was a Humanist, and therefore derives part at least of his educational ideal from the example of Greece and Rome. The two influences combined to establish the training of the body as an integral element of a complete discipline. Indeed the highest level of Humanist culture was only attained when the full personality had received a cultivation duly proportioned to the three sides of human nature. So that it is not enough to say that Vittorino attached importance to the outdoor life as a means to brisk intellectual activity. No doubt this was in his mind. He always paid serious attention to the health of the scholars. Their life out of doors was carefully organised. Whatever the weather, daily exercise in some form was compulsory. There was ample space for games, riding, running, and all the athletic exercises then popular. We hear that he specially encouraged certain games at ball, leaping, and fencing. He prized excellence in sports as only less praiseworthy than literary power, for in such powers he found a sound corrective to self-indulgence and effeminacy. If we turn to three typical treatises upon education due to the Renaissance, those of Vergerius, of

Castiglione, and of Milton, we see that each lays special stress upon the practice of martial exercises: each of them presents that union of the Courtly with the Humanist ideal to which reference has just been made. But although Vittorino undoubtedly kept such martial exercises in view, he seems to have taken generally a wider view of physical training, aiming rather at strengthening the frame, inducing habits of hardiness, and power of bearing fatigue, than at any special athletic skill. Thus he watched with peculiar care the health of the younger children, providing due supervision for them in their games and walks. In the summer heats he would take certain of them to the Castle of Goito, some twelve miles out of Mantua toward Verona. We know this pleasant spot where Sordello's youth was spent, and may wonder if Vittorino, who in his early Paduan days had had his lyrical moods, felt the associations of the place.[2] We find Ambrogio visiting him there one hot September day. "Vittorino is staying at Goito in charge of the Gonzaga children. We found him at breakfast with them; he comes out to meet us, greeting us with tears of joy. He entertains us right royally. The children seem to be on the happiest terms with him. We talked together for several hours. Then one of the boys declaims some two hundred lines which he had composed upon the state entry of the Emperor Sigismund into Mantua. I was astonished by the taste and scholarship displayed not less than by the grace and propriety of delivery. Two younger brothers and their sister were of the party, all bright and intelligent children. . . . After a morning's most enjoyable intercourse several other youths of distinction were introduced, and after courteous greetings escorted us some distance on our way." The mountains above the Lake of Garda formed an accessible and favourite field for longer excursions, lasting several days, when Vittorino, wiry and active to the last, in company with his elder boys, explored that most striking of all the gateways of the Alps.

In all this we see Vittorino consciously carrying out a definite aim of developing the physical not less than the intellectual side of his scholars. Free, on the one hand, from the sensuous cult of the body which marks a later stage of the Renaissance, he had even less

2   "just a castle built amid
      A few low mountains; firs and larches hid
      Their main defiles, and rings of vineyard bound
      The rest."
                                      Browning's *Sordello.*

sympathy with that neglect of all that concerns its vigour and grace which was still characteristic of much of the education of his time. Something of the finest temper of the antique world shews itself in this love of the simplicity of the open air and the tried discipline of the body.

But we must again remind ourselves of the depth of religious conviction upon which his own educational ideal ultimately rested. Reverence, piety and religious observance formed the dominant note of Vittorino's personal life. The dignity of human life was with him based upon its relation to the Divine. Hence the transparent sincerity of his religious teaching; the insistence upon attendance at the ordinances of the Church; the inculcation of forgiveness and humility. He himself accompanied the boys to Mass; he set the example of regular Confession. Part of the religious instruction he himself took every day. Apart from the light that is thus thrown upon his personality, what is of chief interest in this aspect of Vittorino is its relation to his Humanism. This was with him no nominal reconciliation between the new and the old. Christianity and Humanism were the two coordinate factors necessary to the development of complete manhood. There is no reason to suppose that Vittorino was embarrassed by a sense of contradiction between the classical and the Christian ideals of life. To him, and to men of his temper since, the thought and morals of the ancient world were identified with the ethical precepts of the Stoics and the idealism of Plato: and it was easy for them to point to the consistency of this teaching with the broader aspects of the Christian life.

Further Readings

BURKHARDT, JAKOB, *The Civilization of the Renaissance in Italy*. New York: Harper & Row, Publishers, 1958.

BUTTS, R. FREEMAN, *A Cultural History of Education*. New York: McGraw-Hill, Inc., 1947.

HASKINS, CHARLES H., "The Greek Element in the Renaissance of the Twelfth Century," *American Historical Review*, vol. 25 (1920), pp. 603–615.

LAURIE, S. S., *Studies in the History of Educational Opinion from the Renaissance*. Cambridge: The University Press, 1905.

OGBURN, CHARLTON, *The Renaissance Man of England.* New York: Coward-McCann, Inc., 1955.

PESTALOZZI, JOHANN H., *The Education of Man: Aphorisms,* translated by Heinz and Ruth Norden. New York: Philosophical Library, Inc., 1951.

SELLERY, GEORGE C., *The Renaissance: Its Nature and Origins.* Madison, Wisc.: University of Wisconsin Press, 1950.

Questions for Discussion

1. What were the central purposes of Vittorino da Feltre in establishing *La Giacosa?*
2. How did this school differ from others of the same time?
3. After you read Section II, return and answer the question: To what school of philosophy does da Feltre belong?
4. Do you know of any schools in the United States that are organized along the same lines as da Feltre's? Where are they? How are they similar?

F. L. JAHN

Preparatory Exercises*

German Physical Education. We move from the Renaissance to the eighteenth century and to another major historical influence on American physical education. Gymnastics developed in Germany as an outgrowth of the culture of the Germanic people. Among the characteristics that distinguish Teutonic culture is an interest in power and in military and religious authority. This should be kept in mind for an understanding of the formality of German physical education programs.

In 1774, during the reign of Frederick the Great, Johann Bernhard Basedow (1723–1790) opened the Philanthropinum at Dessau. This later was known as the Dessau Educational In-

---

* Reprinted from *Treatise on Gymnasticks* by F. L. Jahn, translated by Charles Beck. Northampton, Mass.: Simeon Butler, 1828, pp. 1–7.

stitute. Rousseau's *Émile* (see Section II) provided the stimulus for Basedow's work in gymnastics. The school included a "plan of work," exercises, apparatus, games, and manual training. Johann Christoph Friedrich Guts-Muths (1759–1839), generally called the "Grandfather of German Gymnastics," also spent his life developing gymnastics. One of the most intriguing men at this time was Friedrich Ludwig Jahn (1778–1852). Jahn was not only the "Father of Modern Gymnastics" but also a popular leader and political agitator. Among other accomplishments he founded the Turnverein (German exercise club). Gymnastics in Germany influenced both education and the national spirit, and after the German participation in the defeat of Napoleon in 1813–14, everyone appreciated the effect of gymnastic training because the strength, agility and physical fitness of the soldiers made possible their success. Then came a political reaction against gymnastics and the gymnasiums were closed. Jahn was jailed for his political activity, and those wishing to participate in gymnastics did so only surreptitiously.

The next selection presents in Jahn's own words a description of his preparatory exercises.

Gymnastick Exercises

I. PREPARATORY EXERCISES

All preparatory exercises have for their object to strengthen and to render limber the lower extremities, and to accustom the body to a good carriage in general, as well as in single exercises. They cannot be sufficiently recommended, not only on account of their being preparatory to several other exercises, especially leaping and vaulting, but also on account of their being exceedingly useful in forming and strengthening the body. All instruction in gymnastick exercises ought to begin with them, and every individual to have acquired some facility and duration in performing them, before he passes over to other exercises. They are the more valuable because they can be practised without any instruments, and by a large number at a time.

Posture:

Feet and knees must always be as close as possible.

Body erect, belly inwards, breast outwards. Particular care must be taken to maintain the posture of the upper part of the body. In this way alone the back can be drawn in, the shoulders recede, and a firm and noble posture of the body be effected.

Hands flat upon the hips, the thumb backwards, the fingers forward. Keeping the hands so prevents an unsteady wavering motion of the body.

Lips close.

Standing on tiptoe or, to speak more correctly, on the forepart of the foot. The gymnick raises the heels from the ground, and stands firmly on the forepart of the feet. The joints of the toes are strongly bent, and the knees stretched. This is to be practised for some time.

Hopping. The starting of the body from the ground in the posture on tiptoe.

a. With the knees stiff; the body is raised by the elastic motion of the joints of the toes.

b. With bending the knees; the knees bend a little, but are stretched, as soon as the toes have left the ground. At coming down upon the ground, the knees bend but a little.

Both these kinds of hopping are to be practised.

a. on the spot,

b. moving from the place
forwards,
backwards,
laterally to the right and left.

Kicking, striking the breech with the heels. This motion exercises the flexibility of the knees still more than hopping with bending the knees.

a. In running, forwards, backwards and laterally. While one foot touches the ground, the other strikes the breech, the right foot the right side, the left, the left. The running must be slow, but the start from the ground high and in quick succession.

b. In apparent running. The preceding exercise, except that the gymnick remains on the spot.

c. Standing on one leg; the other leg is stretched forwards, before it strikes against the breech.

d. Standing upon one foot and striking the breech with it: the most difficult kind of kicking. This exercise, repeated twenty times in succession, produces great fatigue.

Crouching. The contracted posture of the body, the knees approaching the breast.

 a. With sitting. The upper part of the body is perpendicular, the thighs horizontal, and the heels close to the breech.

  1. On the spot.

  2. Moving from the place
   forwards,
   backwards,
   laterally, to the right and left.

This exercise is very fatiguing on account of the strong bend of the knees; but at the same time, it very much increases their flexibility.

 b. In leaping. Both knees are drawn at once towards the breast; it is done on the spot. Attention is to be paid to the upright carriage of the upper part of the body.

 c. The same exercise with this difference, that one knee is drawn up towards the breast, while the other foot is standing on the ground.

Straddling is the motion of both thighs to each side. The beginner places himself first before a chair or any other solid object, and takes hold of it, to avoid slipping; then slowly separates his feet; the toes are kept inwards, the knees stretched, and the soles pressed against the ground. This exercise must never be practised violently, but frequently.

If he has gained dexterity in this, the exercise is performed in springing, that is, he hops, with the hands placed on the hips, throws his legs to each side, observing the position before described, descends with legs closed, springs again without delay, and so on.

Stretching, when the body, from head to heels, forms a straight line. The different exercises of this kind consist either in preserving that position, or in moving in it, wherein the hands either assist, or rest close to the body. All of them are extremely strengthening to the joints of the back.

 a. Stretching with the assistance of the hands. Rising on tiptoe, crouching, hands extended forwards, falling forwards of the body without touching the ground with the knees, stretching of the body, so that it does not bend, but forms a straight line. The arms are in a right angle with the body. To stretch them out in a larger angle, tires too soon. Remaining for some time in this posture.

1. With the hands. The gymnick turns in the posture described above, so that the hands describe a circle, the feet forming the centre. The motion is first made to the right, then to the left. Great care must be taken not to sink or raise the back.

2. With the feet. The hands are in the centre, and the feet describe the circumference.

This circling can be performed:

1. the face towards the ground, and the feet resting upon the toes, or

2. the back towards the ground, and the feet resting on the heels. The latter is very difficult, but very exercising.

b. Stretching without the assistance of the hands. The hands are kept close to the body.

1. To be raised from the ground by another person in a straight and stretched posture.

2. To rest in a stretched posture over an excavation. This may be practised with three chairs, the middle one being taken away by the person himself: or upon a narrow joist resting on two chairs, with or without a balancing-pole.

3. To stretch out one's self, when the legs, up to the knees, are held by another person on a bench or chair; the body is bent at the hips, so as to form a right angle, the knees being stretched at the same time.

Further Readings

BOYKIN, JAMES, *History of Physical Training.* (Report of U.S. Commissioner of Education, vol. 1 (1891–1892), pp. 483–504.

DAMBACH, JOHN, *Physical Education in Germany.* New York: Teachers College, Columbia University, 1937.

LEONARD, FRED E., "The Beginnings of Modern Physical Training in Europe," *American Physical Education Review,* vol. 9, pp. 89–110.

———. "Jahn," *American Physical Education Review,* vol. 10, pp. 1–19.

VAN DALEN, D. B., ELMER MITCHELL and BRUCE BENNETT, *A World History of Physical Education.* Englewood Cliffs, N.J.: Prentice-Hall, Inc., 1953.

Questions for Discussion

1. Try to execute the exercises Jahn describes. What similarities do you see between these and some advocated currently, e.g., the Royal Canadian Air Force Exercises, Isometric Exercises?
2. What are the objects of Jahn's preparatory exercises?
3. What uses do we make today of warm-up exercises? Are these similar to the uses Jahn suggests?
4. What are some current theories of warm-up exercises?

PIERRE DE COUBERTIN

The Olympic Games of 1896*

At the same time that Jahn was working in Germany, Ling from Sweden and Nachtegall from Denmark made a definite contribution to the formalization and discipline of exercise. Before we can consider the pattern of the modern Olympic games, we must turn to a brief account of their work.

Swedish Physical Education. Ancient Swedish history shows no particular contribution to physical education. But from the nineteenth century, through the later work of Ling, Branting, Nyblaeus, and Ling's son, Sweden has contributed to physical education. Per Henrik Ling (1776–1839) based his gymnastic system upon rational and scientific foundations. To perpetuate his system, he founded the Royal Gymnastic Central Institute in Stockholm in 1814. The school later became the Stockholm Normal School of Gymnastics. Early in his student days, Ling found satisfaction in studying literature and foreign languages. After graduating from the University of Stockholm, he studied with the Danish gymnasts. He became interested in fencing and introduced this sport in the University of Lund in 1805, when

* Reprinted and abridged from *The Century Magazine*, vol. 80. New Series: vol. 31, November, 1896, pp. 39–53.

he became the fencing master. He stayed there until 1812. Because of a defect in one of his arms, he discovered the curative effects of fencing. His intense study of anatomy and physiology compelled Ling's belief that exercises should be planned for the individual rather than for large groups. He also believed in the importance of a citizenry ready for military combat. His whole system was based on the idea of therapeutic gymnastics.

Danish Physical Education. The development of Swedish and Danish gymnastics are parallel. Two main pioneers of popular gymnastics are important in Danish physical education. Franz Nachtegall (1777–1847) was inspired by the writings of Guts-Muths. He opened a private gymnasium in Copenhagen in 1799. It was the first institution of modern times to devote itself exclusively to physical "training." The news of Nachtegall's work spread, and it became very popular in both the city and the country. As a result of Nachtegall's work, Denmark became the first country formally to adopt gymnastics for the schools and the army. Gymnastics became compulsory in the public schools in 1828. Nachtegall was held in such high esteem that in 1821 the King appointed him the Director of the Civil, Army and Navy schools. Niels Bukh (1880–1950) was appointed the Director of Gymnastics in the People's School at Ollerup, Denmark. He reinterpreted Ling's gymnastics. He wanted to produce perfect exercises to bring about perfect development of the body. He directed his exercises toward the elimination of all bad posture habits and functional deformities. His exercises emphasized sustained movements without any "held" positions. Definite rhythmical bases can be seen in his gymnastics. Although much of the emphasis on apparatus is absent from Danish gymnastics, observation of contemporary Danish gymnasts reveals vestiges of Bukh's contributions.

Modern Olympic Games. Implicit in all the preceding readings is the fact that the national character of the Greek, Roman, English, and German peoples has been, in part, revealed through their sports, games, wars, and exercises.

Nationalism prompted the work of many of the early European pioneers in professional physical education. The desire and need to build strong men for military purposes stimulated new "systems" of physical education. Several decades after Jahn's work flourished in Germany, a young Frenchman, Baron

Pierre de Coubertin (1863–1937), dreamed of reawakening the national pride of France. France had lost the Franco-Prussian War to Germany and was in a state of internal strife. De Coubertin hoped to find a means to insure universal peace and to restore his country's self respect. He believed that international competition in sports might be the avenue through which to accomplish these objectives. Consequently, he worked diligently, travelling, talking, and persuading people all over the world to revive the Olympic games. Finally, in 1896 his goal materialized.

In the engrossing narrative about the first modern Olympic games from the pen of de Coubertin himself, one is reminded of the ancient Greek Olympic pattern. Observe how closely the games followed the ancient festival.

The Olympic Games of 1896
by Their Founder, Baron Pierre de Coubertin,
Now President of The International Committee

The Olympic games which recently took place at Athens were modern in character, not alone because of their programs, which substituted bicycle for chariot races, and fencing for the brutalities of pugilism, but because of their origin and regulations they were international and universal, and consequently adapted to the conditions in which athletics have developed at the present day. The ancient games had an exclusively Hellenic character; they were always held in the same place, and Greek blood was a necessary condition of admission to them. It is true that strangers were in time tolerated; but their presence at Olympia was rather a tribute paid to the superiority of Greek civilization than a right exercised in the name of racial equality. With the modern games it is quite otherwise. Their creation is the work of barbarians [the Greek name for all non-Greeks]. It is due to the delegates of the athletic associations of all countries assembled in congress at Paris in 1894. It was there agreed that every country should celebrate the Olympic games in turn. The first place belonged by right to Greece; it was accorded by unanimous vote; and in order to emphasize the permanence of the institution, its wide bearings, and its essentially cosmopolitan character, an international committee was appointed, the members of which were to represent the various nations, European and American, with whom athletics are held in honor. The presidency of this committee falls to the country in which the next games are to be held. A Greek, M. Bikelas, has presided for the last two years. A Frenchman now presides, and will continue to do so until 1900, since the next games are to take place at Paris during the Exposition. Where will those of 1904 take place? Perhaps at New York, perhaps at Berlin, or at Stockholm. The question is soon to be decided.

It was in virtue of these resolutions passed during the Paris Congress that the recent festivals were organized. Their successful issue is largely owing to the active and energetic cooperation of the Greek crown prince Constantine. When they realized all that was expected of them, the Athenians lost courage. They felt that the city's resources were not equal to the demands that would be made upon them; nor would the government (M. Tricoupis being then prime minister) consent to increase facilities. M. Tricoupis did not believe in the success of the games. He argued that the Athenians knew nothing about athletics; that they had neither the adequate grounds for the contests, nor athletes of their own to bring into line; and that, moreover, the financial situation of Greece forbade her inviting the world to an event preparations for which would entail such large expenditures. There was reason in these objections; but on the one hand, the prime minister greatly exaggerated the importance of the expenditures, and on the other, it was not necessary that the government should bear the burden of them directly. Modern Athens, which recalls in so many ways the Athens of ancient days, has inherited from her the privilege of being beautified and enriched by her children. The public treasury was not always very well filled in those times any more than in the present, but wealthy citizens who had made fortunes at a distance liked to crown their commercial career by some act of liberality to the mother-country. They endowed the land with superb edifices of general utility—theaters, gymnasia, temples. The modern city is likewise full of monuments which she owes to such generosity. It was easy to obtain from private individuals what the state could not give. The Olympic games had burned with so bright a luster in the past of the Greeks that they could not but have their revival at heart. And furthermore, the moral benefits would compensate largely for all pecuniary sacrifice.

This the crown prince apprehended at once, and it decided him to lend his authority to the organizing of the first Olympic games. He appointed a commission, with headquarters in his own palace; made M. Philemon, ex-mayor of Athens and a man of much zeal and enthusiasm, secretary-general; and appealed to the nation to subscribe the necessary funds. Subscriptions began to come in from Greece, but particularly from London, Marseilles, and Constantinople, where there are wealthy and influential Greek colonies. The chief gift came from Alexandria. It was this gift which made it possible to restore the Stadion to its condition in the time of Atticus Herodes. The intention had been from the first to hold the contests in this justly celebrated spot. No one, however, had dreamed that it might be possible to restore to their former splendor the marble seats which, it is said, could accommodate forty thousand persons. The great inclosure would have been utilized, and provisional wooden seats placed on the grassy slopes which surround it. Thanks to the generosity of M. Averoff, Greece is now the richer by a monument unique of its kind, and its visitors have seen a spectacle which they can never forget. . . .

While the Hellenic Committee labored over the scenic requirements, the international committee and the national committees were occupied in recruiting competitors. The matter was not as easy as one might think. Not only had indifference and distrust to be overcome, but the revival of the Olympic games had aroused a certain hostility. Although the Paris Congress had been careful to decree that every form of physical exercise practised in the world should have its place on the program, the gymnasts took offense. They considered that they had not been given sufficient prominence. The greater part of the gymnastic associations of Germany, France, and Belgium are animated by a rigorously exclusive spirit; they are not inclined to tolerate the presence of those forms of athletics which they themselves do not practise; what they disdainfully designate as English sports have become, because of their popularity, especially odious to them. These associations were not satisfied with declining the invitation sent them to repair to Athens. The Belgian federation wrote to the other federations, suggesting a concerted stand against the work of the Paris Congress. These incidents confirmed the opinions of the pessimists who had been foretelling the failure of the fetes, or their probable postponement. Athens is far away, the journey is expensive, and the Easter vacations are short. The contestants were not willing to undertake the voyage unless they could be sure that the occasion would be worth the effort. The different associations were not willing to send representatives unless they could be informed of the amount of interest which the contests would create. An unfortunate occurrence took place almost at the last moment. The German press, commenting on an article which had appeared in a Paris newspaper, declared that it was an exclusively Franco-Greek affair; that attempts were being made to shut out other nations; and furthermore, that the German associations had been intentionally kept aloof from the Paris Congress of 1894. The assertion was acknowledged to be incorrect, and was powerless to check the efforts of the German committee under Dr. Gebhardt. M. Kemeny in Hungary, Major Balck in Sweden, General de Boutonski in Russia, Professor W. M. Sloane in the United States, Lord Ampthill in England, Dr. Jiri Guth in Bohemia, were, meantime, doing their best to awaken interest in the event, and to reassure the doubting. They did not always succeed. Many people took a sarcastic view, and the newspapers indulged in some pleasantry on the subject of the Olympic games. . . .

The Greeks are novices in the matter of athletic sports, and had not looked for much success for their own country. One event only seemed likely to be theirs from its very nature—the long-distance run from Marathon, a prize for which has been newly founded by M. Michel Breal, a member of the French Institute, in commemoration of that soldier of antiquity who ran all the way to Athens to tell his fellow-citizens of the happy issue of the battle. The distance from Marathon to Athens is 42 kilometers. The road is rough and stony. The Greeks had trained for this run for a year past. Even in the remote districts of Thessaly young peasants prepared to enter as contestants. In three cases it is said that the enthusiasm and the inexperience of these young fellows cost them their lives, so exaggerated were their preparatory efforts. As the great day approached, women offered up prayers and votive tapers in the churches, that the victor might be a Greek!

The wish was fulfilled. A young peasant named Louës, from the village of Marousi, was the winner in two hours and fifty-five minutes. He reached the goal fresh and in fine form. He was followed by two other Greeks. The excellent Australian sprinter Flack, and the Frenchman Lermusiaux, who had been in the lead the first 35 kilometers, had fallen out by the way. When Louës came into the Stadion, the crowd, which numbered sixty thousand persons, rose to its feet like one man, swayed by extraordinary excitement. The King of Servia, who was present, will probably not forget the sight he saw that day. A flight of white pigeons was let loose, women waved fans and handkerchiefs, and some of the spectators who were nearest to Louës left their seats, and tried to reach him and carry him in triumph. He would have been suffocated if the crown prince and Prince George had not bodily led him away. A lady who stood next to me unfastened her watch, a gold one set with pearls, and sent it to him; an innkeeper presented him with an order good for three hundred and sixty-five free meals; and a wealthy citizen had to be dissuaded from signing a check for ten thousand francs to his credit. Louës himself, however, when he was told of this generous offer, refused it. The sense of honor, which is very strong in the Greek peasant, thus saved the non-professional spirit from a very great danger.

Needless to say that the various contests were held under amateur regulations. An exception was made for the fencing-matches, since in several countries professors of military fencing hold the rank of officers. For them a special contest was arranged. To all other branches of the athletic sports only amateurs were admitted. It is impossible to conceive the Olympic games with money prizes. But these rules, which seem simple enough, are a good deal complicated in their practical application by the fact that definitions of what constitutes an amateur differ from one country to another, sometimes even from one club to another. Several definitions are current in England; the Italians and the Dutch admit one which appears too rigid at one point, too loose at another. How conciliate these divergent or contradictory utterances? The Paris Congress made an attempt in that direction, but its decisions are not accepted everywhere as law, nor is its definition of amateurship everywhere adopted as the best. The rules and regulations, properly so called, are not any more uniform. This and that are forbidden in one country, authorized in another. All that one can do, until there shall be an Olympic code formulated in accordance with the ideas and the usages of the majority of athletes, is to choose among the codes now existing. It was decided, therefore, that the foot-races should be under the rules of the Union Francaise des Sports Athletiques; jumping, putting the shot, etc., under those of the Amateur Athletic Association of England; the bicycle-races under those of the International Cyclists' Association, etc. This had appeared to us the best way out of the difficulty; but we should have had many disputes if the judges (to whom had been given the Greek name of ephors) had not been headed by Prince George, who acted as final referee. . . .

Every night while the games were in progress the streets of Athens were illuminated. There were torch-light processions, bands played the different national hymns, and the students of the university got up ovations under the windows of the foreign athletic crews, and harangued them in the noble tongue of Demosthenes. Perhaps this tongue was somewhat abused. That Americans might not be compelled to understand French, nor Hungarians forced to speak German, the daily programs of the games, and even invitations to luncheon, were written in Greek. On receipt of these cards, covered with mysterious formulae, where even the date was not clear (the Greek calendar is twelve days behind ours), every man carried them to his hotel porter for elucidation. . . .

Then there were nocturnal festivities on the Acropolis, where the Parthenon was illuminated with colored lights, and at the Piraeus, where the vessels were hung with Japanese lanterns. Unluckily, the weather changed, and the sea was so high on the day appointed for the boat-races, which were to have taken place in the roadstead of Phalerum, that the project was abandoned. The distribution of prizes was likewise postponed for twenty-four hours. It came off with much solemnity, on the morning of April 15, in the Stadion. The sun shone again, and sparkled on the officers' uniforms. When the roll of the victors was called, it became evident, after all, that the international character of the institution was well guarded by the results of the contests. America had won nine prizes for athletic sports alone (flat races for 100 and 400 meters; 110-meter hurdle-race; high jump; broad jump; pole-vault; hop, step, and jump; putting the shot; throwing the discus), and two prizes for shooting (revolver, 25 and 30 meters); but France had the prizes for foil-fencing and for four bicycle-races; England scored highest in the one-handed weight-lifting contest, and in single lawn-tennis; Greece won the run from Marathon, two gymnastic contests (rings, climbing the smooth rope), three prizes for shooting (carbine, 200 and 300 meters; pistol, 25 meters), a prize for fencing with sabers, and a bicycle-race; Germany won in wrestling, in gymnastics (parallel bars, fixed bar, horse-leaping), and in double lawn-tennis; Australia, the 800-meter and 1500-meter foot-races on the flat; Hungary, swimming-matches of 100 and 1200 meters; Austria, the 500-meter swimming-match and the 12-hour bicycle-race; Switzerland, a gymnastic prize; Denmark, the two-handed weight-lifting contest.

The prizes were an olive-branch from the very spot, at Olympia, where stood the ancient Altis, a diploma drawn by a Greek artist, and a silver medal chiseled by the celebrated French engraver Chaplain. On one side of the medal is the Acropolis, with the Parthenon and the Propylaea; on the other a colossal head of the Olympian Zeus, after the type created by Phidias. The head of the god is blurred, as if by distance and the lapse of centuries, while in the foreground, in clear relief, is the Victory which Zeus holds on his hand. It is a striking and original conception. After the distribution of the prizes, the athletes formed for the traditional procession around the Stadion. Louës, the victor of Marathon, came first, bearing the Greek flag; then the Americans, the Hungarians, the French, the Germans. The ceremony, moreover, was made more memorable by a charming incident. One of the contestants, Mr. Robertson, an Oxford student, recited an ode which he had composed, in ancient Greek and in the Pindaric mode, in honor of the games. Music had opened them, and Poetry was present at their close; and thus was the bond once more renewed which in the past united the Muses with feats of physical strength, the mind with the well-trained body. The king announced that the first Olympiad was at an end, and left the Stadion, the band playing the Greek national hymn, and the crowd cheering. A few days later Athens was emptied of its guests. Torn wreaths littered the public squares; the banners which had floated merrily in the streets disappeared; the sun and the wind held sole possession of the marble sidewalks of Stadion street.

It is interesting to ask oneself what are likely to be the results of the Olympic games of 1896, as regards both Greece and the rest of the world. In the case of Greece, the games will be found to have had a double effect, one athletic, the other political. It is a well-known fact that the Greeks had lost completely, during their centuries of oppression, the taste for physical sports. There were good walkers among the mountaineers, and good swimmers in the scattered villages along the coast. It was a matter of pride with the young *palikar* to wrestle and to dance well, but that was because bravery and a gallant bearing were admired by those about him. Greek dances are far from athletic, and the wrestling-matches of peasants have none of the characteristics of true sports. The men of the towns had come to know no diversion beyond reading the newspapers, and violently discussing politics about the tables of the cafes. The Greek race, however, is free from the natural in-dolence of the Oriental, and it was manifest that the athletic habit would, if the opportunity offered, easily take root again among its men. Indeed, several gymnastic associations had been formed in recent years at Athens and Patras, and a rowing-club at Piraeus, and the public was showing a growing interest in their feats. It was therefore a favorable moment to speak the words, Olympic games. No sooner had it been made clear that Athens was to aid in the revival of the Olympiads than a perfect fever of muscular activity broke out all over the kingdom. And this was nothing to what followed the games. I have seen, in little villages far from the capital, small boys, scarcely out of long clothes, throwing big stones, or jumping improvised hurdles, and two urchins never met in the streets of Athens without running races. Nothing could ex-ceed the enthusiasm with which the victors in the contests were received, on their return to their native towns, by their fellow-citizens. They were met by the mayor and municipal authorities, and cheered by a crowd bearing branches of wild olive and laurel. In ancient times the victor entered the city through a breach made expressly in its walls. The Greek cities are no longer walled in, but one may say that athletics have made a breach in the heart of the nation. When one realizes the influence that the practice of physical exercises may have on the future of a country, and on the force of a whole race, one is tempted to wonder whether Greece is not likely to date a new era from the year 1896. It would be curious indeed if athletics were to become one of the factors in the Eastern question! Who can tell whether, by bringing a notable increase of vigor to the inhabitants of the country, it may not hasten the solution of this thorny problem? These are hypotheses, and circumstances make light of such calculations at long range. But a local and immediate consequence of the games may already be found in the internal politics of Greece. I have spoken of the active part taken by the crown prince and his brothers, Prince George and Prince Nicholas, in the labors of the organizing com-mittee. It was the first time that the heir apparent had had an opportunity of thus coming into contact with his future subjects. They knew him to be patriotic and high-minded, but they did not know his other admirable and solid qualities. Prince Constantine inherits his fine blue eyes and fair coloring from his Danish ancestors, and his frank, open manner, his self-poise, and his mental lucidity come from the same source; but Greece has given him enthusiasm and ardor, and this happy combination of prudence and high spirit makes him especially adapted to govern the Hellenes. The authority, mingled with perfect liberality, with which he managed the committee, his exactitude in detail, and more particularly his quiet perseverance when those about him were inclined to hesitate and to lose courage, make it clear that his reign will be one of fruitful labor, which can only strengthen and enrich his country. The Greek people have now a better idea of the worth of their future sovereign: they have seem him at work, and have gained respect for and confidence in him.

So much for Greece. On the world at large the Olympic games have, of course, exerted no influence as yet; but I am profoundly convinced that they will do so. May I be permitted to say that this was my reason for founding them? Modern athletics need to be *unified* and *purified*. Those who have followed the renaissance of physical sports in this century know that discord reigns supreme from one end of them to the other. Every country has its own rules; it is not possible even to come to an agreement as to who is an amateur, and who is not. All over the world there is one perpetual dispute, which is further fed by innumerable weekly, and even daily, newspapers. In this deplorable state of things professionalism tends to grow apace. Men give up their whole existence to one particular sport, grow rich by practising it, and thus deprive it of all nobility, and destroy the just equilibrium of man by making the muscles preponderate over the mind. It is my belief that no education, particularly in democratic times, can be good and complete without the aid of athletics; but athletics, in order to play their proper educational role, must be based on perfect disinterestedness and the sentiment of honor.

If we are to guard them against these threatening evils, we must put an end to the quarrels of amateurs, that they may be united among themselves, and willing to measure their skill in frequent international encounters. But what country is to impose its rules and its habits on the others? The Swedes will not yield to the

Germans, nor the French to the English. Nothing better than the international Olympic games could therefore be devised. Each country will take its turn in organizing them. When they come to meet every four years in these contests, further ennobled by the memories of the past, athletes all over the world will learn to know one another better, to make mutual concessions, and to seek no other reward in the competition than the honor of the victory. One may be filled with desire to see the colors of one's club or college triumph in a national meeting; but how much stronger is the feeling when the colors of one's country are at stake! I am well assured that the victors in the Stadion at Athens wished for no other recompense when they heard the people cheer the flag of their country in honor of their achievement.

It was with these thoughts in mind that I sought to revive the Olympic games. I have succeeded after many efforts. Should the institution prosper,—as I am persuaded, all civilized nations aiding, that it will,—it may be a potent, if indirect, factor in securing universal peace. Wars break out because nations misunderstand each other. We shall not have peace until the prejudices which now separate the different races shall have been outlived. To attain this end, what better means than to bring the youth of all countries periodically together for amicable trials of muscular strength and agility? The Olympic games, with the ancients, controlled athletics and promoted peace. It is not visionary to look to them for similar benefactions in the future.

Further Readings

COUBERTIN, PIERRE DE, "The Re-establishment of the Olympic Games," *The Chatauquan*, September 1894.

KIERAN, JOHN and ARTHUR DALEY, *The Story of the Olympic Games, 776 B.C.–1960 A.D.*, rev. ed. Philadelphia: J. B. Lippincott Company, 1961.

MEZO, FERENC, *The Modern Olympic Games*. Budapest: Pannonia Press, 1956.

WEBSTER, FREDERICK A., *Olympic Cavalcade*. London and New York: Hutchinson & Co. (Publishers), Ltd., 1948.

WEYAND, ALEXANDER M., *The Olympic Pageant*. New York: The Macmillan Company, 1952.

Questions for Discussion

1. What were some of the reasons for Baron de Coubertin's reviving the Olympic games?
2. Do you think any of his ideas on world-wide peace and greater intercultural understanding have materialized?
3. How does the concept of amateurism described by de Coubertin in 1896 compare with what we believe today?
4. State some results, other than the achievement of athletic prowess, possible from participation in the Olympic games. Discuss the influence of these goals on amateurism.

BENJAMIN FRANKLIN

On Swimming*

Colonial Days in America. Many writings of colonial days refer to the importance of physical exercise. The essays and letters of Benjamin Rush, M.D. (1745–1813), Thomas Jefferson (1743–1826), Noah Webster (1758–1843), and Benjamin Franklin (1706–1790) bear this out. Franklin wrote about his educational ideas, which included some definite notions about the place of physical activity in the people's lives. The following letter to his friend Oliver Neave constitutes a pleasing example of Franklin's ability to analyze. Although swimming teachers may take exception to some of Franklin's statements, they surely must share his interest in this recreational activity, which this letter so well illustrates.

To Oliver Neave

Dear Sir,

I cannot be of opinion with you that it is too late in life for you to learn to swim. The river near the bottom of your garden affords a most convenient place for the purpose. And as your new

* Reprinted from Benjamin Franklin's *Autobiography and Selected Writings*, edited by L. Ziff. New York: Holt, Rinehart and Winston, Inc., 1948, pp. 283–286.

employment requires your being often on the water, of which you have such a dread, I think you would do well to make the trial; nothing being so likely to remove those apprehensions as the consciousness of an ability to swim to the shore, in case of an accident, or of supporting yourself in the water till a boat could come to take you up.

I do not know how far corks or bladders may be useful in learning to swim, having never seen much trial of them. Possibly they may be of service in supporting the body while you are learning what is called the stroke, or that manner of drawing in and striking out the hands and feet that is necessary to produce progressive motion. But you will be no swimmer till you can place some confidence in the power of the water to support you; I would therefore advise the acquiring that confidence in the first place; especially as I have known several, who, by a little of the practice necessary for that purpose, have insensibly acquired the stroke, taught as it were by nature.

The practice I mean is this. Choosing a place where the water deepens gradually, walk coolly into it till it is up to your breast, then turn round, your face to the shore, and throw an egg into the water between you and the shore. It will sink to the bottom, and be easily seen there, as your water is clear. It must lie in water so deep as that you cannot reach it to take it up but by diving for it. To encourage yourself in order to do this, reflect that your progress will be from deeper to shallower water, and that at any time you may, by bringing your legs under you and standing on the bottom, raise your head far above the water. Then plunge under it with your eyes open, throwing yourself towards the egg, and endeavouring by the action of your hands and feet against the water to get forward till within reach of it. In this attempt you will find, that the water buoys you up against your inclination; that it is not so easy a thing to sink as you imagined; that you cannot but by active force get down to the egg. Thus you feel the power of the water to support you, and learn to confide in that power; while your endeavors to overcome it, and to reach the egg, teach you the manner of acting on the water with your feet and hands, which action is afterwards used in swimming to support your head higher above water, or to go forward through it.

I would the more earnestly press you to the trial of this method, because, though I think I satisfied you that your body is lighter than water, and that you might float in it a long time with your mouth free for breathing, if you would put yourself in a proper posture, and would be still and forbear struggling; yet till you have obtained this experimental confidence in the water, I cannot depend on your having the necessary presence of mind to recollect that posture and the directions I gave you relating to it. The surprise may put all out of your mind. For though we value ourselves on being reasonable, knowing creatures, reason and knowledge seem on such occasions to be of little use to us; and the brutes, to whom we allow scarce a glimmering of either, appear to have the advantage of us.

I will, however, take this opportunity of repeating those particulars to you, which I mentioned in our last conversation, as, by perusing them at your leisure, you may possibly imprint them so in your memory as on occasion to be of some use to you.

1. That though the legs, arms, and head, of a human body, being solid parts, are specifically something heavier than fresh water, yet the trunk, particularly the upper part, from its hollowness, is so much lighter than water, as that the whole of the body taken together is too light to sink wholly under water, but some part will remain above, until the lungs become filled with water, which happens from drawing water into them instead of air, when a person in the fright attempts breathing while the mouth and nostrils are under water.

2. That the legs and arms are specifically lighter than salt water, and will be supported by it, so that a human body would not sink in salt water, though the lungs were filled as above, but from the greater specific gravity of the head.

3. That therefore a person throwing himself on his back in salt water, and extending his arms, may easily lie so as to keep his mouth and nostrils free for breathing; and by a small motion of his hands may prevent turning, if he should perceive any tendency to it.

4. That in fresh water, if a man throws himself on his back, near the surface, he cannot long continue in that situation but by proper action of his hands on the water. If he uses no such action, the legs and lower part of the body will gradually sink till he comes into an upright position, in which he will continue suspended, the hollow of the breast keeping the head uppermost.

5. But if, in this erect position, the head is kept upright above the shoulders, as when we stand on the ground, the immersion will,

by the weight of that part of the head that is out of water, reach above the mouth and nostrils, perhaps a little above the eyes, so that a man cannot long remain suspended in water with his head in that position.

6. The body continuing suspended as before, and upright, if the head be leaned quite back, so that the face looks upwards, all the back part of the head being then under water, and its weight consequently in a great measure supported by it, the face will remain above water quite free for breathing, will rise an inch higher every inspiration, and sink as much every expiration, but never so low as that the water may come over the mouth.

7. If therefore a person, unacquainted with swimming and falling accidentally into the water, could have presence of mind sufficient to avoid struggling and plunging, and to let the body take this natural position, he might continue long safe from drowning till perhaps help would come. For as to the clothes, their additional weight while immersed is very inconsiderable, the water supporting it, though when he comes out of the water, he would find them very heavy indeed.

But, as I said before, I would not advise you or any one to depend on having this presence of mind on such an occasion, but learn fairly to swim; as I wish all men were taught to do in their youth. They would, on many occurrences, be the safer for having that skill, and on many more the happier, as freer from painful apprehensions of danger, to say nothing of the enjoyment in so delightful and wholesome an exercise. Soldiers particularly should, methinks, all be taught to swim; it might be of frequent use either in surprising an enemy, or saving themselves. And if I had now boys to educate, I should prefer those schools (other things being equal) where an opportunity was afforded for acquiring so advantageous an art, which, once learned, is never forgotten.

I am, sir, &c.
B. Franklin

Further Readings

JEFFERSON, THOMAS, *A Jefferson Profile As Revealed in His Letters*, selected and arranged by Saul K. Padover. New York: The John Day Company, Inc., 1956. (Letter to Peter

Carr, Jefferson's nephew, p. 24, and letter to William Short, p. 306.)

RUSH, BENJAMIN, *Essays, Literary, Moral and Philosophical.* Philadelphia: Thomas and William Bradford, 1806, pp. 60–61.

WEBSTER, NOAH, *A Collection of Essays and Fugitiv Writings.* Boston: I. Thomas and E. T. Andrews, 1790, p. 388.

Questions for Discussion

1. Which of the admonitions given by Franklin to Neave have validity for the teaching of swimming today?
2. What is Franklin's basis for analyzing skills? Does he believe in gradual progression in skill development from the simple to the complex; or does he use the "whole method"? Explain your answer.
3. What significance do you find in the fact that men like Jefferson, Rush, Webster, and Franklin took a vital interest in the necessity for physical education?

MARSHALL B. DAVIDSON

America Learns to Play*

Recreational Life in America. This section of the book has stressed historical development to demonstrate what elements in life have shaped attitudes toward physical education over the centuries. From these selections the student should conclude that common problems concerning physical education exist throughout the history of Western man.

To make the student aware of the important place of physical activity in our country and the preferences Americans express

* Reprinted and abridged with permission of the publisher from Marshall B. Davidson, *Life in America.* Boston: Houghton Mifflin Company. Copyright © by Marshall B. Davidson, 1951. Vol. 2, pp. 6–16, 22–37.

in their leisure-time pursuits, we turn to an account of recreation in the early development of our country.

Games played with a ball may, as Thomas Jefferson observed, stamp no character on the mind but, in one form or another they have provided an immemorial pastime for American children, men, and occasionally, even women.

"Let any one visit Washington Parade, or indeed any of the fields in that neighborhood," reported the New York *Evening Post* in 1828, "and he will find large groups of men and boys playing ball and filling the air with their shouts and yells . . . the annoyance has become absolutely intolerable . . . and ought to be put an end to without delay." The complaint could have been written almost any time in any American community; the end is not yet in sight.

In spite of its danger to health ("by sudden and alternate heats and cold"), to limbs, and to the propriety of gentlemen scholars, college students played their games with sticks and balls on most early campuses and commons. Cricket enjoyed popularity where English influence lingered. But the time required to complete a game, two days on an average, was a handicap to American participants. Leisure in the new republic was not yet so abundant nor, according to high opinion, without a serious menace to the morals. morals.

Off campus and on, in the fall of the year, football of one sort or another was popular by the end of the eighteenth century. "Before winter comes on the Foot Ball," wrote William Bentley, the noted Salem divine and diarist, in 1791, "which is differently pursued in different places. In Marblehead, even heads of families engage in it, & all the fishermen while at home at this season. The bruising of shins has rendered it rather disgraceful to those of better education." The game was, he added, "unfriendly to clothes, as well as safety."

The ball used might have been a leather-covered bladder or a bag filled with sawdust. The game itself was highly informal and unsystematized and attracted few spectators. It was, and remained for long years, purely a participant's sport. President Timothy Dwight of Yale College was allegedly, (watched) . . . his students play football in tall hats and swallowtail coats, hardly constituted a cheering section. In 1822, as a matter of fact, the college prohibited the game in its buildings or yard under pain of a fine "not exceeding fifty cents."

Golf, in one form or another, seems to have been a pastime of New Yorkers from the seventeenth century. The inventory of Governor Burnet in 1729 mentions "Nine Gouff Clubs, one iron ditto and seven dozen balls." This may possibly have referred to a form of midget golf more closely related to hockey than modern golf, . . . a game played with a crooked club, a small ball, and holes in the turf of an enclosure. Fifty years later the *Royal Gazette* of New York carried an advertisement for what was probably a more familiar version of the game: "To the Golf Players. The season for this pleasant and healthy Exercise now advancing, Gentlemen may be furnished with excellent Clubs and the veritable Caledonian Balls, by enquiring at the Printers'." After the Revolution, the game was for a while played in other colonies as well, although interest then lapsed for almost a century.

During the hot seasons people of all rank sought refreshment in and by the water. As ever, men and boys took their dips with complete informality, at the risk of "exposing themselves to the walks of gentlemen and ladies." Ladies were more circumspect but no less eager for the plunge. At New Lebanon in 1792, Mary Palmer Tyler recalled: "Several of my companions . . . would swim like mermaids . . . The swimmers would dive off the platform and after sporting around like a bevy of boys skip up the stairs and dress themselves, telling me I was foolish not to share so great a luxury."

Most early cities had provisions for public bathing in the form of highly popular floating baths with showers, attendants, and other conveniences. In such places the proprieties were more strictly regarded. "We saw the females," wrote William Bentley in his diary for 1819, "not uncovered, enjoying the water of the cove." He probably meant they were completely clothed. A swimming school started in Boston in 1827 won immediate success, attracting such patrons as Audubon and John Quincy Adams who, at sixty-one, took occasional dives from its six-foot springboard.

Of all leisure-time pursuits dancing enjoyed the greatest popularity with both sexes in country and city alike. The Reverend Andrew Burnaby, an early British critic of American ways, had complained that the dancing he saw in the country districts of

Virginia before the Revolution was "without method or regularity." "A gentleman and lady stand up," he wrote, "and dance about the room, one of them retiring, the other pursuing, then perhaps meeting, in an irregular fantastical manner. After some time, another lady gets up, and then the first lady must sit down, she being as they term it, cut out: the second lady acts the same part which the first did, till somebody cuts her out. The gentlemen perform in the same manner."

New steps introduced into the cities spread rapidly even into rural and inland regions. Reactionaries who protested against "the abomination of permitting a man who was neither your lover nor your husband to encircle you with his arms, and slightly press the contour of your waist," were powerless to discourage such exciting new diversions as the polka and the waltz.

The public rooms of such magnificent new establishments as the Tremont House in Boston, the first "modern" hotel of America, provided large, novel arenas for those who must dance. While the elders frowned at this fresh invitation to popular, public amusement, dancing provided rare and irresistible occasions for the sexes to mix in their recreation. At a public ball in Cincinnati Mrs. Trollope was surprised to find "a large room filled with extremely well-dressed company, among whom were many very beautiful girls. . . . I had not yet been long enough in Western America," she added, "not to feel startled at recognizing in almost every full-dressed *beau* that passed me, the master or shopman that I had been used to see behind the counter, or lolling at the door of every shop in the city."

In the still farther West dancing could be a riotous revel that attracted people from many miles about and that lasted through the night if not through the entire week. On the distant frontier Indian squaws substituted for their white sisters on the dance floor and, from some reports, went through their steps with quite as much grace. . . .

In spite of . . . observations [to the contrary] it was growing increasingly difficult for the ordinary city dweller to find the right place and time to indulge in outdoor sports and other active leisure-time pursuits. To those with a country background, and they were many, such limitations canceled out much of the advantage of urban life. "The physical deterioration of the Americans, as a people," dolefully commented *Harper's Weekly,* is remarked upon by almost every traveler who comes among us. . . . The employments of American women, especially of those resident in cities, are so entirely sedentary, that they do continual violence to the laws of nature." In 1832 *Atkinson's Casket* recommended to city-bound females the calisthenic exercises . . . which were "calculated to give strength, not only to the arms and shoulders, but also to the back."

The portrait of the urban male, as drawn by *The People's Magazine* in 1835, was even more grim. "How often do we see a young man with an intelligent but very pale countenance," the periodical asked, "whose legs have hardly strength to support the weight of his bent and emaciated body? He once probably was a strong and active boy, but he came to the city, shut himself up in an office, took no exercise because he was not obliged to take any, grew nervous and bilious . . . and may probably linger out a few years of wretched existence, when death will be welcomed as his best friend."

Some Americans felt with John Adams that the bloom of life was lost indoors at the billiard table. To play the ancient game well was a clear sign of ill-spent youth. But the game had its many devotees over the years, including one woman who wrote to *The Ladies' Billiard Messenger* (a periodical "Devoted to Literature and Billiards") that the game made her forget all her troubles, and that she could play it confident that she was not sacrificing health to a morbid appetite for amusement.

A sport criticized along with billiards was pin bowling, of which the first recorded match in America was held at the Knickerbocker Saloon, Broadway, New York—"the largest bowling saloon in the world," it was reported—in 1840, although bowling on the green was an old sport. The air of dissipation that hung heavy over the alleys made them a public nuisance, the press remarked. The game was prohibited in several places and popular interest did not develop elsewhere on a large scale until late in the century.

A quarter of a century after the complaints of invalidism registered in *Atkinson's Casket* and *The People's Magazine*, the situation had apparently worsened. "I am satisfied," wrote Oliver Wendell Holmes in an *Atlantic Monthly* of 1858, "that such a set of black-coated, stiff-jointed, soft-muscled, paste-complexioned youth as we can boast in our Atlantic cities never before sprang from loins of Anglo-Saxon lineage . . . and as for any great athletic feat performed by a gentleman in these latitudes, society would drop a man who should run round the Common in five minutes." Another writer in the same magazine commented on the current belief that physical vigor and spiritual sanctity were incompatible. In a sporting match the best preacher would be chosen last since athletic capacity was in inverse ratio to spiritual accomplishment. There were clergymen, however, who recognized the importance of a sound constitution if their work in improving humanity was to be successful and who lent both their approval and attendance to gymnasiums. The strengthening of the flesh, it was hoped, might encourage more "willingness of the spirit."

The first gymnasium in the United States was opened at the Round Hill School in Northampton, Massachusetts, by Dr. Karl Beck, a German refugee, in 1825. In the years immediately following, first-class establishments were set up in the larger cities and enjoyed the patronage of the best people. Supporting the cause, the New York *Evening Post* advised its readers in 1830 that it could "be assumed that a physically healthy population is likewise a moral one and vice versa. Morality being thus closely linked with and dependent upon health, and a dense population unfavorable to the latter, it ought to be a popular sentiment in all our large cities to establish and support institutions intended to develop our physical power and give health and vigor to the human frame." The instructor at the New York gymnasium was a well-known English pugilist who taught boxing as a gymnastic art and manly science, not to be confused with the brutal sport of prize fighting.

An instructor in Boston had proposed to teach the art of boxing as early as 1798. It was, said a slightly later teacher, a gentleman's necessary defense against the ungovernable passions of ruffians. As practised professionally, however, the sport was more offensive, in every sense of that word, then defensive. Fighting with bare knuckles and with few rules stated or observed fell little short of the mayhem of frontier fighting. Death or disfiguration was not unusual. It remained popular largely as a spectator's sport, although much of the press railed against it as a brutal, uncivilized importation from England, all of which it was.

In 1835 the New York *Mirror* printed an alarm stating that "the detestable practise of prize-fighting threatens to take root within the soil of our native land." Twenty-four years later *Leslie's Illustrated Newspaper* identified the sport with the "lowest vice of our cities" but played safe by sending a special correspondent and an artist to London to cover the famous international bout between John C. Heenan, America's favorite "Benicia Boy," and Tom Sayers, the English champion in 1860.

Laws prohibiting fights in America were numerous, but a growing public found the excitement it craved in watching or even often in reading about such contests. In 1849 when Yankee Sullivan fought Tom Hyer, the bout was held in the backwoods of Maryland to escape the law, but by 1860 when the champion, Heenan, held an exhibition at Jones Wood outside New York, the crowd had grown to thirty thousand spectators. . . .

Further Readings

DULLES, FOSTER RHEA, *America Learns to Play*. New York: Appleton-Century-Crofts, Inc., 1940.

LYND, ROBERT S. and HELEN M., *Middletown: A Study in Contemporary American Culture*. New York: Harcourt, Brace & World, Inc., 1929.

STEINER, JESSE F., *Americans at Play*. New York: McGraw-Hill Inc., 1933.

TUNIS, JOHN R., *Sport for the Fun of It*. New York: A. S. Barnes & Co., Inc., 1940.

WHITE, WILLIAM ALLEN, "A Typical Kansas Community," *Atlantic Monthly*, vol. 80 (1897), pp. 171–77.

Questions for Discussion

1. How did recreational interests in Colonial America differ from those of today?

2. What evidence, in addition to Holmes' observation, can you find that youth and adults sorely needed physical activity in the early days of our country?

3. To what extent are the major recreational interests in our country today similar to the ones described for early America?

GRANTLAND RICE

Notre Dame's Cyclone
Beats Army, 13 to 7*

As the previous article suggests, gymnastics were first inaugurated at the Round Hill School in Northampton, Massachusetts, in 1825. A follower of Jahn's German system, Charles Beck (1798–1866) became the director of this school. Gymnastics were introduced in the New York High School in 1825, and the first American college to include gymnastics was Harvard College in 1826. Charles Follen (1796–1840) directed this program. The first noteworthy public gymnasium in the United States was Boston Gymnasium established in 1826. Charles Follen also served as the director of this school until he was succeeded by Francis Lieber (1800–1872) in 1827. These men all emigrated from Germany and brought Jahn's gymnastic system with them.

Between the years 1830 and 1860 gymnastics programs were dormant. The revival of gymnastics is credited to the efforts of Dio Lewis (1823–1886). He became the director of the Boston Normal Institute for Physical Education in 1861. This school lasted for only ten years.

The advent of the Civil War checked the wide-spread interest in gymnastics generated by Lewis' work and furthered by the many contributions of Catherine Beecher (1800–1878). After the war, there was little popular interest in gymnastics. As time went on, however, people renewed their love for outdoor sports. Colleges built expensive gymnasiums, and ethnic groups in many cities felt the need to perform and promulgate their cultural games, dances and exercises. Arguments ensued over whether Swedish or German gymnastics should be used in schools and colleges. A significant conference, the *Conference in the Interests of Physical Training*, was called in Boston on November 29–30, 1889. This major dispute was resolved at the conference, which approved Swedish gymnastics. Mrs. Mary Hemenway, whose generosity had made the conference possible,

---

* From the *New York Herald Tribune*, October 19, 1924. © 1924, New York Herald Tribune Inc. Reprinted with permission.

was an advocate of the Swedish system, and she donated funds
for the establishment of the Boston Normal School of Gymnastics in 1889. This marked an epoch in "physical training" in
America. Development of physical education in the United
States had many pioneers. The student is directed to the work of
such educators as Edward Hartwell, Dudley Sargent, Luther
Gulick, William Anderson, Nils Posse, Watson Savage, Del-
phine Hanna, Mary Channing Coleman, Amy Morris Homans,
Frederick Cozens, Edward Hitchcock, Joseph Lee, Senda Ber-
enson, and James McCurdy.

In the early 1900's, Clark Hetherington, Thomas Wood, and
later Jesse Feiring Williams, among others, revolted against the
formalized systems of gymnastics of Jahn and Ling. They
initiated the transition to what we might call a "naturalized"
program of physical education. Games and sports originally
transplanted from other countries, mainly from England,
gradually became popular in America. The development and
inclusion of American football and baseball, among other
sports and games, in the physical education programs of schools
and colleges began to change the character of American physical
education.

The interest and devotion to sports by the American people is
vividly portrayed in the classic account by Grantland Rice of
the great Notre Dame–Army football game of 1924. In this
piece note the intense emotionalism surrounding the game.
Compare this with the attitudes toward games seen in the selections from the *Iliad* and the first Olympic games. Observe the
crafty Stuhldreher and how he exemplifies the same attributes
as Odysseus in Homer's *Iliad*. The reiteration of the deep interest in the contestants, in the performance, the environment
brings about the preoccupation with the kinds of entertainment
people want and obviously need runs through all the historical
selections. Despite apparent changes in emphasis, usage, and
purpose, the persistent underlying significance of sports and
games cannot be denied.

Outlined against a blue-gray October sky, the Four Horsemen
rode again. In dramatic lore they are known as Famine, Pestilence,
Destruction and Death. These are only aliases. Their real names
are Stuhldreher, Miller, Crowley and Layden. They formed the

crest of the South Bend cyclone before which another fighting Army football team was swept over the precipice at the Polo Grounds yesterday afternoon as 55,000 spectators peered down on the bewildering panorama spread on the green plain below.

A cyclone can't be snared. It may be surrounded, but somewhere it breaks through to keep on going. When the cyclone starts from South Bend, where the candle lights still gleam through the Indiana sycamores, those in the way must take to storm cellars at top speed. Yesterday the cyclone struck again, as Notre Dame beat the Army, 13 to 7, with a set of backfield stars that ripped and crashed through a strong Army defense with more speed and power than the warring cadets could meet.

Marvelous Backfield

Notre Dame won its ninth game in twelve Army starts through the driving power of one of the greatest backfields that ever churned up the turf of any gridiron in any football age. Brilliant backfields may come and go, but in Stuhldreher, Miller, Crowley and Layden, covered by a fast and charging line, Notre Dame can take its place in front of the field.

Coach McEwan sent one of his finest teams into action, an aggressive organization that fought to the last play around the first rim of darkness, but when Rockne rushed his Four Horsemen to the track they rode down everything in sight. It was in vain that 1,100 gray-clad cadets pleaded for the Army to hold. The Army line was giving all it had, but when a tank tears in with the speed of a motorcycle, what chance has flesh and blood to hold? The Army had its share of stars in action, such stars as Garbisch, Farwick, Wilson, Wood, Ellinger and many others, but they were up against four whirlwind backs who picked up top speed from the first step as they swept through scant openings to slip on by the secondary defense. The Army had great backs in Wilson and Wood, but the Army had no such quartet, who seemed to carry the mixed blood of the tiger and the antelope.

Cyclone Starts Like Zephyr

Rockne's light and tottering line was just about as tottering as the Rock of Gilbralter. It was something more than a match for the Army's great set of forwards, who had earned their fame before.

Yet it was not until the second period that the first big thrill of the afternoon set the great crowd into a cheering whirl and brought about the wild flutter of flags that are thrown to the wind in exciting moments. At the game's start Rockne sent in almost entirely a second string cast. The Army got the jump and began to play most of the football. It was the Army attack that made three first downs before Notre Dame had caught its stride. The South Bend cyclone opened like a zephyr.

And then, in the wake of a sudden cheer, out rushed Stuhldreher, Miller, Crowley and Layden, the four star backs who helped to beat the Army a year ago. Things were to be a trifle different now. After a short opening flurry in the second period, Wood, of the Army, kicked out of bounds on Notre Dame's 20-yard line. The cloud in the west at this point was no larger than a football. There was no sign of a tornado starting. But it happened to be at just this spot that Stuhldreher decided to put on his attack and begin the long and dusty hike.

Dynamite Goes Off

On the first play the fleet Crowley peeled off fifteen yards and the cloud from the west was now beginning to show signs of lightning and thunder. The fleet, powerful Layden got six yards more and then Don Miller added ten. A forward pass from Stuhldreher to Crowley added twelve yards and a moment later Don Miller ran twenty yards around the Army's right wing. He was on his way to glory when Wilson, hurtling across the right of way nailed him out of bounds. Crowley, Miller and Layden—Miller, Layden and Crowley—one or another, ripping and crashing through, as the Army defense threw everything it had in the way to stop this wild charge that had now come seventy yards. Crowley and Layden added five yards more and then on a split play, Layden went ten yards across the line as if he had just been fired from the black mouth of a howitzer.

In that second period Notre Dame made eight first downs to the Army's none, which shows the unswerving power of the Western attack that hammered relentlessly and remorselessly without easing up for a second's breath. The Western line was going its full share, led by the crippled Walsh with a broken hand.

But always there was Miller or Crowley or Layden, directed through the right spot by the cool and crafty judgment of Stuhldreher, who picked his plays with the finest possible generalship. The South Bend cyclone had now roared eighty-five yards to a touchdown through one of the strongest defensive teams in the game. The cyclone had struck with too much speed and power to be stopped. It was the preponderance of Western speed that swept the Army back.

The next period was much like the second. The trouble began when the alert Layden intercepted an Army pass on the 48-yard line. Stuhldreher was ready for another march.

Once again the cheering crowds began to call for a rallying stand. They are never overwhelmed by any shadows of defeat as long as there is a minute of fighting left. But silence fell over the cadet sector for just a second as Crowley ran around the Army's right wing for 10 yards, where Wilson hauled him down on the 33-yard line. Walsh, the western captain, was hurt in the play but soon resumed. Miller got 7 and Layden got 8 and then, with the ball on the Army's 20-yard line, the cadet defense rallied and threw Miller in his tracks. But the halt was only for the moment. On the next play Crowley swung out around the Army's left wing, cut in and then crashed over the line for Notre Dame's second touchdown.

On two other occasions the Notre Dame attack almost scored. Yeomans saving one touchdown by intercepting a pass on his 5-yard line as he ran back thirty-five yards before he was nailed by two tacklers. It was a great play in the nick of time. On the next drive Miller and Layden in two hurricane dashes took the ball forty-two yards to the Army's 14-yard line, where the still game Army defense stopped four plunges on the 9-yard line and took the ball.

Army Line Outplayed

Up to this point the Army had been outplayed by a crushing margin. Notre Dame had put under way four long marches, and two of these had yielded touchdowns. Even the stout and experienced Army line was meeting more than it could hold. Notre Dame's brilliant backs had been provided with the finest possible interference, usually led by Stuhldreher, who cut down tackler after tackler by diving headlong at some rival's flying knees. Against this each Army attack had been smothered almost before it got under way. Even the great Wilson, the star from Penn State, one of the great backfield runners of his day and time, rarely had a chance to make any headway through a massed wall of tacklers who were blocking every open route.

The sudden change came late in the third quarter, when Wilson, raging like a wild man, suddenly shot through a tackle opening to run thirty-four yards on to midfield before he was finally collared and thrown with a jolt. A few moments later Wood, one of the best of all the punters, kicked out of bounds on Notre Dame's 5-yard line. Here was the chance. Layden was forced to kick from behind his own goal. The punt soared up the field as Yeomans called for a free kick on the 35-yard line. As he caught the ball he was nailed and spilled by a Western tackler, and the penalty gave the Army fifteen yards, with the ball on Notre Dame's 20-yard line.

At this moment Harding was rushed to quarter in place of Yeomans, who had been one of the leading Army stars. On the first three plays, the Army reached the 12-yard line, but it was now fourth down, with two yards left to go. Harding's next play was the feature of the game.

As the ball was passed he faked a play to Wood, diving through the line, held the oval for just a half breath and then, tucking the same under his arm swung out around Notre Dame's right end. The brilliant fake worked to perfection. The entire Notre Dame defense had charged forward in a surging mass to check the line attack and Harding, with open territory, sailed on for a touchdown. He traveled those last twelve yards after the manner of food shot from guns. He was over the line before the Westerners knew what had taken place. It was a fine bit of strategy, brilliantly carried out by every member of the cast.

The cadet sector had its chance to rip open the chilly atmosphere at last, and most of the 55,000 present joined in the tribute to football art. But this was the Army's last chance to score. From that point on it was see-saw, up and down, back and forth, with the rivals fighting bitterly for every inch of ground. It was harder now to make a foot than it had been to make ten yards. Even the all-star South Bend cast could no longer continue a romp for any set distances, as Army tacklers, inspired by the touchdown, charged harder and faster than they had charged before.

The Army brought a fine football team into action, but it was beaten by a faster and smoother team. Rockne's supposedly light, green line was about as big as the Army's and every whit as aggressive. What is even more important, it was faster on its feet, faster in getting around.

It was Western speed and perfect interference that once more brought about Army doom. The Army line couldn't get through fast enough to break up the attacking plays, and once started the bewildering speed and power of the Western backs slashed along for eight, ten and fifteen yards on play after play. And always in front of these offensive drives could be found the whirling form of Stuhldreher, taking the first man out of the play, as cleanly as if he had used a hand grenade at close range. This Notre Dame interference was a marvelous thing to look upon.

It formed quickly and came along in unbroken order, always at terrible speed, carried by backs who were as hard to drag down as African buffaloes. On receiving the kick-off, Notre Dame's interference formed something after the manner of the ancient flying wedge and they drove back up the field with the runner covered for twenty-five and thirty yards at almost every chance. It was speed that beat the Army, speed plus interference. And when a back such as Harry Wilson finds few chances to get started you can figure upon the defensive strength that is barricading the road. Wilson is one of the hardest backs in the game to suppress, but he found few chances yesterday to show his broken field ability. You can't run through a broken field until you get there.

One strong feature of the Army play was its headlong battle against heavy odds. Even when Notre Dame had scored two touchdowns and was well on its way to a third, the Army fought on with fine spirit until the touchdown chance came at last. And when this chance came Coach McEwan had the play ready for the final march across the line. The Army has a better team than it had last year. So has Notre Dame. We doubt that any team in the country could have beaten Rockne's array yesterday afternoon East or West. It was a great football team brilliantly directed, a team of speed, power and team play. The Army has no cause for gloom over its showing. It played first class football against more speed than it could match.

Those who have tackled a cyclone can understand. . . .

Questions for Discussion

1. Why is this news story considered a classic in journalism?
2. What comparisons can be made between the game and en-

vironment described by Rice in 1924 and the actions of the
crowd and players in a game today?

3. Compare the chronicle of Homer with this piece of modern
   writing. How are the actions of the contestants, onlookers,
   of officials similar for the two periods?

4. What are some of the main purposes of physical activity or
   sports and games down through the ages?

[SECTION II]

Philosophical Backgrounds

Philosophic differences underlie many of the heated discussions about physical education. Superficially, many current disagreements appear to be the result of peculiarly modern problems. However, a knowledge of western philosophy reveals the ancient lineage of many modern educational debates. Surely the present debate about the place and significance of physical education in the school and college reflects traditional philosophical differences.

As physical educators we must assume that our field has a rightful place, whatever its nature and scope, in the curriculum. We prefer to argue in the cause of physical education at a more sophisticated level—not to justify its *raison d'être* but to demonstrate its most useful function. At this level we discover that physical educators are hardly in full agreement. A central issue seems to be the educational objectives of physical education programs. Should these programs focus primarily on the education of the physical—on motor learning and muscle building? Should the programs be primarily oriented toward recreation and the appreciation of nature? Should they contribute to the social development of the individual? And, finally, should they contribute to the student's intellectual development as well as to his physical development?

This statement of the issues is greatly simplified, but in it we can see several traditional lines of philosophical argument. Those physical educators most interested in motor skill learning and physical fitness may be designated philosophical realists in approach. In fact, modern psychology, which is realistic in its empirical orientation, is also concerned with motor skill learning. Those physical educators who stress the value of outdoor education and harmony with nature rather clearly reflect the naturalism (and even the romanticism) of late- eighteenth- and nineteenth-century thought. Physical educators who stress the social learning that results from physical education, the unity of play and work, of school and society, rather clearly reveal philosophical pragmatism. Finally, there are the Platonists among us who see the primary purpose of physical education in its contribution to the development of intellect. Physical educators who seek a fusion of the ideal and the real, as guided by the ideal, reflect the Hegelian point of view. Hegelians, akin to the Platonists, see the Idea or Spirit controlling the physical world.

These basic philosophic differences are represented in the selection of readings for this section. The readings are arranged by schools of thought, with frequent pairing of a philosopher and a modern physical educator who reflects at least in part his philosophical viewpoint. There cannot be precise correspondence because the modern physical educator must cope with problems and expectations that often lie beyond the scope of traditional philosophy.

The exercise in comparing the old and the new that this section poses for the student should expand his philosophical perspective on the field of physical education. In undertaking this exercise the student should keep in mind these major concepts: (1) the idealism of Plato; (2) the pragmatic idealism of Oberteuffer; (3) the naturalism (romanticism) of Rousseau; (4) the dynamic idealism of Hegel; (5) the modern naturalism of Brightbill; (6) the realism of Locke; (7) the dualism of Descartes; (8) the realism of McCloy; (9)the pragmatism (experimentalism) of Dewey; (10) the social pragmatism of Williams; (11) and the aesthetics of Spencer and H'Doubler.

PLATO

Physical Education*

As the progenitor of the philosophy of idealism, Plato's thought
will always have a major place in Western thought. He demands
more than Juvenal's *mens sana in corpore sano* (a sound mind
in a sound body). What is important is the sound mind, which,
as Plato states in the following article, will make the bodily
condition as perfect as it can be. Plato is idealistic as well in
his description of a sound body. It is the body beautiful of
Hellenic sculpture—not the real body, but the ideal body.

The following selection suggests that as ends in themselves the
care of the body and the preservation of health are hardly
worthy of our attention. Overindulgence or neglect of the body,
however, leads to distractions from what should be our central
occupation—the cultivation of the mind and the use of the intellect in study.

Frequently, physical educators' choices of such educational
objectives as the development of "personality," the "good life,"
or even the "intellect," may reflect Platonic idealism.

*Plato does not go into detail but makes it clear that he is thinking
of a military rather than an athletic training: which is why, perhaps, he tends to regard it, as appears later, as a* stage *of education,
lasting approximately from the eighteenth to the twentieth year,
rather than as something which accompanies the secondary education which he has just finished describing. Young men at Athens,
in fact, spent two years, from eighteen to twenty, doing a course of
compulsory military training, and it is of military training as much
as of physical education in our sense that Plato is thinking.*

*The passage proceeds to criticize certain developments of con-
temporary medicine of which Plato disapproved (criticisms which*

* Reprinted with permission of the publisher from Plato's *The Republic*, translated
by H. D. P. Lee. Baltimore, Maryland and Harmondsworth, England: Penguin
Books, 1955, pp. 145–155.

*read oddly to us), and to condemn litigiousness (Plato undoubtedly
has contemporary Athens in mind); it ends by emphasizing that
physical, as much as literary, education is aimed primarily at the
development of character.* [H. D. P. Lee]

"The next stage in the training of our young men will be physical education. And here again they must be carefully trained from
childhood onwards. I have my own opinions about it: let me see if
you agree. In my view physical excellence does not of itself produce
good character: on the other hand, excellency of mind and character *will* make the best of the physique it is given. What do you
think?"

"I agree."

"We should do well then to leave the elaboration of rules for
physical training to minds that have been thoroughly educated: all
we need do, for brevity's sake, is to give a rough outline."

"Yes."

"We have already forbidden drink. A guardian is the last person
in the world to get drunk and not know where he is."

"It would be absurd," he replied, "for a guardian to need someone to look after him."

"What about diet? Our guardians, you will agree, are competing
in the most important of all contests. Should they train like ordinary athletes?"

"Perhaps so."

"But the athlete in training is a sleepy creature and his health
delicately balanced. Haven't you noticed how they sleep most of
their time, and how the smallest deviation from their routine leads
to serious illness?"

"Yes, I've noticed that."

"So we shall need a better adjusted form of training for our
soldier-athletes. They must be as wakeful as watchdogs, their sight
and hearing must be of the keenest, and their health must not be
too delicate to endure the many changes of food and drink, and the
varieties of temperature that campaigning entails."

"I agree."

"And do you not also agree that the best form of physical training would be one akin to the simple education we have just been
describing?"

"What do you mean?"

"I mean a suitably simple physical training, concentrating particularly on training for war."

"In what way?"

"Even Homer can tell you that," I replied. "For you know that when his heroes are on campaign he does not give them fish to eat, although they are on the shore of the Hellespont, nor boiled meat, but only roast. That is what suits soldiers best, because it is, generally speaking, easier to cook something direct on the fire than carry round pots and pans for the purpose."

"Much easier."

"And Homer, I think, never mentions seasonings. Indeed, even the ordinary athlete knows that if he is to be fit he must keep off them."

"And he is quite right to do so."

"In that case I assume that you don't approve of the luxury of Syracusan and Sicilian cooking."

"I should think not."

"And what about Corinthian girl-friends? Do you disapprove of them for men who want to keep fit?"

"I certainly do."

"And Attic confectionery, which is supposed to be so good, must go too?"

"It must."

"We might, I think, with justice compare these luxurious ways of living and eating with the music and song which used a wide range of harmony and rhythm. Elaborate music, we found, produces indiscipline, and elaborate food produces disease. But simplicity in music produces discipline of character, and simplicity in physical education health of body."

"Very true."

"And the prevalence of indiscipline and disease in a community leads, does it not, to the opening of law courts and surgeries in large numbers, and law and medicine begin to give themselves airs, especially when they are paid so much attention even by free men."

"That is bound to happen."

"And when not only the lower classes and workers, but also those who have some pretensions to education, need skilled doctors and lawyers, that is a pretty conclusive proof that the education in a state is thoroughly bad. For is it not a scandalous sign of a bad education if one's sense of right and wrong is so deficient that one has to seek justice at the hands of others as one's masters and judges?"

"I can't think of anything worse," he said.

"Yet it's worse still, don't you think," I replied, "when a man not only spends most of his life in court as plaintiff or defendant, but is even ignorant enough to be proud of it; when he is convinced that he is an expert law-breaker, up to every kind of twist, and that he knows all the tricks to wriggle out of a conviction? And all this for mean and unworthy ends, without any idea how far better it is to arrange one's life so that one has no need of a judge dozing on the bench."

"Yes," he agreed, "that's still worse."

"And it's disgraceful too to need a doctor not only for injury or regular disease, but because by leading the kind of life we have described we have filled our bodies with gases and discharges, like a stagnant pool, and driven the medical profession to invent names for our diseases, like flatulence and catarrh. Don't you agree?"

"I do indeed," he replied, "these new-fangled names for diseases are very far-fetched."

"And I don't think you would have found them in the days of Asclepius,"[1] I added. "Or so I should judge from the fact that when Eurpylus was wounded at Troy, and given Pramnian wine mixed with barley-meal and grated cheese to drink—a mixture you would have thought would have given him a fever—thesons of Asclepius had no fault to find with the women who gave him the drink, or with Patroclus who prescribed it."

"And yet it was an odd prescription for a wounded man," he said.

"I don't think so," I replied, "for it was not till the days of Herodicus, so they say, that doctors made use of modern methods of nursing disease. Herodicus was an athletic trainer, whose health failed, and he proceeded to make first and foremost himself, and then many others after him, miserable by a combination of medicine and physical training."

"How did he do that?"

"By dying a lingering death. His whole attention was devoted to a disease that was mortal; he could not cure himself of it, but spent the rest of his life busy doctoring himself and being made wretched

---

[1] Mythical patron of doctors.

by any departure from his routine treatment. And his skill prolonged the struggle till he was an old man."

"What a reward to win!"

"And quite a suitable one for a man who did not know that it was not from ignorance or lack of skill that Asclepius did not reveal this method of treatment to his successors, but because he knew that in a well-run society each man has a job which he must do, and has no time to spend his life being ill and undergoing cures. We see that this applies to the working class, and it is absurd not to see that it also applies to the wealthy and privileged, as we think them."

"Explain," he said.

"If a carpenter is ill," I replied, "and goes to a doctor he expects to be given an emetic or purge and be cured, or to get rid of the trouble by an operation. If he is ordered to undergo a long cure, wrapping his head up and all that sort of thing, he will probably say that he's no time to be ill and that a life in which one must give all one's attention to one's ailments and none to one's proper job simply is not worth living. Then he will dismiss the doctor who has given the advice, go back to his normal routine, and either regain his health and get on with his job, or, if his constitution won't stand it, die and be rid of his troubles."

"That's the right way for that sort of man to treat medical advice," he agreed.

"The reason being," I said, "that he has a job to do, and if he does not do it, life is not worth while."

"Yes, clearly."

"But hasn't the rich man a job to do, which will make his life not worth living if he can't do it?"

"He isn't usually reckoned to have."

"You haven't listened to Phocylides," was my reply, "who said that when a man no longer has to work for his living, he should 'practice excellence.' "

"I should have thought he might start even earlier," he said.

"Don't let's quarrel with him about that," I returned, "but let us ask ourselves whether the rich man should make this his job, and whether his life is worth living if he can't carry on with it. Valetudinarianism prevents a man giving his attention to carpentry and similar occupations: is it also a hindrance to obeying Phocylides' orders?"

"It certainly is a hindrance. There's nothing worse than this fussiness about one's health, in excess of normal healthy exercise. It's tiresome in the home, as well as in the army, or in any civilian office."

"Worst of all, it makes any kind of study or thought or meditation difficult. If you are always wondering if you've got a headache or are feeling giddy, and blaming your studies for it, you will never be able to exercise your mind or test your abilities. You'll always think you're ill, and never stop worrying about your health."

"That's what's likely to happen."

"Let us say, then, that Asclepius too knew all this, and therefore introduced medical treatment for those who have a good constitution and lead a healthy life. If they get some specific disease, he gets rid of it by drugs or surgery, but tells them to go on leading their normal life so as not to make them less useful to the community. But he makes no attempt to cure those whose constitution is basically diseased; the result of treating them with all the refinements of dosing and diet can only be an unhappy prolongation of life, and the production of children as unhealthy as themselves. No, he thought that no treatment should be given to the man who cannot survive the routine of his ordinary job, and who is therefore of no use either to himself or society."

"You talk as if Asclepius was a real political scientist!"

"Of course he was," said I, "and that is why we find that his sons are good soldiers at Troy, and doctor people in the way I am describing. You will remember how, when Menelaus was wounded by Pandarus, they 'sucked out the blood and skillfully applied soothing ointments.'[2] But they gave him no further orders about diet, any more than they did to Eurypylus; for they thought that 'ointments' were enough to cure a man who had lived a normal healthy life, whatever he drank after treatment. The life of a man whose constitution was bad and undermined by loose living was, they thought, of no use to them or to anyone else; it was not their business to use their skills on such cases or cure them, even if they were richer than Midas."

"Discerning men, these sons of Asclepius."

"Which is as it should be," I said. "But Pindar and the tragedians don't believe us, and say that Asclepius was a son of Apollo, that

[2] *Iliad*, IV, 218.

he was bribed by a large fee to cure a rich man who was at death's door, and blasted by a thunderbolt in consequence. But we cannot, if we are to be consistent, agree with them on both counts; if he was a god he was not out for profit, and if he was out for profit he was not a god."

"All that is very true. But tell me, Socrates," he asked, "surely we shall need good doctors in our state. And good doctors are those who have the widest experience in treating patients both in health and sickness, just as good judges are those who have mixed with all sorts of people."

"We certainly need good doctors," I answered, "but do you know what I mean by good?"

"I shall if you tell me."

"I will try. But your question does not admit of a single answer."

"What do you mean?"

"The best way for a doctor to acquire skill is to have, in addition to his knowledge of medical science, as wide and as early an acquaintance as possible with serious illness; in addition he should have experienced all kinds of disease in his own person and not be of an altogether healthy constitution. For doctors don't use their bodies to cure other people—if so, they could not allow their health to be bad—they use their minds; and if they're defective mentally their treatment can't be good."

"True."

"But with a judge it's a matter of mind controlling mind. And the mind must not be brought up from its youth to associate with wickedness, or to run through a whole range of crimes in order to get first-hand experience on which to judge them in other people, as the doctor did with diseases of the body: on the contrary, the mind must, while it is still young, remain quite without experience or contact with bad characters, if its moral development is to be good and its moral judgment sound. That is why people of good character seem simple when they are young, and are easily taken in by dishonesty—because they have in themselves nothing to give them a sympathetic understanding of vice."

"That's a common experience," he agreed.

"Which is why a good judge must not be a young man," I replied, "but an old one to whom knowledge of wickedness has come late in life, not as a feature he perceives in his own character, but as an evil whose effects he has learned after long practice to discern in other people, something about which he knows but of which he has no personal experience."

"A man like that would be a real judge indeed."

"And a good one, which is what you asked," I pointed out; "for he has the qualities of mind that are needed. But your wily, knowing type, who has been up to all sorts of tricks and has a reputation for super-smartness, looks pretty formidable so long as he is dealing with men like himself, against whom his own bad principles put him on his guard; but when he comes up against men of good character he looks very silly with his untimely suspicions and the unawareness of what honesty is that he owes to his own bad principles. But he meets more rogues than honest men, and so appears a clever fellow and not a silly one, both to himself and others."

"That's perfectly true," he said.

"We must not look to this type, then, for our good and wise judge, but to the other. Vice can never know either itself or virtue, but virtue, when instruction is added to natural endowment, can in course of time acquire knowledge of vice as well as of itself. It is the good man, therefore, and not the bad man who will, in my opinion, make our wise judge."

"I agree with you."

"These then are the kind of doctors and judges for whom you will legislate in your state. They will treat those of your citizens whose physical and psychological constitution is good; as for the others, they will leave the unhealthy to die, and those whose psychological constitution is incurably warped they will put to death."

"That seems to be the best thing both for the individuals concerned and for society."

"And so," I said, "your young men, so long as they maintain their simple form of education, which, as we have said, breeds discipline, will take care not to need judicial treatment."

"True."

"And if they successfully follow on the same track in their physical training, they will never need a doctor except in cases of necessity."

"I agree."

"It is, of course, to stimulate their energy and initiative that they undergo these severities in their training, not merely to make themselves tough, which is the object of the diet and exercises of the ordinary athlete. And that, my dear Glaucon," I went on, "is why I say that the purpose of the two established types of education (literary and physical) is not, as some suppose, to deal one with the mind and the other with the body."

"What is it then?" he asked.

"I think that perhaps in the main both aim at training the mind."

"And how do they do that?"

"Have you noticed," I asked, "how a lifelong devotion to physical exercise, to the exclusion of anything else, produces a certain type of mind? Just as a neglect of it produces another type? One type tends to be tough and uncivilized, the other soft and oversensitive, and . . ."

"Yes, I have noticed that," he broke in; "excessive emphasis on athletics produces a pretty uncivilized type, while a purely literary and academic training leaves a man with less backbone than is decent."

"It is the energy and initiative in their nature that may make them uncivilized," I said; "if you treat it properly it should make them brave, but if you overstrain it it turns them tough and uncouth, as you would expect."

"I agree," he said.

"The philosophic temperament, on the other hand, is gentle; too much relaxation may produce an excessive softness, but if it is treated properly the result should be civilized and humane."

"That is so."

"Now we agreed that our Guardians must have both these elements in their nature, did we not?"

"Yes."

"And must not the two elements be combined to produce a mind that is civilized and brave, as opposed to cowardly and uncivilized?"

"That is so."

"So when a man surrenders to the charms of music and lets the sound of the sweet, soft, mournful strains we have described flood into his soul, and gives up all his time to the pleasures of song, the effect at first on his energy and initiative of mind, if he has any, is to soften it as iron is softened in a furnace, and made workable instead of hard and unworkable: but if he does not break the enchantment, the next stage is that it melts and runs, till the spirit has quite run out of him and his mental guts (if I may so put it) are entirely removed, and he has become what Homer calls 'a feeble fighter.' "

"That is all very true."

"This result is one that follows quickly if he is naturally spiritless in the first place. But if he is a man of spirit, the effect is, by weakening his spirit, to make him unstable, a man who flies into a rage at a trifle and calms down as quickly. His energy has degenerated into peevishness and ill-temper and constant irritability."

"Exactly."

"On the other hand, there is the man who takes a lot of strenuous physical exercise and lives well, but has little acquaintance with literature or philosophy. The physical health that results from such a course first fills him with confidence and energy, and increases his courage. But if he devotes himself exclusively to it, and never opens a book, any capacity he may have for learning is weakened by being starved of instruction or enquiry and by never taking part in any intelligent discussion, and becomes deaf and blind, because its perceptions are never cleared and strengthened by use."

"That is what happens."

"And so he becomes an unintelligent philistine, with no use for reasoned conviction, and an animal addiction to settle everything by brute force. His life is one of clumsy ignorance, unrelieved by grace or beauty."

"That describes him exactly."

"What I should say therefore is that these two methods of education seem to have been given by god to men to train our initiative and our reason. They are not intended, one to train body, the other mind, except incidentally, but to ensure a proper harmony between energy and initiative on the one hand and reason on the other, by turing each to the right pitch. And so we may venture to assert that anyone who can produce the best blend of the physical and intellectual sides of education and apply them to the training of character, is producing harmony in a far more important sense than any mere musician."

"A very reasonable assertion."

"We must therefore ensure, my dear Glaucon," I said, "that there is always someone like this in charge of education in our state, if its constitution is to be preserved."

"We most certainly must."

Further Readings

BAIR, DONN E., "An Identification of Some Philosophical Beliefs Held by Influential Leaders in American Physical
Education," Ph. D. dissertation, University of Southern California, 1956.

BURKE, ROGER, "Idealism and Physical Education," *The Philosophic Process in Physical Education*, edited by E. C. Davis.
Philadelphia: Lea and Febiger, 1961.

ZEIGLER, E. F., *Philosophical Foundations for Physical, Health,
and Recreation Education*, Englewood Cliffs, N.J.: Prentice-
Hall, Inc., 1964, Part V.

Questions for Discussion

1. Of what should the best physical education for young men consist? Do you agree?
2. Why does Plato consider doctors and lawyers evils?
3. According to Plato, what are the consequences of overemphasizing either mental or physical development?
4. To what extent do you subscribe to an idealist position in physical education?
5. Can the discipline of the body contribute to mental discipline? How?

DELBERT OBERTEUFFER

Some Contributions of Physical Education to an Educated Life*

In American physical education one of the outstanding leaders is Delbert Oberteuffer. His views can not be identified with any one school of philosophical thought. His explanation of the re-

* Reprinted with permission of the author and publisher from *The Journal of
Health, Physical Education and Recreation*. Washington, D.C.: American Association for Health, Physical Education and Recreation. January 1945, vol. 16, no. 1,
pp. 3–5, 56–57.

lationship of work and play and the important contribution of physical education to socialization are consistent with the philosophy of Dewey. One is particularly struck, however, by the lofty note of Platonic idealism that frequently appears in Oberteuffer's writing.

In the article presented here, Oberteuffer takes a broad view of the school and physical education. His emphatic statements that the learning resulting from physical education is both intellectual and physical, and that the ultimate contribution is self-fulfillment and the educated life, identify him with the Platonic school. Those physical educators who occupy themselves solely with the development of muscle and skill may not find much solace in Oberteuffer's broad and liberal views of their field.

All living things use movement as an instrument of expression and impression. The amoeba under the glass will react to varying stimuli by moving around. The collie will express his joy at the return of his master by convulsive waggings and affectionate leaps. The runabout child learns that table legs are hard by toddling full tilt into one. Of the unpredictable number of sensory stimuli received by any living organism a good share of them are made possible because that organism has the capacity to move about, to alter his environment by moving, and thus to create new and different worlds for himself which teach him important lessons. Likewise ideas conjured up within find their efferent expression in movements as diverse as the flicker of an eye or the mad stampede of a frightened mob. Ideas, feelings, emotions, drives, or moods frequently can find their most satisfactory expression only through a movement of parts coordinated so as to bring satisfaction as a return for its doing.

Mankind always has used this capacity for coordinated movement to serve his purposes. The savage ran to capture or escape, the primitive tribesman swung a club to beat off an attacker, the Indian danced to invoke the favor of the gods, and the early Greeks wrestled for fun and for the beauty of body development. Later on the middle Europeans danced to the folk songs of their festivals, the Swedes invented exercises for therapeutic purposes, and the English played games and hunted because it was such good sport. But as civilization has progressed it has made less and less urgent the need for movement as necessary to survival. Bullets take the place of clubs, carpenters build our houses for us; and the more these labor-saving substitutions develop, the more dancing, playing, swimming, and climbing we do just for the fun of it. We are neither inclined from choice nor pre-destined biologically to give up our capacity for muscular effort and retire to the armchair. If we do, we die.

What has happened in American education? Our schools and colleges were begun originally to train the mind. The early Puritanic philosophy held play as vulgar and schools would have none of it. The early pattern for American higher education was cut in the form of devotion to a dualistic intellectualism in which mind was an entity unrelated to the remainder of the organism. Actually the boys whose minds were trained at Harvard in the 17th century were not unlike the boys there now; so they played games, and when the lads at Princeton kicked an early American football through the chapel window they thus intruded the fact of their singleness of being into the sacred halls of this unsound intellectualism.

Shortly thereafter, in the 19th century, but unrelated to these impulses to play, physical training came into our schools. It had a Scandinavian and German ancestry. The English games were not a part of the beginnings of school physical training. German exercises and Swedish gymnastics prevailed. In community life, however, our pioneers hunted and fished and later on they danced a little. They played games, either domestic or imported, and soon the school was doing one thing as physical training and people at large were doing others. The schools were at quite a loss to know what was the best for its children. The fatherlands all gave purpose to their physical training. Their exercise was for health, to discipline the youth of the land, or to celebrate an occasional festival. The American games seemed all for fun and amusement. Which of these purposes should the school adopt and develop its program to meet?

The 20th century has made the answer clear. We will have little of imported programs and purposes. We will choose some of the English rugby and develop American football, we will preserve and teach some old folk dances, we will run foot races as did the ancient Greeks but we forget soccer, are bored with calisthenics, use the Swedish horse to play on, and applaud but not perform the ballet.

We are enthusiastic about tennis and golf, imported products, we invent baseball, and we ride and hunt and fish as all human beings do the world over. But we insist on our own purposes and our own development and these are compatible with essential purposes of all education in this particular democracy. If American education aims at normal adjustment of the individual to his world then so does modern physical education in American schools. If the production of integrated personalities possessed of those qualities which make for effective living within a democracy is the general purpose then the activities which educate through these motor avenues must contribute to these ends. A physical education is productive of more than organic or "physical" gains. *These* are important but other outcomes can and must be sought if one is to appraise fairly the place of physical education in the American program of education.

To gain such a view of the part motor activities play in the education of a man one must begin, of course, with a broad view of education itself. It must be seen as education for living rather than just schooling. The boundaries of blackboards, recitations, and lectures must not define academic respectability. The broad view sees education as a series of living experiences and if books, or trips, or chalk, or games, or a tonsillectomy are necessary to enrich that life then those things are organized and arranged by skillful teachers as a part of the educational process. We are just beginning to understand what Dewey years ago pointed out—that it is the *whole* child we are educating—not just his memory centers. No picture of an educated life which has for its colors only the bright hues of poetry or the perspectives of mathematics will do. What a Hutchins or a Flexner may describe as their ideal of an educated life vanishes in the face of such rudimentary knowledge as science has given us about the relation of the psyche to the soma. Or as Williams[1] has aptly put it,

> This view sees life as a totality . . . and the modern spirit in physical education seeks the education of man through physical activities as one aspect of the effort for human enlightenment. . . . The 'cult of music' becomes as ludicrous as those who worship at the altar of mental development. Neither point of view suffices, neither is accurate.

[1] Williams, J. F., "Education Through the Physical," *Journal of Higher Education* (May 1930), p. 279.

Culture must be judged in terms of totality of expression. There is nothing new about that. Plato argued it in his *Republic* and John Locke urged the recognition of motor activities as a way of living. Herbert Spencer clamored for the development of a physical education for men and women and contemporary thinkers such as Dewey, Bode, Horn, Jacks, and others all have pronounced the validity of motor experiences as contributors to education.

But it is necessary to particularize. Muscular strength is surely not the only outcome of a physical education. Just what kinds of learning accrue? There are, potentially, five, all of which may be classified by other names perhaps and surely all of which depend for their existence in large measure upon the quality of leadership which seeks them. From participation one learns, first, the skills and strategy of the activity at hand; second, the hygiene or health implications of the activity; third, the behavior controls involved in the activity situations; fourth, the satisfactions from self-expression, through the activity as a means; and fifth, the history, contemporary status, and relationships of the activity. These values, along with the health or organic values which we are not discussing here, are all potential. They may or may not accrue. Their fullest attainment depends upon good organization and expert teaching.

The first one can be disposed of quickly. It is obvious that one must learn how to *play* golf and that the strategy of tennis or football is not learned except through participation. The skills, the rules, and the plan for any game or dance are fundamental to the other values. Such learning is obviously as much of an "intellectual" exercise as it is a "physical" one. For our purposes let us assume an optimum mastery and move on to the other values.

From the activities, if properly taught, we can get an insight into hygiene. Ringworm of the foot has spread because people are in ignorance of hygienic procedures following exercise. Success in athletics is dependent in some measure upon diet, sleep, and freedom from dissipation. Old lessons about healthful living spring normally and forcefully from such participation, and the refinements of the 20th century have not as yet developed an adequate substitute for a normal metabolism. If participation in activities calls up this kind of associate learning then the activities have added profitably to the sum of knowledge.

Third, the behavior controls involved in the activity may need some elaboration. Somewhere in the first year of life the behavior of the infant begins to take on social implications. His intra-uterine aloneness begins to disappear. He becomes related to others, first to his mother, then to family, then to playmates, and eventually he may develop a vision of the relation of himself to the world of people. This socializing process is not done without pain. The self-preservative drive is strong and the competition or aggression manifested against other individuals is the result of it. In view of this Timme[2] holds it the duty of civilization in general and the school as its agent to modify this aggression into behavior useful in group life. The hitting, shoving, and biting of the child must be modified as he grows older.

Therein can be seen the effect of a physical education. "Play is training in socialization. By far the best and perhaps the only means of socializing the child," according to Timme.[3] Play weans him from self-centeredness to material objects, to playthings, to playfellows, to the group, to the world of people. This process goes on all the time, with or without leadership, with or without the school. The important thing is to give direction to it, plan its outcomes, and the school and its teachers are responsible for such direction-giving and behavior-planning. Note that we have not said this responsibility was solely that of the physical education teacher. No such position is tenable. The physical education teacher and program are in the vortex of such a socializing process but the influence of *all* teachers affects these changes.

Furthermore, these modifying changes go on continuously through life and play always is an instrument. We may grow too old to participate so we watch; and the spectator, through the well known process of identification expresses behaviors of a social nature and has modifications made of his conduct. He will live through the players he watches.

Kimball Young adds further evidence to this. He says,

> Recognition of the fact that the self arises from building up roles and the status that others require of us should convince us that a full life is possible only when we recognize the anticipation or claims of others upon us. This is exactly what socialization . . . means.[4]

[2] Timme, Arthur R., "The Significance of Play and Recreation in Civilized Life," *Mental Hygiene* 18: 1 (January, 1934), p. 51.
[3] *Ibid.*, p. 52.
[4] Young, Kimball, "Freedom, Responsibility, and Self-Control," *Mental Hygiene*, 21:2 (April, 1937), p. 177.

Thus the activities of physical education may become a remarkable instrument for socialization. In games, and in sports, we learn to expect things of our friends and we know our friends are expecting things of us. We take on status; we become persons. We rise and fall as we try to meet these expectations. We learn to judge and to be judged and when a friend fails to measure up, lets us down in a tight foursome, or fumbles at a crucial moment, we, because others have expected things of us, are more tolerant of him. We recognize his weakness and his despair because we share them. We do, that is, if we have played, if our physical education has been a full one. It is usually the person whose physical education has been neglected who is intolerant enough to shout his abuse when players make mistakes.

The full life is possible only when we accurately gauge our role, and know where we stand with reference to our friends. We play hide-and-go-seek or dodge-ball, tennis, or squash-racquets and if we disappoint others we can either correct our mistake, withdraw from the game, or have our errors forgiven. We insist on one of the three happening. Life is uncomfortable until one does. We will go to lengths to make one of these happen. The alibi has its origin in these circumstances. Where the act has failed we attempt to verbalize away its consequences. We try to explain. We always want to be right, to be well thought of, and we do not always succeed. The recognition of the claims others have on us, or of the role others expect us to play becomes strikingly apparent through the materials with which organized physical education deals.

The technique of socialization then begins to appear. The teacher must make clear what is expected; he must instruct us in the use of the tools which will meet this expectancy, and when failure attends our efforts, he must provide opportunity suitable to our capacity for establishing a satisfying equilibrium with our fellows.

Young makes it even more explicit when he says that "social and emotional maturity is achieved only if the sense of freedom has a corresponding sense of responsibility."[5] In games or in a folk dance the participant has freedom *and* responsibility. He cannot evade either. It was he who was caught off the bag, or flubbed his mashie shot, or missed his block, or who forgot to "set and turn single." When one enters an activity of this sort, he has freedom, and if it takes responsibility to produce maturity, then he has that

[5] *Ibid.*, p. 178.

also. His own actions become important to the team, the set, or even to the whole pageant. The player who errs can find few alibies to help him evade his own responsibility, and the teacher must see that he finds none save the true ones. These games are stern tests yet rich in opportunity for producing maturity. They help discipline and develop the weakling, they provide a growth opportunity for the "fringer," and they provide a yardstick for the one who is uncertain where he stands. Likewise they present a temptation for the egocentric who is expert at them, and splendid and useful stimuli for the normally maturing personality.

It is within these spheres that good teaching is important. Bad teaching will be blind to this socializing process. It will permit egotism to take charge of some, cowardice and unhappiness born of consistent failure to spread in others, and complete lack of participation to be the lot of a few. Good teaching will by paying attention to the individual differences, select and teach those activities holding most promise for socialization; it will be impatient with mass activities and prefer small groups where individual growth can be noticed, and it will help each individual undergo the socializing process to the end that he attains his full share of maturity.

In a republic where democratic personal relationships are expected to be the basis of the culture it is not too much to expect that all of the areas within a curriculum will be capable of making a very real and demonstrable contribution to such democratic behavior in the individual. Can a contribution be made to such democratic living through physical education?

If the inter-play of personality constantly found on the play field can be properly directed, the field, the court, the pool, the out-of-doors can be most significant as laboratories of the democratic process. Conversely men can be taught to hate each other, to hold others in disrespect, to take advantage, to "get the other guy," to nurse racial prejudices, to seek advantage, all through sport. In war, some of these latter qualities are necessary. American men cannot fight the enemy with kid gloves on. Because we must win this war we may have to forsake some of our notions of clean combat. Activities can be chosen and taught in physical education in such a way as to produce these fighting skills. But if the essence of the democratic way is to be measured by the quality of our respect for the other personality then organized school and college physical education programs should be held strictly accountable for the kind and quality of teaching through their activities. Nothing may be tolerated which does not guide the student into a deepened and widened understanding of the democratic culture in which he lives.

Fourth, and irrevocably bound up with this socializing process is the opportunity for normal personality adjustment and integration through and by the satisfactions arising out of self-expression. The very nature of physical education throws it into the vortex of this kind of learning. Physical education activities has a rich potential objectivity about them. Children play prisoner's base with all the realism they can muster. Sense of self in a handball game virtually disappears. Casting in a rushing stream gives small chance for any thoughts save those of the catch. All such activities which are rightfully the material of a school-organized physical education can, when properly taught, produce an outward direction of consciousness judged helpful to normal adjustment. The player becomes so absorbed in what he is doing that he has little or no time for himself and his worries. Through such efforts, particularly when they are creative as in the dance, the objectivity of the activities makes some contribution to psychic integration. Richards is quoted as saying that play is our greatest ally in helping the personality that has become ingrowing to be outgrowing in its interest, desires, and responses.[6]

Some of these results occur strikingly through the use of a physical education for the handicapped. Victims of infantile paralysis, tuberculosis of the bone, heart defects, and others too frequently judged to be unfit to receive a physical education are sometimes put on the shelf. There they disintegrate not only whatever muscular tissue and strength may be left, but also they develop those complexes and grievances characteristic of the handicapped. It appears possible to allay all this through an individualized physical education. The victim of paralysis who hates all things athletic, who is almost completely introverted and thus selfish and intolerant, is taught to swim. He mingles with other swimmers, he becomes a man among men, he finds a new way of living. He is well along towards a social rehabilitation which he needed badly. The blind can be taught to dance, the deaf to play games, the nervously unstable to catch and throw. The end results seem to be im-

6 Powell, Margaret, "Activity and the Mental Hygiene Program," *Journal of Health and Physical Education*, 7:9 (November, 1936), p. 556.

proved, in some instances, remade personalities. There are unexplored opportunities ahead in the field of physical education of the
handicapped. We have only begun to experiment with it.

Less subtle of the values which a well planned physical education
will bring to the individual are the simple fun one gets from playing and dancing and the elemental satisfactions from having used
one's leisure without having been bored. Fun, in itself, is valuable.
Life need not all be serious business. We pay a heavy price for a
laugh. We seem to welcome joy when it comes our way. Those
things are obviously attainable through physical education activities.

The fifth type of learning, suggested as the history and contemporary status and relationships of the activities, holds some promise in
its contribution to an educated life. Bode is reported to have said,
"Give me thirty children at the gates of the stadium and I will reveal the world to them." He referred, no doubt, to the contemporary relationships of the activities that went on in the stadium and
the stadium itself. Of what design is the building? What were its
antecedents? Why do people build and use stadiums? What values
have games? What of the history of the world is reflected in the
structure and the uses to which it is put? It behooves the teacher to
explore, to miss no opportunity to further the process of integrating
all knowledge and activity. The dance, alone, provides as rich an
opportunity for concomitant learnings as any other aspect of a
physical education. Dancing in any form requires music, employs
design, may be itself a creative art and in its interpretative aspects
draws it ideas from life and expresses them through the artistry of
its movements.

From a class in physical education or social science may come the
need for knowing of the nature and extent of recreational facilities in a community. Some one, somewhere, may ask of the relationship between playgrounds and juvenile delinquency. An insight
into the study of human behavior under stress may be an outgrowth
of the relationships between physical education and psychology.
There is material here, not all of it vital, not all of it interesting to
all persons. The possibilities, however, have barely been touched.

The sum and substance of these potential contributions to an
educated life point unmistakably to one thing. If the school har-
nesses these natural activities, uses them as a fundamental avenue
of learning, calls the teaching of them "physical education" then

it must recognize the importance of skilled leadership with sound scientific training. Wipe out every teacher and every program of physical education in schools today and the physical education of the race would still go on—albeit in a primitive fashion. The organized school is a product of civilization. It bends man's drives into social uses; it hopes to make the man himself integrated and complete. This hope makes necessary the teaching of physical education. But games alone will not do it. Just play without a plan, without thought, without direction, will make little contribution beyond the organic values to some of the more complicated problems of personality which we face in today's school or college. Physical education teachers should know what they are doing. They should be students of the science of human development and educationists in the best sense of the word.

Thus physical education makes its contributions to the educated life. To attain them the program must be democratically administered and individually based; its games must be free from false values and unsound practices; its activities must have values which are most readily harvested by the participant. If we can develop that game, that contest, that activity in which the individual is used "not as a means merely but as an end" then the foundation upon which the superstructure of educational value may be raised will be safe.

For through a physical education we have the opportunity to help to bring man into possession of himself, to provide him with means for enjoying life, to give him friends and fun and the eminent satisfactions of doing something well. The educated life surely holds these things valuable.

Further Readings

COWELL, C. C. and FRANCE, W. L., *Philosophies and Principles of Physical Education*. Englewood Cliffs, N.J.: Prentice-Hall, Inc., 1963.

OBERTEUFFER, D., "Idealism in Physical Education," *Philosophies Fashion Physical Education*, edited by E. C. Davis. Dubuque, Iowa: William C. Brown Company, Publishers, 1963, pp. 16–24.

OBERTEUFFER, D. and CELESTE ULRICH, *Physical Education*. New York: Harper & Row, Publishers, 3d ed. 1962.

Questions for Discussion

1. Compare the views of Plato and Oberteuffer and list specific similarities.
2. How is Oberteuffer's emphasis on socialization closer to Dewey's than to Plato's philosophy?
3. What are the five major categories of learning that can result from physical education?
4. To which of these does Oberteuffer give primary emphasis?

JEAN JACQUES ROUSSEAU

Emile*

In point of time, it is a considerable leap from Plato to Rousseau. As for their philosophical positions, they occupy opposite ends of a continuum. Whereas Platonic values are rooted primarily in the mind or spirit, the values of Rousseau seem based on the body or nature. Rousseau is a product of the Enlightenment, an eighteenth-century intellectual movement that attacked the idealism of the Greeks and the medieval church. As historians have pointed out, nature was deified, and God was either obscured by the deists or discarded by the atheists.

That Rousseau romanticizes, even idealizes, nature can hardly be denied. His educational philosophy as expressed in *Emile* puts as much trust in nature as the medieval monk put in God. For Rousseau, society is a corrupting influence separating man from nature. Education must attempt to re-establish the unity of child with nature. In the final analysis nature is the best and only teacher. Formal education, as a social product, should be avoided.

---

* From *Emile* by Jean Jacques Rousseau. Translated by Barbara Foxley. Everyman's Library. Reprinted and abridged by permission of E. P. Dutton & Co., Inc.

When physical educators speak about the "innate wisdom of the body," "naturational processes," and the "child-directed curriculum," they are reflecting the philosophy of Rousseau.

The body is strengthened by this constant exercise under the guidance of nature herself, and far from brutalising the mind, this exercise develops in it the only kind of reason of which young children are capable, the kind of reason most necessary at every age. It teaches us how to use our strength, to perceive the relations between our own and neighbouring bodies, to use the natural tools, which are within our reach and adapted to our senses. Is there anything sillier than a child brought up indoors under his mother's eye, who, in his ignorance of weight and resistance, tries to uproot a tall tree or pick up a rock. The first time I found myself outside Geneva I tried to catch a galloping horse, and I threw stones at Mont Salève, two leagues away; I was the laughing stock of the whole village, and was supposed to be a regular idiot. At eighteen we are taught in our natural philosophy the use of the lever; every village boy of twelve knows how to use a lever better than the cleverest mechanician in the academy. The lessons the scholars learn from one another in the playground are worth a hundredfold more than what they learn in the class-room.

Watch a cat when she comes into a room for the first time; she goes from place to place, she sniffs about and examines everything, she is never still for a moment; she is suspicious of everything till she has examined it and found out what it is. It is the same with the child when he begins to walk, and enters, so to speak, the room of the world around him. The only difference is that, while both use sight, the child uses his hands and the cat that subtle sense of smell wich nature has bestowed upon it. It is this instinct, rightly or wrongly educated, which makes children skilful or clumsy, quick or slow, wise or foolish.

As a man's first natural impulse is to measure himself with his environment, to discover in every object he sees those sensible qualities which may concern himself, so his first study is a kind of experimental physics for his own preservation. He is turned away from this and sent to speculative studies before he has found his proper place in the world. While his delicate and flexible limbs can adjust themselves to the bodies upon which they are intended to act, while his senses are keen and as yet free from illusions, then is the time to exercise both limbs and senses in their proper business. It is the time to learn to perceive the physical relations between ourselves and things. Since everything that comes into the human mind enters through the gates of sense, man's first reason is a reason of sense-experience. It is this that serves as a foundation for the reason of the intelligence; our first teachers in natural philosophy are our feet, hands, and eyes. To substitute books for them does not teach us to reason, it teaches us to use the reason of others rather than our own; it teaches us to believe much and know little.

Before you can practise an art you must first get your tools; and if you are to make good use of those tools, they must be fashioned sufficiently strong to stand use. To learn to think we must therefore exercise our limbs, our senses, and our bodily organs, which are the tools of the intellect; and to get the best use out of these tools, the body which supplies us with them must be strong and healthy. Not only is it quite a mistake that true reason is developed apart from the body, but it is a good bodily constitution which makes the workings of the mind easy and correct.

While I am showing how the child's long period of leisure should be spent, I am entering into details which may seem absurd. You will say, "This is a strange sort of education, and it is subject to your own criticism, for it only teaches what no one needs to learn. Why spend your time in teaching what will come of itself without care or trouble? Is there any child of twelve who is ignorant of all you wish to teach your pupil, while he also knows what his master has taught him."

Gentlemen, you are mistaken. I am teaching my pupil an art the acquirement of which demands much time and trouble, an art which your scholars certainly do not possess; it is the art of being ignorant; for the knowledge of any one who only thinks he knows, what he really does know is a very small matter. You teach science; well and good; I am busy fashioning the necessary tools for its acquisition. Once upon a time, they say the Venetians were displaying the treasures of the Cathedral of Saint Mark to the Spanish ambassador; the only comment he made was, "Quì non c'e la radice." When I see a tutor showing off his pupil's learning, I am always tempted to say the same to him.

Every one who has considered the manner of life among the ancients, attributes the strength of body and mind by which they are distinguished from the men of our own day to their gymnastic exercises. The stress laid by Montaigne upon this opinion, shows that it had made a great impression on him; he returns to it again and again. Speaking of a child's education he says, "To strengthen the mind you must harden the muscles; by training the child to labour you train him to suffering; he must be broken in to the hardships of gymnastic exercises to prepare him for the hardships of dislocations, colics, and other bodily ills." The philosopher Locke, the worthy Rollin, the learned Fleury, the pedant De Crouzas, differing as they do so widely from one another, are agreed in this one matter of sufficient bodily exercise for children. This is the wisest of their precepts, and the one which is certain to be neglected. I have already dwelt sufficiently on its importance, and as better reasons and more sensible rules cannot be found than those in Locke's book, I will content myself with referring to it, after taking the liberty of adding a few remarks of my own.

The limbs of a growing child should be free to move easily in his clothing; nothing should cramp their growth or movement; there should be nothing tight, nothing fitting closely to the body, no belts of any kind. The French style of dress, uncomfortable and unhealthy for a man, is especially bad for children. The stagnant humours, whose circulation is interrupted, putrify in a state of inaction, and this process proceeds more rapidly in an inactive and sedentary life; they become corrupt and give rise to scurvy; this disease, which is continually on the increase among us, was almost unknown to the ancients, whose way of dressing and living protected them from it. The hussar's dress, far from correcting this fault, increases it, and compresses the whole of the child's body, by way of dispensing with a few bands. The best plan is to keep children in frocks as long as possible and then to provide them with loose clothing, without trying to define the shape which is only another way of deforming it. Their defects of body and mind may all be traced to the same source, the desire to make men of them before their time.

There are bright colours and dull; children like the bright colours best, and they suit them better too. I see no reason why such natural suitability should not be taken into consideration; but as soon as they prefer a material because it is rich, their hearts are already given over to luxury, to every caprice of fashion, and this taste is certainly not their own. It is impossible to say how much education is influenced by this choice of clothes, and the motives for this choice. Not only do short-sighted mothers offer ornaments as rewards to their children, but there are foolish tutors who threaten to make their pupils wear the plainest and coarsest clothes as a punishment. "If you do not do your lessons better, if you do not take more care of your clothes, you shall be dressed like that little peasant boy." This is like saying to them, "Understand that clothes make the man." Is it to be wondered at that our young people profit by such wise teaching, that they care for nothing but dress, and that they only judge of merit by its outside.

If I had to bring such a spoilt child to his senses, I would take care that his smartest clothes were the most uncomfortable, that he was always cramped, constrained, and embarrassed in every way; freedom and mirth should flee before his splendour. If he wanted to take part in the games of children more simply dressed, they should cease their play and run away. Before long I should make him so tired and sick of his magnificence, such a slave to his gold-laced coat, that it would become the plague of his life, and he would be less afraid to behold the darkest dungeon than to see the preparations for his adornment. Before the child is enslaved by our prejudices his first wish is always to be free and comfortable. The plainest and most comfortable clothes, those which leave him most liberty, are what he always likes best.

There are habits of body suited for an active life and others for a sedentary life. The latter leaves the humours an equable and uniform course, and the body should be protected from changes in temperature; the former is constantly passing from action to rest, from heat to cold, and the body should be inured to these changes. Hence people, engaged in sedentary pursuits indoors, should always be warmly dressed, to keep their bodies as nearly as possible at the same temperature at all times and seasons. Those, however, who come and go in sun, wind, and rain, who take much exercise, and spend most of their time out of doors, should always be lightly clad, so as to get used to the changes in the air and to every degree of temperature without suffering inconvenience. I would advise both never to change their clothes with the changing seasons, and that would be the invariable habit of my pupil Emile. By this I do not mean that he should wear his winter clothes in summer like many people of sedentary habits, but that he should wear his summer clothes in winter like hard-working folk. Sir Isaac Newton always did this, and he lived to be eighty.

Emile should wear little or nothing on his head all the year round. The ancient Egyptians always went bareheaded; the Persians used to wear heavy tiaras and still wear large turbans, which according to Chardin are required by their climate. I have remarked elsewhere on the difference observed by Herodotus on a battle-field between the skulls of the Persians and those of the Egyptians. Since it is desirable that the bones of the skull should grow harder and more substantial, less fragile and porous, not only to protect the brain against injuries but against colds, fever, and every influence of the air, you should therefore accustom your children to go bareheaded winter and summer, day and night. If you make them wear a night-cap to keep their hair clean and tidy, let it be thin and transparent like the nets with which the Basques cover their hair. I am aware that most mothers will be more impressed by Chardin's observations than my arguments, and will think that all climates are the climate of Persia, but I did not choose a European pupil to turn him into an Asiatic.

Children are generally too much wrapped up, particuarly in infancy. They should be accustomed to cold rather than heat; great cold never does them any harm, if they are exposed to it soon enough; but their skin is still too soft and tender and leaves too free a course for perspiration, so that they are inevitably exhausted by excessive heat. It has been observed that infant mortality is greatest in August. Moreover, it seems certain from a comparison of northern and southern races that we become stronger by bearing extreme cold rather than excessive heat. But as the child's body grows bigger and his muscles get stronger, train him gradually to bear the rays of the sun. Little by little you will harden him till he can face the burning heat of the tropics without danger.

Locke, in the midst of the manly and sensible advice he gives us, falls into inconsistencies one would hardly expect in such a careful thinker. The same man who would have children take an ice-cold bath summer and winter, will not let them drink cold water when they are hot, or lie on damp grass. But he would never have their shoes water-tight; and why should they let in more water when the child is hot than when he is cold, and may we not draw the same inference with regard to the feet and body that he draws with regard to the hands and feet and the body and face? If he would have a man all face, why blame me if I would have him all feet?

To prevent children drinking when they are hot, he says they should be trained to eat a piece of bread first. It is a strange thing to make a child eat because he is thirsty; I would as soon give him a drink when he is hungry. You will never convince me that our first instincts are so ill-regulated that we cannot satisfy them without endangering our lives. Were that so, the man would have perished over and over again before he had learned how to keep himself alive.

Whenever Emile is thirsty let him have a drink, and let him drink fresh water just as it is, not even taking the chill off it in the depths of winter and when he is bathed in perspiration. The only precaution I advice is to take care what sort of water you give him. If the water comes from a river, give it him just as it is; if it is spring-water let it stand a little exposed to the air before he drinks it. In warm weather rivers are warm; it is not so with springs, whose water has not been in contact with the air. You must wait till the temperature of the water is the same as that of the air. In winter, on the other hand, spring water is safer than river water. It is, however, unusual and unnatural to perspire greatly in winter, especially in the open air, for the cold air constantly strikes the skin and drives the perspiration inwards, and prevents the pores opening enough to give passage. Now I do not intend Emile to take his exercise by the fireside in winter, but in the open air and among the ice. If he only gets warm with making and throwing snowballs, let him drink when he is thirsty, and go on with his game after drinking, and you need not be afraid of any ill effects. And if any other exercise makes him perspire let him drink cold water even in winter provided he is thirsty. Only take care to take him to get the water some little distance away. In such cold as I am supposing, he would have cooled down sufficiently when he got there to be able to drink without danger. Above all, take care to conceal these precautions from him. I would rather he were ill now and then, than always thinking about his health.

Since children take such violent exercise they need a great deal of sleep. The one makes up for the other, and this shows that both are necessary. Night is the time set apart by nature for rest. It is an established fact that sleep is quieter and calmer when the sun is below the horizon, and that our senses are less calm when the air is warmed by the rays of the sun. So it is certainly the healthiest plan to rise with the sun and go to bed with the sun. Hence in our country man and all the other animals with him want more sleep in winter than in summer. But town life is so complex, so unnatural, so subject to chances and changes, that it is not wise to accustom a man to such uniformity that he cannot do without it. No doubt he must submit to rules; but the chief rule is this—be able to break the rule if necessary. So do not be so foolish as to soften your pupil by letting him always sleep his sleep out. Leave him at first to the law of nature without any hindrance, but never forget that under our conditions he must rise above this law; he must be able to go to bed late and rise early, be awakened suddenly, or sit up all night without ill effects. Begin early and proceed gently, a step at a time, and the constitution adapts itself to the very conditions which would destroy it if they were imposed for the first time on the grown man.

In the next place he must be accustomed to sleep in an uncomfortable bed, which is the best way to find no bed uncomfortable. Speaking generally, a hard life, when once we have become used to it, increases our pleasant experiences; an easy life prepares the way for innumerable unpleasant experiences. Those who are too tenderly nurtured can only sleep on down; those who are used to sleep on bare boards can find them anywhere. There is no such thing as a hard bed for the man who falls asleep at once.

The body is, so to speak, melted and dissolved in a soft bed where one sinks into feathers and eider-down. The reins when too warmly covered become inflamed. Stone and other diseases are often due to this, and it invariably produces a delicate constitution, which is the seed-ground of every ailment.

The best bed is that in which we get the best sleep. Emile and I will prepare such a bed for ourselves during the daytime. We do not need Persian slaves to make our beds; when we are digging the soil we are turning our mattresses. I know that a healthy child may be made to sleep or wake almost at will. When the child is put to bed and his nurse grows weary of his chatter, she says to him, "Go to sleep." That is much like saying, "Get well," when he is ill. The right way is to let him get tired of himself. Talk so much that he is compelled to hold his tongue, and he will soon be asleep. Here is at least one use for sermons, and you may as well preach to him as rock his cradle; but if you use this narcotic at night, do not use it by day.

I shall sometimes rouse Emile, not so much to prevent his sleeping too much, as to accustom him to anything—even to waking with a start. Moreover, I should be unfit for my business if I could not make him wake himself, and get up, so to speak, at my will, without being called.

If he wakes too soon, I shall let him look forward to a tedious morning, so that he will count as gain any time he can give to sleep. If he sleeps too late I shall show him some favourite toy when he wakes. If I want him to wake at a given hour I shall say, "To-morrow at six I am going fishing," or "I shall take a walk to such and such a place. Would you like to come too?" He assents, and begs me to wake him. I promise, or do not promise, as the case requires. If he wakes too late, he finds me gone. There is something amiss if he does not soon learn to wake himself.

Moreover, should it happen, though it rarely does, that a sluggish child desires to stagnate in idleness, you must not give way to this tendency, which might stupefy him entirely, but you must apply some stimulus to wake him. You must understand that is no question of applying force, but of arousing some appetite which leads to action, and such an appetite, carefully selected on the lines laid down by nature, kills two birds with one stone.

If one has any sort of skill, I can think of nothing for which a taste, a very passion, cannot be aroused in children, and that without vanity, emulation, or jealousy. Their keenness, their spirit of imitation, is enough of itself; above all, there is their natural liveliness, of which no teacher so far has contrived to take advantage. In every game, when they are quite sure it is only play, they endure without complaint, or even with laughter, hardships which they would not submit to otherwise without floods of tears. The sports of the young savage involve long fasting, blows, burns, and fatigue of every kind, a proof that even pain has a charm of its own, which may remove its bitterness. It is not every master, however, who knows how to season this dish, nor can every scholar eat it without making faces. However, I must take care or I shall be wandering off again after exceptions.

It is not to be endured that man should become the slave of pain, disease, accident, the perils of life, or even death itself; the more familiar he becomes with these ideas the sooner he will be cured of that over-sensitiveness which adds to the pain by impatience in bearing it; the sooner he becomes used to the sufferings which may overtake him, the sooner he shall, as Montaigne has put it, rob those pains of the sting of unfamiliarity, and so make his soul strong and invulnerable; his body will be the coat of mail which stops all the darts which might otherwise find a vital part. Even the approach of death, which is not death itself, will scarcely be felt as such; he will not die, he will be, so to speak, alive or dead and nothing more. Montaigne might say of him as he did of a certain king of Morocco, "No man ever prolonged his life so far into death." A child serves his apprenticeship in courage and endurance as well as in other virtues; but you cannot teach children these virtues by name alone; they must learn them unconsciously through experience.

But speaking of death, what steps shall I take with regard to my pupil and the smallpox? Shall he be inoculated in infancy, or shall I wait till he takes it in the natural course of things? The former plan is more in accordance with our practice, for it preserves his life at a time when it is of greater value, at the cost of some danger when his life is of less worth; if indeed we can use the word danger with regard to inoculation when properly performed.

But the other plan is more in accordance with our general principles—to leave nature to take the precautions she delights in, precautions she abandons whenever man interferes. The natural man is always ready; let nature inoculate him herself, she will choose the fitting occasion better than we.

Do not think I am finding fault with inoculation, for my reasons for exempting my pupil from it do not in the least apply to yours. Your training does not prepare them to escape catching smallpox as soon as they are exposed to infection. If you let them take it anyhow, they will probably die. I perceive that in different lands the resistance to inoculation is in proportion to the need for it; and the reason is plain. So I scarcely condescend to discuss this question with regard to Emile. He will be inoculated or not according to time, place, and circumstances; it is almost a matter of indifference, as far as he is concerned. If it gives him smallpox, there will be the advantage of knowing what to expect, knowing what the disease is; that is a good thing, but if he catches it naturally it will have kept him out of the doctor's hands, which is better.

An exclusive education, which merely tends to keep those who have received it apart from the mass of mankind, always selects such teaching as is costly rather than cheap, even when the latter is of more use. Thus all carefully educated young men learn to ride, because it is costly, but scarcely any of them learn to swim, as it costs nothing, and an artisan can swim as well as any one. Yet without passing through the riding school, the traveller learns to mount his horse, to stick on it, and to ride well enough for practical purposes; but in the water if you cannot swim you will drown, and we cannot swim unless we are taught. Again, you are not forced to ride on pain of death, while no one is sure of escaping such a common danger as drowning. Emile shall be as much at home in the water as on land. Why should he not be able to live in every element? If he could learn to fly, he should be an eagle; I would make him a salamander, if he could bear the heat.

Further Readings

LUCRETIUS, *Of The Nature Of Things*, translated by W. E. Leonard. London: J. M. Dent and Sons, Ltd., 1921.

SPENCER, H., *Education: Intellectual, Moral, and Physical*. New York: Appleton-Century-Crofts, Inc., 1889.

ZEIGLER, E. F., "Naive Naturalism in Philosophy and Education," *Philosophical Foundations for Physical, Health, and Recreation Education*. Englewood Cliffs, N.J.: Prentice-Hall, Inc., 1964.

Questions for Discussion

1. What illustrations does Rousseau use to support his opinion that nature is the best teacher of physical education? To what extent do you agree with him?
2. What contribution does physical development make to the intellect?
3. How would the adoption of the child-rearing practices described by Rousseau modify current physical education programs?
4. To what extent do you subscribe to the naturalistic position in physical education?

GEORG WILHELM FRIEDRICH HEGEL

Outlines of Logic*

Hegel's grandiloquence frequently obscures his meaning. He is also difficult to follow because there is considerable circularity in his philosophy. Moreover, new terms are defined by other new and equally obscure terms. Yet, his influence on philosophical and political thought of the nineteenth century, especially on the "dialectical materialism" of Karl Marx, was momentous.

A chief characteristic of Hegelian logic is the dialectic method, in which every thesis has its antithesis. According to Hegel all ideas generate their opposites. This mutual antagonism finally creates a new and higher-order *synthesis*, a reconciliation of thesis and antithesis. In this way ideas advance from lower to higher meaning. This dialectic applies to concepts (ideas) but not material things. Marx claimed to have turned Hegel's philosophy upside down when he declared that antagonisms between ideas are the results of the concrete, material, economic antagonisms between socio-economic classes.

Hegel's position is one answer to Platonic idealism, Cartesian dualism, and the romanticism of his period. Mind and body do not exist in separate spheres: mind controls body. Ideas propel and control history. This book of readings is partly Hegelian in its attempt to give an intellectual rationale for physical education and in its implication that the conceptual frameworks of our students in physical education exercise control of their choices of activity and level of development. And the dialectic itself suggests, perhaps, the necessary tension between mind and body, the resolution of which may make for a higher-order human being.

---

* Reprinted with permission of the publisher from J. Loewenberg, ed., *Hegel: Selections*, translated by W. T. Harris. Chicago: Charles Scribner's Sons, 1929, pp. 98–116; 124–128. Paragraphs 73. through 86. are omitted.

Introduction

1. The Science of Logic has for its object the thinking activity and the entire compass of its determinations. "Natural Logic" is a name given to the natural understanding which man possesses by nature, and the immediate use which he makes of it. The Science of Logic, however, is the Knowing of the Thinking in its truth.

Explanatory.—Logic considers the province of thought in general. The thinking activity is its peculiar sphere. It is a whole (complete sphere) for and by itself. Logic has for its content the determinations peculiar to the thinking activity itself—which have no other ground than the Thinking. The "heteronomical" to it, is what is given to it through representation. Logic is, therefore, true science. A distinction must, of course, be made between pure thought and reality; but thought has reality in so far as *true actuality* is understood by this term. In so far, however, as sensuous external existence is meant by "the Real," Thought has a far higher reality. The thinking activity has therefore a content (namely, itself) through its autonomy. Through the study of Logic we also learn to think more correctly; for since we think the Thinking of Thinking, the mind increases thereby its power. We learn the nature of the thinking activity, and thus we can trace out the course in which it is liable to be led into error. It is well to know how to give an account of one's deed. Thereby one gains stability, and is not liable to be led astray by others.

2. The thinking activity is, in general, the apprehension and bringing together of the Manifold into unity. The Manifold as such belongs to externality in general—to feeling and sensuous intuition.

Explanatory.—The thinking activity consists in bringing the Manifold into unity. When the mind thinks upon things, it brings them into simple forms, which are its pure determinations. The Manifold is, at first, external to the Thinking. In so far as we merely seize the sensuous Manifold, we do not yet "think"; but it is the *relating* of the same that is properly called Thinking. The immediate seizing of the Manifold we call *feeling* or *sensation*. When I feel, I merely know somewhat; in "intuition" [*Anschauen*], however, I look upon something as external to me in space and time. Feeling becomes "intuition" when it is determined in space and time.

3. The thinking activity is *Abstraction* in so far as intelligence, beginning with concrete intuitions, neglects one of the manifold determinations, selects another, and gives to it the simple form of thought.

Explanatory.—If I neglect *all* the determinations of an object, *nothing* remains. If, on the contrary, I neglect *one* and select *another,* the latter is then abstract. The *Ego,* for example, is an abstract determination. I know of the *Ego* only in so far as I exclude all determinations from myself. This is, however, a negative means. I negate the determinations of myself, and leave myself as such, alone by myself. The act of abstraction is the *negative* side of the thinking activity.

4. The *content* of representations [*Vorstellungen* = notions] is taken from experience, but the *form of unity* itself, and its further determinations, have not their source in the Immediate as such, but in the thinking activity.

Explanatory.—The Ego signifies, generally, the thinking activity. If I say: "I think," this is something tautological. The Ego is perfectly simple. The Ego is a thinking activity, and that always. We could not say, however: "I always think." Though *potentially* so, yet what we think is not always *actually* Thought. We could however say, in the sense that we are Ego's: "We always think," for the Ego is always the simple identity with itself, and this simple identity with itself is Thinking. As Ego, we are the ground of all our determinations. In so far as the object is thought it receives the form of thinking and becomes a thought-object. It is made identical to the Ego, i.e. it is thought.

5. This must not be understood as though this unity was added to the Manifold of objects by the thinking activity, and thereby the act of uniting was done externally; but the unity must be conceived as belonging likewise to the object, and as constituting with its determinations the proper nature thereof.

6. Thoughts are of three kinds: (1) The Categories; (2) Determination of Reflections; (3) Comprehension, The science of the first two constitutes the objective logic in metaphysics; the science of Comprehensions (concepts or notions) constitutes the proper or subjective logic.

Explanatory.—Logic contains the system of pure Thinking, Being is (1) the Immediate, (2) the Internal; the determinations of Thinking go back again into themselves. The objects of the common system of metaphysics are the *Thing,* the *World, Mind,* and *God* through which the different metaphysical sciences arise Ontology, Cosmology, Pneumatology, and Theology (3) The Comprehension (concept, notion, or idea) presents us with what is *existent* and at the same time *essential.* Being stands in relation to essence as the Immediate to the Mediate. Things *are* in general, but their Being consists in this: that they manifest their Essence. Being goes over into Essence; one can express it thus: "Being presupposes Essence." But although Essence, in comparison with Being, appears as that which is *mediated,* yet Essence is the true Primitive, notwithstanding. Being goes back, in it, into its ground; Being cancels itself (takes itself up) into Essence. Its Essence is in this form a *Become* or *Produced,* but what appears as "Become" is rather the Original or Primitive. The Perishable has in Essence its basis, and originates from it. We make comprehensions (i.e. exhaustive concepts). These are somewhats *posited* by us, but they contain also the Reality in and for itself. As compared with the comprehension, Essence in its turn is a "mere posited," but "the posited" in this relation still stands for the true. The comprehension is partly subjective, partly objective. The IDEA is the union of Subjective and Objective. If we say, "It is a mere conception (*blosser Begriff*)," we mean that it is without reality. The mere Objectivity is devoid of the comprehension. But the Idea is the reality determined through the comprehension. Everything actual is an IDEA.

7. Science presupposes that the separation of itself from Truth is already cancelled, or that the mind is no longer in a phenomenal stage as it was in the *Science of Consciousness* (Phenomenology of Spirit). The certitude of itself comprehends all that is object of consciousness (whether it be an external thing, or a thought produced in the mind), in so far as it does not contain in itself all moments of the *Being-in-and-for-itself:* (1) to be *in itself,* or simple identify with itself; (2) to have determinate Being or determinateness, Being for others; and (3) to be *for itself,* i.e., in its relation to others to be simple, reflected into itself, and by itself. Science does not *seek* Truth, but is *in* the Truth, and *is* the Truth itself.

Part First—Being.

FIRST DIVISION—QUALITY.

8. Quality is the immediate determinateness, whose change is the transition into a Different.

A.—BEING, NAUGHT, BECOMING.

9. Being is the simple empty immediateness which has its opposite in *pure Naught,* and whose union therewith is the Becoming: as transition from Naught to Being, it is Beginning; the converse is Ceasing.

(The "sound common sense," as one-sided abstraction often calls itself, will not admit the union of Being and Naught. "Either it is Being, or it is not. There is no third." "What *is,* does not begin; what is not, is *not.*" It asserts, therefore, the impossibility of Beginning.)

B.—DETERMINATE BEING.

10. Determinate Being is *become* or *determined* Being, a Being which has a relation to another—hence to its non-being.

11. (a) Determinate Being is, consequently, a somewhat divided in itself: *firstly,* it is *in-itself* (i.e. potential); *secondly,* it is relation to others. Determinate Being, thought with these two determinations is *Reality.*

12. (b) A somewhat which is definite has a relation to another. The "other" is a definite Being as the non-being of the somewhat. It has, consequently, a boundary or restraining limit and is finite. What a somewhat ought to be in itself, is called its Destination (determination).

13. The mode in which a somewhat is for another, or in which it is connected with another, and hence immediately posited through another, is called its *state* or *condition.*

14. The mode in which a somewhat is *in-itself,* as well for itself as for another, is its *determinateness* or *quality.* The limit is not only the point where the somewhat ceases, but it belongs to the somewhat in itself.

15. (c) Through its quality, through *what* it is, the somewhat is exposed to CHANGE. It changes in so far as its determinateness comes into connection with another and thereby becomes state or condition [*Beschaffenheit*].

C.—BEING FOR-ITSELF.

16. Inasmuch as the "state or condition" is cancelled through change, change itself also is cancelled. Being, consequently, with

this process, has gone back into itself and excludes otherness from itself. It is FOR ITSELF.

17. It is ONE, and relates only to itself, and stands in a repellent relation towards others.

18. This excluding is at the same time a *bringing-into-relation* to others, and hence it is likewise an *attracting*. No Repulsion without attraction and *vice versa*.

19. Or, with the act of repulsion on the part of the One, many ones are immediately posited. But the many ones are not distinct from each other. Each one is what the other is. Hence their cancelling, i.e. their attraction, is likewise posited.

20. The One is the "Existent-for-itself," which is absolutely distinct from others. But since this distinction (in which Repulsion is cancelled by Attraction) is the distinction posited as cancelled, for that reason it has passed over into another determination—QUANTITY.

("Somewhat" without limits has no meaning. If I change the limits of a somewhat, it remains no longer what it is; if I change the limits of a field, it still remains a field as before though somewhat larger or smaller. In this case I have not changed its limits as field, but as a given quantity. To change its qualitative limit as ploughed field means, e.g., to make it a forest.)

SECOND DIVISION—QUANTITY.

21. Through quality a somewhat is *what* it is. Through change of quality, there is changed not merely a determination of the somewhat—or of the Finite—but the Finite somewhat, itself changes. Quantity, on the contrary, is the determination which does not constitute the nature of the object itself; it is rather an *"indifferent* distinction," which may be changed, while the object remains the same.

22. Quantity is the cancelled Being-for-itself (or One). It is, therefore, an unbroken CONTINUITY in itself. But since it contains the One, moreover, it possesses also the "moment" of DISCRETENESS.

23. (A) *Magnitude* is either *continuous* or *discrete*. But each of these two kinds of magnitude contains discreteness AND continuity in it; and their difference is this only, that in the discrete magnitude, it is Discreteness which constitutes the main principle, while in the continuous it is Continuity.

24. (B) *Magnitude* or *Quantity* is as limited quantity, a *"Quantum."* Since this limit is nothing fixed in its nature, it follows that a *"quantum"* [i.e. a given quantity] can be changed indefinitely; it can be increased or decreased at pleasure.

25. The limits of the *"quantum"* in the form of "Being-in-itself" give INTENSIVE quantity; and in the form of externality give EXTENSIVE quantity. But there is no intensive Being which does not likewise at the same time possess the form of extensive Being; and conversely.

26. (C) *"Quantum"* has no in-itself determined limit. There is, hence, no quantum [given quantity] beyond which a larger or smaller cannot be posited. The "quantum" which is, by hypothesis, the *last* one—the one which has no greater or no smaller (as the case may be)—is generally called the infinitely great or the infinitely small [Maximum and Minimum].

27. But in this shape it ceases to be a "quantum" at all, and is by itself = 0. It has then significance only in a RATIO wherein it no longer possesses any magnitude by itself, but only in relation to another. This is the correct comprehension (conception) of the MATHEMATICAL INFINITE.

28. The Infinite in general, when seized in the form of the Infinite Progress, is the process of cancelling the restraining limit whether it be qualitative or quantitative, so that this restraining limit passes for something positive, and continually reappears after its negation. The true Infinite, however, is the NEGATION OF NEGATION, inasmuch as the restraining limit is to be understood as really a negation. In it the progress beyond the Finite does not posit again a new restraining limit, but through the cancelling of the restraining limit, the Being is restored to identity with itself.

29. While the "quantum" cancels itself in the Infinite, in the same process the indifferent, external determination which constitutes the "quantum," is cancelled and becomes an internal, a *qualitative* determination.

THIRD DIVISION—MEASURE.

30. "Measure" is a SPECIFIC QUANTUM in so far as it is not external, but is determined through the nature of the object, through quality.

31. In the change of a "quantum," in its increase or decrease, which goes on within its "measure," there enters likewise a specifying process, in which the indifferent, external movement of magnitude up and down the scale, is determined and modified through the nature of the thing itself.

32. When the "measure" of a thing is changed, the thing itself changes and ceases to be the particular somewhat that it was, through the passing beyond its "measure,"—increasing or decreasing beyond it.

Part Second—Essence.

33. Essence is Being which has returned from its immediateness and its indifferent relation to others into simple unity with itself.

FIRST DIVISION—THE DETERMINATIONS OF ESSENCE IN ITSELF.

34. Essence (*"Wesen"*) appears to itself (*"scheint in sich selbst"*) and determines itself. But its determinations are in unity. They are only "posited-being," i.e. they are not immediately for themselves, but only such as exist in unity. They are therefore RELATIONS. They are "determinations of Reflection."

35. (1) The first determination is the essential unity with itself—IDENTITY. Expressed as a proposition—namely, as a universal determination—it is the proposition "A = A," "everything is identical with itself"; negatively, as the proposition of contradiction: "A cannot be at the same time A and not-A."

36. (2) The second determination is DISTINCTION (a) as the determination of DIFFERENCE—of Beings indifferent to each other, but distinguished through some determinateness or other. The proposition which expresses it, reads: "There are no two things which are perfectly identical with each other"; (b) as the determination of OPPOSITION (*antithesis*), the positive against the negative, in which a determinateness is posited only by means of another determinateness, and each of these determinatenesses is only in so far as the other is, but at the same time is only in so far as it is *not* the other. The proposition through which this is expressed reads: "A is either B or not-B, and there is no third."

37. (3) The third in which the posited determination are cancelled in general is Essence, which is, in this phase, GROUND.

The proposition of Ground reads: "Every somewhat has its sufficient (reason or) ground."

38. In so far as immediate Being is regarded as a merely "Posited," it has gone back into essence or into its ground. The former (i.e. Being) is here the first—that from which we started. But in this "going back" we retract that position, and recognize the ground rather as the first and essential.

39. The Ground contains that which is grounded through it according to its essential determinations. But the relation of the Ground to the grounded is not a pure transition into the opposite, although the grounded existence has a different shape from its ground, which is likewise an existence, and the chief determination is their common content.

SECOND DIVISION—PHENOMENON.

A.—THING.

40. The Ground, through its internal determination, posits its Being, a Being which, as proceeding from the Ground, is EXISTENCE.

41. As a totality of its determinations, the existing somewhat is a THING.

42. The properties of a Thing are determinations of its existence which are different from each other, but at the same time independent of each other; and moreover a Thing is, as simple identity with itself (undetermined and) indifferent towards them as determinations.

43. The determinations are through the *thingness* identical with themselves, and the Thing is nothing but this identity of its properties with themselves. Through this circumstance, the Thing dissolves into its properties, as into matters which subsist for and by themselves.

44. Since, however, the "matters" are united in the unity of a thing, they interpenetrate each other reciprocally and cancel each other. The Thing is consequently this contradiction in itself, or it is posited as a mere self-dissolving, as Phenomenal.

B.—THE PHENOMENAL.

45. Essence has gone out of *Ground* into *Existence*. The Existing posited as not in-and-for-itself, but as grounded in another, is THE

PHENOMENAL. Essence *must* manifest itself in so far as it is, as ground, simple immediateness, and hence Being in general.

46. On account of the Identity of the Ground and the Existent, there is nothing in *the Phenomenal* which is not in the Essence, and conversely nothing in the Essence which is not in the Phenomenal.

47. (The identity with itself in the Phenomenal is the Undetermined, the determination a mere CAPACITY—the PASSIVE MATTER. The identity of determinations in their relation to each other, constitutes the ACTIVE, the FORM. Since Matter is determined by Form, the two presuppose each other. There is however, in general, no Matter without Form and no Form without Matter. Matter and form give rise to each other reciprocally.) The essential relation in the determinations of the Phenomenal is the LAW thereof.

48. Since the determinations manifest themselves also in the form of independent existence, the Relation of the same as being determined through each other constitutes the mutual relation [*Verhältniss*].

C.—MUTUAL RELATION.

49. The MUTUAL RELATION is a relation to each other of two sides which have partly an indifferent subsistence, but partly each is only through the other and in this unity which determines both.

50. The determinations are posited first in the form of mutual relation, secondly they are only in themselves and manifest themselves as independent, immediate Existence. They are in this respect presupposed somewhats and internally, already in themselves, contain the totality of form, which can have existence only through that presupposition; or they are in so far conditions, and their mutual relation is a conditional mutual relation.

51. In the conditions and the conditioned mutual relation, the Phenomenal begins to return into Essence and Being-in-itself, but there exists still the difference of the Phenomenal as such, and the former (Essence, &c.) in so far as they are *"in themselves."*

52. (1) The immediately conditioned Mutual Relation is the WHOLE and the PARTS. The parts as existing outside of the Relation, and subsisting for themselves, are mere matters, and, in so far, not parts. As parts they have their determination only in the

whole, and the whole is what makes them to be parts, and conversely it is the parts that make it to be the whole.

53. (2) The whole, as internally active Form, is FORCE. It has no external matter as its condition, but is in the matter itself. Its condition is only an external "occasion" which solicits it. The latter is itself the utterance of a Force and demands in turn a solicitation for its manifestation. It is a reciprocal conditioning and being conditioned, and this is as a Whole, therefore, unconditioned.

54. According to content, Force exhibits in its utterance that which it is in itself, and there is nothing in its utterance which is not in its Internal.

55. (3) The content is consequently, in respect to the distinction of Internal and External, unconditioned. It stands in mutual relation as internal, only to itself as external. The external and internal are therefore the same, only considered from different sides. The internal is the perfection of content-determinations as conditions which themselves have determinate existence. The becoming-external is the reflection of the same or the uniting of the whole, which through this receives existence.

THIRD DIVISION—ACTUALITY.

A.—SUBSTANCE.

56. Substance is the unconditioned, in-and-for-itself-subsisting Essence in so far as it has immediate Existence. (*Substantia est— causa sui: id quod par se conciptur sive cujus conceptus involvit existentiam—Spinoza.*)

57. In its existence it has manifold determinations distinct from it = ACCIDENTS. In their Totality they constitute substance, which is the subsistence, and hence the POWER of Accidents.

58. The accidents, in so far as they are contained in the substance, are POTENTIAL.

59. When anything is thought merely in the form of "Being-in-itself," or as not self-contradictory, it is called potential (possible). Everything in so far as it is determined as a Being-in-itself which is only a posited, is called *merely* potential. Such a Possibility, isolated from the Actuality, has an individual content.

60. *Truly* potential is somewhat as a totality of its in-itself-existent determinations. Whatever possesses this internal perfect potentiality is not merely a posited-Being, but in-and-for-itself and

immediately *actual*. The potentiality of substance is, therefore, its actuality. (God, e.g., is not only in general but truly potential. His potentiality is a necessary one. He is absolutely Actual.)

61. The combination of accidents in the substance, is their necessity. It is the unity of Possibility and Actuality. Necessity is blind in so far as the combination is merely an internal one, or in so far as the actual is not previously extant as an in-itself-existent unity of its determinations, but results first from the relation of the same.

B.—CAUSE.

62. Substance manifests itself in the origination and vanishing of its accidents. It is in so far active, or CAUSE.

63. As Cause, substance makes its original content into EFFECT, i.e. into a "posited through another."

64. There is nothing in the effect which is not in the cause, and the cause is cause only in the Effect.

(It is said: the fall of a brick is the cause of the death of a man: the miasma of a region is the cause of fevers. But the former was the cause only of the blow, the latter only of excessive moisture. But the effect in an actual existence which has other determinations, besides, continues to other results.)

65. Cause passes over into effect. Since the cause itself has a definite content and is to be posited as effect, we obtain a regress of causes and effects in an infinite series. Conversely, in so far as that upon which the effect takes place is itself a primitive, it is a cause, and produces an effect in another, through which a progress *ad infinitum* results.

C.—RECIPROCAL ACTION.

66. In so far as the effect returns to the cause, it is itself cause. It makes the cause a Posited. It is REACTION. "Action and Reaction are equal."

67. The Reaction takes place against the first cause, which consequently is posited as effect, through which nothing else happens except that it is posited as it is in itself, namely, as a not truly original (primitive) but as a *Transitory*.

68. Reciprocal action consists in this: that which is effect is conversely cause, and that which is cause is conversely effect. Or the

reciprocal relation is the mediation of the Thing with itself, in which the Primitive determines itself or makes itself a Posited; and therein reflects itself into itself, and exists first as this reflection into itself, and is therein true Primitiveness.

Appendix—The Antinomies.

69. The categories, the determinations of Being are simple; but the determinations which do not constitute the primitive elements, i.e. the determinations of Essence, are simple only in so far as their antithetical moments are reduced to simplicity. Whenever such a category is predicated of a subject and is developed through the analysis of those antithetic moments, the two are predicable of the subject, and there arise antithetic propositions, both of which have equal truth.

70. Kant especially has drawn attention to the Antinomies of Reason, although he has not exhausted them, since he has made an exposition of the forms of only a few.

I. The antinomy of the Finitude or Infinitude of the world in regard to Space and Time.

(1) The antinomy in respect to Time.

(a) THESIS: The world has a beginning in Time.

71. *Proof:* Let one assume that the world has no beginning in respect to time; then, up to any given point of time, an eternity has elapsed, and consequently an infinite series of successive conditions of things in the world. The infinitude of a series consists, however, in this, that it can never be completed by successive synthesis; therefore an infinite series of conditions in the world is impossible; hence a beginning of the same in time is necessitated.

(b) ANTITHESIS: The world has no beginning in time, and is infinite in respect to time.

72. *Proof:* Let one suppose that it had a beginning, then there would be assumed an empty time before that beginning—a time in which the world was not. In an empty time, however, nothing can originate, for in it there is no condition for existence, since one Being always has another as its condition, i.e. is limited by finite Being only. Therefore the world can have no beginning, but every determinate Being presupposes another, and so on *ad infinitum.* . . .

87. This antinomy contains, on the whole, the same antithesis as the previous one. With the Conditioned a condition is posited, and indeed a condition *as such,* or an absolute condition, i.e. one which has not its necessity in something else. Since, however, it is in connexion with the Conditioned, or since the Conditioned lies in its comprehension (or complete definition), it belongs itself to the sphere of the Conditioned, or is a Conditioned itself. According to the former side, an absolutely necessary Being is posited, but according to the latter only a *relative* necessity, and hence *contingence.*

Part Third—Comprehension.

88. The science of the Comprehension (concepts), or subjective logic, has for its object the Comprehension, and not the Categories, and determinations of Reflection. The Category posits Being in a determinateness as limit; Reflection posits essence in a determination which is mediated through the presupposition of another. The Comprehension [conception?], on the other hand, is the in-and-for-itself Existent, the simple totality out of which all its determinations flow.

89. Subjective logic treats of three chief objects, (1) the Comprehension, (2) the Final Cause, (3) the Idea; namely: (1) the formal Comprehension, or the Comprehension as such; (2) the Comprehension in relation to its realization or its Objectivity (the Final Cause); (3) the Idea as the real or objective Comprehension.

FIRST DIVISION—THE COMPREHENSION.

90. Formal Logic contains (1) the comprehension as such, (2) the judgment, and (3) the syllogism.

91. (1) The COMPREHENSION contains the moments of *individuality, particularity,* and *universality.* Individuality is the negative reflection of the comprehension into itself, through which something is in-and-for-itself, and the determinations as moments inhere in it. Universality is the positive, not excluding, unity of the comprehension with itself, which contains the opposite in itself, so that it remains indifferent and undetermined toward it. Particularity is the relation of individuality and universality to each other. It is the Universal reduced to a determination; or, conversely, the individual elevated into universality.

92. As these determinations are distinguished from each other as moments of the Comprehension, so are they distinguished by the

different content they may have, as comprehensions of something universal, something particular, and something individual.

93. The Universal subsumes or includes the Particular and Individual under it. The individual has the same, and at the same time several more, determinations than the Particular and Universal. Likewise the same relation exists on the part of the Particular toward the Universal. What, therefore, possesses validity with regard to the Universal, possesses validity for the Particular and Individual; and what is valid of the Particular is valid of the individual, *but not conversely.*

94. The particular determinations which belong to the same Universal are COORDINATED to each other. The same thing applies also to those which belong to the same individual. But these determinations which are coördinated in a Universal cannot be coördinated in one individual.

95. (2) In the JUDGMENT the implicit unity in which the moments are grasped together in the comprehension, is cancelled. It (the judgment) is the *relation* of the determinations of the Comprehension in so far as each is valid by itself as a self-subsisting and consequently as a particular comprehension.

96. The Judgment contains: (1) the subject as the side of individuality or particularity; (2) the predicate as the side of universality, which is at the same time a determined universality, or also particularity; (3) the simple relation (devoid of content) which the subject has to the predicate, is the COPULA.

97. The species of Judgments indicate the different stages in which the external relation of subject and predicate becomes an internal relation of the comprehension. The subject is, *first,* in immediate identity with the predicate—the two are one and the same determination of content; *secondly,* they are distinguished one from the other. The subject is a more complex content than the abstract predicate, and is in regard to form contingent.

98. (3) In the Judgment two determinations of the Comprehension are related immediately to each other. The SYLLOGISM is the Judgment with its ground. The two determinations are connected in the Syllogism by means of a third which is their unity. The Syllogism is, therefore, the perfect positing of the Comprehension.

99. According to determined form, the two extremes of the Syllogism are the Individual and the Universal; the Particular, on the contrary, for the reason that in it these two determinations are

united, is the middle term of the same. If a determination A belongs to the determination B, and the determination B belongs to a determination C, then the determination A belongs to C.

100. The relation of the two extremes (*termini extremi*) of the syllogism to the middle term is a two-fold one, and forms two judgments (*propositiones praemissae*), each of which contains the moment of particularity—the middle term (*terminus medius*). The one premise contains, moreover, the extreme of universality (*terminus major*) as predicate (*propositio major*); the other contains the extreme of individuality (*terminus minor*) as subject (*propositio minor*); the relation of the two extremes is the third judgment; the inference (*conclusio*), "conclusion," is mediated.

SECOND DIVISION—THE FINAL CAUSE, OR TELEOLOGICAL COMPREHENSION.

101. In the Final Cause, that which is mediated, or the Inference, is at the same time *immediate, first,* and *ground.* The Produced, or that which is posited through mediation, has the act of producing and its immediate determination for presupposition, and conversely the act of producing happens on account of the result which is the ground, and hence is the first determination of the activity. The teleological act is a syllogism in which the same whole is brought into unity (its objective form with its subjective form, the comprehension with its reality) through the mediation of teleological activity, and the Comprehension is ground of a reality determined through it.

102. External conformity to end exists in so far as a somewhat possesses the comprehension through which it is determined, not in itself, but is subordinated to it by another subject as an external form or relation.

103. Internal conformity to end is this: an existence possesses its comprehension in itself and is at the same time its own object and means—self-realising and self-realised final cause in itself.

THIRD DIVISION—THE IDEA.

104. The IDEA is the unity of the Comprehension and Reality, the comprehension in so far as it determines itself and its reality, or the Actuality which is what it ought to be, and contains its comprehension itself.

105. (1) The idea in so far as the comprehension is united with its reality immediately, and does not directly distinguish itself from, and elevate itself out of it, is LIFE. The same exhibited as *physical* and likewise *spiritual* life, and freed from all the conditions and limitations of contingent existence is the BEAUTIFUL.

106. (2) In the Idea of COGNITION and PRACTICAL ACTIVITY is the reality of the Comprehension; or the Subjective is opposed to the Objective and their union is brought about. In *Cognition* Reality lies at the basis as the *first* and as *Essence; Practical Activity,* on the other hand, makes actuality conform to the Comprehension so that the GOOD is produced.

107. (3) The ABSOLUTE IDEA is the content of SCIENCE, namely, the consideration of the universe, as it is in conformity with the Comprehension in-and-for-itself [*"sub specie aeternitatis"*], or the rational Comprehension as it is in-and-for-itself, and as it is in the objective or real world.

Further Readings

HARRIS, WILLIAM T., *Hegel's Logic.* Chicago: S. C. Griggs and Company, 1890.

HEGEL, G. W. F., *Reason in History. A General Introduction to the Philosophy of History,* translated (and introduced) by R. S. Hartman. New York: The Liberal Arts Press, 1953.

ORYNSKI, WANDA, *Hegel. Highlights: An Annotated Selection.* New York: Philosophical Library, Inc., 1960.

Questions for Discussion

1. How do Hegel's views compare with those of Plato, Descartes, and Locke?
2. What are the major theses and antitheses of physical education?
3. For what new logical synthesis may physical education result?
4. How is Dewey's philosophy opposed to Hegel's?

CHARLES K. BRIGHTBILL

What Comes Naturally*

In the writing of Brightbill we find the most eloquent expression of Rousseau's love of and respect for nature. Brightbill may think of himself more as a recreationist than as a physical educator, largely because he is less concerned with the institutional form of our physical activities than are Oberteuffer and Williams. He believes, however, that outdoor education does not occupy its rightful position in our schools. The widespread concern for our forests and parks and the enthusiastic interest in camping attest to the current popularity of Brightbill's views.

A comparison of Rousseau and Brightbill reveals many similarities. Brightbill personifies "nature" as a source of beauty and security in much the same way as does Rousseau. The need to escape the pressures of urban living echoes Rousseau's distrust of civilization and society. In his belief that nature is a classroom, he assigns to it the same pedagogical role as did Rousseau.

The Laurel Is for Learning

Wherever plants grow, the wind blows, animals live, the sun, moon, and stars shine, and the snow and rain fall, we find, along with the chance for adventure, the opportunity for learning. Sometimes instruments such as microscopes and binoculars help, but mostly we need use only our own eyes, ears, and other native senses.

If outdoor education, or nature study as it has been often called, comes slowly into the educational curriculum we should not be surprised. The scholar or educator, with the notable exception

* Reprinted and abridged from Charles K. Brightbill, *Man and Leisure: A Philosophy of Recreation.* © 1961 by permission of Prentice-Hall, Inc., Englewood Cliffs, N.J., pp. 140–144, 151–154.

of the modern scientist, has never been known to startle the world with his willingness to quickly accept the new. Why learning through outdoor living and nature study should encounter such obstacles, however, is difficult to understand, because it is, in fact, an American heritage. The American Indian was the product of the forest, and the Pilgrims lived close to the land. Washington practiced husbandry at Mount Vernon, and Lincoln was a woodsman of the first order. Theodore Roosevelt championed conservation, and naturalist John Burroughs wrote inspiringly at "Slabsides." These stalwarts had roots deep in the land. As Louis Agassiz, the great Swiss naturalist, said, "May we not be daring enough today to be concerned about soil, water, forests, wildlife, and people as practical biological problems? Or shall we pass the way of early civilization in China and the Nile Valley?"[1]

It would be a serious error, however, to assume that those who favored conservation, including the men named above, along with such persons as the late, progressive Senators Robert Marion LaFollette and George W. Norris, and conservationists John Muir and Stephen T. Mather, were either in the majority or that their road was easy. More typical through the years has been the kind of thinking reflected by the articulate voice of Secretary of the Interior Richard A. Ballinger who in 1912 said,

> You chaps who are in favor of this conservation program are all wrong. You are hindering the development of the West. . . . In my opinion, the proper course to take is to divide it up among the big corporations and the people who know how to make money out of it, and let the people at large get the benefit of the circulation of the money.[2]

When "Cap'n Bill" Vinal suggested, during World War II, that colleges provide courses in "outdoor survival," his plea was rejected on the basis that such a course of study was not *basic* to learning. At that very mometn, soldiers in the Pacific Theater were trying to return to their lines, "navigating" as best they could by the sun and stars. If survival is not basic to learning, what is? It is more than probable that nature study and outdoor education once held a most prominent place in learning and in early circles of for-

[1] William Gould Vinal, *The Outdoor Schoolroom for Outdoor Living.* (Cohasset, Mass.: Published by the author, 1952), p. 6.
[2] Richard L. Neuberger, "Guarding Our National Heritage," *The Progressive*, Vol. 23, No. 1 (January 1959), p. 37.

mal education. But gradually its name was dropped from educational curricula, and both its content and attractiveness were smothered in the attitude and methods of modern teaching. Nature, of course, has been and is being studied in the search for truth and increased knowledge, but has yet to come into its own as a study to increase the joy of living. However, the time has arrived in our attempts to improve education that we should, figuratively and literally, "come down to earth."

Nevertheless, there has been progress. As stated earlier, school camping in the United States has become an integral part of the school curriculum in such states as Michigan and California. Educators in these places have come to realize that some learning experiences can be provided best in the outdoors. Less emphasis these days is being placed upon how many pounds a child gains when his parents send him to camp than in what he has learned in the way of getting along with his fellow campers, making do with little, and acquiring new skills. Nature's laboratory of learning is the greatest of them all! Our 35 million children and three to four million college students in the United States could profit immensely by learning from Nature in parks, forests, refuges, camps, gardens, and other outdoor settings. In the process, they would not only improve their health and become better citizens, they would also learn quickly about science, conservation, safety, and full living. Here are agronomy, meteorology, geography, botany, and zoology in their rawest forms. Here we may learn first hand how to preserve, conserve, and strengthen our natural resources. Here the problems of handling fire, harnessing the elements, and using native materials, can actually be experienced. Here, too, we may find valuable experience in adjustment and resourcefulness.

In the outdoors, it is surprising how varied conditions and environment can be within a relatively small area. Californians need not travel the world in order to experience a half-dozen different climates. (In fact, this can all be done within the boundaries of San Francisco alone.) One need not beat a path across an entire continent to experience great extremes in climate and ecology. The Olympic Peninsula in the State of Washington has such extremes. Here there are the mountains and the sea, the rain and the snow, the alpine plateau and the dripping jungle. But what of our own neighborhoods? Has Nature overlooked us at home? Are there not natural texts from which we can learn at our own back-door steps?

Do not most of us have Nature to thank for being able to experience the beauty of the sunrise and sunset? The dewy morning, the warm afternoon, and the cool evening? The Spring, Summer, Fall and Winter? The flowers, fruits, and vegetables? The rain or snow? The trees, the streams, the fields—and, if we are fortunate, the sea or the mountains?

Our colleges and universities have learned how to use Nature as a classroom. Field trips into the outdoors have been common on college campuses for many years—and some have even put their classes "on the road." The University of Idaho, for example, has a class in painting—a workshop on wheels—that travels through some of the West's most magnificent scenic spots. As the head of the University's Art and Architectural Department says, "Idaho has scenes that have been waiting to be painted since the land began. And there are persons who have had the urge to paint almost since *they* began. We simply decided to bring the two together."[3]

With Companionship Abounding

Not a few people through the years have turned to the land, to Nature in order to elude the company of other humans. Others have sought the woods and open fields not so much to escape social intercourse but because they thought the pace of living in an artificial environment much too high. Henry David Thoreau is a fine example of the latter point of view. Thoreau had been a scholar, school teacher, surveyor, carpenter, and pencil maker, but found satisfaction in none of them. He believed that if one lived simply and wisely in the midst of Nature, he could also live fully. And so, with borrowed tools, he built his cabin on the shores of Walden Pond. Here he grew what little food he needed and bartered his services for clothes and some of the foodstuffs he could not raise. Whatever leisure he had was spent with the creatures and beauties of nature, or in thinking and writing about them. With his *Walden,* he gave to the world one of its greatest works on Nature. It is doubtful if others got any closer to life, and life any closer to them, than did Thoreau. This talented naturalist, who never used a trap or a gun to find and keep what he wanted, brought the woods, the birds, the beasts, and even the fish closer to all of us. He made

[3] Rafe Gibbs, "Art Trails Through Idaho," *Ford Times*, Vol. 50, No. 5 (May 1958), p. 53.

it possible for any one of us to plunge deeply and immediately, at any time, into Spring, Summer, Autumn, or Winter simply by turning his pages.

Yet as Thoreau and others have found solitude in Nature, some of us, if we wish, may find in it a great source for companionship—human and otherwise. After the authorities in Tyler, Texas turned a farm into a public-school camp, and it had been in use for a while, they were anxious to see what effects, if any, these camping experiences were having upon the children. Those responsible for investing the taxpayers' money in such an unconventional program were particularly interested in the matter of personal relationships. Before the children were sent to camp, they were asked to name those among their classmates they considered to be their friends. After the youngsters had been to camp, the question was repeated. Interestingly, after their camp experience, the majority of the boys and girls named *more* of their classmates as friends, having added new ones. A large number of them even included their teachers, whom they had come to know under the decidedly different atmosphere of the camp setting.

Camping, of course, is as old as man and as extensive as the places man has chosen to live all over the world. It includes everything from youngsters sleeping in a pup tent in the back yard and hardy people "roughing it" in the wilderness to the concentration of thousands of boys and girls in the highly organized *agency* and *private* camps with their professional staffs and parent-provided "allergy" charts. In the United States, alone, there are more than 1,000 public camping grounds and 12,000 organized camps attended by more than 4 million campers who pay $8 million in fees each year.

When I was growing up, it was my good fortune to have been able to spend six summers in the camp of a voluntary youth-serving agency. This was in the days when the "Y" moved its camp location each year, and camping was done, not in permanently built cabins, but in tents without flooring and with kerosene lamps. We even courted ill health by washing our tin tableware in muddy streams. There was little in the way of an organized program, and often what was done looked too much like a gymnasium program transferred to the outdoors or the duplication of a community-center schedule. There was little chance to learn the pioneer skills and the outdoor-related arts and crafts—woodcraft, Indian lore, nature study, and the like. But one very real attraction in those years of camping stands out in my mind—the companionship and fellowship that I found there while living under somewhat primitive conditions. We joined around the campfire under the starry sky, singing until our voices were hoarse. We plunged into the creek, thirty kids strong, shouting, "The last one in is a monkey," as the gigantic splash sprayed everyone. We jumped from our canvas cots in the middle of the night with our bunk mates to dig a trench around the tent lest the rains come pouring in. All of these experiences resulted in a common bond of good fellowship which I still feel today.

And what was true in my experiences as a boy, I found to be true after I became a man. When our son was fourteen and our daughter, eleven, my wife and I decided to take an extended camping trip with them in tow. Our equipment was not fancy. We had inexpensive sleeping bags, an old tent, a kerosene stove, and a small refrigerator. Several months prior to the trip, we spent a few evenings a week together planning our outdoor excursion. With little previous experience outside of some organized camping, we set out on a camping journey which was to take us 9,000 miles and into state and national parks and forests all over the Western United States. We marveled at the sunsets, rode horses, studied the birds, climbed mountains, and huddled around campfires watching the crimson glow of the embers until we could no longer hold open our eyes. We collected driftwood and shells on the seashore, and threw snowballs at one another in the high mountain passes. We hiked and fished and swam and usually ate like hungry bears. We listened to a naturalist in a national forest tell the story of the changing geology and tried our own hands at being naturalists by attempting to identify wildlife specimens for one another. To be sure, in the cramped quarters of a small tent, when driven inside by the rain, our associations with each other were not always without turbulence. On one occasion, for example, we made the mistake of setting up our camp in the Cibala National Forest after nightfall, at an altitude of over 4,000 feet, and at a time when we were all very tired. The task of pitching our tent and preparing supper would not have been insurmountable if we had not all been so fatigued. Then, all within a period of minutes, the power of our lights was gone; my son, in an effort to help, unintentionally burned his mother with the hot extension of the camp stove; my daughter accidentally spilled wet cereal inside her brother's shoes, and I fell over a tent stake which someone (probably myself) had placed in the wrong location. What followed in the way of family *dis*organization and mutual disgust is not pleasant to recall. Such incidents, however, were the exceptions. All of us have since agreed that our family will never be any closer physically, educationally, socially, and spiritually than we were in those wonderful nine weeks of camping. The gains which came from it were by no means temporary. It was during such adventures that our children developed what will certainly be life-long interests in various phases of nature. We came to know our real selves and each other. It was like rediscovering an entirely new companionable spirit in a strange land and bringing it home to freshen up the living room.

Parents and children who enjoy the outdoors together seem also to enjoy the best in one another. We can teach our children how trees grow, where the waters that feed our lakes come from, and how the animals protect their young, but we cannot make them appreciate these things. This appreciation must come from an inner interest on the part of the child which is nourished by the companionable interests of his parents. It comes easiest in a *natural* setting!

The natural environment, too, teaches us how to be secure without being overprotected, how to grow without merely conforming, and how to look above and beyond—to spread our intellectual and spiritual wings, thus bringing us closer to God and His works.

Further Readings

COWELL, C. C. and FRANCE, W. L., *Philosophies and Principles of Physical Education*. Englewood Cliffs, N.J.: Prentice-Hall, Inc., 1963.

DAVIS, E. C., editor, *The Philosophic Process in Physical Education*. Englewood Cliffs, N.J.: Prentice-Hall, Inc., 1963.

ZEIGLER, E. F., "Naive Naturalism in Physical, Health, and Recreation Education," *Philosophical Foundations for Physical, Health, and Recreation Education*. Englewood Cliffs, N.J.: Prentice-Hall, Inc., 1964.

Questions for Discussion

1. What role in the curriculum does Brightbill assign to outdoor education?

2. What evidence does he present to support his opinion that there has been progress in outdoor education?
3. How can outdoor living influence our social relationships?
4. How would Oberteuffer and Williams evaluate the Brightbill view?
5. How are Rousseau's and Brightbill's positions similar? How do they differ?

RENÉ DESCARTES

Of the Real Distinction between the Mind and Body of Man*

In positing a dualistic world of mind and body, Descartes made his contribution to both philosophical idealism and philosophical realism. His idealism is reflected in his statement, *Cogito ergo sum* (I think; therefore, I am). The statement implies the supremacy of the mental over the physical world. It also implies that the mind (or self) can know itself more directly than it can perceive anything in the physical world. The analysis of experience must begin with the self.

Descartes' philosophical realism, however, may be his major contribution. By establishing the distinction between mind and body, which is partially elaborated in the next reading, he enabled many philosophers and scientists who followed him to concern themselves more completely with speculation about and study of the physical world. Descartes tried to explain physical phenomena in terms of mechanical and mathematical laws, and, in this way, he was the forerunner of much scientific thought.

Most prominent physical educators, such as Oberteuffer, Williams, Brownell, Scott, Metheny, and Abernathy, are concerned with the relationship of the mind and body, and their views often show the combination of philosophical realism and idealism evidenced in this selection from Descartes' *Meditations*.

* From René Descartes: *Meditations*, translated by Lawrence J. LaFleur, copyright © 1951, 1960, by The Liberal Arts Press, Inc. Reprinted by permission of the Liberal Arts Press Division of the Bobbs-Merrill Company, Inc., pp. 81-85.

[To begin this examination,] I first take notice here that there is a great difference between the mind and the body, in that the body, from its nature, is always divisible and the mind is completely indivisible. For in reality, when I consider the mind—that is, when I consider myself in so far as I am only a thinking being—I cannot distinguish any parts, but I (recognize [and) conceive (very clearly)] that I am a thing which is (absolutely) unitary and entire. And although the whole mind seems to be united with the whole body, nevertheless when a foot or an arm or some other part (of the body) is amputated, I recognize quite well that nothing has been lost to my mind on that account. Nor can the faculties of willing, perceiving, understanding, and so forth be [any more properly] called parts of the mind, for it is (one and) the same mind which [as a complete unit] wills, perceives, and understands [, and so forth]. But just the contrary is the case with corporeal or extended objects, for I cannot imagine any [, however small they might be,] which my mind does not very easily divide into [several] parts, and I consequently recognize these objects to be divisible. This (alone) would suffice to show me that the mind [or soul of man] is altogether different from the body, if I did not already know it sufficiently well for other reasons.

I also take notice that the mind does not receive impressions from all parts of the body directly, but only from the brain, or perhaps even from one of its smallest parts—the one, namely, where the senses in common have their seat. This makes the mind feel the same thing whenever it is in the same condition, even though the other parts of the body can be differently arranged, as is proved by an infinity of experiments which it is not necessary to describe here.

I furthermore notice that the nature of the body is such that no one of its parts can be moved by another part some little distance away without its being possible for it to be moved in the same way by any one of the intermediate parts, even when the more distant part does not act. For example, in the cord A B C D [which is thoroughly stretched], if we pull [and move] the last part D, the first part A will not be moved in any different manner from that in which it could also be moved if we pulled one of the middle parts B or C, while the last part D remained motionless. And in the same way, when I feel pain in my foot, physics teaches me that this sensation is communicated by means of nerves distributed through the foot.

When these nerves are pulled in the foot, being stretched like cords from there to the brain, they likewise pull at the same time the (internal) part of the brain [from which they come and] where they terminate, and there produce a certain movement which nature has arranged to make my mind feel pain as though that pain were in my foot. But because these nerves must pass through the leg, the thigh, the loins, the back, and the neck, in order to extend from the foot to the brain, it can happen that even when the nerve endings in the foot are not stimulated, but only some of the (intermediate) parts [located in the loins or the neck], (precisely) the same movements are nevertheless produced in the brain that could be produced there by a wound received in the foot, as a result of which it necessarily follows that the mind feels the same pain [in the foot as though the foot had been wounded]. And we must make the same judgment about all our other sense perceptions.

Finally, I notice that since each one of the movements that occurs in the part of the brain from which the mind receives impressions directly can only produce in the mind a single sensation, we cannot [desire or] imagine any better arrangement than that this movement should cause the mind to feel that sensation, of all the sensations the movement is [70] capable of causing, which is most effectively and frequently useful for the preservation of the human body when it is in full health. But experience shows us that all the sensations which nature has given us are such as I have just stated, and therefore there is nothing in their nature which does not show the power and the goodness of [the] God [who has produced them].

Thus, for example, when the nerves of the foot are stimulated violently and more than is usual, their movement, passing through the marrow of the backbone up to the (interior of the) brain, produces there an impression upon the mind which makes the mind feel something—namely, pain as though in the foot—by which the mind is [warned and] stimulated to do whatever it can to remove the cause, taking it to be very [dangerous and] harmful to the foot.

It is true that God could establish the nature of man in such a way that this same brain event would make the mind feel something quite different; for example, it might cause the movement to be felt as though it were in the brain, or in the foot, or else in some other (intermediate) location [between the foot and the brain], or finally it might produce any other feeling [that can exist]; but none of those who have contributed so well to the preservation of the body [as that which it does produce].

In the same way, when we need to drink, there results a certain dryness in the throat which affects its nerves and, by means of them, the interior of the brain. This brain event makes the mind feel the sensation of thirst, because under those conditions there is nothing more useful to us than to know that we need to drink for the conservation of our health. And similar reasoning applies to other sensations.

From this it is entirely manifest that, despite the supreme goodness of God, the nature of man, in so far as he is composed of mind and body, cannot escape being sometimes [faulty and] deceptive. For if there is some cause which produces, not in the foot, but in some other part of the nerve which is stretched from the foot to the brain, or even in the brain (itself), the same effect which ordinarily occurs when the foot is injured, we will feel pain as though it were in the foot, and we will naturally be deceived by the sensation. The reason for this is that the same brain event can cause only a single sensation in the mind; and this sensation being much more frequently produced by a cause which wounds the foot than by another acting in a different location, it is much more reasonable that it should always convey to the mind a pain in the foot rather than one in any other part [of the body]. And if it happens that sometimes the dryness of the throat does not come in the usual manner from the fact that drinking is necessary for the health of the body, but from some quite contrary cause, as in the case of those afflicted with dropsy, nevertheless it is much better that we should be deceived in that instance than if, on the contrary, we were always deceived when the body was in health; and similarly for the other sensations.

And certainly this consideration is very useful to me, not only so that I can recognize all the errors to which my nature is subject, but also so that I may avoid them or correct them more easily. For knowing that each of my senses conveys truth to me more often than falsehood concerning whatever is useful or harmful to the body, and being almost always able to use several of them to examine the same object, and being in addition able to use my memory to bind and join together present information with what is past, and being able to use my understanding, which has already discovered all the causes of my errors, I should no longer fear to encounter falsity in the objects which are most commonly represented to me by my senses.

And I should reject all the doubts of these last few days as exaggerated and ridiculous, particularly that very general uncertainty about sleep, which I could not distinguish from waking life. For now I find in them a very notable difference, in that our memory can never bind and join our dreams together [one with another and all] with the course of our lives, as it habitually joins together what happens to us when we are awake. And so, in effect, if someone suddenly appeared to me when I was awake and (afterward) disappeared in the same way, as [do images that I see] in my sleep, so that I could not determine where he came from or where he went, it would not be without reason that I would consider it a ghost or a phantom produced in my brain [and similar to those produced there when I sleep], rather than truly a man.

But when I perceive objects in such a way that I distinctly recognize both the place from which they come and the place where they are, as well as the time when they appear to me; and when, without any hiatus, I can relate my perception of them with all the rest of my life, I am entirely certain that I perceive them wakefully and not in sleep. And I should not in any way doubt the truth of these things if, having made use of all my senses, my memory, and my understanding, to examine them, nothing is reported to me by any of them which is inconsistent with what is reported by the others. For, from the fact that God is not a deceiver, it necessarily follows that in this matter I am not deceived.

But because the exigencies of action frequently [oblige us to make decisions and] do not [always] allow us the leisure to examine these things with sufficient care, we must admit that human life is very often subject to error in particular matters; and we must in the end recognize the infirmity [and weakness] of our nature.

Further Readings

BREED, F. S., *Education and the New Realism.* New York: The Macmillan Company, 1929.

BROUDY, H. S., *Building a Philosophy of Education,* 2d ed. Englewood Cliffs, N.J.: Prentice-Hall, Inc., 1961.

BRUBACHER, J. S., *Modern Philosophies of Education,* 3d ed. New York: McGraw-Hill, Inc., 1962.

Questions for Discussion

1. What "evidence" does Descartes offer to support his statement that the mind is unitary or indivisible?
2. What evidence does he offer for his statement that the body
   is divisable?
3. How are the mind and body connected?
4. Although our senses occasionally deceive us, why can we
   usually trust them?
5. In creating a philosophy of physical education, would you
   posit a separation of the mind and body, a mere relationship
   between the mind and body, or a unity of mind and body?
   For each position above, what would be the roles of physical
   fitness, intellectual study, and self-awareness?

JOHN LOCKE

Some Thoughts Concerning Education*

John Locke is often described as a philosophical realist. His
belief that man's mind at birth is a *tabula rasa,* that it is blank,
is a conscious reversal of Plato's view. Plato believes that knowledge is innate—that the pursuit of knowledge is merely its
recollection. Locke believes that we acquire knowledge through
experience or sensory perception. There is a real world, the
existence of which is independent of the mind. Conveniently
enough, the mind faithfully reflects the physical environment in
a photographic sense.

Locke's statement, "A sound mind *in* a sound body is a short
but full description of the happy state of the world," offers a
slightly different philosophical position to the potential physical
educator. Certainly Locke's notion of the *tabula rasa* suggests

* Reprinted with permission of the publisher from John Locke, *On Politics and
Education.* Roslyn, New York: Walter J. Black, Inc., 1947, pp. 210–225.

that the natural athlete could not exist. The development of the physical education curriculum would be quite differently conceived if it were assumed that natural ability did not exist.

Although modern psychologists describe perception as a means of interpreting rather than of simply recording the environment, Locke's views were a reflection of the interest in the physical world *per se* that characterized the Renaissance and the early development of science. His advice on child-rearing is free of Plato's extreme concern for the intellectual life on the one hand and yet avoids Rousseau's mystical attachment to nature on the other.

1. A sound mind in a sound body is a short but full descriptiion of a happy state in this world. He that has these two has little more to wish for; and he that wants either of them will be but little the better for anything else. Men's happiness or misery is most part of their own making. He whose mind directs not wisely will never take the right way; and he whose body is crazy and feeble will never be able to advance in it. I confess there are some men's constitutions of body and mind so vigorous and well framed by nature that they need not much assistance from others; but by the strength of their natural genius they are from their cradles carried towards what is excellent; and by the privilege of their happy constitutions are able to do wonders. But examples of this kind are but few; and I think I may say that of all the men we meet with, nine parts of ten are what they are, good or evil, useful or not, by their education. 'Tis that which makes the great difference in mankind. The little or almost insensible impressions on our tender infancies have very important and lasting consequences: and there 'tis, as in the fountains of some rivers, where a gentle application of the hand turns the flexible waters in channels, that make them take quite contrary courses; and by this direction given them at first in the source, they receive different tendencies, and arrive at last at very remote and distant places.

2. I imagine the minds of children as easily turned this or that way as water itself: and though this be the principal part, and our main care should be about the inside, yet the clay cottage is not to be neglected. I shall therefore begin with the case, and consider first the health of the body, as that which perhaps you may rather expect from that study I have been thought more peculiarly to have ap-

plied myself to; and that also which will be soonest dispatched, as lying, if I guess not amiss, in a very little compass.

3. How necessary health is to our business and happiness, and how requisite a strong constitution, able to endure hardships and fatigue, is to one that will make any figure in the world, is too obvious to need any proof.

4. The consideration I shall here have of health, shall be, not what a physician ought to do with a sick and crazy child, but what the parents, without the help of physic, should do for the preservation and improvement of a healthy, or at least not sickly constitution in their children. And this perhaps might be all dispatched in this one short rule, viz., that gentlemen should use their children as the honest farmers and substantial yeomen do theirs. But because the mothers possibly may think this a little too hard, and the fathers to short, I shall explain myself more particularly; only laying down this as a general and certain observation for the women to consider, viz., that most children's constitutions are either spoiled, or at least harmed, by cockering[1] and tenderness.

5. The first thing to be taken care of, is, that children be not too warmly clad or covered, winter or summer. The face when we are born is no less tender than any other part of the body. 'Tis use alone hardens it, and makes it more able to endure the cold. And therefore the Scythian philosopher gave a very significant answer to the Athenian, who wondered how he could go naked in frost and snow. "How," said the Scythian, "can you endure your face exposed to the sharp winter air?" My face is used to it," said the Athenian. "Think me all face," replied the Scythian. Our bodies will endure anything, that from the beginning they are accustomed to.

An eminent instance of this, though in the contrary excess of heat, being to our present purpose, to show what use can do, I shall set down in the author's words, as I met with it in a late ingenious voyage.

> The heats, says he, are more violent in Malta, than in any part of Europe: they exceed those of Rome itself, and are perfectly stifling; and so much the more, because there are seldom any cooling breezes here. This makes the common people as black as gypsies: but yet the peasants defy the sun; they work on in the hottest part of the day, without intermission, or sheltering themselves from his scorch-

---

[1] Coddling or pampering.

ing rays. This has convinced me, that nature can bring itself to many things, which seem impossible, provided we accustom ourselves from our infancy. The Malteses do so, who harden the bodies of their children, and reconcile them to the heat, by making them go stark naked, without shirt, drawers, or anything on their heads, from their cradles till they are ten years old.

Give me leave therefore to advise you not to fence too carefully against the cold of this our climate. There are those in England, who wear the same clothes winter and summer, and that without any inconvenience, or more sense of cold than others find. But if the mother will needs have an allowance for frost and snow, for fear of harm, and the father, for fear of censure, be sure let not his winter clothing be too warm: And amongst other things, remember, that when nature has so well covered his head with hair, and strengthened it with a year or two's age, that he can run about by day without a cap, it is best that by night a child should also lie without one; there being nothing that more exposes to headaches, colds, catarrhs, coughs, and several other diseases, than keeping the head warm.

6. I have said *he* here, because the principal aim of my discourse is, how a young gentleman should be brought up from his infancy, which in all things will not so perfectly suit the education of daughters; though where the difference of sex requires different treatment, 'twill be no hard matter to distinguish.

7. I will also advise his feet to be washed every day in cold water, and to have his shoes so thin that they might leak and let in water, whenever he comes near it. Here, I fear I shall have the mistress and maids too against me. One will think it too filthy, and the other perhaps too much pains, to make clean his stockings. But yet truth will have it that his health is much more worth than all such considerations, and ten times as much more. And he that considers how mischievous and mortal a thing taking wet in the feet is, to those who have been bred nicely, will wish he had, with the poor people's children, gone barefoot, who, by that means, come to be so reconciled by custom to wet in their feet that they take no more cold or harm by it than if they were wet in their hands. And what is it, I pray, that makes this great difference between the hands and the feet in others, but only custom? I doubt not, but if a man from his cradle had been always used to go barefoot, whilst his hands were constantly wrapped up in warm mittens, and covered

with *hand-shoes,* as the Dutch call gloves; I doubt not, I say, but such a custom would make taking wet in his hands as dangerous to him as now taking wet in their feet is to a great many others. The way to prevent this is to have his shoes made so as to leak water, and his feet washed constantly every day in cold water. It is recommendable for its cleanliness, but that which I aim at in it, is health; and therefore I limit it not precisely to any time of day. I have known it used every night with very good success, and that all the winter, without the omitting it so much as one night in extreme cold weaher; when thick ice covered the water, the child bathed his legs and feet in it, though he was of an age not big enough to rub and wipe them himself, and when he began this custom was puling and very tender. But the great end being to harden those parts by a frequent and familiar use of cold water, and thereby to prevent the mischiefs that usually attend accidental taking wet in the feet in those who are bred otherwise, I think it may be left to the prudence and convenience of the parents, to choose either night or morning. The time I deem indifferent, so the thing be effectually done. The health and hardiness procured by it would be a good purchase at a much dearer rate. To which if I add the preventing of corns, that to some men would be a very valuable consideration. But begin first in the spring with luke-warm, and so colder and colder every time, till in a few days you come to perfectly cold water, and then continue it so winter and summer. For it is to be observed in this, as in all other alterations from our ordinary way of living, the changes must be made by gentle and insensible degrees; and so we may bring our bodies to anything, without pain, and without danger.

How fond mothers are like to receive this doctrine is not hard to foresee. What can it be less than to murder their tender babes, to use them thus? What! put their feet in cold water in frost and snow, when all one can do is little enough to keep them warm? A little to remove their fears by examples, without which the plainest reason is seldom hearkened to: Seneca tells us of himself, *Epistles,* 53, and 83, that he used to bathe himself in cold spring water in the midst of winter. This, if he had not thought it not only tolerable but healthy too, he would scarce have done, in an exorbitant fortune that could well have borne the expense of a warm bath, and in an age (for he was then old) that would have excused greater indulgence. If we think his stoical principles led him to this severity, let it be so, that this sect reconciled cold water to his sufferance. What made it agreeable to his health? For that was not impaired by this hard usage. But what shall we say to Horace, who warmed not himself with the reputation of any sect, and least of all affected stoical austerities? Yet he assures us, he was wont in the winter season to bathe himself in cold water. But, perhaps, Italy will be thought much warmer than England, and the chillness of their waters not to come near ours in winter. If the rivers of Italy are warmer, those of Germany and Poland are much colder, than any in this our country, and yet in these, the Jews, both men and women, bathe all over, at all seasons of the year, without any prejudice to their health. And everyone is not apt to believe it is miracle, or any peculiar virtue of St. Winifred's Well, that makes the cold waters of that famous spring do no harm to the tender bodies that bathe in it. Everyone is now full of the miracles done by cold baths on decayed and weak constitutions, for the recovery of health and strength; and therefore they cannot be impracticable or intolerable for the improving and hardening the bodies of those who are in better circumstances.

If these examples of grown men be not thought yet to reach the case of children, but that they may be judged still to be too tender, and unable to bear such usage, let them examine what the Germans of old, and the Irish now, do to them, and they will find that infants too, as tender as they are thought, may, without any danger, endure bathing, not only of their feet, but of their whole bodies, in cold water. And there are, at this day, ladies in the Highlands of Scotland who use this discipline to their children in the midst of winter, and find that cold water does them no harm, even when there is ice in it.

8. I shall not need here to mention swimming, when he is of an age able to learn, and has anyone to teach him. 'Tis that saves many a man's life; and the Romans thought it so necessary, that they ranked it with letters; and it was the common phrase to mark one ill-educated, and good for nothing, that he had neither learnt to read nor to swim: *Nec literas didicit nec natare*. But, besides the gaining a skill which may serve him at need, the advantages to health by often bathing in cold water during the heat of summer are so many that I think nothing need be said to encourage it; pro-

vided this one caution be used, that he never go into the water when exercise has at all warmed him, or left any emotion in his blood or pulse.

9. Another thing that is of great advantage to everyone's health, but especially children's, is to be much in the open air and as little as may be by the fire, even in winter. By this he will accustom himself also to heat and cold, shine and rain; all which if a man's body will not endure, it will serve him to very little purpose in this world; and when he is grown up, it is too late to begin to use him to it. It must be got early, and by degrees. Thus the body may be brought to bear almost anything. If I should advise him to play in the wind and sun without a hat, I doubt whether it could be borne. There would a thousand objections be made against it, which at last would amount to no more, in truth, than being sunburnt. And if my young master be to be kept always in the shade, and never exposed to the sun and wind for fear of his complexion, it may be a good way to make him a *beau,* but not a man of business. And although greater regard be to be had to beauty in the daughters; yet I will take the liberty to say that the more they are in the air, without prejudice to their faces, the stronger and healthier they will be; and the nearer they come to the hardships of their brothers in their education, the greater advantage will they receive from it all the remaining part of their lives.

10. Playing in the open air has but this one danger in it that I know; and that is, that when he is hot with running up and down, he should sit or lie down on the cold or moist earth. This I grant; and drinking cold drink, when they are hot with labor or exercise, brings more people to the grave or to the brink of it, by fevers and other diseases, than anything I know. These mischiefs are easily enough prevented whilst he is little, being then seldom out of sight. And if, during his childhood, he be constantly and rigorously kept from sitting on the ground, or drinking any cold liquor whilst he is hot, the custom of forbearing, growing into habit, will help much to preserve him, when he is no longer under his maid's or tutor's eye. This is all I think can be done in the case: for, as years increase, liberty must come with them; and in a great many things he must be trusted to his own conduct, since there cannot always be a guard upon him, except what you have put into his own mind by good principles and established habits, which is the best and surest, and therefore most to be taken care of. For, from repeated cautions

and rules never so often inculcated, you are not to expect anything either in this, or any other case, farther than practice has established them into habits.

11. One thing the mention of the girls brings into my mind, which must not be forgot; and that is, that your son's clothes be never made strait, especially about the breast. Let nature have scope to fashion the body as she thinks best. She works herself a great deal better and exacter than we can direct her. And if women were themselves to frame the bodies of their children in their wombs, as they often endeavor to mend their shapes when they are out, we should as certainly have no perfect children born, as we have few well-shaped that are strait-laced, or much tampered with. This consideration should, methinks, keep busy people (I will not say ignorant nurses and bodice-makers) from meddling in a matter they understand not; and they should be afraid to put nature out of her way in fashioning the parts, when they know not how the least and meanest is made. And yet I have seen so many instances of children receiving great harm from strait-lacing, that I cannot but conclude there are other creatures as well as monkeys, who, little wiser than they, destroy their young ones by senseless fondness, and too much embracing.

12. Narrow breasts, short and stinking breath, ill lungs and crookedness, are natural and almost constant effects of hard bodice, and clothes that pinch. That way of making slender waists and fine shapes serves but the more effectually to spoil them. Nor can there indeed but be disproportion in the parts, when the nourishment prepared in the several offices of the body cannot be distributed as nature designs. And therefore what wonder is it, if, it being laid where it can, on some part not so braced, it often makes a shoulder or hip higher or bigger than its just proportion? 'Tis generally known that the women of China (imagining I know not what kind of beauty in it) by bracing and binding them hard from their infancy, have very little feet. I saw lately a pair of China shoes, which I was told were for a grown woman: they were so exceedingly disproportioned to the feet of one of the same age among us, that they would scarce have been big enough for one of our little girls. Besides this, 'tis observed that their women are also very little and short-lived; whereas the men are of the ordinary stature of other men, and live to a proportionable age. These defects in the female sex in that country are by some imputed to the unreasonable bind-

ing of their feet, whereby the free circulation of the blood is hindered, and the growth and health of the whole body suffers. And how often do we see that some small part of the foot being injured by a wrench or a blow, the whole leg or thigh thereby lose their strength and nourishment, and dwindle away? How much greater inconveniences may we expect, when the thorax, wherein is placed the heart and seat of life, is unnaturally compressed, and hindered from its due expansion?

13. As for his diet, it ought to be very plain and simple; and, if I might advise, flesh should be forborne as long as he is in coats, or at least till he is two or three years old. But whatever advantage this may be to his present and future health and strength, I fear it will hardly be consented to by parents, misled by the custom of eating too much flesh themselves, who will be apt to think their children, as they do themselves, in danger to be starved, if they have not flesh at least twice a day. This I am sure, children would breed their teeth with much less danger, be freer from diseases whilst they were little, and lay the foundations of an healthy and strong constitution much surer, if they were not crammed so much as they are by fond mothers and foolish servants, and were kept wholly from flesh the first three or four years of their lives.

But if my young master must needs have flesh, let it be but once a day, and of one sort at a meal. Plain beef, mutton, veal, etc., without other sauce than hunger, is best; and great care should be used that he eat bread plentifully, both alone and with everything else; and whatever he eats that is solid, make him chew it well. We English are often negligent herein; from whence follow indigestion and other great inconveniences.

14. For breakfast and supper, milk, milk-pottage, water-gruel, flummery, and twenty other things that we are wont to make in England, are very fit for children; only, in all these, let care be taken that they be plain, and without much mixture, and very sparingly seasoned with sugar, or rather none at all; especially all spice, and other things that may heat the blood, are carefully to be avoided. Be sparing also of salt in the seasoning of all his victuals, and use him not to high-seasoned meats. Our palates grow into a relish and liking of the seasoning and cookery which by custom they are set to; and an over-much use of salt, besides that it occasions thirst and over-much drinking, has other ill efforts upon the body. I should think that a good piece of well-made and well-baked brown bread,

sometimes with, and sometimes without butter or cheese, would be often the best breakfast for my young master. I am sure 'tis as wholesome and will make him as strong a man as greater delicacies; and if he be used to it, it will be as pleasant to him. If he at any time calls for victuals between meals, use him to nothing by dry bread. If he be hungry more than wanton, bread alone will down; and if he be not hungry, 'tis not fit he should eat. By this you will obtain two good effects: 1. That by custom he will come to be in love with bread; for, as I said, our palates and stomachs too are pleased with the things we are used to. 2. Another good you will gain hereby is, that you will not teach him to eat more nor oftener than nature requires. I do not think that all people's appetites are alike; some have naturally stronger and some weaker stomachs. But this I think, that many are made gourmands and gluttons by custom, that were not so by nature; and I see in some countries men as lusty and strong that eat but two meals a day, as others that have set their stomachs by a constant usage, like alarums, to call on them for four or five. The Romans usually fasted till supper, the only set meal even of those who eat more than once a day; and those who used breakfast, as some did, at eight, some at ten, others at twelve of the clock, and some later, neither eat flesh, nor had anything made ready for them. Augustus, when the greatest monarch on the earth, tells us he took a bit of dry bread in his chariot. And Seneca, in his 83rd Epistle, giving an account how he managed himself, even when he was old, and his age permitted indulgence, says that he used to eat a piece of dry bread for his dinner, without the formality of sitting to it, though his estate would as well have paid for a better meal (had health required it) as any subject's in England, were it doubled. The masters of the world were bred up with this spare diet; and the young gentlemen of Rome felt no want of strength or spirit because they eat but once a day. Or if it happened by chance that anyone could not fast so long as till supper, their only set meal, he took nothing but a bit of dry bread, or at most a few raisins, or some such slight thing with it, to stay his stomach. This part of temperance was found so necessary, both for health and business, that the custom of only one meal a day held out against that prevailing luxury which their Eastern conquests and spoils had brought in amongst them; and those who had given up their old frugal eating, and made feasts, yet began them not till the evening. And more than one set meal a day was thought so monstrous that it was a reproach as low down as Caesar's time, to make an entertainment or sit down to a full table, till towards sunset; and therefore, if it would not be thought too severe, I should judge it most convenient that my young master should have nothing but bread too for breakfast. You cannot imagine of what force custom is; and I impute a great part of our diseases in England to our eating too much flesh and too little bread.

15. As to his meals, I should think it best that as much as it can be conveniently avoided they should not be kept constantly to an hour: for when custom has fixed his eating to certain stated periods, his stomach will expect victuals at the usual hour, and grow peevish if he passes it; either fretting itself into a troublesome excess, or flagging into a downright want of appetite. Therefore I would have no time kept constantly to for his breakfast, dinner, and supper, but rather varied almost every day. And if betwixt these, which I call *meals,* he will eat, let him have, as often as he calls for it, good dry bread. If anyone think this too hard and sparing a diet for a child, let them know that a child will never starve nor dwindle for want of nourishment, who, besides flesh at dinner, and spoon-meat, or some such other thing, at supper, may have good bread and beer as often as he has a stomach. For thus, upon second thoughts, I should judge it best for children to be ordered. The morning is generally designed for study, to which a full stomach is but an ill preparation. Dry bread, though the best nourishment, has the least temptation; and nobody would have a child crammed at breakfast, who has any regard to his mind or body, and would not have him dull and unhealthy. Nor let anyone think this unsuitable to one of estate and condition. A gentleman in any age ought to be so bred as to be fitted to bear arms and be a soldier. But he that in this breeds his son so, as if he designed him to sleep over his life in the plenty and ease of a full fortune he intends to leave him, little considers the examples he has seen, or the age he lives in.

16. His drink should be only small beer; and that too he should never be suffered to have between meals, but after he had eat a piece of bread. The reasons why I say this are these.

17. 1. More fevers and surfeits are got by people's drinking when they are hot than by any one thing I know. Therefore, if by play he be hot and dry, bread will ill go down; and so if he cannot have drink but upon that condition, he will be forced to forbear; for,

if he be very hot, he should by no means drink; at least a good piece of bread first to be eaten, will gain time to warm the beer blood-hot, which then he may drink safely. If he be very dry, it will go down so warmed, and quench his thirst better; and if he will not drink it so warmed, abstaining will not hurt him. Besides, this will teach him to forbear, which is a habit of greatest use for health of body and mind too.

18. 2. Not being permitted to drink without eating, will prevent the custom of having the cup often at his nose; a dangerous beginning, and preparation to good-fellowship. Men often bring habitual hunger and thirst on themselves by custom. And if you please to try, you may, though he be weaned from it, bring him by use to such a necessity again of drinking in the night that he will not be able to sleep without it. It being the lullaby used by nurses to still crying children, I believe mothers generally find some difficulty to wean their children from drinking in the night, when they first take them home. Believe it, custom prevails as much by day as by night; and you may, if you please, bring anyone to be thirsty every hour.

I once lived in a house where, to appease a froward child, they gave him drink as often as he cried; so that he was constantly bibbing. And though he could not speak, yet he drank more in twenty-four hours than I did. Try it when you please, you may with small, as well as with strong beer, drink yourself into a drought. The great thing to be minded in education is, what *habits* you settle; and therefore in this, as all other things, do not begin to make anything customary, the practice whereof you would not have continue and increase. It is convenient for health and sobriety to drink no more than natural thirst requires; and he that eats not salt meats, nor drinks strong drink, will seldom thirst between meals, unless he has been accustomed to such unseasonable drinking.

19. Above all, take great care that he seldom, if ever, taste any wine or strong drink. There is nothing so ordinarily given children in England, and nothing so destructive to them. They ought never to drink any strong liquor but when they need it as a cordial, and the doctor prescribes it. And in this case it is that servants are most narrowly to be watched and most severely to be reprehended when they transgress. Those mean sort of people, placing a great part of their happiness in strong drink, are always forward to make court to my young master by offering him that which they love best them-

selves; and finding themselves made merry by it, they foolishly think 'twill do the child no harm. This you are carefully to have your eye upon, and restrain with all the skill and industry you can, there being nothing that lays a surer foundation of mischief, both to body and mind, than children's being used to string drink, especially to drink in private with the servants.

20. Fruit makes one of the most difficult chapters in the government of health, especially that of children. Our first parents ventured Paradise for it; and 'tis no wonder our children cannot stand the temptation, though it cost them their health. The regulation of this cannot come under any one general rule; for I am by no means of their mind, who would keep children almost wholly from fruit, as a thing totally unwholesome for them: by which strict way, they make them but the more ravenous after it, and to eat good or bad, ripe or unripe, all that they can get, whenever they come at it. Melons, peaches, most sorts of plums, and all sorts of grapes in England, I think children should be wholly kept from, as having a very tempting taste, in a very unwholesome juice; so that if it were possible, they should never so much as see them or know there were any such thing. But strawberries, cherries, gooseberries, or currants, when thorough ripe, I think may be very safely allowed them, and that with a pretty liberal hand, if they be eaten with these cautions: 1. Not after meals, as we usually do, when the stomach is already full of other food, but I think they should be eaten rather before or between meals, and children should have them for their breakfast. 2. Bread eaten with them. 3. Perfectly ripe. If they are thus eaten, I imagine them rather conducing than hurtful to our health. Summer-fruits, being suited to the hot season of the year they come in, refresh our stomachs, languishing and fainting under it; and therefore I should not be altogether so strict in this point as some are to their children; who being kept so very short, instead of a moderate quantity of well-chosen fruit, which being allowed them would content them, whenever they can get loose, or bribe a servant to supply them, satisfy their longing with any trash they can get, and eat to a surfeit.

Apples and pears too, which are thorough ripe, and have been gathered some time, I think may be safely eaten at any time, and in pretty large quantities, especially apples; which never did anybody hurt, that I have heard, after October.

Fruits also dried without sugar, I think very wholesome. But sweetmeats of all kinds are to be avoided; which whether they do more harm to the maker or eater, is not easy to tell. This I am sure, it is one of the most inconvenient[2] ways of expense that vanity has yet found out; and so I leave them to the ladies.

21. Of all that looks soft and effeminate, nothing is more to be indulged children than sleep. In this alone they are to be permitted to have their full satisfaction; nothing contributing more to the growth and health of children than sleep. All that is to be regulated in it, is, in what part of the twenty-four hours they should take it; which will easily be resolved, by only saying that it is of great use to accustom 'em to rise early in the morning. It is best so to do, for health; and he that from his childhood has by a settled custom made rising betimes easy and familiar to him, will not, when he is a man, waste the best and most useful part of his life in drowsiness and lying a-bed. If children therefore are to be called up early in the morning, it will follow of course that they must go to bed betimes; whereby they will be accustomed to avoid the unhealthy and unsafe hours of debauchery, which are those of the evenings; and they who keep good hours, seldom are guilty of any great disorders. I do not say this as if your son, when grown up, should never be in company past eight, nor ever chat over a glass of wine till midnight. You are now, by the accustoming of his tender years, to indispose him to those inconveniences as much as you can; and it will be no small advantage, that contrary practice having made sitting up uneasy to him it will make him often avoid and very seldom propose midnight revels. But if it should not reach so far, but fashion and company should prevail, and make him live as others do above twenty, 'tis worth the while to accustom him to early rising and early going to bed, between this and that, for the present improvement of his health and other advantages.

Though I have said a large allowance of sleep, even as much as they will take, should be made to children when they are little; yet I do not mean that it should always be continued to them in so large a proportion, and they suffered to indulge a drowsy laziness in their bed, as they grow up bigger. But whether they should begin to be restrained at seven or ten years old, or any other time, is impossible to be precisely determined. Their tempers, strength,

---

[2] Improper (obsolete).

and constitutions, must be considered. But some time between seven and fourteen, if they are too great lovers of their beds, I think it may be seasonable to begin to reduce them by degrees to about eight hours, which is generally rest enough for healthy grown people. If you have accustomed him, as you should do, to rise constantly very early in the morning, this fault of being too long in bed will easily be reformed, and most children will be forward enough to shorten that time themselves, by coveting to sit up with the company at night; though if they be not looked after, they will be apt to take it out in the morning, which should by no means be permitted. They should constantly be called up and made to rise at their early hour; but great care should be taken in waking them that it be not done hastily, nor with a loud or shrill voice, or any other sudden violent noise. This often affrights children and does them great harm; and sound sleep thus broke off, with sudden alarms, is apt enough to discompose anyone. When children are to be wakened out of their sleep, be sure to begin with a low call, and some gentle motion, and so draw them out of it by degrees, and give them none but kind words and usage, till they are come perfectly to themselves, and being quite dressed, you are sure they are thoroughly awake. The being forced from their sleep, how gently so ever you do it, is pain enough to them; and care should be taken not to add any other uneasiness to it, especially such that may terrify them.

22. Let his bed be hard, and rather quilts than feathers. Hard lodging strengthens the parts; whereas being buried every night in feathers melts and dissolves the body, is often the cause of weakness, and forerunner of an early grave. And, besides the stone, which has often its rise from this warm wrapping of the reins, several other indispositions, and that which is the root of them all, a tender weakly constitution, is very much owing to down-beds. Besides, he that is used to hard lodging at home will not miss his sleep (where he has most need of it) in his travels abroad, for want of his soft bed and his pillows laid in order. And therefore, I think it would not be amiss to make his bed after different fashions, sometimes lay his head higher, sometimes lower, that he may not feel every little change he must be sure to meet with, who is not designed to lie always in my young master's bed at home, and to have his maid lay all things in print, and tuck him in warm. The great cordial of nature is sleep. He that misses that will suffer by it; and he is

very unfortunate who can take his cordial only in his mother's fine gilt cup, and not in a wooden dish. He that can sleep soundly takes the cordial; and it matters not whether it be on a soft bed or the hard boards. 'Tis sleep only that is the thing necessary.

Further Readings

BROUDY, H. S., *Building a Philosophy of Education*, 2d ed. Englewood Cliffs, N.J.: Prentice-Hall, Inc., 1961.

BRUBACHER, J. S., *Modern Philosophies of Education*, 3d ed. New York: McGraw-Hill, Inc., 1962.

REINHARDT, K. F., *A Realistic Philosophy*. Milwaukee: The Bruce Publishing Company, 1944.

Questions for Discussion

1. To what may the modern parent object in Locke's advice on how to dress children in cold weather?
2. What is the relationship between health education and physical education as conceived by Locke?
3. How consistent is his advice on diet with modern advice on nutrition?
4. To what might Rousseau and Plato object in Locke's advice to parents?
5. How do the rearing practices he prescribes for boys differ from those he prescribes for girls?

C. H. McCLOY

New Wine in New Bottles*

The long career of the late Professor McCloy spanned the years of significant developments in American physical education. McCloy's scientific training in biology and his legacy of German and Scandanavian gymnastics seem to identify him with the school of philosophical realism. The realism of Descartes and Locke opened the way to scientific thought and research. In this article, McCloy emphasizes the scientific search for facts, as opposed to opinion alone, as a basis for practice.

The differences in the positions of McCloy and Oberteuffer are interesting to explore. Both men argue strongly the importance of physical education in the curriculum. Oberteuffer, on the one hand, argues for the intimate interweaving of physical education and the liberal arts for the purpose of developing the fully educated man. McCloy, on the other, stresses the specialized and unique role of the field—its physical and biological role, although he also encourages the closer relationship of physical education to other disciplines. McCloy's emphasis upon education of the physical and his emphasis upon empirical research suggest his classification as a philosophical realist.

While the principles, methods, and philosophy of general education have, in the past thirty years, been growing in definiteness and content, adding convolutions and general height of brow, the principles, practice, and philosophy of physical education have been an educational Island of Reil, buried at the bottom of the Fissure of Archaic Tradition, their functions and educational con-

---

* Reprinted and abridged with permission of the publisher from Charles H. McCloy, *Philosophical Bases for Physical Education.* Copyright 1940, F. S. Crofts & Co., Inc., New York: Appleton-Century-Crofts, Inc., 1940, pp. 21–27. Adapted from an article published under the same title in the *Journal of Physical Education,* vol. 25: 43–52 (October 1927).

nections more than dubious, and apparently all too well protected from the external stimuli of research and experiment to be forced to progress except through the slow process of accidental contact with the overwash from the teachings of the more vigorous of the philosophers of general education. The fact that they possessed their share of the educational cortex was apparently almost overlooked. We shall endeavor, within the limits of this chapter, to uphold the thesis that there are sufficient bases at this time for the construction of a system of physical education which could be an integral and necessary part of the educational process, and to present briefly some of the more important fundamental principles involved in the formulation of such a system.

The older systems of physical education in current use are, in most cases, educational anachronisms—hang-overs from the semimilitary European systems of physical education; developed in nations constantly exposed on all sides to threats of war; invented by and for militarists, and impregnated throughout with the angular never-to-be-used-in-life movements devised by the orthodox military mind. Some of these systems were then elaborated by anatomists with no knowledge of the psychology of learning or of modern educational principles, who thought only in terms of anatomical parts, not in terms of living, dynamic man. These older systems were further complicated by teachers of gymnastics, few of whom were scholars, who too often thought in terms of stunts and exercises, of inventing new movements to do, most of which were of no conceivable educational value.

Since the development of the modern educational philosophy, there have been three general types of reactions on the part of physical educators: (1) One group stood pat, defiantly closing their minds to the demonstrated facts of modern educational science, and making changes only when forced to do so by a waning attendance upon voluntary activities. (2) A second group, who became imbued with the new wine of educational philosophy, tried to put it in the old bottles, patching up the old skins, and "adapting" until the old medieval warrior—to change the figure—became outwardly dressed in modern clothing and talked the modern educational jargon, but still retained so much of the rigid soul and the inefficient educational outlook of the old, as largely to sterilize the result. (3) A third group could see no other hope than to throw away everything formal and turn the physical-educational period into anything which might carry the name of being "natural"—dancing, games, athletics, all too often poorly selected, and frequently the product of little constructive thought. Whatever faults might be found in the old systems, they at least showed thoroughness of preparation in the selection of the activities which they thought should be used, even though these might be based upon wrong premises.

It is not flattering to physical educators in general that such a condition still exists, for there are sufficient facts available from the modern general educational sciences to build far better than we have done. There are some notable exceptions to the general pessimistic situation outlined above, but, in the main, the statements there made can be successfully defended. After careful consideration of the facts involved, one is convinced that the educators in this field of education would do well to scrap much of the present philosophy of physical education and to start afresh with a study of modern educational philosophy and put the new wine into new bottles.

Good marksmanship is usually accompanied by careful aiming at the right target, and not by shooting with closed eyes and then ascertaining what was hit. It would seem that the formulation of an intelligent and scientific system of physical education should rest upon the same basis, that the objectives possible and desirable of attainment should first be carefully determined, with the limitations and the demands of the environment of present-day civilization kept in mind.

With the objectives outlined, it would further seem that the teaching material of physical education should then be surveyed, to decide upon a content which would accomplish the objectives in the most efficient manner. From the selection of this material, however, it would be necessary first to formulate the important criteria essential to a scientific selection of this teaching material.

After these steps, the next thing should be to formulate a technique of teaching which would make possible and probable the accomplishment of the desired results, educationally. It would seem even more important to learn how to secure results with the teaching material than simply to formulate the curriculum.

The term "physical education" tells its own story. It is, or should be, education through big-muscle, psychomotor experience. Far from being a handicap, this is its real strength. Big-muscle, psychomotor experience goes back to the taproots of human education and beyond. From the time when man as a species first saw the light of day, even until years after the founding of this country, he learned the great lessons of life in association with those racial activities connected with hunting and fighting and with playing at hunting and fighting, such as the activities of running, chasing, jumping, throwing, striking, pouncing upon, vaulting over or upon, climbing, defense from attack, kicking, swimming, and others of the same type which need not be enumerated here. He learned facts associated with the exercise of these activities in response to situations, and developed traits, characteristics, and adaptive habits of muscle and mind, those elements of that mosaic which we designate by such terms as character and personality. From those prehistoric times, man formed these traits by reacting to situations where action was demanded. The successful response was often necessary to survival; but the relative success, and the satisfaction or annoyance proceeding from it, determined the direction of future reaction, and eventually crystallized into the individual's character and personality. Physical education was the *sole* form of education in those days; it was a project-laboratory course in character and personality. Our psychomotor instinct patterns are still tuned in on this racial wave length and we "get" the educational character and personality response best by seeking it through the physical approach.

In the situation of twentieth-century city civilization, factual education, or what may be called intellectual content-education, has developed with amazing speed. We have developed many devices for giving a laboratory education in mental skills. From the laboratory work in handwriting, the carefully elaborated systems of problem-solving in arithmetic, and the drill and repetition of reading—a type of laboratory work—in the elementary school, through the science of the college and university, these devices for efficiently attaining the mental educational content-objectives have been carefully and systematically sought; but we have given much less thought and experimentation to evolving a physical-educational laboratory curriculum of such physical activities as will ensure the maximum development of character and personality as well as assist in the development of a strong body and organic health. The educator of today is too often content to rely upon occasional exhortations to "be manly," to "be a real American"—whatever

that may be—given in "that peculiarly unsuccessful method of instruction," the lecture. Others pass the responsibility on to the
home, which all too often has no system at all, leaving it in turn to
the mercies of an all-wise Providence, which, if not totally negligent
in the matter, is at least wholly inexpert in the devising of an educational method with which to attain results in character and personality. The school system of today devotes years of time and
thousands of dollars to reformulating an arithmetic curriculum
which will be a 5 per cent improvement on what was used in the
past, and then dismisses the task of developing curricula in character and personality to the ministrations of individuals with little
training in the educational fundamentals involved, and gives almost no thought to the result, or depends upon the incidental
overflow of such results from the general situation. It is not meant
to imply that character and personality are not developed or given
attention in general education, for they not infrequently are given a
large place. It is believed, however, by the writer that the physical-
education content, especially in the lower grades, gives a much
better opportunity to stimulate the development of this phase
of the individual than does the mental-educational content, and
that physical education should stress this much more than it does,
even now. It would seem that this situation in physical education
should be given more urgent attention. Physical education should
be educationally recognized for what it *can* be, not for what it
seems to be now. It should be organized as a laboratory course of
natural big-muscle activities, formulated and taught in such a
manner as will give abounding health and organic vigor and, by
demanding suitable expression, will ensure the exercise and development of such traits and characteristics essential to a well-
rounded character and personality as can be developed through
physical education. Such a curriculum, scientifically formulated and
taught, often under the emotional stress of keen competition, with
its deep and swift instinctive and emotional undercurrents, offers
possibilities of character education not often present in a classroom. I believe that the content of the physical-education curriculum should be limited to the attainment of the above ends.
Dramatics and pageantry and similar activities should be taken
care of by other departments. The department of physical education shall, of course, co-operate in such activities, but they should
not unduly encroach upon the small amount of time that physical

education is likely to secure in this decade, with the limited equipment usually available.

Further Readings

BRUBACHER, J. S., *Modern Philosophies of Education,* 3d ed. New York: McGraw-Hill, Inc., 1962.

MCCLOY, C. H., *Philosophical Bases for Physical Education.* New York: Appleton-Century-Crofts, 1940.

WILD, J., "Education and Human Society: A Realistic View," *Modern Philosophies and Education,* edited by N. B. Henry. Chicago: University of Chicago Press, 1955.

Questions for Discussion

1. What does McCloy mean by "new wine in new bottles"?
2. What are his objections to an emphasis upon the "natural" and to progressive education?
3. What contribution can research make to physical education?

JOHN DEWEY

Work, Play, and Leisure*

In his *Democracy and Education,* from which the following excerpts are taken, Dewey fully states his pragmatic philosophy. Of the philosophic schools so far delineated, Dewey seems much closer to the realism of Locke than to either the idealism of Plato or the naturalism of Rousseau. According to Dewey, neither sensory perception nor intellectual speculation can reveal the essential (or ideal) character of the physical universe. It cannot, therefore, ever be known. However, we can, and should, learn by experience. Dewey's model for problem solving

* Reprinted and abridged with permission of the publisher from *Democracy and Education* by John Dewey. Copyright 1916 by the Macmillan Company, renewed 1944 by John Dewey. New York: The Macmillan Company, 1930, pp. 237–242, 293–305.

is a prototype of scientific methodology and results occasionally in the labeling of his philosophy as experimentalism.

The this-worldly aspect of Dewey's philosophy seems in the tradition of philosophical realism. Rejecting Platonic idealism, he is able to assert the unity of the physical and mental, of work and play, and of school and society. Rather than discuss physical education, he talks about recreation, a word which avoids the connotation of drudgery associated with work and the empty stimulation associated with leisure.

Dewey was particularly sensitive to the social implications of his philosophy. Physical educators who emphasize the relationship between physical education and social adjustment, social integration, and social change often reflect the philosophical pragmatism of John Dewey.

Work and Play

What has been termed active occupation includes both play and work. In their intrinsic meaning, play and industry are by no means so antithetical to one another as is often assumed, any sharp contrast being due to undesirable social conditions. Both involve ends consciously entertained and the selection and adaptations of materials and processes designed to effect the desired ends. The difference between them is largely one of time-span, influencing the directness of the connection of means and ends. In play, the interest is more direct—a fact frequently indicated by saying that in play the activity is its own end, instead of its having an ulterior result. The statement is correct, but it is falsely taken, if supposed to mean that play activity is momentary, having no element of looking ahead and none of pursuit. Hunting, for example, is one of the commonest forms of adult play, but the existence of foresight and the direction of present activity by what one is watching for are obvious. When an activity is its own end in the sense that the action *of the moment* is complete in itself, it is purely physical; it has no meaning. . . . The person is either going through motions quite blindly, perhaps purely imitatively, or else is in a state of excitement which is exhausting to mind and nerves. Both results may be seen in some types of kindergarten games where the idea of play is so highly symbolic that only the adult is conscious of it. Unless the children succeed in reading in some quite different idea of their own, they move about either as if in a hypnotic daze, or they respond to a direct excitation.

The point of these remarks is that play has an end in the sense of a directing idea which gives point to the successive acts. Persons who play are not just doing something (pure physical movement); they are *trying* to do or effect something, an attitude that involves anticipatory forecasts which stimulate their present responses. The anticipated result, however, is rather a subsequent action than the production of a specific change in things. Consequently play is free, plastic. Where some definite external outcome is wanted, the end has to be held to with some persistence, which increases as the contemplated result is complex and requires a fairly long series of intermediate adaptations. When the intended act is another activity, it is not necessary to look far ahead and it is possible to alter it easily and frequently. If a child is making a toy boat, he must hold on to a single end and direct a considerable number of acts by that one idea. If he is just "playing boat" he may change the material that serves as a boat almost at will, and introduce new factors as fancy suggests. The imagination makes what it will of chairs, blocks, leaves, chips, if they serve the purpose of carrying activity forward.

From a very early age, however, there is no distinction of exclusive periods of play activity and work activity, but only one of emphasis. There are definite results which even young children desire, and try to bring to pass. Their eager interest in sharing the occupations of others, if nothing else, accomplishes this. Children want to "help"; they are anxious to engage in the pursuits of adults which effect external changes: setting the table, washing dishes, helping care for animals, etc. In their plays, they like to construct their own toys and appliances. With increasing maturity, activity which does not give back results of tangible and visible achievement loses its interest. Play then changes to fooling and if habitually indulged in is demoralizing. Observable results are necessary to enable persons to get a sense and a measure of their own powers. When make-believe is recognized to be make-believe, the device of making objects in fancy alone is too easy to stimulate intense action. One has only to observe the countenance of children really playing to note that their attitude is one of serious absorption; this attitude cannot be maintained when things cease to afford adequate stimulation.

When fairly remote results of a definite character are foreseen end enlist persistent effort for their accomplishment, play passes into work. Like play, it signifies purposeful activity and differs *not* in that activity is subordinated to an external result, but in the fact that a longer course of activity is occasioned by the idea of a result. The demand for continuous attention is greater, and more intelligence must be shown in selecting and shaping means. To extend this account would be to repeat what has been said under the caption of aim, interest, and thinking. It is pertinent, however, to inquire why the idea is so current that work involves subordination of an activity to an ulterior material result.

The extreme form of this subordination, namely drudgery, offers a clew. Activity carried on under conditions of external pressure or coercion is not carried on for any significance attached to the doing. The course of action is not intrinsically satisfying; it is a mere means for avoiding some penalty, or for gaining some reward at its conclusion. What is inherently repulsive is endured for the sake of averting something still more repulsive or of securing a gain hitched on by others. Under unfree economic conditions, this state of affairs is bound to exist. Work or industry offers little to engage the emotions and the imagination; it is a more or less mechanical series of strains. Only the hold which the completion of the work has upon a person will keep him going. But the end should be intrinsic to the action; it should be *its* end—a part of its own course. Then it affords a stimulus to effort very different from that arising from the thought of results which have nothing to do with the intervening action. As already mentioned, the absence of economic pressure in schools supplies an opportunity for reproducing industrial situations of mature life under conditions where the occupation can be carried on for its own sake. If in some cases, pecuniary recognition is *also* a result of an action, though not the chief motive for it, that fact may well increase the significance of the occupation.

Where something approaching drudgery or the need of fulfilling externally imposed tasks exists, the demand for play persists, but tends to be perverted. The ordinary course of action fails to give adequate stimulus to emotion and imagination. So in leisure time, there is an imperious demand for their stimulation by any kind of means; gambling, drink, etc., may be resorted to. Or, in less extreme cases, there is recourse to idle amusement; to anything which passes time with immediate agreeableness. Recreation, as the word indicates, is recuperation of energy. No demand of human nature is more urgent or less to be escaped. The idea that the need can be suppressed is absolutely fallacious, and the Puritanic tradition which disallows the need has entailed an enormous crop of evils. If education does not afford opportunity for wholesome recreation and train capacity for seeking and finding it, the suppressed instincts find all sorts of illicit outlets, sometimes overt, sometimes confined to indulgence of the imagination. Education has no more serious responsibility than making adequate provision for enjoyment of recreative leisure; not only for the sake of immediate health, but still more if possible for the sake of its lasting effect upon habits of mind. Art is again the answer to this demand. . . .

Aristotle was certainly permanently right when he said that "any occupation or art or study deserves to be called mechanical if it renders the body or soul or intellect of free persons unfit for the exercise and practice of excellence." The force of the statement is almost infinitely increased when we hold, as we nominally do at present, that all persons, instead of a comparatively few, are free. For when the mass of men and all women were regarded as unfree by the very nature of their bodies and minds, there was neither intellectual confusion nor moral hypocrisy in giving them only the training which fitted them for mechanical skill, irrespective of its ulterior effect upon their capacity to share in a worthy life. He was permanently right also when he went on to say that "all mercenary employments as well as those which degrade the condition of the body are mechanical, since they deprive the intellect of leisure and dignity,"—permanently right, that is, if gainful pursuits as matter of fact deprive the intellect of the conditions of its exercise and so of its dignity. If his statements are false, it is because they identify a phase of social custom with a natural necessity. But a different view of the relations of mind and matter, mind and body, intelligence and social service, is better than Aristotle's conception only if it helps render the old idea obsolete in fact—in the actual conduct of life and education.

Aristotle was permanently right in assuming the inferiority and subordination of mere skill in performance and mere accumulation of external products to understanding, sympathy of appreciation, and the free play of ideas. If there was an error, it lay in assuming the necessary separation of the two: in supposing that there is a natural divorce between efficiency in producing commodities and rendering service, and self-directive thought; between significant knowledge and practical achievement. We hardly better matters if we just correct his theoretical misapprehension, and tolerate the social state of affairs which generated and sanctioned his conception. We lose rather than gain in change from serfdom to free citizenship if the most prized result of the change is simply an increase in the mechanical efficiency of the human tools of production. So we lose rather than gain in coming to think of intelligence as an organ of control of nature through action, if we are content that an unintelligent, unfree state persists in those who engage directly in turning nature to use, and leave the intelligence which controls to be the exclusive possession of remote scientists and captains of industry. We are in a position honestly to criticize the division of life into separate functions and of society into separate classes only so far as we are free from responsibility for perpetuating the educational practices which train the many for pursuits involving mere skill in production, and the few for a knowledge that is an ornament and a cultural embellishment. In short, ability to transcend the Greek philosophy of life and education is not secured by a mere shifting about of the theoretical symbols meaning free, rational, and worthy. It is not secured by a change of sentiment regarding the dignity of labor, and the superiority of a life of service to that of an aloof self-sufficing independence. Important as these theoretical and emotional changes are, their importance consists in their being turned to account in the development of a truly democratic society, a society in which all share in useful service and all enjoy a worthy leisure. It is not a mere change in the concepts of culture—or a liberal mind—and social service which requires an educational reorganization; but the educational transformation is needed to give full and explicit effect to the changes implied in social life. The increased political and economic emancipation of the "masses" has shown itself in education; it has effected the development of a common school system of education, public and free. It has destroyed the idea that learning is properly a monopoly of the few who are predestined by nature to govern social affairs. But the revolution is still incomplete. The idea still prevails that a truly cultural or liberal education cannot have anything in common, directly at least, with industrial affairs, and that the education which is fit for the masses must be a useful or practical education in a sense which opposes useful and practical to nurture of appreciation and liberation of thought.

As a consequence, our actual system is an inconsistent mixture. Certain studies and methods are retained on the supposition that they have the sanction of peculiar liberality, the chief content of the term liberal being uselessness for practical ends. This aspect is chiefly visible in what is termed the higher education—that of the college and of preparation for it. But it has filtered through into elementary education and largely controls its processes and aims. But, on the other hand, certain concessions have been made to the masses who must engage in getting a livelihood and to the increased rôle of economic activities in modern life. These concessions are exhibited in special schools and courses for the professions, for engineering, for manual training and commerce, in vocational and prevocational courses; and in the spirit in which certain elementary subjects, like the three R's, are taught. The result is a system in which both "cultural" and "utilitarian" subjects exist in an inorganic composite where the former are not by dominant purpose socially serviceable and the latter not liberative of imagination or thinking power.

In the inherited situation, there is a curious intermingling, in even the same study, of concession to usefulness and a survival of traits once exclusively attributed to preparation for leisure. The "utility" element is found in the motives assigned for the study, the "liberal" element in methods of teaching. The outcome of the mixture is perhaps less satisfactory than if either principle were adhered to in its purity. The motive popularly assigned for making the studies of the first four or five years consist almost entirely of reading, spelling, writing, and arithmetic, is, for example, that ability to read, write, and figure accurately is indispensable to getting ahead. These studies are treated as mere instruments for entering upon a gainful employment or of later progress in the pursuit of learning, according as pupils do not or do remain in school. This attitude is reflected in the emphasis put upon drill and practice for the sake of gaining automatic skill. If we turn to Greek schooling, we find that from the earliest years the acquisition of skill was subordinated as much as possible to acquisition of literary content possessed of æsthetic and moral significance. Not getting a tool for subsequent use but present subject matter was the emphasized thing. Nevertheless the isolation of these studies from practical application, their reduction to purely symbolic devices, represents a survival of the idea of a liberal training divorced from utility. A thorough adoption of the idea of utility would have led to instruction which tied up the studies to situations in which they were directly needed and where they were rendered immediately and not remotely helpful. It would be hard to find a subject in the curriculum within which there are not found evil results of a compromise between the two opposed ideals. Natural science is recommended on the ground of its practical utility, but is taught as a special accomplishment in removal from application. On the other hand, music and literature are theoretically justified on the ground of their culture value and are then taught with chief emphasis upon forming technical modes of skill.

If we had less compromise and resulting confusion, if we analyzed more carefully the respective meanings of culture and utility, we might find it easier to construct a course of study which should be useful and liberal at the same time. Only superstition makes us believe that the two are necessarily hostile so that a subject is illiberal because it is useful and cultural because it is useless. It will generally be found that instruction which, in aiming at utilitarian results, sacrifices the development of imagination, the refining of taste and the deepening of intellectual insight—surely cultural values—also in the same degree renders what is learned limited in its use. Not that it makes it wholly unavailable but that its applicability is restricted to routine activities carried on under the supervision of others. Narrow modes of skill cannot be made useful beyond themselves; any mode of skill which is achieved with deepening of knowledge and perfecting of judgment is readily put to use in new situations and is under personal control. It was not the bare fact of social and economic utility which made certain activities seem servile to the Greeks but the fact that the activities directly connected with getting a livelihood were not, in their days, the expression of a trained intelligence nor carried on because of a personal appreciation of their meaning. So far as farming and the trades were rule-of-thumb occupations and so far as they were engaged in for results external to the minds of agricultural laborers and mechanics, they were illiberal—but only so far. The intellectual and social context has now changed. The elements in industry due to mere custom and routine have become subordinate in most economic callings to elements derived from scientific inquiry. The most important occupations of to-day represent and depend upon applied mathematics, physics, and chemistry. The area of the human world influenced by economic production and influencing consumption has been so indefinitely widened that geographical and political considerations of an almost infinitely wide scope enter in. It was natural for Plato to deprecate the learning of geometry and arithmetic for practical ends, because as matter of fact the practical uses to which they were put were few, lacking in content and mostly mercenary in quality. But as their social uses have increased and enlarged, their liberalizing or "intellectual" value and their practical value approach the same limit.

Doubtless the factor which chiefly prevents our full recognition and employment of this identification is the conditions under which so much work is still carried on. The invention of machines has extended the amount of leisure which is possible even while one is at work. It is a commonplace that the mastery of skill in the form of established habits frees the mind for a higher order of thinking. Something of the same kind is true of the introduction of mechanically automatic operations in industry. They may release the mind for thought upon other topics. But when we confine the education of those who work with their hands to a few years of schooling devoted for the most part to acquiring the use of rudimentary symbols at the expense of training in science, literature, and history, we fail to prepare the minds of workers to take advantage of this opportunity. More fundamental is the fact that the great majority of workers have no insight into the social aims of their pursuits and no direct personal interest in them. The results actually achieved are not the ends of *their* actions, but only of their employers. They do what they do, not freely and intelligently, but for the sake of the wage earned. It is this fact which makes the action illiberal, and which will make any education designed simply to give skill in such undertakings illiberal and immoral. The activity is not free because not freely participated in.

Nevertheless, there is already an opportunity for an education which, keeping in mind the larger features of work, will reconcile liberal nurture with training in social serviceableness, with ability to share efficiently and happily in occupations which are productive. And such an education will of itself tend to do away with the evils of the existing economic situation. In the degree in which men have an active concern in the ends that control their activity, their activity becomes free or voluntary and loses its externally enforced and servile quality, even though the physical aspect of behavior remain the same. In what is termed politics, democratic social organization makes provision for this direct participation in control; in the economic region, control remains external and autocratic. Hence the split between inner mental action and outer physical action of which the traditional distinction between the liberal and the utilitarian, is the reflex. An education which should unify the disposition of the members of society would do much to unify society itself.

Further Readings

BODE, B. H., *How We Learn*. Boston: D. C. Heath and Company, 1940.

DEWEY, J., *Education Today*, edited by J. Rather. New York: G. P. Putnam's and Sons, 1929.

KILPATRICK, W. H., *Philosophy of Education*. New York: The Macmillan Company, 1951.

Questions for Discussion

1. What distinction does Dewey make between work and play?
2. Why does Dewey object to the subordination of work to remote goals?
3. If play is considered an end in itself, what would be the relationship of play to physical fitness, social development, or intellectual experience?
4. In Dewey's view, what is the role of liberal studies?
5. What objections would Dewey have to making the training of "star" athletes the major purpose of physical education?
6. In what ways, according to Dewey, have we failed to transcend Greek philosophy in our thinking about work and education?
7. Can play be a means to other learning as well as an end in itself? If so, explain.

JESSE FEIRING WILLIAMS

Education Through the Physical*

Williams' objection to the "cult of muscle" and the deification of the mental helps to distinguish his position from that of the naturalist and the extreme idealist respectively. His belief that physical education is a way of living reflects the social pragmatism of John Dewey. It is also an emphatic assertion of the unity between mind and body, and, as such, the philosophic position of many leading physical educators.

In this article Williams laments current abuse of our leisure time. When we do "play," it is too often for profit and health rather than for enjoyment. Here, Williams applies to physical education many of Dewey's general statements on work, play, and leisure. In his concern that physical education make its contribution to later as well as the present life of the student by encouraging physical skills and social development through sports, Williams expresses the sentiments of several educational critics who point to the abuses of the big stadium and national collegiate competition.

Although this article was written in 1930, its central thesis remains as valid as it was when first conceived.

None can examine earnestly the implications of physical education without facing two questions. These are: Is physical education an education *of* the physical? Is physical education an education *through* the physical? It is clear that an education of the physical would have some concomitant learnings in addition and also that an education through the physical would produce some distinct physical gains. Nevertheless, there are in these two questions

* Reprinted with permission of the author and the publisher from *Journal of Higher Education*, 1930. Columbus: The Ohio State University Press, vol. 1, no. 5, pp. 279–282.

two points of view, two emphases, two ways of looking at physical education.

Education of the physical is a familiar view. Its supporters are those who regard strong muscles and firm ligaments as the main outcomes. Curiously enough this restricted view is not heeded alone by physical educators but also by those who talk about educational values, objectives, and procedures. In effect, such view is a physical culture and has the same validity that all narrow disciplines have had in the world. The cult of muscle is merely another view of the narrowness that fostered the cult of mind or the cult of spirit.

Modern physical education with its emphasis upon education through the physical is based upon the biologic unity of mind and body. This view sees life as a totality. Correct in their appraisement that the cult of muscle is ludicrous, those who worship at the altar of mental developments too frequently neglect the implications of unity. "Socrates with a headache" is always preferable to a brainless Hercules, but the modern spirit in physical education seeks the education of man through physical activities as one aspect of the social effort for human enlightenment. It is the plain truth of the matter that no individual, no community, no nation can depend upon one aspect of life for the whole of living. Deification of only the physical, or the mental, or the spiritual leads to disaster.

This recasting of the scene for physical education is no superficial move but a tendency toward deeper growth. It holds that we need to aim higher than health, than victorious teams, than strong muscles, than profuse perspiration. It sees physical education primarily as a way of living, and seeks to conduct its activities so as to set a standard that will surpass the average and the commonplace. There is in such a view something of the loftier virtues of courage, endurance, and strength, the natural attributes of play, imagination, joyousness, and pride, and through it all, the spirit of splendid living—honest, worthy, and competent—so much desired by each individual.

Physical education, however, stands not alone in the dilemma of special disciplines. Education has been, and still is, confronted with the problem. The old scholastic doctrine that separated mind from body, that held the body as essentially evil has emphasized the contrast today between an education for life and an education for death. A child born in sin, destined to do evil unless transformed by grace, made the chief business of education a salvation of man from the destiny of his own nature. In this view education is a reclamation project, a corrective endeavor. There are few today to espouse such a view openly, but it underlies the practice of many. On the contrary, educational theory today is dedicated to the proposal of education for life here and now. The child is viewed as a being of varying possibilities. The psychology of behavorism has more forcibly established the fact of plasticity and unformed qualities of the young; the function of education as developed stands approved by science and common sense.

Education for life, or modern education, and education through the physical, or modern physical education, have mutual supports and confidences. On the one hand, education for life can hardly be conceived without generous allowance for this kind of physical education, and physical education pointed to its own culture, its own minor objectives, becomes not an education for life at all. The identity, then, of education for life (modern education) and education through the physical (modern physical education) requires understanding by educators of the aim, scope, and objectives of modern physical education and by physical educators of the objects and concerns of modern education.

From the view of living as it goes on among people, and not as the view of a specialist or expert in physical education, it would appear that education for life requires the development of those skills, attitudes, knowledges, and habits that make for fine living. The part to be played by physical education in the lives of boys and girls, men and women, in this enterprise of fine living must be studied increasingly. Perhaps its greatest value will be in the interests it arouses, in the values it emphasizes, in the attitudes it forms. Whereas at one time, its chief values were supposed to be posture, health, and strength, these may become obscure in the prominence given to motives, purposes, and incentives for life.

There is a drama of civilization enacted in every community. The play is still to be written and yet its dramatis personae are all trained for their parts. The drama, if written, would show the lives of people who lack the ability to use leisure wholesomely, either because of a great ignorance of serviceable skills or because of intense occupations with the industrial or business world—losing the ability to live wholesomely, and neglecting the very objects for which it is worth while to acquire riches in a feverish preoccupation with the means by which riches are acquired.

We are unable to use for human happiness the magical liberation from the bond of labor undreamed of by our ancestors and striven for since the first log was used as material for a wheel and beasts domesticated for man's work. We fail again and again to use this glorious thing, leisure, because of habits, preoccupation with small things, lack of education for leisure, and the mood of strenuosity that sits so heavily upon us.

Doubtless we will make little gain in the use of leisure until we overcome the notion that play must be profitable. In physical education we have been ready to recommend golf or tennis for their health values when they were of value in themselves—precisely as sitting in the sun, or fishing, or walking along the river bank. All of us have been indoctrinated by the school teacher not to let the golden hours slip by when it would have been the part of wisdom to understand that they are only golden when we let them slip.

Education through the physical will be judged, therefore, even as education for life will be judged—by the contribution it makes to fine living. The ability to punt 60 yards is on a par with some of the esoteric emphases in general education. It should therefore be declared that physical education seeks to further the purposes of modern education when it stands for the finest kind of living.

This declaration of allegiance of physical education to the legitimate purposes of general education demands rather than forbids a statement that will interpret its understanding of that relationship. Such statement will need amplification or modification from time to time as new relationships appear.

Physical education in the university, first, is responsible for the organized physical activities of students. This responsibility is primarily an educational one in which the plans and purposes of physical education are to be reviewed in the light of legitimate instructional purpose. It is obvious, therefore, that varsity sports must come under the complete direction of the university.

The university is, also, responsible for the interests, activities, and development of its students. No university today can cut itself off from the large, vital, social aspects of the life of the students by insisting that the purpose of the college is to train the mind. It

is obvious, therefore, that a rational program of physical education
is required in every university to the end that men and women
may acquire not only mental, but also physical skills with which
to live an abundant life.

Physical education is responsible for the teaching of skill and
the development of interests in types of activity that will serve the
students in the college and the graduates after collegiate days are
over. Thus a physical education characterized by neglect of minor
sports through undue attention to major ones, or with a chief reliance upon gymnastic drills should be recognized for its limitations. It is precisely this principle of thorough going function
in young people's lives that tests the quality of physical education.

The university is responsible for providing adequate space,
equipment, and time facilities so that the capacities of young
people for leisure-time skills may be developed. A state university
making plans for a stadium has at present only four tennis courts
for all the students. In the past, in many universities, play facilities for all the students have been provided largely out of surpluses
of varsity athletics. The partnership of modern education and
education through the physical requires recognition of the need
for space, equipment, and facilities. Education for life means
vigorous life.

Physical education is responsible as well for leadership in combating all purely professional and educationally poor activities in
the field. Therefore athletics, games, sports, dancing, gymnastics,
et cetera, must be viewed and organized with reference to significant functions in life. The whole program must be examined to
determine major emphases and to eliminate undesirable practices.

Again, the university is responsible for the establishment of
standards of fine living. Those engaged in teaching sports and
games especially should be selected with reference to their ability
to influence the daily preferences of young men and young women.
A university conscious of the need to promote the physical education of all its students in types of activity that may serve in living
more completely will not appoint as director one who is interested
only in the teams or gymnastic uniformity.

Jointly with the university, physical education is responsible for
leadership in setting up among boys and girls those standards of
behavior that represent the best social tradition of the day. The
responsibility rests heavily on this special department because its

activities present so many situations where the individual is impelled to act selfishly or anti-socially. The leadership is vital to favorable growth in desirable social and moral values, in wholesome attitudes toward play and generous reactions to opponents. While the reciprocal relationships have been indicated in the above items, the joint responsibility of the university and physical education is clear at this point.

Further Readings

BRUBACHER, J. S., *Modern Philosophies of Education,* 3d ed. New York: McGraw-Hill, Inc., 1962.

WILLIAMS, J. F., *The Principles of Physical Education,* 8th ed. Philadelphia: W. B. Saunders Company, 1964.

WILLIAMS, J. F. and W. L. HUGHES, *Athletics in Education.* Philadelphia: W. B. Saunders Company, 1937.

Questions for Discussion

1. To what social and moral values does Williams believe physical education can contribute?
2. What distinction does he make between education *through* the physical and education *of* the physical?
3. What distinction does he make between his philosophic position and that of old scholastic doctrine?
4. Describe and evaluate the place which Williams gives to physical education in the school and college curriculum.

HERBERT SPENCER

Aesthetic Sentiments*

The influence of Darwinian evolution on the thought of Spencer was profound. In fact, Spencer is called the social evolutionist, because he applied a theory of evolution based primarily on

* Reprinted and abridged from *Synthetic Philosophy.* New York: D. Appleton and Company, 1885, vol. 2, chapter IX, pp. 627–648.

biology to society and human behavior. Our basic concern as human beings is the maintenance of life—of ourselves and our offspring. Next, we must devote ourselves to building the social and political order. After we have completed these tasks, we can cultivate the "aesthetic sentiments."

In the succeeding article Spencer deals with two topics: (1) the origin of the "play-impulse" and (2) the source and character of aesthetic pleasure. Play begins for both animals and men when they have time left over from the struggle for survival. Play largely imitates that struggle and is motivated by the same competitive need to beat the adversary. Play, then, has its origin in our "lower but more essential powers." Aesthetic activities are a higher but less essential aspect of our existence. Sensations of taste are not aesthetic because they are strongly connected with hunger and survival. However, the perception of color and pleasant scents, when divorced from the useful, can be primitive aesthetic sensations.

Many years ago I met with a quotation from a German author to the effect that the æsthetic sentiments originate from the play-impulse. I do not remember the name of the author; and if any reasons were given for this statement, or any inferences drawn from it, I cannot recall them. But the statement itself has remained with me, as being one which, if not literally true, is yet the adumbration of a truth.

The activities we call play are united with the æsthetic activities, by the trait that neither subserve, in any direct way, the processes conducive to life. The bodily powers, the intellectual faculties, the instincts, appetites, passions and even those highest feelings we have lately dealt with, have maintenance of the organic equilibrium of the individual, or else maintenance of the species, as their immediate or remote ends. Arrest one of the viscera, and the vital actions quickly cease; prevent a limb from moving, and the ability to meet surrounding circumstances is seriously interfered with; destroy a sense-organ, paralyze a perceptive power, derange the reason, and there comes more or less failure in that adjustment of conduct to conditions by which life is preserved; and if those egoistic sentiments which prompt care of property and liberty, or those ego-altruistic and altruistic ones which regulate conduct towards others, do not act, impediments to complete life are caused by absence of means or by the alienation of fellow-men. But while the primary actions of the faculties, bodily and mental, with their acompanying gratifications, are thus obviously related to proximate ends that imply ulterior benefits, those actions of them which constitute play, and those which yield the æsthetic gratifications, do not refer to ulterior benefits—the proximate ends are the only ends. It is, indeed, true that activities of these orders may bring the ulterior benefits of increased power in the faculties exercised; and that thus the life as a whole may be afterwards furthered. But this effect is one that pairs off with the like effect produced by the primary actions of the faculties—leaving the difference just where it was. From the primary action of a faculty there results the immediate normal gratification, *plus* the maintained or increased ability due to exercise, *plus* the objective end achieved or requirement fulfilled. But from this secondary action of a faculty exhibited in play or in an aesthetic pursuit, there results only the immediate gratification *plus* the maintained or increased ability.

Before dealing with the æsthetic sentiments as thus distinguished and thus classed, we must go a little deeper,—asking whence arises the play-impulse, and how there finally comes that supplementary activity of the higher faculties which the Fine Arts imply.

Inferior kinds of animals have in common the trait, that all their forces are expended in fulfilling functions essential to the maintenance of life. They are unceasingly occupied in searching for food, in escaping from enemies, in forming places of shelter, and in making preparations for progeny. But as we ascend to animals of high types, having faculties more efficient and more numerous, we begin to find that time and strength are not wholly absorbed in providing for immediate needs. Better nutrition, gained by superiority, occasionally yields a surplus of vigour. The appetites being satisfied, there is no craving which directs the overflowing energies to the pursuit of more prey, or to the satisfaction of some pressing want. The greater variety of faculty commonly joined with this greater efficiency of faculty, has a kindred result. When there have been developed many powers adjusted to many requirements, they cannot all act at once: now the circumstances call these into exercise and now those; and some of them occasionally remain unexercised for considerable periods. Thus it happens that in the more-evolved creatures, there often recurs an energy somewhat in excess of immediate needs, and there comes also such rest, now of this faculty and now of that, as permits the bringing of it up to a state of high efficiency by the repair which follows waste. . . .

Every one of the mental powers, then, being subject to this law, that its organ when dormant for an interval longer than ordinary becomes unusually ready to act—unusually ready to have its correlative feelings aroused, giving an unusual readiness to enter upon all the correlative activities; it happens that a simulation of those activities is easily fallen into, when circumstances offer it in place of the real activities. Hence play of all kinds—hence this tendency to superfluous and useless exercise of faculties that have been quiescent. Hence, too, the fact that these uncalled-for exertions are most displayed by those faculties which take the most prominent parts in the creature's life. Observe how this holds from the simplest faculties upwards.

A rat, with incisors that grow continuously in adaptation to the incessant wear they undergo, and with a correlative desire to use these incisors, will, if caged, occupy itself in gnawing anything it can get hold of. A cat, with claws and appended muscles adjusted to daily action in catching prey, but now leading a life that is but in a small degree predatory, has a craving to exercise these parts; and may be seen to satisfy the craving by stretching out her legs, protruding her claws, and pulling at some such surface as the covering of a chair or the bark of a tree. And still more interestingly in the giraffe, which when free is all day long using its tongue to pull down branches of trees, there arises, when in confinement, so great a need for some kindred exercise that it perpetually grasps with its tongue such parts of the top of its house as can be laid hold of—so wearing out the upper angles of doors, &c. This useless activity of unused organs, which in these cases hardly rises to what we call play, passes into play ordinarily so called where there is a more manifest union of feeling with the action. Play is equally an artificial exercise of powers which, in default of their natural exercise, become so ready to discharge that they relieve themselves by simulated actions in place of real actions. For dogs and other predatory creatures show us unmistakably that their play consists of mimic chase and mimic fighting—they pursue one another, they try to overthrow one another, they bite one another as much as they dare. And so with the kitten running after a cotton-ball, making it roll and again catching it, crouching as though in ambush and then leaping on it, we see that the whole sport is a dramatizing of the pursuit of prey—an ideal satisfaction for the destructive instincts in the absence of real satisfaction for them. It is the same with human beings. The plays of children—nursing dolls, giving tea-parties, and so on, are dramatizings of adult activities. The sports of boys, chasing one another, wrestling, making prisoners, obviously gratify in a partial way the predatory instincts. And if we consider even their games of skill, as well as the games of skill practised by adults, we find that, significantly enough, the essential element running through them has the same origin. For no matter what the game, the satisfaction is in achieving victory—in getting the better of an antagonist. This love of conquest, so dominant in all creatures because it is the correlative of success in the struggle for existence, gets gratification from a victory at chess in the absence of ruder victories. Nay, we may even see that playful conversation is characterized by the same element. In banter, in rapartee, in "chaff," the almost-constant trait is some display of relative superiority—the detection of a weakness, a mistake, an absurdity, on the part of another. Through a wit-combat there runs the effort to obtain mental supremacy. That is to say, this activity of the intellectual faculties in which they are not used for purposes of guidance in the business of life, is carried on partly for the sake of the pleasure of the activity itself, and partly for the accompanying satisfaction of certain egoistic feelings which find for the moment no other sphere.

But now mark that this which holds of the bodily powers, the destructive instincts, and those emotions related to them that dominate in life because they are directly concerned in the struggle by which life is maintained, holds of all other faculties. Their organs undergoing repair during rest, similarly tend to become more excitable, to pass into ideal action in the absence of real action, and readily fall into any artificial mode of exercise substituted for the natural mode of exercise, when that is not to be had. The higher but less essential powers, as well as the lower but more essential powers, thus come to have activities that are carried on for the sake of the immediate gratifications derived, without reference to ulterior benefits; and to such higher powers, æsthetic products yield these substituted activities, as games yield them to various lower powers.

When we rise from simple sensations to combinations of them, of kinds that awaken ideas and feelings of beauty, we may, I think, discern the same general and special truths. The primitive source of æsthetic pleasure, is that character in the combination which makes it such as to exercise the faculties affected in the most complete ways, with the fewest drawbacks from excess of exercise. Joined to this comes, as before, a secondary source of pleasure—the diffusion of a normal stimulus in large amount, awaking a glow of agreeable feeling, faint and undefinable. And, as before, a third source of pleasure is the partial revival by this discharge of the various special gratifications connected in experience with combinations of the kind presented. Let us pause a moment before each of these. Illustrations of the primary cause will be furnished us by combinations of movements, combinations of forms, combinations of lights, shades, and colours, and combinations of tones.

Movements of the body pleasurable to self, and associated with the consciousness of gracefulness (as in skating), are movements of a kind that bring many muscles into moderate harmonious action and strain none. An awkward motion is one that implies sudden change of direction, angularity, destruction of much momentum, excess of muscular effort; whereas a motion called graceful—a motion in curved lines, flowing one into another without break, is a motion in which little momentum is destroyed, no undue exertion thrown on any muscle, no power lost. And while in the actor the æsthetic consciousness is mainly constituted by this feeling of moderate but efficient muscular action without check, without strain, without loss, the consciousness of gracefulness in the observer, arises in large measure from sympathy with the feelings implied by such motions. Turning to forms, we observe that the delight in flowing outlines rather than in outlines which are angular, is partly due to that more harmonious unstrained action of the ocular muscles, implied by perception of such outlines: there is no jar from sudden stoppage of motion and change of direction, such as results on carrying the eye along a zig-zag line. Here again, then, we have a feeling accompanying an activity that is full, but contains no element of pain from excess. In the more complex combinations, including many forms presented together, it is relatively difficult to trace out the principle; but I see sundry reasons for suspecting that beautiful arrangements of forms, are those which effectually exercise the largest numbers of the structural elements concerned in perception, while over-taxing the fewest of them. Similarly with the complex visual wholes presented by actual objects, or by pictorial representations of objects, with all their lights and shades and colours. The requirements for harmony, for subordination, and for proportion—the demand for a variety sufficient to prevent monotony, but not a variety which too much distracts the attention, may be regarded as all implied by the principle that many elements of perceptive faculty must be called into play, while none are overexerted: there must be a great body of the feeling arising from their moderate action, without the deduction of any pain from extreme action. The pleasure excited by sequences of sounds, such as form musical phrases and cadences, though not mainly due to this cause, is partly due to it. Song differs from speech by using a much wider range of tones, and so exercising many auditory agents in succession; not over-taxing any one in the way that monotonous speech over-taxes it. The like holds in respect to variations of strength. To be artistic, that is, to excite the feeling of beauty effectually, the notes must not be all *forte* or all *piano;* and the execution is the finer the more numerous the gradations—supposing these are such as to satisfy other requirements. So is it too with contrasts in emphasis, with rhythm, and with *timbre*. Due regard being paid to meaning, the rendering is the better the more heterogeneous it is; and, other things equal, its greater heterogeneity implies greater variety of excitements in the percipient, and avoidance of that over-excitement of some perceptive agency which uniformity implies.

Of the supplementary pleasures of perception above named, that which arises from the diffused nervous discharge proceeding from perceptive faculties normally exercised, needs no further illustration. But something must be added in elucidation of the third kind of æsthetic pleasure accompanying perceptive activity—that more special kind which results from the special associations formed in experience.

The feelings from time to time received along with perceptions of graceful movements were mostly agreeable. The persons who exhibited such movements were usually the cultivated, and those whose behaviour yielded gratification. The occasions have usually been festive ones—balls, private dances, and the like. And the places with which graceful motions are associated, such as theatres and the houses of friends, are places where enjoyments of various kinds have been received. Hence the diffused excitation that follows the perception of graceful movements, becomes one by which pleasures derived from these sources are ideally revived in a confused way. With beautiful forms much the same happens. Persons having figures that satisfy the æsthetic requirements, are more frequently than not, connected in experience with agreeable recollections. So, too, are the fine shapes of art-products—architectural, plastic, pictorial: the occasions on which these have been contemplated have mostly been occasions of happiness, social or other. This is a reason why the æsthetic pleasure derived from form, though not great in the uncultured, becomes relatively voluminous in the cultured, by wealth of association. When from simple forms we pass to complex combinations of them with colours, and lights, and shades, as for instance in landscape, this indirect source of æsthetic gratification becomes distinguishable as a large one. The connexion between perception of a grand view and the multitudinous agreeable feelings brought by freedom and relaxation, mostly experienced at the same time, is too clear to permit doubt that a considerable part of the delight given, is caused by this partial revival of many past joys—some within individual experience, and some deeper than individual experience. And then, in the pleasure derived from a skilful representation of a landscape, we have a still more remote result of these associations. For beyond the direct æsthetic satisfaction given by the picture, there is this dim consciousness of enjoyments that have accompanied the actual presence of scenes like the one represented. Once more, it is to be observed that the like holds of the melodic element in music. The expressiveness of musical cadences depends on their relations to cadences of the human voice under emotion. When the emotion suggested by a cadence is a joyous one, opportunity is given for pleasurable sympathy; and when a painful emotion is suggested, there comes an opportunity for the pleasurable pain of pity. Song is distinguished from speech, by various traits that result from idealization of the traits of strong feeling as vocally expressed. And the indirect æsthetic pleasure which melody yields, is due to this derived power of exciting the feelings connected in experience with such traits.

Further Readings

SPENCER, H., *First Principles of a New System of Philosophy,*
2d ed. New York: Appleton-Century-Crofts, 1896.

SPENCER, H., *The Synthetic Philosophy.* New York: Appleton-
Century-Crofts, 1900.

SPENCER, H., *Education: Intellectual, Moral, and Physical.* New
York: Appleton-Century-Crofts, 1889.

Questions for Discussion

1. According to Spencer, what are the three sources of pleasure
   as aesthetic experience?
2. How does his view of play compare with those of Dewey and
   Williams?
3. In what way is aesthetic pleasure a product of feeling?
4. What would Spencer want included in most physical education programs?
5. Should play be defined as what one does when he has time
   free from work? Explain your answer.

MARGARET N. H'DOUBLER

Dance: A Creative Art Experience*

Margaret H'Doubler's article is important because it suggests a
significant relationship between education, including physical
education, and the arts, particularly dance. Much of our traditional instruction, she states, is for impressing or informing
the mind. The arts, on the other hand, give the student the opportunity for the integration and expression of what he has
learned through impression.

* Reprinted with permission of the copyright owner, the Regents of the University
of Wisconsin, Margaret H'Doubler. *Dance: A Creative Art Experience,* Madison:
The University of Wisconsin Press, 1959, pp. 61–66.

H'Doubler's views reflect much of Platonic idealism. The purpose of dance education, she avers, must be intellectual and spiritual as well as physical. The body is only the external aspect of personality. Dancing involves the power to think and feel as well as to act. This article views the individual as an organic whole and the "basic sources of life" as the origin of creative expression. In this manner it reflects Spencer's view of aesthetic sentiment.

Education should be a building toward the integration of human capacities and powers resulting in well-adjusted, useful, balanced individuals. The desire to find peace within ourselves and to bring about an adequate adjustment to the life around us is the basis for all mental and physical activity. From birth to death life is a series of changing behavior patterns because life itself is an unfolding process. Just as the growth of man in civilization is the growth of man in consciousness, so is the educated, cultured, individual life dependent upon the growth and function of the mind, upon its capacity to know, will, imagine, create, and execute.

Everywhere educators are realizing that what is needed more than pedagogical preaching is intelligent stimulation to self-activity. There are, and always will be, many different theories of education. Often the education defined as "a preparation for life" has been so interpreted as to make it no more than a means of bettering one's economic condition. On the other hand, some critics seem to feel that the aim of education is success in living—quite a different matter. For this reason some thinkers and writers, especially those not in intimate touch with the actualities of education, have questioned the importance of creative activity and give but little place to the appreciation of beauty or the cultivation of artistic values. The reply to such attacks lies in a knowledge of the nature of the arts and in recent advances in educational theory.

No one who understands the relation of the arts to human personality can question their values in education, nor can those who have followed educational science during recent years fail to see that provision for the arts must be made in any adequate educational plan. If we go to one of the first masters of educational theory, Plato, we are told that "the purpose of education is to give to the body and soul all the beauty and all the perfection of which they are capable." This definition of purpose still holds, but today we would qualify Plato's statement in some such manner as that suggested by Spencer in his definition of life as "the conscious adjustment of internal relations to external." Both views, it is clear, focus upon the development and growth of the individual, and both imply self-activity, which we may take as the keynote of current educational speculation. The higher aim of education today is the development to the fullest extent of the growth of the individual, based upon a scientific understanding of all his needs and capacities. In so doing we try to attune our own thinking to harmonize with the student's particular interests because we realize that in his interests lies the key to his needs and capacities. Education cannot supply individual capacities—these must be inborn; but it can stimulate and aid in their growth; it can educate the student by giving him the opportunity to develop himself.

There are two aspects to education: one, the capacity to take in, to become impressed; the other, the capacity to give out, to express. To receive impressions informs the mind, but to express its reactions to these impressions requires co-ordination and cooperation of all the mental powers. Power to perceive and to evaluate experience is a high faculty, but of little use unless put into execution. Mere perception and comprehension of knowledge are not sufficient for the fullest development of the mind. To know is the essential first step, but it is the expression of what we know that develops character and a sense of values. It is through perception, intuition, feeling, and conception that our personalities assimilate experience and work it up into our own substance and the world of thought, emotion, and will.

Without this metabolism of experience damage is done to the emerging personality. It is likely to become overburdened and disorganized with undigested and unassimilated information, and inner spontaneity becomes hampered. If dance education is to contribute to this psychic integration, it is essential that the student experience movement in forms characteristic of human responses; that he be led, consciously, from the more natural movement types determined by structure to those responses that are variable and individually modifiable and under the control of higher associative processes; and, finally, it is essential that he experience and evaluate, as he progresses, the accompanying feeling tones of emotional enrichment.

In other words, dance education must be emotional, intellectual, and spiritual, as well as physical, if dance is to contribute to the larger ams of education—the developing of personality through conscious experiencing. It should capitalize every possible resource, selecting and integrating the contributions into a totality.

If we accept the belief in the organic wholeness of man, it is evident that the development of his energies must be interdependent. Our emotions and desires need intelligent selection and guidance, and to be carried to their fullest expression they demand skillful execution.

In such a concept of human development the body should be considered as the outer aspect of personality, for it is the agent through which we receive impressions from the external world and by which we communicate our meaning. Thus the body should be given as careful a study and as high a perfection of technique as the associated processes of thought and feeling. The most completely developed person is the one who has trained all his powers with equal dignity and consideration, in order that he may be physically, intellectually, and emotionally integrated. We may restate the meaning of education as the disciplining and training of our powers and the attainment of skill in execution.

The very nature of the arts makes them especially adapted to this ideal of education, for it is only in art that all the aspects of man's complex nature are united in expression. In art, as in reality, the drives are of the emotional nature; when subjected to the restraint and directions of the intellect and executed by the physical, they result in a fusion of all our energies with the focal point centered in the personality.

The place of dance in developing such individual growth is understood if personality is defined as the expressive total of all our physical, emotional, intellectual, and spiritual energies. These energies are in a constant state of reacting to and being acted upon by the social order in which we live. Of all the arts, dance is peculiarly suited to such a fulfillment of the personality. It serves all the ends of individual growth; it helps to develop the body; it stimulates the imagination and challenges the intellect; it helps to cultivate an appreciation for beauty; and it deepens and refines the emotional nature.

In the teaching and studying of dance we should not be concerned whether or not students develop into professional or re-

cital dancers. The concern should be to develop the power of expression through the study of dance. It may be asked whether the
expression of ordinary people has any particular value. It is true
that expression is of special interest in professional art. We go to
the works of the greatest artists for the wisdom and beauty and
emotion they can communicate to us. But expression, execution,
and sharing also belong to general education, and they are needs
felt by all normal people.

Too often the tendency is to center dance education in performance, with the emphasis on technical skill, instead of studying
the subject as a whole and using creative motor experience as the
basis of instruction. In considering dance as an educational and
creative art experience and not as performance, we should take
care that students know dance as a special way of re-experiencing
aesthetic values discovered in reality. Everyone has within himself
the same potentialities as the artist dancer, but perhaps to a
lesser degree. Everyone has intellect, emotion, spirit, imagination,
ability to move, and educable responses. Every normal person is
equipped with power to think, feel, will, and act. Anyone can dance
within the limits of his capacities. To bring this to the realization
of our youth necessitates an approach that is based on these fundamental human capacities. One of our problems is how to keep the
creative impulse alive through the maturing years and how to help
carry this impulse over into the realities of adult life with heightened power and more enlightened purpose. The basic forces underlying all living forms must be realized as the source of the creative
impulse which impels to expression.

If dance is to realize these educational possibilities, it must take
upon itself a form that is suited to them. It should base its movement forms on the laws of bodily motion, and the study of motion
should include movement in all the forms characteristic of human
responses. At the same time its techniques should be simple enough
to afford the amateur student sufficient mastery of the body as his
instrument of expression, and complex enough to prove interesting and valuable to those who wish to make dance their chosen
profession. The rhythmic scope of dance will need to be sufficiently
broad to include the varying personal rhythms of the students,
and its forms and content will need to be flexible enough to provide opportunity for widely different expressions of widely different
individuals.

Although such an approach to dance does not insist on artistic perfection from the professional critic's point of view, it can insist on high amateur standards and, in so doing, build a foundation for the development of a keen artistic integrity and appreciation. From such a background of study will arise those who are destined by original endowment to become our artist dancers. Our first concern is to teach boys and girls and men and women by means of dance, to teach dance as an experience that contributes to a philosophy and scheme of living.

It is to be expected that not everyone will be a great dancer, and that dancing, of course, will be experienced as a complete art form more by some than by others; but, as every child has a right to a box of crayons and some instruction in the fundamental principles of drawing and in the use of color, whether or not there is any chance of his becoming a professional artist, so every child has a right to know how to achieve control of his body in order that he may use it to the limit of his ability for the expression of his own reactions to life. Even if he can never carry his efforts far enough to realize dance in its highest forms, he may experience the sheer joy of the rhythmic sense of free, controlled, and expressive movement, and through this know an addition to life to which every human being is entitled. If the interest in giving instruction in dance is to produce dancers only, dance as a creative and pleasurable art experience, possible to all, is doomed.

It is because of this tendency that those who are convinced of the value of dance are striving to restore to society a dance that is creative, expressive, communicable, and social, a dance form that in every way will qualify as art.

Further Readings

ASHTON, DUDLEY, "Contributions of Dance to Physical Education" (Parts I–II), *Journal of Health, Physical Education, and Recreation*, vol. 36 (1955) and vol. 27 (1956).

HAYES, ELIZABETH R., *An Introduction to the Teaching of Dance*. New York: The Ronald Press Company, 1964.

LARRABEE, E. and R. MEYERSOHN, *Mass Leisure*. New York: The Free Press of Glencoe, 1958.

MARTIN, JOHN, *The Dance*. New York: Tudor Publishing Co., 1946.

Questions for Discussion

1. Why does H'Doubler discourage the emphasis on technique in dance instruction?
2. Why is the acquisition of knowledge as the single educational objective undesirable?
3. What does the article suggest for the inclusion of the arts in programs of physical education?

Psychological Backgrounds

In selecting papers on the psychological bases of physical education, the editors have been guided by a particular view of the relationship between the two fields. American psychology is becoming more and more empirical and has now eschewed the philosophical speculation of the past for the rather rigorous accumulation of evidence. Whereas "theories" of personality, "theories" of child development, and clinical observation and practice have dominated the past, presently the experimental method and the psychology of learning are in ascendancy. This change in emphasis reflects the growth of psychology from mainly a speculative and descriptive discipline to one that now on the basis of evidence, seeks the causes of behavior.

This transition has important implications for physical education. By using experimental methods in the search for the conditions that *cause* behavior, we obtain the knowledge we need to *control* behavior. A purely speculative and descriptive psychology cannot with much precision and success tell the physical education teacher how to arrange for classroom conditions that promote the changes in behavior he seeks to effect. Accordingly the editors' choice of readings for this section avoids the psychological mysticism of the clinic and child-study center and focuses on research that may prove most useful for physical education.

Paralleling the emphasis on the psychology of learning has been the growing interest in the psychology of individual differences. Unfortunately, these two major areas of inquiry developed in isolation. A rapprochement now seems both possible and desirable, especially for education. Although teachers are aware of individual differences among their students, they still subject them, partly out of economic necessity, to group, as opposed to individual, instruction. Until this past decade, in fact, no systematic attempts were made to classify these differences, as is done in the work of Fleishman reported below. A classification and assessment of students' abilities and knowledge *before* instruction begins, along with a careful specification of what it is we want them to learn, would go a long way toward solving our teaching problems.

The first four readings deal with conditions important for the learning of motor skills, most of which involve the co-ordination of hand and eye movement. Motor learning is basic to physical education and, fortunately, it is an area of major research interest in psychology. Bilodeau and Bilodeau discuss the importance of feedback (or knowledge of results) in learning. This seems to be a learning condition of major concern. Ammons and his associates tried to find out how the amount and distribution of practice affect memory (or retention) over a period as long as two years. Knapp and Dixon are also interested in the practice and rest variables but in the context of original learning. And finally, Colville attempts to relate transfer of learning with the acquisition of skills.

To avoid the confusion that exists in the current psychological speculation on the study of motivation, we have chosen an article discussing a related topic—stress. The experimental study of stress is separated from the study of motivation and can be dealt with more concretely. The articles by Fleishman and Hempel are among the most important in the section. Their classification of abilities and their study of vital changes brought about in abilities as practice continues should have rich implications for physical education programs. Both Paterson and Anastasi review evidence on physique and psychological characteristics. Their conclusions should make us less glib and certain about the relationships which may exist. Finally, the article by Piaget raises play to a high level as crucial in the development of the child's language and thought.

The prospective physical education teacher should find these studies relevant. Although further research and development is necessary, all of these articles have fairly clear implications for testing and teaching. For testing, there are some interesting implications for properly placing students in appropriate sections of their physical education classes. For teaching, there are some fairly specific implications for arranging practice sessions.

In his perusal of the readings in this section, the student should be mindful of these major concepts: (1) the learning of *motor skills;* (2) the *retention* of these skills and the effects of *practice* schedules; (3) training for *transfer;* (4) the effect of *stress* on performance; (5) psychomotor and physical *abilities;* and (6) the relationship of physique to various psychological characteristics, e.g., height and temperament.

EDWARD A. BILODEAU and INA McD. BILODEAU

Motor-Skills Learning: Feedback*

The following selection is part of an excellent review on motor-skills learning. Motor-skills learning, roughly speaking, refers to acquiring manual skills, skills in which the hand is holding or moving some physical apparatus. Development of perception is important for the acquisition of perceptual-motor skills, skills that involve the co-ordination of eye and hand movement. The skills central to physical education are largely perceptual-motor skills.

The process of learning a skill is much the same as that for any other learning. For example, the same aspects of verbal learning and skill learning are studied in experimental psychology. The study of both is equally complex and elusive. Skill learning can be very complex, as, for example, such particular skills as playing a concerto or driving in golf, and it generally involves cognitive as well as muscular learning.

What the following authors call "feedback," or knowledge of results, is the most important variable controlling skilled performance. Like other topics in psychology, it is defined in quite different and even contradictory ways. The student should note the three definitions of the roles of feedback. He should also

* Reprinted and abridged with permission of the author and publishers from the *Annual Review of Psychology*, vol. 12, 1961, pp. 243–259.

note the differential effects of delayed versus immediate feedback, of supplemental feedback, and of the form in which the feedback is given.

S tudies of feedback[1] or knowledge of results (KR) show it to be the strongest, most important variable controlling performance and learning. It has been shown repeatedly, as well as recently, that there is no improvement without KR, progressive improvement with it, and deterioration after its withdrawal. A number of studies show that performance is seriously disrupted or made impossible by lags in feedback of even less than 1.0 sec. Furthermore, behavior is greatly enhanced with supplementary KR (70) and quickened KR. Other kinds of KR studies show that E can elicit R_a, R_b, . . . or R_n at will, depending upon how he regulates the cueing feedback (13). No other independent variable offers the wide range of possibilities for getting man to repeat, or change his Rs immediately or slowly, by small or large amounts.

History and Comment. Laws consisting of statements relating R variations to feedback variations, as expressed by the general mathematical equation, $R = f\ (KR)$, have been sought by some. Though most Es would agree that R is some function of feedback, there is no agreement on the definition, never mind the function. Indeed, there is not even widespread agreement as to name; knowledge and feedback represent the core words, modified by other words such as results, performance, psychological, achievement, intrinsic, extrinsic, extra, supplementary, augmented, degraded, proprioceptive, incentive, social, etc. Feedback appears to be the more descriptive and harmless appellation. Whatever it is, and whatever it may be called, the work of the 1950s can be divided into three broad areas: (*a*) transformations, (*b*) temporal delay, and (*c*) supplements to the standard. A fourth area, frequency schedules, has hardly been touched. Before reviewing the data, we must note how various authors have dealt with or dodged the definitional problems.

Brown (22), Ammons (1), Annett & Kay (6), and Fitts *et al.* (28) take somewhat different positions on knowledge of results. All

[1] The following abbreviations and symbols will be used: S (subject) ; E (experimenter) ; R (response) ; S-R (stimulus-response) ; KR (knowledge of results or feedback) ; I_R (reactive inhibition) ; sI_R (conditioned inhibition).

would include external events that depend upon what S has done and that are directed back towards S. They disagree on whether S's knowledge or habits enter the definition. They also do not all face, recognize, or take a stand on what types of external stimulus feedback are admissible feedbacks. Apparently there is no present limit on what may be a legitimate feedback. After drawing a line, S might hear: "Too low," "$\frac{1}{4}$ unit low," "$\frac{1}{4}$ in. low," ".245 in. low," or "You moved $2\frac{3}{4}$ in." Thus, numbers, signs, units, and goals are most certainly involved. E's evaluations of all these may be involved (and also even higher order codes, or orders of KR), i.e., "Here's a cookie," "Good," "In the top decile," 'Ha, ha," and "Unh ha," the only limitation being E's ingenuity.

Brown (22) says that giving KR is the process of providing the learner with information as to how good or how accurate his reactions are. In an earlier era, Seashore & Bavelas (67) argued that correct and incorrect conceptions of one's performance were included in KR. Ammons (1) refers to "knowledge of various kinds which the performer received about his performance." Annett & Kay (6) insist that it is S's perception of his KR that really counts. Taylor (74), Fitts *et al.* (28), and Bilodeau (14) use R error as if it were the essence of feedback and have so far managed to duck the question of the boundaries. A look at their work suggests that they are unhappy with R evaluation by either S or E as a basic element of feedback. They restrict feedback to observable, quantifiable events, as would Norbert Wiener. They believe that S's overt Rs to feedback are the objects of the inquiry and that the word "knowledge" in the phrase, knowledge of results, should not have the implication of a response to feedback.

When feedback is reduced to a number or represented on a display, it is an independent variable or stimulus coded and transformed in some way by E. It is either some function (f) of R or of error in R. In either case, KR refers to external events on spatial and temporal co-ordinates. Feedback in simple pursuit tracking, for example, consists of two events: the locus of the control (limb, stylus, or cursor) and the locus of the goal stimulus; these events can be coded any number of ways, either within or between sensory modalities. For example, even the loci of stylus and target on the rotor could be represented numerically instead of visio-spatially, or, still visually, on a cathode ray tube at half of true scale (69). In the case of compensatory pursuit, feedback consists of one event, a representation of R error, that has multiple determinants. That is, the error displayed is some coded function of both the locus of the control and the programmed locus of the goal stimulus. A single signal thus represents the S-event (Rs) and E-event (goal-stimulus input). Because the feedback consists of the difference between these two, it is difficult for the naive operator to dissociate the effect of R from that of the program. . . .

The typical tracking task involves at least two, possibly three, primary sources of information. The display produces the first, the control R the second. Both of these are intrinsic loops for the system in that there is no system without them. The display loop is external, whereas the control loop is proprioceptive and internal. Bahrick (9) and Noble & Bahrick (59) review their own excellent work and that of others on the difficult problem of the proprioceptive loop. Gordon (34) evaluates tracking performance under the impoverished conditions of no target, no follower, and standard conditions of pursuit and compensatory display. The third loops, those not directly originating in R and display, are more expendable, extra, or supplementary. Lincoln (44) compares the learning achieved under different varieties of extra loops.

When feedback involves a function of R, there is no such thing as the KR for a particular response. Probably all external feedback is arbitrary inasmuch as E calls the tune. . . . This has been amply shown for simple, discrete response-learning systems . . . ; and for tracking tasks with cathode ray tube, it is quite obvious that E decides the amount of magnification and other properties of the feedback. . . . Or, in the classical line-drawing task, imagine that S's pencil moves two inches or two glubs. . . . If we let KR equal $f(X)$, then KR is equal to whatever E wishes it to be: aX, $aX + b$, X^a, or $^a\sqrt{X}$, etc., even X itself. Notice that KR may, with great propriety, be a "hit," "one glub," "nine glubs," etc. Those Es who round off a KR have, in effect, given up the notion of "true KR." Some transformations are interesting, practical, or analytic; others are of limited or no value. . . .

Feedback, KR, reward, and reinforcement are usually cross-indexed in textbooks; too often, only studies of reward with animals will be found. Many skills people use reward and KR interchangeably, others use reinforcement and KR as equivalents. To name only a few: Saltzman, Kanfer & Greenspoon (65) speak of "delay of reward" for wrong and right in line drawing, Noble & Alcock

(53) use "delayed reward" to denote the delay of the green light on
their switch-pushing task, and Reynolds & Adams (62) use the word
"reinforcement" to represent the click event when their rotor stylus
is on target. The writers (17) have discussed, though much too
briefly, the similarities and differences between occurrence and
nonoccurrence of KR and food and have found sufficient reason to
believe that, in almost every case, E's use of reward with his animals differs substantially from his use of KR with human Ss. This
does not invalidate the work on either side of the fence, but it does
mean that there is no special virtue in generalizing theoretical
similarities *ad infinitum* in the absence of data obtained under comparable procedures. Identical procedures will not be easily come
by, however, because "23 units low" was not evolved as a substitute
for the function of food. When feedback is an error event, the
prior R is weakened. This type of feedback certainly has a function
more in common with no food than with food. Another difference
lies in the typical R—animal Ss seldom being taught skills such as
how to track and move.

Rewards have been varied in a thousand ways, and temporal-fre-
quency schedules can be generated endlessly, as Skinner's work
shows so emphatically. Theories of reward and reinforcement run
not too far behind. We seem to be in for the same empirical and
theoretical treats in the field of KR, for many variations in reward
. . . can be copied with KR. If anything, KR variations will prove
to be much more numerous; they may even, in turn, lead to some
attempts at parallel manipulations with animal reward.

The outstanding thinking on KR in the 1940s was done by Brown
(22) who discussed three now-famous roles of KR: reward, information, and motivation. That is, like primary reward, KR might serve
to reinforce (strengthen) habits, evoke already established habits
(cue properties), and provide the motivation (incentive) for learning or performing. These ideas were generalizations from the issues of reward research, and even today there is no methodology to
differentiate between the alleged effects. It must be said, however,
that KR research is not yet overly concerned with theory, since it
is more or less acknowledged that suitable probes are wanting.
Identifying relevant variables and finding functional relationships
are much more militantly pursued. Brown also made 12 statements
on variables and their probable effects. The first four concern the
delay of feedback. For example, he identifies certain conditions

where delay of KR might be superior to its immediate administration. This may be a bit of foolishness to those skills investigators who confuse KR with food; but it shows that Brown can tell a rat from a human being, and one experimental variable from another. Other statements deal with the specificity of KR, the effect of interpolating activity between R and KR, and independent scheduling of R and KR frequencies. Reward parallels of these last two have been hot topics in animal research for some time, but are comparatively cold for human KR.

Ammons (1) provides the only summary of KR research during the 1950s. After reviewing 56 articles, he formulated 11 generalizations and eight summary statements as a beginning theory. These are a melange of intuition and conservatism and well represent the chaos and achievements of the field. He stays clear of definition, except to say that studies of level of aspiration and of incentives with human Ss are not included. Some of his generalizations are good: "In the case of discontinuous tasks where knowledge of performance is given, small intervals between trials are generally better for learning than are longer ones." Many others are vague, even if they make a certain amount of sense: "The more specific the knowledge of performance the more rapid the improvement and the higher the level of performance," and "For all practical purposes, there is always some knowledge of his performance available to the human performer."

Ineffective Delays of KR. Ammons' Generalization 6 states: "The longer the delay in giving knowledge of performance, the less effect the given information has." The clunk of the pellet dispenser is loud and clear: "It is quite possible that the learner might not be able to use the information given more than 15 or 20 seconds after the response. . . ." It would have been better had these been supported by reference to the literature on delay of reward and by equating food and KR, as Wolfle (79) made no bones about doing in an earlier review; Ammons actually cited studies with human Ss, most of which were null. Among these was the classic by Lorge & Thorndike (45). Actually there are many other studies with no difference between immediate and delayed KR: Saltzman, Kanfer & Greenspoon (65), Noble & Alcock (53), and Denny *et al.* (26). McGuigan (47), too, had a null result, but because of design naivetes and strange statements, his data might well be discounted. Greenspoon & Foreman (35) published a significant difference that Bilodeau & Ryan (19) were unable to reproduce. All in all, it is clear that to delay or to give immediate KR can be quite immaterial for learning to make relatively simple Rs (when the periods between Rs are relatively free of specially interpolated Rs).

The writers (18) reported the results of five studies (800 Ss) with unusually long intervals—hour, day, or week—between successive Rs and between R and KR. The major finding was that the more massed the Rs the better, a result in accord with an earlier study in England (25) and a follow-up study by Denny *et al.* (26). Generally, the temporal position of KR did not matter, except in one of the five experiments where the delayed group was best. Ryan (64), too, got no effect of delay in a study in which E progressively shifted the required amplitude of R, delaying KR a week or not at all for each of eight weeks.

The many failures to obtain significant differences cannot be explained by complaining that traces of R last but a few moments, or by insisting that Ss instruct themselves. The writers do not question the null data; they do doubt the value of the classical role of the trace of R. Traces of the last KR and of the effects of past KRs on past Rs (alternative Rs) are also involved. Delayed groups have some advantage from more recent KR; for example, "Lift the cross-hairs 3.75° higher than you normally would" may be delayed and used as an effective cue for immediate action. Delay of KR is not necessarily bad.

Terminal KR and Instructions. Miller (48) and Annett & Kay (6) use the term "action" feedback to contrast with "learning" feedback. If action feedback has the cue properties of a conditioned stimulus, it has something in common with instructions and commands to perform. Feedbacks such as "Pay half as much attention as usual to display-control A, twice as much attention to display-control B," have been used sparingly (15). They alter the part-performance profile for a time, as does announcing "Your poorest performance is 'throttle'." Similarly, Goldstein & Rittenhouse (33) tell S the sign of his constant ranging errors and get improved performance on a gunnery trainer. Telling S which switch is paired with which light speeds learning [Noble, Alcock & Frye (55)].

Work on continuous, action feedback has been going on for years, but it is difficult to find it compared to learning feedback in the same experiment. Using a pressure stick, Annett (5) compared visual feedback while R was in progress to announcing the result after R was completed. The terminal KR he calls "delayed KR," the action feedback he calls "immediate KR," though it is not as simple as the names imply. Removing the visual feedback during the test period produced a quick and dramatic fall in the accuracy of the visual group, but not the terminal group. During its training, however, the terminal group had improved gradually; the visual group hit the target every time. Obviously, the delayed group learned something that the other group did not. Annett is sorely troubled by the lack of learning in the visual group. Among several alternatives he suggests is that S has learned to move the light and when this visual cue is removed he cannot reproduce the pressure he has not attended, i.e., learned. The results of Pearson & Hauty (61) really pose a difficult explanatory problem since their Ss learned to right themselves in a lateral tilt chair without any identifiable external sources of feedback. The improvement they attribute to proprioceptive learning and not to sensory adaptation. Holding (38) maintains that in full guided practice there is no KR, only knowledge of the correct R and that such kinesthetic cues as there may be are irrelevant. More cases of no learning with KR and learning without KR can be expected in the 1960s along with increases in the loudness of claims and counterclaims.

Effective Delay of KR. Not all delays of KR produce null results, as delays of speech or handwriting (75) show so dramatically. It depends upon what happens between R and KR. In all of the preceding studies of delay, S learned simple, discrete positioning movements such as line drawing and lever moving. Nothing special was interpolated between R and KR or between KR and the next R. When something is interpolated, performance is of a different order of magnitude, and Es such as Noble & Noble make learning as difficult as they wish (58). There is a whole spate of evidence, most of it in the context of human-factors engineering. Representative studies of display and control lags, without large overlays of learning theory, are those of Garvey, Sweeney & Birmingham (31), and Conklin (23), (24). Holland & Henson (39) show that performance improves immediately upon a change from delayed to immediate feedback. Bilodeau (20), following Lorge & Thorndike (45), has used a trials-delay technique to effect a compromise between the tasks of continuous tracking and discrete positioning. In trials delay, discrete events run off about as follows: R1, R2, R3, KR1, R4, KR2, etc. This sequence is illustrative of but one simple type of delay with serious consequences for learning and performance.

In the much too typical tracking task, S continues to track during a lag, for his flow of information is still continuous—merely displaced in time. Habituated to sampling on-going action feedback, S adjusts the control as if that feedback represented his on-going error. In terms of system output, of course, this is all wrong, and more wrong, the longer the lag. As in steering a car, airplane, or submarine, one must anticipate. On-going feedback must be interpreted as a function of Rs preceding the immediate past and as cues related to future events.

More of Verbal and Mechanical Instructions. Instructions and tuitions have the appearance of belonging to the feedback family and are administered before, during, or after R. Below, we deal with the more derivative feedbacks, from initial verbal instructions to S, through feedbacks while R is in progress, to feedbacks summarizing preceding responses. The topic is also divisible, but unnaturally, into studies that make use of verbal instruction and those that employ mechanical surrogates for the spoken word.

Everyone knows how important "motivational" instructions and environments are, yet most Es who undertake a demonstration come up with null results or the thinnest of data [Bayton & Conley (11); Bell (12); Fleishman (29); Noble (50, 57); Williams (78); Zimny (80)]. Others get positive results (205), and the most important of these is Wegner & Zeaman (77). Walton & Begg (76) found that incentives improved the performance of imbeciles on a dull routine task. The whole area of motivation is a dreadful mess with no promising way of straightening it out. Too often, one group is advised to "try hard" and a second group to "try very hard." It is also fashionable to award a nickel, a gum drop, or to threaten a weak shock; it is not the thing to give your Ss KR or instructions such as "stop walking and start running." Surwillo (73) lists nine techniques alleged to vary motivations in the laboratory. Still, he misses some. French (30) has good ideas on individual differences and finds that performance is more closely related to motivation test scores than to experimental conditions.

One can give S some extra indication of decent or poor performance beyond the standard without using "good," smiles, or cookies; the color of the target, a tone, or a special lamp can convey an additional bit of information about on-off target events. The extra KRs that work best are those that attract attention (warning lights) and those that carry relatively specific information about which R has gone wrong. Vague and redundant KRs are readily produced and just as quickly attached to training devices.

Payne & Hauty (60) showed S his relative standing, or a light to signal that an error was in progress. The Ss, under the influence of analeptic or depressant drugs, spent more than four hours at four-dimensional tracking on a splendid apparatus, the Multidimensional Pursuit Test. The Ss paid their toll, but the feedbacks helped performance throughout. The feedbacks, however, were no better at sustaining performance late in practice than early. Hauty & Payne (36) show very nicely that extra signals will serve to raise the entire performance curve during a hard day's work under trying circumstances. Showing better performance with extra cues is not the same as demonstrating greater learning. The training people naturally hope that the extra stimulus will promote learning of the standard task (transfer of training). The unwanted alternatives are that the extra cue (*a*) elicits on-target Rs with no particular transfer to the standard cues and (*b*) motivates S to emit Rs at a greater rate, and thus, of course, to perform better only with the extra cue (i.e., increased motivation), but not without it. Obviously, the learning-performance distinction is the heart of the matter.

Studies shortly after World War II used filters to redden the normally white target of a gunnery trainer. The filters operated when S was on target and they greatly improved performance. Later, switching to no-filter feedback showed that removing the cue produced an immediate and large letdown. There was no large amount of positive transfer, although there was usually some. An experiment by Annett (5) typifies the techniques now in routine use: the extra cue is withdrawn after training; during training its frequency is varied, patterned, or randomized, in an attempt to shift the properties of the extra cue to the standard ones. Stockbridge & Chambers (71) also did work of this sort, but McCormack (46) did not bother to use a test period. Smode's (70) discussion and ideas on extra KR are especially good. In his study, groups with extra KR were deliberately loaded with several supplements. As usual, there were large differences during training and rapid shifts in level of performance with transfer testing, but there was more than the usual evidence for some transfer. Smode says S is not learning more, but is being motivated to do more. Very wisely, he also included groups switched from one model to another. The combined effect of changing model and eliminating the extra cue is always greater than the loss attributable to either one. Apparently the extra cue teaches the idiosyncrasies of the training unit, and this finding adds another limitation to training devices with or without extra cues.

The results of Archer, Kent & Mote (7) on a gunnery trainer and of Archer & Namikas (8) on the rotor are different in that the extra cue did not even produce a performance difference during training. The study on the rotor was a badly needed check of an earlier one by Reynolds & Adams (62), who found positive training differences using a delayed cue or tone to indicate that Rs for the last X seconds were correct. Archer & Namikas used college Ss; Reynolds & Adams, basic airmen trainees. The reviewers think the latter study a fluke, although Archer & Namikas prefer the sampling population hypothesis.

Studies with extra KR can be expected more often, with disagreement about their reinforcing properties. There is, however, no dispute about certain extra KRs producing improved responses. Someone can be expected to use this technique to teach his Ss more about the criterion task. In the meantime, we can expect a number of failures.

Numerical Transformation of KR. When S's error or response (X) can be expressed numerically, a transformation of the number, $f(X)$, can be the feedback. By deliberate, systematic, and arbitrary manipulation of these numbers, E can vary and regulate feedback to study the relations between R and KR. Transformations are standard practice with Es who use trainers and simulators because the electronic linkage between R and display must necessarily be arbitrary. Nearly all of the tracking literature can be organized around $f(X)$, all the transformations being either spatial or temporal in character (2, 10, 24, 74). In the section on Apparatus, Table I shows very clearly that most of the newer edvices, electronic or not, are built so that E must decide the nature of f in $f(X)$. Noble & Bahrick (59), for example, use $4(X)$ with their pressure stick; even in the line-drawing experiment, E need not equate KR with the marks on the ruler. The use of transformations of numerical feedback for discrete Rs was formally opened by Bilodeau in 1953 and was followed three years later by a survey of the transformation literature (16).

Commonplace transformations deal with such variables as rounding, target size, error amplification, specificity, or other ways in which R is coded. A transformation equation shows how the whole KR scale is related to the entire dimension of R. For example, when

KR is set equal to $aX + b$, KR varies with X in a positive and linear manner, the value of KR depending upon the values of slope and intercept E selects. The subject's behavior can be regulated by variations within the equation as Schumsky (66) has done, or by variation of the type of equation as Noble & Broussard have reported (56). Noble & Broussard taught S to make a certain amplitude of R, using different curvilinear relationships between KR and R.

The independent variable, target size, is well handled by the transformation technique. The size of a target is fixed by transformations about some critical value of X, a number of quantitatively different Rs being converted to a single value of KR representing the goal or target. In such systems S can be told he is on target and yet scored as in error. Responses seem remarkably insensitive to rather wide variations of target. . . . When the target is wide, S usually repeats his Rs and avoids the edge. . . .

The major trouble with most psychomotor tasks such as line drawing is that too little learning is produced. Subjects do much too well on Trials 1 and 2, having a decent R for "quarter-inch error" and a pretty good three-inch line-drawing R before encountering the experimenter. The task is not worthy of human learning abilities. Transformations show promise for slowing or speeding the learning process as required for line drawing and many other tasks. Transforming the error fed to S, by adding or subtracting a constant (k), does regulate the speed of learning. In such an experiment, . . . the sign and magnitudes of k have pronounced effects on certain variances and central tendencies. By comparison with $-k$, $+k$ had the effect of minimizing (a) mean absolute error of R and (b) individual differences, while maximizing (c) within-individual variance (i.e., hunting). The transformation $-k$ had quite the opposite multiple effects. The implications are two: (a) the dominant effect of feedback is upon variances; (b) there is no way to minimize (or maximize) all criteria of response.

Our major conclusion on feedback is obvious: to control behavior, regulate functions of error.

Literature Cited

1. AMMONS, R. B. Effects of knowledge of performance: a survey and tentative theoretical formulation. *J. Gen. Psychol.*, 54, 279–99 (1956).
2. ANDREAS, B. G., FINCK, A., GREEN, R. F., SMITH, S., and SPRAGG, S. D. S. Two-

dimensional compensatory tracking performance as a function of control-display movement relationships, positioning vs. velocity relationship, and miniature vs. large stick control. *J. Psychol.,* **48,** 237–46 (1959).

3. ANDREAS, B. G., GERALL, A. A., GREEN, R. F., and MURPHY, D. P. Performance in following tracking as a function of the sensitivity of the airplane-type stick. *J. Psychol.,* **43,** 169–79 (1957).

4. ANDREAS, B. G., GREEN, R. F., and SPRAGG, S. D. S. Transfer effects in compensatory tracking (Modified S A M Two-Hand Pursuit Test) as a function of reversal of the display-control relationships on alternate blocks of trials. *J. Psychol.,* **40,** 421–30 (1955).

5. ANNETT, J. Learning a pressure under conditions of immediate and delayed knowledge of results. *Quart. J. Exptl. Psychol.,* **11,** 3–15 (1959).

6. ANNETT, J. and KAY, H. Knowledge of results and skilled performance. *Occupational Psychol.,* **31,** 69–79 (1957).

7. ARCHER, E. J., KENT, G. W., and MOTE, F. A. Effect on long-term practice and time-on-target information feedback on complex tracking task. *J. Exptl. Psychol.,* **51,** 103–12 (1956).

8. ARCHER, E. J., and NAMIKAS, G. A. Pursuit rotor performance as a function of delay of information feedback. *J. Exptl. Psychol.,* **56,** 325–27 (1958).

9. BAHRICK, H. P. An analysis of stimulus variables influencing the proprioceptive control of movements. *Psychol. Rev.,* **64,** 324–28 (1957).

10. BATTIG, W. F., NAGEL, E. H., and BROGDEN, W. J. The effects of error-magnification and marker-size on bidimensional compensatory tracking. *Am. J. Psychol.,* **68,** 585–94 (1955).

11. BAYTON, J. A., and CONLEY, H. W. Duration of success background and the effect of failure upon performance. *J. Gen. Psychol.,* **56,** 179–85 (1957).

12. BELL, A. H. Effects of experimentally-induced muscular tension and frequency of motivational instructions on pursuit rotor performance. *Perceptual Motor Skills,* **9,** 111–15 (1959).

13. BILODEAU, E. A. Acquisition of two lever-positioning responses practiced over several periods of alternation. *J. Exptl. Psychol.,* **46,** 43–49 (1953).

14. BILODEAU, E. A. Motor performance as affected by magnitude and direction of error contained in knowledge of results. *J. Psychol.,* **40,** 103–13 (1955).

15. BILODEAU, E. A. Variations in knowledge of component performance and its effects upon part-part and part-whole relations. *J. Exptl. Psychol.,* **50,** 215–24 (1955).

16. BILODEAU, E. A. Studies of target size and the control of psychomotor behavior through systematic transformation of knowledge of results. In *Symposium on Air Force Human Engineering, Personnel and Training Research,* 17–24 (Finch, G., and Cameron, F., Eds., Natl. Acad. Sci.–Natl. Research Council, Publ. 445, Washington, D.C., 316 pp., 1956).

17. BILODEAU, E. A., and BILODEAU, I. MCD. Variable frequency of knowledge of results and the learning of a simple skill. *J. Exptl. Psychol.*, **55**, 379–83 (1958).

18. BILODEAU, E. A., and BILODEAU, I. MCD. Variation of temporal intervals among critical events in five studies of knowledge of results. *J. Exptl. Psychol.*, **55**, 603–12 (1958).

19. BILODEAU, E. A., and RYAN, F. J. A test for interaction of delay of knowledge of results and two types of interpolated activity. *J. Exptl. Psychol.*, **59**, 414–19 (1960).

20. BILODEAU, I. MCD. Accuracy of a simple positioning response with variation in the number of trials by which knowledge of results is delayed. *Am. J. Psychol.*, **69**, 434–37 (1956).

21. BIRCH, D. A model for response tendency combination. *Psychometrika*, **22**, 373–80 (1957).

22. BROWN, J. S. A proposed program of research on psychological feedback (knowledge of results) in the performance of psychomotor tasks. In *Research Planning Conference on Planning and Motor Skills. AFHRRC Conf. Rept.* 49–2, 81–87. (U.S. Air Force, San Antonio, Tex., 98 pp., 1949).

23. CONKLIN, J. E. Effect of control lag on performance in a tracking task. *J. Exptl. Psychol.*, **53**, 261–91 (1959).

24. CONKLIN, J. E. Linearity of the tracking performance function. *Perceptual Motor Skills*, **9**, 387–91 (1959).

25. DEES, V., and GRINDLEY, G. C. The effect of knowledge of results on learning and performance: IV. The direction of the error in very simple skills. *Quart. J. Exptl. Psychol.*, **3**, 36–42 (1951).

26. DENNY, M. R., ALLARD, M., HALL, E., and ROKEACH, M. Supplementary report: delay of knowledge of task, and the intertrial interval. *J. Exptl. Psychol.*, **60**, (1960).

27. FARESE, F. J., and NOBLE, C. E. Trial-and-error vs. mixed-selective learning in man. *Perceptual Motor Skills*, **10**, 115–22 (1960).

28. FITTS, P. M., NOBLE, M. E., BAHRICK, H. P., and BRIGGS, G. E. *Skilled Performance—Part II. AF WADC Final Report.* (U.S. Air Force, Dayton, Ohio, 236 pp., 1959.)

29. FLEISHMAN, E. A. A relationship between incentive motivation and ability level in psychomotor performance. *J. Exptl. Psychol.*, **56**, 78–81 (1958).

30. FRENCH, E. G. Some characteristics of achievement motivation. *J. Exptl. Psychol.*, **50**, 232–36 (1955).

31. GARVEY, W. D., SWEENEY, J. S., and BIRMINGHAM, H. P. Differential effects of "display lags" and "control lags" on the performance of manual tracking systems. *J. Exptl. Psychol.*, **56**, 8–10 (1958).

32. GERALL, A. A., and GREEN, R. F. Effect of torque changes upon a two-hand coordination task. *Perceptual Motor Skills*, **8**, 287–90 (1958).

33. GOLDSTEIN, M., and RITTENHOUSE, C. H. Knowledge of results in the acquisition and transfer of a gunnery skill. *J. Exptl. Psychol.*, **48**, 187–96 (1954).

34. GORDON, N. B. Learning a motor task under varied display conditions. *J. Exptl. Psychol.,* 57, 65–73 (1959).

35. GREENSPOON, J., and FOREMAN, S. Effect of delay of knowledge of results on learning a motor task. *J. Exptl. Psychol.,* 51, 226–28 (1956).

36. HAUTY, G. T., and PAYNE, R. B. Mitigation of work decrement. *J. Exptl. Psychol.,* 49, 60–67 (1955).

37. HECKER, D., GREEN, D., and SMITH, K. U. Dimensional analysis of motion: X. Experimental evaluation of a time-study problem. *J. Appl. Psychol.,* 40, 220–27 (1956).

38. HOLDING, D. H. Guidance in pursuit tracking. *J. Exptl. Psychol.,* 57, 362–66 (1959).

39. HOLLAND, J. G., and HENSON, J. B. Transfer of training between quickened and unquickened tracking systems. *J. Appl. Psychol.,* 40, 362–66 (1956).

40. JAHNKE, J. C., and DUNCAN, C. P. Reminiscence and forgetting in motor learning after extended rest intervals. *J. Exptl. Psychol.,* 52, 273–82 (1956).

41. KRENDEL, E. S. *Manpower.* ONR *Final* TR F-A1982 (U.S. Navy, Washington, D.C., 56 pp., 1958).

42. LEWIS, D., and LOWE, W. F. Retention of skill on the SAM Complex Coordinator. *Proc. Iowa Acad. Sci.,* 63, 591–99 (1956).

43. LEWIS, D., MCALLISTER, D. E., and ADAMS, J. A. Facilitation and interference in performance on the Modified Mashburn Apparatus: I. The effects of varying the amount of original learning. *J. Exptl. Psychol.,* 41, 247–60 (1951).

44. LINCOLN, R. S. Learning and retaining a rate of movement with the aid of kinesthetic and verbal cues. *J. Exptl. Psychol.,* 51, 199–204 (1956).

45. LORGE, I., and THORNDIKE, E. L. The influence of delay in the after-effect of a connection. *J. Exptl. Psychol.,* 18, 186–94 (1935).

46. MCCORMACK, P. D. Performance in a vigilance task with and without knowledge of results. *Can. J. Psychol.,* 13, 68–71 (1959).

47. MCGUIGAN, F. J. The effect of precision, delay, and schedule of knowledge of results on performance. *J. Exptl. Psychol.,* 58, 79–84 (1959).

48. MILLER, R. B. *Handbook on Training and Training Equipment Design.* AF WADC TR 53–136 (U.S. Air Force, Dayton, Ohio, 1953).

49. NEUMANN, E., and AMMONS, R. B. Acquisition and long-term retention of a simple serial perceptual-motor skill. *J. Exptl. Psychol.,* 53, 159–61 (1957).

50. NOBLE, C. E. An attempt to manipulate incentive-motivation in a continuous tracking task. *Perceptual Motor Skills,* 5, 65–69 (1955).

51. NOBLE, C. E. The length-difficulty relationship in compound trial-and-error learning. *J. Exptl. Psychol.,* 54, 246–52 (1957).

52. NOBLE, C. E. Human trial-and-error learning. *Psychol. Rept.,* 3, 377–98 (1957).

53. NOBLE, C. E., ALCOCK, W. T. Human delayed-reward learning with different lengths of task. *J. Exptl. Psychol.,* 56, 407–12 (1958).

54. NOBLE, C. E., ALCOCK, W. T., and FARESE, F. J. Habit reversal under differential instructions in compound trial-and-error learning. *J. Psychol.*, 46, 253–64 (1958).

55. NOBLE, C. E., ALCOCK, W. T., and FRYE, R. L., JR. The joint influence of practice and instructions on discrimination reaction time. *J. Psychol.*, 48, 125–30 (1959).

56. NOBLE, C. E., and BROUSSARD, I. G. Effects of complex transformations of feedback upon simple instrumental behavior. *J. Exptl. Psychol.*, 50, 381–86 (1955).

57. NOBLE, C. E., FUCHS, J. E., ROBEL, D. P., and CHAMBERS, R. W. Individual vs. social performance on two perceptual-motor tasks. *Perceptual Motor Skills*, 8, 131–34 (1958).

58. NOBLE, C. E., and NOBLE, J. L. Human trial-and-error learning under joint variation of locus of reward and type of pacing. *J. Exptl. Psychol.*, 56, 103–09 (1958).

59. NOBLE, M. E., and BAHRICK, H. P. Response generalization as a function of intratask response similarity. *J. Exptl. Psychol.*, 51, 405–12 (1956).

60. PAYNE, R. B., and HAUTY, G. T. Effect of psychological feedback upon work decrement. *J. Exptl. Psychol.*, 50, 343–51 (1955).

61. PEARSON, R. G., and HAUTY, G. T. Role of postural experiences in proprioceptive perception of verticality. *J. Exptl. Psychol.*, 59, 425–28 (1960).

62. REYNOLDS, B., and ADAMS, J. A. Motor performance as a function of click reinforcement. *J. Exptl. Psychol.*, 45, 315–20 (1953).

63. REYNOLDS, B., and BILODEAU, I. MCD. Acquisition and retention of three psychomotor tests as a function of distribution of practice during acquisition. *J. Exptl. Psychol.*, 44, 19–26 (1952).

64. RYAN, F. J. The modification of a response under conditions of immediate and a week's delay of knowledge of results (Master's thesis, Tulane Univ., New Orleans, La., 1959).

65. SALTZMAN, I. J., KANFER, F. H., and GREENSPOON, J. Delay of reward and human motor learning. *Psychol. Rept.*, 1, 139–42 (1955).

66. SCHUMSKY, D. A. The use of transformations of knowledge of results with negative slope on a simple motor response (Master's thesis, Tulane Univ., New Orleans, La., 1959).

67. SEASHORE, H., and BAVELAS, A. The functioning of knowledge of results in Thorndike's line-drawing experiment. *Psychol. Rev.*, 48, 155–64 (1941).

68. SIMON, J. R., and SMITH, K. U. Theory and analysis of component errors in aided pursuit tracking in relation to target speed and aided-tracking time constant. *J. Appl. Psychol.*, 40, 367–70 (1956).

69. SMITH, W. M., SMITH, K. U., STANLEY, R., and HARLEY, W. Analysis of performance in televised visual fields: preliminary report. *Perceptual Motor Skills*, 6, 195–98 (1956).

70. SMODE, A. F. Learning and performance in a tracking task under two levels of achievement information feedback. *J. Exptl. Psychol.*, 56, 297–304 (1958).

71. STOCKBRIDGE, H. C. W., and CHAMBERS, B. Aiming, transfer of training, and knowledge of results. *J. Appl. Psychol.*, **42**, 148–53 (1958).
72. STRAHM, C. L. The influence of instruction on performance of a complex perceptual motor task. *Can. J. Psychol.*, **9**, 168–72 (1955).
73. SURWILLO, W. W. A new method of motivating human behavior in laboratory investigations. *Am. J. Psychol.*, **71**, 432–36 (1958).
74. TAYLOR, F. V. Simplifying the controller's task through display quickening. *Occupational Psychol.*, **31**, 120–25 (1957).
75. VANBERGEIJK, W. A., and DAVID, E. E., JR. Delayed handwriting. *Perceptual Motor Skills*, **9**, 347–57 (1959).
76. WALTON, D., and BEGG, T. L. The effects of incentives on the performance of defective imbeciles. *Brit. J. Psychol.*, **49**, 49–55 (1958).
77. WEGNER, N., and ZEAMAN, D. Team and individual performances on a motor learning task. *J. Gen. Psychol.*, **55**, 127–42 (1956).
78. WILLIAMS, D. C. S. Effects of competition between groups in a training situation. *Occupational Psychol.*, **30**, 85–93 (1956).
79. WOLFLE, D. Training. In *Handbook of Experimental Psychology*, Chap. 34, 1267–86. (Stevens, S. S., Ed., John Wiley & Sons, Inc., New York, N.Y., 1436 pp., 1951.)
80. ZIMNY, G. H. Effect of various motivational techniques upon learning and performance tasks. *J. Exptl. Psychol.*, **52**, 251–57 (1956).

Questions for Discussion

1. What are the three roles of feedback (or knowledge of results) described by Brown? Which role seems most important?

2. What may determine whether or not delayed feedback (or knowledge of results) is effective?

3. Why are the authors skeptical about the research on motivation and motor skills?

4. What distinction between "action" feedback and "learning" feedback does Annett make?

5. How can behavior be controlled by regulating the functions of error?

R. B. AMMONS, R. G. FARR, EDITH BLOCH,
EVA NEUMANN, MUKUL DEY, RALPH MARION,
and C. H. AMMONS

Long-Term Retention
of Perceptual Motor Skills*

Perceptual-motor skills involve the coordination of hand and
eye movements. In the next study the skill in question is a procedural task. Each subject must manipulate in particular sequences a number of switches, handles, buzzes, and so forth.
Student subjects, some of whom are from the department of
physical education, found this procedural task interesting.
Because about half of the physical education activities involve hand-eye coordination, this study has particular relevance.

The study is important in several respects. First, it concerns
long-term retention of what is learned—a perennial problem in
education generally and physical education in particular. Working for retention of skills from week to week and season to season often perplexes many teachers and coaches. In physical
education we hope that students will not only acquire skills but
also retain and develop them in the course of a lifetime. This
study points to the fact that to return to an earlier level of proficiency, a person takes more trials the longer the interval
without practice and the greater the amount of previous training. Second, the study is monumental in that 1,000 subjects (for
both experiments) were trained and 650 were retrained up to
two years later. One of the most difficult problems in conducting
studies on long-term forgetting is arranging for the return of
subjects, a task rather successfully managed in this study. Third,
the "no-practice" intervals ranged from one minute to two
years, an impressive range for the testing of this variable.
Finally the effects of the amount of training were investigated.

* Reprinted and abridged with permission of the senior author and the publisher
from the *Journal of Experimental Psychology*, vol. 55, No. 4, 1958, pp. 318–328.

It is commonly believed that perceptual-motor skills are well retained over no-practice intervals and are quickly relearned. Detailed information about the retention of such skills may be found in McGeoch and Irion (5). Of particular interest are studies reported by Tsai (9), Van Dusen and Schlosberg (10), and Jones and Bilodeau (3).

Several preliminary studies were carried out preparatory to the two major ones reported in the present paper.† There was no detectable loss of a procedural skill over a no-practice interval of 1 day (2), or of a compensatory pursuit skill over a no-practice interval of 1 month (1). On the other hand, half of the learned proficiency in performing another procedural skill was lost over a 2-day no-practice interval; and, after a 1-year no-practice interval, proficiency was little or no higher than on the first learning trial, with almost complete, even if transitory, loss of the skill (7). This indicates that not all perceptual-motor skills are well retained.

The purpose of the present studies was to measure the retention of two representative perceptual-motor skills following different amounts of initial training and following no-practice intervals up to approximately two years.

GENERAL PROCEDURE

In order to increase the generality of the findings as much as possible, it was decided to use one task which called for a fairly complex type of compensatory pursuit skill (Airplane Control Test) and another which called for the sequential manipulation of a series of "controls." "Pursuit" and "following a sequence" were judged to be important components of a great many activities.‡

† In order to simplify the reading of this paper, we will suggest some rough definitions of frequently used terms. *Perceptual-motor* (or *motor*) *skill*—a temporally and spatially patterned movement of body musculature, the perception of whose accuracy and timing partially determine whether attempts will be made to decrease the discrepancy between the actual movement and the "ideal" pattern. *Procedural* (or *sequential*) *skill*—a perceptual-motor skill that calls for the making of a series of simple movements in a particular order. *Compensatory pursuit skill*—a perceptual-motor skill that calls for subject movements to match movements of a piece of equipment, where subject movements alter and thus partially determine those of the equipment.

‡ Experiment II on the Airplane Control Test has been omitted.

It was necessary to control variables that might be correlated with particular times during the 3-yr. training and retraining period. The principal problem areas were those related to apparatus, *Es*, and composition of groups. Preliminary work (1, 2) had shown that certain maintenance procedures were sufficient to keep the apparatus fairly constant in properties.

The *Es* were all carefully trained by one supervisor, and were constantly supervised by him in order to insure consistent treatment of *Ss*.

Particular attention was paid to the composition of the groups. Only male university students served as *Ss*. Inspection of early results indicated that there were no detectable differences between *Ss* associated primarily with ages (college classes), so the main control was the source. An approximately equal proportion of each group came from the college of engineering, the physical education department, lower division general social science courses, psychology classes, and campus fraternities. The *Ss* were paid for work on the Airplane Control Test, but not for the procedural task, as the latter took much less time and was reported as more interesting and hence self-motivating.

Return of *Ss* for retraining was also an important problem. At the completion of training, a special effort was made to see that *S* released tensions and left with a good feeling, as this had been shown to be important in an earlier study in the laboratory (4). As many *Ss* as possible were persuaded to serve in both experiments.

Experiment I

PROCEDURE

The equipment for studying the learning and retention of a procedural task has been described in detail elsewhere (2). It consisted of a large vertical panel on which 17 control units were mounted (e.g., a knife switch, a toggle switch, an automobile turn indicator, an automobile door handle, a rotary switch, a doorbell buzzer, a sliding door latch), so arranged that an *S* sitting in position in front of the board could easily reach each one. Only 15 of the items were actually used in the training and retraining. These items were arranged in three different sequences, and each S was assigned randomly to one of the sequences which was then used for him in both the training and retraining sessions. No significant differences in performance on the three sequences had been found in a preliminary study.

The correct sequence was indicated on a schematic chart hanging on the panel. When S manipulated an item incorrectly (manipulative error) or out of order (sequential error), a large red signal light, mounted in the top center of the panel, went out. The S's task was to correct himself and turn the light on before proceeding, working as rapidly as possible. Each time through the sequence was counted as a trial, and 1-min. rests were given between trials. Time and errors were recorded for each trial. Preliminary work had indicated that there would be little or no reminiscence with this duration of intertrial rest. It should also be noted that Reynolds and Bilodeau (8) found that condition of distribution during training had little effect on performance, during the retraining period, of several perceptual-motor skills.

In one of the preliminary studies, verbal reports were elicited from a number of Ss in order to obtain some idea of the nature of the learning. Reports were in agreement that the first few trials were used to learn to identify the items and their correct sequence, as well as how to manipulate them correctly. The next step was to speed up the run, still using the schematic chart as a guide. Finally, S learned to go quickly through the sequence from memory without looking at the chart. In a preliminary study (2) it had been observed that, when items were identified by number, some Ss used these numbers in learning the sequence. For the present study, a chart was used which showed the correct sequence in terms of simplified line drawings of the items themselves.

Groups of from 40 to 47 Ss (total $N = 538$) were trained under each of 12 conditions representing two degrees of learning (5 trials and 30 trials) combined with six durations of no-practice interval (1 min., 1 day, 1 mo., 6 mo., 1 yr., 2 yr.). The Ss were tested for retention and retrained for 10 trials after the no-practice interval. Theoretical and actual mean durations of no-practice intervals for matched groups are given in Table 1.

Table 1
PERFORMANCE OF MATCHED GROUPS ON PROCEDURAL TASK

No-Practice Interval			Means (Min.)			Mean Retraining Trials to Reach Final Training Level
Theoretical	*Actual*	*N*	*First Training Trial*	*Last Training Trial*	*First Retraining Trial*	
Groups with 5 Training Trials.						
1 min.	1 min.	35	1.728	.370	.443	1.61
24 hr.	23.8 hr.	36	1.714	.371	.495	2.19
1 mo.	30.8 da.	31	1.752	.393	.749	3.39
6 mo.	189.0 da.	28	1.710	.397	.796	3.39
1 yr.	355.5 da.	23	1.835	.395	1.267	3.88
2 yr.	704.4 da.	25	1.784	.406	1.294	4.68
Groups with 30 Training Trials.						
1 min.	1 min.	35	1.773	.189	.206	2.46
24 hr.	24.3 hr.	31	1.750	.214	.261	4.35
1 mo.	30.4 da.	35	1.779	.203	.544	8.11
6 mo.	180.8 da.	20	1.688	.206	.922	8.60
1 yr.	353.8 da.	25	1.750	.202	.831	9.67
2 yr.	695.4 da.	23	1.616	.202	.866	8.88

RESULTS

Figure 1 shows the mean time per trial during training for 5-trial and for 30-trial matched groups. It can be seen that a very rapid

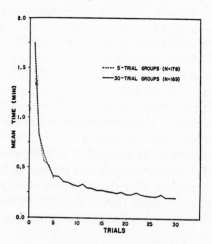

FIG. 1. Sequential Task: Performance during training period

decrease in time per trial takes place during the first few trials, and that later in practice performance levels off.

Mean time per trial during retraining is shown in Figs. 2 and 3. In general the longer the no-practice interval the greater the loss in performance, and relearning is rapid. Mean performance on the first trial after the no-practice interval for the various groups is given in Table 1. With the scores arranged in a 2×6 table, the variance was analyzed. It was found that both amount of training and duration of no-practice interval had significant effects, but that their interaction was not significant (F's of 20.44, 26.38, and 2.03,

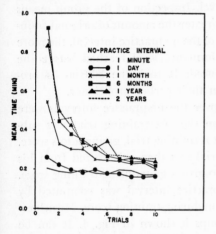

FIG. 2. Sequential Task: Performance of 5 training trial groups during retraining

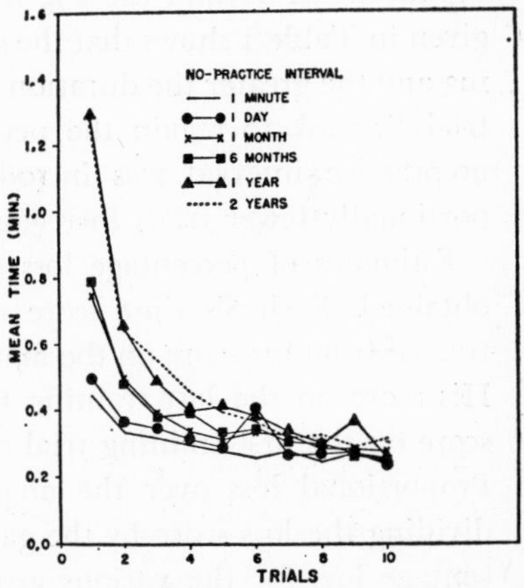

FIG. 3. Sequential Task: Performance of 30 training trial groups during retaining

respectively). The Bartlett test showed heterogeneity significant at far beyond the 1% level, the variance within groups being roughly correlated with the mean level of performance. For this reason, separate nonparametric tests were made for the groups with 5 and those with 30 training trials. The Ss in each of the 5-trial groups were classified as to whether they were above or below the Trial 6 median for the total 5-trial group. The χ^2 computed on the basis of this table was 78.52 with 5 df. The comparable χ^2 on Trial 31 for the 30-trial groups was 103.59. When less training is given before the no-practice interval and there is a greater duration of that interval, absolute performance level is lower immediately after an interval of no practice. This is quite clear from the graphs, the analyses of variance, and the χ^2 analyses.

Number of trials to relearn to the level reached on the last training trial was computed for each S. Where that level had not been reached by the end of retraining (Trial 10), S was arbitrarily given a score of 11 trials. These scores were arranged into a 2×6 table, and their variance analyzed to give a rough estimate of the effects of amount of training and duration of no-practice interval. The F's for both variables and their interaction were significant at far beyond the 1% level. The Bartlett test showed a heterogeneity significant at beyond the 1% level. Inspection of the group means given in Table 1 shows that the greater the amount of original training and the greater the duration of the no-practice interval, the more trials it took to regain the performance level reached before the no-practice interval was introduced. It took the 30-trial Ss proportionally fewer trials to regain their earlier proficiency.

Estimates of percentage loss over the no-practice intervals were obtained. Each S's time score on the last training trial was subtracted from his score on the first retraining trial, giving a loss score. His score on the last training trial was then substracted from his score on the first training trial to give a gain-during-training score. Proportional loss over the no-practice interval was computed by dividing the loss score by the gain-during-training score. Mean percentage loss for the various groups is shown in Fig. 4. It can be seen that proportional loss, when practice is interrupted, is greater the longer the no-practice interval and the less training given before that interval is introduced.

Inspection of Figs. 2 and 3 suggests that the effects of the longer no-practice intervals have not been completely overcome during the relearning, even after 10 trials. Analysis of variance (2×6 table) of the time scores at Trial 10 provides a rough check on this observation, even though score distributions are highly skewed and heterogeneous (Bartlett χ^2 of 129). The F's for amount of training, duration of no-practice interval, and their interaction, using the within-groups variance estimate as the error term, are respectively 39.46, 8.24, and .92. Thus, the results of the analysis of variance are consistent with the observation.

Although no formal analysis was made, records of errors were inspected for clear trends. It was observed that there was an over-all reduction in number of errors paralleling the reduction in time per trial. At the start of training, errors tended to be of the manipulative type, while later errors were almost all of the sequential type. After the no practice interval, Ss tended to show increased sequential but not manipulative errors, at least on the first trial.

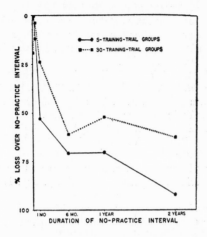

FIG. 4. Sequential Task: Performance loss over no practice interval

Summary

Twenty-two groups, ranging in size from 20 to 36 male college students, were trained to either a moderate or a high level of proficiency on a procedural task or on a compensatory pursuit task, then retrained after no-practice intervals up to 2 yr. in duration. Learning, retention, and relearning were measured. It was found that, on the bases of mean time taken per trial or percentage time on target per trial, absolute loss in level of proficiency was apparently not affected by amount of training and was greater the longer the no-practice interval. A greater *proportion* of proficiency was lost by groups receiving less training and groups receiving longer no-practice intervals. Retraining to the earlier level of proficiency took more trials the longer the no-practice interval and the greater the amount of training.

Literature Cited

1. FARR, R. G., DEY, M. K., and BLOCH, E. The Airplane Control Test: a compensatory pursuit task. *Percept. mot. Skills*, 1956, 6, 77–80.
2. FARR, R. G., RUSSELL, C. H., and MARION, R. Apparatus for studying serial motor learning. *Percept. mot. Skills*, 1956, 6, 93–96.
3. JONES, E. I., and BILODEAU, E. A. *Retention and relearning of a complex perceptual-motor skill after ten months of no practice.* San Antonio, Tex.: Human Resources Research Center, Lackland Air Force Base, June, 1953. (*Res. Bull.* 53–17).
4. LOWE, W. F. Post-experimental discussion and attitude toward psychology. *Percept. Mot. Skills Res. Exch.*, 1952, 4, 145–150.
5. MCGEOGH, J. A., and IRION, A. L. *The psychology of human learning.* (2nd ed.) New York: Longmans, Green, 1952.
6. MELTON, A. W. (Ed.) *Apparatus tests.* AAF Aviation Psychology Program Research Report No. 4, Restricted Supplement (Declassified). Washington, D.C.: U.S. Government Printing Office, 1947.
7. NEUMANN, E., and AMMONS, R. B. Acquisition and long-term retention of a simple serial perceptual-motor skill. *J. exp. Psychol.*, 1957, 53, 159–161.
8. REYNOLDS, B., and BILODEAU, I. M. Acquisition and retention of three psychomotor tests as a function of distribution of practice during acquisition. *J. exp. Psychol.*, 1952, 44, 19–26.
9. TSAI, C. A comparative study of retention curves for motor habits. *Comp. Psychol. Monogr.*, 1924, 2, No. 11.
10. VAN DUSEN, F., and SCHLOSBERG, H. Further study of the retention of verbal and motor skills. *J. exp. Psychol.*, 1948, 38, 526–534.

Questions for Discussion

1. Why is there rapid decrease in amount of time per trial after the first few trials?
2. What is the effect of increasing the length of the rest period on performance and relearning?
3. What is the effect of the amount of training on performance and relearning?
4. What implication does this study have for the following physical education program areas?
   a. curriculum planning
   b. spring practice
   c. swimming

CLYDE G. KNAPP and W. ROBERT DIXON

Learning to Juggle: I.
A Study to Determine the Effect
of Two Different Distributions
# of Practice on Learning Efficiency*

The length of the rest period is an important variable in the study by Ammons and his associates. In that study the primary focus is on long-term retention. The following study concerns original learning. It is designed to help answer two questions: (1) How long should a practice session be? (2) How long a rest should there be between sessions?

The reader will note that a definite relationship exists between the length of the practice sessions and rest periods.

The study has great relevance for physical education. As the authors explain, juggling employs a type of eye and hand coordination essential in many sports. The study also demonstrates how important physical skills can be studied experimentally to discover teaching conditions that make their acquisition easier. Most useful of all, inferences may be made regarding the desirable length and frequency of physical education classes.

Practice is one of the key conditions which must be considered in learning motor skills. This condition may be viewed in the light of at least seven variables whose influence seems to determine the amount of benefit derived from practice: 1) duration of the practice session; 2) length of the rest period between practice ses-

* Reprinted with permission of the senior author and the publisher from the *Research Quarterly*. Washington, D.C.: American Association for Health, Physical Education and Recreation, vol. 24, 1950, pp. 331–336.

sions; 3) practice method; 4) speed of movement during practice; 5) characteristics of the learner; 6) activity of the learner during the time between practice periods; and 7) complexity of the skill. These and other variables are the subject of much research by those interested in performance improvement.

Since practice does play such a prominent role in the learning of motor skills, it is essential that those charged with teaching these skills have a thorough understanding of the role played by the above mentioned variables during practice. The present study is concerned chiefly with the first two of these, specifically, duration of and the rest between practice periods. How long should a practice session be? How much time should elapse before the session may be repeated for the greatest efficiency? The earlier research on these questions was planned so as to identify the separate effect of each of the two variables. Thus, an experiment would be designed to measure the effect of different lengths of practice periods by maintaining a constant amount of rest between practice sessions and changing the length of the practice. By reversing the above arrangement the effect of different amounts of interpractice rest was studied.

As research on these two variables has continued it has become increasingly clear that there is a realtionship between them. Travis, who used a manual pursuit oscillator to study motor learning, states that "the length of the practice periods and the length of the interpractice rest are fundamentally related."[1] He infers that a longer practice period must be followed by a longer rest period for efficient learning. More recently Nance has found distributed paced practice superior to massed unpaced, distributed unpaced, and massed paced practice. He adds that "it is probable that the superiority of distributed practice is based upon the magnitude of the work-rest ratio and not upon absolute length of trial or rest taken separately."[2] Further evidence of the interrelationship between practice and rest may be found in the study by Spence, Buxton, and Melton.[3] As

[1] Travis, Roland. "Length of the Practice Period and Efficiency in Motor Learning," *Journal of Experimental Psychology*, **24** (March 1939), 339–45.

[2] Nance, R. Dale. "The Effects of Pacing and Distribution on Intercorrelations of Motor Abilities." Unpublished Ph.D. Dissertation, State University of Iowa, June, 1946.

[3] Spence, K. W., C. E. Buxton, and A. W. Melton. "The Effect of Massing and Distribution of Practice on the S.A.M. Complex Coordination Test." Civil Aeronautics Authority, Division of Research, December 1945, No. 53.

reported by Nance[4] these investigators used four different distributions of practice to measure learning on the S.A.M. Complex Coordination Test. At the end of the work period all the groups using distributed practice were superior to the continuous group. However, the group using the shortest work-rest ratio was *not* the most superior. Dore and Hilgard also emphasize the relationship when they state, "the optimum distribution of practice obviously lies somewhere between that overcrowding which disrupts practice and that separation which allows a loss of previous gains before practice is resumed."[5]

The present writers were interested in testing the inference made by Travis that longer work periods should be followed by longer rest periods for efficient learning. Would such an arrangement be as efficient as a shorter work-rest distribution? Incidentally, many persons inadvertently adopt the longer work-rest distribution when learning motor skills; they are unwilling or unable to practice regularly and attempt to compensate by engaging in long practice sessions with several days to a week intervening. We wanted to find an experimental situation which would employ a type of coordination closely associated with many sports activities and which would permit easy demonstrations to students. The motor skill of juggling was finally selected as a learning situation which would meet these requirements. Juggling or ball-tossing was a favorite subject of study among early psychological researchers, Swift[6] and Pederson[7] being two who reported using this technique. They were primarily concerned with discovering the nature of the learning curve.

PROCEDURE

Selection of Subjects. The subjects in the experiment were University of Illinois male seniors majoring or minoring in physical education. All of these men were doing student teaching in physical education.

Prior to the establishment of the experimental groups the number of potential subjects was cut down by eliminating those who

4 Nance, R. Dale, *op. cit.*

5 Dore, Leon R. and Ernest R. Hilgard. "Spaced Practice and the Maturation Hypothesis," *Journal of Psychology*, 4 (October 1937), 245–59.

6 Swift, Edgar James. *Mind in the Making.* New York: Charles Scribners Sons, 1909, viii–329.

7 Pederson, Joseph. "Experiments in Ball-tossing: The Significance of Learning Curves," *Journal of Experimental Psychology*, 2 (June 1947), 178–224.

already possessed some juggling skill. In a pre-test, consisting of three trials, each subject tried to juggle three paddle tennis balls. Subjects who made five or more consecutive catches on any one of the three trials were eliminated from the experiment.

By means of random selection, the subjects were placed in *two* groups of 35 men each. After the composition of the groups had been established, the backgrounds were studied to determine whether the groups were equal in athletic experience and competence. In terms of such criteria as high school letters, college squads, and college varsity letters the groups were well matched.

Practice Preparations and Instructions. An effort was made to orient the subjects in the juggling situation. For example, several demonstrations of juggling were presented. Also, a number of rules and suggestions were given to each subject. These were mimeographed and time was spent in class discussion of the items until each subject felt he fully understood how to proceed. The following is a duplicate of the above mentioned mimeographed material:

A. Rules
1. Only the whole method is permissible.
   a. You may not practice the hand movements without using balls.
   b. You may not practice the toss and catch using less than three balls.
2. During a juggle at least one ball must be in the air at all times. If two balls touch a hand simultaneously the count must stop.
3. Time and distribution of practice sessions, as stipulated for your group, must be followed exactly.

B. Suggestions
1. Start with two balls in the dominant hand.
2. Toss and catch the balls with rhythmical movements.
3. In tossing let the ball leave the hand approximately in front of the chin with the head facing forward.
4. Toss the ball to a height approximately equal to the top of your head.
5. Toss the ball so that it may be caught about six inches to the left, or right, of the sternum line at a height slightly above the belt.
6. Toss the ball to the inside of the ball about to be caught.

7. Watch the balls with a minimum of eye movement.
8. Concentrate on your task.
9. Relax.

Group I was instructed to practice juggling the three balls for *five minutes each day*, while Group II was to practice for *fifteen minutes every second day*. Subjects recorded the greatest number of consecutive catches made in each practice schedule until they had succeeded in making 100 consecutive catches. This was the criterion used to measure when the subject had learned to juggle. It will be noted that the above arrangement provides two different ratios of practice and rest: 1) a short practice followed by 24 hours rest; 2) a longer practice followed by a longer rest. This should permit us to ascertain whether or not the longer practice-rest ratio is as conducive to learning as the shorter ratio.

RESULTS

Table 1 presents a comparison of the average time required by the subjects in the two groups to learn to juggle. The mean score for Group I was 69.86 minutes and for Group II was 125.80 minutes. The significance of the difference between the two means was computed by using the Student-Fisher t test. A t value of 3.84 was derived which is significant at the 1 per cent level of confidence.

It will be noted that there are 35 subjects reported for Group I and only 31 subjects for Group II. Actually there were 4 more subjects in Group II when the experiment started, however, 4 gave up after they had spent over 200 minutes in trying to learn. Hence,

Table 1

COMPARISON OF THE FIVE MINUTE DAILY AND THE FIFTEEN MINUTE EVERY
SECOND DAY GROUPS IN TERMS OF THE MEAN NUMBER OF MINUTES
REQUIRED TO LEARN TO MAKE 100 CONSECUTIVE CATCHES
IN JUGGLING THREE BALLS

Group	N	Mean	σ	Diff.	$\sigma_{diff.}$	t	P
Five Minute Daily	35	69.86	48.20	55.94	14.98	3.84	< .01
Fifteen Minutes on Alternate Days	31	125.80	68.60				

their scores would not make the difference between the performances of the two groups less significant.

Inspection of the individual learning times of the subjects revealed wide differences. The range in Group I was from 19 minutes to 210 minutes while in Group II it was from 40 minutes to 270 minutes. The fastest subject in Group I learned more than eleven times as fast as the slowest subject in that group. Such wide variation in individual performance within these groups would seem to be as noteworthy as the difference between the average group performances.

Discussion of Results. The magnitude of the difference between the average performances of the two groups was startling to the authors. Whereas a substantial amount of individual variation might have been predicted, it is doubtful whether anyone would have forecast such a significant difference between the average group scores. The longer practice-rest ratio was certainly not as conducive to efficient learning as the shorter ratio. But, it should be noted that the subjects using the longer ratio learned to juggle in only 8 plus periods while it took the subjects using the shorter ratio 13 plus periods to reach our criterion. On the basis of these data it seems probable that one can compensate for missed practice sessions by engaging in longer work periods, at least as far as the number of such periods is concerned. Nevertheless, this procedure is relatively inefficient in terms of the amount of actual practice time.

To what shall this difference in learning rate be attributed? If Franklin and Brozek's[8] evidence relating to the ineffectiveness of changing the rest interval is accepted then the length of the work period must be the important factor. However, Travis[9] has equally good evidence which indicates that the length of the rest interval does play an important role in motor learning. Just why the shorter work-rest sessions facilitated more rapid learning remains a moot question. Possible determiners might be found in several of the concepts most frequently used to explain such results. Fatigue may have played a part. Motivation also undoubtedly entered the picture since the subjects' attitudes during the longer work periods were noticed to change. Frequently the men became tense, poorly coordinated, and irritated because of their inability to master the skill. Perhaps, too, the shorter work-rest ratio permitted differential forgetting to operate more effectively.

[8] Franklin, Joseph C. and Josef Brozek. "The Relation between Distribution of Practice and Learning Efficiency in Psychomotor Performance," *Journal of Experimental Psychology*, 37, No. 1 (February 1947), 16–24.
[9] Travis, Roland C. "Effect of the Length of the Rest Period on Motor Learning," *Journal of Psychology*, 3 (January 1937), 189–94.

Attention should be directed to the usefulness of the demonstration experiment technique as a teaching procedure. It may confidently be stated that the men learned much more than just juggling during the course of the experiment. For example, a constructive attitude toward experimentation and research was developed by most of the students. Numerous comments were made to the effect that "maybe there is something to this research business after all." Certainly there was noticeable improvement in the interest and zest with which the students approached the study of teaching methods.

SUMMARY AND CONCLUSIONS

The present study has described a demonstration of the effect of two different practice-rest conditions in learning to juggle. College seniors in physical education were selected as subjects. After eliminating those who were able to make five or more consecutive catches on a pre-test, the men were placed in one of two groups by means of random selection. The groups possessed an equivalent amount of athletic experience, as measured by high school letters and college varsity letters. The subjects in Group I practiced juggling 3 paddle tennis balls for five minutes daily until they were able to make 100 consecutive catches, while Group II practiced the same skill for fifteen minutes every second day.

The data from this demonstration indicate that: 1) the five minute daily practice sessions facilitated more rapid learning than the fifteen minute every second day sessions, one minute of practice in Group I proving to be as effective as 1.80 minutes in Group II; 2) fewer practice periods will be needed to learn a motor skill when a longer work-rest distribution is used; 3) wide individual differences may be expected in the learning of motor skills even among subjects who have had wide experience in related skills.

Questions for Discussion

1. How do the learning conditions for Group I and Group II differ? Express these relationships as ratios.
2. What is the advantage of the *longer* practice-rest rates?
3. What is the advantage of the shorter practice-rest ratio?

4. Are these findings consistent with those of Ammons and his associates?

5. In view of this research, would it be the reader's opinion that a beginning class in tennis should meet for practice daily or, as do most college classes, two times a week?

FRANCES M. COLVILLE

The Learning of Motor Skills as Influenced by Knowledge of Mechanical Principles*

The most rigorous tests for determining how much and how well students have learned are tests for transfer of learning. Transfer occurs when whatever is learned in one situation is applied to another, similar or different, situation. Educators try to promote conditions that favor transfer of learning among the various school subjects. Principles of democracy learned on the playing field hopefully transfer to social situations. Tests for transfer provide evidence that the student can not only respond appropriately to the stimuli used in the original teaching but also make (or generalize) the new response to a wide range of novel but related stimuli. The fact that learning does generalize frees us from the futility to which we would be condemned if a discrete response had to be acquired for each discrete stimulus. Transfer also has implications for the well-rounded as opposed to the specialized education.

The following experiment attempts to improve the learning of particular motor skills: rolling a ball against a surface from which it will rebound, catching a tennis ball in a lacrosse stick and catching a badminton bird on a tennis racquet, and, finally,

* Reprinted with permission of the author and publisher from *The Journal of Educational Psychology*, vol. 48, no. 6, October 1957, pp. 321–327.

the skill of archery. The experimental group studied selected physical principles as a substitute for part of its practice. For example, elementary physical education curriculum is based on the transference of this generalized learning concept. A student who learns how to kick a ball in the first grade should be able to generalize this learning, at least in part, to kicking of a football in the sixth grade. Also, as this study implies, transfer involves discrimination as well as generalization. Negative transfer, for example, applying inappropriately what is learned in bat swinging to golf club swinging, interferes with learning.

Many general principles of mechanics are relevant to the teaching, learning, and performance of activities included in the physical education curriculum. These principles may describe the motion of objects such as balls and racquets, movement of the body itself, or a combination of both.

The question has been raised as to whether knowledge of these general principles and an understanding of their application to these activities will facilitate the learning and improve the performance of pupils in physical education classes. Also of interest are questions concerning the influence of knowledge of these principles as applied to one activity upon subsequent learning of other activities to which the same principles apply. Results of a few experiments suggest that a pupil who understands a principle related to one skill may master a related skill more readily than the pupil whose experience has been restricted to specific instruction in technique without explanation of pertinent principles.

With reference to the teaching of a motor skill in which a specific principle of mechanics is involved, then, two questions have been raised:

1. What is the effect of knowledge of a principle upon immediate learning of a skill to which the principle applies?

2. What is the effect of knowledge of a principle learned in relation to one skill upon subsequent learning of a different or more complicated skill to which the same principle is applicable?

Reported investigations bearing on the acquisition and transfer of principles are limited, and although most authorities agree that general principles are probably transferable, little strong experimental evidence is available to support such a claim. Apparently, little or no experimentation has been done in the field of physical education on the effect of knowledge of principles of mechanics in learning situations involving body movement and large muscle activities.

Judd (7), and Hendrickson and Schroeder (4) reported that knowledge of the principle of refraction was beneficial in dart throwing and rifle shooting at a target under water. Cox (2) found that knowledge of principles involved in manipulating electrical equipment facilitated the assembling and stripping of such equipment. Other experimenters have reported similar results from investigations involving mathematics, mental games, spelling, card tricks, and mechanical puzzles (13, 11, 15, 10, 14, 8, 2). In contrast to these findings are a number of investigations in which the method of including instruction in the principles involved did not appear to be more effective. In studying the effect of drill versus the learning of generalizations related to addition and subtraction, Olander (9) found that the two methods appeared to be equally effective. Babitz and Keys (1) found similar results with college chemistry classes, and Hendrix (6) reported only one difference, significant at the 12% level, in her experiment with teaching algebraic generalizations.

With the exception of the experiments by Judd, Hendrickson and Schroeder, and Cox, all of the reported investigations have dealt with various types of learning other than motor learning, and only Judd's experiment involved skills requiring the coordinated use of large muscles of the body as well as fine coordinations of the fingers. Judd, and Hendrickson and Schroeder, while reporting a difference in favor of instruction in principles, included this instruction in such a way that additional time was allotted to the group receiving the instruction. Thus, the experimental groups had the advantage of additional time as well as additional information. Furthermore, Judd supplied no statistical analysis of his early experiment, and the other differences reported were significant at a statistical level below that which is usually considered acceptable.

In the present investigation, an attempt was made to control these ambiguities by using an experimental design which insured that both the experimental and the control groups spent equal amounts of time in learning and performing and by considering only those differences which were significant at the 5% level of confidence or above.

Method

PURPOSE OF THE STUDY

It was the purpose of this study to investigate certain questions related to the teaching of physical education activities in which specific principles of mechanics are involved. This problem was approached by: (a) selecting three principles of mechanics which are pertinent to motor skills; (b) selecting three motor skills, each of which utilizes one of the principles; (c) establishing for each skill two comparable groups of Ss, one of which was taught without reference to the principle involved, and the other of which was taught to understand and apply the principle; (d) comparing for each skill the performance of the two groups, one of which spent the entire time practicing the skill without reference to the principle involved, and the other of which spent part of the time practicing the skill and part of the time in learning the principle; (e) comparing for each skill the performance of the two groups in a similar or more complicated form of the skill to which the same general principle applies.

SELECTED PRINCIPLES AND SKILLS

The selected principles and the skills in which they are utilized were as follows:

Principle I. The angle of incidence is approximately equal to the angle of reflection. Skill: Rolling a ball against a surface, or surfaces, from which it would rebound.

Principle II. In stopping a moving object, the force opposing the momentum must be equal to the force of the momentum, and if the object is to be caught, this momentum must be dissipated by reducing the resistance of the catching surface. Skill: Catching a tennis ball in a lacrosse stick and catching a badminton bird on a tennis racquet.

Principle III. An object set in forward motion through the air by an external force is acted upon by the force of the momentum and by gravital acceleration. Skill: Archery.

PROCEDURE

Three parallel experiments were devised, each of which was designed to investigate performance of one of the three skills. The Ss for all three experiments were undergraduate women students at the University of Southern California. There were 36 Ss in the Ball Rolling experiment, 40 in the Catching experiment and 42 in the Archery experiment. (The Ss in the Archery experiment included some men whose scores were treated separately from those of the women.) For each of the experments the Ss were divided into two groups, one of which spent the entire time learning and practicing the skill, and the other of which spent part of the time learning about the principle and the rest of the time learning and practicing the skill. Each experiment consisted of two tests. During the First test the Ss of the nonprinciple group learned the skill and practiced. The Ss of the principle group learned the principle, and the skill, and practiced. The total amount of time spent by both groups was the same. During the Second test both groups practiced a similar or more complicated skill. Each group spent the same amount of time and no mention was made of the principle involved.

The Ball Rolling Experiment. The Ball Rolling experiment was designed to illustrate the principle describing the rebound of a ball. The apparatus consisted of a modified pinball machine plunger, a squash ball, a felt-covered table surface four feet wide and six feet long, and a target made of colored construction paper. The overall size of the target and each of its scoring divisions was determined by recording the hits made by a group of comparable Ss who were not used in the experiment. These Ss rolled the ball so that it would rebound from one side of the table as close as possible to the center of the adjacent side which was marked with a square of white paper. The rest of the side was covered with brown wrapping paper, and spots on this paper to which the ball rolled were marked in red pencil. This scoring sheet provided the basis for establishing a six-standard deviation scale, and from this scale the scoring areas of the target were derived.

The Ss were asked during the First test to roll the ball against one side of the table in such a manner that it would rebound to the target placed against the adjacent side. For the Second test they

were asked to roll the ball so that it would rebound from two
adjacent sides to the target set at right angles on the third side.

The Catching Experiment. The Catching experiment consisted of
two tests each involving the skill of catching a moving object. The
First test involved catching a tennis ball in a lacrosse stick. For
the Second test, they caught a badminton bird on a tennis racquet.
The apparatus for this experiment, in addition to balls, birds,
crosse, and racquet, included a homemade device for projecting
the tenn is ball and the badminton bird. This device proved to
have high reliability.

The Archery Experiment. The Archery experiment was planned
to illustrate the principle of gravital acceleration and its action
on arrow flight and the relation of line of flight to line of sight.
The First test involved shooting from 20 yards. The Second test
included ends shot from 30 yards, from 40 yards, and a Junior
Columbia Round.

Analysis of Data. In each experiment, the reliability of the
scores was established by use of the split-half technique, the odd
scores being correlated with the even scores. Use of the Spearman-
Brown Prophecy Formula for predicting reliability of the whole
test resulted in coefficients which ranged from .81 to .94 and thus
it was felt that these scores were sufficiently reliable to permit
further analysis and comparison.

All of the data were analyzed by means of analysis of variance
using Edwards' (3) technique for repeated measurements of the
same subjects. This technique tests differences between methods,
between trials, and between the interaction of trials and methods.
In each experiment the initial ability of the two groups, as evidenced by preliminary trials, was tested and found not to differ
significantly.

Findings

In the Ball Rolling experiment, no significant difference in the
performance levels of the two groups was found on either test. A
difference between trials significant at the 1% level of confidence
was found on both tests.

In the Catching experiment, no significant differences were
found in performance levels, and a difference between trials significant at the 5% level of confidence was found only on the First test.

In the Archery experiment no significant difference in performance levels was found. A difference significant at the 1% level for men and at the 5% level for girls was found on the Second test at all distances except forty yards.

The following general findings were noted:

1. A significant amount of learning took place under both methods of instruction.

2. This learning was not only similar in amount but also in pattern. Exceptions occurred in the Second test of the Catching experiment where no significant increase in scores occurred in either group, and in the Junior Columbia Round for men in the Archery experiment, where both groups increased in scoring ability, but the group which had been taught the principle was significantly better at twenty yards.

These findings are in general agreement with those of some published investigations and are opposed to those of some others. However, most of the reported experiments have dealt with various types of learning other than motor learning. The ability to use understood principles in performing a motor skill presents a complex problem since more than one type of learning is involved. As Ragsdale (12) has pointed out, a learner may understand a principle when applied to inanimate objects, but he may not understand and be able to apply it to his own movements. In general, it seems that the findings of this study support Ragsdale's observation, at least in the initial stages of acquiring an unfamiliar motor skill.

Conclusions

Within the limitations of the three parallel experiments which constitute the present investigation, there is no evidence:

1. That instruction concerning mechanical principles utilized in the performance of a motor skill facilitates the initial learning of the skill to any greater extent than an equivalent amount of time spent in practicing the skill.

2. That such knowledge facilitates subsequent learning as evidenced in the performance of a similar or more complicated skill to which the same principle is applicable.

However, since it appears that some part of the learning period may be devoted to instruction concerning general principles with out detriment to the motor learning of the students, it would seem desirable to include such instruction in order to provide this additional opportunity for acquiring some related knowledge about principles of mechanics and the application of forces.

Literature Cited

1. BABITZ, M., and KEYS, N. Experiment in teaching pupils to apply scientific principles. *Sci. Educ.,* 1939, **23**, 367–370.
2. COX, J. W. Some experiments on formal training in the acquisition of skill. *Brit. J. Psychol.,* 1933, **24**, 67–87.
3. EDWARDS, A. L. *Experimental design in psychological research.* New York: Rinehart, 1950.
4. HENDRICKSON, G., and SCHROEDER, W. H. Transfer of training in learning to hit a submerged target. *J. Educ. Psychol.,* 1941, **32**, 205–213.
5. HENDRICKSON, G., and SCHROEDER, W. H. Transfer of training. In R. G. Kuhlen and G. G. Thompson (Eds.), *Psychological studies of human development.* New York: Appleton-Century-Crofts, 1952.
6. HENDRIX, GERTRUDE. A new clue to transfer of training. *Elem. Sch. J.,* 1947, **48**, 197–208.
7. JUDD, C. H. Special training and general intelligence. *Educ. Rev.,* 1908, **36**, 38–42.
8. KATONA, G. *Organizing and memorizing.* New York: Columbia Univer. Press, 1940.
9. OLANDER, H. T. Transfer of learning in simple addition and subtraction. *Elem. Sch. J.,* 1931, **32**, 358–369; 427–437.
10. OVERMAN, J. R. Experimental study of the effect of the method of instruction on transfer of training in arithmetic. *Elem. Sch. J.,* 1930, **31**, 183–190.
11. PETERSON, J. C. The higher mental processes in learning. *Psychol. Monogr.,* 1920, **28**, No. 7 (Whole No. 129).
12, RAGSDALE, C. E. How children learn the motor types of activities. In N. B. Henry (Ed.) *Yearb. nat. Soc. Stud. Educ.,* **49**, Part I. *Learning and Instruction.* Chicago: Univer. of Chicago Press, 1950.
13. RUGER, H. A. The psychology of efficiency. *Arch. Psychol.,* 1910, **2**, No. 15.
14. THIELE, C. L. The contribution of generalization to the learning of addition facts. *Teach. Coll. Contr. Educ.,* 1938, No. 763.
15. WATERS, R. H. The influence of tuition upon ideational learning. *Psychol. Monogr.,* 1920, **28**, No. 7 (Whole No. 129).

Questions for Discussion

1. Why did the experimenter use three different skills? Were the results the same for each of the three?

2. Specifically, what changes were made for the transfer (or second) tests?
3. Why may the teaching of principles have failed to benefit the experimental group?
4. Why may the control group have beneficial work with practice?
5. Would you expect some transfer of learning between tennis and the following:
   a. Badminton?
   b. Lacrosse?
   c. Batting?
6. Explain your answers. List several general skills of physical education that might be identified and taught.

JAMES DEESE

Skilled Performance
and Conditions of Stress*

There is no area of psychology in greater confusion than the area of motivation. Both the layman and the teacher have confused learning and motivation. They frequently believe that motivation, whatever this is, inevitably leads to learning. One is almost ready to declare that much discussion of motivation in the journals represents the last of the major linguistic fictions in the study of human behavior.

To avoid this confusion and controversy and yet to deal with a more relevant, clearly defined, and useful concept, the editors have selected the following reading. It deals with the concept of stress (or, roughly speaking, discomfort) and its influence on the learning of skills. The major thesis is that stress is related to the skill rather than to personality traits or motivational

* Reprinted and abridged with permission of the author, editor and publisher from *Training Research and Education*, edited by R. Glaser. Pittsburgh, Pa.: The University of Pennsylvania Press, 1962, pp. 204–217.

states. The psychomotor abilities to which Deese refers will be described more fully in Fleishman and Hempel's articles.

The reader is encouraged to consider the implications of these data for stress and heart disease, stress and athletic skill performance, and stress and individual skill performance.

The emphasis just given to the stimulus definition of stress is by way of preparation for the presentation of a somewhat different approach to the analysis of the effects of stress upon skilled behavior. Much of what has been said thus far has concerned the stability of individual reactions to stress. This, however, is not the context in which concern over the question of stress and skilled behavior arose. Indeed, from the standpoint of the problem of the relationship between stress and skilled behavior, the assumption of *stable patterns* of reactivity to stress need not arise.

The usual assumptions that have been made about the relationship between the external stimulating conditions of stress and skilled performance may be stated as follows:

1. The most common assumption made by the layman concerning stress is that the conditions responsible for discomfort have in common a deleterious influence upon the performance of skilled acts. It is known, of course, that this assumption cannot be generally correct. The fact is, however, that much of the experimental work on stress and skilled performance has made the assumption of deterioration under stress something to be taken for granted. Indeed, a good deal of the earlier work on stress and skill could be characterized as a search for "sensitive" measures, i.e., measures that showed deterioration under stress. This preoccupation has led to a neglect of some of the important effects of stress.

2. A more sophisticated assumption says that there is a specific task component part of a great number of skills and that either positive or negative effects of stress can be predicted from the presence or absence of this component. This is the kind of assumption that provides the basis for the work of Spence, Taylor and others on the influence of anxiety drive upon performance during acquisition. Specifically these investigators have assumed an interaction between drive level and intratask interference and, by extension, an interaction between these and stress.

3. A more general assumption would be to assert that the effects of stress upon skilled performance are specific to particular components of the performance under consideration. This is the general viewpoint taken in this article. There are a variety of ways in which such an assumption could be correct. It could be correct if one assumed no generality across tasks. That is to say, it would be true if skilled behavior consisted of a large number of uncorrelated elements or dimensions. Such a situation would be very discouraging. The fact is, of course, that such extreme specificity is not the case. What is more, some general components seem to contribute to the performance of perceptual motor skills as well as to more general kinds of skills (Fleishman, 1956). Thus, it is safe to assume some generality of components of ability across a wide variety of tasks. The problem is then to determine how important each task component may be in reaction under stress. Consideration of this problem can lead to a "synthesis" of the influence of stress upon the performance of a particular task. This means that a study of the effects of stress upon task components rather than the tasks themselves is what is required. While this assumption—that stress may affect different components of skilled acts in different ways—cannot be dignified by the term theory, nevertheless it does lead to some interesting hypotheses. Before discussing some of the consequences of this notion, however, a brief discussion of the rationale of the notion itself may be useful.

One may arrive at the present view by considering the effects of stressful stimuli to be twofold. For one thing stressful stimuli arouse specific responses which may be either compatible with the components of a certain skill (and thus facilitate performance of that skill) or they may arouse responses which are incompatible and thus inhibit or interfere with the performance of the skill. It is this property of stressful stimuli that is most important to the present analysis. In addition, however, it can be assumed that stressful stimuli arouse tendencies to eliminate the stressful stimuli. The empirical grounds for this assertion are well enough known so that it is not necessary to review them here. This assumption does describe a motive state, and a word needs to be said about the motive, since something quite different from the traditional view is involved. Consider the possibility that the *escape or avoidance motive does not interact in any significant way with any of the components of the skill as such.* This view, of course, is in contrast with the views of the sort presented in the anxiety drive theory (Spence, 1958) or by those found in the more general theories relating motive states to need-achievement scores, etc. In these theories the aversive motive state directly influences performance.

The notion presented here implies that the motivational state aroused by the discomfort associated with stressful stimuli determines only the choice behavior of the individual with respect to the task he is performing. That is to say, an individual can choose to work faster, work slower, abandon the task altogether or to ignore stoically his discomfort. While one would suppose that an individual's choice of behavior would be influenced by his estimate of the likely outcome of the task (and hence of his own level of performance on the task), such an influence should have little or nothing to do with the specific components of the task. All other things equal, an individual should be just as ready to abandon one task as another under conditions of stress. Thus, an individual's choice about how to go about working at a task under stress should have nothing to do with whether the task is highly saturated with psychomotor coordination, or whether it demands the use of spatial relations, but should only be the result of the events likely to influence choice. If this notion is correct, then what is indicated is study of the influence of the motivational component of reactions to stress independently of any particular skill.

This separation of the influence of discomfort and the influence of the avoidance motive upon performance through choice behavior has been implied in some earlier work (see, for example, Conrad, 1950), but not much attention has been paid to it. There are, of course, many implications of this separation, but the major one for present purposes is that it permits concentrating directly upon the effects of discomfort arousal upon performance. Thus, it is implied that the major effects of stress upon performance of a particular task operate through the stimulus conditions of the moment. This emphasis upon stimulus conditions leads to the characterization of the present approach as dynamogenic.

In turning to the basic problem of the prediction of the effects of stress upon perceptual motor skills we may take as a point of departure Fleishman's (1954) analysis of the dimensions in psychomotor abilities. Fleishman's data and his analysis can be used to illustrate the general approach to the problem suggested here. The account presented here can only be regarded as an example, since the analysis is not independent of the particular tests used and cannot, therefore, be generalized to tests and skills at large. The method of analysis, however, can be generalized, and it is the method that is emphasized here.

Fleishman identifies ten relatively independent factors in the battery of tests he used. These are (*a*) wrist-finger speed, (*b*) finger dexterity, (*c*) rate of movement, (*d*) manual dexterity, (*e*) arm-hand steadiness, (*f*) reaction time, (*g*) aiming, (*h*) psychomotor coordination, (*i*) postural discrimination and (*j*) spatial relations. He presents a table of the loadings on the factors for the 40 tests he employed in his battery. These factor loadings will be used, in conjunction with the assumptions about the effects of stress on the motor components of behavior, to make some rough predictions about the effects of stress upon the skills represented by the test scores.

How this is done may be illustrated by some examples. Consider the four tests which have the highest loading on Factor I (wrist-finger speed, or speed of ballistic movement). According to the assumptions made above about stress and motor arousal, ballistic movements should have a shorter latency under the dynamogenic influence of stress. Therefore, the speed of ballistic movement should be greater. Thus, stress would result in a facilitation of a pure Factor I test. These four tests with high loadings on Factor I, however, also have loadings on other factors. It is quite possible that these other factors would lead to a prediction of deterioration under stress. Therefore, before a prediction may be made with respect to a test having significant loadings for more than one factor, it is necessary to take into account the other factors. In Fleishman's data, the first two of the four tests having a high loading on Factor I are two tapping tests. Both have loadings of .74 on Factor I, and neither have appreciable loadings on any other factor. One would therefore predict facilitation under stress for these two tests.

Stress and Training

The problem of stress and training presents a suitable area for the application of the kind of analysis suggested here. Any such application, it is well to remember, must take into account the fact that the distribution of skill components (the factor loadings) will change with practice at a task (Fleishman & Hempel, 1954 . . .). One thing is clear from the existing data; no simple idea about the effects of stress during training is adequate. Deese and Lazarus (1952) put forward the hypothesis, supported by some experimental evidence, that the effects of stress would be deleterious early in practice but not so later in practice. Aside from the fact that any such effect would be probably more easily described as the result of adaptation than anything else, there is no real evidence for accepting a general hypothesis of this sort. The point of the present account is that the effect of stress will depend upon the components involved in the skill being performed, and since the relevant components change as a function of practice, it is impossible to say generally what effects will happen early in training compared with late in training, or, indeed, whether or not there will be any differences between early and late practice. Knowing, however, how the components do change (and taking into account adaptation) it should be possible to predict the relative effects of stress upon early and late practice.

From time to time it has been suggested that the appropriate way to look at the problem of stress in training is by means of the transfer paradigm. Such an approach appears to be very reasonable, particularly if one accepts the identification of the concept of stress with stimulus conditions. The essential step in the analysis of stress from the point of view of transfer is in the identification of stimulus and response components. If either the case of stress present during training but not during later performance or the case of stress absent during training but present during later performance is considered, the principle is the same. The response components are the same[1] but the stimulus components change because stress is either absent or present. Classical transfer theory leads to the prediction of a decrement due to altered stimulus conditions. This stimulus generalization can be called decrement. Thus, if stress is absent during either training or performance but present for one of them, learning theory suggests the operation of stimulus generalization decrement and hence poorer performance.

Despite the general usefulness of the concept of stimulus generalization decrement, it will probably not be fruitful to try to make

---

[1] This statement may not be strictly true. Both the factor analytic work and some recent experimental and theoretical work in learning suggests the possibility that the response components of a given task actually do change during learning. Thus, it may not be possible to speak in strict accuracy of the "same" responses being performed during and after training.

use of this notion in understanding the problem of stress and training. The prediction of decrement will probably not hold with any degree of cross-task generality. This is partly because of the loose stimulus character of stress. While any stressful stimulus has a stable component that gives rise to the condition of stress, the specific components of such stimuli vary widely in their composition. Thus, the question of stimulus patterning must enter any predictions about the effects of stress made from the point of view of the transfer paradigm. Therefore, it appears that the occasionally stated view that stress should be deliberately introduced during training if it is to be expected during performance is not so sound as it first appears.

Another difficulty with the application of the transfer paradigm to the problem of stress and training is more important and also more complicated. Furthermore, the extent to which the difficulty is significant depends upon some assumptions about the nature of transfer in motor skills, assumptions that are not universally agreed upon. It can be stated, however, that any stimulus generalization decrement of the sort that could be involved in stressful stimuli and skills may be primarily influential over what can be called the cognitive control of psychomotor skills. If this is so, stimulus generalization decrement would be mainly influential over the verbal and stimulus pre-differentiation aspects of particular tasks. Little is known about such influences, particularly with the kind of complicated skills to which predictions must eventually be addressed. . . .

In summary, the present analysis does not suggest anything unique about the training situation. The components of skill do change as a function of practice, and hence the specific predictions about the effects of stress upon a particular skill must change. Thus, the training situation would demand nothing more than the reapplication at successive levels of skill of the kind of analysis of the factor structure of tasks suggested earlier. If the notion of stimulus generalization decrement turns out to be significant for a particular set of tasks, the question of whether or not original training was done under conditions of stress like those to be expected in actual performance may be important. It is likely, however, that other sources of differences between the training and performance situation will be so much more important as to swamp any effects due to generalization decrement.

Finally, a word needs to be said about the autonomic concomitants of stress and arousal. These do occur, and a variety of theorists have given them crucial roles in the influence of stress upon behavior. Little attention has been paid, however, to the question of skills and autonomic arousal. It has always been assumed that any effects autonomic arousal had upon performance were indirect ones achieved through changes in the motivational state. It may be, however, that there are more direct influences. The present author has suggested elsewhere (Deese, 1958) that autonomic arousal may be responsible for direct interference with the performance of certain skilled acts. The hypothesis is that such interference was the result of distraction. If this hypothesis is correct, certain kinds of effects are to be expected. Those skills which involved a high level of vigilance should suffer by the distracting stimuli arising from autonomic arousal, whereas those skills which involve repetitive performance of simple movements should not.

Such guesses do little more, however, than emphasize the need for an analytic approach to the problem of stress and skilled performance. It is necessary to know the details of the effects of stressful stimuli upon behavior generally (the sort of details that come from the studies of autonomic and skeletal activity as well as the studies of mood changes under stress), and it is necessary to know the components of particular skills to be performed under stress. The contribution of specific research on stress and skills should be directed towards the correlation between the general patterns of arousal under stress and the relevancy of particular components of skill. The fundamental difficulty with much of the experimental work thus far on stress and skilled behavior is a deficiency in analysis and synthesis. This article has had the purpose of suggesting the usefulness of factor analysis of tasks in trying to understand the variable influence of stress upon skilled behavior.

Further Readings

CONRAD, R., "Speed and Load Stress in a Sensory-motor Skill," *Appl. Psychol. Res. Unit* (Cambridge), 1950, APU 134/50.

DEESE, J., *Psychology of Learning*, 2d ed. New York: McGraw-Hill, Inc., 1958.

DEESE, J., and R. S. LAZARUS, *The Effects of Stress Upon Psychomotor Performance. USAF Hum. Resour. Res. Cent. Res. Bull.*, 1952, No. 5219.

FLEISHMAN, E. A., "Dimensional Analysis of Psychomotor Abilities," *J. Exp. Psychol.*, vol. 48 (1954), pp. 437–454.

FLEISHMAN, E. A., "Psychomotor Selection Tests: Research and Applications in the U.S. Air Force," *Personnel Psychol.*, vol. 9 (1956), pp. 448–467.

FLEISHMAN, E. A. and W. E. HEMPEL, "Changes in Factor Structure of a Complex Psychomotor Test as a Function of Practice," *Psychometrika*, vol. 19 (1954), pp. 239–252.

MEYER, D. R., "On the Interaction of Simultaneous Responses," *Psychol. Bull.*, vol. 50 (1953), pp. 204–220.

SPENCE, K. W., "A Theory of Emotionally Based Drive (D) and Its Relation to Performance in Simple Learning Situations," *Amer. Psychologist*, vol. 15 (1958), pp. 131–141.

TAYLOR, JANET A., "Drive Theory and Manifest Anxiety," *Psychol. Bull.*, vol. 53 (1956), pp. 303–320.

TAYLOR, JANET A., "The Effects of Anxiety Level and Psychological Stress on Verbal Learning," *Abnorm. Soc. Psychol.*, vol. 57 (1958), pp. 55–60.

Questions for Discussion

1. What would one infer from this article about the difference between learning a skill under little stress, and performing the same skill in actual competition under stress?

2. Of what level of organization are those activities regarded as "low stress yielding"?

3. Do these data purport to substantiate any position on the effect of stress and little-league performance?

4. Do diet, rest, and general health conditions relate to stress as well as to psychological condition? If so, how?

5. How does Deese's analysis of stress differ from that of the layman?

6. What two tendencies do stressful situations arouse in individuals?

7. What distinction does Deese make between the influence of stress and the influence of motive?

8. Why is it difficult to predict whether stress will have a deleterious effect either early or late in practice?

EDWIN A. FLEISHMAN
and WALTER E. HEMPEL, JR.

Changes in Factor Structure
of a Complex Psychomotor Test
as a Function of Practice*

The following article has major significance for ability testing
and training programs in physical education. It represents the
first in a series of studies that tries to develop a way of classifying skills in terms of the abilities necessary for their performance. The *abilities* to which the authors refer are stable traits
of individuals and apply to the performance of a wide variety
of skills. For example, as Fleishman has suggested, spatial
visualization, the name given to one ability, is related to such
diverse tasks as aerial navigation and dentistry.

Factor analysis is a sophisticated statistical technique and
requires more explanation and study than can be provided here.
It is used to enable the researcher to handle many correlations
at the same time and to see if these correlations can be accounted for *by a single ability factor or by several different
factors.* Factor analysis involves the administration of several
different tests so that eventually a minimum number of discrete
abilities are identified. This technique as applied to athletic
ability is illustrated in the reading following this one.

In this study the authors identify all the psychomotor ability
factors previously discussed in psychological journals. The illusion that there are general skill abilities (such as manual
dexterity), any one of which may govern a given skill, should
be laid to rest. Also, the recognition that different abilities are

* Reprinted with permission of the authors and the publisher from *Psychometrika,*
vol. 19, no. 3, September 1954, pp. 239–252.

important in the different phases of learning a skill should discourage attempts to predict future success in terms of initial performance.

In some previous studies . . . evidence was found that even during the short time of administration of a single psychomotor test, the ability or abilities sampled may shift materially in importance. This was indicated by variations in the factor patterns and in the weights of particular factors at various stages of practice on the particular tests investigated. Similar results also had been found earlier in factorial studies of extended practice on printed tests. . . . The problem appears more crucial in the psychomotor area, however, since measures of such skills typically show quite rapid and extensive improvement with even brief amounts of practice. It then becomes important to establish what abilities are being sampled at different stages in performance as practice is continued on particular psychomotor tasks. Such knowledge would have implications for future test development in this aptitude area as well as for questions concerning the processes involved in the learning of complex perceptual-motor skills.

Purpose

The study to be reported here was designed to investigate further the nature of these changes in ability patterns which seem to occur as practice continues on a complex psychomotor test. More specifically, an attempt was made to *identify* the factors involved at different stages of performance on a criterion psychomotor task, through the inclusion of well-established reference variables in the analysis. The interpretation of the nature of the factors involved at various practice stages has been limited in the earlier studies by the absence of such sufficiently well-defined reference variables. Moreover, in the present study practice on the criterion task was continued over a considerably longer time period than had been investigated previously.

The analysis also was aimed at identifying (1) the stages of practice in which the task is most complex (in terms of the number of abilities sampled), (2) the stages at which systematic changes in factor structure occur, (3) the stage at which the factor structure becomes stabilized, (4) the relative importance of "motor" versus "non-motor" factors at early and late stages of practice.

Method

A factor analysis of performance at various stages of practice on the criterion task together with selected reference tests was carried out by the Thurstone Centroid Method (4). The analysis is based on a sample of 197 basic airmen tested at Lackland Air Force Base. Variables in the analysis are described below.

THE CRITERION PRACTICE TASK

The Complex Coordination Test, Model E, was the criterion task learned. The test has been described in detail elsewhere by Melton (2). Essentially, the subject is required to make complex motor adjustments of an airplane-type stick and rudder in response to successively presented patterns of visual signals. A correct response (movement of stick and rudder controls to proper positions) is not accomplished until both the hands and feet have completed the appropriate movements. A new pattern appears as each correct response is completed. Score is the number of correct responses completed in a given test period. This task was selected since it has a high learning ceiling, shows no appreciable decrease in relative variability between subjects as practice is continued, and was suspected to be factorially complex. The acquisition curve for this task has been presented elsewhere. . . .

Practice on the test was continued over 64 two-minute trials. For each subject, testing was accomplished over a two-day period, each day involving a morning and afternoon session. Each session included 16 trials separated by one-minute rest intervals.

Scores obtained during the following eight segments of the total practice period were selected for inclusion in the present analysis:

1. Stage 1—Trials 1–5.
2. Stage 2—Trials 12–16.
3. Stage 3—Trials 17–21.
4. Stage 4—Trials 28–32.
5. Stage 5—Trials 33–37.

6. Stage 6—Trials 44–48.
7. Stage 7—Trials 49–53.
8. Stage 8—Trials 60–64.

These stages of practice on the criterion task, which represent the first eight variables in the present analysis, include the first and last ten minutes of practice during each of the four testing sessions.

TEST VARIABLES

The following printed tests were included in the analysis. They have been described in detail by Guilford (1).

9. Numerical Operations—II. A highly speeded test requiring simple subtraction and division operations.
10. Dial and Table Reading. A series of instrument dials and mathematical tables from which information must be read accurately and quickly.
11. Mechanical Principles. Pictorial items which require the comprehension of principles and mechanisms, such as leverage, and rotation and transformation of motion, involved in the action and uses of various mechanical devices.
12. General Mechanics. Verbally presented items of practical mechanical information dealing with the use and operation of familiar mechanical methods and devices.
13. Speed of Identification. Pictorial items in which the silhouette of an object must be identified quickly when it is rotated and imbedded in a group of similar silhouettes.
14. Pattern Comprehension. A series of drawings requiring visualization of relationships between components of solids and their unfolded flat projections.
15. Visual Pursuit. From a series of mazes of irregularly curved lines, the task is to trace each line visually from its beginning to its proper termination point.
16. Decoding Test. A series of short words, written in a code of flag symbols, must be decoded by relating the position of repeated symbols to the positions of repeated letters.
17. Instrument Comprehension. For each item which presents views of cockpit instruments the examinee must determine the proper position or orientation of an airplane.
18. Spatial Orientation. From a large aerial photograph or map,

the examinee must find the area that matches each of a series of small photographs.

19. Speed of Marking. The examinee marks an IBM answer sheet in the indicated spaces as rapidly as possible.

20. Log Book Accuracy. On an IBM answer sheet, the examinee marks as quickly and accurately as possible the proper letter indicated in a separate test booklet.

The following apparatus tests were included. They have been described in detail by Melton (2).

21. Rotary Pursuit. The examinee attempts to keep a stylus in contact with a small metallic target set in a rapidly revolving disk.

22. Plane Control. The task is to make compensatory adjustments of stick and pedal controls in order to keep a model plane straight and level.

23. Discrimination Reaction Time. The examinee manipulates one of four toggle switches as quickly as possible in response to a series of visual stimulus patterns differing from one another with respect to the spatial arrangement of their component parts.

Three additional apparatus tests which have not been described elsewhere were also included.

24. Nut and Bolt. The task is to insert and fasten as many nut and bolt assemblies as possible through a series of holes in an upright metal plate.

25. Reaction Time. A series of reactions in which the examinee must move his hand six inches as quickly as possible to a switch in response to a light stimulus which appears at varying intervals.

26. Rate of Movement. The examinee's task is to break the beams between a series of photoelectric cells, one after another, by making scalloped movements of his hand as rapidly as possible.

Results

INTERPRETATION OF FACTORS

The intercorrelations (Pearson product-moment) among the 26 variables are presented in Table 1. Ten factors were extracted from this matrix. The complete centroid factor matrix obtained is presented in Table 2. Orthogonal rotations were made using Zimmerman's graphical method (7). Table 3 presents the orthogonal solution of rotated factor loadings obtained using the criteria of simple structure and positive manifold.

Variables having orthogonal projections of .30 or larger on the rotated axes were considered in defining a factor. However, loadings of .25 or higher are considered significant (see Table 3). Interpretations given certain of the factors have drawn on several previous Air Force analyses. . . .

Factor I is common only to stages of practice on the criterion task, the Complex Coordination Test. Moreover, it can be seen (Table 3) that the loadings increase progressively through stage 4 and then remain at about the same level through the remaining practice stages. For the present, this factor is called the *Complex Coordination Test Specific.*

Factor II is common to all eight stages of practice on the Complex Coordination Test and to the Rotary Pursuit Test. It also shows a low loading in the Plane Control Test. This factor appears to be the same as the factor called *Psychomotor Coordination* in many previous analyses of the Aircrew Classification Batteries. It has consistently been identified in all analyses which have included the Rotary Pursuit and Complex Coordination Test (the latter represented by stage 1 in the present analysis). The factor has been defined rather broadly as representing either coordination of the large muscles of the body, in movements of moderate scope, or coordination of such movements with the perception of a visual stimulus.

The present analysis indicates that this factor is most adequately sampled in stages 2 and 3 of the Complex Coordination Test, but that it maintains its importance at all stages of practice on the test.

Factor III is defined primarily by the two apparatus tests, Reaction Time and Rate of Movement, which are practically pure measures of this factor. Significant loadings are also evidenced by the Rotary Pursuit, Plane Control, and Discrimination Reaction Time Tests. It seems clear that this factor may be defined as *Rate of Movement.* It is possible that this factor extends beyond rate of arm movement to leg and feet movements as well.

With respect to the importance of this factor at different stages of practice on the criterion task, we may again refer to Table 3. It

Table 1
INTERCORRELATIONS AMONG TEST AND PRACTICE TASK VARIABLES[a]

Test	1	2	3	4	5	6	7	8	9	10	11	12	13	14	15	16	17	18	19	20	21	22	23	24	25	26
1. Practice Stage 1, Complex Coordination	—	75	73	66	64	57	63	59	28	51	49	38	50	55	43	50	44	47	46	33	51	40	50	36	08	25
2. Practice Stage 2, Complex Coordination		—	85	85	84	79	77	79	30	46	40	31	45	41	47	38	38	39	41	32	51	45	44	30	22	32
3. Practice Stage 3, Complex Coordination			—	85	83	79	81	79	30	45	39	29	46	44	45	39	42	46	44	35	59	44	48	31	27	31
4. Practice Stage 4, Complex Coordination				—	85	83	86	85	30	45	39	27	41	44	42	32	40	40	40	34	51	44	42	32	30	28
5. Practice Stage 5, Complex Coordination					—	90	88	86	22	37	36	25	37	37	39	34	31	38	36	33	50	42	38	28	30	34
6. Practice Stage 6, Complex Coordination						—	90	86	22	34	29	20	31	27	34	24	27	31	33	28	47	39	33	25	27	37
7. Practice Stage 7, Complex Coordination							—	85	23	36	33	25	32	33	36	29	28	39	39	31	50	39	35	24	33	37
8. Practice Stage 8, Complex Coordination								—	24	34	30	24	35	29	38	29	30	35	34	28	49	36	33	26	27	30
9. Numerical Operations—II									—	63	32	23	44	34	23	45	42	31	37	40	22	08	39	13	09	12
10. Dial and Table Reading										—	54	43	61	59	40	61	51	54	49	50	38	22	54	28	05	24
11. Mechanical Principles											—	52	46	52	34	43	30	44	33	26	27	22	37	27	-05	12
12. General Mechanics												—	29	30	17	32	30	32	17	23	26	29	30	30	15	04
13. Speed of Identification													—	57	44	58	40	58	55	48	31	23	52	31	03	22
14. Pattern Comprehension														—	43	60	44	49	45	39	39	31	54	30	10	26
15. Visual Pursuit															—	33	35	46	32	32	29	20	38	24	08	16
16. Decoding																—	53	59	41	32	24	19	55	22	11	18
17. Instrument Comprehension																	—	46	34	22	28	29	47	31	06	24
18. Spatial Orientation																		—	49	37	40	21	41	26	14	15
19. Speed of Marking																			—	55	26	18	43	20	23	28
20. Log Book Accuracy																				—	27	19	43	18	26	28
21. Rotary Pursuit																					—	35	34	28	20	28
22. Plane Control																						—	36	20	23	20
23. Discrimination Reaction Time																							—	22	05	25
24. Nut and Bolt																								—	05	14
25. Reaction Time																									—	30
26. Rate of Movement																										—

[a] Decimal points omitted.

Table 2

CENTROID FACTOR LOADINGS OF TEST AND PRACTICE TASK VARIABLES[a]

Test	I	II	III	IV	V	VI	VII	VIII	IX	X	h^a
1. Practice Stage 1, Complex Coordination	79	04	20	-17	-09	-11	-13	13	07	10	76
2. Practice Stage 2, Complex Coordination	83	34	12	03	-07	-05	-16	08	14	-13	90
3. Practice Stage 3, Complex Coordination	85	33	07	01	-08	-07	-05	13	04	-05	87
4. Practice Stage 4, Complex Coordination	83	43	13	13	02	04	-06	-04	-09	-12	93
5. Practice Stage 5, Complex Coordination	80	48	13	10	03	10	-05	-10	-01	01	92
6. Practice Stage 6, Complex Coordination	75	52	07	14	09	13	-02	-09	05	-02	89
7. Practice Stage 7, Complex Coordination	77	48	09	15	06	08	05	05	-06	14	90
8. Practice Stage 8, Complex Coordination	76	48	14	15	07	11	10	04	-02	02	87
9. Numerical Operations – II	49	-35	-21	21	21	19	-11	19	09	-10	59
10. Dial and Table Reading	71	-44	-08	07	22	10	-10	12	14	04	80
11. Mechanical Principles	56	-29	33	-14	23	-04	-12	-10	07	05	62
12. General Mechanics	45	-20	13	-26	36	-15	-06	07	-22	-05	53
13. Speed of Identification	68	-37	02	15	-17	-08	-03	-10	-05	-03	66
14. Pattern Comprehension	65	-35	07	-17	-14	05	-10	-17	11	15	67
15. Visual Pursuit	55	-11	12	10	-18	-08	14	-04	14	-13	43
16. Decoding	62	-41	06	-03	-17	27	-05	17	-12	14	72
17. Instrument Comprehension	57	-25	-08	-17	-09	19	14	15	-04	-15	53
18. Spatial Orientation	64	-31	14	07	-11	-08	20	08	-10	15	63
19. Speed of Marking	60	-23	-14	24	-13	-14	-08	-07	-05	19	57
20. Log Book Accuracy	53	-21	-25	30	05	-22	-08	-18	-04	11	58
21. Rotary Pursuit	60	17	-10	-13	04	-17	15	13	10	08	50
22. Plane Control	47	16	-07	-29	-03	-07	-09	-03	-13	-09	38
23. Discrimination Reaction Time	64	-22	-15	-12	-18	12	-16	03	-07	-10	58
24. Nut and Bolt	41	-07	10	-18	08	-10	15	-09	-03	-11	27
25. Reaction Time	27	24	-39	03	-05	03	10	-11	-19	-04	34
26. Rate of Movement	39	13	-31	-06	-08	06	08	-21	14	13	36
$\Sigma a^2/k$	41	10	03	02	02	02	01	01	01	01	

[a] Decimal points omitted.

Table 5

ROTATED FACTOR LOADINGS OF TEST AND PRACTICE TASK VARIABLES[a]

Test	Factors										h[a]
	I CC	II PC	III RM	IV SR	V P	VI Vz	VII ME	VIII N	IX PS	X Res	
1. Practice Stage 1, Complex Coordination	24	48	10	39	20	38	28	03	22	02	76
2. Practice Stage 2, Complex Coordination	45	62	26	24	26	17	21	04	15	-15	90
3. Practice Stage 3, Complex Coordination	41	60	33	29	27	16	19	03	18	01	88
4. Practice Stage 4, Complex Coordination	62	45	38	20	25	06	25	00	18	-03	93
5. Practice Stage 5, Complex Coordination	65	46	40	11	16	13	22	00	15	01	92
6. Practice Stage 6, Complex Coordination	63	47	43	02	15	12	20	06	09	-01	89
7. Practice Stage 7, Complex Coordination	60	48	40	12	13	13	16	06	17	21	90
8. Practice Stage 8, Complex Coordination	62	47	37	10	22	10	18	04	08	17	88
9. Numerical Operations – II	07	07	05	21	25	03	16	66	09	-05	59
10. Dial and Table Reading	07	13	03	26	32	30	30	60	21	00	79
11. Mechanical Principles	17	06	-14	15	24	41	49	14	20	-02	60
12. General Mechanics	-03	05	00	26	14	06	62	08	16	13	52
13. Speed of Identification	12	01	10	35	47	29	08	21	37	-09	65
14. Pattern Comprehension	07	04	10	33	23	60	19	18	21	-11	60
15. Visual Pursuit	15	20	09	16	50	24	02	04	11	-06	42
16. Decoding	17	-03	01	59	22	36	06	35	10	11	71
17. Instrument Comprehension	02	09	20	46	35	20	16	24	-12	03	52
18. Spatial Orientation	10	07	04	35	45	32	09	12	27	26	61
19. Speed of Marking	10	09	20	23	26	24	-03	26	50	00	56
20. Log Book Accuracy	03	05	27	04	27	12	07	31	55	-05	58
21. Rotary Pursuit	03	48	34	12	21	18	18	06	10	17	51
22. Plane Control	07	25	33	29	04	09	29	-10	07	-09	38
23. Discrimination Reaction Time	08	12	25	52	22	23	13	24	12	-18	58
24. Nut and Bolt	03	08	14	12	29	17	32	-07	03	03	26
25. Reaction Time	06	08	54	08	03	-11	-03	03	07	01	33
26. Rate of Movement	03	17	48	-01	04	28	-03	12	07	-05	36
Σa²/k	10	10	08	08	07	06	06	05	05	01	

[a] Decimal points omitted.

can be seen that the first stage of practice shows an insignificant loading on this factor, but that subsequent stages show a progressive increase to a point later in training, where the loadings become stabilized.

Factor IV appears to be a *Spatial Relations* factor. Most direct evidence for this interpretation is found in the significant loadings of the Discrimination Reaction Time, Instrument Comprehension, Complex Coordination, and Dial and Table Reading Tests, which have consistently been found saturated with this factor. The loadings of the remaining tests on this factor are not inconsistent with the interpretation of this factor as primarily Spatial in nature. A possible exception is the relatively high loading of the Decoding Test. It is, thus, possible that Factor IV may be a composite of Reasoning and Spatial Relations factors. However, the remaining tests are primarily spatial in nature. This factor seems to involve the ability to relate different responses to different stimuli, where either stimuli or responses are arranged in spatial order. Emphasis in this Spatial factor appears to be on decision as to direction of movement.

It can be seen in Table 3 that this factor is most importantly involved in the fist stage of practice on the Complex Coordination Test and is not found in later stages of practice.

Factor V is defined primarily by the Visual Pursuit, Speed of Identification, and Spatial Orientation Tests, and also by Instrument Comprehension and Dial and Table Reading. This factor is readily defined as *Perceptual Speed*. It involves the rapid comparison of visual forms and the notation of similarities and differences in form and detail.

It is found in the Complex Coordination task only to a low degree with a loading of .25 or above only in certain of the earlier stages of practice.

Factor VI is defined principally by Pattern Comprehension and Mechanical Principles and also by Decoding, Spatial Orientation, and Dial and Table Reading. The tests with the two highest loadings have consistently identified a factor called *Visualization*. It appears to represent the ability to make "mental" manipulations of visual images or to comprehend imaginary movements. It is found, for example, in tests requiring the examinee to imagine the rotation of depicted objects in three-dimensional space, the folding or unfolding of flat patterns, the relative changes in position of objects in space, and the motion of machinery. In the present analysis, the Complex Coordination Test was found to sample this factor only in the first stage of practice.

Factor VII is readily identified from its high loadings in the General Mechanics and Mechanical Principles Tests. It has been called *Mechanical Experience* in previous analyses. In the present study this factor also contributes somewhat to the Nut and Bolt, Plane Control, and Dial and Table Reading Tests.

With respect to the Complex Coordination Test, the factor appears more involved in the early stages of practice, but only to a low degree. Loadings are not significant in the later stages of practice.

Factor VIII is identified from the high loadings of the Numerical Operations and Dial and Table Reading Tests as the *Numerical Facility* factor. The presence of this factor in tests involving the location and use of numbers as well as in those tests involving computation confirms a previous suggestion (6) that the definition of this factor must be broadened to include more than computational facility. This factor was not common to the Complex Coordination Text at any of the stages of practice.

Factor IX is most strongly sampled by the Log Book Accuracy and Speed of Marking Tests. These two tests have previously defined a factor labeled *Psychomotor Speed* (1). It appears, however, that this factor is confined to printed tests which require simple, rapid movements (marking an answer sheet). It is not common to any of the apparatus tests and is distinct from the Rate of Movement factor. The name Psychomotor Speed, thus, appears too broad since many kinds of tasks involve speed. Whether this factor is broader than speed of marking or whether it represents speed in very simple restricted movements as contrasted with the more gross movement involved in the Rate of Movement factor must await additional data.

Factor X is a residual factor.

Factor Pattern in Relation to Practice

The results indicate clearly that considerable changes occurred in the factor structure of the criterion task as practice on the task was continued. It also is evident that these changes were quite systematic. It appears useful to examine the nature of these changes more closely.

The results indicate that the Complex Coordination Test was most complex (showed higher loadings on more factors) during the first stage of practice, and that the test became less complex factorially as practice was continued. Thus, the last four stages of practice show significant loadings on only three factors, while during the first two stages significant loadings were obtained on seven different factors.

Moreover, the somewhat lower communality (h^2) of Stage 1 (.76) relative to those of the remaining seven stages (.88-.95) suggests the presence of more unexplained variance ($1 - h^2$) at Stage 1 than at the later stages. Since the reliabilities (Hoyt) of each of the eight stages are high and quite constant (.95-.98), the differences between communalities cannot be explained on the basis of increased error variance during the first practice stage. Thus, the presence of still additional factors during this first stage of practice is suspected.

There was also a shift in the *nature* of the factors contributing variance at early and later stages of practice. For example, the factors primarily involved early in practice were Psychomotor Coordination, Spatial Relations, Visualization, and to some extent Mechanical Experience. Perceptual Speed also appeared to a low degree in certain of the early stages. From the fifth through the last stage of practice, the only factors with significant loadings in the test were the Psychomotor Coordination and Rate of Movement factors and a factor common only to the criterion task itself. This suggests that at early stages of practice on the task, certain "non-motor" factors play a major role, but as practice is continued these become less and less important as contributors to individual differences in performance. At the same time, certain "motor" factors increase in importance as practice is continued until these are the only factors that enter to a significant degree at late stages of practice.

Figure 1 presents this shift graphically. The shaded areas represent the percentage of the total variance in performance accounted for by each factor at each of the eight stages of practice. By combining percentages of variance accounted for by various factors, it can be seen quite clearly that during the first stage of practice on the Complex Coordination Test, so-called "non-motor" factors are contributing 46.1 per cent of the variance, while the three "motor" factors contribute but 29.5 per cent. However, as practice continues there is a systematic decrease in "non-motor" variance accompanied by an increase in "motor" variance until approximately stage 5, beyond which little appreciable change occurs. By the final stage of practice, the non-motor factors account for only 10.5 per cent of the variance while the motor factors now account for 74.5 per cent.

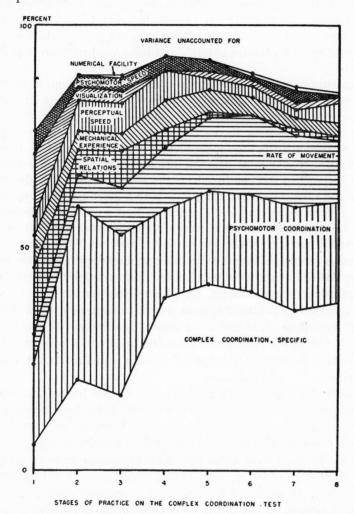

FIG. 1. Percentage of variance (shaded area) represented by each factor at different stages of practice on the Complex Coordination test.

Discussion

In general, these changes in factor loadings at different stages of performance on the criterion task indicate that the quantitative pattern of abilities determining differences in goodness of performance changes with practice. In other words, individual differences in performance on the task after certain amounts of practice are likely to depend more on certain abilities and less on others than they did initially.

Learning theorists have given relatively little attention to the relationships of individual differences to the principles of learning. It is therefore difficult to relate the results of the present study to any specific learning theory. However, a few investigators have given some attention to the problem. Reynolds, for example, found decreasing correlations between printed test and a psychomotor test as practice was continued on the latter test. He hypothesized that the subject's early performance is to a great extent a function of previous experience and therefore reflects a number of abilities. As learning continues, the subject's performance depends more upon his experience with the particular task employed. To an increasing extent, he learns the specific responses required by the task. The abilities or aptitudes associated with these specific habits being acquired, it is hypothesized, are progressively restricted in extent and generality. This view appears related to Seashore's "work methods" hypothesis (3) as well as to some of the findings of Woodrow (cf. 5). In factor analyses of extended practice on printed tests, Woodrow found that loadings of practice gains scores are often specific to the particular test.

Some of the data of the present study are not inconsistent with these previous interpretations. For example, it has been noted that as practice was continued on the Complex Coordination Test there was a progressive increase in loadings on a factor common only to the test itself. Also consistent with these hypotheses is the shrinkage in the number of factors contributing to performance as practice is continued. However, such "specificity hypotheses" imply that a sizable portion of the between-subjects variance observed at advanced levels of proficiency in a task is not ascribable to variation along any other dimension other than that established by the task itself.

At present, however, this view is regarded as overly pessimistic, especially with respect to the problem of predicting more advanced and terminal proficiency in psychomotor skills. It is felt, rather, that the problem is one of identifying what variables predict such advanced proficiency levels. The present study indicates that it is possible to isolate variables which predict performance at advanced stages. For example, the Rate of Movement and Psychomotor Coordination factors were found to contribute a sizable portion of the variance at advanced stages. The factor found specific to only the trials of the practice task may be broken down still further, with additional experimentation including other variables. Perhaps the most encouraging results regarding the predictability of advanced stages of psychomotor performance are found in recent work by Adams. He found that a combination of certain test measures yielded a multiple correlation with advanced levels of performance on this criterion task that exceeded the correlation between the first and last stages of practice on the task itself. This gives further indication that the abilities sampled at late stages of practice on a psychomotor task are not necessarily specific to the task, but may represent common factors definable by other test variables.

For the present, performance at any stage of practice is regarded as determined by a *set* of cooperating but independently variable abilities. This view is similar to that proposed by Woodrow (6). Continuation of practice on the task does not result in an equal increase or decrease in favorableness for the operation of all the cooperating determining factors contributing to individual differences. For example, in the early stages of performing the task, learning the spatial relationships of the different stimuli to the different responses may be an important contributor to individual differences. Once this is learned to a sufficiently high degree and no further improvement in this skill is possible (or necessary), within the limits of the task, other features of the task may assume increasing importance (e.g., completing the proper sequence of movements quickly). However, the important point is that earlier in the learning period the use of certain skills is a minimal but necessary requirement for achieving a certain amount of progress in performing the task. At this stage, individual differences in these skills affect the rise in the acquisition curve. Later in training, individual differences in other combinations of skills may be the chief contributors to performance. The rise in the performance curve may be considered to be a resultant of systematic transformations in the particular combination of abilities contributing variance at different stages of practice.

Implications

The results of the present study would appear to have certain implications for test development in this aptitude area and for certain problems of criterion analysis. For example, the fact of changes in factor pattern with practice points up the importance of establishing for such tests what abilities are contributing variance at different stages of performance on the test. The problem appears especially crucial in regard to psychomotor tests which are included as parts of larger, rather comprehensive classification batteries. The need for excluding from such apparatus tests variance measurable by printed tests has been pointed out earlier. Knowledge about factorial content at different stages should enable one to specify how much practice to give on such tests in the operational test situation in order to reach the stage of performance at which it would be most desirable to score the test; that is, performance up to a given stage would be purely "practice" for the subject and scoring would begin *after* this stage is reached and for a specific period. This would include the stage at which (1) the factors measured by the test which are also measured by the other tests are at a minimum, and (2) the loadings of the remaining valid factors in the test are at a maximum. This would presumably maximize the unique contribution of such tests to the predictive power of the total battery.

The findings of the present study are indirectly related to certain problems of criterion development in operational situations. For example, testing programs are most often evaluated against more immediate criteria of proficiency in lieu of more intermediate or ultimate criteria of performance. Thus, the tests used in the Aircrew Classification Battery were, without exception, designed to predict the success of candidates *in training* for the specialty to which they were assigned. Similarly, in the industrial situation, test validation is often conducted against proficiency at relatively early stages of training in place of validation against the more elusive on-the-job criteria. Aside from the several reasons supporting the use of the more immediate criteria (and there are many), the data of the present study at least suggest the need for criterion analyses of more advanced levels of proficiency, especially in jobs emphasizing perceptual-motor skills. It is quite conceivable that the abilities contributing to individual differences in earlier stages of skill attainment in such jobs may be somewhat different than those contributing variance at more advanced and terminal levels of proficiency. Thus, the relative size of test regression weights determined against immediate criteria may be expected to shift, when the same battery is evaluated against more advanced criteria. Similarly, tests rejected from the battery because of insignificant validity against immediate criteria may have turned out to possess considerable validity for advanced levels of proficiency. As a corollary of these possibilities, there is a need for developing tests which predict individual differences at more advanced and terminal levels of proficiency in such situations.

Literature Cited

1. GUILFORD, J. P., FRUCHTER, B., and ZIMMERMAN, W. S. "Factor Analysis of the Army Air Forces Shepard Field Battery of Experimental Aptitude Tests." *Psychometrika,* 1952, **17,** 45–68.
2. MELTON, A. W. (Ed.) Apparatus Tests. AAF Aviation Psychology Program Research Report No. 4, 1947.
3. SEASHORE, R. H. "Work and Motor Performance." In Stevens, S. S. (Ed.) *Handbook of Experimental Psychology.* New York: Wiley, 1951.
4. THURSTONE, L. L. *Multiple-factor Analysis.* Chicago: Univ. Chicago Press, 1947.
5. WOODROW, H. "Factors in Improvement with Practice." *J. Psychol.,* 1939, **7,** 55–70.
6. WOODROW, H. "The Ability to Learn." *Psychol. Rev.,* 1946, **53,** 147–158.
7. ZIMMERMAN, W. S. "A Simple Graphical Method for Orthogonal Rotation of Axes." *Psychometrika,* 1946, **11,** 51–55.

Questions for Discussion

1. What nine factors are identified? How may these factors be related to certain skills in physical education?
2. What is the major shift in the importance of various abilities in the later stages of practice?
3. What happens to the number of factors contributing to performance as practice continues?
4. What are the implications of this report for test development and administration in physical education?

WALTER E. HEMPEL, JR.
and EDWIN A. FLEISHMAN

A Factor Analysis
of Physical Proficiency
and Manipulative Skill*

The following study employs the same theoretical base and
method of analysis described in the previous reading (by the
same authors). This study, however, has more immediate relevance for physical education because it deals with what is described by the layman as athletic ability. This analysis indicates
that there is no general athletic ability.

This paper represents one in a series of factorial studies . . . concerned with the organization of abilities in certain of the relatively
unexplored aptitude areas of motor skill. In the present study primary attention was given to the areas of gross physical proficiency
and fine manipulative performance. Specifically, the analysis was
undertaken (a) to investigate the interdependence of abilities contributing to individual differences in these two areas; and (b) to
identify possible ability categories which might be useful and meaningful in describing performance in these areas.

Procedure

The analysis is based on the intercorrelations among 46 tests of a
battery originally developed in this laboratory by J. B. Reynolds,
J. A. Adams, and Ina McD. Bilodeau. The tests fell into three general categories: (a) seventeen manipulative apparatus tests; (b) six
printed tests; and (c) twenty-three gross physical performance tests.

* Reprinted with permission of the authors and the publisher from *The Journal
of Applied Psychology*, vol. 39, no. 1, 1955, pp. 12–16.

The physical performance tests are similar to those given in school physical education departments or military training situations to evaluate physical proficiency. However, the tests in this battery were highly standardized. All the tests were pretested on samples of airmen and scored on a pass-fail basis. The pass-fail cutoff point, determined from the pretest results, was located so that approximately 50% of the examinees would pass each test. The complete battery had been administered to a sample of 400 basic trainee airmen. The list of tests and very brief descriptions of the operations required by each test follow.

MANIPULATIVE TESTS

1. *Cox pin board.* Wrap a cord in a prescribed manner around pins closely spaced in rows on a board.
2. *Cox eye board.* Thread a cord through a small hole in each of a series of pegs arranged in rows on a board.
3. *Santa Ana peg turning.* Lift, rotate, and replace a series of pegs in a pegboard.
4. *Nut and bolt.* Complete a series of nut and bolt assemblies through holes in a panel.
5. *Track steadiness.* Trace through an irregular slot pathway with a stylus, without touching the sides of the path.
6. *Hex nut steadiness.* Stack a series of small hexagonal nuts one on top of the other.
7. *Pin punch, right.* Punch a tack through each of a series of tiny holes arranged in a pattern on a template, using the right hand.
8. *Pin punch, left.* Same as 7, except using left hand.
9. *Speed of manipulation "A."* Remove a number of small washers from a series of pegs.
10. *Speed of manipulation "B."* Replace the small washers on the pegs.
11. *Ball and pipe.* Drop a small ball through a pipe, catch it as it emerges from the bottom of the pipe, and repeat the process.
12. *Speed of reaction.* Catch a strip of metal with the thumb and forefinger as quickly as possible when it is released.
13. *Rotary aiming.* Strike a series of buttons arranged in a circle, as rapidly as possible, with the end of the index finger.
14. *Marble board.* Place marbles, one at a time, in grooves in a board.

15. *Dowel manipulation.* Arrange a series of suspended pieces of dowel so as to make a continuous strip of dowel.

16. *Restricted manipulation.* Insert bolts through a series of holes in a panel by reaching behind it and avoiding the baffles encountered.

17. *VDL rings.* Remove small rings from a small pole.

PRINTED TESTS

18. *Circle dotting.* Place three dots in each of a series of small circles.

19. *Irregular dotting pursuit.* Place one dot in each of a series of small circles arranged in an irregular pattern.

20. *Speed of square marking.* Place an "X" precisely in each of a series of small squares.

21. *Two-hand coordination (printed).* Draw a line through a pair of vertical lines with one hand, while drawing a line through a pair of horizontal lines with the other hand.

22. *Pattern discrimination.* From the shape and shade of combinations of geometric figures, respond according to prearranged directions.

23. *Discrimination square marking.* Mark the correct number of squares for each of a series of problems, according to a two-digit code.

PHYSICAL PERFORMANCE TESTS

24. *Chinning.* While hanging by the arms from a bar, pull the body up until the chin is above the bar, and repeat.

25. *Jump and click heels.* Jump and click heels as often as possible before returning to the floor.

26. *Jump and turn.* Leap in the air and turn around as far as possible before returning to the floor.

27. *Push-ups.* Push up body from prone position, until arms are fully extended, and repeat.

28. *Cable jump.* Jump through a cable held in the hands and land on both feet in front of the cable.

29. *Two-foot rail balance.* Maintain balance with both feet placed heel to toe on a 1-in. board.

30. *Foot balance I.* Maintain balance on the left foot, with the right foot resting on the inside of the left knee.

31. *Foot balance II.* Maintain balance on the left foot, with the right foot behind the left knee.

32. *Rail walking.* Walk on a 1-in. rail, heel to toe, with hands on back of hips.

33. *Circular tie walking.* Move around a circle in a specified manner with feet spread apart on the edge of a circular rail.

34. *Rising from supine.* From supine position, rise to standing position without using hands or arms.

35. *Leg bend.* Squat slowly on the right leg only, until the thigh touches the calf of the leg.

36. *Leg raising.* Raise legs to the level of the head while in an upright sitting position.

37. *Backing down wall.* Bend backwards as far as possible.

38. *Table vault.* Vault over a table.

39. *Kicking height.* Kick one foot as high as the head.

40. *Backward jump.* Jump backwards as far as possible.

41. *Abdominal pivot.* Push body around with hands while lying on stomach and keeping back arched.

42. *Hurdle jump.* Accomplish an ordinary standing high jump with certain specifications.

43. *Jump and balance.* Jump onto the edge of a box and maintain balance.

44. *Rate of jump.* Jump forward up several steps and then backward down the steps, keeping feet together.

45. *Toe touching.* Bend forward and downward as far as possible without bending knees.

46. *Jump and touch.* Jump up and make a mark on the wall as high as possible.

Results

The tetrachoric correlations among the test variables . . . were subjected to a Thurstone centroid factor analysis. Factor extraction was continued well beyond the point where any meaningful factor variance was suspected to be present. The 17 centroid factors [were] extracted. . . . Orthogonal rotations of the primary axes were accomplished by Zimmerman's graphical method (9) until simple structure and positive manifold were closely approximated. . . .

Interpretation of Factors

Rotated loadings of .30 or greater were considered significant in defining the factors.

Factor I appears to be the same as that factor called *Aiming* in some previous studies.

No.	Variable	Loading
19	Irregular dotting pursuit (printed)	.82
20	Speed of square marking (printed)	.71
18	Circle dotting (printed)	.69
21	Two-hand coordination (printed)	.58
13	Rotary aiming	.38
22	Pattern discrimination (printed)	.36
3	Santa Ana peg turning	.33
9	Speed of manipulation "A"	.32
1	Cox pin board	.31

It is defined as the ability to perform quickly and precisely a series of directed movements requiring eye-hand coordination. The largest loadings on this factor are for printed tests requiring rather exact visual alignment of the response. Loadings are highest as the area to be marked in becomes smaller.

Factor II is defined as *Limb Strength*.

No.	Variable	Loading
27	Push-ups	.57
24	Chinning	.55
46	Jump and touch	.33

Primary emphasis in both the tests with highest loadings on this factor is on strength of the arms. The presence of "Jump and touch" suggests that this factor may extend to leg strength as well.

Factor III is defined as *Gross Body Coordination*.

No.	Variable	Loading
34	Rising from supine	.57
28	Cable jump	.56
42	Hurdle jump	.52
24	Chinning	.52
30	Foot balance I	.36
32	Rail walking	.31

It appears to involve the ability to coordinate movements where more of the entire body is involved. The tests most highly loaded on this factor require that the trunk as well as the limbs be employed simultaneously in accomplishing the task.

Factor IV is defined as *Equilibrium Balance.*

No.	Variable	Loading
31	Foot balance II	.56
29	Two foot rail balance	.47
30	Foot balance I	.40

It represents the ability to maintain balance while in an abnormal stance or position. This feature is the crucial characteristic of all the tests loaded on this factor.

Factor V is identified as *Energy Mobilization.*

No.	Variable	Loading
46	Jump and touch	.65
40	Backward jump	.46
42	Hurdle jump	.39
43	Jump and balance	.35
44	Rate of jump	.35
38	Table vault	.34

All the tests most heavily loaded on this factor are tests in which the objective is to jump as far or as fast as possible, where no accuracy is required. It appears that this factor involves the ability to mobilize quickly and effectively a maximum of energy or force. In the present analysis it is involved primarily in tasks of jumping.

Factor VI is defined as *Trunk Strength.*

No.	Variable	Loading
41	Abdominal pivot	.64
27	Push-ups	.43
36	Leg raising	.43

It is defined by three tests in which the starting position is either prone or supine and in which performance is dependent on the strength of the trunk muscles. This factor, therefore, appears to involve the strength potential of the trunk muscles.

Factor VII is identified as a *Doublet* with doubtful psychological significance.

No.	Variable	Loading
7	Pin punch, right	.71
8	Pin punch, left	.69
13	Rotary aiming	.32

The significant loadings on this factor are primarily those of the "Pin punch" subtests which involve either the right or left hand on the same task. Variance in these tests is therefore obscure.

Factor VIII appears to be a *Reasoning* factor.

No.	Variable	Loading
23	Discrimination square marking (printed)	.68
22	Pattern discrimination (printed)	.46
16	Restricted manipulation	.46

The tests defining it each require the interpretation of relatively complex relationships in arriving at a successful solution to the problem. This is true of both the printed tests as well as the apparatus test. It appears that this factor represents a nonverbal reasoning factor.

Factor IX is identified as *Leg Suppleness or Flexibility*.

No.	Variable	Loading
45	Toe touching	.63
39	Kicking height	.62
35	Leg bend	.51
34	Rising from supine	.38
37	Backing down wall	.33

It is defined primarily by three tests that require the leg muscles to endure considerable strain or distention. It seems, therefore, that this factor involves the capacity of the leg muscles to resist deformity and to recover quickly from undue strain.

Factor X is defined as *Arm-Hand Steadiness*.

No.	Variable	Loading
5	Track steadiness	.56
2	Cox eye board	.47
6	Hex nut steadiness	.42
3	Santa Ana peg turning	.32

Tests defining this factor best are manipulative apparatus tests which require the ability to make precise, steady arm-hand movements of the kind that minimize speed and strength. The "Track steadiness" test has defined this factor in a previous study (2).

Factor XI is tentatively identified as *Trunk Flexibility*.

No.	Variable	Loading
37	Backing down wall	.50
38	Table vault	.37

It is rather poorly defined with only two tests having significant loadings on the factor. Both these tests, however, require the back and abdominal muscles to endure strain through either bending the body backwards or twisting it around. It therefore seems probable that this factor involves the ability of the trunk muscles to endure strain and distortion.

Factor XII is identified as *Manual Dexterity*.

No.	Variable	Loading
14	Marble board	.51
17	VDL rings	.44
15	Dowel manipulation	.40

It appears to involve the ability to make skillful, well-coordinated arm-hand manipulations, and is best measured by certain of the manipulative apparatus tests.

Factor XIII is tentatively defined as *Performance* or *Dynamic Balance*.

No.	Variable	Loading
25	Jump and click heels	.54
43	Jump and balance	.53
44	Rate of jump	.46

In each test defining this factor the crucial feature appears to be maintaining balance while in the process of some other performance, such as jumping. This is distinguished from Factor IV (Equilibrium Balance) which involves a more static kind of balance. Whether or not the present balance factor is restricted to jumping activities remains to be tested by future studies.

Factor XIV is identified as *Finger Dexterity*.

No.	Variable	Loading
9	Speed of manipulation "A"	.45
11	Ball and pipe	.45
4	Nut and bolt	.39
16	Restricted manipulation	.35

It appears in tasks which emphasize skillful manipulations primarily with the fingers. It is distinguished from Manual Dexterity (Factor XII) which does not emphasize such finger movements. The separation of these two factors confirms previous findings (e.g., 2, 4, 8).

Factor XV is very tentatively identified as *Jump Performance*.

No.	Variable	Loading
26	Jump and turn	.57
25	Jump and click heels	.50
42	Hurdle jump	.33
38	Table vault	.32
46	Jump and touch	.32

The identifying characteristic of the tests with highest loadings on this factor appears to be jumping and completing some performance after jumping and before landing. It appears, therefore, that this factor involves the ability to perform a task while in the process of jumping. However, a more psychologically meaningful interpretation is lacking at present.

Factor XVI and *Factor XVII* are *Residual* factors with no apparent psychological meaning.

Summary and Conclusions

Fifteen factors were identified to account for performance on the 46 experimental tests. While the precise nature of several of the factors is yet uncertain, some general conclusions appear possible.

1. The results indicate that the abilities contributing to performance on gross physical tasks are quite independent of those contributing to fine manipulative skill. No factors were found that overlapped these areas.

2. Pending the indentification of additional factors or clarification of the present ones, the factors identified suggest a possible classification of ability areas primarily involved on a wide range of

motor tasks, especially those of a gross physical nature. They at least point up a way of organizing more meaningfully the hodgepodge of such tests generally used in evaluating physical proficiency.

The nine factors identified in the physical performance tests appear to fit under five general categories:

a. *Strength*—of the limbs (Factor II) and of the trunk (Factor VI).

b. *Flexibility* (ability of the muscles to endure and recover from strain and distortion)—of the legs (Factor IX) and of the trunk (Factor XI).

c. *Balance*—static or equilibrium balance (Factor IV) and dynamic or performance balance (Factor XIII).

d. *Gross Body Coordination* (Factor III)—ability to coordinate muscular movements where the trunk as well as the limbs are employed simultaneously.

e. *Energy Mobilization* (Factor V)—ability to mobilize quickly and effectively a maximum of energy or force.

While better tests of these factors could be developed, these categories at least provide a functional classification of areas that might receive attention in assessing physical proficiency and deficiency, or in sectioning classes for further training and development.

3. The four factors identified in the manipulative tests have each been identified in previous studies. These were defined as:

a. *Manual Dexterity* (Factor XII)—ability to make skillful, coordinated arm-hand movements.

b. *Finger Dexterity* (Factor XIV)—ability to make skillful manipulations with the fingers.

c. *Arm-Hand Steadiness* (Factor X)—ability to make precise, steady, arm-hand movements of the kind that minimize speed and strength.

d. *Aiming* (Factor I)—ability to make accurately directed positioning movements requiring precise, visual alignment and motor control (eye-hand coordination).

4. In addition, an independent *nonverbal reasoning factor* (Factor VIII) was identified in certain of the printed tests.

5. Future research should be directed at validating the factors obtained against more complex motor performance. Such research might possibly lead to a better indication of the unique contribution of tests in these areas to problems of classification and selection as well as to problems of evaluation and training.

Literature Cited

1. FLEISHMAN, E. A. A factor analysis of intra-task performance on two psychomotor tests. *Psychometrika,* 1952, **18,** 45–55.
2. FLEISHMAN, E. A. A factorial study of psychomotor abilities. *USAF, Personnel Train. Res. Cent., Res. Bull.,* 1954, No. 54–15.
3. FLEISHMAN, E. A. Testing for psychomotor abilities by means of apparatus tests. *Psychol. Bull.,* 1953, **50,** 241–262.
4. FLEISHMAN, E. A., and HEMPEL, W. E., JR. A factor analysis of dexterity tests. *Personnel Psychol.,* 1954, **7,** 15–32.
5. FLEISHMAN, E. A., and HEMPEL, W. E., JR. Changes in factor structure of a complex psychomotor test as a function of practice. *Psychometrika,* 1954, **19,** 239–252.
6. FLEISHMAN, E. A., and HEMPEL, W. E., JR. Factorial analysis of complex psychomotor performance. *USAF, Personnel Train. Res. Cent., Res. Bull.,* 1954, No. 54–12.
7. GREENE, E. B. An analysis of random and systematic changes with practice. *Psychometrika,* 1943, **8,** 37–52.
8. *Staff, Division of Occupational Analysis, W. M. C.* Factor analysis of occupational aptitude tests. *Educ. Psychol. Measmt.,* 1945, **5,** 147–155.
9. ZIMMERMAN, W. S. A simple graphical method for orthogonal rotation of axes. *Psychometrika,* 1946, **11,** 51–55.

Questions for Discussion

1. What implications has this report for sectioning classes in physical education?
2. Apply this analysis in describing the "all-around" athlete.
3. How could this analysis be applied to your favorite sport?
4. What are the five general categories in which the nine factors can be identified?
5. What significance has this article's conclusion for transfer of training or general skill learning as opposed to specific skill learning?

DONALD G. PATERSON

Height and Weight
in Relation to Intellect*

The psychology of individual differences has contributed significantly to the abandonment of stereotypes. We frequently describe the intellectual as having an unimpressive if not puny physique. Having no body, to speak of, to develop, he is forced to turn all his attention to matters of the mind. Similarly, the athlete is described as devoid of mind but large of body. He stands taller and he weighs more, but he thinks less. Like his counterpart, the intellectual, he develops not out of choice but out of necessity what limited resources nature has bestowed. There is also the stereotype, best articulated by Nietzsche, of the superman, one of a few who have been blessed by nature. They are the benefactors of all her gifts, both physical and mental. The evidence presented in the next two articles should be used to examine all the stereotypes involving physique and intellect.

With such a minimum of evidence and with that evidence itself shaky it is difficult to see what justification exists for Baldwin's continued adherence to belief in a strikingly close relationship between physical development and mental development. Unfortunately, his views have received wide circulation, especially among educators, through an article published in a yearbook of the National Society for the Study of Education.[1]

* Reprinted and abridged with permission of Mrs. Donald G. Paterson and the publisher from *Physique and Intellect.* New York: Appleton-Century-Crofts, 1930, pp. 48–52.
[1] B. T. Baldwin, "Methods of Selecting Superior or Gifted Children," *Twenty-third Yearbook of the National Society for the Study of Education* (Public School Publishing Co., Bloomington, Ill., I, 1924), 25–47.

It is a satisfaction to report one of the most recent studies which utilizes straightforward correlation technique upon data secured in such a way as to control adequately the troublesome factor of age. Our reference is to the admirable study of Murdock and Sullivan in Honolulu.[2] This work differs from most of the previous studies in utilizing on a large scale more minutely graduated measures of intelligence, namely standard intelligence tests such as the Otis Primary Test for grades 1–3, National Intelligence Test for grades 3–9, and the Terman Group Test of Mental Ability for grades 9–12. These tests were all administered by Katherine Murdock in the capacity of school psychologist. The physical measurements were secured by Louis R. Sullivan, anthropologist representing the American Museum of Natural History in New York. In a sense it is fortunate that the physical data and the mental data were obtained in entire independence of each other and for other purposes than that of correlating the two. The subjects were some 600 pupils of old American, British, German, or Scandinavian descent constituting a "fairly homogeneous race group."

Scores on the mental tests were converted into I.Q.'s and in a similar manner the absolute physical measures were converted into relative measures by expressing each physical measure as a quantitative deviation from the average of each age-sex group. Both techniques thus eliminate the age factor and permit direct comparison for all subjects. The chief correlations are as follows:

$$r \text{ between weight and I. Q.} = +.16 \pm .03 \ (N = 595)$$
$$r \text{ between height and I. Q.} = +.14 \pm .03 \ (N = 597)$$

There is thus shown to be a slight positive correlation between height and weight and intelligence. The fact that that (probability errors) are small in relation to the size of the coefficients tends to emphasize the significance of the latter. Recomputation of the correlation between weight and intelligence for boys and girls separately did not reveal any effect of lumping the two sexes together in the original computations.

The evidence obtained by McHale regarding the association between weight and intelligence is consistent with that already cited.[3]

[2] K. Murdock and L. R. Sullivan, "A Contribution to the Study of Mental and Physical Measurements in Normal Children," *Am. Phys. Educ. Rev.*, 1923, 28:209–215; 276–280; 328–330.

[3] Kathryn McHale, *Comparative Psychology and Hygiene of the Overweight Child.* Teachers College, Columbia University, Contributions to Education, No. 221, 1926, especially ch. VII, pp. 66–72.

It takes on added significance, however, because this investigator made a thoroughgoing study of a number of psychological traits which might be associated with adiposity and the finding of a negligible relationship between weight and I. Q. was incidental to a comprehensive and well controlled study of overweight, normal weight, and underweight children. In all, 312 eleven-year-old children evenly divided into three weight groups were studied. Children who were 15 per cent or more over the weight standard for their height and age were classified as overweight; those who were within 5 per cent plus or minus were included in the normal-weight group; and those who were 8 per cent and below were placed in the under-weight group. The mean I. Q.'s for these three weight groups in order were 107, 102, and 102. The author properly concluded: "The results of the measurement of intelligence by the Stanford-Binet test indicated that body-weight had little to do with the possession of certain degrees of intelligence" (p. 72).

Abernethy's study of girls in the University of Chicago Laboratory Schools, likewise reveals relatively low correlations between height and weight and Stanford-Binet mental age.[4] For 120 girls between 6 and 12 years of age the partial correlation for constant age was +.34 ±.05 between height and mental age and +.39 ±.05 between weight and mental age. But when chronological age was controlled experimentally by computing the Pearson coefficient of correlation between weight and height and mental age for each group separately for ages 13 to 17 inclusive the correlations turn out to be consistently lower, The results are shown in Table 1.

Table 1

COEFFICIENTS OF CORRELATION BETWEEN WEIGHT AND STANFORD-BINET MENTAL AGE AND BETWEEN HEIGHT AND STANFORD-BINET MENTAL AGE FOR UNIVERSITY OF CHICAGO LABORATORY SCHOOL GIRLS AT EACH AGE FROM THIRTEEN TO SEVENTEEN INCLUSIVE. (AFTER ABERNETHY.)

Correlation between Mental Age and:		Chronological Age Groups				
		13	14	15	16	17
Weight	N	44	61	29	45	37
	r	−.06 ±.10	+.10 ±.08	+.15 ±.12	+.21 ±.10	+.18 ±.11
Height	N	44	62	29	45	37
	r	+.01 ±.10	+.07 ±.08	+.11 ±.12	+.02 ±.10	+.25 ±.10

[4] E. M. Abernethy, "Correlations in Physical and Mental Growth," *J. of Educ. Psychol.*, 1925, 16:458–466 and 539–546.

The small number of cases at each age is responsible for the relatively high probable errors of each coefficient of correlation, which prevent placing much credence upon the exact size of any of them. The trend, however, points to a low positive correlation between each of these physical traits and mental age for homogeneous age groups.

Finally, we may mention Gates' study published in 1924 and the study of Pearson and Moul published in 1925. Gates showed that the correlation between height and Standford-Binet mental age is +.06 and between weight and Stanford-Binet mental age is +.10 for children in the kindergarten and in the fourth grade.[5] These two correlations represent the average of four correlation coefficients each with age held constant. The partial correlation technique itself was really unnecessary since each correlation was derived from very homogeneous age groups. Pearson and Moul conducted a very elaborate biometrical study of 616 alien Jewish boys and 580 alien Jewish girls residing in London and found a negligible correlation (correlation ratio) between estimated intelligence and height and weight.[6]

We may summarize the general trend of this critical review of the studies on the relation between height and weight and intelligence in normal children by stating that a slight positive correlation seems to exist between stature or weight and intelligence. The emphasis can be on either of two points: on the one hand, we would emphasize the fact that the relationship, even though slight, is positive; on the other hand, in view of the exaggerated notions which have been current in the past and which persist even at the present time, it is important to emphasize the fact that physical status and mental status are to a great extent independent of one another.

[5] A. I. Gates, "The Nature and Educational Significance of Physical Status and of Mental, Physiological, Social, and Emotional Maturity," *J. of Educ. Psychol.*, 1924, 15:329–358.

[6] Karl Pearson and Margaret Moul. "The Problem of Alien Immigration into Great Britain, Illustrated by an Examination of Russian and Polish Jewish Children." Part II, "On the Intelligence of the Alien Jewish Children." *Annals of Eugenics*, 1925–26, 1:56–127.

ANNE ANASTASI

Physique and Temperament*

Type theories have a history that stretches from Hippocrates to Kretschmer and, more recently, Sheldon. Such theories assume that (1) there are basic physical types, and (2) there exists precise relationships between physical and psychological characteristics. There is also the underlying assumption that behavior is more a product of heredity than environment.

Since the layman and the educator frequently accept these assumptions, it may be well to examine the evidence upon which they are based. In the following article, the leading psychologist of individual differences reviews the evidence for one of the newest constitutional typologies—that of W. H. Sheldon.

In examining the article, the student should note not only the basic typology, but also, the method used in rating both physique and behavior.

Sheldon's Typology

A more recent system of constitutional typology is that developed by Sheldon and his co-workers (11, 12, 13). The distinctive feature of this system is that every individual is rated on a 7-point scale in each of the three categories of physique and in each of the three corresponding categories of temperament. Rather than being characterized in terms of the type he most closely resembles, the individual is thus placed along a continuum with respect to each of the three components of physique and of temperament.

The three components of physique were chosen and defined through detailed observations of the photographs of 4000 college

* Reprinted and abridged with permission of the publisher from *Differential Psychology* by Anne Anastasi. Third Edition. The Macmillan Company, 1958, pp. 171–77.

men. . . . Each person was photographed in the nude and in a standardized posture, from the frontal, lateral, and dorsal positions. Once the three components had been suggested by this inspectional analysis, suitable anthropometric measures were selected by trial and error. The measurements were made directly on the photographs with needle-point dividers.

A parallel procedure was followed in arriving at the basic components of temperament. First, the authors assembled a list of 650 alleged temperamental "traits" described in the literature, most of them being related to introversion-extroversion. After adding a few from their own observations, arranging, and condensing, they were able to reduce the list to 50 terms which seemed to embody all the essential characteristis. A group of 33 young men, mostly graduate students and instructors, were then rated on a 7-point scale for each of these 50 traits. The ratings were based upon a series of 20 intensive interviews by the experimenter, extending over a period of one year and supplemented by everyday observations. All the 1225 intercorrelations among the ratings of the 50 traits were computed. Inspection of this correlation table suggested to the authors that the traits fell into three principal "clusters," such that the tests within each cluster were positively correlated with one another and negatively correlated with the tests in the other clusters. At this point it was decided to keep only those traits, or items, that had a positive correlation of .60 or more with other items within their cluster and a negative correlation of .30 or more with items outside the cluster. On this basis 22 of the original 50 traits were retained. In the course of subsequent studies on more subjects, the investigators undertook to sharpen and redefine the initial 22 traits and to add others which also satisfied the above correlational criterion. The final scale developed by this technique consisted of 60 traits, 20 in each cluster.

The three components of physique and the corresponding temperamental components may be briefly described as follows:

PHYSIQUE

1. *Endomorphy*—predominance of soft roundness; relative over-development of digestive viscera

TEMPERAMENT

1. *Viscerotonia*—tendency toward relaxation, love of physical comfort, pleasure in eating, sociability

PHYSIQUE

2. *Mesomorphy* — predominance of bone, muscle, and connective tissue; heavy, hard, rectangular physique

3. *Ectomorphy* — predominance of linearity and fragility; relative to his mass, the ectomorph has greatest sensory exposure and largest brain and nervous system

TEMPERAMENT

2. *Somatotonia*—tendency toward assertiveness, energetic activity, love of power and risk, physical courage

3. *Cerebrotonia*—tendency toward restraint, introversion, love of privacy and solitude, inhibition

Each individual's *somatotype* consists of three numbers, representing his ratings in endomorphy, mesomorphy, and ectomorphy, respectively. Thus a 7–1–1 represents extreme endomorphy. A 2–6–2 and a 3–6–2 are both highly mesomorphic, but the latter shows more endomorphy than the former. Theoretically, there are 210 somatotype combinations which could be obtained with three components rated on a 7-point scale. But some of these combinations are physically impossible, such as the hypothetical 7–7–7 or 1–1–1. Sheldon (12) describes 88 somatotypes that have been actually observed. The use of a 7-point scale is of course arbitrary and only a matter of convenience. Five, 10, or any other number of steps could be substituted, in which case the total number of somatotypes would decrease or increase.

Sheldon's system was originally developed on men. Extension of the system to women is in progress and it is planned to prepare an *Atlas of Women* to parallel the recently published *Atlas of Men*. Applying the original somatotyping system to women, Sheldon reports that women tend to be more endomorphic than men. Six new somatotypes in the endomorph group, not previously found in male samples, have been identified among women. The most frequent somatotype among the 4000 college women so far surveyed is 5–3–3. . . . The most common physique among the college men who were Sheldon's original subjects was 3–4–4. In somatotyping an individual, the three components are rated in at least five different bodily regions and then averaged. . . . The predominant endomorph . . . corresponds to Kretschmer's pyknic type, while the predominant mesomorph and ectomorph represent the athletic and leptosome types, respectively. . . .

Each of the three temperamental components in Sheldon's system is also rated on a 7-point scale. The primary evidence for the association between somatotype and temperament ratings was derived from a study of 200 university men between the ages of 17 and 31, observed by Sheldon over a five-year period (13). Correlations between corresponding components of physique and temperament in this group were as follows:

Endomorphy and viscerotonia	.79
Mesomorphy and somatotonia	.82
Ectomorphy and cerebrotonia	.83

From a further analysis of the same subjects, the authors suggest the hypothesis that certain *discrepancies* between somatotype and temperamental index may predispose the individual to maladjustment and interfere with his achievement. . . .

The correlations between structural and temperamental components reported by Sheldon are certainly much higher than those found previously. Sheldon and his co-workers attribute this difference to their own reliance upon "essential underlying components" of both physique and temperament, in place of what they regard as the relatively superficial or fragmentary measures of earlier investigators. Sheldon argues, for example, that aptitude or personality tests may not reveal the "deeper and more enduring aspects" of temperament which he claims to have reached through his series of interviews (2, p. 33). For this reason, test scores might not yield such high correlations with somatotype as were found by Sheldon through the use of ratings. A counter-argument is that the well-known "halo effect" may have produced artificially high correspondences between physique and temperamental index, since the same observer assigned both sets of ratings. As the strongest defense against the halo effect, Sheldon offers the fact that the experimenter was aware of its nature and was therefore on guard against it. The effectiveness of such a safeguard is of course debatable.

Subsequent studies by other investigators have failed to corroborate the high degree of association between physique and temperament reported by Sheldon. When ratings were correlated with somatotypes, significant correlations were generally obtained, although they were usually much lower than those found by Sheldon (1, 6, 9, 10). Significant correlations were likewise obtained when scores on the Allport-Vernon Study of Values were compared with somatotypes based on self-ratings for physical qualities (9). In all such studies, the possibility of spurious correlation resulting from halo effect, social stereotypes, self concepts, and similar factors remains. Those investigations in which independent measures of somatotypes were compared with scores on personality or ability tests, on the other hand, yielded few if any significant correlations (2, 4, 7, 14). In the light of such findings, it can only be concluded that Sheldon's primary claim regarding the association of somatotype and temperament among normal persons remains unproved.

In a further extension of his theory, Sheldon has applied his constitutional classification to psychiatric patients and to delinquents (11, 16). For these purposes, he has devised categories that represent a pathological deficiency in the previously described temperamental components. Utilizing the suffix "-penia" to characterize these negative traits, he proposes the following classification:

Cerebropenia—lack of inhibition
Visceropenia—lack of compassion and of relaxed, soft qualities
Somatopenia—lack of energy and of drive for overt action

At the psychotic level, Sheldon links manic-depressive conditions with cerebropenia, paranoid states with visceropenia, and hebephrenic schizophrenia with somatopenia. Milder forms of the same deficiencies, he maintains, produce the corresponding neuroses, traditionally known as hysteria, psychasthenia, and neurasthenia, respectively.

Some evidence in support of this theory is provided by a study conducted on 167 male patients at Elgin State Hospital (16; 11, pp. 66–78). Significant correlations in the expected directions were found between ratings for psychiatric reaction types, on the one hand, and both somatotype and temperament ratings, on the other. In this investigation, the psychiatric ratings were obtained independently of the somatotype and temperament ratings, so that halo effect was ruled out of the correlations. Some of the association, however, may have resulted from differences in age, socioeconomic level, and other uncontrolled factors among the psychiatric groups. No data on these factors are given in the report of the study.

In a ten-year study of 200 delinquent boys in a rehabilitation home, Sheldon (11) found a predominance of endomorphic mesomorphs. The greatest clustering of somatotypes fell between the mesomorphic and endomorphic extremes, but was distinctly closer to mesomorphy. There was a decided absence of ectomorphy. Sheldon regards these findings as further confirmation of his hypothesis, since the most prevalent somatotype in the delinquent group is that which in his system would be associated with cerebropenia, or lack of inhibition. At the same time, somatotype cannot be regarded as an indicator of delinquency. As Sheldon himself points out, endomorphic mesomorphy is also characteristic of eminent generals, statesmen, and business leaders. Moreover Sutherland (15), in a reanalysis of Sheldon's published data, found no significant association between somatotype and *degree* of criminality as determined from the case histories.

In a somewhat better-controlled study, the Gluecks (5) compared 500 delinquent boys with 500 nondelinquents approximately matched with the delinquents in age, IQ, national origin, and residence in underprivileged neighborhoods. In general, their results on body build confirmed those of Sheldon. There was a significantly larger percentage of mesomorphic and a significantly smaller percentage of ectomorphic physiques among the delinquents than among the controls. Furthermore, one of the largest group differences occurred in the case of endomorphic mesomorphs, who were four times as numerous in the delinquent as in the control group.

The evidence cited by Sheldon in support of his system of classifying personality traits, as well as that purporting to show a close relationship between physique and personality, needs to be carefully examined. The possible operation of halo effect when physique and temperament are rated by the same observer has already been mentioned. Reference has also been made to the presence of such uncontrolled factors as age and socioeconomic level in the study of psychiatric patients.

The original identification of the three temperamental components (viscerotonia, somatotonia, and cerebrotonia) can likewise be questioned because of inadequacy of data. Ultimately, the entire structure of evidence for the presence of these particular components stands or falls with the adequacy of the initial experiment on 33 college men. To be sure, subsequent studies were conducted on larger groups. But these studies were designed simply to redefine, sharpen, and expand the originally chosen list of 22 "traits" for measuring the three temperamental components, rather than to check the adequacy of the components themselves. This is clearly indicated by the authors' procedure. The criterion for adding a new trait to the list was that the trait must correlate highly and positively with the traits in one of the original clusters, and negatively with the traits in the other two clusters. Subsequent modification or addition of traits thus depended in a very intimate way upon the results of the initial experiment. The small number and highly unrepresentative nature of the subjects employed in this initial experiment make it ill-suited to play such a fundamental part in the development of the entire schema of temperament classification.

Moreover, the technique of identifying components by *inspection* of a correlation table leaves too much to subjective judgment. In so far as the major contribution of Sheldon's approach is its emphasis upon components rather than types, the best available objective techniques for identifying such components ought to be applied. These techniques, known collectively as "factor analysis," are based upon further statistical analysis of a table of intercorrelations. . . . In the present connection it will suffice to note that other investigators have begun to employ these techniques in the analysis of body build as well as personality characteristics, with results that offer little support to Sheldon's tripartite classification. Even more disconcerting is Lubin's (8) finding that, in Sheldon's published table of intercorrelations among temperamental ratings, some of the reported coefficients are arithmetically impossible. It thus appears that the basic data from which the temperamental components were derived contain computational errors!

In reference to the classification of *physique,* it is relevant to note that age and nutritional status (2) do affect the somatotype, despite Sheldon's original claim to the contrary. Sheldon argued, for example, that loss of weight will not change endomorphs into mesomorphs or ectomorphs—"they become simply emaciated endomorphs." In more recent writing, he has qualified such assertions somewhat, pointing out that the somatotype is an indication of the individual's body build "under standard conditions of nutrition and in the absence of grossly disturbing pathology" (12, p. 19).

Apart from specific criticisms of the *evidence,* there are more fundamental questions which can be raised regarding Sheldon's whole approach. Is the three-component schema the most efficient system for classifying people in either physique or personality? Are the observed relationships between body build and behavioral characteristics—in so far as reliably established—indications of a basic, hereditary, "constitutional" connection, as Sheldon maintains? Or are there alternative explanations for the obtained correspondences?

Literature Cited

1. CHILD, I. L. "The Relation of Somatotype of Self-ratings on Sheldon's Temperamental Traits." *J. Pers.*, 1950, **18**, 440–453.
2. CHILD, I. L., and SHELDON, W. H. "The Correlation between Components of Physique and Scores on Certain Psychological Tests." *Char. and Pers.*, 1941, **10**, 23–34.
3. COFFIN, T. E. "A Three-component Theory of Leadership." *J. Abnorm. Soc. Psychol.*, 1944, **39**, 63–83.
4. FISKE, D. W. "A Study of Relationships to Somatotype." *J. Appl. Psychol.*, 1944, **28**, 504–519.
5. GLUECK, S., and GLUECK, ELEANOR T. *Unraveling Juvenile Delinquency.* N.Y.: Commonwealth Fund, 1950.
6. HANLEY, C. "Physique and Reputation of Junior High School Boys." *Child Develpm.*, 1951, **22**, 247–260.
7. JANOFF, IRMA Z., BECK, L. H., and CHILD, I. L. "The Relation of Somatotype to Reaction Time, Resistance to Pain, and Expressive Movement." *J. Pers.*, 1950, **18**, 454–460.
8. LUBIN, A. "A Note on Sheldon's Table of Correlations Between Temperamental Traits." *Brit. J. Psychol., Statist. Sect.*, 1950, **3**, 186–189.
9. SANFORD, R. N. "Physical and Physiological Correlates of Personality Structure." In C. Kluckhohn and H. A. Murray (Eds.), *Personality.* (2nd Ed.) N.Y.: Knopf, 1953. Ch. 5.
10. SELTZER, C. C., WELLS, F. L., and MCTERNAN, E. B. "A Relationship Between Sheldonian Somatotype and Psychotype." *J. Pers.*, 1948, **16**, 431–436.
11. SHELDON, W. H. *Varieties of Delinquent Youth.* N. Y.: Harper, 1949.
12. SHELDON, W. H. *Atlas of Men.* N.Y.: Harper, 1954.
13. SHELDON, W. H., and STEVENS, S. S. *The Varieties of Temperament.* N.Y.: Harper, 1942.
14. SMITH, H. C. "Psychometric Checks on Hypotheses Derived from Sheldon's Work on Physique and Temperament." *J. Pers.*, 1949, **17**, 310–320.
15. SUTHERLAND, E. H. "Critique of Sheldon's Varieties of Delinquent Youth." *Amer. Sociol. Rev.*, 1951, **16**, 10–13.
16. WITTMAN, PHYLLIS, SHELDON, W. H., and KATZ, C. J. "A Study of the Relationship Between Constitutional Variations and Fundamental Psychotic Behavior Reactions." *J. Nerv. ment. Dis.*, 1948, **108**, 470–476.

Questions for Discussion

1. What seems to be the chief methodological weakness of Sheldon's original identification of three temperaments?
2. What implication would this research have for the classification of students on the basis of height, weight, strength, and age?
3. What environmental factors may explain why certain constitutional types become athletes, leaders, or even juvenile delinquents?
4. What pessimistic implications does Sheldon's typology have for physical education programs?
5. How can body build be a result of behavior?

JEAN PIAGET

Explanation of Play*

More than any other contemporary psychologist, Piaget has contributed to our knowledge of the development of thought and language in children. In the succeeding selection he describes the role of play (or ludic function) in the child's cognitive development. The elementary school teacher recognizes the importance of the make-believe play of the young child for the learning of physical activities just as the high-school teacher values the student's accomplishment of a touchdown in football.

For Piaget, *"adaptation"* refers to the processes of *"assimilation"* and *"accommodation." "Assimilation"* occurs whenever something new is seen or thought of in terms of something familiar. It is, in part, analogous to the ingestion of food, at the physical level, and to transfer of learning and generalization, at the psychological level. *"Accommodation"* is analogous to the learning of new responses, responses made as accommodation to the impact of environmental occurences. *"Adaptation,"* then,

* Reprinted with permission of the publisher from *Play, Dreams and Imitation in Childhood*. London: William Heinemann, Ltd., 1951, pp. 161–168.

involves one or both processes, the combining the new with the familiar or simply acquiring the new. These concepts are basic to the following reading and are defined and elaborated in it.

An Attempt to Interpret Play through the Structure of the Child's Thought

A baby sucks his thumb sometimes as early as the second month, grasps objects at about four or five months, shakes them, swings them, rubs them, and finally learns to throw them and retrieve them. Such behaviours involve two poles: a pole of accommodation, since there must be adjustment of movements and perceptions to the objects, but also a pole of assimilation of things to the child's own activity, since he has no interest in the things as such, but only in so far as he finds them useful for a behaviour learnt earlier or for one he is in process of acquiring. This assimilation of reality to sensory-motor schemas has two complementary aspects. On the one hand it is active repetition and consolidation (hence the "circular reaction" described by Baldwin), and in this sense it is essentially functional or reproductive assimilation, *i.e.*, growth through functioning. On the other hand, it is mental digestion, *i.e.*, perception or conception of the object in so far as it is incorporated into real or possible action. Each object is assimilated as something "to be sucked," "to be grasped," "to be shaken," etc., and is at first that and nothing more (and if it is "to be looked at" it is still being assimilated to the various focusings and movements of the eyes and acquires the "shapes" which perceptive assimilation gives it). It is obvious that in the actual activity these two functions of assimilation become one, for it is by repeating his behaviours through reproductive assimilation that the child assimilates objects to actions and that these thus become schemas. These schemas constitute the functional equivalent of concepts and of the logical relationships of later development. At all stages of the development of intelligence we find both accommodation and assimilation, but they are increasingly differentiated, and consequently more and more complementary in their increasing equilibrium. In scientific thinking, for instance, accommodation to reality is nothing but experiment, while assimilation is deduction, or incorporation of objects into logical or mathematical schemas. But there are two important differences between this rational assimilation and the initial sensory-motor assimilation. In the first place, rational assimilation is not centred in the individual, the mental activity in this case being only an assimilation of things one to another,[1] while the initial assimilation is centred in the individual, and is therefore non-operational, *i.e.*, it is egocentric or distorting. In the second place, and this second difference explains the first, rational assimilation is complementary to accommodation to things, and therefore in almost permanent equilibrium with experience, while sensory-motor assimilation is as yet undifferentiated from accommodation and gives rise to a fresh "displacement of equilibrium" with every new differentiation. Phenomenism and egocentrism are the two undissociated aspects of elementary consciousness as distinct from experimental objectivity and rational deduction.

This being so, children's play is merely the expression of one of the phases of this progressive differentiation: it occurs when assimilation is dissociated from accommodation but is not yet reintegrated in the forms of permanent equilibrium in which, at the level of operational and rational thought, the two will be complementary. In this sense, play constitutes the extreme pole of assimilation of reality to the ego, while at the same time it has something of the creative imagination which will be the motor of all future thought and even of reason.

Play begins, then, with the first dissociation between assimilation and accommodation. After learning to grasp, swing, throw, etc., which involve both an effort of accommodation to new situations, and an effort of repetition, reproduction and generalisation, which are the elements of assimilation, the child sooner or later (often even during the learning period) grasps for the pleasure of grasping, swings for the sake of swinging, etc. In a word, he repeats his behaviour not in any further effort to learn or to investigate, but for the mere joy of mastering it and of showing off to himself his own power of subduing reality. Assimilation is dissociated from accommodation by subordinating it and tending to function by itself, and from then on practice play occurs. Since it requires neither thought nor social life, practice play can be explained as the direct result of the primacy of assimilation. The "functional

---

[1] It is, of course, real activity, and the assimilation of things one to another therefore amounts to assimilating them to "operations," *i.e.*, to active schemas constructed by the mind.

pleasure" and pleasure of being the cause, which accompany this type of play, raise no particular problem, since the first comes from the *sui generis* character of this assimilation for the sake of assimilation, with no need for new accommodation, and the second from the fact that when the child has overcome the difficulties inherent in the corresponding "serious" action, the assimilation is more concentrated on his own activity.

The appearance of symbolism, on the other hand, is the crucial point in all the interpretations of the ludic function. Why is it that play becomes symbolic, instead of continuing to be mere sensory-motor exercise or intellectual experiment, and why should the enjoyment of movement, or activity for the fun of activity, which constitute a kind of practical make-believe, be completed at a given moment by imaginative make-believe? The reason is that among the attributes of assimilation for assimilation's sake is that of distortion, and therefore to the extent to which it is dissociated from immediate accommodation it is a source of symbolic make-believe. This explains why there is symbolism as soon as we leave the sensory-motor level for that of representational thought.

Although the distinction between practice play and symbolic play is greater than is generally thought (even Buytendijk supports Groos's ideas on this point), since their respective origins are to be found on two quite different levels of behaviour, there is still an undeniable relationship between them: *symbolic play is to practice play as representational intelligence is to sensory-motor intelligence.* And to this correspondence at two different levels must be added one at the same level: *symbolic play is to representational intelligence what practice play is to sensory-motor intelligence, i.e.,* a deviation in the direction of pure assimilation.

Representative thought, as distinct from sensory-motor activity, begins as soon as the "signifier" is differentiated from the "signified" in the system of significations which constitutes the whole intelligence and indeed the whole conciousness. In the process of adaptation through sensory-motor schemas there are already "signifiers." They are the "indices" which enable the child to recognise objects and relationships, to assimilate consciously and even to imitate. But the index is only one aspect of the object or of the situation, and is therefore not a "signifier" which is differentiated from the "signified." Language, on the other hand, provides the prototype of a system of distinct signifiers, since in verbal behaviour the signifier is the collective "signs" or words, while the signified is the meaning of the words, *i.e.,* the concepts which at this new level take the place of the preverbal sensory-motor schemas. Verbal, properly conceptual intelligence occupies this privileged position in representational thought by virtue of the fact that verbal signs are social, and that through their use the system of concepts attains sooner or later (later than is usually supposed) a high degree of socialisation. But between the index and the sign, or between the sensory-motor schema and the logical concept, the symbolic image and imaged or pre-conceptual representation have their place. As we have seen, the image is interiorised imitation, *i.e.,* the positive of accommodation, which is the negative of the imitated object. The image is therefore a schema which has already been accommodated and is now used in present assimilations, which are also interiorised, as "signifier" for these "signified." The image is therefore a differentiated signifier, more so than the index since it is detached from the perceived object, but less so than the sign, since it is still imitation of the object, and therefore is a "motivated" sign, as distinct from verbal signs which are "arbitrary." Moreover, the image is a signifier which is within the scope of individual thought, while the pure sign is always social. For this reason there is in all verbal and conceptual thought a stratum of imaged representation which enables the individual to assimilate for himself the general idea common to all, and for this reason also, the nearer we get to early childhood the more important is the role of imaged representation and intuitive thought. Each image has a corresponding object (*i.e.,* the concept of this object) which, even in the adult, serves as a representative or example of the general class of which it is a part, and which in the child is a partial substitute for the general class which is not yet constructed.

This then being the mechanism of adapted thought, which is the equilibrium between assimilation and accommodation, we can understand the role of the symbol in play, where accommodation is subordinated to assimilation. The ludic symbol also is an image, and therefore imitation, and therefore accommodation. But the relationship between assimilation and accommodation in play differs from that in cognitive or adapted representation precisely because play is the predominance of assimilation and no longer an equilibrium between the two functions. (1) In the case of the adapted image there is exact imitation, or at least imitation which aims at exactness, *i.e.*, a one-one correspondence with the object signified. For instance, the representation of a triangle can be obtained by a real imitation (a drawing, or an indication of the figure by movement of a finger), or by a purely mental imitation (an interior image or "intuition" of a triangle), but there is then correspondence between the parts of the drawing, those of the image and those of the object represented. But when in play one thing is symbolised by another, *e.g.*, a cat walking on a wall by a shell moved with the hand along a cardboard box, there is a whole series of signifiers, related one to another, but further and further removed from the real situation. First there is the shell representing the cat and the box representing the wall; then there is imitation through gesture, *i.e.*, the movement of the hand representing the cat walking; finally there is presumably the mental image of the cat on the wall, an image which may be vague and undifferentiated since it is supported by motor imitation and the symbol-object. (2) The representation of a triangle is adequate and exact in so far as the triangle raises a problem, *i.e.*, gives rise to a need for adaptation to reality, with accommodation to the object and assimilation of the object to a system or relationships not centred in the ego, while the evocation of the cat on the wall has no other purpose than temporary satisfaction of the ego: it is a "pathic" and not a "gnostic" attitude, to use Buytendijk's terms, but it is at the same time egocentric and not objective. We have here the explanation of the difference seen in (1). (3) In cognitive representation the mental or material image represents a particular object whose concept (the particular class) serves as a single representative or example of the general class of which it is a part. For instance, the triangle which is drawn represents all triangles, or at least all triangles of that class. But in play, the symbol-object is not only the representative of the signified, but also its substitute (the shell becomes for the moment a cat), whether the signified is general (any cat) or particular (a definite cat). In cognitive representation, therefore, there is adaptation to the signified (*i.e.*, equilibrium between assimilation and accommodation), while the signifier consists of images, which are exactly accommodated or imitated, and whose corresponding object is only one representative of a general class. In the symbolic representation of play, on the contrary, the signified is merely assimilated to the ego, *i.e.*, it is evoked for temporary interest or for immediate satisfaction, and the signifier is then less exact mental imitation than imitation by means of material pictures in which the objects are themselves assimilated to the signified as substitutes, by reason of resemblances which may be extremely vague and subjective. In a word, while in cognitive representation there is a permanent equilibrium between assimilation and accommodation, in ludic symbolism there is a predominance of assimilation in the relationship between the child and the signified, and even in the construction of the signifier.

This being so, the connection between symbolic assimilation, which is the source of make-believe play, and functional assimilation, which is the source of practice play, is at once obvious. Both symbol and concept already exist, in a sense, in sensory-motor assimilation. When the baby who has learnt to swing an object swings other objects, this generalised schema is the functional equivalent of the concept, because each particular case belongs to the general class of things "to be swung" of which it has become a representative or example. The same applies in the case of things "to be sucked," etc. But when the baby wants to go on sucking after his meal is over, and finds compensation in sucking his thumb, the thumb is more than a representative example. It becomes a substitute, and could even be considered a symbol if it were possible for the baby to evoke his mother's breast at the same time. But in spite of the Freudians, for whom such symbols exist as early as the age of two months, and in spite of K. Groos, who sees make-believe in all practice play, in our opinion there cannot be symbolism, consciousness of make-believe, before there is representation, which begins and gradually develops at the beginning of the second year, when sensory-motor assimilation becomes mental assimilation through differentiation between signifier and signified. When J. pretended to be asleep, holding a corner of the sheet and bending her head, the sensory-motor schema thus set in motion resulted in more than mere exercise, since it served to evoke a past situation, and the corner of the sheet became a conscious substitute for the absent pillow. With the projection of such "symbolic schemas" on to other objects, the way is clear for the assimilation of any one object to another, since any object can be a make-believe substitute for any other.

The causality of symbolic play now becomes clear, since it derives essentially from the structure of the child's thought. Symbolic play represents in thought the pole of assimilation, and freely assimilates reality to the ego. As we said earlier, it is therefore to practice play what adapted thought is to sensory-motor intelligence, and it is to adapted thought what practice play is to sensory-motor intelligence, *i.e.*, the assimilating pole. But why is there assimilation of reality to the ego instead of immediate assimilation of the universe to experimental and logical thought? It is simply because in early childhood this thought has not yet been constructed, and during its development it is inadequate to supply the needs of daily life. Moreover, the most adapted and most logical thought of which the young child is capable is still pre-logical and egocentric, its structure being intermediate between the symbolic thought of play and adult thought.[2]

To sum up what has already been said, symbolic play is merely egocentric thought in its pure state. The essential condition for objectivity of thought is that assimilation of reality to the system of adapted notions shall be in permanent equilibrium with accommodation of these same notions to things and to the thought of others. It is obvious that it is only by the constitution of systems of logical operations (reversibility of transformations of thought), of moral operations (preservation of values) and spatio-temporal operations (reversible organisation of elementary physical notions), that such an equilibrium can be achieved, for it is only through operational reversibility that thought becomes capable of preserving its notions despite the fluctuations of reality and incessant contact with the unexpected. The reversible operation is at the same time an expression of the modifications of reality and the regulated transformations of thought, and is therefore both accommodation and assimilation. As elementary operations only begin to be "grouped" towards the end of early childhood it is natural that in the preceding stages the child's mind should be in a constant state of flux between three states: temporary equilibrium (liable to continual "displacements") between assimilation and accommodation, intermittent accommodation displacing the previous equilibrium, and assimilation of reality to the ego, *i.e.*, to that aspect of thought which is still centred on itself because correlative accommodation is lacking. It follows that for the child assimilation of reality to the ego is a vital condition for continuity and development, precisely because of the lack of equilibrium in his thought,

[2] See our article, 1923. La pensée symbolique et la pensée de l'enfant, *Arch. de Psych.*, Vol. XVIII, p. 273.

and symbolic play satisfies this condition both as regards signifier and signified. From the point of view of the signified, play enables the child to relive his past experiences and makes for the satisfaction of the ego rather than for its subordination to reality. From the point of view of the signifier, symbolism provides the child with the live, dynamic, individual language indispensable for the expression of his subjective feelings, for which collective language alone is inadequate. The symbol-object, being a real substitute for the signified, makes it actually present in a way that the verbal sign can never achieve. Since the child's whole thought is still egocentric and intuitive even in its states of maximal adaptation, and is thus linked at every intermediate stage with symbolic play, this form of play can be considered to be one of the poles of thought as a whole: the pole at which assimilation is dissociated from accommodation, or in other words, from egocentric thought in its pure state.

Symbolic play, then, is only one form of thought, linked to all the others by its mechanism, but having as its sole aim satisfaction of the ego, *i.e.*, individual truth as opposed to collective and impersonal truth, but we are still faced by the question of why the use of the symbol as opposed to the verbal concept results in make-believe and not in belief. The natural attitude of the mind is belief, and doubt or hypothesis are complex, derived behaviours whose development can be traced between the ages of seven and eleven up to the level of formal operations, at which there is a real distinction between thought and spontaneous acceptance. But although none of the conditions for this hypothetical-deductive thought obtain in the play of very young children, they make statements for the sake of stating, without believing in the game they are playing. It is a commonplace that children make the distinction between pretence and reality very early. How, then, is pretence to be explained, and why is it that ludic symbolism is divorced from belief, in contrast to the symbolism of dreams and delirium and the religious symbolism of primitive tribes? It is a complicated question, for as Janet has shown, there are various types of belief. At the level of early childhood there are two contrasting types, the one connected with social, and more particularly adult behaviours, the other with spontaneous and egocentric individual behaviours. The first is Janet's "promise-belief" an acceptance of others and of the adult, and therefore adherence to the reality which is generally

approved. The second is Janet's "assertive belief," which precedes
the distinction between what is certain and what is doubtful, and
is linked with any impact of reality on the mind. At a later stage
there is "reflective belief," associated with the mechanism of intellectual and affective operations, as for example, belief as a result
of a deduction, or a deliberate, considered decision. When the
child plays, he certainly does not believe, in the sense of socialised
belief, in the content of his symbolism, but precisely because
symbolism is egocentric thought we have no reason to suppose
that he does not believe *in his own way* anything he chooses. From
this point of view the "deliberate illusion" which Lange and Groos
see in play is merely the child's refusal to allow the world of adults
or of ordinary reality to interfere with play, so as to enjoy a private
reality of his own. But this reality is believed in spontaneously,
without effort, merely because it is the universe of the ego, and
the function of play is to protect this universe against forced accommodation to ordinary reality. There is no question, therefore,
in the early stages of symbolic play, of consciousness of make-believe like that of drama or poetry.[3] The two- to four-year-old child
does not consider whether his ludic symbols are real or not. He is
aware in a sense that they are not so for others, and makes no serious effort to persuade the adult that they are. But for him it is a
question which does not arise, because symbolic play is direct
satisfaction of the ego and has its own kind of belief, which is a
subjective reality. Moreover, as the symbol-object is a substitute
for the reality it signifies, there develops, during the first stages, a
kind of co-operation between the two, analogous to that between
the image and the object it represents.

The question then is whether collective symbolic games result in
the strengthening or weakening of belief, and the answer depends
on age. In the case of very young children, collective play either has
no effect on the egocentric symbolism or, when there is imitation, it
enhances it. In the case of older children, in whose play the symbols
are replaced by rules, it is obvious that the effect of social life is to
weaken ludic belief, at least in its specifically symbolic form.

Games with rules remain to be considered in the light of what has
been said above. We have seen that they mark the decline of children's games and the transition to adult play, which ceases to be a

---

[3] It is only after the age of seven that play really becomes make-believe in contrast
to "reflective belief."

vital function of the mind when the individual is socialised. In games with rules there is a subtle equilibrium between assimilation to the ego—the principle of all play—and social life. There is still sensory-motor or intellectual satisfaction, and there is also the chance of individual victory over others, but these satisfactions are as it were made "legitimate" by the rules of the game, through which competition is controlled by a collective discipline, with a code of honour and fair play. This third and last type of play is therefore not inconsistent with the idea of assimilation of reality to the ego, while at the same time it reconciles this ludic assimilation with the demands of social reciprocity.

Questions for Discussion

1. Piaget writes that play begins with the first dissociation between assimilation and accommodation. Based on the reading, give some specific examples of this dissociation.
2. How is representational thought (or language) different from sensory-motor activity?
3. How is make-believe play (symbolic assimilation) different from representational or mature thought?
4. Why is symbolic play necessary in the child's development?
5. What implications have Piaget's views for children's physical education programs?

BERNICE E. LOTT and ALBERT J. LOTT

The Formation of Positive Attitudes toward Group Members*

An interesting current development in social psychology is the application of the concept of social reinforcement to the description and explanation of group behavior. The importance of

* Reprinted and abridged with permission of the authors and the publisher from the *Journal of Abnormal and Social Psychology*, vol. 61, no. 2, 1960, pp. 297–300.

studying group behavior—morale, cooperation, and competition—is obvious for physical education. However, the experimental manipulation of conditions that foster desirable behavior in the team and in each member has been undertaken only recently.

The next study concerns the promotion of group cohesiveness. It is based upon learning theory and the rewarding (or reinforcement) of responses. In terms of classical conditioning, stimuli that are paired with the original stimulus also become conditioning stimuli, as in the case of the bell and the food in the Pavlov experiments. In this experiment the good feeling of an individual rewarded in the presence of members of his group extends to the group itself.

In an attempt to predict group behavior on the basis of general psychological principles as contrasted with formulations specific to the area, the concept of group cohesiveness has been re-examined and reformulated within a learning theory framework (Lott). Within this framework, cohesiveness is defined as *that group property which is inferred from the number and strength of mutual positive attitudes among the members of a group.* The concept of attitude is used, instead of the more usual one of attraction, because of its precise and particular meaning within learning theory, i.e., an implicit anticipatory response having cue and drive properties (Doob, 1947). By defining cohesiveness in terms of mutual positive attitudes among group members, the assumption is made that the members who comprise a group constitute its most significant components.

A number of hypotheses regarding both the antecedents and consequents of cohesiveness, as defined above, have been derived from learning theory (Lott). The problem of this experiment has been to test the most fundamental of these hypotheses, one which concerns the conditions under which positive attitudes toward group members may be formed.

It is predicted that if a person is rewarded in the presence of others (fellow group members), he will develop positive attitudes toward them. This proposition rests upon the following assumptions:

1. Persons may be conceptualized as discriminable stimuli to which responses may be learned.

2. A person who experiences reinforcement or reward for some behavior will react to the reward, i.e., will perform some observable or covert goal response (R_g or r_g).

3. This response to reward will become conditioned, like any other response, to all discriminable stimuli present at the time of reinforcement.

4. A person (group member) who is present at the time that Individual X, for example, is rewarded thus becomes able, in a later situation, to evoke R_g or, what is more likely, its fractional and anticipatory component, $r_g — s_g$. This latter response, which Hull has called "expectative" (1952, Ch. 5), was earlier interpreted by Doob (1947) as the underlying mechanism of an attitude.

The specific prediction tested by this study is that members of three-person groups who are rewarded for their performance in the presence of their fellow group members will more likely develop positive attitudes toward them than will members of such groups who are not rewarded. Positive attitudes are inferred, here, from choices made on a sociometric test subsequent to, and outside of, the experimental situation.

Method

SUBJECTS

Forty-eight children from the University of Kentucky Elementary School, 24 each from Grades 3 and 5, served as Ss.

PROCEDURE

The Ss were divided into 16 three-member groups, following the administration of two sociometric tests. These tests were given, by the regular classroom teachers, on two consecutive days, several days before the actual experimental situation. On the basis of the test results the groups were formed so that each group was made up of children who had *not chosen each other* on either of the tests. Four all male and four all female groups were formed from Grade 3; five male and three female groups were formed from Grade 5.

Omitting the preliminary instructions, the criterion question asked in the first test was as follows:

Test I. Let us suppose that each one of you gets picked to take a trip to the moon in a rocket ship. This is a very special trip. . . . It is important for everyone who is on the same ship to get along well with each other. . . . Because of this you get a chance to pick two children to go along with you. Now, of all the children in this class, which two would you pick to travel in the same rocket ship with you?

Test II. [For this test the children were asked to think of themselves as visitors from Mars and to choose two classmates whom they would like to have waiting for them when their spaceship landed on Earth.]

For a group situation in which rewards and non-rewards could be manipulated, a board game called "Rocket Ship" was devised. The object of the game, played by groups of three, is to land cardboard rocket ships on planetary objectives. Each objective is reached by traversing a separate path containing four danger zones, at each of which a choice between a white and a striped subpath (one "safe" and the other "dangerous") must be made. By having the children in a group take turns crossing the danger zones first, the *E*s could arrange to have some children succeed and others fail in reaching the planets safely. The manner in which this was accomplished will be described below.

On the day of the experiment proper (separate days for the two classes), the *E*s were introduced to *S*s as having developed a children's game which they wished to test. One group at a time was called upon (in a predetermined random order) to play the game in a room adjoining the regular classroom. The following instructions, given to each group by one of the investigators (E_1), describe the manner of playing:

. . . You three are rocket ship pilots. Each one of you has your own ship but you are going to take a trip into outer space together, side by side. The first trip you are to take is to ____. In order to get there you must follow this path which scientists have decided is the safest way to go. The scientists also know that, at a few points along the way on this path, there is great danger. When you get to one of these dangerous points you are going to have to stop and decide whether the striped path or the white path is the dangerous one. One of the paths will get you past the danger safely. If you take the wrong path your rocket ship will be blown up and you'll have to parachute to Earth. . . . When you get to a danger point you'll have to decide which one of the group will take a chance and be the first to try either the striped or white path. If he gets through safely, the other two rockets may follow him. If his ship should get blown up, though, the other two ships will take the other path which you will know to be safe. You'll know that a ship has been blown up when you hear the sound of a bell, like this [sounded by E_2]. . . . Remember, you must take turns being first.

. . . It's possible for all three of you to get through to a planet safely, but it may be that only two of you will make it, and maybe just one or none of you will make it. . . . If you reach a planet safely you will be able to choose one of these prizes [small plastic auto models] which you may keep. . . . We'll play half the game this morning and half this afternoon.

Each group tried for three objectives in the morning and three in the afternoon. Half the total number of Ss was permitted to land safely on four planets (two at each session) while half was prevented from reaching any of them. "Reward" was thus defined as the receipt of four plastic car models (one for each successful landing). A child was either "rewarded" or "not-rewarded," i.e., made no successful landings at all and received no prizes; there were no in-between conditions. Prizes won in the morning session were held by the Es until the end of the afternoon session at which time the rewarded Ss returned to their classroom with four model cars and the nonrewarded Ss returned with none.

Rewarded and nonrewarded Ss were selected on a random basis prior to the game. A nonrewarded S always had his ship "blown up" when, at his chance to go first at a danger point, he took either the striped or white path.[1] As soon as he made his choice of path, the "blow up" bell was rung by E_2 who sat somewhat apart from the game area.

Each group had been randomly assigned, prior to the game situation, to one of the following conditions which describe the number of group members who were to be rewarded during the game: zero, one, two, all. Four groups, two from each class, were assigned to each condition. This aspect of the design was intro-

---

[1] Each child was in the position of "being first" at a danger point at least once on his way to each of the planets since Ss had been instructed to take turns and there were four danger zones per path and three children in a group. It was always possible, therefore, to "blow up" nonrewarded Ss without interfering with a group's spontaneous behavior regarding which child would go first at which point.

duced to avoid having the Ss suspect that the game was "rigged." The natural flavor of the game was maintained by having Ss know that it was possible for all three group members to be successful, or only two, etc.

Shortly before the close of the school day, approximately one hour after the last group had played the game, the classroom teacher administered another sociometric test (III), as follows:

> Suppose your family suddenly got the chance to spend your next vacation on a nearby star out in space . . . you can invite two children to go on the trip . . . and spend the holiday with you on the star. Which two children in this class would you choose to take with you?

After the choices were collected by the teacher, E_2 appeared before the class to thank the Ss for their cooperation and help. And, because everyone had been such "good sports," four prizes were distributed to each of the youngsters who had not won them during the game.

Results

The results of the final sociometric test (III), which succeeded the play-group experience, are presented in Table 1. The proportion

Table 1
CHOICES MADE BY SUBJECTS ON SOCIOMETRIC TEST III

Subjects	Choices		
	Play-group Member	Non-play-group Member	N^a
Rewarded	11	37	48
Nonrewarded	3	45	48

[a] N = number of choices made; each S made two choices.

of play-group members chosen by rewarded Ss was found to be significantly greater than the proportion chosen by nonrewarded Ss. The obtained critical ratio, corrected for continuity, is 2.14 ($p = .03$; two-tailed). This confirms the prediction that Ss who had been rewarded would choose members of their groups, on the final sociometric test, significantly more often than Ss who had not been rewarded.

Discussion

The present findings indicate that the formation of positive attitudes toward persons is predictable from learning theory principles and can be studied in the laboratory. This study thus extends the applicability of a general S-R framework to significant social behavior.

The prediction that positive attitudes toward persons can be formed by experiencing reward in their presence, was clearly confirmed. Since it is in terms of such positive attitudes among the members of a group that cohesiveness has been defined, the present experiment is seen to be concerned with the antecedents or determinants of cohesiveness even though no attempt was made to measure the variable directly. The specific concern of this first study was with the development of positive attitudes toward group members and not with the group property that results from such attitudes when they are mutual.[2]

There have been comparatively few experimental attempts to vary group cohesiveness other than by suggesting to the members of a group that they will like each other. One investigation in which determinants were experimentally manipulated (Thibaut, 1950) found a positive relationship between cohesiveness and group status. In another study, more relevant to the present one (Bovard, 1951), a significantly greater level of interpersonal affect was found in group-centered as compared with traditional leader-centered classes. Bovard suggested that this result was due to the fostering, in group-centered classes, of member-to-member interaction which produces greater accuracy in intermember perception, creating, according to Bovard, a situation conducive to "need satisfaction." That the experience of need satisfaction (reward) in the presence of group members can, indeed, result in positive affect toward those group members has been demonstrated in the present experiment.

The results obtained in this study should be evaluated in the light of the following factors which could only have tended to work against substantiation of the hypothesis:

1. Play-group members were, by design, neutral or negative stimuli for one another at the beginning of the experimental situa-

2 An operational measure of cohesiveness which follows directly from the definition of the concept given earlier has been developed by the investigators and will be reported in connection with its use in another study.

tion. This was assured by placing, in a group, only *S*s who had not chosen one another on two previous sociometric tests.

2. The amount of reward experience received by rewarded *S*s in the presence of others was extremely small when compared with the amount of daily contact our *S*s typically had with each other in the classroom, playground, and after school. (Practically all the *S*s in each of the classes had been together for their entire schooling, beginning with kindergarten.)

3. The choices made on the two pre-experimental sociometric tests (I and II) were found to be unexpectedly stable for third and fifth graders, indicating relatively reliable friendship ties[3] which the experimental experience was able to disrupt, however temporarily.[4]

Despite the above factors the prediction, that positive attitudes toward persons will be developed as a result of the receipt of reward in their presence, was clearly supported. Though the results were obtained with children, there is no reason to expect that they would not hold with adults as well. Such generalization must, of course, await adequate test.

The variable manipulated in the present study was simply reward vs. nonreward. Future research might profitably deal with variations in reward frequency, delay, and schedule, for example, as these affect the conditioning of attitudinal responses, and, consequently, as these affect the development of cohesiveness in small groups. That the results obtained in this study were predicted from general behavior principles increases our confidence in the promise which this kind of an approach holds for the general area of small group behavior.

Summary

Three-member groups of children played a game in which some members were rewarded and others were not. On a later sociometric test, outside of the game situation, rewarded *S*s chose a significantly

---

[3] Forty percent of the *S*s made the same two choices on both tests; another 42% of the *S*s repeated one choice on both tests.

[4] No follow-up test was given since there was no reason to expect that the positive attitudes formed during the brief game situation would last, in the absence of continued reward experience in the presence of the same individuals.

greater proportion of their fellow group members than did the nonrewarded *S*s. These results were predicted from general principles of S-R learning theory.

Literature Cited

1. BOVARD, E. W. The experimental production of interpersonal affect. *J. abnorm. soc. Psychol.,* 1951, 46, 521–528.
2. DOOB, L. W. The behavior of attitudes. *Psychol. Rev.,* 1947, 54, 135–156.
3. HULL, C. A. *A behavior system.* New Haven: Yale Univer. Press, 1952.
4. LOTT, BERNICE E. Group cohesiveness: A learning phenomenon. *J. soc. Psychol.,* 1961, 55, 275–286.
5. THIBAUT, J. An experimental study of the cohesiveness of underprivileged groups. *Hum. Relat.,* 1950, 3, 251–278.

Questions for Discussion

1. How did the treatment differ for rewarded and non-rewarded subjects?
2. How is cohesiveness defined in this experiment?
3. What application of these methods could be made to promote team cohesiveness?
4. What are the rewards offered by teachers to students?
5. Would blame put upon an individual tend to extend to the group?

[SECTION IV]

Biological Backgrounds

Each area of subject matter in the school curriculum plays its part to fulfill the main purpose of education, the fullest possible development of the total individual. The unique contribution of physical education to the education process is made through the medium of human movement, or large muscle activity. It is the only field of study offering physical exercise as a means to complete education.

Two interrelated generalizations emerge from the analysis of this unique contribution: (1) that exercise has a direct bearing upon growth and development, and (2) that exercise is needed for the maintenance of physical fitness.

These generalizations are no longer mere assumptions. Supporting evidence is found in the research biology, anthropology, genetics, nutrition, physiology, medicine, kinesiology, and biochemistry. These fields constitute the biological backgrounds of physical education.

Knowledge of exercise and its contribution to physical growth and development is meaningful for predicting sequential skill development, graded activities, classification systems, and levels of competition. The effects of vigorous exercise on muscle and bone development and on the heart and other vital organs also demand the student's attention.

Equally important is the maintenance of physical fitness once body growth and development are completed. Physical fitness in adulthood becomes more problematic today than ever before as modern life becomes more sedentary. Activities once viewed as leisure-time sports now become health necessities; this has important implications for physical education.

The central purpose of this section is the presentation of important research from the biological backgrounds of physical education in order to assist the student in understanding the special contribution of his field.

Although it is generally assumed that exercise is necessary for minimum growth, controversy has surrounded discussions of this subject among physical educators. This controversy bears on a variety of issues, ranging from the amount of actual physical growth ensuing from certain amounts of exercise to the advisability of athletic competition for elementary school children.

The following article is one of the best statements of the relationship between physical growth and exercise and presents important scientific evidence to support its conclusions.

G. LAWRENCE RARICK

Exercise and Growth*

Exercise as a Factor Affecting Growth of Muscle

Physiologists have repeatedly verified the commonplace observation that muscles increase in size as a result of regular periods of heavy physical exercise. Gains in strength also accompany increases in muscle size although the strength increments are usually proportionately greater than the increases in muscle girth. As Morpurgo (25) demonstrated almost 60 years ago, the muscular hypertrophy of exercise is due to an increase in the sarcoplasm of the individual muscle fibers and not to any increase in the number or

* Pp. 450–461, "Exercise and Growth" by G. Lawrence Rarick from *Science and Medicine of Exercise and Sports* edited by Warren R. Johnson. Copyright © 1960 by Warren R. Johnson.
Reprinted with the permission of Harper & Row, Publishers.

length of the fibers. It is now believed that the increase in size and strength of muscles which accompanies training is largely due to the development of latent fibers called into play by heavy exercise and not to the additional growth of fibers normally used (17). As muscular hypertrophy occurs there is also an increased vascularization of muscle tissue, more particularly an increase in the capillary bed of the exercised part. Petren (27) believes that exercises of endurance bring on additional capillarization whereas activities requiring considerable strength result in hypertrophy of muscle fibers.

The stimulant for growth of muscle tissue is more closely related to the intensity of exercise than to the duration. This was demonstrated by Siebert (34), who forcibly exercised rats over a period of six months on motor-driven drums. In his experiment all rats ran the same distance, but the speed of running was systematically varied for different animals. Siebert found that the greatest muscular hypertrophy occurred in the leg muscles of the animals which were forced to run at high speeds. Only mild hypertrophy was produced at moderate speeds of long duration and only when the rate was markedly increased did additional hypertrophy occur. There seems to be little doubt that muscular hypertrophy is a function primarily of the rate at which the work is performed, and that mild activity even though conducted over long periods of time accomplishes little in the way of building muscle tissue or developing strength.

Accompanying the hypertrophy of exercise chemical changes occur in the muscle tissue which include substantial increases in muscle protein, muscle glycogen, phosphocreatine, and muscle hemoglobin (17). The question as to whether the stimulus for the hypertrophy of exercise is the mechanical involvement of tension and pressure or a chemical phenomenon is not as yet clear. Hettinger and Müller (12) present the view that exercise triggers the growth mechanism in the muscle fiber only when an oxygen deficit occurs. The data presented by these researchers indicate that strength increases most rapidly when the training load is increased from $\frac{1}{3}$ to $\frac{2}{3}$ maximum tension. The hypothesis proposed is that only when the load is approximately $\frac{2}{3}$ maximum are "all" the muscle fibers experiencing some oxygen want. Early work by Müller had indicated that approximately 20 percent of maximal strength could be held almost indefinitely and that strength building effects were not noted until static contractions reached ⅓ the maximum level. In stimulating muscle growth and building strength Hettinger and Müller believe that sustained isometric contractions are more effective than isotomic contractions and that for each muscle there is a range of exercise loads for building strength, the lower level being sufficient to throw only a few fibers into oxygen debt, while at the upper limit (approximately ⅔ maximal strength) all fibers are placed in oxygen debt.

The possibility that chemical agents formed in the contracting muscle may activate growth should not be overlooked; for Steinhaus (36) cites evidence that the feeding of tetanized muscle tissue to tadpoles is effective in stimulating muscle growth. The effects of testosterone and the androgens upon muscle growth have been previously mentioned. Increased activity of certain of the endocrine glands during periods of training has been suggested as a possible stimulus for growth of muscle tissue. Again the immediate stimulating factor is elusive. As will be pointed out in the next section, a considerable body of evidence is aligned on the side of mechanical tension as the most significant factor in initiating the reactions resulting in the maintenance and growth of muscle tissue.

STRESS AS A GROWTH STIMULANT

Athletic coaches and physical educators base training programs on the belief that when the human body is repeatedly placed under conditions of physical stress the organs and tissues involved tend to react by overcompensating both structurally and functionally in such a way that gradual improvement in performance results. The validity of this concept has been established not only in respect to the muscular hypertrophy associated with heavy physical activity but also in the compensatory responses of the body to biological stresses of many kinds. As one example, in embryological development stress is recognized as a major morphogenetic factor particularly for tissues of mesenchymal origin. In the structural development of cartilage, bone, blood vessels, fascia, and muscles the orientation of the cells and the intercellular fiber systems is dependent upon the mechanical tensions involved, such orientation occurring in the direction of the applied stress. Weiss (44) states that many of the tensions occurring during normal development are from intrinsic sources and are the result of the interplay of local shifts in intensities of growth involving stresses brought on by expanding or contracting areas. This does not preclude the influence of extrinsic tensions in orienting the form and direction of growth. In fact, it is recognized that any physical force which affects the orientation of the molecular matrix of the cells may alter structural design.

While it is recognized that physical stress is important in shaping the structural arrangement of tissues, it must be realized that tension is not the determining factor in cell differentiation. It may, however, be a significant factor in enabling the cells to achieve terminal transformations for which they were originally predisposed, for as Weiss points out myoblasts will not develop into muscle cells in the absence of stretch. However, stretch cannot transform a non-myoblast into a muscle fiber. Stresses then of either intrinsic or extrinsic origin appear to be capable of not only altering the orientation of structure during early development, but appear to be important in helping cells, particularly those of mesenchymal origin, realize their destiny in the growth of normal body structures.

Hellebrandt and Houtz (11) point out the importance of overload stress in increasing the capacity of the human body to perform severe exercise. They believe that the increased capacity for work brought about by overload stress is in a large measure due to changes in the central nervous system and not, at least initially, to changes in basic structure. The fact that performance changes seem to occur more rapidly than modifications in structure gives support to this point of view.

DENERVATION ATROPHY AND ATROPHY OF DISUSE

Additional insight into the matrix of factors which affects the growth and maintenance of muscle tissue has been gained from observations which have been made on denervation atrophy and atrophy of disuse. In cases where the nerve supply to the muscle is lost there is a gradual wasting-away of the active muscle tissue. As Fischer points out, the loss is characterized by a decline in muscle wet weight and muscle-phase volume, a reduction in myogen, actin, and myosin and an increase in fibrous tissue and myoalbumin. It should be noted that Kosman and others found that in the case of denervated muscle, loss in tension occurred more rapidly

and to a greater extent than weight loss. The fact that these workers noted that tension returned more rapidly on re-innervation than
the increase in weight, suggests that the gains in the protoplasm-
fixing power of the muscle are in some way enhanced as the muscle
regains its tension-producing powers. The importance of activity
to the normal well-being of muscle tissue and to its protein-retain-
ing power is indicated by the effect of daily galvanic stimulation
on denervation atrophy. As Hines (13) demonstrated, daily weak
galvanic stimulation had only a mild effect in retarding the weight
loss of denervation atrophy, whereas prolonged and strong daily
galvanic or faradic stimulation not only markedly retarded muscular weight loss, but also accelerated the return of muscle to its
original size after re-innervation. There is general agreement that
electrical treatment can slow down the weight loss in denervated
muscle. Present research has also demonstrated that the use of electrical treatment with denervated muscles has the effect of maintaining larger and stronger muscle fibers at the time of initial re-
innervation than would have occurred without the treatment.
Those who hold to the theory that the tension effects are important
in stimulating growth of muscle can point to the evidence of Fischer
and Ramsey in which stimulation of a loaded extremity proved to
be more effective than stimulation of an unloaded muscle in preventing loss of muscle protein in denervation atrophy.

The rate at which the muscle atrophies with denervation is relatively rapid, for the muscle loses approximately 40 percent of its
dry weight in 2 weeks, 50 percent in 4 weeks, and 60 percent in 12
weeks. The rapid loss in muscle tissue brought on by denervation is
believed by some to be due to the energy used in the endless, haphazard contractions of muscular fibrillation which begins 7 to 10
days after denervation and continues as long as contractile tissue remains. However, Abramson cites evidence that electrical stimulation retards the rate of atrophy without reducing the fibrillation.
This would suggest that the atrophy is not entirely a function of the
muscular fibrillation which is brought on by denervation.

In atrophy of disuse resulting from immobilization of a part the
rate of atrophy approaches that of denervation. When the muscle
is made completely quiet by cutting all dorsal roots and transection
of the cord, the rate of atrophy is the same as that under conditions
of denervation. Likewise, in tenotomy atrophy sets in at the same
rate as in the case of denervation but with no accompanying fibril-

lation. Application of passive tension to the muscle does not in itself prevent atrophy in cases of denervation, nor is atrophy prevented by activation of the muscle under conditions in which the normal tension-producing function of the muscle is lost by severing the tendon of insertion. Therefore the active tension produced by the muscular contraction itself would appear to be the factor which prevents atrophy, for the greater the interference with this function, the more extensive the atrophy. This parallels what is known about the hypertrophy resulting from heavy exercise; the more tension the muscle is called upon to develop, the greater the hypertrophy.

Exercise and Bone Growth

Steinhaus (36) in an early review of research on the chronic effects of exercise found little agreement among research workers concerning the long-term effect of exercise on long bone growth. In citing evidence drawn chiefly from studies conducted in Europe, Steinhaus reported that a substantial body of these data supported the belief that the pressure effects of exercise on the epiphyses of bones had a stimulating effect on growth up to an optimal length, but excessive and prolonged pressure retarded growth. Evidence of the effects of inactivation was presented from studies in which one limb in dogs was inactivated by a stiff bandage, resulting in bones lighter in weight and with less mineral matter than in the bones of the active limbs. However, the bones in the immobilized limb tended to be longer and slenderer with histological evidence of more growth at the epiphyseal line. The accelerated activity of the epiphyseal line was believed to be due to the lack of growth-slowing pressure on the ends of the bones, whereas the slender character of the bones was attributed to the absence of the growth-stimulating effect of muscular tension on lateral bone growth.

Evidence obtained from humans who have become bedfast gives some insight into the role which physical activity plays in maintaining the normal structure of bone tissue. Asher, in pointing out the dangers of prolonged bed rest, states that bones which are not subjected to normal use lose calcium and that the absence of weight-bearing may delay the complete union of fractured bones. According to Abramson, a normal healthy person who is placed in bed in a plaster fixation increases his calcium loss for five to six weeks. There is also an associated nitrogen loss during this period which shows that complete physical inactivity results in a depletion of the normal stores of both calcium and protein. Upon restoration of a program of activity there occurs a positive calcium and nitrogen balance.

In motor paralysis the density of bone declines. Regardless of the cause, muscular atrophy in children brings about a decrease in both bone diameter and density, whereas in the adult only the density decreases (24). Howell (15) in an early study on growing puppies found that with very young dogs the stress and strain of use had little effect on long bone growth early in life, but later the effects of disuse retarded linear growth by as much as 20 to 25 percent. This led Howell to conclude that length of bone and the basic features in bony configuration are determined by inherent factors, whereas growth in diameter of bones is influenced by exercise. Lanier (42) studied the effects of daily exercise on the joint structure of mice in which the animals were run on motor-driven roller cylinders for 1 to 6 hours daily throughout their normal life span. The results of microscopic examinations of the joint structures of the exercised animals and nonexercised controls showed no essential differences. The author concluded that continued daily use in no way contributed to joint degeneration and perhaps prevented or delayed the appearance of early degenerative change.

The effect of neurotrophic action on growing bone has been investigated by Tower under conditions in which the normal nerve supply to the bone was retained but the part under observation was kept inactive. The results eliminated neurotrophic action as a growth stimulant in the absence of nervously initiated activity in muscle. The author concluded that function such as the weight-bearing effect on the lower extremities was the primary factor in the maintenance of bone density. Apparently the tension produced by muscle on bones and the pressure effects of supporting the body weight are of primary importance in maintaining the integrity of bone tissue.

Growth Stimulating Effects of Protracted Exercise Regimens

The previous sections have indicated that certain undefined minima of muscular exercise are necessary for maintaining normal muscle and bone tissue and that muscular hypertrophy can be attained in a matter of a few weeks by intensive muscular training. The importance of recognizing the role which nature plays in shaping developmental design has been emphasized as has the modifying influence of certain environmental factors. Attention will now be given to examining information on the growth effects of extended periods of physical exercise. Obviously controlled experimentation on human subjects in which the exercise variable can be carefully manipulated over a period of 12 to 15 years is impracticable. Hence one must turn to experimental work performed on animals where effective controls can be applied for a lifetime or fall back on more limited evidence obtained from humans where less rigorous controls can be applied.

Observations on Animals. Well-controlled studies on the effects of a lifetime of heavy exercise on the physical growth of animals are limited in number. The work of Donaldson and Meeser, who observed the effects of exercise on two families of albino rats followed through seven generations, is noteworthy. These investigators, using litter mates as control and experimental animals observed the effects of daily exercise begun on the 56th day of life and continued for the next 170 days (human age equivalent, 4.5 year to 19 years). Each experimental animal ran approximately 5 miles per day in a revolving cage, the distance varying from 2.4 miles to 12.6 miles depending on the age of the animal. Each paired control was kept in a stationary cage during the 170 days of the experiment. At the conclusion of the experimental period all experimental and control animals were killed and the various tissues and organs were weighed. The findings of the study showed that exercise in the male did not stimulate growth in either length or weight during this period. However, in the female exercise resulted in rats slightly larger than the controls. As a result of exercise most of the internal organs in both sexes increased in weight more rapidly than did those of the controls. Since the over-all change in weight was slight the authors concluded there must have been some compensating factor which was undergoing loss in weight; this was assumed to be fat. Furthermore, the experimenters concluded that apparently a sex difference in response to exercise did exist, in that the female was more resistant than the male in respect to depletion of body fat. The view was expressed that the rats exposed to ample exercise were living under circumstances favorable for supporting healthful circulatory and metabolic conditions and that the response to exercise was most likely an expression of the capacity of the formed cells to respond. In the view of the writers the capacity for change was limited and therefore the response to a stimulus such as exercise depended on the extent to which the cells of the responding organs had reached the size limits imposed by nature. It is interesting to note that there was a moderate increase in the weight of the musculature which was in part masked by the loss of fat. Increases were large in the weight of the heart, kidneys, suprarenals, and gonads, whereas the thyroid and liver were smaller than in the controls. In making inferences to humans, the authors pointed out that several studies have indicated that in many ways the internal chemistry of man and the rat are similar and that there is reason to believe that man and rat are in like developmental phases at relatively equivalent ages. The authors could find no evidence of cumulative effects of exercise from generation to generation.

Hatai, in an earlier study on albino rats in which the animals were exercised from the third through the sixth month of life (human equivalent, 7 to 14 years), observed that the exercised animals showed slightly greater gains in weight than the unexercised controls but no difference in length. Substantially greater gains were shown by the exercised animals in heart and kidney weight with slightly greater gains in brain weight. The animals which were exercised for only 30 days showed proportionally smaller gains.

One of the questions which is frequently raised concerning exercise and growth is the effect upon growth of the time in the growth cycle when exercise is introduced. Donaldson studied this problem with albino rats starting the exercise program with a small group of experimental animals when they were 25 days old (human equivalent of 2.1 years) and running them 0.6 mile per day in drum cages for a period of 31 days. A second group began exercise at 200 days (human equivalent of 16.6 years), running 1.2 miles per day for a period of 90 days. When compared to the controls the rats beginning the exercise at 200 days showed increases in tissues and organs similar to those given exercise early in life. The percentage deviations were approximately three times as great for the older rats and since the period of training for this group was about three times as long as for the younger animals, the author concluded that the response to exercise was of the same order regardless of age. The deviations were proportional to the duration of the training period and not a function of either age or the normal processes of growth at a particular age level.

Another technique which has proved useful in examining the effects of exercise on the growth of animals is to examine the influence of inducing inactivity into the living regimen of growing animals previously subjected to an extended program of exercise. This procedure was followed by Donaldson and Messer in which 6 male and 6 female albino rats were exercised from the 57th to the 147th day of life while an equivalent number of litter mates previously exercised were kept as controls in stationary cages. At the termination of this period both the exercised animals and the controls were killed and examined. Another series of animals was exercised similarly, but at the end of the 90-day period of activity the rats were moved to stationary cages for 100 days of inactivity. A third group was given 150 days of inactivity following the 90-day period of exercise. In each instance tissue analyses were made of experimental animals and controls at the conclusion of the period of inactivity. This method was used to ascertain the extent to which varied periods of rest would alter any gains brought about by exercise. In general the results showed that for all organs and tissues examined, growth was accelerated during the 90-day period of exercise, but with the subsequent rest period the organ weights of the exercised animals tended to regress toward the weights of the controls. However, following the periods of inactivity the organ weights of the exercised animals were still somewhat the greater. The extent to which the organ weights of the exercised animals returned to "normal" appeared to be a function of the length of the period of inactivity, being greatest following the 150 days of rest. The tendency of the organs and tissues to return to the size of the unexercised controls was not due, according to the investigators, to shrinkage by abstraction of fluid, but rather to retardation of growth during the interval of inactivity. These data would suggest that protracted exercise programs have a favorable effect on the growth of rats which is still apparent after long periods of inactivity.

In summarizing his studies on the effects of exercise on the growth of the albino rat, Donaldson concluded that body weight and body length tended to improve slightly under extended periods of moderate or vigorous exercise, the effects being more noticeable in the female than in the male. The general trend for accelerated growth was attributed to improved nutritional status with an accumulation of muscle tissue and loss of fat. With moderate exercise the gains in weight were marked; however, with excessive exercise there tended to be a loss in total weight.

Most authorities who have experimented on the rat agree that prolonged vigorous exercise results in increase in organ weight, musculature, and bone weight with a drop in body fat. The impetus given to growth by exercise applied during a portion of the period of growth tends to persist even after protracted periods of rest. The characteristically greater gains achieved by the exercised female as compared to the male is attributed by Donaldson to the role which exercise plays in releasing the organs of the female from the inhibiting forces which normally restrain growth. Donaldson's findings that exercise tends to increase the size of leg bones in rats is supported by data presented by Steinhaus (37) in which daily exercise of dogs amounting to 6 miles per day resulted in approximately 5 percent increase in leg bone length.

The importance of exercise in influencing the qualitative aspects of soft tissues should not be underestimated. For example, Mayer (22) found that the difference in the fat content of the tissues of obese and nonobese animals was not so much a difference in caloric consumption as in energy output. Nonfasted nonobese animals were found by Mayer to be 50 to 100 times more active than obese animals, thus providing some evidence of the importance of activity in influencing the deposition of fat in animals. The fact that inactivity usually preceded the development of obesity led Mayer to conclude that inactivity must be considered as a predisposing factor in the etiology of obesity. As has been pointed out earlier one of the major differences in the growth of exercised and unexercised animals is the relatively smaller amount of body fat in the exercised animals and the proportionately greater amounts of active muscle tissue.

Observations on Humans. Most studies concerned with the growth effects of exercise on bodily dimensions of humans have been conducted over a limited period of time and the majority have dealt with subjects at or near their adult body size. Only a few studies are available in which the exercise variable is clearly enough defined and extensive enough in duration to permit even tentative conclusions to be drawn. One of the few attempts to

examine the growth effects of heavy physical activity during childhood is the investigation reported by Adams in which 100 Negro
women, 17 to 21 years of age who had undergone a lifetime of
hard manual labor were compared on the basis of several anthropometric measures with 100 young women of similar age who had engaged in no heavy manual labor. The finding showed that the
women who had engaged in heavy labor from early childhood were
taller and heavier at the conclusion of the growing years than the
nonworking women. The muscle girths, chest dimensions, knee
width, and hip width of the hard-working women were also the
larger. Since the hard-working women labored regularly 10 to 12
hours daily on southern plantations and since the group came
from a lower socioeconomic group than the nonworking Negroes,
the authors concluded that the differential factor was the regimen
of heavy exercise rather than nutritional differences which would
presumably have favored the nonworking women.

Observations on humans in which a single member of the body
has been used extensively over long periods during the growing
years offers a means of examining the more lasting effects of exercise. The view has been expressed that the dominant hand and
arm are frequently larger than the member less often used. It is
known that the gripping strength of the preferred hand is ordinarily
the stronger and there is evidence which indicates that the greater
use favorably influences growth. For example, Van Dusen (70) in
comparing right and left hand and arm size of children in the age
ranges 1 to 4 years and 5 to 8 years found that children in the older
age range tended more frequently to have longer right arms, forearms, forearms and hands, and wider palms than did children in
the 1 to 4 year age range. With college-age adults the author found
that the discrepancies between right and left sides were in the same
direction as for the children, but greater in magnitude. The findings
indicate that the increasing use of the right arm with advancing
age carries with it structural advances favoring the right upper
extremity. This argument is strengthened by the recent findings of
Buskirk, *et al.* (3), in which it was demonstrated that anthropometric and roentgenographic measurement of the hands and forearms of seven nationally ranked tennis players showed significantly
greater osseous and muscular development in the dominant than in
the nondominant member. The investigators also obtained measures on a small sample of non-tennis-playing soldiers and while

differences in size were noted favoring the right over the left hand and arm in these subjects the differences were much less than the laterality differences for the tennis players. Since all of the tennis players had participated in this activity extensively in their teens, the authors expressed the view that exercise must have brought about some alteration in the osseous "growth apparatus" of the adolescent period. These studies provide rather substantial evidence that exercise of the upper extremities does stimulate the growth processes in this region. Whether heavy use of the lower extremities with the added burden of weight-bearing would result in both linear and appositional growth is still open to question.

With advancing age children gradually acquire more effective use of their muscles, not only in respect to improved coördination, but also in regard to the amount of muscular force they can develop. Martin (21) and Kintis (18) noted that with boys in the age range 5 through 11 years gains in body strength occurred at a faster rate than increases in weight. Asmussen and Heebøll-Nielson (1) in checking actual gains in strength of boys in the age range 7 to 17 years against theoretical values based upon computed indices of body mass and muscle cross section, found that the observed gains in strength substantially exceeded the theoretical values based upon indices of size. According to these writers the additional strength over and above that which might be expected to result from normal growth is explained either as a result of qualitative changes in the muscle tissue, or by more effective neural mechanisms which provide an increased ability to mobilize muscular power voluntarily. With advancing age the child is perhaps able to call on more motor units simultaneously in an all-out effort. Most certainly the effects of exercise upon muscle tissue during the growing years cannot be interpreted solely in terms of changes in muscle girths for the increases in functional power surpass the increases in size. Of even greater significance is the improvement in efficiency and economy of muscular movement which according to Steinhaus (36) is the most prominent effect of training.

It is evident from the data now available on the effects of exercise on growth that one must be cautious in drawing conclusions. If growth is used in its broadest sense, there is little doubt that development of neuromuscular skill, improved efficiency of muscular movement, and increased capacity of the organism to perform work are all the direct result of systematic practice and training. However, in respect to the morphological changes brought about by exercise the picture is not so clear. There seems to be little question that certain "minima" of muscular activity are essential for supporting "normal growth" and for maintaining the protoplasmic integrity of the tissues. What these "minima" mean in terms of intensity and duration of activity has not been ascertained. Most certainly, the drive for physical activity in the healthy young child is so strong that these "minima" represent only a fraction of the healthy child's daily exercise program. The gap between these ill-defined "minima" of exercise and that required for optimal growth is probably large, but as yet this question has not been adequately studied.

As might be expected present evidence shows that the most dramatic effect of an exercise regimen during the growing years is upon muscle tissue. While neither the height nor the weight of the organism appear to be noticeably changed, muscle tissue increases as fatty tissue declines. Likewise, heavy exercise appears to favorably affect the growth in weight and diameter of bone tissue. Long bone growth, particularly of the non-weight-bearing segments of the body seems also to be favorably influenced by exercise. In animals the internal organs, such as the heart, kidneys, and suprarenals, which are called upon to act vigorously in stress situations, show positive growth responses to exercise.

Studies on animals indicate that the time of introduction of the exercise program into the life cycle of the animal is of less consequence than the duration or intensity of the program. One might hypothesize that with humans, more should be gained by introducing the program at the time when the growth impulse is the strongest. Limited data on humans would suggest that with boys, exercise should have its greatest growth stimulating effect at adolescence when the body is marshalling its energy in support of growth of somatic tissue.

The way in which exercise triggers the growth mechanisms is not known. There seems to be little doubt that stress in the form of mechanical tension precipitates a chain of phenomena which results in both physical and chemical changes in muscle and bone tissue. There is also some evidence to indicate that oxygen deficiency in the muscle tissue may act as the stimulating agent. It is clearly evident that overload is the key factor in activating growth of body cells and in increasing the work capacity of the body, intensity rather than duration of activity being the critical factor.

In appraising our knowledge of the growth-stimulating effects of exercise, one must keep in mind that the capacity for growth is not the same for all individuals. This is borne out by the limited data now available which indicates that extended periods of exercise bring about more pronounced changes in the pattern of growth for individuals of mesomorphic build than for linear-framed children. However, general observation gives some support to the view that exercise by increasing the desire for food benefits nutrition and plays a supporting role in adding solid tissue to the slender small-boned child. Likewise, the impetus which nature gives to somatic tissue development at adolescence provides the medium through which exercise may rather extensively accentuate the muscle-building powers of the male at this time.

It should be kept in mind that the effects of exercise on growth cannot be entirely isolated from other growth variables, for the demands of exercise require rather extensive circulatory and metabolic adjustments which affect the entire body. While conclusive evidence of the beneficial effects of vigorous exercise upon the growth of all organ systems of the body has not been established, continued use normally produces improved physiological responses in body cells. The possibility that an inactive childhood may be the forerunner of undesirable developmental trends has not been adequately explored. There is, however, some evidence to indicate that obesity may have its roots in childhood and that much of the problem of the slow and insidious accumulation of weight can be traced to physical inactivity (40).

Much remains to be learned concerning the effects of exercise on human growth. At the present time recommendations concerning exercise programs for children are based primarily on experience rather than scientifically derived facts. All too little information is available on the amount of exercise which children of varying maturity levels and different physiques need in order to achieve optimum growth. The effects of exercise on physical growth can best be ascertained by making repeated observations on the same children over a long period of time under conditions in which the exercise variable can be applied under well-controlled conditions. Even under the best of circumstances the problem of controlling nutritional factors and matters of daily routine makes such an undertaking difficult. While only limited generalizations can now be drawn from animal experimentation and from fragmentary data on humans, scientific information is gradually being accumulated which will serve as a guide for developing more adequate programs of physical education for children and youth.

Literature Cited

1. ASMUSSEN, E., and HEEBØLL-NIELSON, K. "A Dimensional Analysis of Physical Performance and Growth in Boys." *J. Appl. Physiol.*, 1955, 6, 585–592.
2. BAYLEY, NANCY. "Individual Patterns of Development." *Child Develpm.*, 1956, 27, 45–74.
3. BUSKIRK, E. R., ANDERSEN, K. L., and BROZEK, J. "Unilateral Activity and Bone and Muscle Development in the Forearm." *Res. Quart.*, 1956, 27, 127–131.
4. DUPERTUIS, C. W., and MICHAEL, NANCY B. "Comparison of Growth in Height and Weight Between Ectomorphic and Mesomorphic Boys." *Child Develpm.*, 1953, 24, 203–214.
5. FITT, A. B. *Seasonal Influence on Growth Function and Inheritance.* Wellington, N.Z.: New Zealand Council for Educational Research, 1941. P. 182.
6. GARN, S. M. "Physical Growth and Development." *Amer. J. Phys. Anthrop.*, 1952, 10, 169–192.
7. GARN, S. M. "Individual and Group Deviations from Channelwise Grid Progression in Girls." *Child Develpm.*, 1952, 23, 193–206.
8. GARN, S. M., and CLARK, L. C., JR. "The Sex Difference in Basal Metabolic Rate." *Child Develpm.*, 1953, 24, 215–224.
9. GREULICH, W. W., and PYLE, S. I. *Radiographic Atlas of Skeletal Development of Hand and Wrist.* Stanford: Stanford Univer. Press, 1950. P. 190.
10. HARDY, MARTHA C. "Frequent Illness in Childhood, Growth and Final Size." *Amer. J. Phys. Anthropol.*, 1938, 23, 241–260.
11. HELLEBRANDT, FRANCES A., and HOUTZ, SARA J. "Mechanisms of Muscle Training in Man." *Phys. Therapy Rev.*, 1956, 36, 1–13.
12. HETTINGER, T., and MÜLLER, E. A. "Muskelleistung und Muskeltraining." *Arb. Physiol.*, 1953, 15, 111–126.
13. HINES, H. M., and WEHRMACHER, W. H. "Physiologic Factors Involved in Atrophy and Regeneration of Skeletal Muscle." *J. Iowa Med. Soc.*, 1944, 34, 142–145.
14. HOWE, P. E., and SCHILLER, MARIA. "Growth Responses of the School Child to Changes in Diet and Environmental Factors." *J. Appl. Physiol.*, 1952, 5, 51–61.
15. HOWELL, J. A. "An Experimental Study of the Effect of Stress and Strain on Bone Development." *Anat. Rec.*, 1917, 13, 233–253.

16. JONES, H. E. *Motor Performance and Growth.* Berkeley: Univer. of California Press, 1949. P. 181.

17. KARPOVICH, P. V. *Physiology of Muscular Activity.* Philadelphia: Saunders, 1953. P. 340.

18. KINITIS, P. V. *Patterns of Growth in Strength of Elementary School Boys.* Unpublished M.A. thesis, Univer. of Wisconsin, 1953. P. 65.

19. KROGMAN, W. M. "Trend in the Study of Physical Growth in Children." *Child Develpm.,* 1940, 11, 279–284.

20. LINDEGARD, B. *Body-build and Physical Activity.* Lund, Sweden: Lunds Universitets Arsskritt. N. F. Avd. 2 Bd. 52, Nr. 8, 1956. P. 17.

21. MARTIN, E. G. "Muscular Strength and Muscular Symmetry in Human Beings." I. In children. *Amer. J. Physiol.,* 1918, 46, 67–83.

22. MAYER, J. "Decreased Activity and Energy Balance in the Hereditary Obesity-diabetes Syndrome of Mice." *Science,* 1953, 117, 504–505.

23. MEREDITH, H. V. "Stature and Weight of Children in the United States. *Amer. J. Dis. Child.,* 1941, 62, 909–932.

24. MEREDITH, H. V., and CARL, LOIS J. "Individual Growth in Hip Width: A Study Covering the Age Period From 5 to 9 Years based Upon Seriatim Data for 55 Non-pathologic White Children." *Child Develpm.,* 1946, 17, 157–172.

25. MORPURGO, B. "Ueber activitats-hypertrophie der willkurlichen muskeln." *Virchow Arch. Patholog. & Physiol. u. f. klin. Med.,* 1897, 150 S, 522–554.

26. OLSON, W. C. *Child Development.* Boston: Heath, 1949. P. 417.

27. PETREN, T., SJOSTRAND, T. and SYLVEN, B. "Der einfluss des trainings auf die haufigkeit der capillaren in herz und skeletalmuskulatur." *Arb. Physiol.,* 1936, 9, 376–386.

28. PRESCOTT, D. A. *Emotion and the Educative Process.* Washington: American Council on Education, 1938. P. 323.

29. RARICK, G. L., and THOMPSON, JOANN JONES. "Roentgenographic Measures of Leg Muscle Size and Ankle Extensor Strength of 7-year-old Children." *Res. Quart.,* 1956, 27, 321–332.

30. REYNOLDS, E. L. "Fat Bone Index as a Sex-differentiating Character in Man." *Human Biol.,* 1949, 21, 199–204.

31. REYNOLDS, E. L. "Sexual Maturation and the Growth of Fat, Muscle and Bone in Girls." *Child. Develpm.,* 1946, 17, 121–144.

32. REYNOLDS, E. L., and SONTAG, L. W. "Seasonal Variations in Weight, Height and Appearance of Ossification Centers." *J. Pediatr.,* 1944, 24, 524–535.

33. SHUTTLEWORTH, F. K. "Sexual Maturation and the Physical Growth of Girls Age 6 to 19." *Soc. Res. Child Develpm., Monogr.,* 1937, 2(5), 252.

34. SIEBERT, W. W. "Untersuchungen uber hypertrophie des skelettmuskels." *Z. klin. Med.,* 1928, 109, 350–359.

35. SIMMONS, KATHERINE, and GREULICH, W. W. "Menarcheal Age and the Height, Weight and Skeletal Age of Girls Age 7 to 17 Years." *J. Pediatr.,* 1943, 22, 518–548.

36. STEINHAUS, A. H. "Chronic Effects of Exercise." *Physiol. Rev.,* 1933, **13,** 103–147.

37. STEINHAUS, A. H., HOYT, LORIS A., and RICE, H. H. "Studies in the Physiology of Exercise. X. The Effects of Running and Swimming on the Organ Weights of Growing Dogs." *Amer. J. Physiol.,* 1932, **99,** 512–520.

38. STUART, H. C., HILL, P., and SHAW, C. "The Growth of Bone, Muscle and Overlying Tissues as Revealed by Studies of Roentgenograms of the Leg Area." *Soc. Res. Child Develpm., Monogr.,* 1940, 5(3).

39. STUART, H. C., and DWINELL, PENELOPE H. "The Growth of Bone, Muscle and Overlying Tissues in Children 6 to 10 Years of Age as Revealed by Studies of Roentgenograms of the Leg Area." *Child Develpm.,* 1942, **13,** 195–213.

40. STUART, H. C. "Obesity in Childhood." *Quart. Rev. Pediatr.,* 1955, **10,** 132–145.

41. TANNER, J. M. *Growth at Adolescence.* Oxford: Blackwell Scientific Publications, 1955. P. 212.

42. VAN DUSEN, C. R. "An Anthropometric Study of the Upper Extremities of Children." *Human Biol.,* 1939, **11,** 277–284.

43. WATERS, H. J. "The Capacity of Animals to Grow Under Adverse Conditions. Influence of Nutrition Upon the Animal Form." *Proc. Soc. Promot. Agricult. Sci.,* 1908, **29,** 71–96; 1909, **30,** 70–98.

44. WEISS, P. "Differential Growth." In A. K. Parpart (Ed.), *The Chemistry and Physiology of Growth.* Princeton: Princeton Univ. Press, 1949. Chap. VII, pp. 135–186.

Questions for Discussion

1. What causes physiological increase in cell size?

2. Should secondary school physical education programs focus upon the contribution of exercise to growth of the body or be primarily interested in the maintenance of physical fitness?

3. What are the complications resulting from the fact that growth retards after temporary illness? Should special programs in physical education be encouraged for those who suffer temporary illness as well as for those who are permanently handicapped?

4. Is the need for physical activity adequately met by the twenty minutes of physical education required daily in many elementary schools?

JOHN L. REICHERT, M.D.

Competitive Athletics
for Pre-Teen-Age Children*

Whenever the topics of exercise, growth, and development are discussed, the question of the advisability of athletic competition for growing children arises. Although many would postulate that athletic competition is important for physical growth as well as for psychological development, others would argue that athletic competition for the elementary age group may result in over-exertion and consequently impair growth. (The latter group fears injury to organs and bones not yet fully matured.)

The student will find the following discussion of the subject by John L. Reichert, a noted pediatrician, to be relevant and helpful to his understanding of this issue.

The concept of the "total child" is an accepted philosophy in the practice of pediatrics. The medical adviser today cannot be satisfied merely with the child's being well; he must be concerned with the well-being of the child. The physician is no longer merely a dispenser of health services; he is also an educator in health for his young patients and for their parents. Health education and health service start in the nursery. When the child enters school the physician surrenders none of his responsibility. Instead, he and the parents are joined by the classroom teacher, the school nurse, and other school health personnel in a continuing program of health education and health supervision. Ideally, the physician enlarges his area of influence to become a health adviser to the educators, while at the same time he learns some of their problems of education so that teacher and physician can work as a team in maintaining and improving the health of children.[1] As the child's spheres of interest

* Reprinted with permission of the late author's son and the publisher from *The Journal of the American Medical Association*, vol. 166, no. 14, pp. 1701–1707.
[1] School Health Policies, Report of Committee on School Health, *Pediatrics* **13**:74–82 (Jan.) 1954.

develop, his community activities claim the attention of the physician with the added responsibility of serving as a medical adviser
in community recreational and sports projects. The literature contains many excellent reports and studies to guide the physician in
this broad area.[2]

Need for Athletic Play

Nowhere is the need for medical guidance and cooperation greater
than in the problems connected with the participation of children
in competitive athletics. Everyone agrees that competition is essential in the growth and development of children into well-
balanced, responsible adults. But there is a distinct difference of
opinion as to the level and intensity of competition in which children should engage at the various stages of their development. The
most vehement arguments center on the question of athletic competition for children under 13 years of age. Unfortunately, much
of the argument has been on an emotional rather than an intellectual basis. While the lines have not been too clearly drawn, on
one side are those who, while believing thoroughly in competition,
would place certain limitations on the intensity and scope of competitive athletics for young children; in this group are the majority
of educators and physicians who have studied the issue. On the
other side are those who maintain that highly organized, highly
competitive, "varsity-type" athletics are a desirable activity for children in their early school years; this group consists largely of sports
promoters, professional athletes, sports fans, and some coaches. Between the two groups are the parents. Some, with a natural ambition
to develop an athletic star in the family, are drawn to the side of
highly organized pressure programs of athletics; others, concerned
primarily with the safety of their children, move toward the opposite camp.

Children's athletic programs can be classified into four groups:
(1) those that are a part of the regular school curriculum; (2) those
outside the school curriculum but a part of community recreation

---

[2] (*a*) Physicians and Schools, Report of the Fourth National Conference on the
Physicians and Schools, edited by F. V. Hein and D. A. Dukelow, A. M. A. Bureau
of Health Education, 1954, pp. 28–56. (*b*) Report of the Fifth National Conference on Physicians and Schools, A. M. A. Bureau of Health Education, 1955, p.
23. (*c*) Boatman, R. H.: Pediatrician and School Health Education, *J. School
Health* **26**:96 (March) 1957.

programs; (3) those organized under independent, special interests related to specific sports or to specific sponsors; and (4) unorganized, pick-up activities, such as "sandlot" and "scrub" games. While athletic programs in schools are more easily regulated, the essential problems of juvenile athletic competition are common to all types of programs. The problems are most apparent in the third, and most rapidly growing group. For example, one of these, Little League Baseball, has a membership of over 750,000 children. About 4,000 Little League baseball games are played every day within the specified season.[3]

Arguments for Competitive Athletics

In considering the arguments for and against highly organized, high-pressure competitive athletics in or out of school, it must be remembered that the problem is here limited to children under 13 years of age. The proponents commonly maintain the following arguments: 1. Competition as a part of life must be taught to children during their formative years, and a highly organized program of intercommunity or interscholastic competitive athletics, patterned after that of older groups, is an essential means of doing this. 2. Physical injuries and emotional disturbances sustained in such a program can be insignificant with intelligent adult supervision of the program. 3. Children engaged in competitive athletics are more physically fit, more poised, more relaxed, more confident, and in general superior both as children and as adults to those whose athletic activities are noncompetitive. 4. Children of all ages will instinctively engage in competitive athletic activity, especially in body contact play, such as boxing, "wrastling," and bare-hand fighting, with no holds barred, and to minimize the dangers of such activities, it is better for adults to organize and direct them. 5. Competitive athletics at this age can act as a feeder program to college and professional sports. 6. Competitive athletic programs promote good public relations for the school and for the community.

Before stating the answers that most parents, educators, and physicians would give to these statements, it would be well to define what is meant by highly organized, highly competitive athletics. This includes sports which are played by teams that have been developed through a series of elimination games and which rep-

[3] Hale, C.: Personal communication to the author.

resent a school or a community in championship schedules of interschool, intercommunity, regional, or national games or tournaments. The reverse of this system consists of many teams in a sport or game, involving many children in a school or community, with athletic activity confined to the school or to the community. Highly competitive athletics has been defined by the school health committee of the American Academy of Pediatrics[4] as competition in which the chief stress is placed on winning, with excessive emotional pressures applies by teachers, parents, and others, and with parental interest going to the point of expressing undue concern over winning.

In reviewing the work reported in the literature, one is impressed by the number of writers who group all sports in the same category. The same criteria for avoiding injury, exhaustion, and abnormal bone and muscle growth cannot be applied equally to body-contact and non-body-contact games, nor can they be transferred without modification from any one sport to another. This, together with a failure to designate clearly the age group under discussion, has led to much unnecessary misunderstanding and argument. Such a lack of definitiveness is difficult to avoid because of the limitations of time and space. One is also impressed by the number of studies in which medical problems are investigated by students without a medical background. Many of these studies could be improved through medical consultation and cooperation. This is not so much a criticism of the researchers as it is a pointed suggestion that more physicians should be interested in making such studies. With these points in mind, let us consider the arguments of the proponents.

"Competition Is a Part of Life"

No informed person will deny that competition is an essential part of every child's education and growth. But it is equally true that competitive drives must be allowed to develop normally and not be overstimulated or suppressed, so that as the child matures competition and cooperation are balanced forces in his personality. A child can best be developed in respect to posture, coordination, strength and control, and emotional balance by a process of gradual

[4] Competitive Athletics, Report of Committee on School Health, *Pediatrics* **18**:672–676 (Oct.) 1956.

training during the years of physiological immaturity, not by the forced development of special skills.[5] B. L. Johnson[6] of Fresno State College, in an experiment on exercise with 59 junior high school boys, found that they worked harder when put under competitive conditions but that their output was not significantly greater than the boys who were not so motivated. In fact, the added stimulus sometimes reduced the achievement. The competitive group, moreover, showed a slower recovery from heart and blood vessel strain than did the control group. In addition, nausea developed in 37% of the subjects in the motivated group either during the exercise or during the period of recovery, but only one case of nausea occurred in the group not under conditions of competition. An extensive study of Cleveland junior high school boys by Rowe[7] showed that a group competing in highly competitive interscholastic athletics did not gain as much in height, weight, and lung capacity as did a comparable group of boys in the same school who were participating in a good program of physical education and intramural athletics.

Physicians least of all want to eliminate competition from the lives of boys and girls. Physicians are not afraid of children being hurt physically or emotionally if the end-result is one that is of benefit to the child. It is done deliberately when their systems are subjected to vaccines and toxoids and when they are allowed to extricate themselves from emotional or social stresses in which they have become involved and which are not beyond their emotional maturity to cope with. But if they are to suffer such insults, these insults should be of the kind that will strengthen them, not those that will permanently harm them.[8] Johnson's study suggests that the stress of strong competition does not improve skills or promote an increased capacity for performance. At times it seems to have an opposite effect, but more investigation under controlled conditions is necessary to clarify this. Until such studies have been made, one must doubt the claim that the stress of competition promotes optimum growth and development. The preponderance of

5 Brindley, E. D.: Interschool Athletics for Elementary School Youngsters, *J. School Health* **23**:209 (Sept.) 1953.
6 Johnson, B. L.: Influence of Puberal Development on Responses to Motivated Exercise, *Res. Quart.* **27**:182–192 (May) 1956.
7 Rowe, R. A., quoted by Brindley.[5]
8 Barba, P. S.: Fitness of American Youth, read before American Academy of Pediatrics, Washington, D.C., April 1957.

opinion is in favor of limiting competition in prepubescent youth to intramural sports programs.[9]

"Injuries Can Be Insignificant"

The statement, "Injuries can be insignificant with adequate and intelligent adult supervision," contains a number of fallacies. Preadolescent and adolescent children are in a vulnerable age. During this age there are periods of rapid growth, with temporary maladjustments and weaknesses. For example, bone growth at this age is more rapid than muscle development, so that temporarily the bones and joints lack the normal protection of covering muscles and supporting tendons. During these periods, the child is particularly susceptible to dislocations of joints and to bone injuries, especially to the epiphyses. There are injuries which can cause permanent damage and can interfere with normal growth. Dr. C. L. Lowman[10] polled about 400 orthopedists on this point. About 75% of them agreed with a statement made by the state directors of health, physical education, and recreation to the effect that interscholastic athletic competition was not good for young adolescents and that body-contact sports should be eliminated. Most of the other 25% qualified their answers so as practically to rule out this type of athletics as it is now being practiced. Fait,[11] on the other hand, reported that he had surveyed the opinion of a group of orthopedic surgeons and found that only 14% believed that junior high school students were so susceptible to epiphysial injuries that the physical education and athletic programs for this group should differ drastically from the activities offered in the high school program. However, his question was so phrased that the physicians questioned were required to state whether they thought these sports should be modified for younger children. This is really a nonmedical decision on which it is difficult for the physician to give an authoritative opinion.

Violent and sustained exercise and the bruising and fatiguing activities of strenuous competition are believed by many authorities

[9] Statement of Society of State Directors of Physical and Health Education, National Education Association, 1939. Two important Resolutions, editorial, *J. Health, Phys. Educ. & Recreation* **9**:488 (Oct.) 1938.

[10] Lowman, C. L.: Vulnerable Age, *J. Health & Phys. Educ.* **18**:635 (Nov.) 1947.

[11] Fait, H.: Read before Annual Meeting of American Association for Health, Physical Education, and Recreation, April, 1956.

to throw a damaging overload on the immature heart, lungs, or kidneys. Often the damage is not evident at the time but manifests itself weeks or even years later.[12] Evidence to the contrary that I have found in the literature is not well controlled and is not impressive.

Another type of damage is more subtle. In developing skill in a particular sport, the child develops some sets of muscles more than others. As a general rule, strenuous athletics tend to strengthen flexor muscles at the expense of extensor muscles. This leads to a shift in stress and weight bearing, which in turn affects the development of the bones to which the muscles are attached. These abnormal changes in bones occur according to what is well known to physicians as Wolff's law (a bone changes its internal architecture and external shape according to the way in which the weight is borne or the stress is applied; in other words, all changes in the function of a bone are attended by definite alterations in its internal structure). The end-result can well be poor posture which in turn may result in a skeletally malaligned individual.

Foster[13] reports 14 cases in which fractures occurred among high school athletes but in which the diagnosis was not made until x-rays revealed that such an injury had occurred. Many of these fractures had been concealed by players because of the feeling that they might be accused of being "sissies" by their coaches or fellow players. Most of the fractures occurred in the hands, wrists, forearms, feet, ankles, and lower legs. Consider the hazards of permanent deformity in unreported fractures involving the growing ends of long bones. Hibbert[14] reports after extensive study of high school football injuries that one out of every five participants will sustain an injury. Of those injured, one out of five can expect a fractured bone. It is widely recognized that the younger and "greener" the boy, the

12 (a) Lowman, C. L.: Relations of Posture States to Competitive Sports, *Phys. Educ.* vol. 9 (Oct.) 1953. (b) Statement on Boxing, Joint Committee on Health Problems of N. E. A. and A. M. A., 1951. (c) Joint High School Football Injury Study: Michigan, Minnesota, and Wisconsin, Wisconsin State High School Athletic Association, Marinette, Wis., 1949. (d) Crowe, H. E.: Orthopedic Facts About Football, *J. School Health* **17**:180 (Sept.) 1947.

13 Foster, W. K., cited by Byrd, O. E.: Unrecognized Fractures in High School Athletes, in *Health Instruction Yearbook*, Stanford, Calif., Stanford University Press, 1950, p. 50.

14 Hibbert, R. W., Jr.: High School Football Injuries, *Rocky Mountain M. J.* **47**:276–278 (April) 1950.

greater the probability and extent of the injury.[15] The following case in point is reported from my practice.

> A 12-year-old postpubescent boy bumped heads violently with another player in the tryouts for a junior high school football team. He concealed the fact of a painful neck which lasted for two weeks, and continued playing on the team. Six weeks later he had a similar collision and developed a wry neck, which he concealed for one week, and continued to play football every school day. Because of continued pain, he finally admitted his disability to his parents. I saw him one week after the second injury. On x-ray examination, he had a subluxation of the first cervical vertebra and an older, partially healed fracture of the seventh cervical vertebra. After six weeks in traction, he made an uneventful recovery with no residual neurological findings.

There is a definite possibility of paralysis or death in injuries of the type reported above. However, the dangers of high-pressure athletics are not limited to physical injury alone. Strong emotional reactions are too often engendered by high-pressure competitive games, especially by intercommunity or interscholastic schedules and championships. Such a response occurs not only in children but also in adults—parents, teachers, coaches, and spectators. These exaggerated reactions can lead to abnormal psychological responses, both in parents and in children, in many ways. The hero worship of the star, the sense of failure in the boy who does not make the team or who fails to make the crucial point in the game, the obvious disappointment of the parent when the boy fails or the excessive pride and praise when he wins, the apparent difference in social acceptance by playmates and adults between the winners and the losers—all these can have a profound effect on a child's emotional development and social adjustment.

Many of the harmful results engendered by highly competitive sports are due to the fact that they are organized on an adult level. The parades, uniforms, prizes, and general spirit of a Roman holiday presumably glorify the child. But these exhibitions are actually aimed at the parent, who is vicariously glorified, an experience he may have craved but missed in his childhood.

One observer has taken the pulse and respirations of the father of the pitcher of the winning team and of the coach at the end of a World Series game and has found them to be higher than those of the boy who pitched the game.

---

[15] Joint High School Football Injury Study, *op. cit.*

Much of the injury, both physical and emotional, could be avoided if the opponents were equally matched. Matching by chronologic age or by size is not adequate. During this age span there are wide variations in the rate of physical and emotional maturation. . . . The studies of Pryor and Smith[16] show the difference in size, body build, and physiological maturity that can exist between girls of the same chronologic age. They have also demonstrated the wide differences in achievement between the lateral and the linear type of girl of the same age. . . . Although there is a difference in time as to maturation in boys and girls, the same physiological principles apply to boys at a somewhat later age. Two 12-year-old boys who are well matched as to height and build may be years apart in their physical development and stamina and, perhaps more important, in the maturity of their judgment. The immature boy is no match for his more mature opponent. Not only is he more likely to lose but also he can be badly injured in the process. A striking example of this was demonstrated in a recent study by Hale.[17] He found that the majority of boys who played in the 1955 Little League World Series, boys of 10, 11 and 12 years, were adolescent and, not as their chronologic age would indicate, preadolescent. In other words, in the elimination games the tendency was for the more mature boys to win out over the immature ones. It is gratifying to know that so large a boys' organization recognizes the lack of correlation between chronologic and developmental age. On the other hand, one wonders about the effects on all of the preadolescent boys who went down to defeat as the members of the world series team climbed to stardom.

There are several technical methods of judging the developmental level of the child. Shaffer[18] classifies boys as prepubescent, pubescent, and postpubescent, depending on the presence or abscence of pubic hair and the amount of kinking or curling of the hair (the Crampton test). This is a good measure of sexual development, but in my experience there is not enough correlation with the stage of intellectual or emotional maturity to make it useful as a

16 Pryor, H. B., and Smith, R. T.: Physical Strength of Adolescent Girls, *J. Pediat.* **14**:610–617 (May) 1939.
17 Hale, C. J.: Physiological Maturity of Little League Baseball Players, *Res. Quart.* **27**:276–284 (Oct.) 1956.
18 Shaffer, T. E.: Examination and Evaluation of High School Athletics, *J. School Health* **21**:51 (Feb.) 1951.

matching test. It has been suggested[19] that bone age, as determined by x-rays of the carpal bones, be used as a guide. This would probably have the same limitations as the Crampton test. Furthermore, until the question of the danger of excessive radiation exposure in the age of nuclear fission has been settled, it would be unwise to institute an additional mass x-ray program.

The boys most likely to be picked for a football team, particularly the linemen, are usually the tallest and heaviest. These "fast growers" may be the least mature physiologically and emotionally and consequently the least able to stand up under bruising contact sports. I know of no test or set of tests as yet developed, applicable for use in the gym or athletic field, which will measure the level of a preteenage child's physical and emotional maturity with sufficient accuracy to match him safely for strenuous athletic competition.

Adequate and intelligent leadership is, of course, of primary importance. The qualifications of leaders have been outlined in the Fourth National Conference on Physicians and Schools.[20] Besides the technical qualifications which the conference advocated, good leaders understand the needs and desires and the limitations of growing children. They have a sound knowledge of physiology and of child (and parental) psychology, and they can at least partially match the participants. Unfortunately, such leaders are less likely to be available for elementary schools or for community groups, especially in rural areas and in the smaller towns. Men and women with these qualifications are quickly drawn into more lucrative positions in larger cities or in high schools, colleges, or professional athletics, leaving the younger children with a series of promising but relatively inexperienced coaches. The value of having medical counsel available in these situations is apparent.

Health of the Child

"Boys engaged in programs of competitive athletics are healthier than those not in such programs." I know of no sound evidence to substantiate this statement. On the contrary, there is evidence to refute it. Seymour[21] of Springfield College, Mass., studied 114 boys

---

[19] Statement of Society of State Directors of Physical and Health Education, *op. cit.*
[20] Physicians and Schools Report of the Fourth National Conference on Physicians and Schools, *op. cit.*
[21] Seymour, E. W.: Comparative Study of Certain Behavior Characteristics of Participant and Non-Participant Boys in Little League Baseball, *Res. Quart.* **27**:338–346 (Oct.) 1956.

from five Little Leagues in and around Atlanta, Ga., and compared them with the same number of nonparticipating boys. He found no significant difference in problems, needs, or behavioral pattern between the two groups, except that the participants scored significantly higher acceptance by their peers. Fait[22] reported that a study of two comparable groups of junior high school boys (one group participating in interscholastic sports and the other not participating) showed that growth in height was the only statistically significant difference between the two groups, and this difference was in favor of the non-athletic group. This is probably significant when one considers that, generally speaking, the athletic type of boy is larger and/or has more physical ability and that subsequent improvement might be expected to be greater in this group even if they had not participated in athletics.

Instinctive Play

The sudden violent contact of two young boys to "wrastle," slug, or otherwise maul each other is usually an expression of the normal paroxysmal surge of energy seen in all growing animals. Such contact serves as a release of excess energy and lasts only until it has accomplished its purpose. Unless one of the children is a bully, it usually stops short of any injury. If one of the boys is a bully or if such activity involves a group and develops into an organized sport, such as tackle football or any other form of mass tackling, it ceases to be harmless or desirable. It then becomes the duty of the adults responsible for the children's activities, parents or physical educators, to direct the children to more appropriate, safe, and beneficial outlets for the needed expenditure of their abundant energies. This does not eliminate training in football as an activity for these children. Anderson,[23] football coach at Holy Cross and formerly at Iowa University, has pointed out that touch football for immature children probably provides a better training program for future football skill than does tackle football. (About 60% of all injuries occurring in tackle football occur while tackling or being tackled.[24] Such injuries, of course, should be eliminated with adequately supervised touch or flag football.)

22 Fait, H., *op. cit.*
23 Anderson, E.: Personal Communication to F. V. Hein.
24 Handbook of the National Federation of High School Athletic Associations, Chicago, 1952–1953, p. 31.

"Professional" Preparation

"Competitive athletics at this age develops college and professional stars." While this may occur in some instances, it is more common to find that a boy who is a star at 12 years of age is fed up with the sport at 16 or before. He has already "had it," and the sport has nothing more to offer. This is fortunate for the boy. It is difficult for an individual who has been a star athlete from the age of 12 through college not to develop a warped sense of values and an unrealistic concept of the type of economic and social competition he will encounter after college.

"Good Public Relations"

The last point, that "competitive athletics produces good public relations" needs only the comment that the school, the community —and the sponsor—should find other means of advertising than the exploitation of children.

Recommendations for an Athletic Program

I would like to submit 11 recommendations as a means of giving preteenagers most of the advantages and a minimum of the disadvantages in athletic programs.

1. Competition is an inherent characteristic of growing, developing children. Properly guided, it is beneficial and not harmful to their development.

2. Children should have an opportunity of developing skills in a wide variety of individual and team activities. A sound athletic program in schools should include competitive and noncompetitive sports and play activities.

3. Athletics should offer opportunity for all of the children in the school to participate in some phase of the program. Many teams are better than a few teams. At this age, the "star" system is bad.

4. Opponents should be matched as carefully as possible as to their physical and emotional level of development, as well as to their age, size, and body build. The sports and other activities selected should be those appropriate for their capacities. In many instances this requires the judgment of a physician as well as a coach.

5. Body-contact sports, particularly tackle football, boxing, and wrestling, are dangerous at this age. Touch and flag football are safe games if properly supervised.

6. The best possible leadership should be obtained; volunteers, however well intentioned, should work under professional supervision. Parents should have a voice in the policies and administration of the program.

7. All competitive athletic programs should be organized with the cooperation of local medical organizations. All children should have a thorough physical examination before entering the program and at specified intervals during the program. There should be continuous medical supervision and individual attention for such factors as injury, response to fatigue, individual emotional needs, and undue emotional strain. Ideally, a physician should be in attendance at all games. A minimum requirement should be that he be quickly available. The medical group should be responsible also for teaching health observations to teachers and coaches. (A detailed plan of medical supervision for athletic events has been adopted by the National Joint Committee on Standards for Boys' Athletics and endorsed by the Joint Committee on Health Problems in Education of the National Education Association and the American Medical Association.[25] Through their role as medical advisor, physicians have been led into important research in this field. Some have also developed an interest which has resulted in their distinguished participation in a variety of sports.[26]

8. Regularly scheduled interschool and intercommunity contests are not recommended for this age group; neither are state, regional, or national tournaments or the bowl, charity, or exhibition type of games. Commercial exploitation in any form is unequivocally condemned.

9. Any athletic program should be so designed as to be of educational as well as recreational value.

10. Provision should be made to include in some phase of the program the child who is either physically or psychologically handicapped. This often requires the active cooperation of private physicians and other specialists.

[25] Basketball in Junior High Schools, Queries and Minor Notes, *J.A.M.A.* **148**:975 (March 15) 1952.
[26] Handbook of the National Federation of High Schools Athletic Association, *op. cit.*

11. Qualified professional leadership should be supplied. It should be such that highly organized, highly competitive programs are avoided. The primary consideration should be a diversity of wholesome childhood experiences.

A community program should also be based on the same principles. It should be entirely voluntary, without undue emphasis on any one sport and without undue emphasis on winning. Here again, many teams are better than one.

In making these recommendations, I have drawn freely from a number of publications, particularly the Report of the Joint Committee on Athletic Competition for Children of Elementary and Junior High School Age,[27] the five national conferences on Physicians and Schools,[28] and a report of the Committee on School Health of the American Academy of Pediatrics.[29] Some of these points may be argued. But they represent the considered judgment of the majority of capable professional educators and physicians who have studied the problem. Until continued and comprehensive objective research has finally settled the points in question, the burden of proof rests with those who disagree.

Summary

It is apparent that today's athletic programs suffer from a lack of competent medical advice and supervision. More objective and qualified medical research is needed. More doctors, interested in children and informed on the basic facts of juvenile athletics, are needed to provide medical supervision for school and community athletic programs for preteenagers. If we as physicians are to work toward our stated goal of leading children to secure, responsible, and well-adjusted manhood and womanhood, here is an area where we must get in and pitch.

Questions for Discussion

1. What are some of the psychological and physiological causes for concern about pre-teen-age athletic competition?

[27] Desirable Athletic Competition for Children. Report of Joint Committee on Athletic Competition for Children of Elementary and Junior High School Age. National Education Association, 1954.

[28] Physicians and Schools Report of the Fourth National Conference on Physicians and Schools.

[29] Completitive Athletics, Report of Committee on School Health Pediatrics, *op. cit.*

2. Why is the age of three utilized by Reichert? Does this age constitute a general physical change or is this age arbitrarily selected?

3. It is stated sometimes that not to allow elementary or pre-teenage athletic competition is merely a product of the protective values of our culture, and there is little physiological or psychological basis for it. What evidence and arguments support or refute this opinion?

4. What type of classification system of children of elementary school age would be desirable to determine the nature and extent of their participation in athletic competition? In what ways is the traditional exponent system of height, weight, age inadequate?

THOMAS E. SHAFFER, M.D.

The Adolescent's Health and Activity Needs*

The reader has noted some of the effects, both social and physical, of strenuous competitive activities on children. These effects are not as intense or dramatic as are those on the health and activity needs of adolescents. For not only does the adolescent need to cope with a constantly changing society but also with a body that is undergoing rapid physiological change. These problems, needs, and activities demand the reader's further attention.

In the following article Shaffer, an eminent pediatrician with a vital interest in sports medicine, devotes his remarks to the health and activity problems of the physically changing

* Reprinted and abridged with permission of the author and the publisher from *Professional Contributions, No. 8, American Academy of Physical Education.* Washington, D.C.: American Association for Health, Physical Education and Recreation, 1963, pp. 57–72.

adolescent. The health problems of this age group have warranted little attention in our society until just recently.

We are meeting today with a common interest, the more than
20 million teenage youths in the United States. They are only the
forward wave of the war and postwar baby boom, the children
born between 1943 and 1949. The adolescent share of the population will be literally and relatively a larger portion in coming
years.

The adolescent has been a concern of parents, educators, writers,
and poets for centuries. Those who have written about the adolescent, as well as teachers and parents, have been most impressed by
his behavior. His health seems to have been taken for granted, even
by physicians, although Cicero, in *De Senectute* makes an observation pertinent even today when he says "A sensual and intemperate
youth delivers a worn out body to old age."

In medical fields as in the classical, attention to the health of
adolescents has not been notable until the past twenty years. Textbooks and medical journals had few references to adolescents'
health problems prior to World War II. In the 1920 *Index to Current Medical Literature* there are only two references to articles
on adolescence in the world medical literature. The 1960 *Cumulative Index Medicus* lists 63 articles on medical aspects of adolescence alone, and in 1960 a book devoted entirely to *The Medical
Care of Adolescents* (8) was published.

Too long, the adolescent was thought of as bristling with social
and emotional problems but as having no real health problems.

There are a number of reasons for the heightening medical interest in adolescents. An obvious one is that successes in dealing
with the health problems of babies and young children had led
naturally to new, untouched fields. Progress in school health has
brought a multitude of new questions about the health of high
school youths. Still another stimulus has been the revelation of
large numbers of physically and emotionally unfit young men and
women as disclosed by failure to meet Selective Service qualifications
for military service. These findings point to the lack of medical attention school-age children received in the pre-war years.

Incentives for serious consideration of adolescents' health and
medical care came about concurrently with modern developments

in the concept of medical services, particularly the growth of the field of preventive medicine. Advances in preventive medicine might have come slowly had they not been acclaimed by a whole generation of Americans who were made "preventive medicine conscious" by what was done for them and what they saw in military service.

In preventive medicine, mortality statistics are not accepted as a valid index of the public's health. Erroneous emphasis on such facts leads to the notion that because the death rate is lower than that at any time in adult life, there are few health problems in the adolescent period. The rate of fatal illness during adolescence actually *is* as low as in childhood, if one excludes the middle-aged child, for whom the lowest mortality rate of any stage of life is recorded.

The occurrence of illness, acute or chronic, existence of physical handicaps and disability, rates of absenteeism, and other measures of morbidity are correctly considered to be more weighty proof of health needs than are death rates. We are ready to pass from a reverence for cold statistics to a concept of preventing *illness* and *disability*, rather than fatal illness, by giving attention to health appraisals, immunizations, sanitation, nutrition, and safety. We can even hope to control the progression of existing illness through early detection and treatment. This concept of preventive medicine has been called "secondary prevention" as contrasted with "primary prevention" of illness; it increases the scope of preventive medicine considerably.

The term preventive medicine has a fairly negative implication when you think about it. Prevention is passive; it hinders but it does not promote; it checks but it does not advance. It is not too much to hope for further development of a new field, which might be called "constructive medicine," as a further step beyond preventive medicine. If it is possible to prevent progression of a physical or mental disorder by early detection, is it not just as feasible, through rehabilitation, to regain maximum fitness. Such a positive approach to health, which reaches beyond prevention, is being expressed and practiced in health planning as the natural step after health appraisal.

Such thinking has helped to awaken interest in adolescents, for while for them the mortality rate is low, the disability rate in adolescence for both physical and emotional impairments may be very high.

Causes of Teenage Deaths

While it is admitted that mortality statistics do not really reflect all significant health problems, there are some interesting and challenging facts about certain fatal illnesses among adolescents. Tuberculosis was the leading cause of death in adolescence until 1940 and was still in second place in 1950. In the short period since, tuberculosis has dropped from the top ten causes of death, completing the story of a victory won by several forces working together. Were it not for skin-testing and X-ray programs which, sometimes after detective work, usually lead to active contagious cases of tuberculosis, these sources of infection would not have been identified and brought to treatment; were it not for the effective drugs now available for treating tuberculosis, the contagious cases would not have recovered and have been able to return to their families without risk of infecting young people in the home. The present program of treating even those who have no more evidence of tuberculosis than a recently positive tuberculin test should result in fewer advanced cases, and the effects on the tuberculosis rate will be more spectacular than those already seen. Tuberculosis could become as rare as typhoid fever and smallpox are today. In our own recent experience among a group of older adolescents, only 8.5 percent have positive tuberculin tests indicating past infection and only two active cases have been seen among more than 2,500 adolescents, most of whom came from underprivileged homes and communities. The average rate of positive tuberculin tests is far below ours, being less than 5 percent in adolescence. This disease could well disappear from illness as well as mortality statistics. The chief of the U.S. Public Health Service tuberculosis program has said that there must be a more rapid fall in the rate of active cases for this to occur however. "It is really a matter of taking our present knowledge and using it promptly and in the best way we know how," said Dr. Edward T. Bloomquist of the Public Health Service (2), and in so stating this problem he voiced the plaint of experts in many fields of medicine, where the final, satisfying results await the education and motivation of the public.

For years we have been accustomed to reassure adolescents and their parents by telling them that a positive tuberculin test does not necessarily mean that a person has tuberculosis, especially when the X-ray of the lungs is normal. Now we are finding out how well our teaching has succeeded. Present recommendations about treatment of tuberculosis are that a child or adolescent who has a recently converted positive tuberculin test should be treated by drugs for at least one year, whether or not the X-ray shows disease. Many intelligent youngsters and their parents now ask, "Why should I have treatment for such a long time when all I have is the positive skin test? I do not really have tuberculosis." So some different health education, hopefully as effective, will be necessary.

It has been said that "Accidents are the price we pay for motion." It is indeed a dear price, for accidents stand as the leading cause of death both in childhood and in adolescence, being responsible for almost two thirds of all the deaths in the latter group. The logical, advantageous place to start in saving children's lives is prevention of accidents. As the Metropolitan Life Insurance Company points out in *Accident Prevention Can Be Learned,* "Safety is the product of good education rather than simple good fortune" (1). It must be true that most accidents are preventable and that the preventive medicine in this case is education.

There has been considerable interest in the chronic victim of accidents, the accident repeater. Among those who have studied the problem, Dr. Flanders Dunbar has promoted the idea that the accident prone and the juvenile delinquent have things in common (6). She points out that impulsive behavior and difficulty with authority have roots in early failure in communication within the family. She suggests that when the inner resources of children and their capacities to communicate have been restricted, many become accident prone or delinquent. The establishment of a steady dynamic relationship with an adult outside the immediate family is imperative in such cases, and it is dangerous for such children to be alone, figuratively and literally.

I too am convinced that failure to relieve stress by communication within the family is predisposing to delinquency in boys and girls. The resulting need to communicate with someone often is clothed in a physical complaint which may be totally unrelated to the true concern. Through the voiced physical ailment the physician, nurse, health counselor, or friend usually is in a good position to relieve the stress and anxiety by his interest and willingness to listen.

Without question, juvenile offenders have more mishaps, more scars, more sprains, than would normally be expected. But just as most juvenile delinquents are not so much in need of psychiatric treatment as of adjustment of their family and neighborhood relationships, so it would seem that most accidents occur to normal, but active, impulsive people who have never come to make safety a part of their lives. Education, and not psychiatric treatment, is the answer to the prevention of most accidents. It must be interesting and acceptable to adolescents—"cool" if you will—as typified by the excellent safety education which is done in swimming and boating clubs, hot-rod clubs, and outing clubs.

Cancer is second to accidents as a leading cause of death in adolescents. The total number of deaths at this age from this source is not large in comparison with those from cancer at other ages, and many cases in this category are leukemia, statistically classified as a malignant disease. At the present time it appears to be possible that before long drug treatment of cancer will succeed in drastically reducing mortality from cancer at all ages.

A weighty problem related to cancer is whether anything can be done to control the beginning of smoking during adolescence. The surgeon general of the U.S. Public Health Service made a statement, based on research findings, in which smoking was implicated as the principal causative factor in the increase of lung cancer (4). Although giving up cigarette smoking is beneficial, persons who have never smoked at all have the least chance of developing lung cancer. It would be the best preventive medicine to influence teenagers against ever starting to smoke. A study of cigarette smoking among high school students in Newton, Massachusetts, recently showed that by the twelfth grade, seven students in ten are either present or discontinued smokers; in the twelfth grade, more girls than boys are regular smokers, but boys smoke more (20).

The proportion of students who were regular smokers was highest in families where both parents were confirmed smokers and lowest in families where neither parent smoked. About half the teenage children in families where both parents smoked were regular smokers also. Only one quarter of the adolescent children in families where neither parent smoked were smokers. The effect of family influence on behavior is an undeniable factor to be reckoned with in health education (19). It will be difficult, but not impossible, to influence adolescent children seriously to consider any course of action which does not at once appear directly or emphatically to benefit their health and one which they believe, from their own observations, has not harmed their parents. Here in the prevention of lung cancer is a real challenge to health education.

The third leading cause of death is from heart disease. This, like the rating of tuberculosis, will be changed in years to come. The heart complications from rheumatic fever could be entirely prevented if what we now know could be put into action, in a workable program to control streptococcal infections. Rheumatic fever, like tuberculosis, could become as rare as typhoid fever or smallpox if we could but apply knowledge we already have. As for congenital heart disease, hardly a week passes without reports of still more technical advances in surgical treatment; there are thousands who now can reach adult life but would have been fatalities in childhood ten years ago.

As tuberculosis, heart disease, and other problems come under control, new problems will come into view. Preventive and treatment medical services will have to be planned and re-planned to meet changing patterns of health needs.

It is notable that three of the five leading causes of death among older adolescents—accidents, homicide, and suicide—have an aspect of violence. They reflect the highly emotional characteristics of this age and different expressions of the aggressive behavior that goes with adolescence.

Teenage Illnesses

Reports from many sources, hospital clinics, adolescent clinics, public and private schools, and college health services, indicate that acute illnesses are at a minimum during adolescence. This is confirmed in a careful, long-term observation of illnesses among 134 children enrolled in the Harvard Longitudinal Studies of Child Health and Development which showed there were fewer illnesses in early and late adolescence than in any other period from birth to 18 years (22).

There has been some concern among public health officials about the increasing infectious venereal disease-rate, which began to rise in 1958. There has been a rise in cases of primary and secondary syphilis and gonorrhea each year, relatively greater for syphilis. In publicity about the situation, adolescents have been credited with a major part in the increase. Actually the rise in rate is chiefly notable as a trend rather than an alarming incidence. Primary and secondary syphilis had reached (1957) a low level amounting to 20 percent of the cases reported in 1950; the most recent statistics show a two-fold rise in reported cases. If the incidence were unchanged the cases would have risen annually with the population increase; the largest increase in syphilis has been in the 20–35 year age group. The rate for gonorrhea has risen only slightly in comparison with syphilis, but reporting is not as thorough.

Only slightly more than 20 percent of infectious venereal disease occurs in the teenage period. The increased incidence is affected by the population increase, but this is not the full story. The public, and especially private and public health workers, have become complacent about searching for related cases when one infected person is found. The problem has been overemphasized as one primarily related to adolescents, as 80 percent of cases occur among adults.

The acute illnesses are chiefly due to respiratory diseases and injuries. In the Harvard Longitudinal Studies, around 90 percent of illnesses in adolescence were due to respiratory disease. There is little to say about these—the respiratory diseases are almost entirely due to viruses, and those viruses which can produce symptoms of "a cold in the head" now number considerably more than twenty. While immunity to any single one of these viruses may be achieved, it would be unlikely that any one person could gain immunity to all or even most of them. Vaccines offer some hope if the manufacturers can figure out how to make them cheaply enough to be practicable. When one considers the time needed to make measles immunization generally available, there appears little hope that acute respiratory diseases will be eliminated soon. As far as effective treatment is concerned, studies at Western Reserve University School of Medicine over the past 15 years have shown that only about 5 percent of the respiratory diseases which occur in northern Ohio are susceptible to available antibiotics or drugs (5).

An interesting aspect of studies of children's illness is the increased incidence of disease among boys at most ages. There may be some sex-linked resistance to illness or there may be greater physical fitness among females, resulting in less illness and greater longevity. It has been observed that the ratio of male to female fetuses at the time of conception is about 130:100. By the end of pregnancy the greater toll of male fetuses through pregnancy loss has reduced the ratio to about 110:100 (4). The females' superiority in this respect persists throughout life, as reflected by illness rates and by women's greater life expectancy. Kipling's immortal statement "The female is deadlier than the male" might be paraphrased to "The female is livelier than the male."

Serious chronic diseases occur during adolescence, but they are not common and the diseases do not differ essentially from their manifestations in adults. It is the host, the adolescent, who is different. By his reaction to any condition requiring a prescribed program or making him feel that he is different, he changes the aspects of the disease. Epilepsy, an example of a chronic disease, is found in about one of 500 children; diabetes occurs once in about 2,500 children. Both epilepsy and diabetes require a moderately supervised program, with medications and some restrictions on activities. The fact that these prescriptions and proscriptions are difficult for the adolescent to accept make medical care arduous for the physician and the family. The adolescent longs for independence and a chronic disease makes him dependent and subject to authority; medications and routines make him appear different to his peers and this is the last thing he wants to happen. Success in managing a chronic disease in an adolescent depends on minimizing authoritative rotuines and avoiding schedules of treatments which the teenager might think would make him appear different.

Adolescents Need Advice on Life Changes

Most of the conditions for which the adolescent wants medical advice are related to variations in growth and physical development, worries about unpleasant side-effects of maturation, or physiological manifestations of inner stresses and anxieties. How advantageous it would be if it were always possible to prepare youngsters in advance for the physical manifestations of puberty and for the normal variations in the rate and amount of change that may occur during adolescence.

This need is more important in the United States than in many other parts of the world because of the wide variations in genetic make-up that exist among the youth of this country. For this reason the curves of normal distribution of the time of onset and the extent of changes during puberty are broad ones for our adolescent population. At a period of their lives when they are overly concerned about acceptance by their peers and are driven to become independent, most adolescents face problems of delay, precocity, or quantitative variations in their maturation which worry them excessively. Those who are precocious in growth or development fret not only themselves but their normally developing peers, who suspect that they are abnormally slow. There is no question that the tardy matures and growers are more than slightly concerned.

If one had the chance it would be so desirable to tell pre-adolescents many things about the stage before them. For example, the onset of growth is earlier in girls than in boys on the average, but some girls do not show signs of puberty until they are 14 or 15 years old. This latter situation usually becomes a reason for seeking medical advice because it is unexpected and unusual.

Girls should know that normal, regular menstruation typically does not occur until two or three years after the menses begin and that in that interim all sorts of irregularities occur, most of which are not serious and do not require treatment. They should know that many girls have intervals of several or even six months between periods during these two or three years. One would like to tell pre-adolescent girls that ordinarily there is no more than mild discomfort with menstruation and particularly, as reassurance for the time of greatest anxiety, that there should be no discomfort at all in the first year or two of the menses because ovulation does not occur and therefore the hormone which sometimes causes uncomfortable uterine contractions later is not formed.

Pre-adolescents should know that acne occurs in 75 per cent or more of all teenagers and that, while it is distressing to those who have it, its very frequency makes their problem appear almost negligible to their friends. One would like to tell them before it is too late that soap and water, used frequently, are the best preventives.

We should tell boys in advance that most of them will experience swelling and tenderness of one or both breasts during early adolescence, with the hope that this knowledge might allay worries about their masculinity and about cancer.

It is not often that anxieties about growth, development, or appearance are the primary outspoken complaint to a physician, a nurse, or a counselor. It is more likely that headache, abdominal pain, fatigue, sleeplessness, pains in the region of the heart, or backache would be the overt reason for seeking attention, for abscence from school or for excuse from some activity.

Those who work with adolescents must keep in mind that over-concerns about developmental changes in personal appearance occur normally and may be divulged when the listener is interested and understanding. The adolescent himself may not even realize his need to voice his concerns and relieve his anxieties until he has such an opportunity with an empathic listener.

Overnutrition and Undernutrition

Obesity, one of the big health problems in the United States, is medically important because of its relationship to cardiovascular disease and diabetes. To adolescents it is a concern only because it makes them appear different and threatens to jeopardize acceptance by their contemporaries. All children who are overweight are not obese, but there are 10 to 15 percent who are definitely in this class.

While obesity is often named as the outstanding nutritional disease in the United States and even the most important health problem of all, it appears that undernutrition in the adolescent period is far more important than is generally known. According to a summary of nation-wide nutrition studies conducted from 1947 through 1958, teenage girls in the United States typically had diets inadequate in or seriously low in calories, protein, calcium, iron, thiamine, and Vitamin C. The average diets of adolescent girls were the most unfavorable of all age periods surveyed, from early childhood through adult life (18). This situation is particularly alarming because of the importance of nutrition to mother and infant during pregnancy.

Food eaten by teenage boys surveyed in this study on the average provided adequate diets except for insufficient Vitamin C and total calories. These conclusions are generalizations, as there were marked geographic variations in dietary intakes.

Overnutrition and undernutrition alike are problems among our adolescent population. The identification and specific treatment of the undernourished is not easy, and the solution of this problem appears to rest on socioeconomic causes and on motivation through education.

It is seldom that any medical cause for obesity is found, although frequently one or both parents are obese. Newer methods of study of the functions of endocrine glands exonerate them in all but the most unusual cases of obesity. Thyroid deficiency has been popularly accepted as a cause of obesity, but this is seldom true and never when growth in height is normal. The cause of obesity in 95 percent or more cases is simply the intake of more calories than are needed for that individual's expenditure of energy. This could be due to excessive eating but, contrary to general opinion, obese children seldom eat more than their more normal colleagues. This surprising observation has been made by Mayer (17), Fry (7), and others.

Among possible causes for imbalance between an intake of calories which exceeds utilization, inactivity appears to be the most significant factor in the etiology of most cases of obesity. The average child has a high level of activity; reasons for the abnormally sedentary habits of some children are not always apparent. They may be part of a family pattern or trait; occasionally the cause is difficulties in getting along with other children; sometimes inactivity simply appears to be part of a placid temperament; frequently the cause is found in our mechanized culture where labor-saving machines are widely used. Not infrequently physical inactivity is due to a fear of failure in an undertaking which makes a child feign indifference. Sometimes inactivity is prescribed by a physician for health reasons, and the child has no responsibility for the obesity which develops. Regardless of the reason, it is now believed that successful control of obesity depends less on low calorie diets than on more exercise.

Two questions are frequently asked about this approach to the treatment of obesity: Does exercise actually expend enough calories to change the caloric balance, and does physical activity not stimulate the appetite so as to increase caloric intake after the exercise? The answer to each of these questions on the basis of good research studies is "No." Regular exercise, even walking slowly for one hour each day, can affect the balance between intake and utilization; the difference each day may be small but in time it becomes appreciable. Sitting at rest uses 15 calories per hour above basal requirements; walking slowly utilizes 200 calories per hour, and tennis uses 500 calories per hour. Highly sedentary living has forced upon most Americans a decision either to increase the level of their activity or to face lifetime hunger, if obesity is to be avoided.

The reason why some adolescents are sedentary and become overweight is not always clear, but such behavior is not normal and should be studied in order to discover the causes. The typical teenager is strenuously active in play, social activities, and work. No one is more aware of the adolescent's need for activity than a physician who has considered it necessary to restrict this activity because of an illness or injury.

The Need for Strenuous Activity

It is tempting to ascribe an adolescent's need for physical activity solely to a physical cause—the rapid growth of the bones which occurs early in adolescence and the subsequent development of the muscle system which occurs in the later stages of physical and sexual maturation. This muscular development takes place to a greater extent in boys but occurs also in girls and is a result of testicular and adrenal hormones which continue to appear in the body after the height-growth spurt is completed. Because this phenomenal growth of bones and muscles during adolescence occurs at the same time as the adolescent's need for activity it is attractive to hypothesize that there is a relationship, but no direct evidence points to this effect. The developing muscles are an important reason for encouraging activity for they must be strengthened by use, even though they do not appear to be a factor in causing activity.

The need for activity is present from earliest infancy but it is heightened in adolescence, I believe, because muscular activity, creative or aggressive, is a mechanism for relief from the stresses and anxieties which occur at this time. As a boy or girl enters adolescence and tries to adjust to changes in the size and shape of his body, in his relationships within his family and to the rest of the world, he experiences stress because of his concerns about himself. Stresses breed anxieties which can be handled in several ways —one is by talking about them as has been mentioned. Another means for managing anxieties is by release of energy in constructive and aggressive activity. The adolescent is filled with personal concerns about his body, his status, his successes, and his failures, and he needs to have releases through activity.

Another matter of considerable importance is the adolescent's need to find his social and emotional satisfactions among his age group—on the "horizontal plane" as it were, as compared with his inadequacy in finding such satisfactions in associations in the "vertical plane" with persons older or younger than himself. The need to be respected by his own age group calls for competitive activity and participation. The adolescent's strongest defense against insecurity is group approval.

Restrictions and rest with limited associations and activity often are recommended for special reasons, without regard for these needs for activity or the harm that results from limitations. Consideration for developmental needs of the individual, exemplified by an adolescent's need for activity, may be, on occasions, more important than optimum treatment of a particular ailment or disease. These needs of the whole individual probably require more attention during adolescence than at any other time of life (9).

Increased rest and restricted activity are contrary to the adolescent's need for exercise to strengthen muscles and to release anxiety and to socialize; all the needs should be considered in their relative importance. Since activity neutralizes emotional stress and tensions, a child's load of anxieties should be particularly considered before placing strict limitations on one of the therapeutic outlets for emotions.

The typical strenuous living of adolescents is paralleled by needs for recognition, acceptance by other adolescents, and independence from authority, all of which make restrictions undesirable at this time of life. When restricted activity is imperative, great effort should be exerted to offer other sources of satisfaction and to provide other ways of releasing emotional tensions. One of the best means for this is talking, with an empathic interested listener.

There are signs that appreciation of developmental needs of children and of effects of changes in routine is gaining acceptance. The abuse of rest as a therapeutic measure for adults has been a subject for discussion for years (21); only recently have there been reports of studies of this kind which apply to children. For example, there now are several reliable reports that the introduction of some activity during convalescence of rheumatic fever is not harmful to the course of the disease and has some beneficial effects on the child's adjustment to a lengthy illness (10, 12). There also are some recent reports on early activity and ambulation for children who are recovering from acute nephritis (14). Such developments affirm an understanding among people who work with young people that children, particularly adolescents, have good reasons for wanting to resume normal activity and that, within reasonable limits, medical treatment should not interfere with personality growth and physical development.

Literature Cited

1. *Accident Prevention Can Be Learned.* New York: Metropolitan Life Insurance Company, 1962.
2. BLOMQUIST, E. T. "Chemotherapy as a Public Health Measure Against Tuberculosis," *Pub. H. Rep.* 75:1069; 1960.
3. BROWN, C. H. "Self-Portrait: The Teen-Type Magazine," *Ann. Am. Acad. Pol. & Soc. Sci.* 338:13; 1961.
4. BURNEY, L. E. "Smoking and Lung Cancer," *J. A. M. A.* 171:1829; 1959.
5. DINGLE, J. H. "The Prevention of Respiratory Infections within Families," *Ann. Int. Med.* 43:518; 1955.
6. DUNBAR, F. "Homeostasis During Puberty," *Am. J. Psych.* 114:673; 1958.
7. FRY, P. C. "A Comparative Study of 'Obese' Children Selected on the Basis of Fat Pads," *J. Clin. Nutrition* 1:453; 1953.
8. GALLAGHER, J. R. *Medical Care of the Adolescent.* New York: Appleton-Century-Crofts, 1960.
9. GALLAGHER, J. R. "Rest and Restriction: Their Conflict with an Adolescent's Development," *A. J. P. H.* 46:1424; 1956.
10. GIBSON, M. L., and FISHER, G. R. "Early Ambulation in Rheumatic Fever," *A. M. A. J. Dis. Child.* 96:575; 1958.
11. LANE, W. K. "Role of Pediatrician in Physical Fitness of Youth," *J. A. M. A.* 169:421; 1959.
12. LENDRUM, B. L., SIMON, A. J., and MACK, I. "Relation of Duration of Bed Rest in Acute Rheumatic Fever to Heart Disease Present 2 to 14 Years Later. *Pediatrics* 24:389; 1959.
13. LUSTED, L. B., and LEDLEY, R. S. "Mathematical Models in Medical Diagnosis," *J. Med. Ed.* 35:214; 1960.
14. MCCRORY, W. W., FLEISHER, D. S., and SOHN, W. B. "Effects of Early Ambulation on the Course of Nephritis in Children," *Pediatrics* 24:395; 1959.
15. MCKENZIE, R. T. *Exercise in Education and Medicine.* Philadelphia: W. B. Saunders, 1909.
16. MASLAND, R. I., SARASON, S. B., and GLADWIN, T. *Mental Subnormality.* New York: Basic Books, 1959.
17. MAYER, J. "Exercise and Weight Control," Chapter XII in *Exercise and Fitness.* Chirago: The Athletic Institute, 1960.
18. MORGAN, A. F. *Nutritional Status U.S.A.* Berkeley, California, Bulletin 769, California Agricultural Experiment Station, 1959.
19. SALBER, E. J., and MACMAHON, B. "Cigarette Smoking Among High School Students Related to Social Class and Parental Smoking Habits," *A. J. P. H.* 51:1780; 1961.
20. SALBER, E. J., and OTHERS. "Smoking Habits of High School Students in Newton, Massachusetts," *N. E. J. Med.* 265:969; 1961.
21. SPEIR, E. B., and OTHERS. "Symposium on Use and Abuse of Bed Rest," *West. J. Surg.* 54:328; 1946.

22. VALADIAN, I., STUART, H. C., and REED, R. B. "Longitudinal Studies of Child Health and Development—Series II; Patterns of Illness Experiences," *Pediatrics* 24:941; 1959.

Questions for Discussion

1. What are the major causes of death among teenagers?
2. What illnesses have the highest incidence among adolescents?
3. What are the relationships between caloric intake and inactivity of youth?
4. What are the causes and effects of strenuous activity upon youngsters?
5. Some people propose that physical education should incorporate the teaching of health education in its program. Can physical education really devote sufficient time to this important field to make it worthwhile or should health education have a special place in the curriculum?

HANS KRAUS, M.D. and RUTH P. HIRSCHLAND

Minimum Muscular Fitness Tests in School Children*

Unfortunately, the maintenance of the body throughout adulthood has only within the last decade become an important aspect of the responsibility of physical education. Even today, too few secondary school programs instruct their students in activities that help maintain physical fitness. The following selections illuminate the need for exercise and its contributions to physical fitness.

After many years of general indifference to physical fitness, the American people were disturbed by the results of the Kraus-Hirschland and Kraus-Weber tests. The evidence indicated the

* Reprinted and abridged with permission of the senior author and the publisher from *The Research Quarterly*. Washington, D.C.: The American Association for Health, Physical Education and Recreation, vol. 25, no. 2, May 1954, pp. 178–188.

unsatisfactory level of physical fitness of our youth and pointed
to the fact that American children are "second best." Much
argument ensued over the types of tests utilized in the battery,
and claims were made, with some justification, that because
American youngsters were unable to perform well on certain
tests, the total score was biased. Nevertheless, these dramatic
reports turned the attention of America to a vital need—
physical fitness.

A *bstract.* Six test movements appraising strength and flexibility
of trunk and leg muscles were given to 4264 American and 2870
European children from comparable urban and suburban communities. 57.9% of the Americans failed and 8.7% of the Europeans.
The poor American showing can be explained by our high degree
of mechanization obviating much physical activity. Since previous
studies have shown that these tests represent minimum muscular
fitness, and that falling below these levels predisposes to orthopedic
and emotional difficulties, it is urged that the physical activities
of our children be increased and that muscle tests be given at regular intervals, and made a part of the child's complete school record,
to assure at least these minimum standards for our children.

The connection between good posture and health has for many
years been an established part of physical education and health education. In the last decades, the concept of posture has shifted more
and more from merely structural to a functional one as well. The
interest in posture has gained added impetus because of the attention paid to flexibility in the present day treatment of poliomyelitis.
Studies on the subject were published by A. D. Gurewitsch and
Margaret A. O'Neill in 1944 (4) and by H. O. Kendall and Florence
P. Kendall in 1948 (5).
In 1945 Hans Kraus and S. Eisenmenger-Weber reported a follow-
up study on 200 posture cases (school children) who had been patients at the posture clinic of Columbia Presbyterian Medical Center (12, 13, 14).
The results reported in the above three papers were evaluated,
not only by structural measurements, but by functional measurements as well. These functional measurements included strength

tests for trunk muscles and flexibility tests for trunk and hamstring muscles.

The key tests were adopted as basic tests in a Low Back Clinic which was organized by Dr. Barbara Stimson at Columbia Presbyterian Hospital under the auspices of Dr. William Darrach in 1946.

The Kraus-Weber Tests for Muscular Fitness are not designed to determine optimum levels of muscular fitness, but rather to determine whether or not the individual has sufficient strength and flexibility in the parts of the body upon which demands are made in normal daily living.

Kraus-Weber Tests for Muscular Fitness

(There should not be any warm-up prior to taking the tests.)

TEST 1.

Purpose: Tests the strength of the abdominals and psoas.
Designation: "Abdominals plus psoas" or *A+*.
Position of Person Being Tested: Lying supine, hands behind neck. The examiner holds his feet down on the table.
Command: "Keep your hands behind your neck and *try to roll up* into a sitting position."
Precaution: If the person being tested is unable to perform this movement at first try, it may be because he has not understood the directions. Help him a little and then let him try again. Watch for a "stiff back sit-up." This may indicate that either he has not understood you and needs a further explanation with emphasis on "rolling up," or that he has *very* poor abdominals and is doing most of the work with his psoas.

Watch also for a twist of the upper body as he sits up. This may be due to unequal development of the back muscles.
Marking: If the person being tested cannot raise his shoulders from the table, the mark is *0*. If unaided, he is able to reach a sitting position, the mark is *10*. If the examiner must help him halfway to the sitting position, the mark would be *5*. The distance from supine to sitting is marked from *0* to *10*.

TEST 2.

Purpose: Further test for abdominals.
Designation: "Abdominals minus psoas" or *A—*.

Position of Person Being Tested: Lying supine, hands behind neck and knees bent. Examiner holds his feet down on the table.

Command: "Keep your hands behind your neck and *try to roll up* into a sitting position."

Precaution: The precautions are the same as for Test 1, but as Test 2 is usually more difficult the tendency toward "stiff back sit up" will be even more pronounced and to it is added the tendency to help with one or the other elbow.

TEST 3.

Purpose: Tests the strength of the psoas, and lower abdominals.

Designation: "Psoas" or *P.*

Position of Person Being Tested: Supine with hands behind neck and the legs extended.

Command: "Keep your knees straight and lift your feet ten inches off of the table. Keep them there while I count." The count is ten seconds. (Adding any three syllable word after each number makes the count fairly reliable as to time. For example, "One chimpanzee, two chimpanzee, three chimpanzee, etc.")

Precaution: If the person tested has not understood your command, he may try to raise his chest when he raises his feet and will need further explanation. Watch for an extremely arched back which may indicate very weak abdominals or postural habits contributing to sway back or lordosis.

Marking: Holding for ten full seconds is passing and is marked as *10.* Anything less is recorded as that part of the ten seconds that was held: *4* for four seconds, or *7* for seven seconds, etc.

TEST 4.

Purpose: Tests the strength of the upper back muscles.

Designation: "Upper back" or "UB."

Position of Person Being Tested: Lying prone with a pillow under his abdomen, but far enough down as to give the body the feeling of being a seesaw which, if weighted at either end, would be able to hold the other end in the air. This is most easily accomplished with these commands:

Command: "Roll over onto your stomach and lift up the middle so that I can slide this pillow under you." (Be sure the pillow is large enough to really support him.) "Now, I am going to hold down your feet while you put your hands behind your neck and raise up

your chest, head, and shoulders. Hold them up while I count."
The count is ten seconds.

Precaution: Do not let the person being tested drop his chest onto
the table or rest his elbows. Watch for pronounced muscular development on one side of the spine. If this condition is present, the
back should be checked from time to time to guard against scoliosis
(curvature of the spine).

Marking: Holding for ten full seconds is passing and is marked as
10. Anything less than ten seconds is recorded as that part of ten
seconds that was held. For example, a person staying up for four
seconds would get the mark of *4*.

TEST 5.

Purpose: Tests the strength of the lower back.
Designation: "Lower back" or *LB*.
Position of Person Being Tested: He remains prone over the pillow,
but removes his hands from behind his neck, places them down on
the table and rests his head on them.
Command: "I am going to hold your chest down on the table; try
to lift your legs up, but do not bend your knees." There may be a
tendency to bend the knees or even to support the legs by keeping
the toes on the table. It may be necessary to assist him to the required position. "Now, hold this position while I count." The count
is ten.
Marking: Holding for ten full seconds is passing and is marked as
10. Anything less is recorded as that part of the ten seconds that was
held, for example, four seconds would be *4*.

TEST 6.

Purpose: Tests the length of back and hamstring muscles.
Designation: "Back and Hamstrings" or *BH*.
Position of Person Being Tested: Standing erect in stocking or bare
feet, hands at his sides.
Command: "Put your feet together, keep your knees straight, now
lean down slowly and see how close you can come to touching
the floor with your finger tips. Stay down as far as you can for a
count of three. DO NOT BOUNCE.
Precaution: Watch out for bouncing. The furthest point reached
without bouncing and held for three counts is the marking point.

The examiner should hold the knees of the person being tested in order to prevent any bend.

Marking: Touch is designated with *T*. *Touch* is only given when the floor-touch is held for three counts. Less than *Touch* is marked by the distance in inches between the floor and the finger tips. For example, a person unable to touch the floor by two inches would be marked, —2".

In the above tests, the words "upper" and "lower" are merely used to indicate test movements rather than any specific areas.

Discussion

Over 4,000 cases of patients with low back pain were thus evaluated. The people were drawn from the Low Back Clinic at Columbia Presbyterian Hospital and from the Low Back Clinic of New York University's Institute for Rehabilitation and Physical Medicine, as well as from private practice.

A high percentage of these cases (approximately 80%) (19), after thorough evaluation by a team of specialists, were found free from organic disease; however, this group failed to pass one or more of the above tests. When treated with therapeutic exercise, they improved as their test results improved. In an 8-year follow-up, it was found that as the patients stopped exercising, their tests failed and their complaints reappeared. This condition could be reversed by resuming either the therapeutic exercise or regular physical activities, but the final outcome—and the permanency of relief—ran parallel with the muscle status (6, 7, 8, 9). These impressions are shared by other authors (17, 18, 19, 20, 21).

These tests represented *minimum-fitness tests;* that is, they were tests which indicated a level of strength and flexibility in certain key muscular groups below which functioning of the whole body as a healthy organism seemed to be endangered. Furthermore, patients whose physical fitness level fell below these *minimum requirements* appeared to be "sick people," individuals who bore all the earmarks of "constant strain" (Selye, 16), and who frequently manifested signs of emotional instability.

This fact seems quite understandable in the light of W. B. Cannon's study on bodily reactions to physical threat or fear, which emphasized the necessity to discharge those energies accumulated as "preparation for flight or for flight" (1).

When the individual is prevented from ridding himself of surplus energies, tension remains. This tension often results in physical discomfort. It is this observation which is of particular interest to those attempting to understand and alleviate muscular pain of obscure origin (15).

Since the percentage of backache sufferers—as well as that of patients suffering from other tensions syndromes—was undoubtedly very high, the question arose as to whether these syndromes were not the result of an imbalance: an imbalance caused by excessive intake of stimuli and by too little outlet, especially too little physical outlet. If this were the case, prevention might well be found in an increase of physical activity (7, 10, 11).

In a first step toward prevention of this disease, it seems logical to develop healthy movement habits in children, as well as attempting to develop their bodies above and beyond minimum standards of flexibility and strength. Children will not immediately feel the impact of relative muscular weakness and stiffness; but as they proceed in life, and as they must draw on reserves and muscle potential, they shall have to fall back on what was formed during their early years. If high muscular standards are present in the first two decades of life, maintaining these standards, or regaining them later on, will be much easier.

When we started to determine the muscular fitness levels of American school children by submitting them to the above tests, we found such a high percentage of failure that we felt it necessary to make comparative studies abroad.

The question arose in our minds whether our minimum standards were not too high to be met by the average school child. Over 10,000 school children have been tested to date both here and abroad. A report on over 4,000 American children and 2,000 European children (Italian and Austrian) was published in the *Journal of the American Association for Health-Physical Education-Recreation* in December 1953 (11). We here submit a more complete study, augmented by information gained from testing 1,156 Swiss children.

The children reported in this study were between the ages of 6 and 16 years, and were from public school systems in suburban and small urban communities. The sizes of these cities, both European and American, were comparable. Every effort was made to keep test conditions identical and to make the tests uniform.

All the tests were made by the authors themselves and were completely standardized. Statistics obtained from sick or disabled children were excluded from the results, although all the children on hand were tested in order to avoid trauma to disabled individuals.

The major difference between these two groups is the fact that European children do not have the "benefit" of a highly mechanized society; they do not use cars, school-buses, elevators, or other labor-saving devices. They must walk everywhere—even to school, frequently a long distance. Their recreation is largely based on the active use of their bodies. In this country the children are generally conveyed in private cars, or by bus, and they engage in recreation as spectators rather than as participants.

Test Results

The following table gives the results of the tests:

	Austrian	Italian	Swiss	American
Number Tested	678	1036	1156	4264
Failure	9.5%	8.0%	8.8%	57.9%
Incidence of Failure	9.7%	8.5%	8.9%	80.0%

The Kendalls reported a very definite variation of results with age (5) and we fully agree with the authors that the ages between 10 and 13 years seem to be "critical" ones. We found, however, that this "critical" period was reached one to two years earlier in Europe.

It is interesting to note that European figures, representing completely different countries, are highly similar. . . . As these countries are effectively separated by frontiers, we consider this of significance. The higher flexibility failure rate in Austrian and Swiss children, as compared with that in Italian children, is due partly to the fact that not much attention is paid to flexibility in an otherwise strict and vigorous physical education program. A one-sided strengthening program, disregarding flexibility and relaxation, could well result in shifts of these figures.

Findings

In our efforts to determine the age at which muscle deficiency first becomes apparent, we were met with a distressing fact: children coming into the first grades of the school system are already seriously deficient.

Furthermore, it appears that we are unable to alleviate this situation during the time the children are in elementary schools. They leave elementary school in very much the same condition as when they entered it—if anything, a little worse. Weakness as well as flexibility failures show that at no time do American statistics approach the fitness levels of the European. These figures are preliminary ones. We have started investigation of rural areas where the preliminary reports yield better results (32%) than those found in suburban areas. Studies in private schools, where more time is given to physical education, also give better results.

At present we are in the process of evaluating tests given to children diagnosed as emotionally unstable. We are trying to determine whether a relationship exists between their emotional condition and their physical fitness levels.

Conclusions

We have the impression that insufficient exercise may cause the dropping of muscular fitness levels below the minimum necessary for daily living. The same lack of exercise may cause inadequate outlet for nervous tension.

Lack of sufficient exercise, therefore, constitutes a serious deficiency comparable with vitamin deficiency. Prevention of this deficiency is an urgent need.

Further research will be necessary to complete and broaden our preliminary survey, and to show the geographical incidence of under-exercise in this country. We may well find large sections where excellent conditions of muscular fitness prevail.

Some form of muscular fitness tests should be a part of every school health examination.[1]

Our physical education is in definite need of expansion so that there can be active and total participation not only in high schools, but even more important, in elementary school and pre-school groups.

Literature Cited

1. CANNON, WALTER B. *The Wisdom of the Body.* New York: W. W. Norton & Co., Inc. 1939. 333 pp.
2. GASTON, SAWNIE R. *Preliminary Report of a Group Study of the Painful Back.* New York: Columbia Presbyterian Medical Center.

[1] The tests presented in this paper determine minimum fitness levels (6) and therefore constitute a good minimum requirement.

3. ———. "The Low Back Syndrome," *Surgical Clinics of North America,* 31:2 (April 1951).

4. GUREWITSCH, A. D., and MARGARET A. O'NEILL. "Flexibility of Healthy Children," *Archives of Physical Therapy,* April 1944.

5. KENDALL, HENRY A., and FLORENCE P. "Normal Flexibility According to Age Groups," *The Journal of Bone and Joint Surgery,* 30A, pp. 690–694 (July 1949).

6. KRAUS, HANS. "Diagnosis and Treatment of Low Back Pain," *GP,* V:4 (April 1952).

7. ———. "Prevention of Low Back Pain," *Journal of the Association for Physical and Mental Rehabilitation,* 6:1 (Sept.-Oct. 1952).

8. ———. "The Role of Therapeutic Exercises in the Treatment of Low Back Pain," *New York State Journal of Medicine,* 49:13 (July 1, 1949).

9. ———. *Principles and Practice of Therapeutic Exercises,* Springfield, Ill.: Charles C Thomas, 1949. 309 pp.

10. ——— and RUTH P. HIRSCHLAND. "Muscular Fitness and Orthopedic Disability." (Paper delivered before medical society of the State of New York, May 30, 1953, Buffalo, N.Y.—To be published in the *New York State Journal of Medicine.*)

11.——— and RUTH P. HIRSCHLAND. "Muscular Fitness and Health," *Journal of the American Association for Health, Physical Education and Recreation,* 24:10:17 (Dec. 1953).

12. ——— and E. EISENMENGER-WEBER. "Evaluation of Posture Based on Structural and Functional Measurements," *Physio-therapy Rev.,* 25:6 (Nov.-Dec. 1945).

13. ——— and E. EISENMENGER-WEBER. "Fundamental Consideration of Posture Exercises," *Physio-therapy Rev.,* 27:6 (Nov.-Dec. 1947).

14. ——— and S. EISENMENGER-WEBER. "Quantitative Tabulation of Posture Evaluation," *Physio-therapy Rev.,* 26:5 (Sept.-Oct., 1946).

15. LORENZ, THOMAS H., and MARC J. MUSSER. "Life Stress and Painful Stiff Shoulders," *Modern Medicine,* March 1, 1953. (From *Ann. Int. Med.,* 37:1232–1244, 1952.)

16. SELYE, HANS. *The Physiology and Pathology of Exposure to Stress.* Montreal (Canada): Medical Publishers, 1950.

17. STIMSON, BARBARA. "The Low Back Problem," *Psychosomatic Medicine,* 9:3 (May-June 1947).

18. ———. "Backache," *American Journal of Nursing,* 51:11 (Nov. 1951).

19. ———. Personal Communications.

20. STINCHFIELD, FRANK. Personal Communications.

21. ——— and WILLIAM SINTON. "Criteria for Spinal Fusion," *Arch. Surgery,* Oct. 1952.

Questions for Discussion

1. Does the Kraus-Weber test battery seem to include exercises pertinent to the education of American youth? If not, what others could be substituted in the battery?

2. Could the scores on the typical physical fitness battery be improved through a general sports and activities program or must youngsters be instructed in just exactly those skills included in the battery? What problems arise in requiring pupils to perform regularly the skills required in the test battery?

3. To what extent is physical fitness over-emphasized in current physical education programs?

4. With all the recent interest in physical fitness, what explanation is there for the fact that only one state in the nation continues to require daily physical education on the secondary school level?

THOMAS K. CURETON

What Is Physical Fitness?*

Part of the controversy surrounding the Kraus-Weber results focuses upon the use of the back-flexibility test in determining general flexibility of the body. Other disagreements relate to the definitions of physical fitness and total fitness. Both controversies are discussed indirectly by Thomas K. Cureton in an article written some ten years prior to the publication of the Kraus-Weber research. This selection contains a good definition of motor capacity, motor ability and motor fitness and a good description of their interrelationships. It should be studied in connection with the previous selection.

What Does Physical Fitness Mean?

Physical fitness means a great deal more than freedom from sickness or passing a medical inspection without a positive prescription for a disability. In addition to freedom from germinal or chronic

* Reprinted with permission of the author and the publisher from the Washington, D.C.: American Association for Health, Physical Education, and Recreation, *Journal of Health, Physical Education and Recreation.* vol. 16, no. 3, March 1945, pp. 111–112, 148, 150.

disease, possessing good teeth, good hearing, good eye sight, and normal mentality, physical fitness means ability to handle the body well and the capacity to work hard over a long period of time without diminished efficiency. Three principal approaches for objective testing of physical fitness (apart from diagnosis of disease) are:

1. Appraisal of physique.
2. Appraisal of organic capacity.
3. Appraisal of motor fitness.

If we break down each of these three approaches into a greater number of specifics, physical fitness takes on characteristics like the following:

Physique (Appearance)

1. Healthy and robust appearance.
2. Muscular development strongly in evidence.
3. Good posture with appearance of ease, alertness, and poise.
4. Good proportions of bone, muscle, fat quotas.
5. Normal bones, joints, and muscles.
6. Good size for age and sex.

Organic Health and Condition (Organic Efficiency)

1. Normal sense organs—sight, hearing, smell, taste, feeling.
2. Fit heart and circulatory system with marked resistance to cardiovascular fatigue.
3. Fit glands of internal secretion and blood.
4. Fit digestive system and good teeth.
5. Fit muscular system in development and tone.
6. Fit nervous system for rhythmic alternation of abundant energy and relaxation.
7. Normal sexual vigor and virility.
8. Normal excretory and evacuation systems.

Motor Capacity (Dynamic Fitness)

1. At least average capacity in a wide variety of fundamental motor abilities—balance, flexibility, agility, strength, power, and endurance activities.
2. Sufficient swimming ability to save life.
3. At least average skill in basic skills of running, jumping, climbing, crawling, throwing.

Total Fitness

Physical fitness is one phase of *total fitness*. It does not include all of the aspects of emotional fitness, mental fitness, or social fitness. In emotional fitness, the feelings are important—love, fear, conflicts, and frustrations. In mental fitness the power of thought is paramount—solving problems, rationalizing, making choices, memorizing, computing, etc. In social fitness adaptability to the group and to particular friends is important—the manners, the morals, etc. Physical fitness is related to these other phases of fitness in addition to being important for itself.

A critical thinker usually asks, fit for what? Fit for my work? Fit for war service? Fit for home life? Fit for athletics? Fit for home defense? In all of these physical fitness looms significantly, as any critical analysis will show.

Definition of Motor Ability

Motor ability is the ability to execute motor skills (not necessarily athletic, as piano playing, typewriting, stringing a tennis racquet, eating, etc., are motor skills). A motor genius may be one who learns easily all motor skills and who rises to exceedingly high levels in some of them. A motor moron is one who learns motor skills with great difficulty and who is definitely retarded in many, far below the average level of performance. His learning "ceiling" is low.

Definition of Motor Fitness

Motor fitness is a limited phase of motor ability which emphasizes: (1) endurance, (2) power, (3) strength, (4) agility, (5) flexibility, (6) balance. It emphasizes the *fundamental* or *gross* big muscle movements that are dominated by muscular energy, kinesthetic sense, and suppleness of the major tissues and joints, i.e., those aspects which are fundamental to athletic or work skills, rather than the higher refinements pertaining to specialized small muscle skills which require years to perfect. Specifically, it means the capacity for efficient performance in the basic requirements of running, jumping, dodging, falling, climbing, swimming, lifting weights, carrying loads, and enduring under sustained effort in a variety of situations. Quick and efficient control of the body in an emergency may save the life of one individual or many. One should be able to change his position quickly to avoid capture, fire, flood, bombs, gas, vehicles, shells, or gun-fire. Obstacles must be overcome, sometimes in a hurry. Speed and endurance in the fundamental locomotion efforts are first essentials. When soldier or naval recruits cannot run speedily or steadily for a long time, when they cannot swim if they are trapped at a river, or fall into the water with clothes and equipment, or fall through the ice; if they cannot jump over obstacles in their path, vault fences, climb out of trenches and shell holes; if they cannot dodge snipers, missiles, or would-be captors; if they cannot bear burdens to form barricades or show strength and endurance to transport their belongings and food; if they cannot endure long hikes, in attack, or in retreat—how then, can they hope to survive? The constituents of motor fitness may be further comprehended by examining some of the fundamental emphases.

Practical Dynamic Emphases in Motor Fitness

Balance represents neuromuscular control paralleling the development of the kinesthetic sense in acts of sitting, skating, riding, tumbling, walking logs or fences, skiing, dancing, and a host of everyday skills. Many people are handicapped because they fall and get hurt at the slightest provocation; they slip on a rug, slip in the shower, or in the pool or tub, or when they dismount from a moving vehicle. The greatest number of serious accidents are due to falls, involving poor awareness of unsteadiness or lack of compensating control. Many adults cannot ride a bicycle, skate, swim, or ski. They are unsteady in shooting or fall easily from moving vehicles. Some do not readjust quickly to experiences in which the body is turned or revolved. Balance in this sense is educable. It can be learned by gradual education of the kinesthetic sense in a variety of balance stunts. The more natural and important these are the better, but good preliminary training is associated with any fundamental gymnastic program. Advanced tumbling and diving require superb development of this ability.

Flexibility emphasizes the ability to move easily in the full range of joint movements, to tuck up tightly, to bend easily in the waist, to twist easily in the spine, to point the toes fully, and to breathe deeply and fully without much extra effort. Good suppleness is a concomitant of gradual and thorough body conditioning. It usually indicates that the joints and muscles are free from abnormal "muscle bound" conditions due to injury or abnormal development. Many events require flexibility directly, such as hurdling obstacles, running under low wires, crawling through culverts and small diameter tunnels, vaulting through the arms, jumping over a stick held in the hands, skinning the cat, fancy diving, etc. Body suppleness also indicates roughly a type of physiological youthfulness, an important characteristic of tissues and healthy blood vessels. Many people are awkward because they lack flexibility. The old person walks jerkily; so may an injured athlete whose torn tissues have healed with adhesions. People with poor flexibility usually tire easily, have little grace in bodily movements, and learn physical skills slowly. Flexibility is synonomous with pliant, supple, limber, and lithe. In the dynamic state it is not easily measurable except by cinematographic analysis. Certain tests of bending, flexing, and twisting have been developed as a start toward appraising this valuable constituent of fitness. Perhaps some of the more important relationships in health involve flexibility of the blood vessels and internal organic tissues, not directly measurable. Blood pressure is a measure of the flexibility of the cardiovascular system.

Agility emphasizes the capacity for fast reaction in controlled, nimble movement, "rabbit-like" in action—the capacity to move quickly, dexterously, and easily. It implies ability to dodge a ball or a missile quickly, to spring quickly to the feet, to climb up a cargo net quickly, to weave through a maze of obstacles quickly, to vault fences or barriers quickly or to zig-zag quickly in running from shell hole to shell hole, to get down and up quickly, to put on a life preserver or parachute quickly, perhaps to climb hurriedly out of a burning plane, or to pull oneself into a moving lifeboat, to climb a rope onto a ship, or to lower oneself by rope from a burning ship or building, or to vault onto a horse or vehicle quickly. Speed in the fundamental locomotion efforts is a first essential along with cat-like sureness of feet all through life. Obviously, accurate coordination is essential in making precise movements with speed. Agility represents one of the highest types of neuromuscular training. Inherently, some people have slow reactions but even these types can be improved. American games like baseball, football, basketball, tennis, handball, squash, badminton, and lacrosse have successfully developed this trait more than some of the others involved in motor fitness.

Strength emphasizes the capacity of the hands, legs, and trunk to exert great force against resistant objects, such as shells, equipment, a partner, a heavy rifle or machine gun. Holding the whole weight of the body suspended from the hands is a severe test if any appreciable time is involved. Swinging upon or climbing ropes requires great strength of the hands, arms, shoulders, and the large depressor muscles of the chest and back. Strength of feet and legs is also important to bear the body weight, armor, pack, and any extra burden. Weak feet and legs are a great handicap in marching under load, in lifting an injured buddy for a carry to safety, for jumping, running, skiing, or pushing a car out of the mud. Most of all the trunk is the base from which the arm and thigh muscles arise. It serves as a base to support forceful movements of the arms and legs. The muscles of the upper back and chest pull the arms downward in chinning or climbing. The muscles of the buttocks give force to all locomotion efforts, as in cycling, running, or jumping. The long back and lateral muscles hold the trunk upright and make it steady in pulling and pushing. The abdominal and thigh flexor muscles reinforce all kicking movements of the legs and all sit-up and leg-lifting movements. A very weak person may be one who cannot sit up at all, or lift the legs from the floor while lying on the back; or again, one who cannot chin the bar once, or lift the equivalent of his own weight from the floor. A strong man could pick up a 200-pound deer, log, or another injured man and put any one of these in a wagon. It is said that Abe Lincoln could tie the hind legs of a 400-pound hog together and then hang the hog on a peg above his head. Strength in its ultimate analysis is a complex human quality involving will power, the number of muscle fibers that can be brought into the act, and the nutritive state of the muscle fibers involved, all developed into coordinated effort against the particular resistance. An important differentiation is that speed and endurance are not primary considerations but only the maximum force capacity is designated as maximum strength.

Power emphasizes the capacity to release great explosive force to execute fast or sudden efforts which move the entire body with maximum effort. Physically, power is *force* x *velocity*. Both elements of force and speed must be present in high-powered acts. Such physical capacity indicates a neuromuscular integration of a superior type. Events are selected in which highly specialized skill is not a major factor but those which are a regular part of day-by-day living, such as: vertical jumping, standing broad jumping, running broad jumping, sprinting, and throwing weights. American track and field athletics have concentrated on power events in the sprint runs, jumps, vaults, and in throwing the weights or javelin. Power is the dominating characteristic in superior performances in these events wherein the whole body is projected or some object is projected with utmost capacity in an all-out explosive effort.

Endurance is capacity for continuous exertion, involving in the first minute or two severe depletion of the oxygen reserve and the development of oxygen debt with severe distress. This is usually overcome by forced ventilation which induces more adequate circulation of blood. When relief comes it is sometimes called "second wind." Local fatigue may develop in particular muscles, such as those of the feet and calves in hopping, or in the arms in chinning without much effect in other parts of the body or in the general circulation. Circulatory (cardiac) fatigue may be due to fast and continued exertion for several minutes or hours. Cramps may develop or the control and rhythm of the movement may be lost. Ability to recuperate to a degree and still continue to run, swim, climb a mountain, or march under load are most obvious tests of endurance. Partial recovery must take place during the exercise, at least enough to attain the "steady state" as it is known to physiologists. In this state the recuperation is sufficient to keep the oxygen debt from mounting any further and enough oxygen is supplied to equal that used in the tissues.

Specific Nature of Various Fitnesses

Considerable confusion exists over attempts to oversimplify the concepts of physical fitness. Physicians do not agree with physical educators about the dominant emphasis. Nutritionists do not agree with other groups. Mental hygienists have their own point of view, too. For convenience and until more research is done it seems reasonable to recognize three major groups of constituent elements, namely, physique, organic efficiency, and motor fitness. This is for the convenience of physical educators. There is some evidence to show that there are many specific elements in each of these categories.

Data on University of Illinois men indicates that the correlations between age, height, weight, and athletic performance are insignificant. Organic condition represented by the Schneider Test correlates insignificantly with age, height, weight, strength tests, power tests, balance exercises, flexibility exercises, and agility exercises. The Schneider Test correlates moderately well with long endurance running times but is not significantly related to muscular endurance items of a highly localized nature in which specific muscles are overloaded, such as hops, floor push-ups, chinning, and bar dips. Intercorrelations between fourteen items of the Illinois Motor Fitness Test gives correlations which are very low among almost all items. This indicates that the total score is a composite of a number of specific elements representing different traits. A test of a few items usually means that not much is measured.

Physique measurements have not correlated well with measures of organic efficiency or motor fitness. Only the Sheldon-Tucker-Stevens body type rating (the somatotype) seems to have much relationship. The Illinois Motor Fitness Test scores correlated .318 with ratings of physique given by inspection and feeling of the muscles. The physique ratings correlated only .200 with the Schneider Test. This does not mean that any one of these dominant aspects is valueless. It means that they are different.

More recently D. M. Hall and J. R. Wittenborn at the University of Illinois completed a factor analysis of 15 tests on boys and concluded that there were four distinctly different groups of factors which are uncorrelated with each other, namely, (1) disease susceptibility (2) size and age, (3) physical development factors, (4) dynamic strength. These workers agree that physique, organic efficiency, and motor fitness represent independent areas of importance and all should be taken into consideration in an all-around fitness program.

A factor analysis by the writer on the separate scores for balance, flexibility, agility, strength, power, and endurance shows that these constituents of the Illinois Motor Fitness Inventory can be resolved into three more primary groups of muscular energy, kinesthetic sense development, and flexibility. All are important.

Prediction of All-round Muscular Endurance

A recent factor analysis of twenty-eight muscular endurance events[1] shows that considerable duplication exists among events of

[1] Cureton, T. K., W. J. Huffman, Lyle Welser, R. W. Kirelis, D. E. Latham, *Endurance of Young Men*. (Research Report in Press.) (Washington, D.C.: National Research Council.)

this sort. Twenty-eight events give four factors which are different from each other, namely: (1) lateral muscles, (2) locomotive muscles of the shoulders and pelvis, (3) extension muscles of the arms and shoulders, (4) endurance of a cardiovascular kind or something different from the specific muscular efficiency that shows up in the 1000-yard drop-off (1000-yd. time—10 x 100-yd. time). A multiple R of .948 is obtained for a combination of three items (in standard scores, 6 σ range):

> .630 (side leg-raisings, left side down) + .448 (time of 300-yd. shuttle run) + .323 (floor pushups).

A slightly better combination is (in standard scores):

> .614 (side leg-raisings, left side down) + .379 (floor push-ups) + .228 (full squat-jumps) + .209 (1000-yd. drop-off).

These equations predict all-round muscular endurance but they do not measure other aspects of motor fitness, such as balance, flexibility, and agility. An appraisal of motor fitness on an all-round basis would include these also.[2] The misconception is to maintain that this type of test is an adequate all-round measure of physical fitness, whereas it estimates only one phase.

Further Readings

CURETON, THOMAS K., *Physical Fitness Appraisal and Guidance.* St. Louis: The C. V. Mosby Company, 1947.

CURETON, THOMAS K., "Physical Fitness—A No. 1 Health Problem," *Hygiea*, March 1945.

CURETON, THOMAS K., "Improvements in Cardiovascular Condition Associated with Physical Training (Persistently Performed Sports and Exercises), *Proceedings of College Physical Education Association*, pp. 82–104, 1957. "The Value of Hand Endurance Exercises and Tests to Produce Changes in Weight, Fat, Metabolism and Cardiovascular Condition," *61st Annual Proceedings, College Physical Education Association*, pp. 162–172, 1958.

RESEARCH COUNCIL OF THE AMERICAN ASSOCIATION FOR HEALTH, PHYSICAL EDUCATION AND RECREATION, *Measurement and*

---

[2] Cureton, T. K., "The Unfitness of Young Men in Motor Fitness," *The Journal of the American Medical Association*, 123:69–74 (Sept. 11, 1943).

Evaluation Materials in Health, Physical Education and Recreation Washington, D.C.: U.S. Government Printing Office, 1950.

Questions for Discussion

1. What are the differences between the Kraus-Weber conception of physical fitness and that of Cureton's? How do their conceptions of body flexibility differ?
2. What would be an adequate list of criteria for the measurement of flexibility? Does the Kraus-Weber flexibility test seem adequate? Explain.
3. How could the "other aspects" of motor fitness described by Cureton be measured? Describe three tests possible in each area.

JOHN F. KENNEDY

The Soft American*

The Kraus-Weber research and the work of physical educators stimulated President Dwight D. Eisenhower to create the President's Council on Youth Fitness and the President's Citizens Advisory Committee on the Fitness of American Youth. The purpose of this executive order of 1956 was to promote a higher level of fitness in American youngsters.

President John F. Kennedy also played a tremendous part in stimulating the physical vitality of our nation and increasing interest in physical fitness. The article that follows expresses his views.

Beginning more than 2,500 years ago, from all quarters of the Greek world men thronged every four years to the sacred grove of Olympia, under the meadow of Mount Cronus, to complete in the

* Reprinted with the permission of Mrs. John F. Kennedy and the publisher from *Sports Illustrated*. New York: Time, Inc., vol. 13, part 2, December 26, 1960, pp. 15–17.

most famous athletic contents of history—the Olympian games. During the contest a sacred truce was observed among all the states of Greece as the best athletes of the Western world competed in boxing and foot races, wrestling and chariot races for the wreath of wild olive which was the prize of victory. When the winners returned to their home cities to lay the Olympian crowns in the chief temples they were greeted as heroes and received rich rewards. For the Greeks prized physical excellence and athletic skills among man's great goals and among the prime foundations of a vigorous state.

Thus the same civilizations which produced some of our highest achievements of philosophy and drama, government and art, also gave us a belief in the importance of physical soundness which has become a part of Western tradition; from the *mens sana in corpore sano* of the Romans to the British belief that the playing fields of Eton brought victory on the battlefields of Europe. This knowledge, the knowledge that the physical well-being of the citizen is an important foundation for the vigor and vitality of all the activities of the nation, is as old as Western civilization itself. But it is a knowledge which today, in America, we are in danger of forgetting.

The first indication of a decline in the physical strength and ability of young Americans became apparent among United States soldiers in the early stages of the Korean War. The second came when figures were released showing that almost one out of every two young Americans was being rejected by Selective Service as mentally, morally or physically unfit. But the most startling demonstration of the general physical decline of American youth came when Dr. Hans Kraus and Dr. Sonja Weber revealed the results of 15 years of research centering in the Posture Clinic of New York's Columbia-Presbyterian Hospital—results of physical fitness tests given to 4,264 children in this country and 2,870 children in Austria, Italy and Switzerland.

The findings showed that despite our unparalleled standard of living, despite our good food and our many playgrounds, despite our emphasis on school athletics, American youth lagged far behind Europeans in physical fitness. Six tests for muscular strength and flexibility were given; 57.9% of the American children failed one or more of these tests, while only 8.7% of the European youngsters failed.

A Consistent Decline

Especially disheartening were the results of the five strength tests: 35.7% of American children failed one or more of these, while only 1.1% of the Europeans failed, and among Austrian and Swiss youth the rate of failure was as low as .5%.

As a result of the alarming Kraus-Weber findings President Eisenhower created a Council on Youth Fitness at the Cabinet level and appointed a Citizens Advisory Committee on the Fitness of American Youth, composed of prominent citizens interested in fitness. Over the past five years the physical fitness of American youth has been discussed in forums, by committees and in leading publications. A 10-point program for physical fitness has been publicized and promoted. Our schools have been urged to give increased attention to the physical well-being of their students. Yet there has been no noticeable improvement. Physical fitness tests conducted last year in Britain and Japan showed that the youth of those countries were considerably more fit than our own children. And the annual physical fitness tests for freshmen at Yale University show a consistent decline in the prowess of young Americans; 51% of the class of 1951 passed these tests, 43% of the class of 1956 passed, and only 38%, a little more than a third, of the class of 1960 succeeded in passing the not overly rigorous examination.

Of course, physical tests are not infallible. They can distort the true health picture. There are undoubtedly many American youths and adults whose physical fitness matches and exceeds the best of other lands.

But the harsh fact of the matter is that there is also an increasingly large number of young Americans who are neglecting their bodies—whose physical fitness is not what it should be—who are getting soft. And such softness on the part of individual citizens can help to strip and destroy the vitality of a nation.

For the physical vigor of our citizens is one of America's most precious resources. If we waste and neglect this resource, if we allow it to dwindle and grow soft then we will destroy much of our ability to meet the great and vital challenges which confront our people. We will be unable to realize our full potential as a nation.

Throughout our history we have been challenged to armed conflict by nations which sought to destroy our independence or threatened our freedom. The young men of America have risen to those occasions, giving themselves freely to the rigors and hardships of warfare. But the stamina and strength which the defense of liberty requires are not the product of a few weeks' basic training or a month's conditioning. These only come from bodies which have been conditioned by a lifetime of participation in sports and interest in physical activity. Our struggles against aggressors throughout our history have been won on the playgrounds and corner lots and fields of America.

Thus, in a very real and immediate sense, our growing softness, our increasing lack of physical fitness, is a menace to our security.

However, we do not, like the ancient Spartans, wish to train the bodies of our youths merely to make them more effective warriors. It is our profound hope and expectation that Americans will never again have to expend their strength in armed conflict.

But physical fitness is as vital to the activities of peace as to those of war, especially when our success in those activities may well determine the future of freedom in the years to come. We face in the Soviet Union a powerful and implacable adversary determined to show the world that only the Communist system possesses the vigor and determination necessary to satisfy awakening aspirations for progress and the elimination of poverty and want. To meet the challenge of this enemy will require determination and will and effort on the part of all Americans. Only if our citizens are physically fit will they be fully capable of such an effort.

For physical fitness is not only one of the most important keys to a healthy body; it is the basis of dynamic and creative intellectual activity. The relationship between the soundness of the body and the activities of the mind is subtle and complex. Much is not yet understood. But we do know what the Greeks knew: that intelligence and skill can only function at the peak of their capacity when the body is healthy and strong; that hardy spirits and tough minds usually inhabit sound bodies.

In this sense, physical fitness is the basis of all the activities of our society. And if our bodies grow soft and inactive, if we fail to encourage physical development and prowess, we will undermine our capacity for thought, for work and for the use of those skills vital to an expanding and complex America.

Thus the physical fitness of our citizens is a vital prerequisite to America's realization of its full potential as a nation, and to the opportunity of each individual citizen to make full and fruitful use of his capacities.

It is ironic that at a time when the magnitude of our dangers makes the physical fitness of our citizens a matter of increasing importance, it takes greater effort and determination than ever before to build the strength of our bodies. The age of leisure and abundance can destroy vigor and muscle tone as effortlessly as it can gain time. Today human activity, the labor of the human body, is rapidly being engineered out of working life. By the 1970s, according to many economists, the man who works with his hands will be almost extinct.

Many of the routine physical activities which earlier Americans took for granted are no longer part of our daily life. A single look at the packed parking lot of the average high school will tell us what has happened to the traditional hike to school that helped to build your bodies. The television set, the movies and the myriad conveniences and distractions of modern life all lure our young people away from the strenuous physical activity that is the basis of fitness in youth and in later life.

Now It Is Time

Of course, modern advances and increasing leisure can add greatly to the comfort and enjoyment of life. But they must not be confused with indolence, with, in the words of Theodore Roosevelt, "slothful ease," with an increasing deterioration of our physical strength. For the strength of our youth and the fitness of our adults are among our most important assets, and this growing decline is a matter of urgent concern to thoughtful Americans.

This is a national problem, and requires national action. President Eisenhower helped show the way through his own interest and by calling national attention to our deteriorating standards of physical fitness. Now it is time for the United States to move forward with a national program to improve the fitness of all Americans.

FIRST: We must establish a White House Committee on Health and Fitness to formulate and carry out a program to improve the physical condition of the nation. This committee will include the Secretary of Health, Education and Welfare and the Secretary of the Interior. The executive order creating the committeee will clearly state its purpose, and coordinate its activities with the many federal programs which bear a direct relation to the problem of physical fitness.

SECOND: The physical fitness of our youth should be made the direct responsibility of the Department of Health, Education and Welfare. This department should conduct—through its Office of Education and the National Institutes of Health—research into the development of a physical fitness program for the nation's public schools. The results of this research shall be made freely available to all who are interested. In addition, the Department of Health, Education and Welfare should use all its existing facilities to attack the lack of youth fitness as a major health problem.

THIRD: The governor of each state will be invited to attend an annual National Youth Fitness Congress. This congress will examine the progress which has been made in physical fitness during the preceding year, exchange suggestions for improving existing programs and provide an opportunity to encourage the states to implement the physical fitness program drawn up by the Department of Health, Education and Welfare. Our states are anxious to participate in such programs, to make sure that their youth have the opportunity for full development of their bodies as well as their minds.

FOURTH: The President and all departments of government must make it clearly understood that the promotion of sports participation and physical fitness is a basic and continuing policy of the United States. By providing such leadership, by keeping physical fitness in the forefront of the nation's concerns, the federal government can make a substantial contribution toward improving the health and vigor of our citizens.

But no matter how vigorous the leadership of government, we can fully restore the physical soundness of our nation only if every American is willing to assume responsibility for his own fitness and the fitness of his children. We do not live in a regimented society where men are forced to live their lives in the interest of the state. We are, all of us, as free to direct the activities of our bodies as we are to pursue the objects of our thought. But if we are to retain this freedom, for ourselves and for generations yet to come, then we must also be willing to work for the physical toughness on which the courage and intelligence and skill of man so largely depend.

All of us must consider our own responsibilities for the physical vigor of our children and of the young men and women of our community. We do not want our children to become a generation of spectators. Rather, we want each of them to be a participant in the vigorous life.

Further Readings

BAUER, W. W., and FRED V. HEIN, "Exercise and Health, A Point of View," *The Journal of the American Medical Association*, 1959.

EISENHOWER, DWIGHT D., *Fitness of American Youth*. White House Executive Order, July 16, 1956.

"Exercise and Fitness," *Colloquium on Exercise and Fitness*, Chicago, Ill.: University of Illinois and The Athletic Institute, 1959.

HEIN, FRED V., and ALLAN J. RYAN, "The Contribution of Physical Activity to Physical Health," *Research Quarterly Supplement*. The American Association for Health, Physical Education and Recreation, May 1960, pp. 263–279.

JOHNSON, WARREN R., *Health Concepts for College Students*. New York: The Ronald Press Company, 1962.

MCCLOY, C. H., "The Significance of the Profit Statistics," *The Physical Educator*. Indianapolis: Phi Epsilon Kappa Fraternity, vol. XV, no. 2 (May 1958), pp. 48–49.

Questions for Discussion

1. What was the Greek position on physical fitness?
2. Why is there a need for physical fitness when machines do most of our work?
3. Has physical fitness become an important area of physical education? Possibly too important? Explain your answer.
4. What are the arguments for developing fitness through formal exercise? Through sports activities?
5. What effect has spectatorship had on the physical fitness of our youth?

WILHELM RAAB, M.D., F.A.C.P.

Degenerative Heart Disease
from Lack of Exercise*

Thus far, the readings in this section have related the need for and contributions of exercise to physical growth, development, and fitness. The readings that follow present expert opinion and scientific evidence concerning the contribution of exercise to the heart, weight control, and aging.

For many years principles of physical education stressed its contributions to life's processes. Recently these claims have been upheld by scientific research.

Discussion of the most vital of human organs, the heart, have included both myth and evidence. Persistent interest in the heart has resulted in excellent cardiac research. Much of this research places an enormous responsibility upon physical educators, for it indicates that lack of exercise has a causal relationship to heart disease.

The two following readings represent the major areas of research on this subject. The article by Raab, a well-known physician of sports medicine, illustrates the great difference between the heart that is regularly exercised and the one that is not. The implication for physical education programs—that regular exercise is important for a healthy heart—is as important as the fact that endurance activities are superior to strength exercises for a healthy heart. Despite this evidence, only California requires daily physical education for secondary school pupils. Furthermore, the majority of activities in the typical physical education program do not stress endurance.

In the decades that have elasped since the first attempts (1) to obtain epidemiological data concerning a possible role of dietary fats and cholesterol in atherogenesis, a great deal of highly suggestive

---

* Reprinted and abridged with permission of the author and the publisher from *Colloquium on Exercise and Fitness.* Chicago: The Athletic Institute, 1960, pp. 10–19.

statistical material has been gathered in favor of this concept (2). However, it has also become clear that dietary factors alone cannot be made fully responsible for the enormously widespread morbidity and mortality from degenerative cardiovascular diseases in this country.

Socio-economic pressures, emotional tensions, anxieties and frustrations have been recognized as contributing their pathogenic share (3, 4), and the steadily increasing lack of physical exercise, as it prevails among the super-civilized, motorized, automatized and TV-sitting populations of the West, has, likewise, come under scrutiny as a possible major factor.

Extensive statistical surveys from England (5), the United States (6, 7, 8), Austria (9) and Finland (10) seem to provide strong support for the assumption of an earlier and greater cardiovascular morbidity and mortality among non-exercising individuals, as compared with those engaged in physically strenuous occupations or sports activities continued into their later age. Such conclusions are, however, regarded with scepticism by some other observers (3, 4, 11, 12), and one must admit that the apparent mutual interferences of several overlapping variables make a decisive evaluation of even the most elaborate statistical data extremely difficult.

It is worthy of note that Morris and Crawford (13), by analyzing 3,800 autopsy reports, found a decidedly reversed proportion between habitual exercise intensity and the occurrence of myocardial fibrosis, whereas no such relationship seemed to exist with respect to coronary atherosclerosis. Altogether, the influence of exercise habits on the functional and structural state of the myocardium is more thoroughly investigated and more solidly established than is the case concerning the vascular system, even though certain experimental (14, 15, 16, 17) and clinical (18) observations do suggest an antiatherogenic effect of prolonged exercise periods.

Without being able to express a definite opinion of his own regarding the conclusiveness of existing statistical data, this reviewer will base his following discussion on the well-known primitive experience that cardiac performance under stress is superior in the trained sportsman and lumberjack compared with the sedentary office clerk or businessman.

It has long been known that the hearts of highly trained athletes, especially of those active in endurance sports such as running, cycling, swimming, etc. (much more than in sports of strength and skill: weight lifting, wrestling, judo, etc. (19, 20) display certain characteristics which distinguish them sharply from those of non athletes. Some of these characteristics, namely a slow heart rate, long isometric (= tension) period of the left ventricle at rest and rapid deceleration after exercise have always been interpreted as the expression of a highly developed tone of the cardiac vagus and of its cholinergic effect on the heart (21, 22, 23). Since the heart rate is directly influenced by the vagus, this concept can be maintained, as far as the athlete's bradycardia is concerned. The negative inotropic prolongation of the isometric ventricular contraction period, however, may be better explained on the grounds of the recently discovered cardiac sympatho-inhibitory mechanisms (24) in view of the fact that the ventricular muscle is devoid of vagal nerve terminals. In the following we shall, therefore, speak of both vagal cholinergic and sympatho-inhibitory forces as prevailing in the typical "athlete's heart."

Considering the familiar cardiac metabolic and functional advantages of the cholinergic-sympatho-inhibitory neurovegative pattern as it exists in the highly trained individual, we decided to compare heart rates and dynamic cycles (isometric periods) of the left ventricle at rest . . . in groups of persons with widely differing exercise habits, ranging from competitive endurance athletes to completely sedentary individuals. With the support of the National Heart Institute, the Vermont Heart Association and the U. S. Department of State Fulbright Commission in Vienna, we examined 360 healthy men, 17 to 50 years old, in Vermont and in the Austrian Alps at the University of Innsbruck, thus, in two territorially, climatically and socially comparable semi-rural urban communities, surrounded by mountainous farmland (25). The test subjects were divided in four groups, namely Group I: American and Austrian sportsmen, mountain peasants and soldiers of élite Mountain Units of the Austrian Army (subgroup I + consisting of competitive endurance athletes); Group II: men engaged in regular light sports or routine military training including daily gymnastics non-motorized farm laborers in the plains, patrols of the Austrian State Police who walk several hours per day; Group III: men with only irregular and scanty sports activities, mechanics, factory workers in nonstrenuous occupations, walking not more than 3 miles per day; Group IV: nearly completely sedentary individuals.

Records of the heart rate and of the isometric period of the left ventricle, which is a sensitive indicator of neurovegetative inotropic influences (26), showed a linear increase of cardiac sympathetic tone (decreasing cholinergic-sympatho-inhibitory activity) with decreasing exercise habits. In the two age categories (17–34 and 35–50 years) which were examined separately, the most active groups displayed the lowest, the least active groups the highest sympathetic tone, the latter being manifested by the fastest average heart rate and shortest average isometric period. . . . Thus, in striking contrast to the prominent cholingeric-sympatho-inhibitory features of "athlete's heart," a sympathetic adrenergic preponderance proved to be characteristic for what we like to call "loafer's heart." The Russian translators of this reviewer's writings on the subject (27) found this expression not enough dignified for scientific purposes and replaced it by the term "detrenyrovannoye syerdce" ("detrained heart").

In order to make certain that the high cholinergic-sympatho-inhibitory activity in athletically inclined individuals is an acquired one and not merely a predisposing constitutional trait, we tested 20 students before and after 6 to 12 weeks of vigorous training, . . . and found in about 75% of them a shift toward the "athlete's heart's" pattern in agreement with other observers (21, 28, 29, 30).

Conversely, the distinctly cholinergic-sympatho-inhibitory features of active sportsmen tend to disappear after cessation of training (20, 21, 31, 32) and in a group of volunteers, tested by Taylor et al. (33), three weeks of complete bed rest were followed by the appearance of marked adrenergic cardiac manifestations which persisted up to one month.

The basic mechanism underlying the above discussed neurovegetative shifts in connection with physical training and with lack of exercise, respectively, is still obscure but it appears most likely that the responsible alterations take place primarily in the central nervous areas of impulse formation which govern cardiac dynamics (24, 34).

Although this problem seems theoreticaly intriguing, its clinical significance is overshadowed by the far-reaching pathogenic implications of a more or less permanent adrenergic preponderance in cardiac metabolism and function.

It took this reviewer nearly 20 years of hard labor until he finally succeeded in directing the attention of clinical cardiologists and pathologists toward the fundamental role played by the biochemical actions of the adrenergic catecholamines, norepinephrine and epinephrine, in the pathogensis of functional and degenerative diseases of the heart, as contrasted with the traditional purely mechanistic concepts which had viewed these derangements almost exclusively as a matter of vascular plumbing.

Under normal circumstances, the adreno-sympathogenic catecholamines do not constitute any threat to the heart, in the regulation of whose function they are purposefully integrated (34, 35). However, they possess certain basic properties which, if unduly exaggerated, become harmful and capable of seriously injuring cardiac metabolism, function and structure. The most important adverse influences exerted by intensified catecholamine action upon the myocardium are: excessive wasteful consumption of oxygen, reduction of energetic efficiency, production of local hypoxia, interference in potassium exchange, and tissue necrotization. All of these factors have been discussed in detail in a monograph on "The Adrenergic-Cholinergic Control of Cardiac Metabolism and Function" (36).

Frequently supervening conditions which are apt to cause a "toxifying" aggrevation of the aforesaid catecholamine effects are the following:

(a) quantitative increase of catecholamine production and liberation, e.g., under prolonged emotional or physical stress;

(b) hormonal potentiation of oxygen-wasting catecholamine action by the thyroid hormone, and of necrotizing effects by adrenal corticoids;

(c) aggravation of the hypoxiating influence of the catecholamines by coronary sclerosis which reduces the oxygen supply of the myocardium, and/or by arterial hypertension (without or with ventricular hypertrophy) which increases cardiac oxygen requirements;

(d) deficiency of cholinergic-sympatho-inhibitory mechanisms, which creates an abnormal sympathetic adrenergic preponderance in myocardial metabolism, thus augmenting the metabolic vulnerability of the heart muscle.

This last-named point (d) is the one with which we are particularly concerned in evaluating the detrimental cardiac consequences of habitual physical inactivity. By itself, the permanent elevation of the sympathetic tone of the "detrained" or "loafer's heart" does not seem to cause any demonstrably pathological manifestations. However, it constitutes a metabolic background situation with highly pathogenic potentialities, going into effect if it coincides with any one or several of the above listed "toxifying" complications. . . .

The most common of these are acute or chronic additional sympathetic-stimulating emotional stresses (possibly accompanied by exaggerated adrenal cortical activity), coronary sclerosis and arterial hypertension. The two last-named conditions themselves are initiated, in part, by atherogenic (37) and vasopressor (38) catecholamine action respectively, owing to the key position occupied by the sympathetic adrenergic system in general cardiovascular pathology (39). Thus, an originally intact "loafer's heart" may remain functionally normal for a long time, but when any of the toxifying factors supervene, its abnormal metabolic vulnerability will predispose it to the development of such largely catecholamine-induced manifestations of hypoxic anginal pain, arrhythmias, necrotic and fibrous myocardial degeneration, and ventricular failure (36).

All of these clinical features can be mitigated or abolished by direct or indirect antiadrenergic therapeutic measures, such as sympathectomy, ganglionic blockade, catecholamine-depleting rauwolfia and catecholamine-inactivating thyrostatic medication, adrenalectomy and vagal stimulating drugs or procedures (36).

Among the latter, prolonged systematic physical training assumes a prominent place. Obviously, for long-range cardiac protection, such training should be begun at an early age, but with consideration of the fact that the cardiac sympathetic tone of the very young is relatively high (40, 41), stressful overtraining should be avoided.

If and when signs of cardiac damage have already developed in the adult, exercise therapy, carried out under appropriate, meticulous precautions, is likely to diminish or even to abolish the important conditioning and contributory factor of an exaggerated sympathetic tone. Under the impression of numerous favorable clinical reports (30, 42, 43, 44, 45, 46, 47, 48, 49, 50) and of experimental evidence to the extent that exercise stimulates the development of collaterals in coronary insufficiency (51), both the medical profession and the general public have assumed a far more optimistic and courageous attitude in this respect than in the past.

In middle-aged and elderly, quietly degenerating sedentary individuals who have not yet developed any overt cardiac pathology, prophylactic reconditioning has proved most gratifying and useful (52, 53, 54). It is being practiced on a large scale in West Germany where insurance companies and big industrial concerns (53) are financing the physical and psychological re-conditioning of thousands of sedentary employees and workers through graded outdoor programs in the Bavarian Alps under the direction of Dr. P. Beckmann (55). We are hoping to develop a similar center in the Green Mountains of Vermont, but we also feel that preparatory careful functional testing (including the study of climatic influences on exercise tolerance) will be necessary. Otherwise we would not dare to assume the responsibility for imposing on aging hearts the acute stresses of vigorous exercising, even though it is intended to achieve a long-range reduction of sympathetic tone. All-year home exercise programs like those proposed by Cureton (31) will, likewise, be required for maintenance of whatever gains are made during the actual training periods. There is no other rational way to bring our civilization and prosperity-ridden, artificially denaturalized so-called "normal" flabby hearts back to that obsolete type of vigorous normalcy which has been the privilege of our ancestors since time immemorial.

In summarizing, it can be stated that habitual lack of physical exercise leads to a deficiency of vagal cholinergic and sympatho-inhibitory mechanisms in cardiac functional regulation. The resulting preponderance of sympathetic adrenergic tone (potentially cardiotoxic catecholamine overactivity) creates a threat to myocardial health in that it increases the metabolic vulnerability of the heart muscle. It is apt to produce oxygen wastage, myocardial hypoxia, focal necrotization and ventricular failure under such commonly supervening catecholamine-"toxifying" circumstances as emotional and other stresses, certain hormonal interferences, coronary sclerosis, arterial hypertension and ventricular hypertrophy.

No one single factor, such as diet, emotional pressures or lack of physical exercise, can be made fully responsible for the present-day high incidence of functional and degenerative heart diseases; rather do their varying combinations become pathogenic through mutual aggravation.

The inactivity-induced neurovegetative imbalance is reversible by appropriate and persistent exercise training. With the necessary precautions, such training is applicable also to overt cardiac patients, and in particular, to seemingly healthy, yet quietly degenerating sedentary adults, for whose benefit the establishment of organized mass-reconditioning centers and programs, like those already existing in other countries, is being urged.

Literature Cited

1. RAAB, W., Alimentäre Faktoren in der Entstehung von Arteriosklerose und Hypertonie, *Mediz. Klinik,* 14, 15, 1932.
2. KEYS, A., Diet and the Epidemiology of Coronary Heart Disease, *J. Am. Med. Ass'n.,* 164: 1912, 1957.
3. RUSSEK, H. I. and B. L. ZOHMAN, Relative Significance of Heredity, Diet, and Occupational Stress in Coronary Heart Disease of Young Adults, *Am. J. Med. Sci.,* 235: 266, 1958.
4. FRIEDMAN, M. and R. H. ROSENMAN, Association of Specific Overt Behavior Pattern With Blood and Cardiovascular Findings, *J. Am. Med. Ass'n.,* 169:97/1287, 1959.
5. MORRIS, J. N., P. A. RAFFLE, C. C. ROBERTS, and J. W. PARKS, Coronary Heart Disease and Physical Activity of Work, *Lancet* 2: 1053, 1953.
6. POMEROY, W. C. and P. D. WHITE, Coronary Heart Disease in Former Football Players, *J. Am. Med. Ass'n.,* 167: 711, 1958.
7. LUONGO, E. P., Health Habits and Heart Disease Challenge in Preventive Medicine, *J. Am. Med. Ass'n.,* 162: 1021, 1956.
8. SPAIN, D. M. and V. A. BRADESS, Relation of Sex, Age and Physical Activity to Sudden Death From Coronary Arterial Occlusion, publ. in F. F. Rosenbaum and E. L. Belknap *Work and the Heart,* p. 283, New York: P. B. Hoeber, 1959.
9. WIENER GEBIETSKRANKENKASSE, *Sterbefälle und Sterbegeld, Jahresbericht d. Weiner Gebietskrankenkasse* (Vienna) p. 168, 1956.
10. KARVONEN, M. J., J. KIHLBERG, J. MÄÄTTÄ and J. VIRKAJÄRVI, Longevity of Champion Skiers, *Duodecim,* 72: 893, 1956.
11. KEYS, A., Occupational and Environmental Factors in the Development of Heart Disease, publ. in F. F. Rosenbaum and E. L. Belknap *Work and the Heart,* p. 103, New York: P. B. Hoeber, 1959.
12. STAMLER, J., Current Epidemiological, Clinical and Laboratory Research Findings on the Etiology of Atherosclerosis, *Nebraska State Med. J.,* 41: 75, 1956.
13. MORRIS, J. N. and M. D. CRAWFORD, Coronary Heart Disease and Physical Activity of Work, *Brit. Med. J.,* 2: 1485, 1958.
14. MYASNIKOV, A. L., Influence of Some Factors on Development of Experimental Cholesterol Atherosclerosis, *Circulation,* 17: 99, 1958.
15. WONG, H. Y. C., F. B. JOHNSON and A. K. WONG, Effect of Exercise and Androgen in Cholesterol-fed Pullets, *Fed. Proc.,* 17: 173, 1958.
16. ORMA, E. J., Effect of Physical Activity on Atherogenesis, *Acta Physiol. Scandinav.,* 41: Suppl. 142, 1957.
17. KOBERNICK, S. D., G. NIWAYAMA and A. C. ZUCHLOWSKI, Effect of Physical Activity on Cholesterol Atherosclerosis in Rabbits, *Proc. Soc. Exp. Biol. and Med.,* 96:623, 1957.
18. WOLFFE, J. B., Continued Vigorous Physical Activity as a Possible Factor in the Prevention of Atherosclerosis. *Circulation,* 16: 517, 1957.

19. REINDELL, H., H. KLEPZIG, K. MUSSHOFF and E. SCHILDGE, Das Sportherz, Ergeb. d. inn. *Med. u. Kinderheilk,* 5: 306, 1954.
20. JOKL, E., Ballistocardiographic Studies on Athletes, *Am. J. Cardiol.,* 4: 105, 1959.
21. MELLEROWICZ, H., Oekonomieprinzip in Arbeit und Leistung des Trainierten Kreislaufs, *Arch. f. Kreislaufforschg.,* 24: 70, 1956.
22. HEINECKER, R., Individualle Unterschiede in der Reaktion von Kreislauf und Gasstroffwechsel auf Dosierte Belastungen und Cold Pressor Test, Flickerlicht, Lärm, Körperhiche Arbeit, *Arch. f. Kreislaufforschg.,* 30: 1, 1959.
23. CURETON, T. K., Comparison of 55 Middle-aged Former Athletic Champions with Some 400 Middle-aged Men and with Normal Young Men, *Am. J. Phys. Anthropology,* 12: 273, 1954.
24. FOLKOW, B., *Hypothalamic Inhibition of Sympathetic Tone, Symposium on Central Nervous System Control of Cardiovascular System,* Nat'l. Research Council, Washington, D.C., Nov. 1–3, 1959.
25. RAAB, W., P. DE PAULA E SILVA, H. MARCHET, E. KIMURA and Y. K. STARCHESKA, Cardiac Adrenergic Overactivity Due to Habitual Lack of Physical Exercise and Its Pathogenic Implications, *Am. J. Cardiol,* 5, March, 1960, pp. 300–320.
26. RAAB, W. P., DE PAULA E SILVA and Y. K. STARCHESKA, Adrenergic and Cholinergic Influences on the Dynamic Cycle of the Normal Human Heart, *Cardiologia,* 33: 350, 1958.
27. RAAB, W., Adrenergychesko-Cholinergycheskaya Regulyacya Obmyena Vyeshchestvy Funktsiy Syerdca, publ, in *Dostyzheniya Kardiologiy,* State Publications, of Medical Literature, Moscow (Medgiz), 1959.
28. PROKOP, L., Vegetatives System and Jurgendtraining, *Sportsmedizin,* 5, No. 10, Oct., 1954.
29. KNEHR, C. A., D. B. DILL and W. NEUFELD, Training and Its Effects on Man at Rest and at Work, *Am. J. Physiol.,* 136: 148, 1942.
30. CURETON, T. K., Improvements in Cardiovascular Condition of Humans Associated with Physical Training, Persistently Performed Sports and Exercises, *Coll. Phys. Educ. Ass'n.,* p. 86, 1957.
31. CURETON, T. K., The Nature of Cardiovascular Condition, *J. Ass'n. Phys. and Mental Rehabil.,* 11: 186, 1957; 12: 8, 41, 113, 1958.
32. JOKL, E., A. KOSKELA, W. MCCUBBIN, P. JOKL and S. R. ARBEIT, Physical Efficiency, One of the Determinators of Ballistocardiographic Patterns, *Am. J. Cardio.,* 1: 4, April, 1958.
33. TAYLOR, H. L., A. HENSCHEL, J. BRŎZEK and A. KEYS, Effects of Bed Rest on Cardiovascular Function and Work Performance, *J. Appl. Physiol.,* 2: 233, 1949.
34. RUSHMER, R. F., O. SMITH and D. FRANKLIN, Mechanisms of Cardiac Control in Exercise, *Circul. Res.,* 7: 602, 1959.
35. SARNOFF, S. J., The Role in Circulatory Regulation of Reflexly Induced Myocardial Catecholamine Changes, Symposium on "The Catecholamines in Cardiovascular Pathology," University of Vermont, Burlington, Vt., Aug. 23–26, 1959.

36. RAAB, W., The Adrenergic-Cholinergic Control of Cardiac Metabolism and Function, in *Advances of Cardiology*, 1: 65, S. Karger, Basel, New York, 1956.

37. RAAB, W., Neurohormonal Atherogenesis, *Am. J. Cardiol.*, 1: 113, 1958.

38. RAAB, W., Transmembrane Cationic Gradient and Blood Pressure Regulation. Interaction of Corticoids, Catecholamines and Electrolytes on Vascula Cells, *Am. J. Cardiol.* 5, April, 1960.

39. RAAB, W., Key Position of Catecholamines in Functional and Degenerative Cardiovascular Pathology, *Am. J. Cardiol.* 5, May, 1960, pp. 571–578.

40. PROKOP, L., Vegetatives System und Jugendtraining, *Sportsmedizin*, 5, No. 10, Oct., 1954.

41. KOVALENO, V., L'electrocardiogramme du Sportif dans le Surmenage Chronique du Système Cardiovasculaire, XII. Sports Medicine Congress, Moscow, May-June, 1958, p. 28.

42. WALKER, W. J., Should the Patient with a Healed Myocardial Infarction Avoid Physical Exercise?, *J. Am. Geriatr. Soc.*, 3: 959, 1955.

43. DURBIN, E. and L. J. GOLDWATER, Rehabilitation of the Cardiac Patient, *Circulation*, 13: 410, 1956.

44. HANSEN, H. and N. K. WEAVER, Arteriosclerotic Hearts at Work, *J. Louisiana State Medical Soc.*, 107: 63, 1955.

45. HOCHREIN, M., Zur Beurteilung der Einsatzfahigkeit von Angina Pectoris-Kranken, *Münch. Med. Wschr.*, 97: 1588, 1955.

46. BISHOP, L. F., Rehabilitation Following Coronary Occlusion, *Brit J. Phys. Med.*, July, 1957.

47. REINDELL, H. and H. KLEPZIG, Schonung oder Uebung bei Koronarleiden, *Wiener Zeitschr. f. inn. Med.*, 39: 340, 1958.

48. MCCLOY, C. H., Home Exercise for Convalescing Cardiac Patients, *J. Ass'n. for Phys. and Mental Rehabil.*, 2: 6, 181, 1957.

49. SLIPYAN, A., Effect of Competitive Industrial Activity on Severely Disabled Cardiac Patients, *J. Am. Med. Ass'n.*, 168: 147, 1958.

50. XII. *International Congress of Sports Medicine, Moscow*, May-June, 1958 (Vogralik, V., p. 84; Oganessian, L., p. 86; Voskanov, M., p. 96; Chestakov, S., p. 102; Vilkovyski, A., p. 103; Porochina, J., p. 104; Lebedeva, V. and Vinokourov, D., p. 105; Lartsev, V., p. 105).

51. ECKSTEIN, R. W., Effect of Exercise and Coronary Arterial Narrowing on Coronary Collateral Circulation, *Circul. Res.*, 5: 230, 1957.

52. CURETON, T. K., Physical Fitness Work with Normal Aging Adults, *J. Ass'n. Phys. and Mental Rehabil.*, 11: 145, 1957.

53. ARBEIT, S. R., E. JOKL, A. KOSKELA and W. E. MCCUBBIN, Ballistocardiographic Changes During a 30-day Physical Training Period, *Am. Heart J.*, 54: 556, 1957.

54. UFER, G., Werkärztliche Erfahrung mit Frühheilverfahren als vorbeugende Gesundheitspflege, *Aerztl. Praxis*, No. 10–38, Sept. 20, 1958.

55. BECKMANN, P., Gesundheitserziehung als Krankenbehandlung, *Internationale Rundschau f. Physikal. Med.*, 11: 1, 1958.

Questions for Discussion

1. Why are activities that stress endurance more important to a healthy heart than strength activities?
2. What, exactly, is a "loafer's" heart?
3. According to this reading, what seem to be the effects of stress on a healthy heart?
4. What are some of the implications for a program of skill teaching in physical education that encourages life-long physical fitness? Should team or individual sports be stressed?
5. What new role for physical education do the reconditioning centers suggest? Would these centers best be placed in schools, recreation departments, or in other agencies?

J. N. MORRIS, F.R.C.P., D.D.H.
and MARGARET D. CRAWFORD, M.D.

Coronary Heart Disease and Physical Activity of Work*

The previous selection discussed research on the effect of and lack of exercise on the heart. The second area of research in this section concerns the effect of occupational activity on the heart. The work of Morris and Crawford, British pioneers in research on this subject, indicates that heart disease is less prevalent in occupations where physical exertion is the greatest than in occupations requiring only mild activity.

Important implications for physical education are to be found in this reading. Not only is there a need for continued fitness education but also for special efforts to cope with the conse- quences of sedentary occupations. This reading could also ap-

* Reprinted and abridged with permission of the authors and the publisher from the *British Medical Journal.* No. 5 iii, Copy 2. December 20, 1958, pp. 1485–1496.

pear in the section on sociological backgrounds because of its relation to automation and the rapid cultural changes accompanying it. Only through proper maintenance of physical skills and activities can we counterbalance the effects of these social changes and retain our national health and vigor.

It has previously been shown that the drivers of London's double-decker buses are more likely to die suddenly from "coronary thrombosis" than the conductors and that Government clerks suffer more often from rapidly fatal cardiac infarction than do postmen. (43) On the basis of these and similar observations a hypothesis has been stated that *men in physically active jobs have a lower incidence of coronary (ischaemic) heart disease in middle-age than men in physically inactive jobs. More important, the disease is not so severe in physically active workers, tending to be present in them in relatively benign forms.*

It is a principle of epidemiological research of this type to seek evidence from as many, as various, and as independent sources as possible (40). The present report deals with the frequency, in relation to occupation, of ischaemic myocardial fibrosis in men dying from causes other than coronary heart disease itself. These myocardial scars are often evidence of early coronary heart disease and of less severe, or at any rate non-lethal, ischaemia. Thus the present study provides a picture of coronary heart disease in one of its simpler forms, and this may help in elucidating social connexions. At the same time another test of the hypothesis is made, using quite different data from the previous inquiries and upon quite another aspect of the condition. The inquiry it was hoped would provide some information on the pathological mechanisms of any differences with physical activity of work that were found; and in particular we sought to learn something about the relationships of occupation to coronary artery disease. In brief, Can the hearts of men be seen to vary with the kind of work they have done? At what phases in the complex of coronary-myocardial disease as a whole can this particular "cause"—physical activity/inactivity—be seen to operate? More generally the inquiry was intended to provide a statistical account of the coronary arteries of the middle-aged British male population, 1954–6 (42).

Method

Through the universities and regional hospital boards we appealed personally to all pathologists in the National Health Service who might regularly be in charge of post-mortem examinations to co-operate in the inquiry, and the pathologists of 206 hospitals or hospital groups—between 85% and 90% of the "possibles"—very kindly agreed. We cannot be more precise about this fraction, because it is not known whether some of those who did not reply at all to our letters were in fact regularly responsible for appreciable numbers of necropsies.

Each pathologist was invited to provide particulars on a standard form of 25 consecutive unselected necropsies on men aged 45–70 years, no matter what the cause of death or how the case came to necropsy. 5,000 reports were sent to us: trial runs with records from 1944 to 1951 in the Pathological Institute of the London Hospital (39, 60) had encouraged the hope that with such numbers stable group patterns would emerge. In all cases *macroscopic details* were requested of *disease in the coronary arteries,* its nature, amount, and distribution, with descriptions of any stenosis; and of *fibrosis of the myocardium of the left ventricle* and *interventricular septum,* using lesions of 1 cm. in any dimension as markers; and the *heart weight.* Particulars were also asked about the main causes of death and other important clinical and pathological findings such as valvular heart disease, including especially aortic stenosis. By appealing for detailed descriptions of lesions seen, discouraging evaluations such as "slight" or "much," and giving guidance on terminology if not on technique, we hoped to reduce the variability of such procedures. It was postulated, moreover, that the variability in observation and recording over so many departments of pathology would be "random" in relation to the main factor with which pathology was to be correlated—physical activity of work.

The pathological data on each record relating to disease in the coronary arteries and fibrosis of the myocardium were graded, agreed, and coded by at least two and often three physicians in the unit. It took many months to define appropriate scales; but finally scales emerged that made pathological sense, were simple in use, having no more than five points, and the gradings on which proved highly reproducible by ourselves and by others.

Pathologists were also invited to give details of the *last occupation* of the deceased, but in many cases this information had to be obtained by the unit from the General Register Office. The last stated occupation, apart from other difficulties (57) is unlikely to be an exact indicator of men's jobs during their middle-age. The present inquiry, however, is concerned only with *type of job* in terms of its characteristic *physical activity*. Some special categories apart, the last job is probably by and large an adequate indicator of this. (Occupational histories of their national series kindly made available to us by Doll and Hill (14, 15) showed on analysis that among 152 fatal cases of lung cancer in men aged 55–64, 80% had been in the same job for more than their last 10 years and a further 10% had changed jobs during the last 10 years of life but remained in the same physical activity category. These proportions over 15 years were 70% and 14% respectively; over 20 years, 61% and 17%.)

The 1,700 different descriptions of occupations included in the 5,000 returns of the present inquiry were classified, in terms of the physical activity habitually involved, by two experts in industrial medicine who first graded all the jobs independently and then presented the unit with an agreed coding. They used a three-point scale: typically "light" jobs (for example, schoolmaster, bus-driver, clerk of any description); "active" jobs (for example, postman, carpenter); or "heavy" jobs (for example, boilermaker, dock labourer). Light jobs, that is, include sedentary; heavy include the heaviest.

The technical problems involved in such studies as the present have already been considered (37, 40, 42), and further comments are included in this and will be given in subsequent papers. There are many imperfections in the data on both biological and social sides of the equations to be attempted. The method used, like any other, and more than most, has its limitations as well as its possibilities. In particular, detailed occupational histories could not be obtained, which may be a considerable loss, and more than occupation-wise, since related economic/nutritional standards varied far more widely in the 1930s than in the 1950s (13, 36, 51). Moreover, considered agreement on pathological techniques, not to say uniformity, has been sacrificed for numbers. The crucial issue was that of range of occupation: only a countrywide and comprehensive survey gathering large numbers of cases from many different centres could include enough men in the diminishing categories of truly "heavy" workers—coal hewers, farm labourers, men in heavy engineering, and the like. The interest of the questions that can be asked only from the present kind of study will, it is hoped, compensate for what has had to be forgone—and suggest what might next be done (41).

Material

Necropsy material may be classified for our present purposes as follows (39, 42):

Group A.—Deaths due to coronary heart disease: coronary heart disease itself; or with hypertension, and/or other pathology; and including slow, congestive cardiac failure as well as the more numerous sudden deaths. There were about 1,200 altogether in Group A.

Group B.—Deaths from conditions associated with a specially high prevalence or severity of coronary artery disease—for example, deaths from hypertension and its complications; deaths from vascular disease in sites other than the coronary arteries, with or without hypertension; ("senile") aortic stenosis; deaths from destructive renal disease; the cases of diabetes. In addition to such well-recognized associations it was noticed that deaths from peptic ulcer in the present material showed a significant excess of occlusive coronary artery disease, and these deaths were therefore included in Group B. This group of 1,000 cases was called the *high coronary artery disease group*.

Group C.—Deaths from other conditions, the remainder and majority of necropsies, including injuries, infections, cancers. No disease or disease-group with 100 cases or over included in Group C showed significantly more or significantly less coronary artery disease at the 5% level than the remainder, as judged by the prevalence and amount of mural disease and the frequency of lumen narrowing of 50% or more in a major artery. This group is therefore called the *basal group* as regards coronary artery disease. There were 2,800 cases in it.

The present report deals with the 3,800 cases in Groups B and C. Brief reference is also made to Group A, but these cases will be fully considered on another occasion.

ISCHAEMIC MYOCARDIAL FIBROSIS

In some 500 of the 3,800 non-coronary deaths fibrosis was reported in the myocardium of the left ventricle and/or septum. All these records were scrutinized, and any subjects with rheumatic heart disease or other possible cause of myocardial fibrosis, the collagen-vascular diseases, for example, or ostial syphilis, were excluded; cases with generalized, "diffuse" fibrosis not otherwise described were also discarded. ("Myocarditis" was rarely mentioned by the pathologists; no microscopical examination was requested.) This left close on 400 cases with scars, commonly in the lower, antero-lateral walls of the left ventricle, in the front of the septum, or high on the posterior wall, which are presumptively ischaemic, will henceforth be regarded as *ischaemic myocardial fibrosis,* and have alone been analysed. In most of these 400 cases there was much coronary artery disease and a report of topical coronary narrowing.[1] The few scars in the right ventricle were ignored.

Scars were classified on two axes, whether they were single or multiple and large or small. Two main types of ischaemic myocardial fibrosis soon identified themselves, and provided a quick first answer to one of the main questions of the inquiry:

Type 1.—The *large, discrete patch* of fibrosis, over 1.5 cm. in one dimension, and often solitary. These patches were commonly transmural, and they are presumably the healed end-result of major and maybe acute infarction—"large healed infarcts"—or sometimes of confluent lesser infarcts. They were usually associated with occlusion or near-occlusion in the related main coronary artery, often high in it, rather than with lesser coronary narrowing. All aneurysmal dilatations have been included here, and also some large areas of fibrosis which were not clearly circumscribed.

Type 2.—*Small, multiple scars,* in the left ventricular wall, the septum, or papillary muscles which were usually thinner and less defined than type 1 and were associated in this material mostly with minor degrees of focal narrowing, low in a main coronary artery, for example, or in smaller branches. These scars are commonly regarded as the product of lesser and more slowly developing coronary insufficiency and myocardial ischaemia. However, some of this "focal myocardial fibrosis" (21) may well be the result of very small infarcts.

It was soon apparent that the occurrence of a large patch was strongly related to physical activity/inactivity of occupation, the occurrence of the small multiple scars less so. Discrete patches of

---

[1]In the minority of scars in which there was no record of topical coronary narrowing the same relationships with physical activity of occupation were observed as among the majority with a record of obstructive arterial disease. Only one tabulation is therefore presented.

0.5–1.5 cm. in diameter, and some very small scars also regarded as ischaemic, were all found to behave much more like type 2 in relation to occupation, to coronary narrowing (and, as seen later, to hypertension) than the large healed infarcts of type 1, and they have therefore been classified to type 2. All type 2 scars will, for convenience, be called "focal myocardial fibrosis." Mixed cases with both types of fibrosis were included with type 1 (1, 21, 47, 65, 69).

Results

As stated, this report deals mainly with the (presumptively) ischaemic myocardial fibrosis found in a national sample of 3,800 non-coronary deaths in middle-aged men. Table 1 sets out the findings, first for the 2,800 miscellaneous deaths from injuries, infections, cancers, etc., and, below, for the 1,000 deaths from hypertensive and other vascular disorders, the deaths in diabetics, etc. Throughout, in each line of Table 1, the rate among the "light" workers (e.g., *2.0%* in the first line) is substantially higher than in the "heavy" (*0.3%* in the first line). The "active" rates mostly fall between, but occasionally are below the "heavy" (as in the second line of the Table). This trend was repeated time after time in the analysis of Group C, Group B, and various pathological, medical, and social subdivisions of these; it was found in Scotland, Wales, Greater London, and the rest of England, separately; in London teaching hospitals, other teaching hospitals, and non-teaching hospitals when these were distinguished; and it was also the main finding of the trial study of the 1944–51 Woods and Russell London Hospital cases.

The results in Table 1 con be summarized thus:

1. Disregarding age, cause of death category, and type of scarring (last line of the Table) there is twice as much ischaemic myocardial fibrosis in the "light" workers as in the "heavy"—*13.4%* compared with *6.8%*.

2. There is a stronger gradient with physical activity of occupation in the cases with large fibrous patches—threefold overall, *3.5%* to *1.2%*—than in those with the smaller/multiple scars—*9.9%* to *5.7%* (second and third last lines of Table 1).

3. This excess of large healed infarcts among the "light" workers is more evident in the younger age group than at 60–70 years. At 45<60 years, in Groups B and C combined, there are four to five

times as many of these scars in "light" workers as in "heavy"; at 60–70, two to three times as many (Table 2).

Numbers are often small, but it seemed preferable to set out all the data instead of amalgamating the active and heavy occupations and comparing these with the light, which was the alternative the data indicated. Table 17 emphasies that even among the heavy occupations there is a good deal of ischaemic myocardial fibrosis; though, in fact, large healed infarcts were as common in light workers aged 45–54 (2.0%) as in heavy aged 65–70 (1.9%).

HYPERTENSION

Pathologists were asked to report any clinical or pathological evidence of hypertension, and much detailed information was provided for us. Using one at least of these criteria—(*a*) a clinical history of hypertension with record of diastolic pressure over 110; often there were particulars of treatment; (*b*) "concentric" left ventricular hypertrophy; or (*c*) in younger cases particularly, left ventricular hypertrophy not otherwise described or explained, together with nephrosclerosis—it was possible to distinguish those with "record or evidence of hypertension" from the "others." Close on 10% of the "basal" Group C had incidental hypertension as so defined. In almost half the cases of the "high coronary artery disease" Group B hypertension was present, and considered usually to be a principal factor in the death—for example, in many of the deaths from cerebrovascular disease.

The prevalence of ischaemic myocardial fibrosis in relation to hypertension is summarized in Table 3, which shows no difference in the large fibrous patches (large healed infarcts) but substantially more of the smaller/multiple scars (focal myocardial fibrosis) among the hypertensive (p < 0.001). This latter excess, it may be noted, held for each of the subtypes of small scars and multiple scars included in type 2; whence the use of the term "focal myocardial fibrosis" for all of type 2 scars.

Table 4 continues this analysis by occupation, and includes all the cases in Groups B and C—that is, all the non-coronary deaths. There is nothing of interest in the large fibrous patches, both the hypertensive (e.g., 4th line, in italics, left half of the table) and the "others" (e.g., first line in italics, right half of the table) showing the expected trend. But the picture is quite different in the smaller/

Table 1

PROPORTIONS WITH ISCHAEMIC MYOCARDIAL FIBROSIS BY PHYSICAL ACTIVITY OF OCCUPATION ("LIGHT," "ACTIVE," "HEAVY"). 3,800 NON-CORONARY DEATHS. MALES AGED 45–70[a]

Age	Ischaemic Myocardial Fibrosis	Occupation		
		Light	Active	Heavy
	Deaths from Conditions in "Basal" Group			
45<60	No. of cases	509	516	324
	With large fibrous patch	10	5	1
	Rate %	2.08%	1.0%	(0.3%)
	With smaller/multiple scars	21	14	9
	Rate %	4.1%	2.7%	2.8%
60–70	No. of cases	486	518	344
	With large fibrous patch	16	12	3
	Rate %	3.3%	2.3%	(0.9%)
	With smaller/multiple scars	45	34	19
	Rate %	9.3%	6.6%	5.5%
45–70	No. of cases	995	1,034	668
	Total with ischaemic myocardial fibrosis	92	65	32
	Rate %	9.2%	6.3%	4.8%
	Deaths from Conditions in "High" Coronary Artery Disease Group			
45<60	No. of cases	193	189	82
	With large fibrous patch	6	4	1
	Rate %	3.1%	(2.1%)	(1.2%)
	With smaller/multiple scars	33	16	5
	Rate %	17.1%	8.5%	6.1%
60–70	No. of cases	252	206	112
	With large fibrous patch	19	7	5
	Rate %	7.5%	3.4%	4.5%
	With smaller/multiple scars	43	32	16
	Rate %	17.1%	15.5%	14.3%

45–70	No. of cases	445	395	194
	Total with ischaemic myocardial fibrosis	101	59	27
	Rate %	*22.7%*	*14.9%*	*13.9%*
		All Non-coronary Deaths		
45–70	No. of cases	1,440	1,429	862
	With large fibrous patch	51	28	10
	Rate %	*3.5%*	*2.0%*	*1.2%*
	With smaller/multiple scars	142	96	49
	Rate %	*9.9%*	*6.7%*	*5.7%*
	Total with ischaemic myocardial fibrosis	193	124	59
	Rate %	*13.4%*	*8.7%*	*6.8%*

[a] National Necropsy Survey, Scotland, England and Wales, 1954–6. Data from 206 hospitals or hospital groups.

The number of non-coronary deaths that were analysed varied slightly around 3,800, depending on the availability of data.

Forty-six cases have been omitted from this and all subsequent tables because information was inadequate, or it was impossible to classify a main cause of death to Groups A, B, or C (e.g., 12 cases of polyarteritis nodosa). In addition 114 non-coronary deaths have been omitted from tables dealing with the physical activity of occupation because the last job was unknown or could not be classified.

Occupations were classified by Dr. R. Murray and Dr. D. Turner.

Throughout these tables rates of ischaemic myocardial fibrosis are printed in italic. Rates based on a numerator of less than 5 cases are bracketed ( ).

45 < 60 years = 45–59 incl. 60–70 years = 60–70 incl. 45–70 years = 45–70 incl.

Because of the similarity of age distributions crude rates have been used throughout the analysis and tables in amalgamations of 45–70 years inclusive.

Tests of Significance.—The test used in this table (and throughout this paper where relevant) is the test for linear trends in proportions (P. Armitage, *Biometrics*, 1955, **11**, 375). A significant value of p indicates that the trend in the proportions (percentages) from "light" through "active" to "heavy" occupations is unlikely to be due to chance. The p values in separate subgroups —e.g., age groups 45 < 60 and 60–70—have usually been combined in the total groups— e.g., aged 45–70—the method of combination allowing for the fact that the trend was in the same direction in each subgroup.

Third last line, $p < 0.001$; 2nd last line, $p < 0.001$; last line, $p < 0.001$.

Table 2

LARGE HEALED MYOCARDIAL INFARCTS. 3,800 NON-CORONARY
DEATHS. MEN

Ages	Occupation		
	Light	*Active*	*Heavy*
45 < 60	2.3%	1.3%	(0.49%)
60–70	4.7%	2.6%	1.8%

Table 3

PROPORTIONS WITH ISCHAEMIC MYOCARDIAL FIBROSIS. FACTOR
OF HYPERTENSION. 3,800 NON-CORONARY DEATHS.
MALES AGED 45–70

Ischaemic Myocardial Fibrosis	Cases with Record or Evidence of Hypertension		Others	
No. of cases	759		3,086	
With large fibrous patch	18		74	
Rate %		2.4%		2.4%
With smaller/multiple scars	122		172	
Rate %		16.1%		5.6%

multiple scars. Among the hypertensives the prevalence of this focal
myocardial fibrosis was very high in light workers—22% of these
patients aged 45–70 (*21.5%* and *21.6%*) showed it. This rate is
higher than that found in the active and heavy workers with hypertension, and much higher than in all with no record or evidence of
hypertension (Others in Table). The effects are again clearer at
45 < 60 years; the light occupations showed these small scars almost
three times more often at this age than the rest with hypertension,
and *six* times more than the others without hypertension. At 60–
70 years the figures are *one and a half* times, and *three* times, respectively. Indeed, this special excess of small, multiple scars *in light
workers* with hypertension is largely responsible for the higher
overall rate of such scars seen in hypertensives as a whole (Table 3)
when they are compared with the "others." (These "others" without
record or evidence of hypertension, it is interesting, showed little
variation of focal myocardial fibrosis with occupation among themselves, but what trend there was is also in the expected direction.)
In brief, however,

The physical activity factor is clearly evident in the occurrence of smaller/multiple scars only in association with hypertension. At ages 45–70, light workers with hypertension showed these scars twice as often as active and heavy workers with hypertension, and five times more than all without record or evidence of hypertension. The excess in light occupations is, again, greater at 45 < 60 years than at 60–70.

CORONARY ARTERY DISEASE

The next question, of course, is whether these various occupational differences in the prevalence of ischaemic heart disease are associated with corresponding differences in the prevalence of coronary artery diseases and, in particular, of coronary narrowing. The pathogenesis of ischaemic myocardial fibrosis may be regarded for the present as coronary insufficiency, and the basic pathology is "atheroma" or "atherosclerosis" (the terms are interchangeable in Britain—and equally unsatisfactory) with focal coronary obstruction. Most ischaemic scars, it will be recalled, were associated with topical coronary narrowing, the large fibrous patches more commonly with complete or near-complete occlusions, the smaller/ multiple scars with lesser degrees of coronary narrowing.

Statistical analysis of the condition of the coronary arteries in the 5,000 reports has only been started, and it will inevitably be on less sure ground than with myocardial fibrosis. Meanwhile, Table 5 presents some preliminary indices of macroscopic disease in the main arteries and large branches (8, 12, 16, 17, 18, 22, 26, 37, 38, 39, 42, 47, 67) firstly for the basal Group C and then for the high coronary artery disease Group B, the main classification of the inquiry as a whole. These are the indices:[2]

(1) The presence of any reported coronary atheroma. Macroscopic intimal disease was reported in 85% of the cases in the light occupations of the basal group, 82% in the active occupations, etc.

(2) The proportion with severe coronary atherosclerosis, using mainly a simple quantitative five-point scale of "none," "little," "moderate," "much," "indefinite" disease. The minimum to qualify as "severe" was (a) "much" atheroma throughout the coronary arteries with large or confluent plaque formation—superficial flecking or streaking alone did not count—showing also (b) some focal obstruction.

(3) The presence of much mural disease without encroachment upon the lumen. Cases with arterial dilatation were also included here.

(4) The presence of calcification.

[2] The Report of the World Health Organization's Study Group on the Classification of Atherosclerotic Lesions (*Wld Hlth Org. techn. Rep. Ser.*, 1958, 143) became available too late for use in this analysis.

Table 4

PROPORTIONS WITH ISCHAEMIC MYOCARDIAL FIBROSIS BY PHYSICAL ACTIVITY OF OCCUPATION. FACTOR OF HYPERTENSION. 3,800 NON-CORONARY DEATHS. MALES AGED 45–70[a]

Age	Ischaemic Myocardial Fibrosis	Cases with Record or Evidence of Hypertension			Others		
		Occupation			Occupation		
		Light	Active	Heavy	Light	Active	Heavy
45 < 60	No. of cases	135	130	41	567	575	365
	With large fibrous patch	2	2	0	14	7	2
	Rate %	(1.5%)	(1.5%)	(0%)	2.5%	1.2%	(0.5%)
	With smaller/multiple scars	29	12	2	25	18	12
	Rate %	21.5%	9.2%	(4.9%)	4.4%	3.1%	3.3%
	Total with ischaemic myocardial fibrosis	31	14	2	39	25	14
	Rate %	23.0%	10.8%	(4.9%)	6.9%	4.3%	3.8%
60–70	No. of cases	194	160	78	544	564	378
	With large fibrous patch	10	3	1	25	16	7
	Rate %	5.2%	(1.9%)	(1.3%)	4.6%	2.8%	1.9%
	With smaller/multiple scars	42	23	11	46	43	24
	Rate %	21.6%	14.4%	14.1%	8.5%	7.6%	6.3%
	Total with ischaemic myocardial fibrosis	52	26	12	71	59	31
	Rate %	26.8%	16.3%	15.4%	13.1%	10.5%	8.2%

[a] This table amalgamates the "basal" and "high" coronary artery disease Groups C and B, and corresponds with Table 1. 0 and 0% = No cases with ischaemic myocardial fibrosis.

Tests were for trends in percentages from "light" through "active" to "heavy" occupations (cf. footnote to Table 1).

TESTS OF SIGNIFICANCE

	Hypertensives	Others
Line 1	—[a]	0.02 > p > 0.01
„ 2	0.01 > p > 0.001	—[a]
„ 3	0.01 > p > 0.001	0.02 > p > 0.01
„ 4	—[a]	0.02 > p > 0.01
„ 5	0.05 > p > 0.02	—[a]
„ 6	0.01 > p > 0.001	0.02 > p > 0.01

[a] Trend not significant—i.e., p > 0.05.

(5) The proportion with coronary obstruction—that is, lumen stenosis or narrowing of any degree; and including

(6) Complete occlusion or near-complete (e.g., "admitting fine probe only") of a main coronary artery (left, left anterior descending, circumflex, right). This alone was called "coronary occlusion."

Diffuse intimal fibrous thickening, by itself, was ignored.

There is much in Table 5, but attention is here paid only to the frequency of coronary artery disease by occupation. Both in the basal group and in the cases of the high coronary artery disease group—Table 5 corresponds to Table 1 but is set out horizontally—gross coronary artery disease (1), (2), (3), and (4) is exceedingly common: however, there is no occupational trend of any interest. Index (5) again reveals no material difference in the overall frequency of coronary obstruction among the occupation groups. In terms of one of the original hopes in the design of the inquiry the stability of these various indices of coronary artery disease is reassuring—if for other reasons disappointing! The first observation of note is in (6), the greater frequency of complete or near-complete occlusions in light occupations (5.8%) compared with heavy (3.2%). The rate of coronary occlusion, as defined, is about the same in light workers aged 45 < 60 as in heavy workers 10–15 years older (Table 6). Straightaway, however, it is obvious that the excess of occlusion in light workers is less than the excess of large healed infarcts already reported in Table 2.

Comparison of the condition of the coronary arteries in cases with *hypertension* and in others showed much more atherosclerosis in the hypertensive throughout 45–70 years of age (6, 26, 54). For example, the proportion with severe coronary atherosclerosis, as previously defined, was as shown in Table 8. The prevalence of coronary occlusions was higher in the hypertensive, and it was

Table 5

CORONARY ARTERY DISEASE BY PHYSICAL ACTIVITY OF OCCUPATION. 3,800 NON CORONARY DEATHS. MALES AGED 45–70[a]

Coronary Artery Disease		"Basal" Group Occupation			"High" Coronary Artery Disease Group Occupation			All Non-Coronary Deaths Occupation		
		Light	Active	Heavy	Light	Active	Heavy	Light	Active	Heavy
	No. of cases:	995	1,034	668	445	395	194	1,440	1,429	862
(1) Coronary atherosclerosis present	Rate %	85	82	82	91	90	86	87	84	83
(2) Much coronary atherosclerosis with focal obstruction ("severe disease")	Rate %	10	9	10	24	17	22	14	11	13
(3) Much coronary atherosclerosis without focal obstruction	Rate %	5.7	6.0	4.6	9.0	8.4	9.3	6.7	6.6	5.7
(4) Calcification present	Rate %	19	18	18	32	26	31	23	20	21
(5) Focal obstruction present including	Rate %	21	16	19	34	28	32	25	19	22
(6) Complete or near-complete occlusion of a main coronary artery	Rate %	3.7	3.0	2.5	10.3	7.3	5.7	5.8[b]	4.2	3.2

[a] The figures in the last panel cannot be used directly as indicators, however crude, of the overall prevalence of coronary artery disease, and of its various manifestations, in the whole middle-aged male population of Britain. Even if the dead can be taken at all to represent the situation in the living, it must be remembered that deaths from clinical coronary heart disease (Group A) have not been considered so far. The great majority of these would of course show severe coronary artery disease, coronary occlusions, etc.; and, whatever proportion of such cases were added to set up a "model" of the total population, the totals of all 6 indicators, except (3), in the last panel would surely be raised. On the other hand, deaths from severe hypertension, as in Group B, are very likely over-represented. However that may be, it seems probable from what is known of the occurrence of clinical coronary heart disease in different occupations that the excess here reported of coronary occlusions among light occupations may be an underestimate. By the same token, there may well be some excess of severe coronary artery disease among light workers in the population as a whole.

[b] 0.02 > p > 0.01.

Table 6

CORONARY OCCLUSION. 3,800 NON-CORONARY DEATHS

MEN

| Ages | Occupation | | |
	Light	Active	Heavy
45 < 60	3.8%	2.8%	2.5%
60–70	7.6%	5.5%	3.9%

Table 7

SEVERE CORONARY ATHEROSCLEROSIS. 3,800 NON-CORONARY DEATHS

MALES AGED 45–70

| Cases | Occupation | | |
	Light	Active	Heavy
With hypertension	22%	19%	19%
No record or evidence of hypertension	12%	9%	12%

greatest again in the light occupations. There was no occupational trend, however, in the frequency of lesser degrees of coronary narrowing among the hypertensives; though, as stated above, these cases showed a strong light-heavy trend in the frequency of focal myocardial fibrosis, and the small/multiple scars are particularly associated with such lesser narrowing.

Fig. 1 illustrates these points in the most interesting cases, men under 60. If all such cases are taken together there is no particular difference with occupation in the prevalence of severe coronary artery disease, or in the overall prevalence of coronary obstruction, but quite a clear trend in ischaemic scarring. There is a gradient with occupation in the frequency of complete or near-complete coronary occlusions—notice the change of scale—but a steeper one in the large healed infarcts. It is striking how, with similar occupational frequencies of coronary obstruction, the hypertensive cases (the most important cases in Group B have been used for this illustration— the deaths actually from hypertensive vascular disease, mostly cerebral) show a marked occupational difference in the frequency of focal myocardial fibrosis. On the other hand, in the cases without hypertension there are again similar prevalences of arterial obstruction in the occupation groups but, now, very little occupational trend in such scars. (The contrast with focal myocardial fibrosis is the same if the prevalence of lesser coronary narrowing alone is included.) It looks, then, as if much of the variation in ischaemic

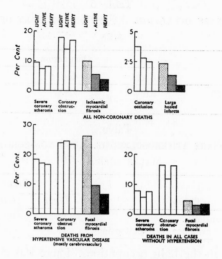

FIG. 1. Coronary artery disease, ischaemic heart disease, and physical activity of occupation. 1,800 non-coronary deaths. Males aged 45 < 60 years.

myocardial scarring with physical activity of work does not depend on occupational differences of, at any rate, *gross* coronary artery disease. Or, another way of looking at the data, there is no suggestion in the present material that habitual physical exertion materially affects coronary atheroma, but an indication that it is related to the frequency of coronary occlusion.[3]

---

[3] *Hypertension.* We have shown that focal myocardial fibrosis was commoner in hypertensive cases than in those without record or evidence of hypertension and that, among the hypertensives, light workers showed substantially more of these small scars than did the active and heavy workers. There is another point of interest. In this material, the proportion of cases with hypertension among heavy workers, throughout 45–70 years of age but more so in the younger men, is smaller than among light workers. In Group C, at 45 < 60, 3% of the men in heavy occupations showed it, compared with 8% in light; in Group B, 39% compared with 50%.(49) "Following through" this observation from the Group C through Group B into Group A, it may be seen in Table 12 (next footnote) that the proportion with hypertension in these deaths *from* coronary heart disease, etc., was lower in heavy occupations than the others. Broadly speaking, in the material as a whole the frequency of hypertension in heavy workers aged 60–70 was the same as in light workers of 45 < 60 years of age.

Occupation and "Social Class"

The distribution, in Britain, of mortality from coronary heart disease by social class is well known. First established in 1930–2 (56) the most recent figures (Table 8) relate to 1949–53.

Table 8

Social Class	Scotland (46 59) Males, Aged 15 and Over	England and Wales (33 57) Males, Aged 20–64
I	167	147
II	119	110
III	109	105
IV	85	79
V	79	89
All classes	100	100

The mortality in social class I (Osler's (52) "better classes") when adjusted for age, as in the above, is much higher than in the rest and about twice that in classes IV and V.

"Social class" is intended to reflect "general standing within the community," social class I including the leading professions and business, class III the craftsmen and skilled workers, and class V the unskilled. Classes II and IV are intermediate. It seems clear that, for men in the age range dealt with, "class" also provides an economic grading.

The 3,800 non-coronary deaths of the present inquiry were analysed by social class (58): the present approach has the advantage that the "level" or "plane" of description and diagnosis is probably the same for all classes. The result in Table 9 shows a steady fall in ischaemic myocardial fibrosis from 13.3% to 7.8%. This trend, however, disappears when the social classes are analysed in terms of the physical activity of the occupations in them. Table 10 (A), read *downwards,* shows that the frequency of the fibrosis in these light workers of similar ages is about the same in social classes I, II, III, and IV—that is, there is no variation with social

Two special factors, then, may be operating in relation to hypertension: heavy workers possibly have less of it; and light workers with hypertension may be specially liable to cardiac damage. The suggestion that the combination of high blood pressure and light occupation may be particularly important, may provide a "way in" for the study of the complicated relations of hypertension with coronary heart disease.

Table 9

PROPORTIONS WITH ISCHAEMIC MYOCARDIAL FIBROSIS BY SOCIAL CLASS
3,800 NON-CORONARY DEATHS. MALES AGED 45–70[a]

Social Class	No.	Proportion with Ischaemic Myocardial Fibrosis
I	98	*13.3%*
II	510	*12.1%*
III	1,847	*10.5%*
IV	605	*9.2%*
V	683	*7.8%*

[a] The trend of the proportions with ischaemic myocardial fibrosis is statistically significant (p < 0.01).

Occupations were allocated to social class in accordance with the General Register Office *Classification of Occupations*, 1950.(58) 102 cases could not be so allocated because of insufficient information.

class and, incidentally, no indication of the particular excess seen in the national mortality data among social class I. There is again no class trend in the active occupations (middle column of Table 10 (A)) and less than none in the heavy. But reading Table 10 (A) *across*, the light-heavy trend previously reported is pretty clear *within* each social class, the light occupations showing more with scars than the active in class II, and the light in class III and class IV a higher prevalence than the active and heavy in these classes. That is to say, among men of comparable social-economic circumstances, those in light occupations showed a clear excess of ischaemic myocardial fibrosis (9, 43). As would be expected—Tables 10 (B) and (C)—the reduction in the frequency of fibrosis that occurs with physical activity of occupation *within* the social classes is more evident for the large healed infarcts; though the numbers in Table 10 (B) are impossibly small.

The irregularities in these tables are also interesting. Social class V stands out on its own, both in showing low rates among light workers and in showing little trend with occupation. It is just in these men that the classification of occupations by "activity" is at its weakest. On the one hand, the light occupations—for example, lift attendant, night watchman—are reserved mostly for disabled persons; therefore the last and "light" job, more than in other classes, is apt to be an inaccurate indicator of the main or usual job during working life. On the other hand, all "general labourers" were perforce graded as "heavy" workers, though, as is well known, many an

Table 10

PROPORTIONS WITH ISCHAEMIC MYOCARDIAL FIBROSIS BY SOCIAL CLASS
AND PHYSICAL ACTIVITY OF OCCUPATION. 3,800 NON-CORONARY
DEATHS. MALES AGED 45–70

Social Class	Light Occupations %	Active Occupations %	Heavy Occupations %	All %
(A) *Ischaemic Myocardial Fibrosis by Social Class and Physical Activity of Occupation:*				
I	13.7	(0)	—a	13.3
II	13.4	9.2	(0)	12.1
III	13.8	8.0	8.2	10.5
IV	13.5	10.1	4.9	9.1
V	8.9	9.0	7.1	7.8
All	13.4	8.7	6.8	10.0
(B) *Large Healed Infarcts by Social Class and Physical Activity of Occupation:*				
I and II	4.3	(2.1)	(0)	3.8
III	3.2	1.8	(1.2)	2.3
IV	(3.6)	2.1	(1.5)	2.3
V	(2.2)	(2.2)	(1.0)	1.5
(C) *Focal Myocardial Fibrosis by Social Class and Physical Activity of Occupation:*				
I and II	9.1	6.9	(0)	8.6
III	10.6	6.2	6.9	8.2
IV	9.9	8.0	3.4	6.8
V	6.7	6.7	6.1	6.3

(The "All" figures for classes I and II in section (A) — 13.3 and 12.1 — are bracketed together with the value 12.3.)

a No cases at all.

elderly "labourer," officially or unofficially disabled, does little more
than odd jobs on a building site and the like, and may have been
so occupied for years before his death. There is an irregularity in
social class III because some very heavy workers—for example,
stonemasons and boilermakers—have a high prevalence of scars,
high for heavy workers; a hint here, perhaps, of the dangers of *too
much* physical activity (48). The rate for heavy occupations in class
IV is particularly low because agricultural workers show little
ischaemic fibrosis—little even for heavy workers. These special features of classes III and IV persist when the prevalence of scarring
in these particular occupations is compared also with that of other
heavy workers in the same sets of necropsy reports, the kind of internal "control" that is so important in this type of study. (40)

In brief, *in this material* there is no evidence of any important
"class" factor. Most of the social class trend in ischaemic myocardial

fibrosis seems to arise from the distribution of "light" and "heavy" workers among the classes (Table 11), though there is evidence also

Table 11

DISTRIBUTION OF OCCUPATIONS WITHIN THE SOCIAL CLASSES

| | Percentage of | | | |
Social Class	Light Occupations	Active Occupations	Heavy Occupations	Total
I	97	3	—	98
II	72	28	1	510
III	42	44	13	1,847
IV	18	47	34	605
V	13	26	60	683

of other and it may be more specific occupational factors affecting the class rates. The association of ischaemic myocardial fibrosis with physical activity of work in these data seems to be independent of standards of living, including obviously in the present instance levels of education and skill and possibly also of responsibility.

Summing up the 3,800 Non-coronary Deaths

Fig. 2 sums up the main findings. In each block the rate of ischaemic myocardial fibrosis in the light occupations is regarded as 100%, and the rates in active and heavy occupations are calculated as proportions of this. In each line the first block illustrates the prevalence of the large fibrous patch, the middle block that of the smaller scars, and the third is the total of ischaemic myocardial fibrosis. (In the first two lines of the second column dealing with hypertensive disease the data have been amalgamated for 45–70 years of age in the large healed infarcts, but distinguished by the two age groups in focal myocardial fibrosis.) There is, of course, considerable overlapping in these various extracts from the data, and some of the numbers—the total is given in each line for light, active, and heavy in that order—are small. The tests of statistical significance apply to the total with scars in each line.

The consistency of the pattern is striking and makes it unlikely that the association of ischaemic myocardial fibrosis, and particularly the large healed infarcts, with physical activity of occupation is the product of some gross bias in this necropsy material. There is quite conceivably an association between ischaemic myocardial fibrosis and the chances of dying and/or undergoing necropsy. But it is less conceivable that such an association could be systematically greater in light occupations than heavy, so that with equal real prevalence of fibrosis among occupations the rate would appear higher in the light. And it is difficult to conceive how such a bias could be effective in the wide variety of disease (and other categories) illustrated in Fig. 2. But, of course, bias can be "built-in" in goodness knows how many ways, and no individual study can deal with all of even the recognized sources. Other studies will need to be done, and also on large numbers, to repeat these observations and to permit still further and quite different subdivisions of the data.

Evidence from 1,200 Deaths from Coronary Heart Disease

As stated before, about 1,200 of the 5,000 reports in the inquiry were on deaths in which coronary heart disease was the main cause—coronary heart disease by itself, or coronary heart disease with hypertension or with other pathology (for example, the post-operative cases)—together with a small number of less-defined though related cardiac conditions. These 1,200 will be described elsewhere. Much less can be made of them because they raise acutely the intractable problem of selection of cases; problems that are of less moment, as just discussed, in conditions like ischaemic myocardial fibrosis which are not the main cause of death and are incidental and often chance findings at necropsy. Moreover, no base or denominator can be defined for the estimations of frequency *rates* of coronary heart disease—for example, by type of occupation. Less effort was therefore made to obtain a good national sample. Thus no request for co-operation was made to the coroners' pathologists in Greater London; though in the provinces many coroners' cases were included in the series of 25, and there were a fair number also, as a matter of fact, in the Metropolitan hospitals' series. However, the 1,200 deaths from coronary heart disease can be classified by occupation and ratios comparing the actual number of cases in each of the three occupation groups can be calculated. This was done.

There were 482 deaths from coronary heart disease and related conditions in light workers, 436 in active workers, and 230 in heavy workers, a ratio of 1.0:0.9:0.48; and there is little doubt, from previ-

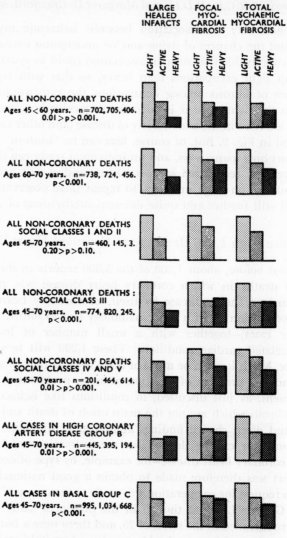

FIG. 2. Frequency of ischaemic myocardial fibrosis, by physical activity of occupation. 3,800 non-coronary deaths. Males aged 45–70 years. In each block of three columns the first column is the rate among light occupations regarded as 100%. In the second column (active occupations) and the third column (heavy) the rates have been recalculated as proportions of the rate among light occupations.

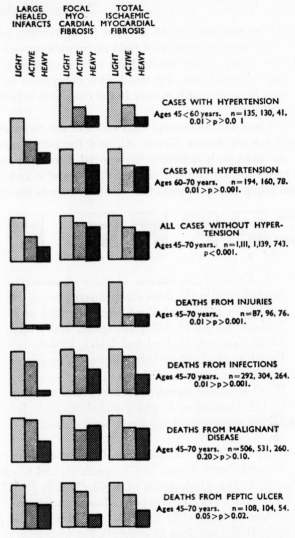

FIG. 2. (cont.) In each line the first block represents the large fibrous patches; the second block represents the smaller/multiple scars; and the third is the total of ischaemic myocardial fibrosis.

n gives the numbers of cases in light, active, and heavy occupations in that order. The test of significance applies to the total of ischaemic myocardial fibrosis. In deaths from injuries active and heavy occupations have been amalgamated.

ous inquiries by the unit, (39 43 45) that if the London area had
been fully represented the excess of light occupations among deaths
from coronary heart disease would have been greater still. Meanwhile it may be noted that the trend with occupation in deaths
from coronary heart disease is greater in the cases with hypertension
than in the others.

Fig. 3a to c sets out the occupational ratios of the coronary heart
disease and related deaths (Group A), and for completeness the
ratios of the cases with ischaemic myocardial fibrosis in the high
coronary artery disease group B, then of the cases with such fibrosis
in the basal group C. Fig. 3d gives the ratio (using again the numbers

LIGHT
ACTIVE
HEAVY

     a   b   c   d   e

FIG. 3. Ratios of the number of cases of ischaemic
heart disease in the three occupational groups, the
number in light occupations being regarded as 1.
National sample of 5,000 necropsies. Males aged
45–70. Scotland, England and Wales, 1954–6. (*a*)
Group A: Deaths from ischaemic heart disease, etc.
(*b*) Ischaemic myocardial scars in cases of Group
B. (*c*) Ischaemic myocardial scars in cases of Group
C. (*d*) Showing *a*, *b*, and *c* added together. (*e*)
All the cases without ischaemic heart disease.

in light, active, and heavy occupations) of all these cases with evidence of ischaemic heart disease in Groups A, B, and C added together—that is, in the whole series of 5,000. This is 1.0:0.84:0.43.
Fig. 3e is for the rest of the 5,000 reports, those showing no evidence
of ischaemic heart disease—1.0: 1.50:0.64; and this ratio is plainly
not of a kind with the previous (p < 0.001). For what such evidence
is worth, then—and this is by no means the right way of asking this
particular question—there is indication of higher mortality from
clinical coronary heart disease among light workers.[4]

Discussion

An association has been demonstrated between physical activity/
inactivity of work and one form of coronary heart disease, ischaemic

[4] Other sums can be done with the data if required.

Table 12
NUMBER OF CASES OF ISCHAEMIC HEART DISEASE IN A NATIONAL SAMPLE
OF 5,000 NECROPSIES. MALES AGED 45–70[a]

Occupation	"Coronary" Deaths, Etc.		Non-Coronary Deaths, with Ischaemic Myocardial Fibrosis		Non-Coronary Deaths, With *No* Ischaemic Myocardial Fibrosis	Total
	Hypertension Present	*Others*	*Large Healed Infarcts*	*Focal Myocardial Fibrosis*		
Light (No.)	145	337	51	142	1,247	1,922
Active (No.)	127	309	28	96	1,305	1,865
Heavy (No.)	51	179	10	49	803	1,092
Total	1,148		376		3,355	4,879

[a] 160 cases were excluded for one reason or another, cf., Table 1.

myocardial fibrosis. Explanation of this may be attempted along several lines. First, that light occupation increases the incidence of ischaemic myocardial fibrosis, heavy jobs are protective. Second, that the association is effect rather than cause; on account of disability from myocardial ischaemia men give up heavy jobs for light ones and a higher prevalence of scarring is thereby created among light workers. Third, that the association is indirect: for example, susceptibility to coronary heart disease and individual choice of job may both be the product of host factors in constitution (and previous experience); or physical activity/inactivity may be reflections merely of the nervous strain of jobs, and it is this that really matters in coronary heart disease. All these processes, it could reasonably be proposed in the present state of knowledge, contribute to the community picture of coronary heart disease; but, of course, the first is the most interesting.

The present study sheds no light on personality factors, though we hope other inquiries in which we are engaged—on somatotype and occupation, for example—will do so (44). No attempt has yet been made to classify the 1,700 different job descriptions in terms, say, of responsibility, of nervous strain—and emotional support. This might be done; but it is an appalling prospect, and the similarity of the rate of fibrosis among the professional and business men of class I to that found in the semi-skilled light workers of class IV does not encourage us to try. The study of psychological stress in relation to coronary heart disease still lacks an appropriate method (we have long thought that a forward-looking study among doctors from their late thirties or early forties is the most helpful). The possibility that the high prevalence of fibrosis in light jobs is the result of transfer by men into these *because* of coronary insufficiency has not been directly considered. It can only be said that the evidence available gives no hint that such transfer, which must surely be common, explains all or even much of the occupational distribution found. Thus the excess of scarring among light workers is no greater at 60–70 years of age than at $45 < 60$, and, indeed, for the large patches it is more evident in the younger men. Moreover, it may again be pertinent that the rate among the light occupations of social classes I and II, drift into which from heavy jobs is unlikely, is just as high as that in class III, where such drift is more likely and class IV, where it is very likely. In social class V itself there was little if any excess among the light occupations, which is as reassuring as it was unexpected; because, as already said, it is just these jobs—messenger, lift attendant, night watchman, and the like— that "disabled" manual workers so often select, and drift into, which for lesser impairment is also very likely. But this difficult and important problem needs to be tackled in other ways: an attempt is now being made in this unit, for example, to determine the prevalence of quite silent coronary heart disease by electrocardiographic study of workers with contrasting physical activity of jobs.

RESTATEMENT OF HYPOTHESIS

Another piece of evidence has thus been provided in this report that confirms the general hypothesis, and using on this occasion quite different material from before. In the present data as a whole, and in every sizable category of it, *there was a lower prevalence of ischaemic myocardial fibrosis among men who had been in physically active and heavy jobs than among those in sedentary and light jobs*. Study of the detailed morbid anatomy of this social difference supports the second part of the original hypothesis. It is particularly in the prevalence of the large, often and for obvious reasons solitary, patch of fibrosis, the probable result it may be said of major and acute infarction (and homologue of sudden death in the bus driver?) that light workers shows an excess. The heavy workers had less ischaemic fibrosis altogether, and relatively more of it took the form of smaller patches and small, often very small, scars. That is to say, in this material *ischaemic myocardial fibrosis is not so severe in physically active and heavy* workers. But the prevalence of these minor forms of myocardial fibrosis also was lower in active and heavy than in light occupations; which rather suggests that the excess of angina previously noted in physically active men (bus conductors and postmen) is more likely to be a matter of symptom formation, of the disease being elicited and made manifest in them by their physical effort, rather than of an absolute excess of any particular pathology in active workers (43).

Evidence can now be advanced relating physical activity of occupation to the incidence of coronary heart disease, to sudden death and other rapidly fatal cardiac infarction, to the prognosis in the survivors of the first clinical episode, to the prevalence of the disease, to total coronary mortality in middle-age, and to several forms of ischaemic myocardial fibrosis. The time seems to have come, in view of the convergence of such varied and independent evidence, for a restatement of the general hypothesis in causal terms: *Physical activity of work is a protection against coronary (ischaemic) heart disease. Men in physically active jobs have less coronary heart disease during middle-age, what disease they have is less severe, and they develop it later than men in physically inactive jobs.*

It must be emphasized, however, that, overall, the evidence on this problem is quite conflicting (2, 5, 7, 9, 11, 22, 23, 24, 27, 34, 45, 62, 63, 64, 66, 69). In several studies coronary heart disease has been found to be associated with physical activity/inactivity of occupation in the expected way. In as many, no relationship was demonstrated, or an equivocal or opposite one; and why this is so is still quite unclear. Different methods are being used by different investigators and different aspects of the disease are being studied. Moreover, the "epidemic constitution" may be different in the U.S.A. from the U.K.—the important causes may be present in different degrees and in different combinations (22).

Some *speculations* may be worth airing here. The diminishing physical activity of work during the present century may be one of the causes of the increasing incidence of coronary heart disease that seems to be occurring, and, if the increase is as modest as is now often suggested, a principal cause. This question might be studied through the historical experiences of "underdeveloped" populations becoming "westernized." If it is argued that constitution and mesomorphy is the crucial variable, unexpressed mesomorphy, the

disuse of large-muscle masses, may be said to be one of the characteristic biological consequences of industrialization. Then, it may be
asked whether regular physical activity *outside* work protects
against coronary heart disease in middle-age. There is no information, meanwhile, on the relations, if any, between physical exertion
in leisure, for example, and the incidence or prevalence of coronary
heart disease; but plainly this is the main implication of observations such as the present for preventive medicine, and means of
testing such a hypothesis must be found. Typical of to-day's problems in epidemiology, this will involve *ad hoc* studies of large numbers of individuals; and even preliminary indirect studies of coronary heart disease and leisure activities in ready-made social groups
such as the social "classes" cannot be made.

A final speculation may be advanced that *habitual physical activity is a general factor of cardiovascular health in middle-aged
men* since it may be related to blood lipid levels, to clotting and to
fibrinolysis, to diabetes, to hypertension and its complications, to
coronary occlusion, and to ischaemic heart disease (3, 10, 20, 25, 28,
29, 30, 31, 35, 40, 50, 53, 68). Regular physical exercise could be one
of the "ways of life" that promote health in middle-age, and
ischaemic heart disease may be in some degree a deprivation syndrome, a deficiency disease.

MECHANISMS OF THE OCCUPATIONAL DIFFERENCE

Nothing corresponding to the differences with physical activity
which have been found in experimental atherogenesis (31, 50) were
observed in the present material. Clearly the main causes of coronary atherosclerosis in man have to be sought elsewhere—for example, in hypertension and, the principle field of interest at present,
in diet and lipid metabolism. There is more coronary occlusion
among the light occupations, which is particularly interesting because the factor of intracoronary thrombosis may be particularly
associated with these complications of atheroma (16, 17, 18, 38) and
the present findings may be another indication of the relationship
between physical activity and intravascular clotting (3, 25, 29, 30). If,
as many would argue, the pathogenesis of all degrees of coronary
obstruction is the same, then, it would appear, the capacity to cope
and to resolve such obstructions must vary with occupation so that
actual occlusion of large coronary vessels is less common in active
and heavy workers than in sedentary and light workers. However

that may be, the excess of coronary occlusion is inadequate to explain the excess of large healed infarcts in light occupations; and the other indicators of coronary artery disease so far studied do not help at all to account for the occupational distribution of the scarring. Mechanisms of the occupational differences in ischaemic myocardial fibrosis need therefore to be postulated that operate additionally to those of gross coronary artery disease (10, 25, 32, 55, 62) in general and local haemodynamics, it may be, in neuro-hormonal mechanisms, in special relationships with hypertension, in the physiological capacity of the main arteries and branches, in intercoronary collateral circulation (4, 19, 20, 61, 70). Recently it has been observed that effective collateral vessels in dogs with coronary obstruction develop more profusely if the dogs are exercised; functional myocardial hypoxia might be the mechanism relating physical activity to collateral formation (19, 20).

DISTINCTION OF ISCHAEMIC HEART DISEASE FROM CORONARY ARTERY DISEASE

In the first report of the present series (39) it was suggested that the recent history of coronary thrombosis/myocardial infarction on the one hand, and that of coronary atheroma on the other, are different. The former, there is good reason to believe, have increased during this century; there is no evidence whatever in Britain that the latter has, and, indeed, coronary atheroma may have declined here during the past 40 years (39, 60). The historical material, that is to say, suggests that ischaemic heart disease is not a simple, proportional function of coronary atherosclerosis. The evidence now presented goes further in dissociating the heart disease from the arterial disease, because it suggests that even when the latter is analyzed into obstructive and non-obstructive processes nothing like a 1 : 1 relationship emerges between myocardial damage and the *obstructive* arterial disease. Social grouping of the pathological data (by occupation) shows substantial differences in the frequency of myocardial fibrosis which correspond only moderately to the frequency of coronary occlusions and correspond not at all to the frequency of lesser narrowing of the coronary lumen. Such identification of syndromes from undifferentiated clinical material—in this instance of ischaemic heart disease from coronary artery disease —is one of the uses of epidemiology, and theoretically is of much interest (40).

A WORD ON THE METHOD

Finally, it may be remarked that post-mortem reports are just about the most difficult medium for epidemiological analysis: many sources of bias in the material are known; as many, it must be assumed, are quite unknown. The use of necropsy data finds its main warrant in asking questions, such as the present report illustrates, that cannot be asked by any other method. But the limitations of any one set of data, with its inevitably imperfect "population" samples and incomplete ascertainment of disease, make it very necessary that studies are repeated in quite different situations.

Summary and Conclusions

This report is one of a series on the epidemiology of coronary disease, and it continues the study of coronary (ischaemic heart disease in relation to physical activity of work.

The hypothesis was previously stated that *men in physically active jobs have a lower incidence of coronary heart disease in middle-age than men in physically inactive jobs. More important, the disease is not so severe in physically active workers, tending to be present in them in relatively benign forms.* The investigation now reported deals with the relations between physical activity of work and the frequency of ischaemic myocardial fibrosis in a sample of 3,800 middle-aged men dying from causes other than coronary heart disease.

All departments of morbid anatomy in the hospitals of the National Health Service of Scotland, England, and Wales were invited to take part in a national necropsy survey during 1954–6 by sending particulars in standard form of the naked-eye findings on the coronary arteries, the myocardium, and other specified items for a consecutive series of 25 males aged 45–70 years coming to necropsy. 206 departments co-operated, more than 85% of those eligible. About 5,000 reports were received, made up in round numbers thus: 1,200 deaths from coronary heart disease, etc. (Group A); 1,000 deaths from conditions with a specially high prevalence of coronary artery disease—for example, deaths caused by hypertension and its complications, deaths in diabetics, deaths from arterial disease in other sites (Group B); and, the remainder, 2,800 deaths from miscellaneous conditions, their main causes having no particular association with coronary artery disease—for example, injuries, infections, cancer (Group C). Groups B and C comprise 3,800 non-coronary deaths.

Two broad types of *ischaemic myocardial fibrosis* in the left ventricle and interventricular septum are described: (1) the large, discrete, often solitary patch which is probably the end-result of major and acute infarction and is associated particularly with complete or near-complete occlusion in a main coronary artery (90 cases among the 3,800 non-coronary deaths); and (2) smaller, commonly multiple scars, the result, it may be, of more chronic and less severe ischaemia, and occurring in hearts showing usually lesser focal narrowings of coronary arteries or branches (290 cases).

Cases were classified as *"hypertensive"* or *"other"* on the basis of the clinical and pathological information provided. About half the cases in Group B and 10% of those in Group C were thus regarded as hypertensive. The large healed infarcts—type 1 fibrosis above—were found equally in hypertensive and other cases; focal myocardial fibrosis of type 2 was commoner in hypertensive cases than in those without record or evidence of hypertension.

The last *occupation* of each man was graded on a three-point scale in terms of the physical activity the job typically involved as "light," "active," or "heavy."

Relation of Fibrosis to Occupation. Ischaemic myocardial fibrosis in these 3,800 necropsies was commoner in the light occupations than in the active and heavy. Scarring among light workers aged $45 < 60$ was as common as in heavy workers 10 to 15 years older.

The two main types of ischaemic fibrosis were differently related to physical activity of occupation:

The *large healed infarcts,* type 1 above, showed a strong gradient with occupation, being *three* times commoner in light workers than in heavy workers overall; *four to five* times commoner at $45 < 60$ years of age, and *two to three* times commoner at 60–70 years. The excess of these severe ischaemic lesions in light workers was evident in Group B and in Group C, in hypertensive cases as in others, in every sizable medical and social category that was identified.

Focal myocardial fibrosis, type 2, was strongly associated with occupation only in hypertensive cases. Under 60 years of age, the light occupations among the hypertensives showed these small, multiple scars almost *three* times more often than active and heavy workers with hypertension, and about *six* times oftener than all without rec-

ord or evidence of hypertension. The corresponding figures at 60–
70 years of age were *one and a half* and *three* times.

In brief, ischaemic myocardial fibrosis was commoner in light occupations and it appeared earlier in them. It was also more severe
among light workers, particularly at younger ages.

Coronary Artery Disease. The pathological basis of ischaemic
myocardial fibrosis is coronary "atheroma" or "atherosclerosis" with
impairment of the coronary circulation. In the present data the
overall prevalence of coronary atheroma was exceedingly high, and,
little, moderate, or much, it did not vary with physical activity of
occupation. Coronary narrowing was similarly common in all occupation groups. But actual occlusion of a main coronary artery,
complete or near-complete, was commoner in sedentary and light
workers than in the active and heavy. This excess of coronary occlusion was seen in the younger men and older, in hypertensive
cases as in those without record or evidence of hypertension. In general, the frequency of coronary occlusion in light workers aged 45 <
60 was the same as that in heavy workers aged 60–70.

The main results of the inquiry may therefore be stated as follows: atheroma of coronary walls, no relationship with physical activity of occupation; occlusion of coronary lumen, some relationship; ischaemic myocardial fibrosis, much relationship.

Ischaemic Heart Disease and Coronary Artery Disease. The excess
of coronary occlusion among the light occupations was smaller than
the excess of large healed infarcts found in them. Among hypertensive cases there was no trend with occupation in the frequency of
lesser degrees of coronary narrowing, although, as stated, the frequency of focal myocardial fibrosis was greater in light workers with
hypertension than in active and heavy workers with hypertension.
That is to say, in the presence of coronary narrowing and occlusion
light occupations showed more ischaemic lesions of the myocardium
than did active and heavy workers. Analysis of this sample of pathological data by social (occupation) categories thus discloses only
very limited correlation between the frequency of myocardial scarring and the condition of the coronary arteries. This is a further
suggestion that ischaemic heart disease is not a simple function of
coronary artery disease.

Hypertension was less common and occurred at later ages (10–15
years later) in the heavy occupations than in the rest; the excess of
coronary occlusions in light workers was seen in hypertensive cases

as in the others; a specially high prevalence of small ischaemic myocardial scars in light workers with hypertension has been described. There are suggestions thus of multiple connexions between physical activity of occupation and the blood pressure which need to be followed up.

The expected trend of ischaemic myocardial fibrosis with *social class* was found, the rate falling from 13.3% in class I through 10.5% in class III to 7.8% in class V. This trend, however, disappeared when the social classes were broken down into categories of physical activity, and the occupations of which each class is composed were graded as "light," "active," or "heavy." Light workers in classes I, II, III, and IV all had similar prevalence of ischaemic scarring, and there was no class trend in the fibrosis among active workers or in heavy workers. On the other hand, the relationship of fibrosis to physical activity of occupation was independent of social-economic circumstances, being evident within single social classes: light occupations in class II showed more ischaemic fibrosis than the active in that class, light skilled workers a higher rate than the active and heavy occupations in class III, the light occupations of class IV more scarring than the active and heavy in that class. The overall trend with social class in this material is largely a function of the different proportions of light and heavy workers in the different classes.

Evidence has now been produced relating several aspects of clinical and subclinical coronary heart disease to physical activity of work. The general *hypothesis* may therefore be restated in *causal* terms that *physical activity of work is a protection against coronary (ischaemic) heart disease. Men in physically active jobs have less coronary heart disease during middle-age, what disease they have is less severe, and they develop it later than men in physically inactive jobs.* Since there are suggestions of other connexions between physical activity of work and cardiovascular disease of middle-age, and multiplying evidence from laboratory experiment of the beneficial effects of exercise on relevant cardiovascular physiology and pathology, the *speculation* may be advanced that habitual physical activity is a general factor of cardiovascular health in middle-age, and that coronary heart disease is in some respects a deprivation syndrome, a deficiency disease. In the present material the hearts of sedentary and light workers showed the pathology of the hearts of heavy workers 10–15 years older.

Perspective. Coronary *heart disease among heavy workers,* though less common, less severe, and occurring later than among light workers, is nevertheless common enough to constitute a major health problem in them: absolutely; and in comparison with the rest of the population, heavy workers seem to have enjoyed earlier this century and in many countries still enjoy greater freedom from the disease.

Literature Cited

1. ACHOR, R. W. P., FUTCH, W. D., BURCHELL, H. B., and EDWARDS, J. E., *A.M.A. Arch. intern. Med.,* 1956, **98**, 162.
2. *Acta med. scand.,* 1956, Suppl. 315.
3. ASTRUP, T., *Lancet,* 1956, **2**, 565.
4. BAROLDI, G., MANTERO, O., and SCOMAZZONI, G., *Circulat. Res.,* 1956, **4**, 223.
5. BECKER, B. J. P., *Lancet,* 1958, **1**, 1019.
6. BELL, E. T., and HARTZELL, T. B., *J. med. Res.,* 1924, **44**, 473.
7. BIÖRCK, G., OVERBECK, W., and GRÖNVALL, C., *Cardiologia (Basel),* 1954, **25**, 232.
8. BLUMGART, H. L., SCHLESINGER, M. J., and DAVIS, D., *Amer. Heart J.,* 1940, **19**, 1.
9. BROWN, R. G., DAVIDSON, L. A. G., MCKEOWN, T., and WHITFIELD, A. G. W., *Lancet,* 1957, **2**, 1073.
10. BROZEK, J., *Geriatrics,* 1955, **10**, 469.
11. CHAPMAN, J. N., GOERKE, L. S., and LOVELAND, D. B., *Amer. J. publ. Hlth.,* 1957, **47**, Special Suppl., p. 33.
12. CRAWFORD, T., and LEVENE, C. I., *J. Path. Bact.,* 1953, **66**, 19.
13. CRAWFORD, W., and BROADLEY, H., *The People's Food.* Heinemann, London. 1938.
14. DOLL, R., and HILL, A. B., *Brit. med. J.,* 1950, **2**, 739.
15. ———, ibid., 1952, **2**, 1271.
16. DUGUID, J. B., *Lancet,* 1949, **2**, 925.
17. ———, ibid., 1954, **1**, 891.
18. ———, and Robertson, W. B., ibid., 1955, **1**, 525.
19. ECKSTEIN, R. W., *Fed. Proc.,* 1956, **15**, 54.
20. ———, *Circulat. Res.,* 1957, **5**, 230.
21. EDWARDS, J. E. *Bull. N.Y. Acad. Med.,* 1957, **33**, 199.
21a. ENOS, W. F., BEYER, J. C., and HOLMES, R. H., *J. Amer. med. Ass.,* 1955, **158**, 912.
22. ———, HOLMES, R. H., and BEYER, J., ibid., 1953, **152**, 1090.
23. EPSTEIN, F. H., BOAS, E. P., and SIMPSON, R., *J. chron. Dis.,* 1957, **5**, 300.
24. GOPALAN, C., and RAMANATHAN, K. S., *Lancet,* 1956, **2**, 1212.
25. GREIG, H. B. W., ibid., 1956, **2**, 16.
26. HARRISON, C. V., and WOOD, P., *Brit. Heart J.,* 1949, **11**, 205.
27. KENNEDY, A. C., *Scot. med. J.,* 1957, **2**, 420.

28. KEYS, A., ANDERSON, J. T., ARESU, M., BIÖRCK, G., BROCK, J. F., BRONTE-STEWART, B., FIDANZA, F., KEYS, M. H., MALMROS, H., POPPI, A., POSTELI, T., SWAHN, B., and DEL VECCHIO, A., *J. clin. Invest.*, 1956, **35**, 1173.

29. ———, and BUZINA, R., *Circulation*, 1956, **14**, 479.

30. ———, *J. Amer. med. Ass.*, 1957, **164**, 1912.

31. KOBERNICK, S. D., NIWAYAMA, G., and ZUCHLEWSKI, A. C., *Proc. Soc. exp. Biol. (N.Y.)*, 1957, **96**, 623.

32. KRAUS, H., PRUDDEN, B., and HIRSCHHORN, K., *J. Amer. Geriat. Soc.*, 1956, **4**, 463.

33. LOGAN, W. P. D., *Lancet*, 1952, **1**, 758.

34. LUONGO, E. P., *J. Amer. med. Ass.*, 1956, **162**, 1021.

35. MANN, G. V., TEEL, K., HAYES, O., MCNALLY, A., and BRUNO, D., *New Engl. J. Med.*, 1955 **253**, 349.

36. Ministry of Agriculture, Fisheries and Food, Domestic Food Consumption and Expenditure. 1955.

37. BRANWOOD, A. W., and MONTGOMERY, G. L., *Scot. med. J.*, 1956, **1**, 367.

38. MORGAN, A. D., *The Pathogenesis of Coronary Occlusion.* Blackwell Scientific Publ., Oxford. 1956.

39. MORRIS, J. N., *Lancet*, 1951, **1**, 1, 69.

40. ———, *Uses of Epidemiology.* Livingstone, Edinburgh. 1957.

41. ———, *Circulation*, 1958, **17**, 321.

42. ———, and DALE, R. A., *Proc. roy. Soc. Med.*, 1955, **48**, 667.

43. ———, HEADY, J. A., RAFFLE, P. A. B., ROBERTS, C. G., and PARKS, J. W., *Lancet*, 1953, **2**, 1053, 1111.

44. ———, ibid., 1956, **2**, 569.

45. ———, and RAFFLE, P. A. B., *Brit. J. industr. Med.*, 1954, **11**, 260.

46. MORRISON, S. L., ibid., 1957, **14**, 130.

47. MUIR, R., *Textbook of Pathology*, 6th ed. Ed. Cappel, D. F. Arnold, London. 1951.

48. MYASNIKOV, A. L., *Circulation*, 1958, **17**, 99.

49. MIALL, W. E., and OLDHAM, P. D. (1958). *Clin. Sci.*, **17**, 409.

50. ORMA, E. J., *Acta physiol. scand.*, 1957, Suppl. 142.

51. ORR, J. B., *Food, Health, and Income*, Macmillan, London. 1936.

52. OSLER, W., *Lancet*, 1910, **1**, 697.

53. PHIPPS, C., *J. Amer. med. Ass.*, 1936, **106**, 761.

54. PICKERING, G. W., *High Blood Pressure.* Churchill, London. 1955.

55. RAAB, W., *A.M.A. Arch. intern. Med.*, 1958, **101**, 194.

56. REGISTRAR-GENERAL, *Decennial Supplement, England and Wales, 1931. Part IIA. Occupational Mortality.* H.M.S.O., London. 1938.

57. ———, ibid., *1951. Part II. Occupational Mortality.* H.M.S.O., London. 1958.

58. ———, *Classification of Occupations*, 1950.

59. REGISTRAR-GENERAL, Scotland (1957).

60. RUSSELL, D., *J. med. Wom. Fed.*, 1958, **40**, 4.

61. SCHERF, D., and GOLBEY, M., *Amer. Heart J.*, 1954, **47**, 928.

62. SIMONSON, E., *Geriatrics*, 1957, **12**, 28.

63. SPAIN, D. M., and BRADESS, V. A., *A.M.A. Arch. intern. Med.*, 1957, **100**, 228.

64. STAMLER, J., *Neb. St. med. J.*, 1956, 41, 75.
65. GROSS, H., and STERNBERG, W. H., *Arch. intern. Med.*, 1939, 64, 249.
66. THOMAS, A. J., COTES, J. E., and HIGGINS, I. T. T., *Lancet*, 1956, 1, 414.
67. TURNBULL, H. M., *Quart. J. Med.*, 1915, 8, 201.
68. WARNOCK, N. H., CLARKSON, T. B., and STEVENSON, R., *Circulat. Res.*, 1957, 5, 478.
69. YATER, W. M., WELSH, P. P., STAPLETON, J. F., and CLARK, M. L., *Ann. intern. Med.*, 1951, 34, 352.
70. ZOLL, P. M., WESSLER, S., and SCHLESINGER, M. J., *Circulation*, 1951, 4, 797.

Questions for Discussion

1. What are some of the cultural reasons for the prevalence of sedentary occupations in the United States?
2. What is the contribution of hypertension to the incidence of coronary disease? What bearing might physical education have upon hypertension?
3. Projecting present trends in automation, what may be the effect of sedentary occupations on the heart in the year 2000? What can physical education do to reduce this threat to the nation's health?
4. Do physical education programs sufficiently stress activities that may be performed in adulthood? If not, why not? What can be done to change this?

JEAN MAYER and FREDERICK J. STARE, M.D.

Exercise and Weight Control— Frequent Misconceptions*

Research indicates a causal relationship between body weight and heart disease. This evidence has stimulated the study of another frequently raised question: What is the effect of exercise on body weight? This problem was traditionally argued

* Reprinted with permission of the authors and the copyright owners, the American Dietetic Association, from *The Journal of the American Dietetic Association*, vol. 29, no. 4, April 1953, pp. 340–343.

on aesthetic grounds, that is, personal appearance rather than health or physical fitness. The opponents of exercise state that a man would have to run ten miles to lose a pound of body weight and that this activity would serve only to increase the appetite, thereby negating the value of exercise.

In the selection that follows, two nutritionists illuminate the subject of exercise by discussing in some detail three serious misconceptions. Their discussion emphasizes the need for regular physical education in school programs and for adult exercise. The reader should note the type of activities that are most effective and consider whether they are stressed in the usual instructional program.

Three general misconceptions on the relation of muscular exercise and development to weight control are frequently encountered. They are:

(a) Exercise requires relatively little caloric expenditure, and, therefore, increased physical activity is of no particular concern as an aid to weight reduction.

(b) An increase in the physical activity from whatever base level is automatically followed by an increase in appetite and food intake and may, therefore, actually impair reduction of weight.

(c) Body weight is always a reliable measure of degree of obesity, regardless of the degree of muscular development.

May we again state that *these three common statements are misconceptions,* as we shall now attempt to prove.

Energy Expenditure in Exercise

The first misconception, minimizing the caloric expenditure due to physical activity, should be avoided by anyone familiar with the Recommended Dietary Allowances of the National Research Council (1) or any similar table of requirements or allowances. The National Research Council allowances for men vary from 2400 to 4500 calories per day, depending on the level of activity. And, the figure of 4500 calories per day does not represent an upper limit. (Laborers, soldiers in the field, and athletes often require up to or even more than 6000 calories per day.)

In contrast to these comments, one frequently hears or reads such statements as the following: "The caloric equivalent of a pound of fat can only be matched by walking 36 hr., splitting wood for 7 hr., or playing volley ball for 11 hr." These unattainable extremes of physical activity ridicule the possibility of losing weight by exercise. One might answer that, while splitting wood for 7 consecutive hours would be difficult for anyone other than a Paul Bunyan, splitting wood for ½ hr. every day, by no means an impossible task for a healthy man, would add up to 7 hr. in a fortnight and, if it represented a regular practice, would represent the caloric equivalent of 26 lb. body fat in a year. A half hour of hand ball or squash a day would be equivalent to 16 lb. per year.

It seems more useful, however, simply to recall the measured cost of different types of physical exercise. All energy costs quoted here (2) were established for a "mean" man with a body surface of 1.77 sq. m. (this corresponds, for example, to a height of 172 cm. [5 ft. 7 in.] and a weight of 65 kg. [143 lb.]). Energy expenditure, and hence weight loss, would be greater in the case of a larger or heavier man.

For the "mean" man, then, examples of energy expenditure per hour *over that of sitting* are: walking (not running), 100 to 550 calories, depending on the speed; swimming, up to 685 calories per hour; climbing, up to 950 calories per hour; skiing, up to 950 calories per hour; skating, up to 685 calories per hour; and cycling, up to 585 calories per hour. These hourly energy expenditures above the resting level of sitting do not include peaks of activity reached in competition. Here caloric expenditures may approach 1300 calories per hour. A caloric expenditure of 500 to 600 calories per hour above the resting level represents a level of physical activity which can be endured by the average adult not in training for a period of 30 min. without undue discomfort. This rate of expenditure for 30 min. is the caloric equivalent of a piece of apple pie à la mode.

Exercise is an important aid to weight reduction but only if it is carried out frequently, consistently, and in moderation.

In most types of exercise, no heavy object is moved other than the whole or parts of the body; therefore, the energy cost of exercise is proportional to body weight (3, 4). If excess body weight is so great that it impairs body movement, this relationship will not, of course, strictly apply (5).

If the energy cost of exercise is approximately proportional to body weight, it follows that the overweight person will require more energy, and hence burn up more body tissue, for the *same amount* of exercise than the person of desirable weight. Twenty per cent overweight will increase the cost of walking, tennis playing, golfing, and so on by 20 per cent. This represents a much greater proportional increase than that introduced by the increase in basal metabolism due to excess weight, which is proportional only to a fractional power of the body weight (6, 7).

Thus, any increase of the caloric intake above the balance level in a physically active individual will cause only a modest increase in weight because of the energy cost of moving the extra poundage. On the other hand, in a sedentary individual, less energy will be expended moving the extra weight and hence weight gain will be more rapid and more pronounced. A sedentary person will, therefore, be more exposed to the danger of overweight to a much greater extent than an individual who makes a practice of daily— or at least, frequent—physical exercise.

It is amusing in this connection to mention that, in the hereditary obesity-diabetes syndrome of mice that is under study in our laboratory (8, 9), the obese members of the strain who carry the "waltzing" gene and are in nearly constant rotary movement in their cages show a weight gain only about 30 per cent more than the non-obese mice, rather than 200 or 300 per cent shown by the sedentary obese mice. The activity level of the sedentary obese mice is 50 to 100 times less than that of the non-obese animals (10).

Exercise and Appetite

A second frequent misconception concerning the value of exercise in weight reduction is that an increase in physical activity always causes an increase in appetite and food intake which equals or is greater in energy value than that of the energy cost of the exercise.

That appetite generally follows physical activity is true and explains why the weight of most adults is relatively constant. But, this adjustment of caloric intake to caloric expenditure has certain limitations: (a) the mechanism which regulates food intake must function normally; (b) energy expenditure must not be raised above a certain (upper) limiting value; and (c) energy expenditure must not be below a certain (minimal) limiting value.

The first limitation—dependence on regulation of food intake— is almost self-evident. It is paradoxical (although frequently done) in considering an overweight individual, that is, one whose appetite is not adjusted to his energy requirements, to postulate that, if his energy requirement is increased by exercise, his appetite will automatically follow suit to the same extent in energy.

The second limitation is suggested by animal studies. Studies in our own laboratory, as yet unpublished, show that adult rats may be exercised to a moderate degree without any increase in food consumption. On the other hand, it is well known that experimental animals can be exercised to the point where they will lose weight, even if fed *ad libitum*. As far as man is concerned, farm workers at the peak of the harvest season have been repeatedly observed to lose weight in spite of extremes of caloric consumption. The weight loss must be made up during periods of decreased activity. Similar observations have been made in soldiers under strenuous field conditions.

At the opposite end of the caloric scale, a third limitation is due to the fact that a decrease in appetite does not always follow a decrease in physical activity. Experiments (11) have demonstrated that rabbits, when restricted in their activity by confinement in a small cage, will consume more calories than they require and accumulate fat. The excess food consumed is characteristic of the strain; hence an hereditary factor is involved here. The same phenomenon has been strikingly illustrated with rats made obese by immobilization (12). Progressive decrease of the activity of the rat also showed that a level is reached under which no further decrease of caloric intake is noticeable (13). In the light of the glucostatic theory of the regulation of food intake (14, 15), this may correspond to the point where further decrease of an already-low level of activity has no further effect on blood glucose levels. The glucostatic theory of the regulation of appetite, proposed by our laboratory as a result of studies carried out on rats, mice, and man, postulates an appetite-regulating center in the hypothalamus which responds to variations of the "effective level" of available blood glucose.

Greene (16) has studied more than two hundred overweight patients in whom the beginning of obesity could be traced directly to a sudden decrease in activity. This suggests that if activity is depressed below a certain level, probably characteristic of each individual, food intake does not decrease to the same extent from an energy viewpoint. The frequent observation of increase in weight of individuals discharged from active military units tends to confirm Greene's observations. Thus, even if and when heavy physical exercise increases food intake in the overweight individual, it does not necessarily follow that a marked decrease in exercise will depress the appetite below the level corresponding to moderate activity.

While no one questions the fact that overweight is a manifestation of imbalance between caloric intake and energy expenditure, it does not necessarily follow that the etiologic element in the imbalance is excessive intake. It could in some cases be insufficient energy expenditure, i.e., exercise.

The estimate of caloric intake is always difficult (17). In obese patients the difficulties are multiplied (18). Yet only careful determination of both caloric intake and activity could establish, for a given individual, the levels that will result in exact maintenance of weight. A slight but consistent variation in either would result in a change of weight. For example, Conn has shown (19) that for a sedentary individual weighing 75 kg. (165 lb.), a dietary excess of only 80 calories per day will cause an increase of 6 kg. (13 lb.) in five years. Eighty calories also represents the approximate energy cost of walking about 1 mi. at moderate speed for a man of this weight. Thus, one is led to wonder whether there is not a direct relationship between the improvements in transportation in this country and the prevalence of overweight. Certainly "overtransportation" is related to "overconsumption" in mild, "middle-age" overweight. Energy balance can still be re-established by decreasing caloric intake, but at a cost in gastronomic discomfort that a moderate and regular increase in activity would overcome.

Exercise, Body Composition, and Weight

The third aspect of the relation of exercise to weight control concerns the use of changes of body weight as a criterion of fat accumulation or loss, independently of the status of the individual as regards muscular development and exercise. The line of the average college football team contains a number of twenty-year-old boys, averaging 5 ft. 10 in. in height and 200 lb. in weight. According to any tables of desirable weights, these boys would be overweight, and some would be obese. Yet a larger proportion than average of the body tissues of these football players has been shown to be muscle rather than fat (20).

It is likely that when playing is discontinued, muscle tissue will be replaced by fat tissue, and even though weight remains stationary or decreases slightly, the "true" degree of obesity (based on fat content) will increase. A gram of tissue protein is the equivalent of about 5 calories, and its deposition is accompanied by about 3 or 4 gm. water. A gram of tissue fat represents 9 calories and is not accompanied by water. Thus, it is apparent that fat tissue represents gram for gram or pound for pound up to seven or eight times more calories than muscle tissue (21).

It has been repeatedly shown, in particular by Brožek and Keys (22, 23), that weight alone is not an accurate comparison of different individuals from the point of view of fat content, unless the individuals are grossly obese or emaciated or have been at the same approximate exercise level. When a single individual is followed, weight variations will be an index of the decrease or increase of his fat stores only if his level of physical activity has remained fairly constant. Brožek and Keys (24) found that men fifty years of age had a fat content almost double that of twenty-two-year-old men of the same height and weight.

The more widespread use of various devices for the measurement of soft tissues and skinfold thickness (25–27) will no doubt permit the extension of the procedures of classifying individuals simultaneously as overweight or underweight and as lean or fat. This should be a helpful adjunct in weight reduction programs, where a main interest is in reduction of fat tissue.

Conclusion

The intent of this discussion has been to point out three common fallacies concerning exercise and weight control. In many cases of mild overweight and in all cases of obesity, only rigid adherence to caloric restriction will permit successful reduction. Following the weight of the patient is, in most cases, the easiest and most practical way to follow fat accumulation or loss. An increase in physical activity may be impossible in the frequent situations where overweight is accompanied by an already dangerously increased load on the cardiovascular system.

But, when all these limitations have been acknowledged, it still remains that exercise is the only practical way to increase energy expenditure; that a given level of exercise in a person gaining weight, or already overweight, will require more energy, because of the extra weight to move. Hence, an increase in caloric intake tends to produce a self-limiting weight increase if an active exercise level is maintained. And finally, a decrease in physical activity is not necessarily accompanied by a decreased appetite, nor is a moderate increase in exercise accompanied by an increase in appetite.

Strenuous exercise once a year during a vacation, or even weekly, is of no aid in weight reduction and may be harmful to the vascular system, but moderate, frequent, and consistent exercise is a very helpful aid in weight reduction.

Literature Cited

1. FOOD AND NUTRITION BOARD: Recommended Dietary Allowances, Revised. National Research Council *Rep. & Circ. Series* No. 129, October, 1948.
2. ORR, J. B., and LEITCH, I.: The determination of the calorie requirements of man. *Nutrition Abstr. & Rev.* 7: 509, 1938.
3. KEYS, A.: Energy requirements of adults. *J.A.M.A.* 142: 333, 1950.
4. KEYS, A.: The calorie requirement of adult man. *Nutrition Abstr. & Rev.* 19: 1, 1949.
5. NEWBURGH, L. H.: Obesity. 1. Energy metabolism. *Physiol. Rev.* 24: 18, 1944.
6. COMMITTEE ON CALORIE REQUIREMENTS: Calorie Requirements. *FAO Nutritional Studies* No. 5, June, 1950.
7. DUBOIS, E. F.: *Basal Metabolism in Health and Disease.* 3rd ed., rev. Philadelphia: Lea & Febiger, 1936.
8. MAYER, J., BATES, M. W., and DICKIE, M. M.: Hereditary Diabetes in Genetically Obese Mice. *Science* 113: 746, 1951.
9. MAYER, J., RUSSELL, R. E., BATES, M. W., and DICKIE, M. M.: Metabolic, nutritional and endocrine studies of the hereditary obesity-diabetes syndrome of mice and mechanism of its development. *Metabolism.* In press.
10. MAYER, J.: Decreased activity and energy balance in the hereditary obesity-diabetes syndrome of mice. In press.
11. GASNIER, A., and MAYER, A.: Recherches sur la régulation de la nutrition. 1. Qualités et cotes des mécanismes régulateurs généraux. 2. Les mécanismes régulateurs de la nutrition chez le lapin domestique. 3. Mécanismes régulateurs de la nutrition et intensité du métabolisme. 4. Différences entre deux races de lapins domestiques. 5. Caractères individuels. *Ann. Physiol. Physicochim. biol.* 15: 145, 157, 186, 195, 210, 1939.
12. INGLE, D. J.: A simple means of producing obesity in the rat. *Proc. Soc. Exper. Biol. & Med.* 72: 604, 1949.

13. Unpublished observations.
14. MAYER, J., and BATES, M. W.: Blood glucose and food intake in normal and hypophysectomized, alloxan-treated rats. *Am. J. Physiol.* **168:** 812, 1952.
15. MAYER, J.: The glucostatic theory of regulation of food intake and the problem of obesity. *New England M. Center Bull.* **14:** 43, 1952.
16. GREENE, J. A.: Clinical study of the etiology of obesity. *Ann. Int. Med.* **12** (O.S. 17): 1797, 1939.
17. MAYER, J.: Food composition tables and assessment of the caloric content of diets. *J. Am. Dietet. A.* **28:** 308, 1952.
18. BEAUDOIN, R., and MAYER, J.: Food intakes of obese and non-obese women. *J. Am. Dietet. A.* **29:** 29, 1953.
19. CONN, J. W.: Obesity. 2. Etiological aspects. *Physiol. Rev.* **24:** 31, 1944.
20. WELHAM, W. C., and BEHNKE, A. R., JR.: The specific gravity of healthy men. Body weight ÷ volume and other physical characteristics of exceptional athletes and of naval personnel. *J.A.M.A.* **118:** 498, 1942.
21. MAYER, J.: Definition and quantitative expression of ageing. *Growth* **13:** 97, 1949.
22. BROŽEK, J., and KEYS, A.: Evaluation of leanness-fatness in man: a survey of methods. *Nutrition Abstr. & Rev.* **20:** 247, 1950.
23. BROŽEK, J., and KEYS, A.: Limitations of the "normal" body weight as a criterion of normality. *Science* **112:** 788, 1950.
24. BROŽEK, J., and KEYS, A.: Age changes in body composition during maturity. *J. Gerontol.* **6:** 67 (Supp., Proc.), 1951.
25. Body fat in man. *Nutrition Rev.* **9:** 265, 1951.
26. Specific gravity, skinfolds and body fat. *Nutrition Rev.* **10:** 246, 1952.
27. MCCANCE, R. A., and WIDDOWSON, E. M.: A method of breaking down the body weights of living persons into terms of extracellular fluid, cell mass and fat, and some applications of it to physiology and medicine. *Proc. Roy. Soc.,* London, s.B. **138:** 115, 1951.

Questions for Discussion

1. What activities in physical education programs could be regularly performed by adults over forty years of age?
2. Why does regular exercise seem more appropriate for weight control than severe but occasional exercise?
3. According to the typical exponent system used in schools, some obese pupils are classified with older children. How could this be avoided?

PAUL D. WHITE, M.D.

The Role of Exercise
in the Aging*

Physical education expresses the need for life-long activity, which is an important aspect of health. Increased longevity and early retirement have increased popular concern for continued activity in the later years. More of our citizens now than ever before must develop skills for the maintenance of health as well as for the fulfillment of their leisure time.

The paper by Paul Dudley White, the famous physician who treated President Eisenhower after his heart attack, points out the effects of exercise on hypertension, physical recovery, digestion, and aging. Perhaps, physical education programs should provide for the needs of the types of persons White discusses.

As I sit down to write about the role of exercise in the aging, I am conscious of the pleasant and relaxing effect of a brisk walk in the clear cold air of Santa Fe and the hills around. As a senior member of society, I can vouch for this particular positive effect of exercise; for many aging persons this may be its chief value. However, there are other physiological results of exercise which deserve as much emphasis in the aging as they do in the young, and possibly even more.

Though such effects of exercise are frequently referred to in the presentation of health programs, they are but little discussed in planning for the health and happiness of older persons. To be sure, no hard and fast rules about exercise can be laid down for everyone of a certain age, in the first place, because no two persons have exactly the same physical needs or psychological preferences

* Reprinted with permission of the author and the publisher from *The Journal of the American Medical Association*, vol. 165, No. 1, September 7, 1957, pp. 70–71.

and, secondly, because chronological age is not the same as physiological age. Also it is true that some individuals live to be old and free from disease despite the fact that the only exercise they get is in breathing, eating, talking, and in tending to their minimal physiological processes of other nature; what percentage of healthy older persons belong in this category has not been determined, but it appears to be considerably in the minority.

Naturally, in extreme old age, when physical strength and mental ability steadily decline, there comes a time when exercise beyond that of the simplest acts of living is no longer possible, but in the early and middle years of old age exercise can be very beneficial. It is important to recognize that there is a difference between positive health and the mere absence of disease.

At any age, physical exercise, more or less planned, though not as a burdensome or boring program, has certain beneficial effects which can be helpfully reviewed in our discussion of the problems of aging. The kind of exercise is not very important except that it should suit the strength, aptitude, and liking of the particular person. It may vary in strenuousness from that involved in simple deep breathing in short periods several times a day to that involved in heavy wood cutting or snow shoveling or fast tennis.

There should be no age set at which a person long accustomed to vigorous exercise should cease exercising, although it is usually wise to tone down the energy expenditure and the amount of time per day or week with each passing decade. If a man or woman is in good health and enjoys exercise in the open air (or perhaps even if not) the beneficial effects can continue to a very advanced age. I have known of Maine guides and lumbermen, gardeners, sailors, laborers, and sportsmen who have kept up a vigorous program both enjoyably and beneficially well into the 80's.

There are very few adequate statistics concerning the health and longevity of athletes. Some articles and books have been published on the subject; one of these, entitled "University Oars," was written many years ago (1873) by Dr. John E. Morgan, who was an oarsman himself. Dr. Morgan, of Oxford University, made a follow-up study of members of the crews who took part in the annual races between Cambridge and Oxford from 1829 to 1869. His conclusion was that the effect of the rowing was a favorable one, that this type of exercise (some of which was continued for years afterward) had no unfavorable effect on health but rather the reverse, and that the longevity of the oarsmen was slightly greater than that of the average population.

A study not yet reported, which my associates and I made, was a follow-up of Harvard football players who earned their letters between the years 1900 and 1930. This study showed a longevity close to that expected in the population at large. It had been hoped to compare those who continued vigorous exercise throughout their lives with those who took no particular exercise after graduation from college and also those who had gained very much weight with those who had gained practically no weight at all. Evidence on these two points was definitely favorable for those who continued vigorous exercise and who did not gain weight, but the numbers in these extreme groups were hardly adequate for statistical conclusions. One of the difficulties in such a study is that the majority of American males live a standard existence, that is, they eat much the same diet, drink and smoke moderately, get some exercise but not of any considerable degree, and gain a moderate amount of weight through the years (10 to 25 lb. or more in the course of 30 years).

Benefits of Exercise

Exercise has positive effects on the health. In the first place, there is the benefit of establishing or maintaining the general muscular tone throughout the body, including that of the heart itself. Some muscles, of course, become stronger if they are more involved in the exercise, for example, the leg muscles in long walks, golfing, cycling, or tennis, or the arm muscles in wood cutting, gardening, fishing, or housework. One of the muscles that it is important to keep in good tone is the diaphragm; almost any vigorous exercise or even repeated programs of deep breathing will help here.

There are several values that are derived from good muscle tone. One is that which concerns the circulation of the blood itself. Sometimes one forgets that the heart, although the most important factor of course, is not the sole supporter of the circulation. The elasticity of the aorta and other great arteries is of importance in maintaining an even flow of blood. The vasomotor function of the smaller vessels is vital for the selective distribution of the blood to the organs as needed. The peripheral veins with their valves act as local pumps for the return of blood to the heart when they are compressed by the muscles that surround them. The better the tone of the muscles the better is this support to the heart afforded by the veins. For the same reason, peripheral venous stasis of high degree with the development of varicosities, the pooling of blood, and phlebothrombosis is counteracted, to a certain degree at least, by good muscle tone. Finally, good tone of the diaphragm with wide respiratory excursions (aided by the avoidance of obesity) not only greatly helps respiration but also improves the pumping action of the diaphragm in its suction of blood back to the chambers of the right side of the heart.

A second benefit from exercise is that already referred to, namely, its effect on the psyche. Most individuals, old as well as young, are much helped by the relaxation which comes from exercise of the right degree, usually midway in amount and intensity between the extremes of triviality and of exhaustion. For many of us, exercise is a delightful antidote for nervous tension and strains, anxiety, and mental concentration. A pleasant fatigue of the skeletal muscles has time and time again given me mental repose, peaceful sleep, and a sense of equanimity.

A third benefit has been on digestion, partly, in all probability, by reducing nervous tension, which is a common factor in cases of esophageal irritability (cardiospasm) and peptic ulcer, and partly by its favorable effect on the bowel function.

A fourth benefit of exercise at any age, and therefore applicable to the "aging," is its favorable effect in helping to control obesity, a condition widely regarded as inimical to the best of health and longevity. Although it is true that obesity is due to the combined effects of heredity and overnutrition, nevertheless, with the same caloric intake, the increased metabolic requirement resulting from exercise does help to control body weight. It is not the fat deposited under the skin here and there throughout the body or in the omentum that is of most importance but rather a few grams of fat in the wrong places, particularly in the walls of the coronary and other important arteries.

Finally, the deepening of respiration which comes with exercise favors the function of the lungs in gaseous exchange and in the state of the lung tissue itself. Although chronic bronchitis and emphysema are common in old age and limit the amount of exercise possible, they are not a bar in themselves to mild exercise within the reserve of the person affected.

Even in the presence of disease other than in the lungs, suitable exercise can be beneficial. I have seen many patients with heart diseases of various kinds and degree and, except for the most severe cases, slight to moderate exercise can and should be prescribed. Of course, angina pectoris too easily induced or myocardial weakness of considerable degree will demand pro tem absolute rest, but with recovery or in the presence of well-healed myocardial infarction, as in the President's case, a careful program of regular exercise may not only be an important health measure but it may conceivably be helpful, in the absence of important symptoms, in retarding the further progress or increase of coronary atherosclerosis. Further research as to this possibility is in order.

Thus, in conclusion, it may be said that exercise of almost any kind, suitable in degree and duration for the particular individual concerned, can and does play a useful role in the maintenance of both physical and mental health of the aging individual but that no hard and fast rules can be set, because each person requires individual appraisal.

Further Readings

MAYER, JEAN, "Exercise and Weight Control," *Science and Medicine of Exercise and Sports*, edited by Warren Johnson. New York: Harper & Row, Publishers, 1960, pp. 307–308.

NATIONAL EDUCATION ASSOCIATION and AMERICAN MEDICAL ASSOCIATION. Joint Committee on Health Problems, *Health Education*. Washington, D.C.: National Education Association, 1948, pp. 67–68.

SHOCK, NATHAN W., "The Physiology of Aging," *Scientific American*, vol. 206, no. 1 (January 1962), pp. 100–110.

THE GERIATRICS COMMITTEE, MICHIGAN STATE MEDICAL SOCIETY, "Exercise—The First Step Towards Successful Aging," reprinted from *Journal of Michigan State Medical Society*, vol. 56, no. 5 (May 1951).

WHITE, PAUL DUDLEY, "Health and Sickness in Middle Age," *Journal of Health, Physical Education and Recreation*. Washington, D.C.: American Association for Health, Physical Education and Recreation, vol. 31, no. 7 (1960), pp. 21–22.

Questions for Discussion

1. Would regularly performed calisthenics be an effective exercise program for the average person over fifty? Would the average person at this age level be enough motivated to perform regularly a program of this nature?
2. Should some vigorous activity be included in a program developed for persons over fifty? If so, what? Explain.
3. What are the shortcomings of physical education programs that provide only football, volleyball, basketball, and baseball instruction?
4. What types of activities would persons over sixty-five years of age prefer?

[SECTION V]

Sociological Backgrounds

If a central purpose of education is to create, transmit, and maintain the great American culture, certainly each teacher must be familiar with the field of sociology. Sociology describes society and what man learns (culture) as a member of it. The background and character of physical education are largely determined by the values, institutions and social relationships of the culture in which they exist. We can readily see cultural influences in the relationships between teacher and student, coach and quarterback, and in such cultural patterns and ceremonies as Saturday's game and the rooting section.

Five major areas of sociology are particularly applicable here. The first is the study of American values, because values are exemplified and taught through participation in physical education programs. The second consists of the study of the distinct subculture of the school and its importance in motivating the behavior of both teachers and students. A third area is the place of the individual in society, and it has important implications for the role physical education can play in fostering individual as well as group development. Because maintaining a democratic society is part of a teacher's role, he must understand a fourth area, social-class structure. The problems of mobility, leisure activities, and social status are included here. Social change constitutes the fifth and final area. The prospective teacher must be able to direct the philosophy and programs of his field within a rapidly changing culture, all the while keeping in mind the future value of the activities and skills taught.

Anthropology enables the student to acquire cultural perspective and to view his own culture with greater objectivity. Kluckhohn's article presents a direct observation of the American culture, whereas Mead's article adds insight by the comparison of American culture with that of Samoa.

Kluckhohn's *The Great American Culture* suggests many parallels between general American values and the particular principles and attitudes taught in American physical education. For example, the "work counts" theory and the American zeal for progress are both reflected in the "practice makes perfect" concept in skill learning. The American subscription to "getting ahead," "aggressiveness," and "helping the underdog" are as readily found in physical education as are competition, independence, and the quest for vigor.

CLYDE KLUCKHOHN

The American Culture*

American culture has been called a culture of paradoxes. Nevertheless national advertising and a national moving-picture industry would be impossible were there not certain terms in which one can appeal to the vast majority of this capturable people. Though sectional, economic, and religious differences are highly significant in some respects, there are certain themes that transcend these variations. Some life goals, some basic attitudes tend to be shared by Americans of every region and of all social classes.

To start with the commonplace: even the most bitter critics of the United States have conceded us material generosity. In spite of the romanticism of "public-spirited disinterestedness" most Americans

* Reprinted and abridged with permission of the McGraw-Hill Book Co., a division of McGraw-Hill, Inc., from *Mirror for Man* by Clyde Kluckhohn. Copyright © 1949 by the McGraw-Hill Book Company, Inc., pp. 230–244; 246–248; 252–255.

are outgoing and genuinely benevolent. Sometimes, to be sure, American humanitarianism is linked with the missionary spirit—the determination to help others by making the world over on the American model.

Perhaps no huge society has ever had such generalized patterns for laughter. In older civilizations it is commonly the case that jokes are fully understood and appreciated only by class or regional groups. It is true that it is some distance from the sophisticated humor of *The New Yorker* to the slapstick of popular radio programs. But the most widespread formulas reach all Americans. Some of the most characteristic of these are related to the cult of the average man. No one becomes so great that we cannot make fun of him. Humor is an important sanction in American culture. Probably the ridicule of Hitler did more than all the rational critiques of Nazi ideology to make the man in the street contemptuous of Nazism.

All European travelers are struck by American attitudes toward women. They often note that "Americans spoil their women," or that "America is dominated by petticoats." The truth is more complicated. On the one hand, it is clear that a very large number of American women of privileged economic position are freed by labor-saving devices from much household drudgery—particularly after their few children have entered school. Their abundant leisure goes into women's clubs, community activities, "cultural" organizations, unhealthy devotion to their children, other mildly or seriously neurotic activities. It is also true that many American men are so wrapped up in pursuit of the success goal that they largely abdicate control over their children's upbringing to their wives. The responsibility of American women for moral and cultural questions is tremendous. On the other hand, it is too often forgotten that in 1940, 26 out of every 100 women of working age worked outside the home, that almost every girl who graduates from high school or college has had some job training. We interest women in careers but make it difficult for them to attain a full life in one. In a culture where "prestige" is everything we have felt it necessary to set aside Mother's Day as a symbolic atonement for the lack of recognition ordinarily given to domestic duties.

The pattern of the implicit American creed seems to embrace the following recurrent elements: faith in the rational, a need for moralistic rationalization, an optimistic conviction that rational effort counts, romantic individualism and the cult of the common man, high valuation of change—which is ordinarily taken to mean "progress," the conscious quest for pleasure.

Mysticism and supernaturalism have been very minor themes in American life. Our glorification of science and our faith in what can be accomplished through education are two striking aspects of our generalized conviction that secular, humanistic effort will improve the world in a series of changes, all or mainly for the better. We further tend to believe that morality and reason must coincide. Fatalism is generally repudiated, and even acceptance seems to be uncongenial—though given lip service in accord with Christian doctrine.

The dominant American political philosophy has been that the common man would think and act rationally. The same premises are apparent in typical attitudes toward parental responsibility. The individual, if "let alone" and not "corrupted by bad company" will be reasonable. If a child does not turn out well, the mother or both parents tend to blame themselves or to explain the failure by "bad blood"—as if action-guided-by-reason could of itself always produce well-adjusted children when the biological inheritance was adequate.

While many Americans are in some senses profoundly irreligious, they still typically find it necessary to provide moral justifications for their personal and national acts. No people moralizes as much as we do. The actual pursuit of power, prestige, and pleasure for their own sakes must be disguised (if public approval is to be obtained) as action for a moral purpose or as later justified by "good works." Conversely, a contemplative life tends to be considered "idleness."

The American mother offers her love to her child on the condition of his fulfilling certain performance standards. No conversational bromides are more characteristically American than "Let's get going"; "Do something"; "Something can be done about it." Although during the thirties there was wide-spread devaluation of present and future and though pessimism and apathy about the atomic bomb and other international problems are certainly strong currents in contemporary national thinking, the dominant American reaction is still—against the perspective of other cultures—that this is a world in which effort triumphs. A recent public opinion study showed that only 32 per cent of Americans were concerned about social security—for themselves.

Countless European observers have been impressed by "enthusiasm" as a typically American quality. During the war military analysts noted repeatedly that the British were better at holding a position but the Americans at taking one. As Margaret Mead has observed, the British cope with a problem; Americans start from scratch and build completely anew.

Americans are not merely optimistic believers that "work counts." Their creed insists that anyone, anywhere in the social structure, can and should "make the effort." Moreover, they like to think of the world as man-controlled. This view about the nature of life is thus intimately linked with that conception of the individual's place in society which may be called "romantic individualism."

In the English-speaking world there are two principal ideologies of individualism. The English variety (which may be tagged with the name of Cobden) is capitalistic in its basic outlook. American individualism has agrarian roots and may be associated with Jefferson. To this day Americans hate "being told what to do." They have always distrusted strong government. The social roles most frequently jibed at in comic strips are those that interfere with the freedom of others: the dogcatcher, the truant officer, the female social climber (Mrs. Jiggs) who forces her husband and family to give up their habitual satisfactions. "My rights" is one of the commonest phrases in the American language. This historically conditioned attitude toward authority is constantly reinforced by child training patterns. The son must "go farther" than his father, and revolt against the father in adolescence is expected.

However, as de Tocqueville pointed out, Americans are characteristically more interested in equality than in liberty. "I'm as good as the next man," seems at first a contradiction of the American emphasis upon success and individual achievement within a competitive system. It is true that there are relatively few places at the top in a social pyramid—*at any one time*. But the American faith that "there is always another chance" has its basis in the historical facts of social mobility and the fluidity (at least in the past) of our economic structure. "If at first you don't succeed, try, try again." The American also feels that if he himself does not "get a break," he has a prospect for vicarious achievement through his children.

American individualism centers upon the dramatization of the individual. This is reflected in the tendency to personalize achievement, good or bad. Americans prefer to attack men rather than issues. Corporations are personified. Public power projects were advertised as much as a means of beating the Utility Devil as a way of getting better and cheaper service.

The less opportunity the greater the merit of success. "You can't keep a good man down." Conversely, failure is a confession of weakness, and status distinctions and even class lines are rationalized on such grounds as, "he got there by hard work," "it's his own fault that he didn't get on." Such attitudes—and the idealization of the "tough guy" and the "red-blooded American" and the fear of "being a sucker"—derive both from the Puritan ethic and from the American pioneer era. Aggressive activity and rapid mobility were effectual in the rapid development of a new country, and it made sense then that the rewards in money and status should be high.

The worship of success has gone farther than in any known culture, save possibly prewar Japan. This is reflected in countless staple phrases such as "bettering yourself," "getting ahead," and "how are you getting on?" The opposition to Roosevelt's proposal for a taxation program that would limit net income to $25,000, attests to the depth of feeling for slogans like "the sky's the limit." But the striving for money is not simply the pursuit of purposeless materialism. Money is primarily a symbol. The deeper competition is for power and prestige. "Aggressive" is, in American culture, a descriptive adjective of high praise when applied to an individual's personality or character. "You have to be aggressive to be a success." The obvious crudities of aggression are, as Lynd says, explained away by identifying them with the common good.

But there is a defensive note in this aggressiveness which is also symptomatic. Competitive aggressiveness against one's fellows is not just playing a part in a drama. The only way to be safe in American life is to be a success. Failure to "measure up" is felt as deep personal inadequacy. In a phrase, the American creed is equality of opportunity, not equality of man.

The cult of the average man might seem to imply disapproval of outstanding individuals of every sort. Certainly it is true that a great deal of hostility is directed upward. However, under the influence of the dramatic and success aspects of the "romantic individualism" orientation, the typical attitude toward leaders may best be described as one of mixed feelings. On the one hand, there is a tendency to snipe at superior individuals with a view to reducing them to the level of their fellows. On the other hand, their very success is a dramatic vindication of the American way of life and an invitation to identification and emulation.

The cult of the average man means conformity to the standards of the current majority. To de Tocqueville this was "enfeeblement of the individual." A more recent observer, Fromm, who also looked at the American scene from a European viewpoint, likewise finds this conformity repressive to self-expression. But he fails to see that the American is not a passive automaton submitting to cultural compulsives like European provincials. The American voluntarily and consciously seeks to be like others of his age and sex—without in any way becoming an anonymous atom in the social molecule. On the contrary, all the devices of the society are mobilized to glamorize the individual woman and to dramatize every achievement of men and women that is unusual—but still within the range of approved aspirations of the conforming majority. "Miss America" and "the typical American mother" are widely publicized each year, but an announced atheist (no matter of what brilliance and accomplishment) cannot be elected President.

American devotion to the underdog must be linked to this attitude. As Lynd points out, we worship bigness yet we idealize "the little man." "Griping" is a characteristic American trait, but the griping of American soldiers against the officer caste system is to be understood in terms of American egalitarian notions and especially of the cult of the average man. The fact that officers and enlisted men did not have equal access to various facilities for recreation and transportation enraged what were felt to be the most basic sentiments in the American code. To some extent this aspect of the cult of the average man doubtless represents a refuge for those who fail "to rise," a justification for envy of those who do.

Because of the cult of the average man, superficial intimacy is easy in America. People of every social class can talk on common topics in a way that is not so easy in Europe where life is based more on repetition of patterns of early family routines that are differentiated by class. However, American friendships tend to be casual and transitory.

Thanks to our expanding economy and to national folklore created by various historical accidents, the nineteenth-century faith in "progress" became intrenched in the United States as nowhere else. As Lovejoy and Boas have pointed out, America's golden age has been located mainly in the future rather than in the past. To some extent, to be sure, the future has been brought into the present by installment plan buying, the philosophy of "spend, don't save," etc. But the basic underlying notions have been well made explicit by Carl Becker.

> By locating perfection in the future and identifying it with the successive achievements of mankind, the doctrine of progress makes a virtue of novelty and disposes men to welcome change as in itself a sufficient validation of their activities.

Western Europeans and Americans tend to be fundamentally different in their attitudes toward conforming. Americans believe in conforming only to the standards of one's own age group and change-in-time is a strong value; Europeans believe—or have believed—in conforming to a past society and have found security in traditional behavior; yet conformity to a contemporary society is only incidental and not a value. There are, to be sure, wide disparities in American hospitality to change. We take pride in material change but are, on the whole, more hostile than contemporary Europeans to changes in our institutions (say the Constitution or the free enterprise system). In some ways the conformity of middle-class Englishmen, for instance, is more rigid than that of Americans —but in other ways it is less so. American attitudes toward change make generational conflicts more serious. These very generational conflicts, however, make certain types of social change possible. As Mead points out, children can be more "successful" than their parents, hence "better."

Americans publicly state that having a good time is an important part of life and admit to craving "something new and exciting." In terms of this ideology we have created Hollywood, our Forest of Arden type of college life, our National Parks, Monuments, and Forests. Leaders of our entertainment industry are the best paid men and women in the United States. In 1947 the American people spent nearly twenty billion dollars for alcoholic beverages, theater and movie tickets, tobacco, cosmetics, and jewelry. We spend as much for moving pictures as for churches, more for beauty shops than for social service. However, because of the Puritan tradition of "work for work's sake," this devotion to recreation and material pleasure is often accompanied by a sense of guilt—another instance of the bipolarity of many features of American culture. The pleasure principle attains its fullest development in American youth culture. Youth is the hero of the American Dream. Most especially, the young girl ready for marriage is the cynosure of American society.

We have borrowed ideas and values from countless sources. If one takes single features, one can match almost every instance in a dozen or more cultures, including the primitive. For example, during the last war many of our soldiers carried magic amulets, such as a miniature wooden pig which was said to have raised fogs, smoothed out a high sea, commuted an execution, or cured assorted cases of illness. But if one looks at the total combination of premises and attitudes one sees a pattern that has its own special flavor, even though this description is too brief to take account of regional, class, ethnic group, and generational variations.

An anthropological snapshot of the American way of life cannot catch all the details, but, with other cultures in the background, it should highlight some meaningful interplay of light and shadow. And the attempt is needed. No amount of knowledge of Russian or Chinese culture will avail in the solution of our international problems unless we know ourselves also. If we can predict our own reactions to a probable next move in the Russian gambit and have some clues as to why we shall react in that manner, the gain to self-control and toward more rational action will be tremendous. Because of our tradition of assimilating immigrants and because of our overweening pride in our own culture it is particularly difficult to get Amercians to understand other cultures.

Seen in the perspective of the range of human institutions, the following combination of outstanding features define the American scene: consciousness of diversity of biological and cultural origins; emphasis upon technology and upon wealth; the frontier spirit; relatively strong trust in science and education and relative indifference to religion; unusual personal insecurity; concern over the discrepancy between the theory and the practice of the culture.

"The melting pot" is one of the surest catchwords that has ever been applied to the United States. Probably much of the vitality of American life and the increased stature and other evidences of physical superiority for new generations of Americans must be attributed to the mingling of diverse cultural and biological strains as well as to dietary and environmental factors. The "Ballad for Americans" triumphantly proclaims our manifold origins. News-

papers during the war proudly referred to the fact that Eisenhower
was a German name but he was an American, to the fact that another general was an Indian, to the variety of names in American
platoons and in American graveyards overseas. The distinguished
record of Japanese-Americans in the armed services was used to
document the success of the American Way.

Heterogeneity has, in fact, become one of the organizing principles of American culture. Ripley's "Believe It or Not," "Quiz
Kids" programs, "Information Please," and other formal and informal educational devices are evidence that Americans value dis-
connected pieces of information and feel that people must be prepared to live in a world in which generalizations are hard to apply.

Although the definition of an American as a person who is endlessly catching trains is a caricature, the phrase of G. Lowes Dickin-
son "contemptuous of ideas but amorous of devices" remains un-
comfortably correct as a characterization of all save a tiny minority
of Americans. And while we indignantly met the Fascist label of
"plutocracy!" by pointing to our humanitarian organizations, our
numerous foundations dedicated to the spending of untold millions
for lofty aims, and the generosity of individual citizens, it remains
true that not only are we the wealthiest nation in the world but
that money comes closer with us than with any other people to
being the universal standard of value.

This is why the level of intellectual ability is very much higher
in the Harvard Law School than in the Harvard Graduate School
of Arts and Sciences. The ablest undergraduates in Harvard College do not always receive the highest honors. The energies of
many are often, realistically enough, consecrated to "making con-
tacts" through "activities," through a sedulous campaign to acquire
membership in a "final club." This is not necessarily because they
are congenitally uninterested in ideas, but because they have been
effectually conditioned by family pressure and by certain schools.
They have considerable intuitive insight into the structure of our
culture. They know that intellectual endeavor will lead them to
little "recognition" and less salary. They know how vital is "success"
to security in our society. Brilliant young men voluntarily condemn themselves to lives of cutthroat competition and narrow
slavery.

Our economy is a prestige economy to a pathological extent. The
wife must buy fur coats and drive an expensive automobile because

she too is an item of conspicuous consumption. Even in the supposedly uncommercial halls of learning the awed whisper is heard, "Why, he is a $15,000-a-year professor." The numerical system of grading, an unmistakably American invention, is simply another projection of our conviction that all attainments can be expressed in figures.

Suppose that an intellectual Australian aborigine, who was also a trained anthropologist, were to write a monograph on our culture. He would unequivocally assert that machines and money are close to the heart of our system of symbolic logics. He would point out that the two are linked in a complex system of mutual interdependence. Technology is valued as the very basis of the capitalistic system. Possession of gadgets is esteemed as a mark of success to the extent that persons are judged not by the integrity of their characters or by the originality of their minds but by what they seem to be—so far as that can be measured by the salaries they earn or by the variety and expensiveness of the material goods which they display. "Success" is measured by two automobiles—not by two mistresses as in some cultures.

Could our aboriginal anthropologist introduce some time perspective into his study, he would note that this value system has shown some signs of alteration during the last two decades. However, against the background of all known cultures, American culture would still stand out for its quantitative and materialistic orientations.

Americans love bigness—so far as things and events are concerned. Their constant overstatement appears to others as boasting. Americans love to speak in numbers. They like to "get down to brass tacks" and "want the lowdown." Europeans are usually content to rate students according to categories corresponding to "high honors," "honors," "pass." Only Americans think that the relative standing of students in a course can be measured on a continuous scale from zero to 100. This emphasis on the quantitative must not be too easily taken as proof of a thoroughgoing materialism. But Americans do tend to get very excited about things as opposed to ideas, people, and aesthetic creations. "Virtuous materialism" has tended to be part of the American creed.

Status in the United States is determined more by the number and price of automobiles, air-conditioning units, and the like owned by a family than by the number of their servants or the learning and aesthetic skills of family members. In fact, Americans usually are scared out of being artists. There is reverence only for the man who "does *things* in a big way." Most Americans do subscribe to the current Einstein legend, but *Time* has recently pointed out that many did not take this very seriously until they were told that Einstein's "theories" had made the atomic bomb possible. It is significant that Edison is a household name, whereas only the professors have heard of Willard Gibbs. . . .

Assembly-line factories and skyscrapers must, in part, be understood in terms of the frontier. Our so rapid development in invention and technique, our gigantic financial and industrial systems—in general, the fact that we adjusted so completely and quickly, albeit so inharmoniously, to the Technical Age is to be traced to the absence of an ancient order of society and the presence of the frontier where we had to adapt ourselves to vastness with decision, speed, and skill. In an old culture there is a belief in the established order, a rooted opposition to change, a constitutional imperviousness to new ideas which would involve radical alteration in the mode of life. The frontier liberated the American spirit. It developed generosity and radiant vitality, together with a restlessness which was both good and ill, but did certainly bring with it a resiliency of mind, fluidity of idea and of society, a willingness for bold experiment.

Mass education, like mass suffrage and mass production, is a leading trait of our code. During the last generation education has supplanted the frontier as a favorite means of social mobility, for we have continued to define success in terms of mobility rather than in terms of stability. Our educational system has recently been built upon a kind of watery intellectualism. We have too often naïvely assumed that, if people were "well informed" and taught to reason in accord with accepted canons of logic, their characters would take care of themselves, and they would automatically acquire the point of view requisite in the citizen of a great society. Meanwhile, the toughening influences of frontier conditions were becoming steadily more dilute. Children of the economically dominant classes were being brought up in relative luxury. Parents failed to condition their offspring to rigorous standards of conduct because they were themselves confused. Actually many educative functions formerly carried out by the family have been surrendered to the school. The existing educational system is hopelessly irresolute on many fronts. It vacillates between training girls to be housewives or career women; it is torn between conditioning children for the theoretically desirable cooperative objectives or to the existing competitive realities. In spite of the terrific demands made upon them, elementary and high-school teachers are under-paid and lack social status. Psychiatrists are agreed that the elimina-tion of social disorganization, as well as of personal disorganization, can be furthered only by more consistent educational practices both in the home and in the school because automatic actions based on the habits of early life are the most stable.

The anthropologist must also characterize our culture as pro-foundly irreligious. More than half of our people still occasionally go through the forms, and there are rural and ethnic islands in our population where religion is still a vital force. But very few of our leaders are still religious in the sense that they are convinced that prayer or the observance of church codes will affect the course of human events. Public figures participate in public worship and con-tribute financially to a church for reasons of expediency or because they know that churches represent one of the few elements of stability and continuity in our society. But belief in God's judg-ments and punishments as a motive for behavior is limited to a decreasing minority. Feelings of *guilt* are common but the sense of *sin* is rare. . . .

Most thoughtful Americans are concerned about the fact that the theory and the practice of our culture are hopelessly out of line. It is well established that while cultural content often changes rapidly, cultural forms often have extraordinary permanency. Thus it is only the *tradition* of economic independence which truly sur-vives. For all our talk of free enterprise we have created the most vast and crushing monopolies in the world. Although the fable that every boy can become president has been repeatedly scoffed at in recent years, parents and children still act upon the ruling motiva-tion that hard work, training, and aggressiveness can overcome almost all limitations. The result is of course, countless disgruntled or bitter men and women, for as Veblen has shown, in a capitalistic economy the number of places at the top is disappointingly few. A cramping constriction will be felt by individuals so long as our ideal pattern is proclaimed as equality of opportunity for all. "Freedom" likewise has become fertile of disillusioned cynicism because of in-creasing realization of the truth of Durkheim's words, "I can be free only to the extent that others are forbidden to profit from their physical, economic, or other superiority to the detriment of my liberty." And much of the exultation in our "high standard of living" is, as Norman Thomas contends, "ludicrously beside the point. What the workers have a right to demand of the machine age is not that it will give them more bath tubs than Henry VIII had for his troublesome domestic establishment; they have a right to ask that machinery will conquer poverty rather than increase insecurity."

A society may indeed be viewed as a structure of expectancies. Neuroses have been produced experimentally in laboratory animals by causing the relation between stimulus and proper response to be irregular and haphazard. It follows that if the expectancies which are generated by the cultural ideology are notably unrealistic, mass frustration and mass neurosis are the inescapable consequences.

The diversity of ethnic origins in our forming nation provided strong psychological reinforcement of the doctrines of human equality which were the gospel of the Age of Enlightenment and of the Romantic Movement. Had not a belief in mystic equality become part of the official ideology of American culture and offered psychological security to non-Anglo-Saxons, these divergent groups might well have remained tight little islands of transplanted Europeans. But the contrast between this legal and political theory and the private theories and practices of too many American citizens (as symbolized in labels like "wops" and "greasers," in Jim Crow laws and lynchings) constitutes one of the severest strains undermining the equilibrium of the American social system. The Negroes and, to only a slightly lesser extent, the Spanish-speaking Americans constitute caste groups—that is, normal intermarriage does not occur between them and the rest of the population. Segregation in housing and discriminatory practices in our armed services stand out as intolerable contradictions in the institutions of a free society.

In the last fifteen years anthropologists have presented evidence that, in contrast to our official beliefs, a class structure has even now considerably crystallized in at least some parts of the United States. Lloyd Warner and his associates distinguish a six-class system: upper-upper, lower-upper, upper-middle, lower-middle, upper-lower, lower-lower. These groupings are not solely economic. In fact, members of the top class ordinarily have less money than those of the lower-upper group. Nor does stratification correspond entirely to occupational lines. Physicians, for example, are found in all of the first four classes. In Warner's sense a class consists of persons who visit in one another's home, belong to the same social clubs, exchange gifts, and show awareness of themselves as a group set apart from others, and in a subordinate or superior position to others.

Whether the six-class system is generally valid or whether a larger or smaller subdivision better represents the facts in some communities is a factional question that cannot be answered until there have been more studies. The division of labor in a complex society makes some form of class stratification almost inevitable. It just so happens that in American culture recognition of the facts is repugnant to the American creed. Public-opinion polls indicate that 90 per cent of Americans insist that they are "middle class" despite wide variations in income level, occupation, and social habits. One study shows that 70 per cent of low-income groups claim middle-class social position. Warner, however, places 59 per cent of the people in one New England town in the two lower classes.

Under the influence of the depression and of Marxian theories discussion of class in the United States has increased greatly in the past twenty years. When class position is grudgingly recognized, it is often with anger—as something un-American and hence wrong. Some students of American class structure have failed to examine the significance of values—adhered to by almost all Americans—which operate to deny and tear down class divisions. Except possibly in limited areas of the eastern seaboard, the South, and the San Francisco area, the lines are still relatively fluid and everyone hopes to rise. The statement that American culture is dominantly a middle-class culture is something more than an acceptance of popular ideology which glosses over the sometimes ugly facts of differentiation. Hence "class," though a real phenomenon, does not have precisely the sense that it does in Europe. Certainly Americans are increasingly conscious of status, but the ranking of individuals and their immediate families is often still divorced from that of their close relatives. And the place of the whole body of kin in the smaller communities is frequently based primarily on length of residence there. Our society remains in important respects an open society.

Nevertheless the facts indicate that rapid rise through sheer ability and industry is much more difficult than it was a generation or two ago. Status is harder to achieve by one's own initiative and easier to acquire through family connections. In Washington during the war it was noted that considerable communication and power flowed through channels that were not only nonofficial but not those of political or other normal American interest groups. For the first time since the Age of Jackson an upper class appeared to be operating without much reference to regional or political lines. The class problem is also manifesting itself in the schools. Teachers, themselves usually of middle-class position, discriminate against lower-class children. The children sense that they are punished for following the cultural patterns of their parents. If effort and ability are not rewarded, the way to delinquency or stolid escapism is inviting. In short, class typing rather than individual typing has become one American mode of granting or denying recognition to other people. . . .

Further Readings

DU BOIS, CORA, "The Dominant Value Profile of American Culture," *The American Anthropologist*, vol. 57, Part I, (December 1955), pp. 1232–1239.

KLUCKHOHN, CLYDE, *Mirror For Man*. New York: McGraw-Hill, Inc., 1949.

MASLOW, ABRAHAM H., *Toward a Psychology of Being*. Princeton, N.J.: D. Van Nostrand Company, Inc., 1962.

TOCQUEVILLE, ALEXIS DE, *Democracy in America*. New York: Alfred A. Knopf, Inc., 1945.

Questions for Discussion

1. What would be our cultural perception of physical fitness if we lived in the past instead of in the golden age of the future as described by Kluckhohn?

2. In what ways are social and athletic success similar? In what ways different? In what ways are social and athletic failure similar? In what ways different?

3. What is character development? If people are well informed and taught to reason properly, will their character development be ensured?

MARGARET MEAD

The Coming of Age in Samoa*

Next, we take a second look at the American culture by contrasting it with Samoan culture. The distinguished anthropologist, Margaret Mead, states, "We may well examine in turn all
of our institutions thrown into strong relief against the history
of other civilizations, and weighing them in the balance, be not
afraid to find them wanting." In the following article Mead
compares the American educational principles of work, play,
competition, and skill development with those of Samoa.

To achieve a better understanding of his own culture, the
student should attempt to compare and contrast Samoan principles of education with those prevalent in America. He should
consider particularly those principles relevant to physical
education in both cultures.

Among the factors in the Samoan scheme of life which are influential in producing stable, well-adjusted, robust individuals, the organisation of the family and the attitude towards sex are undoubtedly the most important. But it is necessary to note also the general
educational concept which disapproves of precocity and coddles the
slow, the laggard, the inept. In a society where the tempo of life was
faster, the rewards greater, the amount of energy expended larger,
the bright children might develop symptoms of boredom. But the
slower pace dictated by the climate, the complacent, peaceful society,
and the compensation of the dance, in its blatant precocious display
of individuality which drains off some of the discontent which the
bright child feels, prevent any child from becoming too bored. And
the dullard is not goaded and dragged along faster than he is able
until, sick with making an impossible effort, he gives up entirely.

* Reprinted and abridged with permission of the author and the publisher from
   The Coming of Age in Samoa. New York: William Morrow Company, 1928,
   pp. 195; 198–211; 216–220.

This educational policy also tends to blur individual differences and so to minimise jealousy, rivalry, emulation, those social attitudes which arise out of discrepancies of endowment and are so far-reaching in their effects upon the adult personality.

It is one way of solving the problem of differences between individuals and a method of solution exceedingly congenial to a strict adult world. The longer the child is kept in a subject, non-initiating state, the more of the general cultural attitude it will absorb, the less of a disturbing element it will become.

Still another factor in Samoan education which results in different attitudes is the place of work and play in the children's lives. Samoan children do not learn to work through learning to play, as the children of many primitive peoples do. Nor are they permitted a period of lack of responsibility such as our children are allowed. From the time they are four or five years old they perform definite tasks, graded to their strength and intelligence, but still tasks which have a meaning in the structure of the whole society. This does not mean that they have less time for play than American children who are shut up in schools from nine to three o'clock every day. Before the introduction of schools to complicate the ordered routine of their lives, the time spent by the Samoan child in running errands, sweeping the house, carrying water, and taking actual care of the baby, was possibly less than that which the American school child devotes to her studies.

The difference lies not in the proportion of time in which their activities are directed and the proportion in which they are free, but rather in the difference of attitude. With the professionalisation of education and the specialisation of industrial tasks which has stripped the individual home of its former variety of activities, our children are not made to feel that the time they do devote to supervised activity is functionally related to the world of adult activity. Although this lack of connection is more apparent than real, it is still sufficiently vivid to be a powerful determinant in the child's attitude. The Samoan girl who tends babies, carries water, sweeps the floor; or the little boy who digs for bait, or collects cocoanuts, has no such difficulty. The necessary nature of their tasks is obvious. And the practice of giving a child a task which he can do well and never permitting a childish, inefficient tinkering with adult apparatus, such as we permit to our children, who bang aimlessly and destructively on their fathers' typewriters, results in a different attitude towards work. American children spend hours in schools learning tasks whose visible relation to their mothers' and fathers' activities is often quite impossible to recognise. Their participation in adults' activities is either in terms of toys, tea-sets and dolls and toy automobiles, or else a meaningless and harmful tampering with the electric light system. (It must be understood that here, as always, when I say American, I do not mean those Americans recently arrived from Europe, who still present a different tradition of education. Such a group would be the Southern Italians, who still expect productive work from their children.)

So our children make a false set of categories, work, play, and school; work for adults, play for children's pleasure, and schools as an inexplicable nuisance with some compensations. These false distinctions are likely to produce all sorts of strange attitudes, an apathetic treatment of a school which bears no known relation to life, a false dichotomy between work and play, which may result either in a dread of work as implying irksome responsibility or in a later contempt for play as childish.

The Samoan child's dichotomy is different. Work consists of those necessary tasks which keep the social life going: planting and harvesting and preparation of food, fishing, house-building, mat-making, care of children, collecting of property to validate marriages and births and succession to titles and to entertain strangers, these are the necessary activities of life, activities in which every member of the community, down to the smallest child, has a part. Work is not a way of acquiring leisure; where every household produces its own food and clothes and furniture, where there is no large amount of fixed capital and households of high rank are simply characterised by greater industry in the discharge of greater obligations, our whole picture of saving, of investment, of deferred enjoyment, is completely absent. (There is even a lack of clearly defined seasons of harvest, which would result in special abundance of food and consequent feasting. Food is always abundant, except in some particular village where a few weeks of scarcity may follow a period of lavish entertaining.) . . . There is social reward for the industrious, social toleration for the man who does barely enough. And there is always leisure—leisure, be it noted, which is not the result of hard work or accumulated capital at all, but is merely the result of a kindly climate, a small population, a well-integrated social system, and no social demands for spectacular expenditure. And play is what one does with the time left over from working, a way of filling in the wide spaces in a structure of unirksome work.

Play includes dancing, singing, games, weaving necklaces of flowers, flirting, repartee, all forms of sex activity. And there are social institutions like the ceremonial inter-village visit which partake of both work and play. But the distinctions between work as something one has to do but dislikes, and play as something one wants to do; of work as the main business of adults, play as the main concern of children, are conspicuously absent. Children's play is like adults' play in kind, interest, and in its proportion to work. And the Samoan child has no desire to turn adult activities into play, to translate one sphere into the other. I had a box of white clay pipes for blowing soap bubbles sent me. The children were familiar with soap bubbles, but their native method of blowing them was very inferior to the use of clay pipes. But after a few minutes' delight in the unusual size and beauty of the soap bubbles, one little girl after another asked me if she might please take her pipe home to her mother, for pipes were meant to smoke, not to play with. Foreign dolls did not interest them, and they have no dolls of their own, although children of other islands weave dolls from the palm leaves from which Samoan children weave balls. . . .

The intelligibility of a child's life among us is measured only in terms of the behaviour of other children. If all the other children go to school the child who does not feels incongruous in their midst. If the little girl next door is taking music lessons, why can't Mary; or why must Mary take music lessons, if the other little girl doesn't take them. But so sharp is our sense of difference between the concerns of children and of adults that the child does not learn to judge its own behaviour in relationship to adult life. So children often learn to regard play as something inherently undignified, and as adults mangle pitifully their few moments of leisure. But the Samoan child measures her every act of work or play in terms of her whole community; each item of conduct is dignified in terms of its realised relationship to the only standard she knows, the life of a Samoan village. So complex and stratified a society as ours cannot hope to develop spontaneously any such simple scheme of education. Again we will be hard put to it to devise ways of participation for children, and means of articulating their school life with the rest of life which will give them the same dignity which Samoa affords her children.

Last among the cultural differences which may influence the emotional stability of the child is the lack of pressure to make important choices. Children are urged to learn, urged to behave, urged to work, but they are not urged to hasten the choices which they make themselves. The first point at which this attitude makes itself felt is in the matter of the brother and sister taboo, a cardinal point of modesty and decency. Yet the exact stage at which the taboo should be observed is always left to the younger child. When it reaches a point of discretion, of understanding, it will of itself feel "ashamed" and establish the formal barrier which will last until old age. Likewise, sex activity is never urged upon the young people, nor marriage forced upon them at a tender age. Where the possibilities of deviation from the accepted standard are so slight, a few years' leeway holds no threat for the society. The child who comes later to a realisation of the brother and sister taboo really endangers nothing.

This laissez faire attitude has been carried over into the Samoan Christian Church. The Samoan saw no reason why young unmarried people should be pressed to make momentous decisions which would spoil part of their fun in life. Time enough for such serious matters after they were married or later still, when they were quite sure of what steps they were taking and were in less danger of falling from grace every month or so. The missionary authorities, realising the virtues of going slowly and sorely vexed to reconcile Samoan sex ethics with a Western European code, saw the great disadvantages of unmarried Church members who were not locked up in Church schools. Consequently, far from urging the adolescent to think upon her soul the native pastor advises her to wait until she is older, which she is only too glad to do.

But, especially in the case of our Protestant churches, there is a strong preference among us for the appeal to youth. The Reformation, with its emphasis upon individual choice, was unwilling to accept the tacit habitual Church membership which was the Catholic pattern, a membership marked by additional sacramental gifts but demanding no sudden conversion, no renewal of religious feeling. But the Protestant solution is to defer the choice only so far as necessary, and the moment the child reaches an age which may be called "years of discretion" it makes a strong, dramatic appeal. This appeal is reinforced by parental and social pressure; the child is bidden to choose now and wisely. While such a position in the churches which stem from the Reformation and its strong emphasis on individual choice was historically inevitable, it is regrettable that the convention has lasted so long. It has even been taken over by non-sectarian reform groups, all of whom regard the adolescent child as the most legitimate field of activity.

In all of these comparisons between Samoan and American culture, many points are useful only in throwing a spotlight upon our own solutions, while in others it is possible to find suggestions for change. . . . We may well examine in turn all of our institutions, thrown into strong relief against the history of other civilisations, and weighing them in the balance, be not afraid to find them wanting. . . .

Further Readings

GINZBERG, ELI, *Values and Ideals of American Youth.* New York: Columbia University Press, 1961.

KARDINER, ABRAM, *The Psychological Frontiers of Society.* New York: Columbia University Press, 1945.

KROEBER, ALFRED L., The Societies of Primitive Man," *Biological Symposia*, VIII, 1942, pp. 205–216.

LINTON, RALPH, *The Study of Man.* New York: Appleton-Century-Crofts, Inc., 1936.

MALINOWSKI, BRONISLAW, *Argonauts of the Western Pacific.* New York: E. P. Dutton & Co., Inc., 1950.

MASLOW, ABRAHAM H., *Toward a Psychology of Being.* Princeton, N.J.: D. Van Nostrand Company, Inc., 1962.

MEAD, MARGARET, *Coming of Age in Samoa.* New York: William Morrow & Company, Inc., 1928.

Questions for Discussion

1. What implications for curriculum development can be found in the Samoan system? For teaching? For skill development?
2. Should there be a dichotomy between work and play in in our culture? Defend your answer.
3. What are the possibilities that peers will exert pressure on one another in a system where no one may advance until the slowest student learns the lessons? Explain.

WILLARD WALLER

The Separate Culture of the School*

Understanding the separate culture of the school is also of great importance if the teacher is to be successful, for the school's culture is largely responsible for motivating students and determining to what extent they learn, succeed, and fail. This article concerns the characteristics of the school culture and the contribution of physical education to that culture and to the American culture at large.

Because an interaction takes place between certain cultural patterns of the school and the physical education program, the student must know the meaning of the school's bimodal population and understand the highly structured system of roles anticipated and played by each group. He must recognize other characteristics, such as formal and informal groupings, class functions, student government, and athletics. In reading the following essay, he should attempt to project the role of the physical educator into Waller's description of the separate culture of the school.

Teachers have always known that it was not necessary for the students of strange customs to cross the seas to find material. Folklore and myth, tradition, taboo, magic rites, ceremonials of all sorts, collective representations, *participation mystique,* all abound in the front yard of every school, and occasionally they creep upstairs and are incorporated into the more formal portions of school life.

There are, in the school, complex rituals of personal relationships, a set of folkways, mores, and irrational sanctions, a moral code based upon them. There are games, which are sublimated wars, teams, and an elaborate set of ceremonies concerning them. There are traditions, and traditionalists waging their world-old

* Reprinted with permission of the publisher from *The Sociology of Teaching.* New York: John Wiley & Sons, Inc., 1932, pp. 103–112.

battle against innovators. There are laws, and there is the problem
of enforcing them. There is *Sittlichkeit*. There are specialized
societies with a rigid structure and a limited membership. There
are no reproductive groups, but there are customs regulating the
relations of the sexes. All these things make up a world that is
different from the world of adults. It is this separate culture of the
young, having its locus in the school, which we propose to study.
To work out all the details of this culture would be a task long
and difficult, and, for our purpose, not altogether necessary. We
shall be content to mark out the main lines of the cultural background of school life. . . .

We have advanced the notion that the school is a center of cultural diffusion; we have shown that the school serves as a point
from which the cultural standards of the larger group are mediated
to the local community. The organization of higher and lower
schools for the purpose of cultural diffusion may be thought of as
analogous to the organization of wholesale and retail merchandising for the distribution of material goods. The goods, here certain
cultural traits, are sent out from centers in job lots, to be distributed
by retailers by their own methods at their own price. There is a
certain amount of central control of education, as there is central
control of the merchandising of certain material objects. We have
noted also that the school is engaged in the transmission of a vast
body of culture which is passed on from the old to the young. The
school must pass on skills and it must implant attitudes; most of
these are not new in the community. At any time and in any community the major portion of the work of the school is that of imposing these preexistent community standards upon children.

Certain cultural conflicts are at the center of the life of the school.
These conflicts are of two sorts. The first and most obvious is that
which arises from the peculiar function of the school in the process
of cultural diffusion. A conflict arises between teachers and students
because teachers represent the culture of the wider group and students are impregnated with the culture of the local community.
Where the differences concern matters of religion or of fundamental
morality, the struggles which then ensues may become quite sharp
and may seriously affect the relation of the school to the community.
A second and more universal conflict between students and teachers
arises from the fact that teachers are adult and students are not, so
that teachers are the bearers of the culture of the society of adults,

and try to impose that culture upon students, whereas students represent the indigenous culture of the group of children.

The special culture of the young grows up in the play world of childhood. It is worth while to note that it arises in the interstices of the adult social world. Thrasher's *The Gang* is a study of the conflict between the established social order and the interstitial group which has sprung up and grown strong in the sections of society where the adult order does not hold. But this is by no means a complete explanation of the behavior norms of childhood groups. Another fact of importance is that the child does not experience the world in the same manner as does the adult. The child perceives the world differently from the adult in part because he sees it in smaller and simpler configurations. The adult sees social situations as falling into certain highly complex configurations; the child, with a simpler mental organization, does not see these, but breaks up his sensory data into different wholes. The sensory patterns of childhood, then, arise in part from imperfectly experienced adult situations. What the child appropriates from the cultural patterns around him must always be something which it is within his power to comprehend. This is usually one of the simpler and more elementary forms of adult behavior, as the criminal behavior followed out by the gang, or it is a split-off part of a more complex whole common in the culture of adults.

The culture pattern followed out by children may be a survival, for when culture changes it often happens that what was formerly a serious activity for adults is continued in the play of children. Indian fighting, sword play, Hallowe'en festivities, fairy tales, and the use of the bow and arrow have lost their worth in the adult world, but they have retained a certain value in the mental world of childhood. Sometimes economic activities survive and are continued in play because they have great intrinsic interest and have disappeared from the adult world only because they were unable to hold their own in competition with more efficient and prosaic means of getting a living. This has been true of hunting and fishing. There is in the developmental process a gradual evolution in the complexity of social situations and of the adjustment which the person makes to them; the fact that these social situations sometimes reproduce the actual situations of an earlier state of society has led some common-sense observers to believe in the theory of recapitulation.

Between mental processes and the cultural milieu in which they take place there is at all times a nice adjustment. As one's mind approaches the adult form of organization, he is increasingly assimilated to the culture of adults. Koffka, in *The Growth of the Mind,* has ably described the intellectual processes by which the child approaches mental maturity. The very young child sees the red ball against the indifferent background; it sees its mother's face and hears her voice. It is conscious of only the most elementary discomforts. As the child grows older, it acquires more objects in its world, and those objects are more complicated; interrelations appear between those objects in the form of new configurations. Mental life develops by a series of "Aha moments." As a result of these moments of insight, material objects may pass through a long series of metamorphoses. The little round glass backed with mercury is for the very young child something to pound with; a little later it is a mystery, and later yet a thing with which to play a prank upon the teacher; at one time it is a thing that it is slightly disgraceful to be caught looking into; for the adult it is just a pocket mirror. It is this difference in mentality which determines the different uses of cultural products among groups of different age levels.

Age is not the only factor that separates people who nominally drink of the same cultural stream from actual community of culture. Mental ability, education, subtle differences of interests and of personality may likewise sort people into cultural pigeonholes. So completely is the individual immersed in the culture of his own age and social level that he often has difficulty in realizing that any other kind of culture exists. He is separated by invisible walls from those about him who follow different gods. Persons living in different segments of our culture, as determined by age and life situation, may find difficulty in communicating with each other or in understanding each other at all. The old cannot understand the young, the prudent cannot understand the heedless, the married can have little sympathy for the unmarried, parents can never commune with non-parents; each person in the world is surrounded by many with whom he must communicate by smoke signals and by only a few with whom he can converse. But the greatest chasm is that which separates young persons and old.[1]

---

[1] The fact that the world of the child is organized into configurations of a different kind from the configurations composing the base of the adult's universe seems to constitute, by the way, the best justification we have for lying to children. The

The journey from the world of the boy to the world of the man is rarely smooth and continuous. But it has fewer sharp corners to turn if the members of the adult world are able to project themselves back into the psychic world of childhood. The adult who can live in the childish world with sufficient intensity to understand children from within can help them intelligently to develop those complex and unstable syntheses upon which the adult adjustment depends. Teachers have tried to make the transition easier by presenting to children a finely graded and continuously evolving culture, organized into ever more complex configurations. (They have succeeded very well in grading and sorting academic subject matter.) So have arisen those teacher-initiated and teacher-managed "activities," ceremonials, traditions, etc. So were produced, in fact, most of the things which we shall treat in discussing the culture of the school. The purpose of all these things is to soften the conflict of cultures between old and young.

---

greatest argument for the teaching of falsehood seems to be that different orders of truth exist for different mental levels. Children should therefore be taught the kind of truth they are able to understand. There is truth in this argument in that children are likely to break up into simpler configurations the complicated configuration which results for the adult mind in the weighing of virtue against vice, and they are likely to get a final result which is, for the adult, distorted and beside the point. No one who has seen the demoralization produced in some not overly intelligent youths by contact with cynical but well-balanced and earnest adults can fail to see that there is some argument for the simple virtues, even if they are based upon falsehoods. But one wonders whether demoralization is not even more likely to result from building up in the child's mind a structure of beliefs which he is likely to take sometime for complete lies because they are partly false. That such demoralization often occurs will be apparent to all who have ever been in a position to witness the changes wrought in the moral fiber of students when they enter the greater world or make the transition from secondary schools to universities. Nor should we fail to remark in this connection that the policy of lying to children presupposes that one should be intelligent enough and dexterous enough to deceive them completely. This is often not the case at all, for shrewd children, judging their elders by their behavior rather than by their words, are frequently able to cut through the adults' rationalizations to the amoral core of their behavior. Since children, even the shrewdest of them, do not make allowance for rationalizations as rationalizations, as phenomena beyond the conscious control of the individual, they judge their elders more harshly, sometimes, than they deserve. They think their elders both knaves and fools when those elders are in fact too high-minded to admit their selfishness to themselves. Perhaps, when all the alternatives are considered, we shall do better to stick to the simple virtues ourselves, and to speak truth, while taking such precautions as we may against unwarranted generalizations from facts which run contrary to the accepted views of ethics. The virtue that we shall so engender will be a tough-minded virtue. It may be less comprehensive than some would desire, but it will not be brittle.

Though an enlightened pedagogy may ameliorate the conflict of adults and children, it can never remove it altogether. In the most humane school some tension appears between teacher and students, resulting, apparently, from the rôle which the situation imposes upon the teacher in relation to his students. There are two items of the teacher's duty which make it especially likely that he will have to bring some pressure to bear upon students: he must see to it that there is no retrogression from the complexity of the social world worked out for students of a certain age level,[2] and he must strive gradually to increase that complexity as the child grows in age and approximates adult understanding and experience. Activities may reduce conflict, but not destroy it.

Children have something which can be regarded as a culture of their own. Its most important loci are the unsupervised play group and the school. The unsupervised group presents this culture in a much purer form than does the school, for the childish culture of the school is partly produced by adults, is sifted and selected by adults, and is always subject to a certain amount of control by teachers. The culture of the school is a curious mélange of the work of young artisans making culture for themselves and old artisans making culture for the young; it is also mingled with such bits of the greater culture as children have been able to appropriate. In turning to more concrete materials, we may note certain aspects of tradition in the school. It will illustrate well this mingling of cultures if we divide the tradition which clusters about the school into three classes: tradition which comes entirely, or almost entirely, from the outside; tradition which is in part from outside the school and in part indigenous; and tradition which is almost entirely indigenous. It is roughly true that tradition of the first class exists in the community at large, that of the second class among teachers, and that of the third class among students.

Tradition of the first class, that which for the particular school comes altogether from the outside, is a manifestation of a culture complex diffused throughout the whole of West European culture. The historic school has of course had a part in the formation of this complex, but any particular school is largely the creation of it.

---

[2] A strong tendency toward such retrogression in the direction of simpler and easier structures seems to exist, especially in the intermediate stages. This retrogression appears as "silliness." Much conflict between teachers and students arises from the desire of the teacher to eliminate "silliness."

Tradition of this sort governs the very existence of schools, for, without such a culture complex, schools would not exist at all. This traditional culture complex governs also the general nature of the life in the schools. It determines that the old shall teach the young, and not that the young shall ever teach the old, which would be at least equally justifiable in a world that changes so rapidly that an education twenty years old is out of date. Tradition governs what is taught and it holds a firm control upon the manner in which it is taught. Tradition determines who shall teach; we have already discussed some of the traditional requirements for teaching. It is this same sort of tradition also which largely determines how students and teachers shall think of each other.

The best example of a mingled tradition in part absorbed from the general culture of the group and in part produced in the particular institution is the tradition of teachers. In so far as this tradition of teachers is derived from outside a particular school, it is drawn by teachers from the general culture, and from association with members of the teaching profession everywhere. In so far as it is a purely local product, it is produced by the teachers in the institution and is passed on from one teacher to another. We may mention some cardinal points of the teacher tradition as it is usually encountered, making due allowance for local variations. There is a teacher morality, and this morality regulates minutely the teacher's relations with his students and with other teachers; it affects his relations with other teachers especially where the standing of those teachers with students might be affected. There is a character ideal of the teacher; nearly every group which lives long in one stereotyped relation with other groups produces its character ideal, and this ideal for teachers is clearly observable. When teachers say of a colleague, "He's a school teacher," they mean that he conforms to this local character ideal. (It usually implies that the individual puts academic above other considerations, is conscientious in his duties, and exacting in the demands he makes upon himself and others.) There is a taboo on seeking popularity among students, and this taboo operates with dreadful force if it is thought that popularity seeking is complicated by disloyalty to the teacher group. There is a traditional atttiude toward students; this attitude requires that a certain distance be kept between teachers and students. The desire to be fair is very likely not the strongest motive that teachers have for keeping students at a distance, but it is certainly one of the consequences of the policy, and it has in its own right the compelling value of an article of faith. None may violate the code of equality with impunity. Teachers have likewise a certain traditional attitude toward each other. The most obvious manifestation of this traditional attitude is the ceremoniousness of teachers toward each other and toward the administration of the school. It seems clear that this is the ceremoniousness of a fighting group which does not care to endanger its prestige with underlings by allowing any informality to arise within itself. Another interesting observation that has often been made about particular groups of teachers is that they discriminate markedly between veterans and new men. This distinction is in the folkways. Occasionally there is a more or less definite ceremony of initiation, more rarely, actual hazing.

The indigenous tradition of the school is found in its purest form among students. This tradition, when it has been originated on the spot, is passed on, largely by word of mouth, from one student to another. Some of the indigenous tradition has been originated by the faculty, and then imposed upon the students; once it has been accepted by students, however, it may be passed on by student groups. Some of the traditional observances which students follow are not home-grown; there is a great literature of school life, and students occasionally appear who are obviously playing the parts of storybook heroes. Besides, there exists in the culture of any community a set of traditional attitudes toward school and school life, varying from one social class to another, and from family to family; these attitudes influence profoundly the attitudes which students have toward school life. Nevertheless the tradition of students is very largely indigenous within the particular school. Although this sort of tradition varies much in detail from one school to another, we may mention certain characteristics of the fundamental patterns.

Like teacher morality, student morality is the morality of a fighting group, but differences appear in that the student group is subordinate, and its morality is relevant to that situation. Social distance between student and teacher seems as definitely a part of the student code as of the teacher code. The student must not like the teacher too much, for that is naïveté. There is the well-known school-boy code, the rule that students must never give information to teachers which may lead to the punishment of another student.

Certain folkways grow up in every group of school children, as the folkway of riding to grade school on a bicycle or of not riding to high school on a bicycle, and these folkways have a great influence over the behavior of all members of the group. These groups of children are arranged in stair-steps. Membership in the older group implies repudiation of the folkways of the younger group. No one more foolish than the high-school boy on a bicycle, or the college boy wearing a high-school letter! Interlocking groups look forward only, each group aping its elders and despising its juniors. In modern schools, there is a whole complex of traditions pertaining to activities; it seems that all activities are meritorious, that they are in some way connected with the dignity and honor of the school, that some activities are more meritorious than others.

Sometimes a whole social system is carried in the tradition of students, and such social systems are very resistant to change. The fagging system, or a system of any sort of hazing, may persist for decades against the best efforts of highly efficient teachers and administrators to change them. A collegiate institution comes to mind which has conducted such a struggle for upwards of a hundred years. We are led to believe that hazing, at least, having its roots in the desire of those already in the group to dominate new members (and having its parallel on the faculty), would be destined to have some place in the culture which the young work out for themselves even if it had no sanction in tradition. In other words, the manner in which the young experience the universe recreates a hazing problem in every generation of students.

An interesting sidelight upon the importance of tradition is afforded by the fact that certain universities have recently become aware of the beauty of old tradition and have tried to establish traditions overnight. Thus the student daily of one of the great western universities recently announced that it had become a tradition in that university for cowbells to be rung by loyal students in the stands when a touchdown was made by the home team; this tradition, one gathered, had been established on the preceding Saturday. Regulations concerning the wearing of caps by freshmen, likewise, become traditions as soon as the regulations are promulgated. Tradition from time immemorial, that is from time beyond the memory of a particular generation of students, determines the relations of classes, sets the day for the class fight of the freshmen and sophomores, and reserves for seniors the right to sit upon a certain bench or to walk with their sweethearts along a particular path across the campus. In American universities, which have mostly not had a long history, such traditions are rarely aged in the wood.

Less dignified than tradition, and less old, but of a fascinating diversity, are those bits of folklore which circulate among students. A few years ago there walked upon this very spot a marvellous being, a student who defied the school authorities, laughed when the principal flogged him, finally ran away from home and has never been seen again. There was formerly a teacher in this school who was so near-sighted that the boys played leap-frog in the rear of the classroom. Such and such a teacher has a glass eye. The principal has an artificial foot. A certain male teacher once killed a man in a boxing bout. Much of this folklore centers about teachers. By its spread to adults, which occurs only occasionally, it gives rise to some of the fantastic gossip concerning teachers which circulates in the small town.

The cultural anthropologists have taught us to analyze the actions of human beings living in a certain culture into culture patterns. Those partially formalized structures of behavior known as "activities" will serve as excellent examples of culture patterns existing in the school. Among the "activities" to be found in most public schools may be mentioned athletics, work on the school paper, oratory and debating, glee club work, Hi-Y work, dramatics, participation in social clubs, departmental clubs, literary societies, fraternities, etc. Each of these activities may be thought of as representing a more or less ritualized form of behavior carried out by the individual as a member of a group and, often, a representative of the larger group. There is a set form for these activities. There is merit in these activities, and that merit seems to rest ultimately upon the notion that group welfare and group prestige are involved in them; the honor of the high school is damaged if the team loses. ("Our team is our fame protector, On boys, for we expect a touchdown from you—"is unpoetic, but explicit on this point.) But there is intrinsic, irrational merit in them, too, as in the trading of the Trobiand Islanders. There is distinction in these activities for individuals. That distinction rests in part upon the prominence which participation in them gives the individual in the eyes of the school at large, and in part upon the recognition which the adult group accords them. The variety of activities is almost endless, for each of the activities mentioned above has many sub-divisions; these subdivisions are sometimes arranged in something of a hierarchy as in athletics, where the greatest distinction attaches to football, a little less to basketball, less yet to baseball and track. These activities are commonly justified on the grounds that they actually prepare for life, since they present actual life situations; their justification for the faculty is in their value as a means of control over restless students. It is noteworthy that a competitive spirit prevails in nearly all activities. Not all activities are really competitive, but the struggle for places may make them so, and the desirability of having some place in some school activity makes the competition for places keen. One "makes" the school orchestra or glee club quite as truly as one makes the football team.

These culture patterns of activities are partly artificial and faculty-determined, and partly spontaneous. In so far as they have been evolved by the faculty, they have been intended as means of control, as outlets for adolescent energies or substitutes for tabooed activities. They represent also the faculty's attempt to make school life interesting and to extend the influence of the school. Any activity, however, which is to affect the life of students at all deeply, any activity, then, which aspires to a greater influence than is exerted by the Latin Club or the Cercle Français, must have a spontaneous basis, and must appeal to students by presenting to them behavior patterns of considerable intrinsic interest. Each activity usually has some sort of faculty connection, and the status of the faculty adviser is thought to rise or fall with the prosperity or unprosperity of the activity which he promotes. Activities, then, increase in importance and gain recognition from the faculty through the efforts of interested faculty members, as well as through their own intrinsic appeal to students.

Further Readings

BECKER, HOWARD S., "The Career of the Chicago Public School Teacher," *American Journal of Sociology*, vol. 57 (1952), pp. 470–477.

COLEMAN, JAMES S., *The Adolescent Society*. New York: The Free Press of Glencoe, 1961.

GORDON, CALVIN W., *The Social System of the High School*. New York: The Free Press of Glencoe, 1957.

HOLLINGSHEAD, AUGUST B., *Elmtown's Youth*. New York: John Wiley & Sons, Inc., 1949.

LASSWELL, HAROLD D., "The Language of Power," in Lasswell, Harold D. and Nathan Leites and Associates, *Language of Politics*. New York: George W. Stewart, 1949, pp. 3–19.

PECK, ROBERT F., and ROBERT J. HAVIGHURST and ASSOCIATES, *The Psychology of Character Development*. New York: John Wiley & Sons, Inc., 1960.

Questions for Discussion

1. To what extent do athletics teach educational values? To what extent do they merely offer diversion or respite from the educational goals of the school?
2. What are the possible effects of winning or losing upon the total school?
3. What are the possible effects of winning or losing on the individual?

JAMES S. COLEMAN

Athletics in High School*

The greatest contribution physical education makes to school tradition is through the athletic program. Athletics promote students' identification with their schools, for competition with outsiders seems to draw the institution together in spirit as well as in purpose.

Through athletic participation students gain many qualities for effective citizenry. Adherence to the rules, which is essential to most games, carries over to the social order. Fair play and respect for the rights of others constitute a part of the planned athletic program. Certain conflicts do exist, however, as the next article suggests. One conflict is that students are

* Reprinted with permission of the author and the publisher from *The Annals of the American Academy of Political and Social Science*, vol. 338, November 1961, pp. 33–43.

urgently prompted to fight for alma mater, yet are punished if they do so in a manner contrary to stated rules. Detrimental effects of athletic participation should also be noted by the reader.

Coleman recognizes some of the social values generated by athletic events, but he suggests that the organization used for athletic games could be put to better use by debating teams or other "intellectual" groups. As one reads this article, he should ask himself the question: What in the culture of the school makes for such interest in athletic games and *not* in the debate?

The role of interscholastic athletics in high schools is a controversial one. Athletics is castigated as the antithesis of scholastic activity by intellectuals—many of whom have never taken part in interscholastic sports. It is defended and praised as the builder of men by coaches and athletes—most of whom have a vested interest in this proposition.

It is characteristic of athletics to provoke violent and lasting controversies, for it occupies a very special position in high schools. The amount of attention devoted to athletics would be most striking to an innocent visitor to a high school. A visitor entering a school would likely be confronted, first of all, with a trophy case. His examination of the trophies would reveal a curious fact: The gold and silver cups, with rare exception, symbolize victory in athletic contests, not scholastic ones. The figures adorning these trophies represent men passing footballs, shooting basketballs, holding out batons; they are not replicas of "The Thinker." The concrete symbols of victory are old footballs, basketballs, and baseballs, not works of art or first editions of books won as literary prizes. Altogether, the trophy case would suggest to the innocent visitor that he was entering an athletic club, not an educational institution.

Walking further, this visitor would encounter teen-agers bursting from classrooms. Listening to their conversations, he would hear both casual and serious discussions of the Friday football game, confirming his initial impression. Attending a school assembly that morning, he would probably find a large segment of the program devoted to a practice of school yells for the athletic game and the announcement of a pep rally before the game. At lunch hour, he would be likely to find more boys shooting baskets in the gymnasium than reading in the library. Browsing through a school yearbook, he would be impressed in his innocence, with the number of pages devoted to athletics.

Altogether, this visitor would find, wherever he turned, a great deal of attention devoted to athletics. As an impressionable stranger, this visitor might well suppose that more attention is paid to athletics by teen-agers, both as athletes and as spectators, than to scholastic matters. He might even conclude, with good reason, that the school was essentially organized around athletic contests and that scholastic matters were of lesser importance to all involved.

To be sure, his impression would vary from school to school—but, perhaps surprising to him, it would vary little by the social origins and destinations of the adolescents served by the schools. In ten schools recently studied by the author, athletics was about as dominant, by any of several criteria, in middle class schools with a high proportion of their graduates going to college as in working class schools.[1]

Considering his impressions, such a visitor to American high schools might ask himself two questions: First of all, why is it this way? He had assumed, naively, that schools were for learning, yet his impressions led to a different conclusion. He had talked with educators about curriculum, new academic programs, and scholastic standards. Yet, upon visiting the schools, he found the adolescents' attention on athletics, and all the excitement and enthusiasm he found was focused around athletic contests. Why the discrepancy?

The visitor might ask another question: What are the consequences of the attention devoted to athletics? What are the consequences within the school itself, and what are the long-term consequences for these adolescents when they have become adults?

It is to these two questions, the question of consequences and the question of sources, that this paper is directed. The examination will be based upon evidence collected during a study of ten high schools in 1957–1958. These high schools were located in the Middle West. Five were small-town schools with 500 or fewer students; one was a parochial school of 750 boys in a large city; there was a working class, suburban school of 1,000 students; two small-city

[1] See James S. Coleman, *The Adolescent Society* (Glencoe: The Free Press, 1961), pp. 70–71, 88–90.

comprehensive schools were included of 1,400 and 2,000 students respectively; there was an upper middle class, suburban school of 2,000 students. Unless otherwise noted, the generalizations mentioned below apply to all schools.[2] In fact, a striking discovery in this study was the similarity of all schools in the importance attached to athletics. Greater similarity among schools was found in this than in any other dimension of the research.

Consequences

The more difficult question concerns the long-term consequences of attention to athletics. On this question, the study has no evidence, since adolescents were studied only during one year in high school, and there seems to be no systematic evidence on the matter available elsewhere. However, evidence from the research does show some of the short-term consequences, those manifest in the school itself.

IMPACT ON FRESHMEN

The attention focused upon athletics in high schools directly affects the impact of the schools upon their incoming freshmen. Football, which is played in the fall as school begins, is especially important. A major element in the impact of athletics is the visibility of athletic stars. A boy who achieves something, however creditable his achievement, can be a model to emulate only if that achievement is made visible by the structure of activities in the school.

Some idea of the relative visibility of scholastic achievement and athletic achievement can be gained through a finding from the survey of the ten schools. About six weeks after school opened in the fall, each boy in every school was asked to name the boy whom he saw as the best student in his grade and the boy who was the best athlete. This can be a difficult task for freshmen, but it is less difficult in those areas for which school activities focus attention on achievement. Thus, a comparison of the proportions of boys able to answer the questions provides some guide to the relative visibility

[2] In certain cases, random variation due to the small number of students in the smallest school prevents separate conclusions about it.

of scholastic and athletic achievements in each of the four years of school.

Table 1 shows this comparison. The data indicate, in general,

Table 1

COMPARATIVE VISIBILITY OF BEST ATHLETES AND BEST SCHOLARS
TO THEIR CLASSMATES[a]

	Freshmen	Sophomores	Juniors	Seniors
Small Schools:				
Percent naming best athlete	68	75	88	85
Percent naming best scholar	58	66	83	88
Number of cases	317	292	214	205
Large Schools:				
Percent naming best athlete	54	56	48	72
Percent naming best scholar	40	47	57	68
Number of cases	635	1,049	749	557

[a] Percentages are based on the nine public schools.

that the best athletes are more visible than the best scholars. The difference is greatest for the freshmen—the best athlete is known 10 per cent more often than the best scholar in the small schools and 14 per cent more often in the large schools. Only in the junior and senior years does the visibility of the best scholars catch up with that of the best athletes. Thus, for the impressionable freshmen, the achievements that stand out most are those of the athlete, not those of the scholar.[3]

Assuming adolescents desire to be successful, known, and recognized, one consequence of the visibility of achievement in athletics or scholarship would be the desire to achieve in these particular areas. Does the environment and climate of opinion in the school affect these desires? Boys were asked, in the fall shortly after school had started and again in the spring toward the end of the school year, how they would most like to be remembered at school—as a brilliant student, an athletic star, or most popular. One would suppose, if schools focus attention on scholastic endeavors, that the effect of the school year would be to increase the strength of the brilliant-student image relative to that of the athletic-star image. Yet, for the freshmen and sophomores of the schools surveyed, mat-

[3] Other areas of achievement were included in the questionnaire, for example, knowing about cars and being most attractive to the girls. The visibility for both of these was far below that for athletes or scholars.

ters are quite different. Of all those responding either "brilliant student" or "athletic star," 44 per cent in each grade responded "brilliant student" in the fall and only 37 per cent gave this response in the spring.[4] Rather than increasing in strength over the school year, the brilliant-student image declined in strength relative to that of the athlete. It appears, then, that the very functioning of the school itself tends to reduce the initial interest of the adolescent in being seen as a brilliant student, or tends differentially to increase his interest in being seen as an athletic star.

Another effect of athletics upon the incoming freshmen concerns the "leading crowd" in school. Most high schools, other than the very smallest, have a leading crowd in each grade, though schools larger than about 2,000 in enrollment may have more than one. This crowd is recognized by other students and by its own members, and most students can name members of the leading crowd in their grade. This, in fact, was what they were asked to do in the research discussed above. In addition, all boys were asked to name their friends, so that it was possible to reconstruct the actual crowds or cliques in the school. Then, by identifying which of the cliques had as members boys frequently named as members of the leading crowd, it was possible to identify objectively the leading clique or crowd in each grade of each school. Having done this, the question then was asked: What do these boys, who constitute the leading crowds in their grades, have in common?[5]

Among the freshmen in each of the four schools studied for leading cliques, the one attribute shared by every boy in every leading clique—twenty-three boys in all—was being out for either football or basketball. Most of the twenty-three were out for both. No other attribute—in background, activities, or attitudes—so sharply distinguished the leading cliques. In the later years of school, the leading cliques were found to be less uniformly athletic, but, among freshmen, they were found to be totally so.

Athletic participation as a basis for membership in the leading clique is not, of course, characteristic of every freshman class in the country, but it seems likely that the general tendency is widespread.

[4] The number of cases was over 800 in each grade, so the difference reported is significant beyond the .001 level.
[5] This question was studied only in four of the five smallest schools; technical problems prevented it in the large schools, and the smallest school had no distinct crowds.

Sociological Backgrounds

Athletic teams provide a basis for intensive and prolonged association, more than any other activity in school. Thus, the foundation is laid, from the very beginning of high school, for a cohesive, tightly knit group. This, together with the attention directed toward athletic contests and athletic stars in high school, makes it very likely that the athletes will constitute the leading crowd among freshmen. Later, when other activities develop in school and groups form on other bases, there is less dominance of the athletic crowd. But, in the crucial first year, when a boy's aims and aspirations in high school are established, the athletic crowd dominates.

Altogether, then, athletics is a particularly important factor in the impact of the high school upon its freshmen. Through the several mechanisms discussed above, the freshmen get a picture of the school focused even more toward athletic achievement than it actually is.

ATHLETICS IN THE STATUS SYSTEM

One of the most important aspects of any social system is its distribution of status: the way status attaches to different persons and to different activities. The importance of the distribution of status lies partly in its effect as a motivating device, for it motivates people toward those activities which confer status upon them. To the extent that adolescents are concerned with status among their peers—and every indication suggests that the great majority of them are so motivated—their motivations and aspirations in various activities are shaped by the distribution of status.

It is important, then, in assessing the consequences of the attention to athletics in high schools, to examine the position of athletics in the adolescent status system. In the present research, this was done by several means.

Each boy was asked to assess what was required in his school to be a member of the leading crowd, and he was asked to rank various attributes for making a boy popular.

In response to the first question, the two attributes most often mentioned were personality—mentioned by 23 per cent of the boys—and a good reputation—mentioned by 17 per cent. Next in order, however, was athletic ability—mentioned by 16 per cent. This was followed by good looks and success with girls—mentioned by 14 per cent—and good grades or "brains"—mentioned by 12 per cent.

In ranking attributes for their effect in making a boy popular, six attributes were available to be ranked from first to sixth. These attributes, with their average rank in all schools, were the following:[6]

Being an athletic star	2.2
Being in the leading crowd	2.6
Leader in activities	2.9
High grades, honor roll	3.5
Having a nice car	3.9
Coming from the right family	4.5

These answers show the great value that boys attribute to athletic achievement in gaining popularity. It is ranked considerably above any other item and far above good grades, which is fourth among the six.

In addition to these subjective estimates, it is also possible to determine which boys have highest status. In this research, it was done by asking each boy to name another boy he would like to be like, one he would like to be friends with, and who were members of the leading crowd. The status of a boy was determined by the number of such choices he received. Another question had made it possible to identify the boys seen as the best athletes and the best scholars. By comparing the likelihood of the best athletes to receive the status choices with the likelihood of the best scholars to receive such choices, it is possible to examine the objective status of athletic achievement. Table 2 shows the average number of choices on these

Table 2

AVERAGE NUMBERS OF CHOICES RECEIVED BY ATHLETES, SCHOLARS, AND ALL OTHER BOYS ON STATUS CRITERIA[a]

	Be friends with or be like	Member of leading crowd	Number of cases
Athletes	5.6	7.8	272
Scholars	3.4	4.9	278
All Other Boys	0.4	0.8	3,598

a "Athletes" and "scholars" are those named two or more times as best athlete or best scholar in their respective grades by other boys. Percentages are based on the nine public schools.

6 The ranks average to 3.3 rather than 3.5 as they should, because not every boy assigned all ranks.

criteria received by the best athletes, the best scholars, and all other boys in the schools studied.

As in various other tests, athletics scored higher than scholarship, although both athletes and scholars far outdistanced other boys. Stated another way, the star athletes, only 6.6 per cent of the schools' male enrollment, received 47.4 per cent of the "be friends with" and "be like" choices and 36.5 per cent of all the leading crowd nominations.

According to all evidence, then, the status of athletic achievement in the schools surveyed is exceedingly high, considerably higher than that of scholastic achievement. Thus, the attention paid to athletics in American high schools, which would so puzzle an innocent visitor, is paralleled by the status of athletic achievement among adolescents.

OTHER STUDIES

Other research shows that these facts are not limited to the ten schools surveyed nor even to high schools in the Middle West.

In a large, predominantly Jewish, middle class high school in New York City, Abraham Tannenbaum studied evaluations of stereotyped, fictitious students.[7] These fictitious students were distinguished in short descriptive statements on the bases of intelligence, athletic ability, and studiousness. Juniors in the high school were then asked to ascribe traits—some desirable, some undesirable—to each of the eight fictitious characters. Tannenbaum devised a mean acceptability rating from the ascribed traits, and the fictitious students fell in the following order of acceptability, from high to low:

(1) Brilliant nonstudious athlete
(2) Average nonstudious athlete
(3) Average studious athlete
(4) Brilliant studious athlete
(5) Brilliant nonstudious athlete
(6) Average nonstudious nonathlete
(7) Average studious nonathlete
(8) Brilliant studious nonathlete

---

[7] Abraham J. Tannenbaum, "Adolescents' Attitudes Toward Academic Brilliance" (unpublished Ph.D. dissertation, New York University, 1960).

As the order shows, all athletes had higher acceptability ratings than any nonathlete. Brilliance apparently had little effect in increasing acceptability, and studiousness reduced acceptability. Thus, in a school in which, because of its location and student body, one would expect to find brilliance or studiousness outdistancing athletics, the results are otherwise—and consistent with the results in the ten midwestern high schools.

These data on the status of athletic achievement in schools of widely varying types raise even more insistently the question of why there is such a dominance of athletics. Athletics is wholly outside the focus of attention of many educators in schools of education, for whom curriculum variations have overriding importance. Yet athletics is central to the attention of adolescents, far more so than curriculum variations. And, despite educators' professional disinterest, athletics is an activity promoted by the schools themselves—not an outside interest like cars and dates. These inconsistencies and paradoxes all lead to the question: Why does athletics hold a place of such high importance in the high schools?

ATHLETICS, DEMOCRACY, AND LEGITIMACY OF THE SYSTEM

The effect of athletics in forming leading crowds among freshmen was examined earlier; the formation of leading crowds among girls was left unexamined. The cliques of girls among freshmen reflect, much more than for boys, associations from earlier grades. Girls who travel together in the lower grades maintain their cliques in high school and often present an impregnable front to outsiders. Presumably as a result, the leading crowds for girls among freshmen are more completely middle class in background than for boys.

In effect, athletics provides for boys an interruption of this pattern, breaking down the organization based on common background and replacing it with organization based on common activity or achievement. Perhaps as a consequence, boys are more willing than girls to accept the status system of the school and view it as more legitimate. When asked to agree or to disagree that "There are a few who control things in this school, and the rest of us are out in the cold," 43 per cent of the girls agreed with the statement in the fall, and the number increased to 48 per cent by the next spring.

Only 34 per cent of the boys agreed that the statement was true in the fall, and their number decreased to 32 per cent by spring.

Such a democratizing mechanism is particularly important for boys, who, to begin with, are less involved in school than girls and get poorer grades. If it were not for interscholastic athletics or something like it, the rebellion against school, the rate of dropout, and the delinquency of boys might be far worse than they presently are. This can only be a matter of conjecture. It does seem clear, however, that athletics introduces an important democratizing factor in the status system for boys in high school by undercutting social background as a basis for status.

Sources

Clearly, a part of the importance of athletics for adolescents lies in its compatibility with teen-age energy, enthusiasm, and explosive spirits. Were it not for this basic compatibility, the avidity with which teen-agers follow sports contests would be difficult to explain.

But the compatibility does not explain the special place that athletics holds in the activities of a school. As an innocent visitor might observe, the institution itself often seems more oriented toward athletic goals than academic ones. This can hardly be explained by the interests of teen-agers alone, for teen-agers are interested in many things—popular music, cars, dates—which have relatively little place in the high school structure of activities. Nor can the interests of teen-agers explain the fact that, in the ten schools surveyed, the strength of the athletic-star image increased during the school year and, apparently, decreased over the summer.[8]

Athletic contests in schools seem to serve an important function for the institution. Every institution depends for its survival upon capturing a certain portion of the energies of its members. In business organizations, this is done by pay, including incentive pay, and by opportunity for promotion. Among some members of an organization, identification with the achievements of the organization provides additional motivation. In unions, motivation derives from the common goals of the members, which can only be gained through concerted, collective effort.[9]

---

[8] For further discussion of this point, see Coleman, *op. cit.*, p. 303.

[9] When a union becomes merely a business union, no longer actively fighting for collective worker benefits, it survives in name, but it can no longer depend upon its members for active support. This, in fact, is the fundamental problem of many unions at the present time.

Schools, however, provide no comparable motivating devices for their students. Students are forced by family and by law to attend school, but this insures only their physical presence, not their involvement in school activities. The necessary motivation for the expenditure of effort in school arises naturally only for those students whose backgrounds and aspirations make good grades important for them. For some students, that is, grades are comparable to pay for workers in a factory. The crucial difference is that grades are important only for a part of the school population. For many adolescents, high school only delays their access to adult freedoms and pleasures and does not offer any unique and necessary benefits.

But, even for students with the right backgrounds, grades are a poor motivating mechanism, because they are unique to the school and useful only in comparison with grades of fellow students. This generates invidious comparisons, sets each student in competition with his fellows, and is a powerfully divisive force among the students. Direct incentive pay, or piece work, in factories produces the same effect and has sometimes been consciously used by employers to keep employees divided against each other.[10]

In the long run, this is a dangerous mechanism, as the history of incentive pay has shown. Under many conditions, it encourages informal norms restricting production—against the "rate-buster"— just as grade systems in high schools promote informal action against too much studiousness—against "the curve-breaker" or the "D.A.R.," Damned Average Raiser. Finally, piece work systems in factories have led to organized collective activity against the companies, unless the workers feel strongly identified with their companies.[11]

A much more successful mechanism of control in an institution is one which generates strong positive identification with the institution. Churches employ such mechanisms with their revival meet-

---

10 This can be illustrated by the story, perhaps apocryphal, of the employer who paid every second worker on an assembly line a higher rate, so that every worker's neighbors received rates different from his own. A similar mechanism has been documented in department stores, where clerks are given marginal differentiations in title and pay to keep them divided. See Carl Dreyfuss, "Prestige Grading: A Mechanism of Control," in R. K. Merton and Others, *Reader in Bureaucracy* (Glencoe: The Free Press, 1952), pp. 258–264.

11 One of the important reasons that incentive pay, in the form of commissions, has always worked well for salesmen is that their active work in selling the company products to doubtful customers generates in them a positive identification with the company. Another reason, of course, is that they are usually dispersed, not in contact with one another.

ings and special holy day services. Associations and groups of all sorts do the same with rallies and collective events. But schools— apart from their athletic contests and similar activities—are peculiar institutions. There are no collective goals which the students share, and the institution is lifeless. There are only individual goals, individual scholastic achievements, made largely at the expense of other students.

Athletic contests with other schools provide, for these otherwise lifeless institutions, the collective goals that they lack. The common goals shared by all makes the institution part of its members and them part of it, rather than an organization outside them and superimposed upon them. The results are evident to any observer: The adolescent social system is centered at the school, not at the drugstore; the name by which the teen-agers identify themselves is that of the school ("Those are East High kids; I'm from Tech."); the teen-agers think of the school, the team, and the student body as one and use the pronoun "we" in referring to this entity ("We're playing Parkville Friday.").

Such effects are evident as well in the bases of alumni loyalty to many private preparatory schools and colleges. Athletic competition as a basis of loyalty is so dominant that the stereotypical alumnus is a man cheering wildly at a football game, waving a school banner in his hand. Colleges which dropped interscholastic athletics, like University of Chicago, or which never depended on them, like Johns Hopkins, thereby sacrificed the attention and support of many alumni.[12] Historians have noted that colleges in the United States, before the introduction of organized sports, were beset by student violence directed at both the college and other students. Sports seemed to transform the disorganized and explosive student body into a close-knit community with strong common goals.

Thus, the importance of athletic contests in both high schools and colleges lies, at least in part, in the way the contests solve a difficult problem for the institution—the problem of generating enthusiasm for and identification with the school and drawing the energies of adolescents into the school.

[12] This is not to say that the absence of athletic emphasis in these institutions has principally bad consequences. Many colleges have, rather, compromised their original goals through the power and interest of their athletically involved alumni. But the withdrawal from interscholastic athletics without the substitution of other bases for institution-inspired pride and identification leaves the institution weaker and less likely to survive.

In the study of the ten high schools upon which much of this paper is based, all students were asked, "If school were not compulsory and it were completely up to you, would you stay in school until graduation, leave school before graduation, or are you undecided? Very few students, only 3.6 per cent, responded that they would leave, and only 9.3 per cent were undecided. It is hard to imagine that the great body of adolescents in our society which has been brought into high school in such a short period could be so positively oriented to school without some mechanism such as athletic contests for providing common goals.[13]

LACK OF COMMON COMMUNITY GOALS

A force which strengthens the emphasis upon athletics in the high schools comes from outside the schools themselves. Except in the very largest cities, a high school is a community or neighborhood institution. Many communities have only a single high school, whose name is the name of the town. In those cities with several high schools, each school usually represents a community area within the city and often carries the name of that community.

Communities, like schools without interscholastic games, have few common goals. They fight no wars, seldom engage in community rallies, and are rarely faced with such crises as floods or tornadoes that can engender a communal spirit and make members feel close to one another by creating collective goals. One of the few mechanisms by means of which this can occur is that of games or contests between communities. Sometimes these games are between professional teams representing the communities.[14] More often, there are high school games, and these contests serve the purpose admirably. The community supports the team, and the team rewards the community when it wins. The team is a community enterprise, and its successes are shared by the community, its losses mourned in concert.

[13] This suggests that high schools in Europe, which are coming to enroll larger and larger proportions of adolescents, will increase the emphasis upon athletic contests, unless they find another mechanism to accomplish the same end.

[14] The sense of shock and disbelief in Brooklyn when the Dodgers moved to Los Angeles is a measure of Brooklynites' identification of the team with their community. On the other side, it has been said that Los Angeles ceased to be a collection of surburbs and became a city for the first time when "their" Dodgers won a pennant.

The results of this are evident in many ways. One striking evidence is teacher salaries. The school board characteristically pays more to athletic coaches than to other teachers and, occasionally, to keep a winning coach, may pay more than to the principal. When a new principal is to be found among the ranks of teachers, the pattern is common for the athletic coach to be promoted to the job.[15]

Another indicator is buildings. It is often easier to obtain funds for a new gymnasium—especially in "basketball territory"—than for other buildings. In Paris, Illinois, for example, where the high school team won the state basketball tournament a few years ago, the community voted funds for a large new gymnasium, while the high school remained without a library. In one of the ten schools included in the survey, the author found, returning in 1961, that a new gymnasium and a new reading room had been built. Funds for the gymnasium had been donated by a member of the community; the reading room had been added by means of school building funds.

Substitutes for Athletics

It is indisputable that the interscholastic sports function to give the school and the community a collective identity. Few principals would seriously consider dispensing with these games. Yet, it is also indisputable that athletic contests create serious problems for schools. Perhaps the most serious problem is the change they engender in the institution itself. Their very importance to the life of the school transforms the school from an institution devoted to learning into an institution focused, at least partly, on athletics.

It is useful to wonder whether another mechanism might not give the school collective goals without effecting this transformation. Completely to replace athletic contests between schools with something else would possibly have ill effects. To reduce the dominance of athletics in high schools, however, clearly would be desirable. The most obvious course is to keep the game but to

---

[15] This pattern is being replaced by a pattern of promoting assistant principals or guidance counselors, who have administrative training in schools of education. There is no evidence that they make better principals than coaches do.

change the content in the direction of educational goals. Although it is true that athletics fits especially well with the interests and energies of adolescents, other games could fit equally well.

There is some experience with games and contests other than athletics, the most extensive being with debate. In a number of areas where debate leagues have flourished, these contests have generated some of the same community and school enthusiasm and involvement that is evident with athletic games. In a few states, interscholastic leagues promotes competition in fields other than athletics: music, drama, mathematics. Although the effects of these contests have not been adequately evaluated, they do provide examples of what might be done.

There has very recently been another development which promises to make games truly educational in many areas. These are social and economic games which use a complex environment provided by electronic computers. The first to be developed were management games which involve teams of decision-makers representing competing firms. These games have been used by business and are coming to be used in graduate business schools. A political game, with teams representing political candidates in competition for votes, has been programed for a computer and is used in a college course at Johns Hopkins. At least one economic game has been developed—at Washington University in St. Louis—for teaching the course in principles of economics. Experience with these games shows that they generate a high degree of involvement and interest among players and spectators. It is possible that the most valuable use of machines in education will come to be their use for games, rather than programed learning.

These examples indicate that it is possible to change the content of games in an educational direction yet to maintain some of the values athletics provides for school. To do this, however, would require more than sporadic contests. To gain attention and involvement, leagues, schedules, and tournaments would be necessary. Through such means, it might be possible to transform schools back into the educational institutions they were intended to be. An innocent visitor to such an institution, upon examining the trophy case, listening to student conversation, and examining a yearbook, might well conclude that the institution was one devoted to learning.

Further Readings

ALLISON, DAVIS, "Socialization and Adolescent Personality," in *Adolescence*, Forty-Third Yearbook, National Society for the Study of Education, Part I. New York: Harper & Row, publishers, 1944, Chapter 12.

COZENS, FREDRICK W. and FLORENCE STUMPF, *Sports in American Life*. Chicago: University of Chicago Press, 1953.

PARSONS, TALCOTT, *The Social System*. New York: The Free Press of Glencoe, 1951.

Questions for Discussion

1. What does Coleman think about the place of athletics in comparison with that of "intellectual" pursuits in the high school?

2. If so prominent a sociologist as Coleman holds this disparaging point of view toward athletics, what do you believe other, possibly less knowledgeable, people think about the athletic program in a high school?

3. What is your critical view of this article? Implicit in Coleman's writing is a bias, can you identify it and can you suggest steps that physical educators might take to dispel some of these misconceptions?

4. What do you believe would be the effects of substituting debate teams for athletic teams in a high school?

5. Why does the athletic program serve as a major function in motivation? Does this motivation have any influence upon students to do better in their "academic work"? If so, describe.

WILLIAM T. FOSTER

An Indictment of
Intercollegiate Athletics*

The cultural ceremonies that occur in athletic events further the image and traditions of the school. The coach can greatly influence the ceremonies, faculty, and student body of the school. The student should read this "indictment" with attention, for it is, in a sense, an indictment of his profession. Foster's charges should not be rejected without proper study, for many of his criticisms are in complete accord with the principles of modern physical education.

Foster questions how physical education and athletics can be educationally defensible and still constitute a business satisfying to the alumni but not the faculty. It is significant that much of the criticism he leveled at intercollegiate athletics forty years ago remains pertinent today.

I

Intercollegiate athletics provide a costly, injurious, and excessive régime of physical training for a few students, especially those who need it least, instead of inexpensive, healthful, and moderate exercise for all students, especially those who need it most.

Athletics are conducted either for education or for business. The old distinction between amateur and professional athletics is of little use. The real problems of college athletics loom large beside the considerations that define our use of the terms 'professional' and 'amateur.' The aims of athletics reveal the fact that the important distinctions are between athletics conducted for educational purposes and athletics conducted for business purposes.

* Reprinted with permission of the publisher from *The Atlantic Monthly*, vol. 116, no. 5, November 1915, pp. 577–587.

When athletics are conducted for education the aims are (1) to develop all the students and faculty physically and to maintain health; (2) to promote moderate recreation, in the spirit of joy, as a preparation for study rather than as a substitute for study; and (3) to form habits and inculcate ideals of right living. When athletics are conducted for business, the aims are (1) to win games—to defeat another person or group being the chief end; (2) to make money—as it is impossible otherwise to carry on athletics as business; (3) to attain individual or group fame and notoriety. These three—which are the controlling aims of intercollegiate athletics—are also the aims of horse-racing, prize-fighting, and professional baseball.

These two sets of aims are in sharp and almost complete conflict. Roughly speaking, success in attaining the aims of athletics as education is inversely proportional to success in attaining the aims of athletics as business. Intercollegiate athletics to-day are for business. The question is pertinent whether schools and colleges should promote athletics as business.

Nearly all that may be said on this subject about colleges applies to secondary schools. The lower schools as a rule tend to imitate the worst features of intercollegiate athletics, much as the young people of fraternities, in their 'social functions,' tend to imitate the empty lives of their elders that fill the weary society columns of the newspapers.

If the objection arises that intercollegiate athletics have educational value, there is no one to deny it. 'Athletics for education' and 'athletics for business' are general terms, used throughout this discussion as already defined. Exceptions there may be: only the main tendencies are here set forth. The whole discussion is based on my personal observations at no less than one hundred universities and colleges in thirty-eight states during the past five years.

The most obvious fact is that our system of intercollegiate athletics, after unbounded opportunity to show what it can do for the health, recreation, and character of *all* our students, has proved a failure. The ideal of the coach is excessive training of the few: he best attains the business ends for which he is hired by the neglect of those students in greatest need of physical training. Our present system encourages most students to take their athletics by proxy. When we quote with approval the remark of the Duke of Wellington that Waterloo was won on the playing grounds of Eton, we should observe that he did not maintain that Waterloo was won on the grandstands of Eton.

What athletics may achieve without the hindrance of intercollegiate games and business motives is suggested by the experience of Reed College. There the policy of athletics for everybody was adopted five years ago before there were any teachers, students, alumni, or traditions. Last year all but six of the students took part in athletics in the spirit of sport for the sake of health, recreation, and development. Sixty per cent of the men of the college, including the faculty, took part in a schedule of sixteen baseball games. Nearly all the students, men and women alike, played games at least twice a week. There were series of contests in football, baseball, track, tennis, volley-ball, basket-ball, and other out-of-door sports. All of this, according to the report of the athletic association, cost the students an average of sixteen cents apiece. No money for coaches and trainers; no money for badges, banners, cups, and other trinkets; no money for training-tables and railroad fares; no money for grandstands, rallies, brass bands, and advertising. Fortunately, it is the unnecessary expenses that heap up the burdens—the cost of athletics as business. The economical policy is athletics for everybody—athletics for education.

II

Opposed to the three educational aims are the aims of athletics as business—winning games, making money, and getting advertised.

Almost invariably the arguments of students in favor of intercollegiate games stress the business aims and ignore all others. Win games! Increase the gate-receipts! Advertise the college! These are the usual slogans. Thus the editors of one college paper reprimand the faculty for even hesitating to approve a trip of fifteen hundred miles for a single game of football:—

'Contrary to the expectations of the students, the matter of the Occidental football game for next fall has not been acted upon as yet. That such an important matter as this has not received attention so far from the Faculty is unfortunate. While it is generally believed that the Faculty will act favorably in regard to letting the game be scheduled, it is understood that some opposition has developed on the ground that such a long trip would keep the football men away from their classes too long a time.

'From every point of view, there seems no reason why the game should not be played. To state any of the arguments in favor of the offer is unnecessary. Every one knows what it would mean to football next fall, the greater interest it would mean to the game, the incentive it would prove to every football man to work to become one of the seventeen men to take the trip, the advertising it would give to the college, and, perhaps most important, the drawing card it would be to bring new athletes to the college in the fall. These points and others are too well known to need pointing out and too evident to need proof.'

This is a typical football argument. It attempts to prove the necessity of the proposed trip by showing that it would tend to perpetuate the thing the value of which is under dispute.

In like vein the students of Cornell complain because the faculty did not grant an additional holiday in connection with the Pennsylvania football game. It is the familiar cry, 'Support the team! Win games! Advertise the college!'

'Our friends, the professors, will perforce hold forth in their accustomed cells from eight till one of that fair morning. The benches, no doubt, will derive great benefit therefrom. . . .

'We want the football team to have as much support as possible. The faculty should want the football team to have as much support as possible. The faculty should foster true Cornell spirit whenever it can honestly do so, and intercollegiate athletics is the greatest single thing that unites the different colleges into Cornell University. A victory over Penn would mean a lot for Cornell.'

After all, how important is this end for which such sacrifices are made? To hear the yelling of twenty thousand spectators, one might suppose this aim to be the only one of great importance in the life of the university. Yet who wins, who loses, is a matter of but momentary concern to any except a score or two of participants; whereas, if there is one thing that should characterize a university, it is its cheerful sacrifice of temporary for permanent gains,—in Dr. Eliot's fine phrase, its devotion to the durable satisfactions of life.

The making of money, through intercollegiate athletics, continues a curse, not only to institutions, but as well to individual players. Only childlike innocence or willful blindness need prevent American colleges from seeing that the rules which aim to maintain athletics on what is called an 'amateur' basis, by forbidding players to receive pay in money, are worse than useless because, while failing to prevent men from playing for pay, they breed deceit and hypocrisy. There are many ways of paying players for their services. Only one of these, and that the most honorable, is condemned.

There are many subterranean passages leading to every preparatory school notable for its athletes. By such routes, coaches, overzealous alumni, and other 'friends' of a college, reach the schoolboy athlete with offers beyond the scope of eligibility rules. Sometimes payments are made expressly for services as half-back, or short-stop, or hurdler, and no receipts taken, the pay continuing as long as the player helps to win games. Sometimes payments take a more insidious and more demoralizing form. The star athlete is appointed steward of a college clubhouse on ample pay, his duties being to sign checks once a month. Or his college expenses are paid in return for the labor of opening the chapel door, or ringing the bell, or turning out the lights.

Athletes may be paid for their services in other ways that escape the notice of the most conscientious faculties and athletic associations. But there are hundreds of boys who know that they are paid to win games and keep silent; they are hired both as athletes and as hypocrites.

The sporting editor of one of the leading daily papers said recently, 'It is well known that the Northwest colleges are at present simply outbidding one another in their desire to get the best athletes. Money is used like water. It is a mystery where they get it, but they do.'

So common is the practice of paying athletes that they sometimes apply to various colleges for bids. While I was acting as Registrar of Bowdoin College, I received a letter from a man asking how much we would guarantee to pay him for pitching on the college nine. I found out later that he had registered at one college, pitched a game for his class team, left his trunk at a second college awaiting their terms, and finally accepted the offer of a third college, where he played 'amateur' baseball for four years before joining one of the big league professional teams.

At the athletic rallies of a New England college, a loyal alumnus is often cheered for bringing so many star athletes to the college. Officially, the college does not know that he hires men to play on the college teams. And what is to prevent a graduate of the college or any other person from hiring athletes? All but futile are the rules governing professionalism. Is it not a worthy act to enable a boy to go to college? And shall he be denied such aid because he happens to be an athlete? No eligibility committee knows of all these benefactors or even has the right to question their motives. But the objectionable motives themselves can be eliminated by one act—the abolition of intercollegiate athletics. With the subordination of winning games as the chief end in athletics, falls also the money making aim and its attendant evils.

All the serious evils of college athletics centre about the gate-receipts, the grandstand, and the paid coach. Yet the aim of nearly every college appears to be to fasten these evils upon the institution by means of a costly concrete stadium or bowl, and by means of more and more money for coaches. When the alumni come forward to 'support their team,' they usually make matters worse. Typical of their attitude is a letter signed in Philadelphia last fall by some thirty graduates of a small college:—

'The team has just closed the most disastrous season in its history. . . . The alumni will coöperate cheerfully with the undergraduates in increasing the football levy. It only remains, then, to initiate a campaign for procuring the money. . . . We must depart from out time-worn precedents and give *more money for the coaches!* Alumni are tired of reading the accounts of useless defeats!'

The extent to which interest in athletics is deadened by paid coaches was shown last spring, when a track team from one university, after traveling over two hundred and fifty miles—at the expense of the student body—to compete with the team of another institution, took off their running shoes and went home because the *coaches* could not agree on the number of men who should participate in the games. Could there me a more abject sacrifice of the educational purposes of athletics? Consider the spectacle. A glorious afternoon in spring, a perfect playground, complete equipment in readiness, two score of eager youth in need of the health and recreation that come from sport pursued in the fine spirit of sport. Could anything keep them from playing? Nothing but the spirit of modern American intercollegiate athletics and the embodiment of that spirit, the paid coach, who knows that there is but one crime that he can commit—that of losing a contest.

The athletic policy of many an institution is determined by a commercial aim, the supposed needs of advertising, much as the utterances of many a newspaper are dictated by the business manager. But does the advertising gained through intercollegiate athletics injure or aid a college? At one railroad station I was greeted by a real-estate agent who offered to sell me 'on easy terms a lot in the most beautiful and rapidly growing city in America.' (Thus do I safely cover its identity.) Among the attractions, he mentioned the local college. He was proud of it; he said it had the best baseball team in the state. Apart from that he had not an intelligent idea about the institution, or any desire for ideas. The only building he had visited was the grandstand. He could not name a member of the faculty or a course of instruction. College advertising which gets no further than this is paid for at exorbitant rates.

The people of Tacoma discovered recently that college athletics conducted as a business are too costly. They brought college students 1400 miles to play a football game at Tacoma on Thanksgiving Day for the benefit of the Belgian refugees. The charitable object of the game was widely advertised and there was a large attendance. After they had paid the expenses of the 'amateur' teams, the coaches, and the advertising, they announced that there was nothing left for the Belgians.

A writer in the *North American Review* tries to justify the time spent by college boys in managing athletic teams on the plea that it is good training for business. He gives testimony to this effect from a graduate of two years' standing 'engaged in the wholesale coal business in one of the large New York towns.' Following the usual custom, this young graduate returns to his college and gives the admiring undergraduates the benefit of his wisdom, lest they be corrupted by the quaint notions of impractical professors. He has them guess what part of his college work has proved of greatest use; then he assures them that his best training came as manager of the baseball team. Such is the mature judgment of the coal-dealer. And such is the advice of alumni that makes undergraduates resolve anew not to allow their studies to interfere with their college education. But some people raise the question why a boy should be maintained in college for four years, at a great cost to society and to his parents, in order that he may gain a little business experience when he could gain so much more by earning his living.

The conflicts frequently arising between faculties and students over questions of intercollegiate athletics are the natural outcome of the independent control of a powerful agency with three chief

aims—winning games, making money, and getting advertised—
which are antagonistic to the chief legitimate ambitions of a university faculty. No self-respecting head of a department of psychology would tolerate the presence in the university of persons
working in his field, in no way subject to him and with aims sub-
versive of those of the department. No professor of physical education should tolerate a similar condition in his department. It is
one of the hopeful signs in America that several of the men best
qualified to conduct athletics as education have declined to consider university positions, unless they could have control of students, teams, coaches, alumni committees, grandstands, fields,
finances, and everything else necessary to rescue athletics from the
clutches of commercialism.

I have read a letter from one of the ablest teachers in America,
declining to accept a certain university position under the usual
conditions, but outlining a plan whereby, as the real head of the
department of physical education, he might begin a new chapter in
the history of American athletics. His plan was rejected, not because it had any defects as a system of education, but solely because
it would cause a probable decline in victories, gate-receipts, and
newspaper space. That university continued the traditional dual
contest of coaches and physical directors with their conflicting
ideals. Recently I received a letter from the professor of physical
education who *did* accept the position, himself one of the ablest
athletes among its graduates, declaring that he would no longer
attempt the impossible, in an institution that deliberately prosti-
tuted athletics for commercial ends.

We hear much about the value of intercollegiate games for the
'tired business man' who needs to get out of doors and watch a
sport that will make him forget his troubles. It is true that for him
a game of baseball may be a therapeutic spectacle. The question is
whether institutions of learning should conduct their athletics—or
any other department—for the benefit of spectators. Doubtless university courses in history could provide recreation for the general
public and make money, if instruction were given wholly by means
of motion-pictures. But such courses would hardly satisfy the needs
of all students. Is it less important that departments of physical
education should be conducted primarily for all students rather
than for spectators? We do not insist that banks, railroads, factories,

department stores, and legislatures jeopardize their main functions
in order to provide recreation for the tired business man. Universities are institutions of equal importance to society, in so far as
they attend to their main purposes. Athletics for the benefit of the
grandstand must be conducted as business; athletics for the benefit
of students must be conducted as education.

III

It is when we rightly estimate the possibilities of athletics as education that the present tyranny of athletics as business becomes intolerable. Is it not an anomaly that those in charge of higher institutions of learning should leave athletic activities, which are of such
great potential educational value for *all* students, chiefly under the
control of students, alumni, coaches, newspapers, and spectators?
Usually the coach is engaged by the students, paid for by the students, and responsible only to them. He is not a member of the faculty or responsible to the faculty. The faculty have charge of the
college as an educational institution; athletics is for business and
therefore separately controlled. Why not abandon faculty direction
of Latin? Students, alumni, and newspapers are as well qualified
to elect a professor of Latin and administer the department in the
interests of education, as they are to elect coaches and administer
athletics in the interests of education.

A few of the more notable coaches of the country are aware of
the possibilities of athletics controlled by the faculty for educational purposes. Mr. Courtney, the Cornell coach, spoke to the
point when he said,—

'If athletics are not a good thing, they ought to be abolished.
If they are a good thing for the boys, it would seem to me wise
for the university to take over and control absolutely every branch
of sport; do away with this boy management; stop this foolish
squandering of money, and see that the athletics of the university
are run in a rational way.'

Next to the physical development and the maintenance of the
health of all the students and teachers of an institution, the main
purpose of athletics as education is to provide recreation as a preparation for study rather than as a substitute for study. But, intercollegiate athletics having won and retained unquestioned su-

premacy in our colleges, students do not tolerate the idea of a conflicting interest.

Even the nights preceding the great contests must be free from the interference of intellectual concerns. An editorial in one of our college weeklies makes this point clear. If a member of the faculty ventured to put the matter so extremely, he would be charged with exaggeration. But in this paper the students naïvely present their conviction that even the most signal opportunities for enjoying literature must be sacrified by the entire student body in order that they may get together and yell in preparation for their function of sitting in the grandstand. In this case the conflicting interest appeared in no less a person than Alfred Noyes. For a geographically isolated community to hear the poet was an opportunity of a college lifetime. Yet the students wrote as follows:—

The Rally *vs.* Noyes

'Returning alumni this year were somewhat surprised to find the Hall used for a lecture on the eve of our great gridiron struggle, and some were very much disappointed. The student body was only partially reconciled to the situation and was represented in great part by Freshmen [who were required to attend].'

The relative importance of intercollegiate athletics and other college affairs, in the minds of students, is indicated by student publications. There is no more tangible scale for measuring the interests of college youth than the papers they edit for their own satisfaction, unrestrained by the faculty.

Let us take two of the worthiest colleges as examples. The Bowdoin College *Orient,* a weekly publication, is typical. For the first nine weeks of the academic year 1914–15, the *Orient* gave 450 inches to intercollegiate athletics. For the same period, it devoted six inches to art, ten inches to social service, thirteen inches to music, and twelve inches to debating. Judging from this free expression, the students rate the interests of intercollegiate athletics nearly three times as high as the combined interests of art, music, religion, philosophy, social service, literature, debating, the curriculum and the faculty. Second in importance to intercollegiate athletics, valued at 450 inches, are dances and fraternities, valued at 78 inches.

Another possible measure of the student's interest is found in *Harvard of Today from an Undergraduate Point of View,* published in 1913 by the Harvard Federation of Territorial Clubs. The book gives to athletics ten pages; to the clubs, six pages; to debating, five lines,—and that student activity requires sustained thinking and is most closely correlated with the curriculum. The faculty escapes without mention. 'From an undergraduate point of view' the faculty appears to be an incumbrance upon the joys of college life.

These publications appear to be fair representatives of their class. It is probable, furthermore, that the relative attention given by the student papers to intellectual interests is a criterion of the conversation of students.

Not long ago, I spent some time with the graduate students at an Eastern university. Their conversation at dinner gave no evidence of common intellectual interests. They appeared to talk of little but football games.

On a visit to a Southern state university, I found the women's dormitory in confusion. The matron excused the noise and disorder on the ground that a big football game was pending and it seemed impossible for the girls to think of anything else.

'The big game comes to-morrow?' I asked.

'Oh, no, next week,' she said.

Last spring, at a large university on the Pacific Coast, I met one young woman of the freshman class who had already been to thirty-one dances that year. At a state university of the Middle West, I found that the students had decided to have their big football game on Friday instead of Saturday, in order to wrench one more day from the loose grip of the curriculum. When the faculty protested, the students painted on the walks, 'Friday is a holiday'—and it was.

Intellectual enthusiasm is rare in American colleges, and likely to be rarer still if social and athletic affairs continue to overshadow all other interests. Their dominance has given many a college faculty is characteristic attitude in matters of government. They assume that boys and girls will come to college for anything but studies. They tell new students just how many lectures in each course they may escape. A penalty of unsatisfactory work is the obligation to attend all the meetings on their schedule, and the usual reward for faithful conduct is the privilege of 'cutting' more lectures without a summons from the dean. Always the aim of students appears to be to escape as much as possible of the college life provided by the faculty, in order to indulge in more of the college life provided by themselves. Their inventive powers are marvelous; they bring forth an endless procession of devices for evading the opportunities for the sake of which (according to old-fashioned notions) students seek admission to college. The complacent acceptance of this condition by college faculties—the pervasive assumption that students have no genuine intellectual enthusiasm—tends to stagnation. In the realm of thought some appear to have discovered the secret of petrified motion.

The pronounced tendencies in higher education aggravate the disease. Feeble palliatives are used from time to time,—the baseball schedule in one college, after six hours of debate by the faculty, was cut down from twenty-four games to twenty-two,—but the bold and necessary surgeon seldom gets in his good work. When he does operate, he is hung in effigy or elected President of the United States.

Concerning the policy of no intercollegiate games at Clark College, President Sanford says: 'Our experience with this plan has been absolutely satisfactory and no change of policy would be considered. Doubtless some of the less intellectually serious among the students might like to see intercollegiate sports introduced. It is generally understood that in a three-year college there is not time for such extras.' The faculty appear to be unanimously in favor of no intercollegiate games, since the course at Clark College takes only three years. Intercollegiate contests appear to be ruled out chiefly on the ground that, in a three-year course, students cannot afford to waste time. But why is it worse for a young man to waste parts of three years of his student life than to waste parts of four years of it?

The educational effect of our exaggerated emphasis on intercollegiate athletics is shown in the attitude of alumni. It is difficult to arouse the interest of a large proportion of graduates in anything else. At one of the best of our small colleges, in the Mississippi valley, I saw a massive concrete grandstand. This valiant emulation of the Harvard stadium seemed to me to typify the indifference of alumni to the crying needs of their alma mater. For these graduates who contributed costly concrete seats, to be used by the student body in lieu of exercise, showed no concern over the fact that the college was worrying along with scientific laboratories inferior to those of the majority of modern high schools. 'What could I do?' the president asked. 'They would give the stadium and they would not give the laboratories.'

IV

There have been numerous attempts to prove that intercollegiate athletics are not detrimental to scholarship by showing that athletes receive higher marks than other students. Such arguments are beside the point. Though we take no account of the weak-kneed indulgence to athletes in institutions where winning games is the dominant interest, and of the special coaching in their studies provided them because they are on the teams, we must take account of the fact that wherever the student body regards playing on intercollegiate teams as the supreme expression of loyalty, the men of greatest physical and mental strength are more likely than the others to go out for the teams, and these are the very men of whom we rightly expect greatest proficiency in scholarship. That they do not as a group show notable leadership in intellectual activities seems due to the excessive physical training which, at certain seasons, they substitute for study.

But this is not the main point. A large college might be willing to sacrifice the scholarship of a score of students, if that were all. The chief charge against intercollegiate athletics is their demoralizing effect on the scholarship of the entire institution. The weaklings who have not grit enough to stand up on the gridiron and be tackled talk interminably about the latest game and the chances of winning the next one. They spend their hours in cheering the football hero, and their money in betting on him. The man of highest achievement in scholarship they either ignore or condemn with unpleasant epithets.

Further hindrances to scholarship are the periodic absences of the teams. It is said that athletes are required to make up the work they miss during their trips, but is not this one of the naïve ways wherein faculties deceive themselves? They are faced with this dilemma. Either the work of a given week in their courses is so substantial, and their own contribution to the work so great, that students cannot possibly miss it, and 'make it up' while meeting the equally great demands of the following week, or else the work of all the students is so easy that the athletes on a week's absence do not miss much. What actually happens, year in and year out, is that the standards of scholarship of the entire institution are lowered to meet the exigencies of intercollegiate athletics.

To what an illogical position we are driven by our fetish worship of college 'amateur athletics'! We especially provide the summer vacation as a period for play and recreation, and as a time when a majority of students must earn a part of the expenses of the college year. For these purposes we suspend all classes. Yet the student who uses this vacation to play ball and thereby earn some money must either lie about it or be condemned to outer darkness. There are no intercollegiate athletics for him; he has become a 'professional.' It matters not how fine his ideals of sport may be, how strong his character, or how high his scholarship. These considerations are ignored. The honors all go to the athlete who neglects his studies in order to make games his supreme interest during that part of the twelve months which is specifically set apart for studies.

Far more sensible would be an arrangement whereby, if we must have intercollegiate athletics at all, the games could be scheduled in vacation periods, and a part of the gate-receipts, if we must have them at all, could be used for the necessary living expenses of worthy students instead of being squandered, as much of that money is squandered to-day. That this will seem a preposterous plan to those who are caught in the maelstrom of the present collegiate system need not surprise us. An accurate record of the history of intercollegiate athletics shows that, year in and year out, the arrangements desired by students are those that interfere most seriously with study during the days especially intended for study.

The maelstrom of college athletics! That would not seem too strong a term if we could view the age in which we live in right perspective, an age so unbalanced nervously that it demands perpetual excitement. We have fallen into a vicious circle: the excesses of excitement create a pathological nervous condition which craves greater excesses. The advertisement of a head-on collision of two locomotives is said to have drawn the largest crowd in the history of modern 'sport'; next in attractiveness is an intercollegiate football game. It is unfortunate that our universities, which should serve as balancing forces,—which should inculcate the ideal of sport as a counterpoise to an overwrought civilization,—are actually making conditions worse through cultivating, by means of athletics as a business, that passion for excitement which makes sustained thinking impossible and which is elsewhere kept at fever heat by prize-fights, bull-fights, and blood-curdling motion pictures.

V

But even if intercollegiate games are detrimental to the interests of scholarship, is not the college spirit they create worth all they cost? Perhaps so. A university is more than a curriculum and a campus. It is more than the most elaborate student annual can depict. Even in Carlyle's day, it was more than he called it: a true university was never a mere 'collection of books.' It is the spirit that giveth life, and 'college spirit' is certainly a name to conjure with. The first question is what we mean by college spirit. A student may throw his hat in the air, grab a megaphone, give 'three long rahs,' go through the gymnastics of a cheerleader,—putting the most ingenious mechanical toys to shame,—and yet leave some doubt whether he has adequately defined college spirit.

What is this college spirit that hovers over the paid coach and his grandstand—this 'indefinable something,' as one writer calls it, 'which is fanned into a bright flame by intercollegiate athletics'? Shall we judge the spirit by its manifestations in an institution famed above all else for its winning teams and its college spirit? In such an institution, not long ago, every student was cudgeled or cajoled into 'supporting the team,' and many a callow youth acted as though he thought he had reached the heights of self-sacrifice when he sat for hours on the grandstand, watching practice, puffing innumerable cigarettes, and laying up a stock of canned enthusiasm for the big game. A student who would not support his team by betting on it was regarded as deficient in spirit. Every intercollegiate game was the occasion of general neglect of college courses. If the game was at a neighboring city, the classrooms were half empty for two days; but the bar-rooms of that city were not empty, and worse places regularly doubled their rates on the night of a big game. Some of the most enthusiastic supporters of the team went to jail for disturbing the peace. If the contest took place at home, returning alumni filled the fraternity houses and celebrated with general drunkenness. 'An indefinable something'—consisting of college property and that of private citizens—

was 'fanned into a bright flame' in celebration of the victory. Following this came the spectacle of young men parading the streets in nightshirts. For residents of the town who did not enjoy this particular kind of spirit, the night was made hideous by the noises of revelry. All this and much more was tolerated for years on the assumption that students, imbued with college spirit, should not be subjected to the laws of decent living that govern those members of civilized communities who have not had the advantages of a higher education. The most serious difficulties between faculties and students and between students and the police, the country over, for the past twenty years, have arisen in connection with displays of 'college spirit' after the 'big game.' Any college and any community might cheerfully sacrifice this kind of college spirit.

But some men mean by college spirit something finer than lawlessness, dissipation, and rowdyism. They mean the loyalty to an institution which makes a student guard its good name by being manly and courteous in conduct at all times and in all places. They mean the sense of responsibility which aids a student in forming habits of temperance and industry. They mean that eagerness to make a grateful use of his opportunities which leads a student to keep his own body fit, through moderate athletics, and a physical training that knows no season—is never broken. By college spirit some men mean this and far more: they mean that loyalty to a college which rivets a man to the severest tasks of scholarship, through which he gains intellectual power and enthusiasm, without which no graduate is an entire credit to any college; and finally they mean that vision of an ideal life beyond commencement which shows a man that only through the rigid subordination of transient and trivial pleasures can he hope to become the only great victory a university ever wins—a trained, devoted, and inspired alumnus, working for the welfare of mankind. There is no evidence that the intercollegiate athletics of to-day inculcate in many men this kind of college spirit.

Have I exaggerated the evils of intercollegiate athletics? Possibly I have. Exceptions should be cited here and there. But I am convinced that college faculties agree with me in my main contentions. My impression is that at least three fourths of the teachers I have met the country over believe that the American college would better serve its highest purposes, if intercollegiate athletics were no more. At a recent dinner of ten deans and presidents, they declared, one by one, in confidence that they would abolish intercollegiate athletics if they could withstand the pressure of students and alumni.

Is it therefore necessary for all institutions to give up intercollegiate athletics permanently? Probably not. Let our colleges first take whatever measures are necessary to make athletics yield their educational values to all students and teachers. If intercollegiate athletics can then be conducted as incidental and contributory to the main purposes of athletics, well and good. But first of all the question must be decisively settled, which aims are to dominate—those of business or those of education.

Further Readings

DU BOIS, CORA, "The Dominant Value Profile of American Culture," *The American Anthropologist,* vol. 57, part I (December 1955), pp. 1232–1239.

EDUCATIONAL POLICIES COMMISSION, *Moral and Spiritual Values in Public Schools.* Washington, D.C.: 1951.

EDUCATIONAL POLICIES COMMISSION, *School Athletics Problems and Policies.* National Education Association and the American Association of School Athletics. Washington, D.C.: 1954.

Questions for Discussion

1. Why do coaches concern themselves with the alumni, speaking engagements, recruiting, and Saturday's gate receipts if they are educators and not businessmen?
2. Is the time and money spent on eleven players returned in sufficient value to the school? Could greater value accrue if this time, energy, and money were spent on those with poor physical skills? If so, under what circumstances?
3. Can the same justification for grouping based on high scholastic achievement be used in athletics?
4. Should changes be made in athletic budgets so that the play-for-fun principle becomes paramount? If this principle is not acceptable, what effect may television have, especially pay television?
5. Have the criticisms leveled by Foster in 1915 led to the reform of intercollegiate athletic programs?

FRED C. COLE

Intercollegiate Athletics and Higher Education*

The criticisms against intercollegiate athletics by Foster in the previous article are also made, in part, by Cole. Unlike Foster's argument for either business or education, Cole argues for a solely educational perspective in intercollegiate athletics. He also raises the question of whether intercollegiate coaches are being prepared for a future that may have little demand for them.

Formal and organized athletic competition is an established and venerable institution of Western civilization. The association of athletics with educational institutions also is old and is characteristic of British-American culture. Athletics, therefore, have a legitimate place in American colleges and universities; interest and participation in sports is both normal and desirable.

The objectives and standards of a university should, however, be determined by its educational mission; extracurricular interests should be governed in conformance with those objectives and standards. Furthermore, it should be obvious that the future of the world depends upon the effectiveness with which trained intelligence can be brought to bear upon the major problems of man and his universe. The adequacy of our education will be the deciding factor. The results of games will signify nothing.

The American system of higher education is healthily diversified. There are a number of different types of institutions which, though similar in many purposes and objectives, represent different emphases and specific functions. Generally, these are identified

* Reprinted with permission of the author and the publisher from *Current Issues in Higher Education*. Washington, D.C.: National Education Association, 1961, pp. 193–196.

as independent, public, and church-affiliated institutions. Because of variations among institutions, there may be differences which must be taken into consideration in regard to athletic programs and problems. This is not to say that the athletic program should be allowed to influence educational policies in any kind of institution. It is recognized nevertheless that the particular functions and responsibilities of a college or university may affect its athletic as well as its educational activities, and that the effect in the two areas may sometimes be related.

An intercollegiate athletic program should benefit both the participants and the institutions which they represent. For individuals, the advantages and satisfactions of athletic competition might include the development of physique, character and personality, and emotional catharsis. The experience is represented as instilling self-reliance, as fostering simultaneously the desire to excel and a spirit of fair play, and as inculcating the ability to cooperate for mutual ends, even at the sacrifice of immediate self-aggrandizement.

If any of these claims are valid—and at least some of them are in most cases—athletics make a valuable contribution to the educational process. It follows, then, that colleges and universities should provide opportunities for as many students as possible to take part in organized sports. The number of participants will vary, of course, from one school to another, as will the number of intercollegiate sports. There appears to be no necessary correlation between the breadth of the program and the popular identification of the school with emphasis on athletics, or with the strength or type of competition which is normally faced.

Institutional benefits of intercollegiate athletics are usually conceived in vicarious or emphatic terms. Students and alumni identify themselves with the team, exult in its success, despair in its defeat. Interest in the team provides a unifying bond among students in different academic programs, and alumni in diverse occupations living in many places. It also serves as a continuing link between the alumni and their alma mater. This association is wholesome as long as it remains subordinate to and apart from educational considerations, which should always be the chief source of student and alumni pride and affection. There is no evident connection whatever between touchdowns or goals and the quality of teaching in academic classrooms.

Many others besides students and alumni are interested in college sports, and a college or university should provide the spectator accommodations which it reasonably can for persons genuinely interested in its athletic teams and in those of its usual opponents. It is not obligated to conduct entertainment or spectacles with no educational value for the benefit of the general public.

As the objective in any competition is to win or to excel, it is recognized that value must be placed upon victory. But if athletics are to continue as a wholesome influence, victory should never be the overriding consideration in college athletics. It is assumed that words so often used by coaches and others interested in sports —character building, sportsmanship, team spirit, and others of similar import—represent true goals and not mere lip service. A winning athletic team may be a source of great satisfaction; but it is small compensation for loss of integrity by an individual or an institution.

Not more than half the teams which play on a given day can win. Where tie scores can occur, fewer than half will gain victory. If victory is the only gratification to be had, the total of disappointment will always be greater than the total of satisfaction. It would be foolish to support a system which is logically absurd and psychologically damaging. Sports should provide a healthy catharsis of emotions and not a pathological frustration. Victory has, of course, an economic aspect. Winning teams ordinarily draw more spectators than losing ones; and many institutions depend upon gate receipts for most of their athletic income. But it must be remembered that it serves no educational purpose to play winning contests in order to attract crowds large enough to finance winning contests. It is indeed a vicious cycle when this occurs.

There are pressures which are brought to bear on colleges and universities to engage in just this kind of cycle. Pressures vary in kind and intensity and come from various directions, but most seek some compromise of academic standards for anticipated athletic success. At this point in history, it is imperative that the most effective possible use be made of America's educational resources. Any serious hindrance to this purpose may be disastrous, and even minor obstacles are dangerous. The best possible instruction must be given to the best possible student. Universities and colleges of high standards should make every effort to resist pressure upon themselves and to help other institutions to do so. Those seeking athletic pre-eminence are often a small but highly vocal minority, while those who favor educational excellence are a silent majority.

Areas of opinion in favor of academic standards should be sought out and brought forth to at least balance if not subdue the athletic clamor.

The stated admission policy of an educational institution should apply to all applicants. Individual exceptions should be made only for the acceptance of obviously qualified students who may not meet all technical requirements. Certain geographic, religious, or alumni preferences may be permitted, but in such cases, minimum requirements should be uniformly applied. No admission policy should be designed to facilitate the enrollment of persons who wish to attend an institution primarily for purposes other than educational. Admissions pressures will continue to increase. Our civilization cannot afford to deny a superior education to a superior person in order that a boy with little or no scholastic ability may be allowed to play games.

In any institution of higher learning, every curriculum and course should fulfill a genuine educational purpose. Courses which foster good health and physical fitness are a benefit to the individual and society. They have a legitimate place in a college curriculum, but they should be offered as supplementary to the academic program and should never be substituted for courses of intellectual content.

Preparation of students for careers in athletic coaching should be offered in a college or university only if the faculty believes and freely decides that it meets a legitimate obligation of the institution and serves an educational need on the collegiate level. In the coming years, the techniques of coaching and of directing recreation can hardly be given high priority. The need for people with the proper skills in these areas is not challenged; but the question may be raised whether the training should be undertaken in college classes or through other agencies and systems.

Colleges and universities should award financial aid to students on the basis of scholastic aptitude and need. Scholastic aptitude, on a competitive basis, should determine the fact of eligibility for assistance. Actual need should determine the amount. Athletic ability should be considered only insofar as it may indicate physical health and emotional stability contributing to the likelihood of academic success.

Many institutions do offer grants-in-aid to students based primarily on the athletic prowess of the individuals. Pressures which were suggested earlier may prevent any abrupt discontinuance of this policy, but even for these institutions there are certain principles which should be observed. Assistance should be limited to the actual expenses of attending college. The amount of aid to an athlete should be based on financial need. If a student is able to pay his own way to college and then accepts an athletic grant, this amounts to outright compensation for service rendered and constitutes professionalism.

Many will argue that athletic grants should be condoned because they offer the only means by which many young men (and women) can avail themselves of a college education. In the future, this contention will become increasingly less valid. Regardless of the source of fee payments, athletes occupy dormitory rooms and classroom seats, and they demand the attention of faculty members, just as any other enrolled students do. We must instruct our academically qualified young people whether they are all-American halfbacks or whether they can walk only with crutches.

Once in college, all students in any academic program should meet the same requirements for remaining enrolled, progressing through the grade levels, and receiving a degree. Any privileges should likewise apply equally and universally. Any student engaging or expecting to engage in intercollegiate athletics should meet all the requirements for full-time enrollment and progression. When a student is admitted to a college or university, the institution by this action admits a certain responsibility to that student; namely, to provide the opportunity for a proper education in a regular curriculum leading to a degree. If a student is allowed to wallow through an easy succession of vacuous courses which serve no purpose except to keep him eligible for sports competition, then the institution is not meeting this responsibility.

If the academic standards and integrity of an educational institution are to be maintained in regard to athletics, the athletic policies and practices of the institution must be subject to academic authority. The faculty should have full authority for prescribing all curricula, methods, and criteria for instruction, and rules of eligibility for participation in athletics. The athletic director, or similar officer, should be responsible to a principal administrative officer of the institution, on the same basis as any other subordinate administrative officer, and subject to the same policy regarding appointment and removal. The budget of the athletic department should be subject to the approval and audit of the chief fiscal officer of the institution. Any standing executive or advisory committee which functions in the field of athletics should be appointed in the same way and by the same authority as similar committees in other areas of administration, and its members should serve as individuals rather than as representatives of any groups or interests. No organization of students, alumni, or other persons, within or without the institution, should have any more to say about athletic policy and procedure than it has in regard to academic policies, excluding, of course, athletic conference organizations and the National Collegiate Athletic Association.

The proper relationship of intercollegiate sports to the general framework of higher education is a problem, varying in its scope and intensity from one institution to another. But it is not a problem without a solution or solutions.

Further Readings

DU BOIS, CORA, "The Dominant Value Profile of American Culture," *The American Anthropologist,* vol. 57, part I (December 1955), pp. 1232–1239.

EDUCATIONAL POLICIES COMMISSION, *Moral and Spiritual Values in Public Schools.* Washington, D.C.: 1951.

EDUCATIONAL POLICIES COMMISSION, *School Athletics Problems and Policies.* National Education Association and the American Association of School Athletics, 1954.

HUGGETT, ALBERT J. and T. M. STINNETT, *Professional Problems of Teachers.* New York: The Macmillan Company, 1956.

LIEBERMAN, MYRON. *Education as a Profession.* Englewood Cliffs, N.J.: Prentice-Hall, Inc., 1956.

Questions for Discussion

1. Should athletic scholarships be given to students in an educational institution?
2. According to Cole's article, should coaches be trained in educational institutions or can other agencies better prepare them?

   3. What indications are there that the preparation of physical
   education personnel has low priority in the future? What
   biological and social loss may be involved if this occurs?

GEORGE HERBERT MEAD

Self*

Thus far, the American culture and the culture of the school
have been explored. It is the intent of the following three articles to describe the place of the individual in society and the
contributions of physical education to individual development
and adjustment.

   In the contemporary world, man and society mutually depend
upon one another for existence and progress. A balance between
concern for self and society is crucial to each individual's proper
personality development. Consequently, questions arise regarding the development of the self-image through physical education, the effect of society on types of play activities, and the
place of the individual in physical education. In the first instance, G. H. Mead describes how the "self" is discovered
through the interpretations of the play society, and, in the
second, Riesman and his associates discuss how man may be
losing his autonomy in play because of society's heavy dictates.

   A central principle of physical education is that it helps the
individual to develop his "social self." Many students, however, do not understand how and on what basis game situations
help build the self-image. For a full understanding of this fundamental concept, we next turn to the reading on that subject by
the well-known sociologist, G. H. Mead.

   Mead points out two stages of self-development. The first
involves the play patterns of early elementary school children,
where the social roles of others, such as firemen and aviators,
are emulated. Each role is played with little relationship to the
other, and each contributes to the understanding of the self.

* Reprinted with permission of the publisher from *Mind, Self and Society* by
George Herbert Mead. Chicago: The University of Chicago Press, 1934, pp.
229–241.

The second stage refers to the upper elementary and secondary physical education programs, which lend themselves to the full development of the individual's self. In contrast to the first stage of play with its single role emphasis, many attitudes and roles become important. Consider a baseball game. Merely to throw the ball involves the first stage. To throw the ball in relation to its being caught by another implies the understanding of another person's role. In fact, each player must understand the roles and attitudes of *all* others on the team. This is Mead's "generalized other," a concept that allows each of us as adults to utilize our knowledge of others in directing our individual "selves."

This organization is put in the form of the rules of the game. Children take a great interest in rules. They make rules on the spot in order to help themselves out of difficulties. Part of the enjoyment of the game is to get these rules. Now, the rules are the set of responses which a particular attitude calls out. You can demand a certain response in others if you take a certain attitude. These responses are all in yourself as well. There you get an organized set of such responses as that to which I have referred, which is something more elaborate than the rôles found in play. Here there is just a set of responses that follow on each other indefinitely. At such a stage we speak of a child as not yet having a fully developed self. The child responds in a fairly intelligent fashion to the immediate stimuli that come to him, but they are not organized. He does not organize his life as we would like to have him do, namely, as a whole. There is just a set of responses of the type of play. The child reacts to a certain stimulus, and the reaction is in himself that is called out in others, but he is not a whole self. In his game he has to have an organization of these rôles; otherwise he cannot play the game. The game represents the passage in the life of the child from taking the rôle of others in play to the organized part that is essential to self-consciousness in the full sense of the term.

Play, the Game, and the Generalized Other

We were speaking of the social conditions under which the self arises as an object. In addition to language we found two illustrations, one in play and the other in the game, and I wish to summarize and expand my account on these points. I have spoken of these from the point of view of children. We can, of course, refer also to the attitudes of more primitive people out of which our civilization has arisen. A striking illustration of play as distinct from the game is found in the myths and various of the plays which primitive people carry out, especially in religious pageants. The pure play attitude which we find in the case of little children may not be found here, since the participants are adults, and undoubtedly the relationship of these play processes to that which they interpret is more or less in the minds of even the most primitive people. In the process of interpretation of such rituals, there is an organization of play which perhaps might be compared to that which is taking place in the kindergarten in dealing with the plays of little children, where these are made into a set that will have a definite structure or relationship. At least something of the same sort is found in the play of primitive people. This type of activity belongs, of course, not to the everyday life of the people in their dealing with the objects about them—there we have a more or less definitely developed self-consciousness—but in their attitudes toward the forces about them, the nature upon which they depend; in their attitude toward this nature which is vague and uncertain, there we have a much more primitive response; and that response finds its expression in taking the rôle of the other, playing at the expression of their gods and their heroes, going through certain rites which are the representation of what these individuals are supposed to be doing. The process is one which develops, to be sure, into a more or less definite technique and is controlled; and yet we can say that it has arisen out of situations similar to those in which little children play at being a parent, at being a teacher—vague personalities that are about them and which affect them and on which they depend. These are personalities which they take, rôles they play, and in so far control the development of their own personality. This outcome is just what the kindergarten works toward. It takes the characters of these various vague beings and gets them into such an organized social relationship to each other that they build up the character of the little child.[1] The very introduction of organization from outside supposes a lack of organization at this period in the child's experience. Over against such a situation of the little child and primitive people, we have the game as such.

The fundamental difference between the game and play is that in the latter the child must have the attitude of all the others

---

[1] ["The Relation of Play to Education," *University of Chicago Record*, i (1896–97), 140 ff.]

involved in that game. The attitudes of the other players which the participant assumes organize into a sort of unit, and it is that organization which controls the response of the individual. The illustration used was of a person playing baseball. Each one of his own acts is determined by his assumption of the action of the others who are playing the game. What he does is controlled by his being everyone else on that team, at least in so far as those attitudes affect his own particular response. We get then an "other" which is an organization of the attitudes of those involved in the same process.

The organized community or social group which gives to the individual his unity of self may be called "the generalized other." The attitude of the generalized other is the attitude of the whole community.[2] Thus, for example, in the case of such a social group as a ball team, the team is the generalized other in so far as it enters—as an organized process or social activity—into the experience of any one of the individual members of it.

If the given human individual is to develop a self in the fullest sense, it is not sufficient for him merely to take the attitudes of other human individuals toward himself and toward one another within the human social process, and to bring that social process as a whole into his individual experience merely in these terms: he must also, in the same way that he takes the attitudes of other individuals toward himself and toward one another, take their attitudes toward the various phases or aspects of the common social activity or set of social undertakings in which, as members of an organized society or social group, they are all engaged; and he must then, by generalizing these individual attitudes of that organized society or social group itself, as a whole, act toward different social projects which at any given

2 It is possible for inanimate objects, no less than for other human organisms, to form parts of the generalized and organized—the completely socialized—other for any given human individual, in so far as he responds to such objects socially or in a social fashion (by means of the mechanism of thought, the internalized conversation of gestures). Any thing—any object or set of objects, whether animate or inanimate, human or animal, or merely physical—toward which he acts, or to which he responds, socially, is an element in what for him is the generalized other; by taking the attitudes of which toward himself he becomes conscious of himself as an object or individual, and thus develops a self or personality. Thus, for example, the cult, in its primitive form, is merely the social embodiment of the relation between the given social group or community and its physical environment—an organized social means, adopted by the individual members of that group or community, of entering into social relations with that environment, or (in a sense) of carrying on conversations with it; and in this way that environment becomes part of the total generalized other for each of the individual members of the given social group or community.

time it is carrying out, or toward the various larger phases of the general social process which constitutes its life and of which these projects are specific manifestations. This getting of the broad activities of any given social whole or organized society as such within the experiential field of any one of the individuals involved or included in that whole is, in other words, the essential basis and prerequisite of the fullest development of that individual's self: only in so far as he takes the attitudes of the organized social group to which he belongs toward the organized, co-operative social activity or set of such activities in which that group as such is engaged, does he develop a complete self or possess the sort of complete self he has developed. And on the other hand, the complex co-operative processes and activities and institutional functionings of organized human society are also possible only in so far as every individual involved in them or belonging to that society can take the general attitudes of all other such individuals with reference to these processes and activities and institutional functionings, and to the organized social whole of experiential relations and interactions thereby constituted—and can direct his own behavior accordingly.

It is in the form of the generalized other that the social process influences the behavior of the individuals involved in it and carrying it on, i.e., that the community exercises control over the conduct of its individual members; for it is in this form that the social process or community enters as a determining factor into the individual's thinking. In abstract thought the individual takes the attitude of the generalized other[3] toward himself, without reference to its expression in any particular other individuals; and in concrete thought he takes that attitude in so far as it is expressed in the attitudes toward his behavior of those other individuals with whom he is involved in the given social situation or act. But only

---

[3] We have said that the internal conversation of the individual with himself in terms of words or significant gestures—the conversation which constitutes the process or activity of thinking—is carried on by the individual from the standpoint of the "generalized other." And the more abstract that conversation is, the more abstract thinking happens to be, the further removed is the generalized other from any connection with particular individuals. It is especially in abstract thinking, that is to say, that the conversation involved is carried on by the individual with the generalized other, rather than with any particular individuals. Thus it is, for example, that abstract concepts are concepts stated in terms of the attitudes of the entire social group or community; they are stated on the basis of the individual's consciousness of the attitudes of the generalized other toward them, as a result of his taking these attitudes of the generalized other and then responding to them. And thus it is also that abstract propositions are stated in a form which anyone—any other intelligent individual—will accept.

by taking the attitude of the generalized other toward himself, in one or another of these ways, can he think at all; for only thus can thinking—or the internalized conversation of gestures which constitutes thinking—occur. And only through the taking by individuals of the attitude or attitudes of the generalized other toward themselves is the existence of a universe of discourse, as that system of common or social meanings which thinking presupposes at its context, rendered possible.

The self-conscious human individual, then, takes or assumes the organized social attitudes of the given social group or community (or of some one section thereof) to which he belongs, toward the social problems of various kinds which confront that group or community at any given time, and which arise in connection with the correspondingly different social projects or organized co-operative enterprises in which that group or community as such is engaged; and as an individual participant in these social projects or co-operative enterprises, he governs his own conduct accordingly. In politics, for example, the individual identifies himself with an entire political party and takes the organized attitudes of that entire party toward the rest of the given social community and toward the problems which confront the party within the given social situation; and he consequently reacts or responds in terms of the organized attitudes of the party as a whole. He thus enters into a special set of social relations with all the other individuals who belong to that political party; and in the same way he enters into various other special sets of social relations, with various other classes of individuals respectively, the individuals of each of these classes being the other members of some one of the particular organized subgroups (determined in socially functional terms) of which he himself is a member within the entire given society or social community. In the most highly developed, organized, and complicated human social communities—those evolved by civilized man—these various socially functional classes or subgroups of individuals to which any given individual belongs (and with the other individual members of which he thus enters into a special set of social relations) are of two kinds. Some of them are concrete social classes or subgroups, such as political parties, clubs, corporations, which are all actually functional social units, in terms of which their individual members are directly related to one another. The others are abstract social classes or subgroups, such as the class of debtors and the class of creditors, in terms of which their individual members are related to one another only more or less indirectly, and which only more or less indirectly function as social units, but which afford or represent unlimited possibilities for the widening and ramifying and enriching of the social relations among all the individual members of the given society as an organized and unified whole. The given individual's membership in several of these abstract social classes or subgroups makes possible his entrance into definite social relations (however indirect) with an almost infinite number of other individuals who also belong to or are included within one or another of these abstract social classes or subgroups cutting across functional lines of demarcation which divide different human social communities from one another, and including individual members from several (in some cases from all) such communities. Of these abstract social classes or subgroups of human individuals the one which is most inclusive and extensive is, of course, the one defined by the logical universe of discourse (or system of universally significant symbols) determined by the participation and communicative interaction of individuals; for of all such classes or subgroups, it is the one which claims the largest number of individual members, and which enables the largest conceivable number of human individuals to enter into some sort of social relation, however indirect or abstract it may be, with one another—a relation arising from the universal functioning of gestures as significant symbols in the general human social process of communication.

I have pointed out, then, that there are two general stages in the full development of the self. At the first of these stages, the individual's self is constituted simply by an organization of the particular attitudes of other individuals toward himself and toward one another in the specific social acts in which he participates with them. But at the second stage in the full development of the individual's self that self is constituted not only by an organization of these particular individual attitudes, but also by an organization of the social attitudes of the generalized other or the social group as a whole to which he belongs. These social or group attitudes are brought within the individual's field of direct experience, and are included as elements in the structure or constitution of his self, in the same way that the attitudes of particular other individuals are; and the individual arrives at them, or succeeds in taking them, by means of further organizing, and then generalizing, the attitudes of particular other individuals in terms of their organized social bearings and implications. So the self reaches its full development by organizing these individual attitudes of others into the organized social or group attitudes, and by thus becoming an individual reflection of the general systematic pattern of social or group behavior in which it and the others are all involved—a pattern which enters as a whole into the individual's experience in terms of these organized group attitudes which, through the mechanism of his central nervous system, he takes toward himself, just as he takes the individual attitudes of others.

The game has a logic, so that such an organization of the self is rendered possible: there is a definite end to be obtained; the actions of the different individuals are all related to each other with reference to that end so that they do not conflict; one is not in conflict with himself in the attitude of another man on the team. If one has the attitude of the person throwing the ball he can also have the response of catching the ball. The two are related so that they further the purpose of the game itself. They are interrelated in a unitary, organic fashion. There is a definite unity, then, which is introduced into the organization of other selves when we reach such a stage as that of the game, as over against the situation of play where there is a simple succession of one rôle after another, a situation which is, of course, characteristic of the child's own personality. The child is one thing at one time and another at another, and what he is at one moment does not determine what he is at another. That is both the charm of childhood as well as its inadequacy. You cannot count on the child; you cannot assume that all the things he does are going to determine what he will do at any moment. He is not organized into a whole. The child has no definite character, no definite personality.

The game is then an illustration of the situation out of which an organized personality arises. In so far as the child does take the attitude of the other and allows that attitude of the other to determine the thing he is going to do with reference to a common end, he is becoming an organic member of society. He is taking over the morale of that society and is becoming an essential member of it. He belongs to it in so far as he does allow the attitude of the other that he takes to control his own immediate expression. What is involved here is some sort of an organized process. That which is expressed in terms of the game is, of course, being continually expressed in the social life of the child, but this wider process goes beyond the immediate experience of the child himself. The importance of the game is that it lies entirely inside of the child's own experience, and the importance of our modern type of education is that it is brought as far as possible within this realm. The different attitudes that a child assumes are so organized that they exercise a definite control over his response, as the attitudes in a game control his own immediate response. In the game we get an organized other, a generalized other, which is found in the nature of the child itself, and finds its expression in the immediate experience of the child. And it is that organized activity in the child's own nature controlling the particular response which gives unity, and which builds up his own self.

What goes on in the game goes on in the life of the child all the time. He is continually taking the attitudes of those about him, especially the rôles of those who in some sense control him and on whom he depends. He gets the function of the process in an abstract sort of a way at first. It goes over from the play into the game in a real sense. He has to play the game. The morale of the game takes hold of the child more than the larger morale of the whole community. The child passes into the game and the game expresses a social situation in which he can completely enter; its morale may have a greater hold on him than that of the family to which he belongs or the community in which he lives. There are all sorts of social organizations, some of which are fairly lasting, some temporary, into which the child is entering, and he is playing a sort of social game in them. It is a period in which he likes "to belong," and he gets into organizations which come into existence and pass out of existence. He becomes a something which can function in the organized whole, and thus tends to determine himself in his relationship with the group to which he belongs. That process is one which is a striking stage in the development of the child's morale. It constitutes him a self-conscious member of the community to which he belongs.

Such is the process by which a personality arises. I have spoken of this as a process in which a child takes the rôle of the other, and said that it takes place essentially through the use of language. Language is predominantly based on the vocal gesture by means of which co-operative activities in a community are carried out. Language in its significant sense is that vocal gesture which tends to arouse in the individual the attitude which it arouses in others, and it is this perfecting of the self by the gesture which mediates the social activities that gives rise to the process of taking the rôle of the other. The latter phrase is a little unfortunate because it suggests an actor's attitude which is actually more sophisticated than that which is involved in our own experience. To this degree it does not correctly describe that which I have in mind. We see the process most definitely in a primitive form in those situations where the child's play takes different rôles. Here the very fact that he is ready to pay out money, for instance, arouses the attitude of the person who receives money; the very process is calling out in him the corresponding activities of the other person involved. The individual stimulates himself to the response which he is calling out in the other person, and then acts in some degree in response to that situation. In play the child does definitely act out the rôle which he himself has aroused in himself. It is that which gives, as I have said, a definite content in the individual which answers to the stimulus that affects him as it affects somebody else. The content of the other that enters into one personality is the response in the individual which his gesture calls out in the other.

We may illustrate our basic concept by a reference to the notion of property. If we say "This is my property, I shall control it," that affirmation calls out a certain set of responses which must be the same in any community in which property exists. It involves an organized attitude with reference to property which is common to all the members of the community. One must have a definite attitude of control of his own property and respect for the property of others. Those attitudes (as organized sets of responses) must be there on the part of all, so that when one says such a thing he calls out in himself the response of the others. He is calling out the response of what I have called a generalized other. That which makes society possible is such common responses, such organized attitudes, with reference to what we term property, the cults of religion, the process of education, and the relations of the family. Of course, the wider the society the more definitely universal these objects must be. In any case there must be a definite set of responses, which we may speak of as abstract, and which can belong to a very large group. Property is in itself a very abstract concept. It is that which the individual himself can control and nobody else can control. The attitude is different from that of a dog toward a bone. A dog will fight any other dog trying to take the bone. The dog is not taking the attitude of the other dog. A man who says "This is my property" is taking an attitude of the other person. The man is appealing to his rights because he is able to take the attitude which everybody else in the group has with reference to property, thus arousing in himself the attitude of others.

What goes to make up the organized self is the organization of the attitudes which are common to the group. A person is a personality because he belongs to a community, because he takes over the institutions of that community into his own conduct. He takes its language as a medium by which he gets his personality, and then through a process of taking the different rôles that all the others furnish he comes to get the attitude of the members of the community. Such, in a certain sense, is the structure of a man's personality. There are certain common responses which each individual has toward certain common things, and in so far as those common responses are awakened in the individual when he is affecting other persons he arouses his own self. The structure, then, on which the self is built is this response which is common to all, for one has to be a member of a community to be a self. Such responses are abstract attitudes, but they constitute just what we term a man's character. They give him what we term his principles, the acknowledged attitudes of all members of the community toward what are the values of that community. He is putting himself in the place of the generalized other, which represents the organized responses of all the members of the group. It is that which guides conduct controlled by principles, and a person who has such an organized group of responses is a man whom we say has character, in the moral sense.

It is a structure of attitudes, then, which goes to make up a self, as distinct from a group of habits. We all of us have, for example, certain groups of habits, such as the particular intonations which a person uses in his speech. This is a set of habits of vocal expression which one has but which one does not know about. The sets of habits which we have of that sort mean nothing to us; we do not hear the intonations of our speech that others hear unless we are paying particular attention to them. The habits of emotional expression which belong to our speech are of the same sort. We may know that we have expressed ourselves in a joyous fashion but the detailed process is one which does not come back to our conscious selves. There are whole bundles of such habits which do not enter into a conscious self, but which help to make up what is termed the unconscious self.

After all, what we mean by self-consciousness is an awakening in ourselves of the group of attitudes which we are arousing in others, especially when it is an important set of responses which go to make up the members of the community. It is unfortunate to fuse or mix up consciousness, as we ordinarily use that term, and self-consciousness. Consciousness, as frequently used, simply has reference to the field of experience, but self-consciousness refers to the ability to call out in ourselves a set of definite responses which belong to the others of the group. Consciousness and self-consciousness are not on the same level. A man alone has, fortunately or unfortunately, access to his own toothache, but that is not what we mean by self-consciousness.

I have so far emphasized what I have called the structures upon which the self is constructed, the framework of the self, as it were. Of course we are not only what is common to all: each one of the selves is different from everyone else; but there has to be such a common structure as I have sketched in order that we may be members of a community at all. We cannot be ourselves unless we are also members in whom there is a community of attitudes which control the attitudes of all. We cannot have rights unless we have common attitudes. That which we have acquired as self-conscious persons makes us such members of society and gives us selves. Selves can only exist in definite relationships to other selves. No hard-and-fast line can be drawn between our own selves and the selves of others, since our own selves exist and enter as such into our experience only in so far as the selves of others exist and enter as such into our experience also. The individual possesses a self only in relation to the selves of the other members of his social group; and the structure of his self expresses or reflects the general behavior pattern of this social group to which he belongs, just as does the structure of the self of every other individual belonging to this social group.

Further Readings

CANTRIL, HADLEY, *The Psychology of Social Movements*. New York: John Wiley & Sons, Inc., 1941.

ERIKSON, ERIK, *Childhood and Society*. New York: W. W. Norton & Company, Inc., 1950.

FREUD, SIGMUND, *Civilization and Its Discontents*. New York: Doubleday & Company, Inc., 1958.

FROMM, ERICH, *Escape From Freedom*. New York: Holt, Rinehart and Winston, 1941.

KARDINER, ABRAM, *The Psychological Frontiers of Society*. New York: Columbia University Press, 1945.

MASLOW, ABRAHAM H., *Toward a Psychology of Being*. Princeton, N.J.: D. Van Nostrand Company, Inc., 1962.

Questions for Discussion

1. When should the transition of phase one of self-development to phase two take place within the physical education curriculum?

2. What would be some effective ways of integrating a student into phase two of self-development?
3. Why do some persons never develop a feeling for the "generalized other"?
4. Does team work require a sense of the "generalized other"? Explain.

DAVID RIESMAN, NATHAN GLAZER
and REUEL DENNEY

The Problem of Competence:
Obstacles to Autonomy in Play*

In the succeeding article Riesman, Glazer, and Denney argue that play or recreational activities should not be entirely directed by the "generalized other," or Riesman's concept of the "other-directed," but rather by the individual's inner motivation, so that the autonomy or privatization of play can be retained.

Physical educators have long proclaimed the desire to retain a balanced program, one that both appeals to the "other-directed" self, such as most team sports and games, and also gives attention to individual sports.

I. The Play's the Thing

Privatization as an obstacle to play can be thought of as primarily a relic of previous eras of status-dominated leisure; indeed, the immobilization of women, children, and the lower classes harks back to the earlier days of the industrial revolution. Wealth, transport, and education are the great liberators here. But we have also inherited obstacles to leisure from the puritan wing of inner-direction, which succeeded in destroying or subverting a whole his-

* Reprinted with permission of the authors and the publishers from *The Lonely Crowd*. New Haven: Yale University Press, 1953, pp. 326–343.

toric spectrum of gregarious fun-making: sport, drama, feast days, and other ceremonial escapes. Even those ceremonies that survive, or have been newly invented, such as the Fourth of July or Halloween, have had to meet, if not the critique of puritan asceticism, then the critique of puritan rationalism, from which young children have been precariously exempted. For many adults our holidays make work out of fun-making or gift-giving which we have neither the wit to welcome nor the courage to refuse; we know holidays are calculated steps in the distributive economy and that new holidays, e.g., Mother's Day, are foisted on us—there are more commercially sponsored "Weeks" than there are weeks in the year. Here puritanism has proved an Indian giver: it not only gives priority to work and distribution but, what is more, takes back the niggardly holidays it gives us. The scars that puritanism has left on the American, and not only on the Philadelphian, Sunday are well known.

It may take a long time before the damage done to play during the era depending on inner-direction can be repaired. In the meantime other-direction has added new hazards. The other-directed man approaches play, as he approaches so many other areas of life, without the inhibitions but also without the protections of his inner-directed predecessor. Beset as he is with the responsibility for the mood of the play-group, he might like to fall back on fixed and objective play ceremonials, and to some extent he does so—it is a common mistake to assume that American city-dwellers are wholly without rituals. Our various drinks, our various card and parlor games, our various sports, and our public entertainments—all can be arranged in a series from the less to the more intimate, the less to the more fluctuating, innovational, and subjective. Even so, the responsibility of all to all, that each join in the fun and involve himself at a similar level of subjectivity, interferes with spontaneous sociability in the very effort to invoke it. Above all, perhaps, this groupiness shuts off the privacy which the other-directed man, engaged in personalizing in his work, requires (without often knowing it) in his play. Just because he feels guilty if he is not contributing to the fun of the group, he needs to learn to distinguish between the loneliness he understandably fears and the privacy he might occasionally choose.

We have seen that children learn early in their lives that they must have no secrets from companionable peers and adults; and this includes their use of leisure. This is perhaps to be expected from the other-directed, who care more for the mood and manner of doing things than for what is done, who feel worse about an exclusion from others' consciousness than about any violation of property or pride, and who will tolerate almost any misdeed so long as it is not concealed from them. Presumably, parents who want their children to become autonomous may help them very much by letting them learn they have the right to make their choices (by lying if necessary) between those leisure situations in which they wish to be intimate with others and those in which intimacy is merely the demand of an authority, parental or groupish. Obviously an individual who needs, for the autonomous use of leisure, both play which is private, reverie-filled, and fantasy-rich, and play which is sociable, even ceremonial, has a hard time combating all at once the privatizations we have inherited and the personalizations we have newly elaborated.

These are very general considerations, and they must be supplemented by reminding ourselves of the continuing consequences, both for work and play, of the Great Depression. The depression did not lead to a redefinition of work but on the contrary made work seem not only precious but problematic—precious because problematic. It is significant that we have now taken full employment, rather than full nonemployment, or leisure, as the economic goal to which we cling in desperation. This is not surprising when we realize how stunted were the play opportunities for the man unemployed in the depression. We could see then, in the clearest form, how often leisure is defined as a permissive residue left over from the demands of work-time. Even financially adequate relief could not remove this moral blockage of play, any more than retirement pay can remove it for the forcibly retired oldsters. For the prestige of work operates as a badge entitling the holder to draw on the society's idleness fund. Even the adolescent who is engaged in "producing himself" suffers emotional discomfort if he cannot demonstrate that he is at work or training assiduously for narrowly defined work aims. In sum, taking together the young, the unemployed, the postemployment old, the housewife, and the guilty featherbedders, not to speak of the "idle rich," we may have a great number who more or less unconsciously feel some uneasiness in play—because by cultural definition the right to play belongs to those who work.

The same industrial advance which has given us a sometimes intolerable freedom from work has also operated to introduce un-

precedented specialization into the area of play, with similar am-
biguous consequences for many technologically unemployed players. The varied capacities of the medieval entertainer whose boast
is quoted at the chapter head include some amiable virtuosities.
But they would hardly get him a billing on the RKO circuit or television today, and he would certainly not be good enough for Ring-
ling Brothers. The amateur player has to compete with profes-
sionals who are far more professional than ever before—can he tell
Laurence Olivier how to play *Hamlet,* as Hamlet himself could get
away with telling the professional players how *not* to do it? We
saw in Part I that, while the inner-directed man held on tenaciously
to his competence as a player at least in his downward escapes,
the other-directed man is faced with and oppressed by virtuosity
from the omnipresent media wherever he turns.

Thus it looks as if the task of restoring competence to play is
almost, if not quite, as difficult as that of restoring it to work. While
a change income relations, or even in the organization of industry,
might make for fairer distribution of leisure and a lessening of
guilts, it could not of itself teach men how to play who have historically forgotten how and who have turned the business over to pro-
fessionals. Are we right, then, in supposing that play offers any
easier channels to autonomy than work; are not both equally
"alienated"?

I think it is not unreasonable to believe that various types of competence, as yet hardly recognized, are being built up in the play of
the other-directed, in the face of all the obstacles we have listed.
Some of these skills, such as craftsmanship, have old foundations;
others, such as consumership, have new aspects. Even taste-exchanging, that intangible product of the play-work of the other-directed
peer-groups, can be seen as a training ground for leisure skills. Perhaps there is more competence at play than meets the eye—less pas-
sivity, less manipulation, less shoddiness than is usually charged.

II. The Forms of Competence

CONSUMERSHIP: POSTGRADUATE COURSE

The mass media serve as tutors in consumption style, and if we
are looking for straws in the wind, we can begin there. To my mind,
it is symptomatic that a number of recent movies can be inter-

preted as encouraging new leisure and domestic styles among men—
with the implication that freedom from their peers will help them
to increase their own competence as consumers and encourage their
development toward autonomy. In *Letter to Three Wives* and
Everybody Does It the hero (Paul Douglas) is represented as a
power seeker with hair on his chest who is making the "one-class
jump"—the jump from lower-middle class to upper-middle class
which still propels much of our economic and social life. The one-
class jumper, caught as he is between a peer-group he has left and
another he has not quite achieved, is usually too insecure, too
driven, to be a good candidate for autonomy. Douglas begins with
a stereotyped, inner-directed tone of toughness and insensitivity
but ends up by discovering new angles in his own complex emotions when he learns (in *Everybody Does It*) that the singing talent
being sought by his socialite would-be canary wife is actually his
own. The discovery may constitute a commentary on the fact that
men need no longer delegate artistic sensibilities to wives seeking
culture as status or as career, but can if they wish enjoy them as
part of their own competence—a new twist (and one that James M.
Cain and the scenarists must have been perfectly aware of) in the
old comedy-dilemma of the man who meets and surpasses the leisure
ideals of his new, upper-class peer-group.

Still other comedies of manners of recent years tackle a similar
theme of peer-free competence from a different perspective. They
portray with sympathy the style of a man who allows himself the
luxury of being a "generalist" at life, self-educated, eccentric, near-
autonomous. In the *Mr. Belvedere* series, for instance, Clifton
Webb is a thinly disguised intellectual and social deviant who is an
expert at anything he cares to turn his hand and brain to. Yet, like
Beatrice Lillie, he attains his range of skill and competence only in
situations where society permits a high degree of individualism;
and he is allowed to create his breath-taking personal style only
because of his astonishing dexterity. On one level the "message"
of the Belvedere movies is quite different from that of the Douglas
movies, where a heightened expressiveness is suggested as an attractive "extra" in life to the ordinary upper-middle-class man and
not to the nonconformist. But on another level the two types of
pictures are very much alike. Both seem to be saying, among all the
other amusing things they have to say, that the power of the peers
can be overcome. Both characterizations give the individual the

right to explore and elaborate his own personality and sensitivity
with a work-leisure competence that goes beyond the requirements
of the peers.

Surely the great mass-media artists, including the directors, writers, and others behind the scenes who "create" and promote the
artists, make an important contribution to autonomy. The enter-
tainers, in their media, out of their media, and in the never-never
land between, exert a constant pressure on the accepted peer-groups
and suggest new modes of escape from them. The sharpest critics of
American movies are likely to forget this too easily. In their concentration on the indubitable failures of quality in Hollywood movies,
they sometimes miss the point that the movies have multiplied the
leisure styles available to millions. Even the fan who imitates the
casual manner of Humphrey Bogart or the fearless energetic pride
of Katharine Hepburn may in the process be emancipating himself
or herself from a narrow-minded peer-group. Or, to take another
instance, it seems likely that the wild, fantastic suspiciousness of
W. C. Fields may have served many in his audience as a support to
their own doubts concerning the unquestioned value of smooth
amiability and friendliness. I believe that the movies, in many con-
ventionally unexpected ways, are liberating agents, and that they
need defense against indiscriminate highbrow criticism as well as
against the ever-ready veto groups who want the movies to tutor
their audiences in all the pious virtues the home and school have
failed to inculcate.

One of these virtues is "activity" as such, and much current rejection of the movies symbolizes a blanket rejection of our allegedly
passive popular-culture consumership. By contrast, the critics are
likely to place their bets on leisure activities that are individualistic
and involve personal participation. For instance, craftsmanship.

THE POSSIBILITIES OF CRAFTSMANSHIP

The "Belvedere" movies happen to be flashing satire on competence and craftsmanship, in much the way that *The Admirable
Crichton* is a satire on competence and class. Today the craftsman
often seems eccentric because of his fanatical devotion to his craft
or hobby; Mr. Belvedere uses his various craft-skills to flaunt and
enjoy his eccentricity, to rub it in. In this sense his life style is a
new commentary on the question whether craft competence in

leisure is on the decline in America. Certainly many people have the leisure and encouragement to pursue crafts who never did before. We are told that the employees at the Hawthorne plant of the Western Electric Company include thousands of active, eager gardeners; that they run an annual hobby show of considerable size and style; that the factory helps bring together amateur photographers, woodcarvers, model builders—the whole countless range of modern hobbyism—in addition, of course, to the usual sports, music, and dramatic groups. But there are no statistics to show whether hobbies that were once privately pursued are now simply taken over as part of the program of the active, indeed world-famous, industrial relations department. Beyond a few careful exploratory works such as the Lundberg, Komarovsky, and Mc-Inerny book, *Leisure: A Suburban Study,* we do not even begin to know whether craftsmanlike leisure has developed new meanings in modern America.

It seems plausible to assume that the craftsmanlike use of leisure has certain compatibilities with the whole way of life of men dependent on inner-direction: their attention to the hardness of the material, their relative unconcern and lack of training for the more complex forms of peer-group taste-exchanging. Moreover, the inner-directed man who carries into his hobby some of his surplus work impulses might find the maintenance of his technical skill playing directly back into his value on the job, making him, for instance, a better and more inventive gadgeteer. Even today, among many skilled workmen, such interchange between the home hobby shop and the plant suggestion box is not by any means a forgotten folkway. But the craft-skill is valued more than ever before for its own sake, as in the case of the Sunday painter.

The dramatic turn toward craftsmanlike hobbies in an advanced economy, in which it pays to cater to the desires of those reacting against mass production, has its own peculiar problems. The conservatism of the craftsman—in this aspect, part of the conservatism of play itself—finds its ideals of competence constantly threatened by a series of power tools and hobby products that make it possible for the dub to appear like a professional. The home craftsman of real craft aspirations is better off with a power tool than without one. But how many can retain the spontaneous craft aspiration in the face of the temptation to have the machine do it better?

Some of the ambiguities of contemporary craft hobbyism dependent on a power tool are illustrated by a study of automotive hobbyists—especially the hot rodders.[1] In this field, a wide range of standards of technique and design gives room to both the green amateurs and the semi-professional car racers, while all the hobbyists have the comfort of working within an old American tradition of high-level tinkering. Competence and imagination are on the scene in force among the youths who race their quassi-Fords and quasi-Chevrolets on the Dry Lakes of the Far West, in a continuous competition with the mass-produced standards of Detroit. Among these groups there exists an active and critical attitude toward the Detroit car as it is now built, or as it was built until recently. Here, astonishingly enough, the top commercial product of the country, the Detroit car, far from driving out amateur performance, has only stimulated, perhaps even provoked it. Moreover, the individual who remakes cars according to standards of his own devising is obviously not exploiting any questionable social dividend in his pursuit of leisure but is "doing for himself" with what parts and help he can muster on a small bank-roll. The very economy of his means helps give the procedure its atmosphere of high competence and high enjoyment.

But this field too is becoming professionalized and standardized. *The Hot Rod,* a magazine founded to cater to the growing number of auto hobbyists (at the same time standardizing their self-image), reports that the business of supplying the amateurs with parts and tools is becoming a big business—some $8,000,000 in 1948. In the meantime Detroit has found its way to many of the hot-rodder power-plant notions, if not stripped-down body notions.

We see looming upon the horizon of the hot rodder much the same fate that has overtaken other forms of amateur competence, not only in the area of crafts and hobbies but, as we shall see below in the instance of jazz, in the area of taste-exchange and criticism. Those who seek play autonomy in a craft must keep an eye on the peer-groups (other than their own immediate one) and on the market, if only to keep out of their way. But this in turn may involve them in a steady search for difficulties in execution and privacies in vocabulary (in some ways, like the "mysteries" of medieval craftsmen) in order to outdistance the threatening invasion of the crowd. Then what began more or less spontaneously may end up as merely effortful marginal differentiation, with the roots of fantasy torn up by a concern for sheer technique. The paradox of

[1] See "The Hot-Rod Culture," by Eugene Balsley, in the American Quarterly, II (1950), 353.

craftsmanship, and of much other play, is that in order to attain any importance as an enlivener of fantasy it must be "real." But whenever the craftsman has nourished a real competence he also tends to call into being an industry and an organization to circumvent the competence or at least to standardize it.

The man whose daily work is glad handing can often rediscover both his childhood and his inner-directed residues by serious craftsmanship. An advertising man, involved all day in personalizing, may spend his week ends in the craftsmanlike silences of a boatyard or in sailboat racing—that most inner-directed pursuit where the individual racers independently move toward the goal as if guided by an invisible hand! And yet it is clear that these "players" may locate themselves in the craftsmanship pattern for reasons that have nothing to do with the search either for competence or for the more distant goal of autonomy.

It is important to see the limitations of the answer of craftsmanship, because otherwise we may be tempted to place more stock in it than is warranted. This temptation is particularly strong among those who try to deal with the challenge of modern leisure by filling it with play styles drawn from the past in Europe or America. Indeed, there is a widespread trend today to warn Americans against relaxing in the featherbed of plenty, in the pulpy recreations of popular culture, in the delights of bar and coke bar, and so on. In these warnings any leisure that looks easy is suspect, and craftsmanship does not look easy.

The other-directed man in the upper social strata often finds a certain appeal in taking the side of craftsmanship against consumption. Yet in general it is a blind alley for the other-directed man to try to adapt his leisure styles to those which grew out of an earlier character and an earlier social situation; in the process he is almost certain to become a caricature. This revivalist tendency is particularly clear in the type of energetic craft hobbyist we might term the folk dancer. The folk dancer is often an other-directed urbanite or suburbanite who, in search of an inner-directed stance, becomes "artsy and craftsy" in his recreations and consumer tastes. He goes native, with or without regional variations. He shuts out the mass media as best he can. He never wearies of attacking from the pulpit of his English bicycle the plush and chrome of the new-model cars. He is proud of not listening to the radio, and television is his bugbear.

The vogue of the folk dancer is real testimony to people's search for meaningful, creative leisure, as is, too, the revival of craftsmanship. The folk dancer wants something better but does not know where to look for it. He abandons the utopian possibilities of the future because, in his hatred of the American present, as he interprets it, he is driven to fall back on the vain effort to resuscitate the European or American past as a model for play. Like many other people who carry the ancestor within of an inner-directed character and ideology, he fears the dangerous avalanche of leisure that is coming down on the Americans.

In this fear the folk dancer is near-cousin to a number of other contemporary critics who, though genuinely concerned with autonomy, have no hope of finding it in play—not even, for the most part, in the hard play of crafts or sports. These critics go the folk dancer one better; they look to experiences of enforced hardship in work, or even to social and individual catastrophe, as the only practicable source of group cohesion and individual strength of character. They see men as able to summon and develop their resources only in an extreme or frontier situation, and they would regard my program for the life of Riley in a leisure economy as inviting psychological disintegration and social danger. Hating the "softness of the personnel"—not seeing how much of this represents a characterological advance—they want to restore artificially (in extreme cases, even by resort to war[2]) the "hardness of the material."

That catastrophes do sometimes evoke unsuspected potentialities in people—potentialities which can then be used for further growth toward autonomy—is undeniable. A serious illness may give a man pause, a time for reverie and resolution. He may recover, as the hero, Laskell, does in Lionel Trilling's novel, *The Middle of the Journey*. He may die, as does the Russian official in Tolstoy's short story, "The Death of Ivan Ilyitch," who near death, confronts himself and his wasted life honestly for the first time. And the

---

[2] The war experience seemed to establish that there was little "practical" need for such hardship therapies in the interests of production or warmaking. It turned out that characterological other-direction and political indifference did not imply an inability to stand physical hardships. Efforts were made to treat the soldier as if he were in America, with cokes, radio programs, and entertainments from home. Apparently such "softness" did not impede fighting power. The tractability of Americans made it possible to build an army less on hierarchy than on group-mindedness. The tractability, the familiarity with machines, the widespread social skills, and the high educational level made it possible to train men quickly for the fantastically varied services and missions of modern warfare.

swath of the last war does offer repeated evidence that not only individuals but whole groups and communities can benefit from hardship, where not too overwhelming. An example is reported by Robert K. Merton, Patricia Salter West, and Marie Jahoda in their (unpublished) study of a warworkers' housing community in New Jersey. The warworkers found themselves living in a jerry-built morass, without communal facilities, without drainage, without a store. Challenged by their circumstances, they responded by energetic improvisation and managed, against all kinds of obstacles, to make a decent, livable, even a lively community for themselves. The dispiriting sequel is familiar: the community, its major problems of sheer existence surmounted, became less interesting to live in, its cooperative store, built by so much energetic and ingenious effort, folded up.

When one reflects on such instances, one realizes that emergencies in a modern society help recreate social forms into which people can with justification pour their energies. People need justification and, as inner-direction wanes, look for it in the social situation rather than within themselves. European and Asian visitors tell Americans that we must learn to enjoy idleness; they criticize alternately our puritan idealism and the so-called materialism which is a by-product of it. This is not too helpful: for if we are to become autonomous, we must proceed in harmony with our history and character, and these assign us a certain sequence of developmental tasks and pleasures. What we need, then, is a reinterpretation which will allow us to focus on individual character development the puritan demands no longer needed to spur industrial and political organization. We need to realize that each life is an emergency, which only happens once, and the "saving" of which, in character terms, justifies care and effort. Then, perhaps, we will not need to run to a war or a fire because the daily grist of life itself is not felt as sufficiently challenging, or because external threats and demands can narcotize for us our anxiety about the quality and meaning of individual existence.

The Newer Criticism in the Realm of Taste

Craftsmanship, whatever part it may play in the leisure of an individual or a group, is obviously not a complete solution to the problems of leisure among the would-be autonomous. While the inner-directed man could solace himself in these pursuits, the other-directed man in search of autonomy has no choice but to pass into and through—to transcend—taste-exchanging—that characteristic process by which the other-directed person relates himself to the peer-groups. Once he has traversed this stage successfully he may be able to value and develop his own standards of taste, even to criticize the taste-making operations in the society as a whole.

We have already discussed the negative side of this process: the fact, for example, that the other-directed man feels a mistake in taste as a reflection on his self, or at least on what he conceives to be the most vital part of his self, his radar, and that taste-exchanging is consequently often harried and desperate. But now we must look at the positive side of taste-exchanging: the fact that it is also a tremendous experiment, perhaps the most strategic one, in American adult education. The taste of the most advanced sections of the population is ever more rapidly diffused—perhaps *Life* is the most striking agent in this process—to strata, formerly excluded from all but the most primitive exercise of taste, and who are now taught to appreciate, and discriminate between varieties of, modern architecture, modern furniture, and modern art—not to speak of the artistic achievements of other times.[3]

Of course, all the other-directed processes we have decribed play a central role in this development, but I am convinced that real and satisfying competence in taste also increases at the same time. It is interesting to note how "old-fashioned" American movies of only twenty years ago appear to a contemporary audience. In part, again, this is caused only by changes in fllm conventions; but in far greater measure, it is the product of an amazingly rapid growth of sophistication as to human motivation and behavior among movie-makers and their audience.

The speed with which the taste gradient is being climbed has escaped many critics of the popular arts who fail to observe not only how good American movies, popular novels, and magazines frequently are but also how energetic and understanding are some of the comments of the amateur taste-exchangers who seem at first glance to be part of a very passive, uncreative audience. One of the most interesting examples of this is jazz criticism. I speak here

[3] Charles Livermore, formerly a CIO official, recently called my attention to the extremely rapid disavowal by Detroit auto workers of overstuffed, Grand Rapids furniture. Many in the last several years have gone in for modern design.

not of such critics as Wilder Hobson and Panassié but of the large number of young people who, all over the country, greeted jazz affectionately and criticized it fondly, on a level of discourse far removed from the facile vocabulary of "sincerity" or "swell." These people found in jazz, as others have found in the movies or the comic strips, an art form not previously classified by the connoisseurs, the school system, or the official culture. They resisted, often violently, and occasionally with success, the effort of the popular-music industry itself to ticket its products: in the very form of their choices—preference for combos over star soloists, preference for improvisation, distrust of smooth arrangers—they set up their own *standards* in opposition to *standardization*. Much like the hot rodders, they developed their own language and culture to go with their new skill.

Here again, as with the hot rodders, the verbal craftsmanship of jazz lovers' taste-exchange could not long continue to develop among isolated peer-groups. Jazz has long since been parceled out by a cult or a series of cults using increasingly exacting aesthetic criteria which have often become ends in themselves.

Unwilling to see that taste-exchanging in popular audiences often is the basis for increasing competence in criticism, writers on popular culture generally view jazz, soap opera, the movies, and television with the same horror with which the inner-directed man was urged to view the brothel and burlesque. Essentially this critique of mass culture is the same as the critique of mass production. But what the critics often fail to observe is that, while in its earlier stages mass production did drive out fine handicrafts and debase taste, we have now a situation better termed *class*-mass production where our industrial machine has become flexible enough to turn out objects of even greater variety and quality than in the handicraft era. Likewise, the critics of the mass media may fail to observe that, while their first consequences were often destructive of older values, we have today a situation in which it is economically possible for the first time in history to distribute first-class novels and nonfiction, paintings, music, and movies to audiences that can fit them into leisure patterns of great individuality.

It is these developments which suggest to me that the process of taste-exchanging holds the promise of transcending itself and becoming something quite different, and of signally contributing to the development of autonomy in other-directed man.

III. The Avocational Counselors

To bring the individual into unfrightening contact with the new range of opportunities in consumption often requires some guides and signposts. In our urban, specialized society it may demand "avocational counselors."

"Avocational counseling" may seem like a rather clinical term with which to describe the activities undertaken by a number of relatively rapidly growing professions in the United States, including travel agents, hotel men, resort directors, sports teachers and coaches, teachers of the arts, including dancing teachers, and so on. But there are also many counselors who supply advice on play and leisure as a kind of by-product of some other transaction. The interior decorator, for instance, seems at first glance to belong in a different occupational group from the dude-ranch social director. To be sure, most clients of the interior decorator may be looking for the correct design for conspicuous display. But beyond these functions may lie a realm in which the interior decorator is looked to for more basic domestic rearrangements that can facilitate a more comfortable leisure life, more "colorful" literally and figuratively. The sale of the decorating service may conceal the sale of this significant intangible.

This function is perhaps even more evident in the work of the domestic architect for the upper middle-class client. True, like the decorator, he still counsels his clients in providing the correct public façade. But a generation ago he would not have dreamed of counseling his clients about the functional interior relationships in the dwelling in terms of anything more than "gracious living." Today, however, the architect, by interior and exterior planning, can lead as well as follow the play patterns of his clients. Through him and his views there filters a variety of tastes, inclinations, social schemes (as in easily rearranged living rooms), leisure-time ecologies that scarcely existed a generation ago. The architect—and, beyond him, the city planner—brings together play opportunities that might otherwise remain subdivided among a score of specialists.

Another set of avocational counselors is clustered around the chronological center of American leisure habits, the vacation. The vacation itself, frequently involving the meeting of others who are not members of one's own peer-group and who may be located outside one's own experience with the social structure, may be considered as dramatic a symbol of the encounters among people in the population phase of incipient decline as the market place was in the population phase of transitional growth. To be sure, with high wages millions of Americans spend their vacations hunting animals rather than people; other millions putter about that restorative residue of earlier eras—the house-and-garden. But increasingly the vacation serves as a time and place for bringing those who have leisure and money to buy in contact with those who have a leisure skill to sell—riding, swimming, painting, dancing, and so on. But of course avocational counseling here, except perhaps for ship and shore recreational directors, is usually trying to sell a commodity or a service rather than to help the individual find what he wants and might want.

It is easy to foresee, in the next decades, a great expansion among the avocational counselors. The objection remains that to turn the other-directed man over to an avocational counselor to teach him competence in play is merely to increase the very dependence which keeps him other-directed rather than autonomous. Will not any effort at planning of play rob him of such spontaneity and privacy as he may still retain? This is certainly one possible effect. We can counter it by doing our best to make the avocational counselors as good and as available as possible. The avocational counselor might stimulate, even provoke, the other-directed person to more imaginative play by helping him realize how very important for his own development toward autonomy play is.

Further Readings

LINTON, RALPH, *The Cultural Background of Personality*. New York: Appleton-Century-Crofts, Inc., 1945.

MILLER, DANIEL and GUY E. SWANSON, *Inner Conflict and Defense*. New York: Holt, Rinehart and Winston, Inc., 1960.

RIESMAN, DAVID, *Individualism Reconsidered*. New York: The Free Press of Glencoe, Inc., 1954.

RIESMAN, DAVID. *Constraint and Variety in American Education*. Lincoln, Nebraska: University of Nebraska Press, 1956.

Questions for Discussion

1. Often physical education classes disregard individual preferences by not allowing pupils to choose their activities. How
   can this be remedied?
2. Does the right to play belong only to those who work? Explain.
3. What is the philosophical defense of our way of financing
   the training of athletes as opposed to the Russian system of
   subsidization?
4. Do we have autonomy of play? What portions of the physical
   education program provide for it?
5. How does the physical educator determine the extent to
   which play should be individualized?

DAVIS McENTIRE

Patterns of Leisure Activity*

One of the greatest problems facing the American society is preserving an open social structure. Presently, certain culturally and
economically deprived individuals are not being afforded the
opportunities of a great democracy. Although some social ranking is inevitable in a competitive society, mobility within the
class structure must be ensured if democracy is to survive. A
predominant purpose of the American school system and
principle of physical education is the recognition of equal
opportunity. This principle has certainly been exemplified by
athletic programs in most of the nation.

In the article by McEntire, the reader will find how the patterns of leisure opportunities are restricted for some groups.
The article by Havighurst and Neugarten shows how athletics
can be a vehicle for the social mobility of culturally deprived
students. Finally, in the reading by Whyte, the reader will discover how social rank develops in small, informal groups.

* Reprinted and abridged with permission of the author and the publisher from
Leisure Activities of the Youth of Berkeley, California. Berkeley: Council of
Social Welfare, 1952, pp. 10–16.

The following reading illustrates the differences in patterns of leisure activities within different socio-economic and ethnic groups. If it is true that lower socio-economic classes and certain ethnic groups have fewer choices for leisure activities, then physical education should provide a broader spectrum of recreational opportunities.

For purposes of the present survey, the term "leisure time" is used broadly to include all of a youth's waking hours not spent in school. Much of this time is, of course, not available for strictly leisure activities. The first question in every interview "How do you spend your time after school and on Saturdays and Sundays?" This question was designed to include not merely activities of a recreational character, but all activities engaged in during non-school hours. . . .

More than two-fifths of the boys and nearly a third of the girls give some part of their time to paid employment. The intermediate socio-economic groups appear to work more than the youth of either Group 1 [lowest] or Group 4 [highest]. The principal jobs are delivering papers, working in stores, and baby sitting—the last being the major money-making activity of girls. Negro and Mexican youth are not employed nearly as much as the general youth population, a difference probably attributable to the scarcity of jobs for members of these groups. Boys and girls of Oriental parentage, however, have a relatively high employment rate, which is probably a reflection of their work in family businesses.

The tasks of school home-work rest lightly on the majority of high school and junior high school youth of Berkeley. Only a third devote as much as an hour per day on the average to their studies outside of school hours. Girls spend somewhat more time than boys on their studies, and high school students more than junior high pupils. Even in the high school group, however, the majority spend less than an hour per average daily on school home-work.

In the proportion who spend an hour or more per day on studies outside of school hours, there is a consistent progression from the lowest to the highest socio-economic group. . . . The proportion is almost twice as great in Group 4 as in Group 1. A striking difference is also apparent as among the ethnic groups. Oriental youth are more studious than any other group, half of them giving an hour or more per day to their school work outside of school.

Least studious are the youth of Mexican parentage, only one-sixth of whom spend as much as an hour a day in school home-work.

Almost all youth claim to "help at home" but fewer than half spend as much as an hour per day on the average in this activity. As might be expected, girls "help" considerably more than boys. Youth of the lower socio-economic groups give substantially more time to helping at home than do those of the higher groups. Negro and Mexican youth, in this respect, follow the pattern of the lower socio-economic groups, while Orientals approximate the general practice.

The transition from junior high school to the high school age group is marked by declines in church attendance, use of parks and playgrounds, movie attendance, and participation in organized group meetings, and by increases in attendance in sport events, dancing, house parties, talking on the telephone, and use of commercial recreational facilities other than movies. Use of the YM- and YWCA remains about the same in both age groups. As between the sexes, girls are distinguished by more frequent church attendance, participation in church programs, window shopping, talking on the telephone, social dancing, folk dancing, house parties, and music and art lessons. The other activities listed girls engage in less frequently than boys.

Leisure activity tends to be patterned not only by age and sex but also by socio-economic group. . . . The lower socio-economic groups make a much greater use of parks and playgrounds than do the youth at higher socio-economic levels; they go more frequently to the YM- and YWCA, attend more movies, and spend more time watching television. On the other hand, organized group activities, social dancing, and music and art lessons play a far more prominent role in the leisure life of the higher socio-economic groups than in the lower ones. Other activities in which the lower group youth engage more frequently than do the members of Groups 3 and 4 are church attendance, "walking around town," automobile pleasure riding, attending school sport events, and going to soda fountains and drive-ins.

It is difficult to explain these socio-economic group differences entirely in terms of the financial cost of given activities. Although some of the major activities of the lower groups are relatively cost-less, yet movie theater admissions are not free and neither are TV sets. Rather, it would appear that the differences in activity emphases are the reflection of differences in values and ways of life. The most frequent activities of Group 1 and to a lesser extent, of Group 2 are those which can be done on a casual, unplanned, "spur of the moment" basis. They are activities with a minimum of structure, which can be carried on for a short or long period according to the immediate impulse of the doer. From the standpoint of social participation, the most prominent lower group activities tend to be either of the spectator variety (movies, TV, school sport events) or of an unorganized, individualistic type such as going to parks and playgrounds, "dropping in" at the YM- or YWCA, "walking around town," and so forth.

The youth of Group 4, in contrast, put less emphasis on spectator activities, but much more emphasis on participation in organized programs and on activities of a "cultural" nature such as music and art lessons and folk dancing. As previously indicated, these youth also give much more time to their studies outside of school hours than do the members of Groups 1 and 2, but they have fewer home duties.

In the contrasts of activity patterns between the lower and higher socio-economic groups, it must be borne in mind that the differences are only of degree. All activities are engaged in to some extent by the youth of all socio-economic groups, but the *emphases* of the several groups are different. In this respect the youth of Berkeley are by no means unique. The present findings are in general agreement with the results of previous studies in other parts of the country which have demonstrated a marked relationship between the socio-economic background of children and their leisure behavior.

Turning to the activity patterns of the minor ethnic groups, one is immediately impressed with the generally high level of activity characteristic of Negro youth. . . . Only in organized group participation and school home-work are the Negro boys and girls conspicuously low. In the majority of activities, the Negro participation rate is higher than that of any socio-economic groups. In social dancing, music and art lessons, attendance at non-school sports, and pleasure reading,—activities characteristic of the higher socio-economic groups, the Negro rate is exceeded only by that of Group 4. In other activities characteristic of the lower socio-economic groups, including attendance at school sports, soda fountains, helping at home, and watching television, Negro participation is exceeded only by that of Group 1. No group rivals the Negro youth in frequency of resort to parks and playgrounds, YM- and YWCA, and church attendance. In frequency of movie-going, Negroes are exceeded only by the youth of Mexican parentage.

Mexican youth are relatively high in their use of parks and play-grounds, YM- and YWCA, church attendance, "walking around town," automobile pleasure riding, movie attendance, house parties, and television watching. In organized group participation and school home-work their rates are the lowest of any group. They are also low in attendance at sport events, shopping, social danc-ing, folk dancing, and music or art lessons.

The Oriental group contrasts with Negro youth in showing a rela-tively low rate of activities generally. They are high only in use of the YM- and YWCA, participation in church groups and programs other than services, music and art lessons, and in time devoted to study outside of school hours.

The leisure behavior of Negro and Mexican youth in many re-spects resembles that of the lower socio-economic groups. This is not surprising since more than four-fifths of the Negro and Mexi-can youth in the present survey samples fall in Socio-economic Group 1 by the criteria previously described. It is a reasonable inference that the activity patterns characteristic of Negro and Mexican youth are connected primarily not with their race or ethnic group as such, but with their low socio-economic status. This seems particularly true of Negroes who have no background in a foreign culture. The only respect in which the Negro youth differ from *all* other groups is their high, general level of activity. They are an "active" group, engaged in many and frequent enterprises. In distribution of emphasis, however, their pattern is very similar to that of Socio-economic Group 1.

Mexican-American youth exhibit to a high degree the pattern of unorganized, casual, spontaneous activities characteristic of the lowest socio-economic group but with a seeming, added disinclina-tion toward activities involving social participation. The only ac-tivities in which their frequency exceeds that of the lowest socio-economic group are use of parks and playgrounds, automobile pleasure riding, movies, fishing, and house parties. The last item, plainly involving an intimate type of social participation, seems to be out of pattern. However, it is an activity of exceptionally high frequency for both Negroes and Mexicans. It may be that the term was misunderstood by Negro and Mexican interview subjects, or it is possible that house parties may be a popular form of social activity within these ethnic groups, substituting in some measure for the lack of participation in the "social" affairs of the larger community.

The youth of Oriental parentage in the present survey are somewhat concentrated in the lower socio-economic groups but not nearly so much so as the Negroes and Mexicans. About one-fifth of them fall in Groups 3 and 4. They do not fit the pattern either of the lower or the higher socio-economic groups. Their activity pattern seems to reflect partly a withdrawal from the forms of social participation represented in organized group meetings, social and folk dancing and attendance at sport events; partly a culture based de-emphasis of movies, television, house parties, and telephone talking. Probably the large amount of time devoted by Oriental youth to study and part-time jobs has much to do with their limited leisure activity participation. . . .

[Parks, playgrounds and recreation centers] are used to some extent by two-thirds of the youth of Berkeley including more than 85 percent of the boys and 60 percent of the girls. Clearly apparent is the relatively large use of parks and playgrounds by Negro and Mexican youth and by members of Socio-economic Group 1. In sharp contrast is the comparatively infrequent use of these facilities by Oriental youth and those of the higher socio-economic groups. . . . It is evident that the YMCA has been more successful in attracting boys to its program than has the YWCA in reaching girls. The difference is not great in Socio-economic Group 1. It is the girls of the higher socio-economic groups who "stay away from the YWCA in droves." The YMCA also, however, had evidently a much greater appeal to the boys of the lower socio-economic groups than to those of the higher groups. It is notable that nearly two-thirds of the Negro youth and almost half of the Mexican group attend the YM- or YWCA, most of them at least once a week.

This difference among socio-economic groups in use of the Ys is probably more pronounced in Berkeley than elsewhere. A recent study in the School of Social Welfare, as yet unpublished, of junior high school students in the adjacent city of Oakland, failed to find a similar relationship there. Following are the proportions of Oakland junior high school students (white only) who reported attendance at the YM- or YWCA:

Upper middle class	29.3 percent	
Lower middle class	26.5	"
Upper lower class	21.9	"
Lower lower class	23.6	"

The Oakland data actually indicate, for white youth, a social class relationship the reverse of the situation in Berkeley, although less strongly marked.[1]

Undoubtedly the location of the YM- and YWCA buildings in Berkeley plays a large part in determining the type of population served. As previously indicated, both Ys have very active branches in the south Berkeley Negro residential area, and the YMCA also has a branch in west Berkeley. The central downtown buildings in both cases are also rather more readily accessible to the lower status areas than to the "best" residential districts. There are no branches in the Berkeley hills or Claremont district (areas 5 and 6). In addition to location factors, there is reason to believe, from unpublished social studies of Berkeley High School and informal evidence noted in the course of this study, that there are prestige factors operating; and the Ys, by the very fact of attracting many members of the lower socio-economic groups and ethnic minorities, have tended to alienate those of higher status and others seeking to climb the social ladder. . . .

Boys frequenting the YMCA engage in quite different types of activity than do the girls at the YWCA—a difference doubtless mainly reflecting different program emphases in the respective organizations. The large majority of boys go to the YMCA only on a casual, "drop in" basis. Most of the girls, however, engage either in the activities of organized, small groups or mass activities, chiefly dance. In both agencies, the relatively few Group 4 youth who attend do so for casual or mass activities; very few participate in small groups.

Extra-curricular activities at school have not been discussed up to this point. To measure participation in activities of this type an index was constructed by summing the number of activities engaged in, each one being weighted by a measure of its frequency. . . . Approximately three out of five students participate to some extent in extra-curricular activities. No difference is observed in participa-

---

[1] The Oakland survey was based on a virtually complete canvass of all junior high school students in the city. Because the sample sizes are so large, the differences among the percentages cited above are all statistically significant.

tion rates as between boys and girls. The amount of extra-curricular activity, however, increases with rising socio-economic status, particularly among girls. Only half of Group 1 girls take any part in extra-curricular activities as compared with three-fourths of those in Groups 3 and 4. The proportion of girls with high rates of extra-curricular activity is four times as great in Group 4 as in Group 1. It is evident from these comparisons that extra-curricular programs for girls are largely dominated by the girls of higher socio-economic status. This tendency is much less pronounced among the boys.

Negro youth show a characteristically high rate of extra-curricular activity, and the youth of Mexican parentage a low rate expected in view of their general pattern. Oriental youth are in between.

Two attitude questions asked of the youth were (1) "Of all the things you do outside of school hours, which one do you like the best?" and (2) "What other things would you like to do?" . . . .

Sports are the activity best liked by a large plurality of both boys and girls in every socio-economic group. As might be expected, sports are favored by a much higher proportion of boys than of girls. In second place are non-specific peer group activities ("just being with my gang," "my bunch"), followed by dancing and going to movies. Dancing is preferred by more of the higher socio-economic groups than of the lower groups. The Mexican group characteristically contains the highest proportion of individuals favoring peer group activities.

One-fourth of the boys and one-fifth of the girls stated they had no desire for additional activities. In both groups it was the younger ones who most frequently expressed a wish for "more things to do." Curiously, the proportion of youth desiring additional activities increases with each upward step in the socio-economic scale. Nearly one-third of Group 1 but only one-sixth of Group 4 are satisfied with their existing activities to the extent of desiring nothing additional.

With respect to type of additional activity desired, sports are again favored by a plurality of all groups. In second place for girls are music and other artistic activities. Boys show a wide scatter of preferences with no clear pattern, and neither are there any significant differences among the socio-economic groups in this respect.

To the question, "What keeps you from doing additional desired activities?", the stock answer was "lack of time" or "I don't know."

The frequency of these responses suggests that the majority of the youth either had no definite wishes for additional activities or did not attach much importance to the wishes which they expressed. It is worth noting, however, that more than two-fifths of the youth including over half of those in Socio-economic Group 1 were able to verbalize definite obstacles to desired activities. Interestingly, relatively few Negroes, despite their high level of activity generally, seemed to feel that time was a barrier to the things they wished to do. The Mexican group appears to have the clearest perception of obstacles to desired activity. Few of this group gave "don't know" answers, and relatively few alleged lack of time. Nearly one-third mentioned lack of physical facilities in which to carry on desired activities.

Another approach to the question of the adequacy of activities was explored with the question, "Some people say there should be more things for teen-agers to do in their free time. What do you think about this?" The youth were almost evenly divided in their responses, with a slight majority in agreement with the statement. This majority was confined to Groups 1 and 2, however. The greater number of those in the higher socio-economic groups disagreed with the statement, feeling that leisure time opportunities for youth were already sufficient. Curiously, the socio-economic group differential of responses to this question appears to be in conflict with replies to the earlier question on desire for additional activities. . . . The explanation appears to be that youth of the higher groups believe there are sufficient activities available but they lack time to do all that they would like to do. The lower groups, on the other hand, appear to sense an actual lack of "things to do."

Summer Camping Experience

Vacation-time activities were not included within the scope of the present study, the only exception being a question about summer camp experience. Replies indicated that some three-fifths of the boys and half of the girls had attended camp during at least one summer. As might be expected, summer camp experience showed a marked relationship to socio-economic and ethnic status. Three-fourths of the Group 4 youth had had camping experience and nearly one-fourth had attended camp as often as four times. A similar, relatively restricted camping experience was also characteristic of the minor ethnic groups.

Further Readings

BOSEN, B. C., "The Achievement Syndrome, A Psycho-cultural Dimension of Social Stratification," *The American Sociological Review*, vol. 21 (1956), pp. 203–211.

BOTERO, GIOVANNI, "The Greatness of Cities," (translated by Robert Peterson, 1606), in Giovanni Botero, *The Reason of State and the Greatness of Cities*. New Haven: Yale University Press, 1956.

FRAZIER, EDWARD F., *The Negro Family in the United States*, revised and abridged ed. New York: Holt, Rinehart and Winston, Inc., 1948.

FREUD, SIGMUND, *Civilization and Its Discontents*. New York: Doubleday & Company, Inc., 1958.

GLUECK, SHELDON and ELEANOR GLUECK, *Unraveling Juvenile Delinquency*. New York: Commonwealth Fund, 1950.

LINTON, RALPH, *The Cultural Backgrounds of Personality*. New York: Appleton-Century-Crofts, Inc., 1945.

RIESMAN, DAVID, N. GLAZER and R. DENNY, *The Lonely Crowd*. New Haven: Yale University Press, 1950.

Questions for Discussion

1. Why do leisure activities tend to be patterned along socio-economic groupings?
2. Why do differences in values exist between upper and lower socio-economic groups in their regard for sporting activities?
3. Why does there seem to be a greater spectator interest among lower class persons than among other classes?
4. What can physical education do to help eliminate differences in leisure activities for lower and higher socio-economic groups?
5. Why are sports rated "best liked" by a large number of boys and girls in every socio-economic group?

ROBERT J. HAVIGHURST and
BERNICE L. NEUGARTEN

Athletic Prowess and Mobility*

One often discussed effect of physical education is the minimization of cultural and ethnic differences in team sports. Also, athletic prowess offers students an opportunity for social mobility. The description that follows demonstrates how one individual improved his social and economic position through athletics. Athletic prowess is a means of social mobility—as are education, in general, or marriage, and money—; it is important that the physical educator understand the social opportunities presented by his field.

Athletic prowess combined with education often provides a very good base for mobility in a lower-class boy.

Joe Plano was the son of an immigrant factory worker. He grew up in the canalport area of Metropolis, and became known as a tough fighter, a good team member and a reliable friend. His father and mother kept their family under fairly close control, requiring the children to become confirmed in the parish church and to attend Mass every Sunday morning. Though Joe sometimes got into trouble through his neighborhood gang, pilfering fruit from a fruit stand and climbing across fences and garage-tops in the alleys, his father kept him out of any serious trouble with the police by watching him closely and punishing him at times. He made it a point to spend as much time as he could with Joe and his brothers, taking them to the park or to the beach when they were young boys, and later to baseball games whenever he could afford it.

In the sixth grade Joe had an unusually good teacher, and he learned that he could master his reading and arithmetic quite easily if he worked steadily. From that time on he never had any trouble

* Reprinted with permission of the authors and the publishers from *Society and Education*, 2d edition. Boston: Allyn and Bacon, Inc., 1962, pp. 52–54.

with his studies in school or college, though he never got top grades for his work.

Growing into a youngster with strong legs and broad shoulders, Joe began to play basketball in the school gymnasium and football in the park. By the time he reached high school he had the makings of a "natural athlete" and was playing on the light-weight team as a freshman. The coach made a special effort to get acquainted with Mr. Plano, and the two men worked together to make Joe into an all-star backfield man on the football team and a capable basketball guard.

From the coach and several men teachers Joe got the idea that college would be a good place for him. It was mainly a place where he could go on playing football, the thing he liked to do best of all. He knew that college required some effort at study, but his high school experience reassured him that he could make reasonably good grades. He did not think about the future beyond college. College life was unknown territory to him and his father, but it was nothing to worry about when, at the age of 18, Joe's pictures were in the newspapers and he had letters from several universities offering him scholarships.

A big, friendly fellow from X University came to visit Joe and offered him a scholarship and a part-time job, at the same time warning Joe and his father that college meant hard work at the books, and was no place for a boy without ambition. Joe made good in his freshman year, with a B average in his studies, a reputation as a steady fellow who could be depended on by his employer, and a first-class performance in football and basketball on the freshman teams. He was asked to join a fraternity and, after some hesitation because of the cost, did so. He decided he could earn enough money in the summer to meet the extra expense.

In his third and fourth years of college, he made the all-conference football team, and was captain in his senior year. He was popular on the campus, elected to an honorary society, and made good friends with dozens of boys and girls who would return to cities all over the state and feel proud to say, "I was a friend of Joe Plano in college."

The Director of Athletics had a talk with him one day in his office. "Joe," he said, "You can go in several directions next year, all of them good ones. You can play professional football or you can coach football. You can also start executive training with one of the big corporations that will send in their scouts to hire the best fellows in the senior class. Whatever you choose, let me know and I'll do all I can to help you."

Joe chose to become a high school coach and took a job in a town of 10,000. He had average success with his teams the first year, won the respect and affection of his boys, and was well liked by the other teachers. The second year his team won all of its football games, for the first time in a decade. Joe became immensely popular. He was invited to join the Lions Club, and was asked to speak at the football banquets of several neighboring smaller towns.

About this time he married Gertrude Brecht, the home economics teacher, also a Catholic, and the daughter of a farmer who was comfortably well off. She continued to teach for the first year, and they saved money for a house.

The next year Joe moved to a city of 100,000, as football coach and assistant basketball coach in the Central High School. Again he took a year to get himself established. Again he won the allegiance of his boys and the respect of the other teachers by his competent, straight-shooting way of doing his work. Gertrude had a baby that year, and Joe spent a good deal of time working around the yard and in the small ranch-style house in which they had invested their savings.

By his third year his football team won the conference championship. Joe was the most popular man in town. The Kiwanis Club sponsored a football banquet for the team, at which Joe was given the "keys of the town" by the Mayor. Joe later joined the Kiwanis Club. His salary was pushed up so rapidly that he had his house paid for in four years. He and Gertrude went regularly to the parish church, and made friends with other young couples in the section of town where they lived.

Joe at 33 had become a successful athletic coach, the idol of the boys in high school, and well liked by the businessmen. At this time he was offered a job as assistant football coach back at X University, with the promise that he could step into the head coach's shoes in four or five years if he made good. Talking it over with Gertrude and some of his friends in Kiwanis, Joe asked himself for the first time where he was heading in life. A man in the Kiwanis Club, middle-aged and head of the biggest insurance firm in the city, asked Joe to come to see him.

"Joe, you've got the makings of a good insurance man," he said. "I've watched you and I know you've got it. You can meet all kinds of people, with your reputation and your personality. My firm does business mainly with corporations. We sell all kinds of insurance, in big lots. We've got to have big men on our staff, men who can talk with big people. I think you can do it. Pretty soon you'll find that you're losing your magic touch in football. It happens to everybody in that game. But in the insurance game you can grow better and better. We couldn't start you at the salary you're making now, but it wouldn't be long before you would really be in the money."

So Joe left coaching and entered the insurance business. Again he had to build slowly, but after two years he knew he could do it in the insurance business as well as in the coaching business. He and Gertrude moved to a larger ranch-style house near the Country Club. They needed the space for their four children, and Joe had learned that he must have a fine home and good club connections if he was to do business with the top businessmen in the city.

Gertrude was busy and happy at home. She furnished her new house in good style, using what she had learned about the upper-middle-class life-style in her home economics training. Though she never pushed Joe ahead, she kept up with him in his career by keeping herself attractive when they attended social affairs, by keeping her house pleasant for visitors, and by seeing to it that the children were well behaved and well groomed.

Joe Plano gradually became Mr. Joseph Plano during the next twenty years. By the time his athletic reputation had waned, he had acquired a new reputation as an honest, sympathetic man who would do what he thought was best for his customers. He played a first-class game of golf, and wore conservative clothes suggested by the manager of the best men's store in town, a man who was an insurance client of his. He headed an important committee for the Chamber of Commerce. He was a leading layman in the Church. His children attended parochial schools, and his oldest boy was planning to go to Notre Dame where he hoped to make the football team.

Further Readings

CUBER, JOHN F. and WILLIAM KENKEL, *Social Stratification in the United States*. New York: Appleton-Century-Crofts, Inc., 1957.

CUBER, JOHN F. and ROBERT A. HARPER, *Problems of American Society*, revised ed. New York: Holt, Rinehart and Winston, Inc., 1951.

DRAKE, ST. CLAIR and HORACE R. CAYTON, *Black Metropolis*. New York: Harcourt Brace & World, Inc., 1945.

Questions for Discussion

1. What possible means of social mobility are available to people like Joe Plano?
2. What evidence is there that some athletes who have attained mobility through their athletic prowess become very disillusioned when they reach middle age?
3. Is is possible to attribute the mobility and success of Joe Plano only to personal characteristics?

WILLIAM FOOTE WHYTE

Bowling and Social Ranking*

Much of the general sociological interest in subcultural groups was stimulated by Whyte's *Street Corner Society*. His reference to bowling and social recreation has direct meaning for the physical educator. Special attention should be given to how a group or team is fostered, how leadership is changed, and how social ranking within the groups may affect athletic performance, particularly when these social rankings are frozen.

Bowling and Social Ranking

One evening in October, 1937, Doc scheduled a bowling match against the Italian Community Club, which was composed largely of college men who held their meetings every two weeks in the Norton Street Settlement House. The club was designed to be an

* Reprinted with permission of the publisher from *Street Corner Society*. Chicago: The University of Chicago Press, 1943, pp. 14–25.

organization of well-educated and superior men, although Doc was a member, and Angelo, Lou, and Fred of the Nortons had been voted in upon his recommendation. The other Nortons felt that the club was "high-toned," and around the corner it was known as the "Boys' Junior League." They were a little flattered that members of their group could mix with such a club, but their opinion was formed largely from the personalities of Chick Morelli, the president, and Tony Cardio, another prominent member, both of whom they considered snobbish and conceited. Consequently, the Nortons took this match very seriously.

Doc was captain of the Nortons. He selected Long John, Frank, Joe, and Tommy for his team. Danny and Mike were not bowling in this period. Chick and Tony led the Community Club team.

Feeling ran high. The Nortons shouted at the club bowlers and made all sorts of noises to upset their concentration. The club members were in high spirits when they gained an early lead but had little to say as the Nortons pulled ahead to win by a wide margin.

After the match I asked Frank and Joe if there was any team that they would have been more eager to beat. They said that if they could pick out their favorite victims, they would choose Chick Morelli, Tony Cardio, Joe Cardio (Tony's brother), Mario Testa, and Hector Marto. These last three had all belonged to the Sunset Dramatic Club.

Frank and Joe said that they had nothing against the other three men on the Community Club team but that the boys had been anxious to beat that team in order to put Chick and Tony "in their places." Significantly, Frank and Joe did not select their favorite victims on the basis of bowling ability. The five were good bowlers, but that was not the deciding factor in the choice. It was their social positions and ambitions that were the objects of attack, and it was that which made victory over the Community Club so satisfying.

Lou Danaro and Fred Mackey had cheered for the club. Although they were club members, the boys felt that this did not excuse them. Danny said: "You're a couple of traitors—Benedict Arnolds. . . . You're with the boys—and then you go against them. . . . Go on, I don't want your support."

Fred and Lou fell between the two groups and therefore had to face this problem of divided allegiance. Doc's position on the corner was so definitely established that no one even considered the possibility of his choosing to bowl for the Community Club against the Nortons.

This was the only match between the two teams that ever took place. The corner boys were satisfied with their victory, and the club did not seek a return match. Tony Cardio objected to the way in which the Nortons had tried to upset the concentration of his team and said it was no fun to bowl against such poor sports. There were, however, clashes with individual members of the club. One night in November, Doc, Frank Bonelli, Joe Dodge, and I were bowling when Chick Morelli and Lou Danaro came in together. We agreed to have two three-man teams, and Chick and Doc chose sides. Chick chose Lou and me. The match was fairly even at first, but Doc put his team far ahead with a brilliant third string. Toward the end of this string, Chick was sitting next to Joe Dodge and mumbling at him, "You're a lousy bum. . . . You're a no-good bowler."

Joe said nothing until Chick had repeated his remarks several times. Then Joe got up and fired back at Chick, "You're a conceited _____! I feel like taking a wallop at you. I never knew anybody was as conceited as you. . . . You're a conceited _____!"

Doc stood between them to prevent a fight. Chick said nothing, and Doc managed to get the six of us quietly into the elevator. Joe was not satisfied, and he said to me in a loud voice: "Somebody is going to straighten him out some day. Somebody will have to wallop him to knock some of that conceit out of him."

When we were outside the building, Lou walked away with Chick, and the rest of us went into Jennings' Cafeteria for "coffee-ands." We discussed Chick:

> Doc: It's lucky you didn't hit him. They'd be after you for manslaughter. You're too strong for the kid.
> Joe: All right. But when somebody's too tough for me, I don't fool around. . . . He shouldn't fool around me. . . . If he's gonna say them things, he should smile when he says them. But I think he really meant it.
> Doc: The poor guy, so many fellows want to wallop him—and he knows it.
> Frank: I liked him all right until the other night. We went to the Metropolitan Ballroom. . . . He didn't mingle in at all. He just lay down on a couch like he wanted to be petted. He wasn't sociable at all.

After driving Chick home, Lou joined us in Jennings'. He said that Chick felt very bad about the incident and didn't know what it was that made people want to hit him. Lou added: "I know he didn't mean it that way. He's really a swell kid when you get to know him. There's only one thing I don't like about him." Then he told about a time when Chick had started an argument with a dance-hall attendant on some technicality involved in the regulations of the hall. Lou commented: "He was just trying to show how intelligent he was."

A few days later, when Joe's anger had subsided, Doc persuaded him to apologize.

Doc did not defend Chick for friendship's sake. Nor was it because they worked together in the Community Club. In the club Doc led a faction generally hostile to Chick, and he himself was often critical of the manner in which Chick sought to run the organization. But Doc had friends in both groups. He did not like to see the groups at odds with each other. Though friendship between the Nortons and Chick was impossible, it was Doc's function to see that diplomatic relations were maintained.

The Community Club match served to arouse enthusiasm for bowling among the Nortons. Previously the boys had bowled sporadically and often in other groups, but now for the first time bowling became a regular part of their social routine. Long John, Alec, Joe Dodge, and Frank Bonelli bowled several nights a week throughout the winter. Others bowled on frequent occasions, and all the bowlers appeared at the alleys at least one night a week.

A high score at candlepins requires several spares or strikes. Since a strike rarely occurs except when the first ball hits the kingpin properly within a fraction of an inch, and none of the boys had such precise aim, strikes were considered matters of luck, although a good bowler was expected to score them more often than a poor one. A bowler was judged according to his ability to get spares, to "pick" the pins that remained on the alley after his first ball.

There are many mental hazards connected with bowling. In any sports there are critical moments when a player needs the steadiest nerves if he is to "come through"; but, in those that involve team play and fairly continuous action, the player can sometimes lose himself in the heat of the contest and get by the critical points before he has a chance to "tighten up." If he is competing on a five-man team, the bowler must wait a long time for his turn at the alleys, and he has plenty of time to brood over his mistakes. When a man is facing ten pins, he can throw the ball quite casually. But when only one pin remains standing, and his opponents are shouting, "He can't pick it," the pressure is on, and there is a tendency to "tighten up" and lose control.

When a bowler is confident that he can make a difficult shot, the chances are that he will make it or come exceedingly close. When he is not confident, he will miss. A bowler is confident because he has made similar shots in the past and is accustomed to making good scores. But that is not all. He is also confident because his fellows, whether for him or against him, believe that he can make the shot. If they do not believe in him, the bowler has their adverse opinion as well as his own uncertainty to fight against. When that is said, it becomes necessary to consider a man's relation to his fellows in examining his bowling record.

In the winter and spring of 1937–38 bowling was the most significant social activity for the Nortons. Saturday night's intra-clique and individual matches became the climax of the week's events. During the week the boys discussed what had happened the previous Saturday night and what would happen on the coming Saturday night. A man's performance was subject to continual evaluation and criticism. There was, therefore, a close connection between a man's bowling and his position in the group.

The team used against the Community Club had consisted of two men (Doc and Long John) who ranked high and three men (Joe Dodge, Frank Bonelli, and Tommy) who had a low standing. When bowling became a fixed group activity, the Nortons' team evolved along different lines. Danny joined the Saturday-night crowd and rapidly made a place for himself. He performed very well and picked Doc as his favorite opponent. There was a good-natured rivalry between them. In individual competition Danny usually won, although his average in the group matches was no better than that of Doc's. After the Community Club match, when Doc selected a team to represent the Nortons against other corner gangs and clubs, he chose Danny, Long John, and himself, leaving two vacancies on the five-man team. At this time, Mike, who had never been a good bowler, was just beginning to bowl regularly and had not established his reputation. Significantly enough, the vacancies were not filled from the ranks of the clique. On Saturday nights the boys had been bowling with Chris Teludo, Nutsy's older cousin, and Mark Ciampa, a man who associated with them only at the bowling alleys. Both men were popular and were first-class bowlers. They were chosen by Doc, with the agreement of Danny and Long John, to bowl for the Nortons. It was only when a member of the regular team was absent that one of the followers in the clique was called in, and on such occasions he never distinguished himself.

The followers were not content with being substitutes. They claimed that they had not been given an opportunity to prove their ability. One Saturday night in February, 1938, Mike organized an intraclique match. His team was made up of Chris Teludo, Doc, Long John, himself, and me. Danny was sick at the time, and I was put in to substitute for him. Frank, Alec, Joe, Lou, and Tommy made up the other team. Interest in this match was more intense than in the ordinary "choose-up" matches, but the followers bowled poorly and never had a chance.

After this one encounter the followers were recognized as the second team and never again challenged the team of Doc, Danny, Long John, Mark, and Chris. Instead, they took to individual efforts to better their positions.

On his athletic ability alone, Frank should have been an excellent bowler. His ball-playing had won him positions on semiprofessional teams and a promise—though unfulfilled—of a job on a minor-league team. And it was not lack of practice that held him back, for, along with Alec and Joe Dodge, he bowled more frequently than Doc, Danny, or Mike. During the winter of 1937–38 Frank occupied a particularly subordinate position in the group. He spent his time with Alec in the pastry shop owned by Alec's uncle, and, since he had little employment throughout the winter, he became dependent upon Alec for a large part of the expenses of his participation in group activities. Frank fell to the bottom of the group. His financial dependence preyed upon his mind. While he sometimes bowled well, he was never a serious threat to break into the first team.

Some events of June, 1937, cast additional light upon Frank's position. Mike organized a baseball team of some of the Nortons to play against a younger group of Norton Street corner boys. On the basis of his record, Frank was considered the best player on either team, yet he made a miserable showing. He said to me: "I can't seem to play ball when I'm playing with fellows I know, like that bunch. I do much better when I'm playing for the

Stanley A.C. against some team in Dexter, Westland, or out of town." Accustomed to filling an inferior position, Frank was unable to star even in his favorite sport when he was competing against members of his own group.

One evening I heard Alec boasting to Long John that the way he was bowling he could take on every man on the first team and lick them all. Long John dismissed the challenge with these words: "You think you could beat us, but, under pressure, you die!"

Alec objected vehemently, yet he recognized the prevailing group opinion of his bowling. He made the highest single score of the season, and he frequently excelled during the week when he bowled with Frank, Long John, Joe Dodge, and me, but on Saturday nights, when the group was all assembled, his performance was quite different. Shortly after this conversation Alec had several chances to prove himself, but each time it was "an off night," and he failed.

Carl, Joe, Lou, and Fred were never good enough to gain any recognition. Tommy was recognized as a first-class bowler, but he did most of his bowling with a younger group.

One of the best guides to the bowling standing of the members was furnished by a match held toward the end of April, 1938. Doc had an idea that we should climax the season with an individual competition among the members of the clique. He persuaded the owner of the alleys to contribute ten dollars in prize money to be divided among the three highest scorers. It was decided that only those who had bowled regularly should be eligible, and on this basis Lou, Fred, and Tommy were eliminated.

Interest in this contest ran high. The probable performances of the various bowlers were widely discussed. Doc, Danny, and Long John each listed his predictions. They were unanimous in conceding the first five places to themselves, Mark Ciampa, and Chris Teludo, although they differed in predicting the order among the first five. The next two positions were generally conceded to Mike and to me. All the ratings gave Joe Dodge last position, and Alec, Frank, and Carl were ranked close to the bottom.

The followers made no such lists, but Alec let it be known that he intended to show the boys something. Joe Dodge was annoyed to discover that he was the unanimous choice to finish last and argued that he was going to win.

When Chris Teludo did not appear for the match, the field was narrowed to ten. After the first four boxes, Alec was leading by several pins. He turned to Doc and said, "I'm out to get you boys tonight." But then he began to miss, and, as mistake followed mistake, he stopped trying. Between turns, he went out for drinks, so that he became flushed and unsteady on his feet. He threw the ball carelessly, pretending that he was not interested in the competition. His collapse was sudden and complete; in the space of a few boxes he dropped from first to last place.

The bowlers finished in the following order:

1.	Whyte	6.	Joe
2.	Danny	7.	Mark
3.	Doc	8.	Carl
4.	Long John	9.	Frank
5.	Mike	10.	Alec

There were only two upsets in the contest, according to the predictions made by Doc, Danny, and Long John: Mark bowled very poorly and I won. However, it is important to note that neither Mark nor I fitted neatly into either part of the clique. Mark associated with the boys only at the bowling alleys and had no recognized status in the group. Although I was on good terms with all the boys, I was closer to the leaders than to the followers, since Doc was my particular friend. If Mark and I are left out of consideration, the performances were almost exactly what the leaders expected and the followers feared they would be. Danny, Doc, Long John, and Mike were bunched together at the top. Joe Dodge did better than was expected of him, but even he could not break through the solid ranks of the leadership.

Several days later Doc and Long John discussed the match with me.

> LONG JOHN: I only wanted to be sure that Alec or Joe Dodge didn't win. That wouldn't have been right.
> DOC: That's right. We didn't want to make it tough for you, because we all liked you, and the other fellows did too. If somebody had tried to make it tough for you, we would have protected you. . . . If Joe Dodge or Alec had been out in front, it would have been different. We would have talked them out of it. We would have made plenty of noise. We would have been really vicious. . . .

I asked Doc what would have happened if Alec or Joe had won.

> They wouldn't have known how to take it. That's why we were out to beat them. If they had won, there would have been a lot of noise. Plenty of arguments. We would have called it lucky—things like that. We would have tried to get them in another match and then ruin them. We would have to put them in their places.

Every corner boy expects to be heckled as he bowls, but the heckling can take various forms. While I had moved ahead as early as the end of the second string, I was subjected only to good-natured kidding. The leaders watched me with mingled surprise and amusement; in a very real sense, I was permitted to win.

Even so, my victory required certain adjustments. I was hailed jocularly as "the Champ" or even as "the Cheese Champ." Rather than accept this designation, I pressed my claim for recognition. Doc arranged to have me bowl a match against Long John. If I won, I should have the right to challenge Doc or Danny. The four of us went to the alleys together. Urged on by Doc and Danny, Long John won a decisive victory. I made no further challenges.

Alec was only temporarily crushed by his defeat. For a few days he was not seen on the corner, but then he returned and sought to re-establish himself. When the boys went bowling, he challenged Long John to an individual match and defeated him. Alec began to talk once more. Again he challenged Long John to a match, and again he defeated him. When bowling was resumed in the fall, Long John became Alec's favorite opponent, and for some time Alec nearly always came out ahead. He gloated. Long John explained: "He seems to have the Indian sign on me." And that is the way these incidents were interpreted by others—simply as a queer quirk of the game.

It is significant that, in making his challenge, Alec selected Long John instead of Doc, Danny, or Mike. It was not that Long John's bowling ability was uncertain. His average was about the same as that of Doc or Danny and better than that of Mike. As a member of the top group but not a leader in his own right, it was his social position that was vulnerable.

When Long John and Alec acted outside the group situation, it became possible for Alec to win. Long John was still considered the dependable man in a team match, and that was more important in relation to a man's standing in the group. Nevertheless,

the leaders felt that Alec should not be defeating Long John and
tried to reverse the situation. As Doc told me:

> Alec isn't so aggressive these days. I steamed up at the way he was
> going after Long John, and I blasted him. . . . Then I talked to
> Long John. John is an introvert. He broods over things, and some-
> times he feels inferior. He can't be aggressive like Alec, and when
> Alec tells him how he can always beat him, Long John gets to think
> that Alec is the better bowler. . . . I talked to him. I made him
> see that he should bowl better than Alec. I persuaded him that he
> was really the better bowler. . . . Now you watch them the next
> time out. I'll bet Long John will ruin him.

The next time Long John did defeat Alec. He was not able to
do it every time, but they became so evenly matched that Alec
lost interest in such competition.

The records of the season 1937–38 show a very close correspondence between social position and bowling performance. This developed because bowling became the primary social activity of
the group. It became the main vehicle whereby the individual
could maintain, gain, or lose prestige.

Bowling scores did not fall automatically into this pattern.
There were certain customary ways of behaving which exerted
pressure upon the individuals. Chief among these were the manner of choosing sides and the verbal attacks the members directed
against one another.

Generally, two men chose sides in order to divide the group into
two five-man teams. The choosers were often, but not always,
among the best bowlers. If they were evenly matched, two poor
bowlers frequently did the choosing, but in all cases the process
was essentially the same. Each one tried to select the best bowler
among those who were still unchosen. When more than ten men
were present, choice was limited to the first ten to arrive, so that
even a poor bowler would be chosen if he came early. It was the
order of choice which was important. Sides were chosen several
times each Saturday night, and in this way a man was constantly
reminded of the value placed upon his ability by his fellows and
of the sort of performance expected of him.

Of course, personal preferences entered into the selection of
bowlers, but if a man chose a team of poor bowlers just because
they were his closest friends, he pleased no one, least of all his
team mates. It was the custom among the Nortons to have the

losing team pay for the string bowled by the winners. As a rule, this small stake did not play an important role in the bowling, but no one liked to pay without the compensating enjoyment of a closely contested string. For this reason the selections by good bowlers or by poor bowlers coincided very closely. It became generally understood which men should be among the first chosen in order to make for an interesting match.

When Doc, Danny, Long John, or Mike bowled on opposing sides, they kidded one another good-naturedly. Good scores were expected of them, and bad scores were accounted for by bad luck or temporary lapses of form. When a follower threatened to better his position, the remarks took quite a different form. The boys shouted at him that he was lucky, that he was "bowling over his head." The effort was made to persuade him that he should not be bowling as well as he was, that a good performance was abnormal for him. This type of verbal attack was very important in keeping the members "in their places." It was used particularly by the followers so that, in effect, they were trying to keep one another down. While Long John, one of the most frequent targets for such attacks, responded in kind, Doc, Danny, and Mike seldom used this weapon. However, the leaders would have met a real threat on the part of Alec or Joe by such psychological pressures.

The origination of group action is another factor in the situation. The Community Club match really inaugurated bowling as a group activity, and that match was arranged by Doc. Group activities are originated by the men with highest standing in the group, and it is natural for a man to encourage an activity in which he excels and discourage one in which he does not excel. However, this cannot explain Mike's performance, for he had never bowled well before Saturday night at the alleys became a fixture for the Nortons.

The standing of the men in the eyes of other groups also contributed toward maintaining social differentiation within the group. In the season of 1938–39 Doc began keeping the scores of each man every Saturday night so that the Nortons' team could be selected strictly according to the averages of the bowlers, and there could be no accusation of favoritism. One afternoon when we were talking about bowling performances, I asked Doc and Danny what would happen if five members of the second team should make better averages than the first team bowlers. Would they then become the first team? Danny said:

> Suppose they did beat us, and the San Marcos would come up and want a match with us. We'd tell them, those fellows are really the first team, but the San Marcos would say, "We don't want to bowl them, we want to bowl you." We would say, "All right, you want to bowl Doc's team?" and we would bowl them.

Doc added:

> I want you to understand, Bill, we're conducting this according to democratic principles. It's the others who won't let us be democratic.

Further Readings

HARE, ALEXANDER, ed., *Small Groups, Studies in Social Interaction.* New York: Alfred A. Knopf, Inc., 1955.

LINDZEY, GARDNER, ed., *Handbook of Social Psychology.* Reading, Mass.: Addison-Wesley Publishing Company, Inc., 1954.

REISS, ALBERT J., "The Sociology of Urban Life: 1946–1956," *Cities and Society: The Revised Reader in Urban Sociology,* Paul K. Hatt and Albert J. Reiss, Jr., eds. New York: The Free Press of Glencoe, Inc., 1957.

WHYTE, WILLIAM, *The Organization Man.* New York: Simon and Schuster, Inc., 1956.

Questions for Discussion

1. Why did there seem to be such a close relationship between social position in the "street corner" society and bowling performance?
2. Was the author able to achieve any mobility within the group when he won the bowling tournament? If so, what is the difference between this type of mobility and that of Joe Plano?
3. Why did Alec triumph over Long John? How did the expectations of the other bowlers influence Alec's winning?

GEORGE SOULE

Work, Productivity and Leisure*

Physical education will be confronted with a number of changes in the future. In the last forty years the base of our society has changed from agrarian to industrial. Soon the base will become one of service. The speed with which society changes causes many problems for the physical educator. Two major problems of the future will be finding a meaningful philosophy of leisure and counteracting the increasingly sedentary character of our lives.

The last article of this section is a brief explanation of how we have so much spare time, more by far than was possible in any previous culture. Soule asks whether leisure is necessary only as a respite from work, whether it is valuable in itself as an end to which work is directed. Compare the discussion here with the views of Dewey, Oberteuffer, Spencer, and Williams in Section II, Philosophical Backgrounds.

Leisure is a word often used but seldom defined. It is likely to be regarded as rest, idleness, play, or recreation. Any or all of these pursuits may at times occupy leisure, but surely they are not identical with it. People in their leisure time may engage in concentrated effort as in outdoor sports or taxing intellectual activity. They may be occupied in producing for themselves or others as in gardening, home construction or repair, useful social activities, painting, drama, music.

Recreation implies play of a sort which fits one for better performance on the job, but leisure is valued for its own sake. A member of the leisure class—that is, one not compelled to work for his living at all—surely does not devote his time solely to

* Reprinted with the permission of the author and publisher from *The Economics of Leisure*. Annals of the American Academy of Political Science, vol. 313, 1957, pp. 16–17; 21–22; 23–24.

recreation. He may be a "play boy"; but if so, for what endeavor his play re-creates him might be hard to say. Those who have means to live without working often find work to do, whether in private life or in public; "leisure classes" have produced many leaders in war, politics, philosophy, science, the arts, and letters.

There is an overtone in the word leisure which involves the absence of being driven by material necessity. In leisure, ideally, one does what one chooses and does it with interest, often with ease and freedom. Individually chosen goals pursued with disregard of economic and social pressures have characterized some of man's finest achievements.

To discuss the economics of leisure, one must think of it in economic categories. Such categories are production and consumption, demand and supply, the allocation of scarce resources to the end of fulfilling wants in the order of their importance. In this sense, leisure is a function of the demand for and supply of time. In the culture to which we are accustomed, most people sell part of their time to others—employers or customers—time to be occupied in producing what others want. People sell time primarily so that they may acquire enough money income to buy products sold by others. What one does in sold time is "the job." Time sold is commonly thought of as work. Time not sold, "one's own time," "free time," is thought of as leisure, no matter what one does with it. Let us adopt this common distinction as a working definition of leisure because, as I hope will appear, it is well suited to economic analysis.

Leisure, then, is time not sold; time not to be used at the direction of others; but rather time during which the individual is, or may be, master of his own living. It is in essence a nonpecuniary, nonmarket element in our largely commercial culture, though it may be strongly conditioned by that culture.

Leisure and Production

In past civilizations, leisure was enjoyed only by a small proportion of the population. These few were typically owners of great landed estates who received the goods and services they consumed by virtue of their station and heritage. As commercial and, later, industrial civilization grew, some persons accumulated other forms of income-yielding property, such as money capital lent at interest or directly owned business establishments. Meanwhile the great majority toiled long hours for little more than enough to sustain life. The wide disparity in wealth and privilege was not, however, the primary cause of lack of leisure for the masses. Even more basic was the lack of enough production to sustain the population at more than a minimum level. The total income of the rich, since they were relatively few, if distributed evenly among all, would have added little to the incomes of those at lower levels in the social pyramid.

This situation has been altered only during the past century of rapid technological development. General enjoyment of both higher income and more leisure has been made possible because the output of goods and services has grown much faster than the population.

According to the most reliable satistical estimates, the real net national product in the United States grew about thirteenfold between the decade 1869–78 and the decade 1944–53. During the same period the population increased only threefold. Real product per capita of the population therefore grew about four times in a little less than eighty years. The rate of its growth averaged about 1.9 per cent a year.

Net national product means, of course, the dollar value of all goods and services purchased by final users, excluding repair and replacement of existing productive equipment. It includes the products not only of manufacture, agriculture, and mining, but of transportation, distribution, construction, and services of all types. In real net national product the dollar figures are corrected for price changes, so that the totals of all years are approximately the same as if average prices had not fallen or risen at all.

Productivity

In 1850 the average worker, it is estimated turned out about 34 cents' worth per hour having the same purchasing power in cents as in 1950. By 1950 the average worker produced about $1.94 worth per hour, or more than five times as much as a century earlier. The total man-hours worked grew somewhat less than five times between 1850 and 1950. The real value of the total output thus increased about twenty-five times, while the population was growing at a much slower rate. Obviously this gain permitted a rapid rise in consumption of goods and services by the average American.

At the same time it made possible a reduction of the average hours worked. The standard working week in 1870 was about 70 hours; in 1950 it was about 40 hours, a reduction of about two-fifths.

Market Demand and Leisure

The fact that so many people have gained access to so much time away from the machine or the desk has of course stimulated numerous industries which make goods usable in free time. Perhaps the first of these to feel a marked effect from growing leisure was the automobile—at the beginning sold to the well-to-do or the eccentric and used by others, when it was used, mainly for transportation to or from the job or as a substitute for the traditional carriage drive on Sunday afternoons. The motor car, of course, has been employed increasingly for utilitarian transportation; but after the 48-hour week became general during World War I, it also became virtually a necessity in getting to and from places where recreation facilities were available. On increasingly longer weekends and vacations, Americans have taken to the road. In 1950 vacation travel topped the list of American expenditures for recreation; it is estimated that 12 billion dollars was spent. The American Automobile Association states that 66 million people take annual automobile vacations. About 85 per cent of vacation travel is by motor car.

Many others depend for a large proportion of their sales on the automobile manufacturing industry. The use of automobiles leads to a demand not only for private resorts, service stations, and motor inns that line the main highways, but for governmentally financed facilities such as roads, bridges, parks, golf courses, camping sites, swimming pools, and the like.

Radio was perhaps the next great industry to develop under the intensive stimulus of the enlarged free time of consumers. It did not appear on the civilian market until after 1918, and its growth was extremely rapid. Together with its cousins or offshoots—television, phonographs, records, and musical instruments it accounted in 1950 for more than 31 per cent of the 10.5 billion dollars spent for strictly recreation goods and services. Reading, hobbies—including the wide range of do-it-yourself aids and pets—took 19 per cent of the 10.5 billion dollars; sports equipment 18.2 per cent; theaters, entertainment, and amusements—most of this classification consists of motion pictures—absorbed 16.6 per cent. Few of these products are newcomers on the market, but their rise to great industries could scarcely have occurred without the increase in leisure.

Participant recreation services, it was estimated, absorbed about 7.5 per cent of the strictly recreation market; organizations and clubs, 5.0 per cent; and spectator sports such as admissions to ball parks, hockey rinks and racetracks, a mere 2.6 per cent.

If one should include in recreation, in addition to vacation travel and strictly recreation goods and services, such things as governmental recreation facilities, liquor, tobacco, sport clothes, candy, soft drinks, and chewing gum, the total consumer expenditure in 1950 would be 40.5 billion dollars or considerably more than 10 per cent of the gross national product for that year.

In a rather materalistic sense, therefore, the access of huge amounts of free time has paid its way by providing expansion of markets and employment opportunity. It is unlikely that the demand for food or clothing—two of the basic human necessities— would have grown more rapidly than it actually did grow if consumers had not used so large a part of their disposable incomes for recreation products. In fact, the demand for basic food products has not risen faster than the population over a recent period; the expansion of food-processing and marketing industries has been a response mainly to the desire of people, and of housewives particularly, to save time for other things than home preparation of meals. Clothing and textiles have not been classified among the most rapidly growing industries. The expansion of leisure is a factor of the first importance in the structure and growth of the American economy.

Use of Free Time by Americans

Unfortunately we do not have as good figures showing how Americans spend their free time as the figures which reveal their spending of money. Sociologists have made partial observations of limited groups and have reached, now and then, conclusions that are disquieting to persons who adhere to the traditional values on which Western civilization is supposed to be founded. It is said that individual choice is at a discount; that persons do, not so much what their innermost selves might lead them to do, as what conformity requires in order to rise in the social or economic scale. It is charged that great opportunities to increase knowledge, wisdom, or aesthetic enjoyment are wasted because, although people read much, they do not read many books; instead they choose literature desired for ephemeral entertainment. Even the books they do read are said to be largely sex thrillers and detective stories.

Great industries compete for the free time of the citizen, and in doing so they often use the same kind of sales methods that are employed to merchandise soap, proprietary medicines, cigarettes. Thus a commercial culture, it is said, warps the tastes and values of the public, ignoring the minorities none of whom is large enough to repay attention by those intent on exploiting a mass market.

It used to be said—though not so often of late years—that people in general act as passive spectators of games rather than engaging in sports and games themselves. Spectatorship is not always entirely passive; it depends on what one is looking at. And in any case, what facts we have indicate that participant sports are widespread and popular; spectator activities often find it difficult to draw audiences. About three times as much was spent in recent years on participant recreation activities as on spectator sports. More is spent on concerts than on professional baseball games. More than 2,000 towns and cities regularly offer good music; there are 200 symphony orchestras in the country.

Figures do show that people choose a large variety of occupations for their leisure. There are some 34 million cameras in the possession of amateur photographers. In 1952, 60 million dollars' worth of tools were bought for home workshops. Fishermen bought 18 million fishing licenses in 1953. There are, it is estimated, 18 million bicyclists, 17 million roller skaters, 20 million bowlers, and 5 million horseshoe players. One estimate is that 4 million own power boats and a half million own sailboats. Golf, which used to be played only at country clubs by the well-to-do, is now played by persons in almost all income levels—4 million of them.

These are only a few of the hundreds of ways in which Americans spend leisure time. Leisure occupations include amateur practice of all the fine arts; building, repairing, and decoration of houses and furniture; fabricating of products requiring special skills— though as a rule not for sale—like short-wave wireless sets, high-fidelity phonograph receivers, model boats and trains; unpaid social service and political activities; study in schools, colleges, and adult education courses.

Further Readings

BENEDICT, RUTH, "Transmitting Our Democratic Heritage in the Schools," *American Journal of Sociology,* vol. 48 (May 1943), pp. 722–727.

BRIGHTBILL, CHARLES K., *Man and Leisure, A Philosophy of Recreation.* Englewood Cliffs, N.J.: Prentice-Hall, Inc., 1961.

DAVIS, KINGSLEY, *Human Society.* New York: The Macmillan Company, 1949.

KEPLER, MAX, *Leisure in America: A Social Inquiry.* New York: John Wiley and Sons, Inc., 1960.

MACIVER, ROBERT M. and CHARLES H. PAGE, *Society: An Introductory Analysis.* New York: Holt, Rinehart and Winston, Inc., 1949.

Questions for Discussion

1. What philosophy of leisure is implied in the word recreation? What is this philosophy?
2. Is the "time not sold" definition of leisure accepted in the United States of America?
3. Does there seem to be the same increase in leisure for persons in the professions as there is for skilled and semi-skilled workers?
4. Why does our culture generally demand one to be productive and attain some preconceived goal in his leisure?

INDEX